Reading Greek
Grammar, vocabulary and exercises

Γράμματα μαθεῖν δεῖ καὶ μαθόντα νοῦν ἔχειν

Menander

THE JOINT ASSOCIATION OF
CLASSICAL TEACHERS' GREEK COURSE

Reading Greek

GRAMMAR, VOCABULARY
AND EXERCISES

CAMBRIDGE UNIVERSITY PRESS
CAMBRIDGE
LONDON · NEW YORK · NEW ROCHELLE
MELBOURNE · SYDNEY

Published by the Press Syndicate of the University of Cambridge
The Pitt Building, Trumpington Street, Cambridge CB2 IRP
32 East 57th Street, New York, NY 10022, USA
296 Beaconsfield Parade, Middle Park, Melbourne 3206, Australia

First published 1978
Reprinted with corrections 1979, 1980
Reprinted 1982, 1983

Printed in the United States of America

Library of Congress cataloguing in publication data

The Joint Association of Classical Teachers' Greek Course
Reading Greek (Grammar, Vocabulary and Exercises).

1. Greek language — Grammar — 1870 — I. Title.

PA258.J59 1978 488'.2'421 77-91090
ISBN 0-521-21977-9

CONTENTS

Cover picture: Athene with stylus and writing tablet. (Photograph reproduced by permission of the Staatliche Antikensammlungen and Glyptothek, Munich.)

PREFACE

This book is written to be used in step with *Reading Greek (Text)* of the Joint Association of Classical Teachers' Greek Course. In it will be found:

(A) Running vocabularies (in alphabetical lists) and learning vocabularies for each sub-section of the text; and at various points, grammatical explanations and exercises, which state clearly and reinforce the grammar which will have been met in reading the Text (pp. 1–258).

It is essential to note here that the grammar and exercises have been written on the assumption that the text with which they go has already been read. Consequently, the grammar and exercises should not be turned to until that point is reached in the reading.

(B) A Reference Grammar, which summarises and expands upon the essential features of the grammar met in the Course (pp. 259–307).

(C) A number of Language Surveys which look in detail at some of the more important features of the language (pp. 308–34).

(D) A total vocabulary of all words that should have been learnt, followed by a list of proper names (pp. 335–55).

(E) A vocabulary for the English–Greek exercises (pp. 356–62).

(F) An index to the grammar (pp. 363–7).

It would be impracticable to produce an exhaustive grammar of the whole Greek language. Students and teachers should bear in mind that the first aim of this grammar is to help students to translate from Greek into English, and that we have therefore concentrated attention on the most common features of the language.

Acknowledgements of the debt we owe to the Steering Committee and Advisory Panel are to be found in *Reading Greek (Text)*, p. xii.

J.A.C.T. Greek Course
Hughes Hall
Cambridge CB1 2EW, England

Peter V. Jones (Director)
Keith C. Sidwell (Second Writer)
Frances E. Corrie (Research Assistant)
November 1977

ABBREVIATIONS

abs.(olute)
acc.(usative)
act.(ive)
adj.(ective)
adv.(erb)
aor.(ist)
art.(icle)
aug.(ment)
cf. (=confer) (Latin: 'compare')
comp.(arative)
cond.(itional)
conj.(ugated, ugation)
contr.(acted, action)
dat.(ive)
decl.(ension)
def.(inite)
del.(iberative)
dir.(ect)
f.(eminine)
fut.(ure)
gen.(itive)
imper.(ative)
impf. (=imperfect)
inc.(luding)
ind.(icative)
indec.(linable)
indef.(inite)
indir.(ect)
inf.(initive)
irr.(egular)
lit.(erally)
m.(asculine)
mid.(dle)
n.(euter)
nom.(inative)

opt.(ative)
part.(iciple)
pass.(ive)
perf.(ect)
pl.(ural)
plup.(erfect)
prep.(osition)
pres.(ent)
prim.(ary)
pron.(oun)
q.(uestion)
redupl.(icated, ication)
rel.(ative)
s.(ingular)
sc.(ilicet) (Latin: 'presumably')
sec.(ondary)
seq.(uence)
sp.(eech)
str.(ong)
subj.(unctive)
sup.(erlative)
tr.(anslate)
uncontr.(acted)
unfulf.(illed)
vb. (=verb)
voc.(ative)
wk. (=weak)
1st, 2nd, 3rd refer to persons of the verb, i.e.
  1st s.   = 'I'
  2nd s.   = 'you'
  3rd s.   = 'he, she, it'
  1st pl.   = 'we'
  2nd pl. = 'you'
  3rd pl. = 'they'

A Grammar, Vocabularies and Exercises for Sections One–Nineteen

---

Simplified alphabet and pronunciation

$A \alpha$ (alpha) pronounced 'c*u*p' or 'c*a*lm'
$B \beta$ (beta) pronounced 'b' as in English
$\Gamma \gamma$ (gamma) a hard 'g', like '*g*ot'
$\Delta \delta$ (delta) a clean 'd', like '*d*ot'
$E \epsilon$ (epsilon) short 'e' like 'p*e*t'
$Z \zeta$ (zeta) like 'wi*sd*om'
$H \eta$ (eta) pronounced as in 'h*ai*r'
$\Theta \theta$ (theta) – blow a hard 't' ('*t*are')
$I \iota$ (iota) like 'b*ea*d' or like 'b*i*n'
$K \kappa$ (kappa) a clean 'k' like 's*k*in'
$\Lambda \lambda$ (lambda) like '*l*ock'
$M \mu$ (mu) like '*m*ock'
$N \nu$ (nu) like '*n*et'
$\Xi \xi$ (xi) like 'bo*x*'
$O o$ (omicron) a short 'o', like 'p*o*t'
$\Pi \pi$ (pi) a clean 'p', like 's*p*ot'
$P \rho$ (rho) a rolled 'r', like '*rr*at'
$\Sigma \sigma \varsigma$ (sigma) a soft 's', like '*s*ing'
$T \tau$ (tau) a clean 't', like '*t*ing'
$\Upsilon \upsilon$ (upsilon) French 'l*u*ne' or German 'M*ü*ller'
$\Phi \phi$ (phi) – blow a hard 'p', like '*p*ool'
$X \chi$ (khi) – blow a hard 'c', like '*c*ool'
$\Psi \psi$ (psi) as in 'la*ps*e'
$\Omega \omega$ (omega) like 's*aw*'

*Note 'clean' indicates no 'h' sound; 'blow hard' indicates plenty of 'h' aspiration
(e.g. ϕ as in 'top-hole').*

The most common diphthongs and double-consonants

αι as in 'high'
αυ as in 'how'
ει as in 'fiancée'
ευ (pronounce both elements *separately*)
οι as in 'boy'
ου as in 'too'
γγ as in 'finger'

Dwell on all double consonants, e.g. ττ as 'rat-trap', λλ as 'wholly' etc.

Sigma and iota subscript

Observe that ς is used as the *end* of words, while σ is used elsewhere (see next example). Sometimes ι is printed *underneath* a preceding α (ᾳ), η (ῃ) and ω (ῳ).

Breathings

‘ above a vowel indicates the presence of an 'h' sound: ’ above a vowel indicates the absence of 'h' sound, e.g.

ὅσος = 'hosos'
οἷος = 'oios'

Note

(i) This is a purposely simplified pronunciation chart. Fuller and more accurate information is given in the Reference Grammar A.2 on p. 260.
(ii) The mark which indicates where a doubtful vowel (α, ι, υ) is pronounced long (ᾱ, ῑ, ῡ) is only used on the endings in the Reference Grammar.
(iii) Greek uses · for a colon and ; for a question-mark.

The alphabet – exercises

---

1. Write the following Greek words in their English form. Some will just require transliteration, others will need a few moments' thought.
   Key:

ζ = sd *or* z	κ = c *or* k	χ = ch *or* kh
η = e	-ον = -um	ψ = ps
θ = th	υ = y *or* u	

Βυζάντιον   Παρθενών
Δικαιόπολις   Χίος
Εὔβοια   ἀκρόπολις
Ζηνόθεμις   ἐμπόριον
Ἡγέστρατος

2. Write the following English words in their Greek form:
(ē = η; -us = -ος; -um = -ον)
drama, panthēr, crocus, geranium, hippopotamus, ibis, asbestos, charactēr

PART ONE

Section One

Running vocabularies and learning vocabularies

Running vocabularies

The vocabulary of each sub-section is given in alphabetical order. Note carefully that *phrases joined in the text by a linking device (‾ or ⌐⌐) will be found under the first word of the phrase.*

Learning vocabularies

At the end of each running vocabulary and after the Grammar of One A–G, Two, Three and Four A–B, you will find a list of words to be learnt. *These will not appear again in the running vocabularies.*

Notes

(i) If you find that the running vocabulary does not contain a word you need, look it up in the Total Vocabulary (pp. 335–55), which contains all words that should have been learnt, including place names and personal names.

(ii) If you are in doubt about the name of a person, turn to the list of proper names (p. 353–5).

(iii) In running vocabularies, the accentuation of words is as in the text, except where words are given in their lexicon form. In learning vocabularies, words are accented in lexicon form.

(iv) In running vocabularies One to Ten, hyphens are freely used to split words up into their constituent parts (prefixes, stems, endings, etc.). The learning vocabularies present the unhyphenated form.

Vocabulary for Section One A

ἀκού-ουσι(ν) (they) hear
βαίν-ει (he) goes
βλέπ-ει (he) looks
βλέπ-ουσι(ν) (they) look
δέ and; but
εἰς to, into
εἰς Εὔβοιαν to Euboia
εἰς τὸ πλοῖ-ον onto the ship
εἰς Χί-ον to Chios
εἰσ-βαίν-ει (he) embarks
εἰσ-βαίν-ουσι(ν) (they)
  embark
ἐν in, on
ἐν Βυζαντίῳ in Byzantium
ἐν Εὐβοίᾳ in Euboia
ἐν Χίῳ in Chios
ἐξαίφνης suddenly
ἔπειτα then, next

ἐστι(ν) (it/there) is
καί and
καί ... καί both ... and
μέν ... δέ on the one
  hand ... on the other
ὁ the
ὁ Δικαιόπολις Dikaiopolis
ὁ Ζηνόθεμις Sdenothemis
ὁ Ἡγέστρατ-ος Hegestratos
ὁ κυβερνήτης the captain
ὁ ῥαψῳδ-ός the rhapsode
οἱ the
οἱ ναῦται the sailors, crew
ὁρ-ᾷ (he) sees
ὁρ-ῶσι(ν) (they) see
οὖν so, therefore
πλ-εῖ (it) sails
πρός towards

πρὸς τὰς Ἀθήνας towards
  Athens
πρὸς τὴν γῆν towards the
  land
πρὸς τὸν Πειραιᾶ towards
  the Piraeus
τε ... καί both ... and
τέλος finally
τήν the
τὴν ἀκρόπολιν the Acropolis
τί; what?
τὸν the
τὸν Παρθενῶνα the
  Parthenon
τό the
τὸ πλοῖ-ον the ship, vessel
ψόφ-ον a noise

Vocabulary to be learnt

δέ and; but
ἔπειτα then, next
καί and

τε ... καί A and B, both A
and B

Vocabulary for Section One B

ἀκού-ω I hear
ἀκού-εις you (s.) hear
ἀκού-ομεν we hear
ἄκου-ε listen! (s.)
ἀληθῆ the truth
ἀλλά but
ἆρα ?
αὖθις again
βλέπ-ε look! (s.)
γάρ for
δεῦρο here, over here
Δικαιόπολι Dikaiopolis
ἐγώ I
ἔγωγε I at least
ἐλθ-έ come! (s.)

ἐστι(ν) (it) is
Ζεῦ Zeus
Ζηνόθεμι Sdenothemis
ἡ the
ἡ ἀκρόπολις the Acropolis
ἡμεῖς we
ἰδού here! hey! look! (s.)
καί also
καλ-ός beautiful
καλ-ή beautiful
καλ-όν beautiful
κυβερνῆτα captain
κυβερνήτης captain
λέγ-εις you (s.) are speaking
μὰ Δία by Zeus

μή don't
ναί yes
νῦν now
ὁ Παρθενών the Parthenon
ὁ Πειραιεύς the Piraeus
ὁρ-ῶ I see
ὁρ-ᾷς you (s.) see
οὐ no
οὐδέν nothing
οὖν so, therefore
οὐχ not
ὁ ψόφ-ος the noise
ποῦ; where?
σαφ-ῶς clearly
σύ you (s.)

τὴν ἀκρόπολιν the Acropolis
τίς; what?
τὸ νεώριον the naval dockyard
τὸν Παρθενῶνα the Parthenon

τὸν Πειραιᾶ the Piraeus
τὸν ψόφον the noise
φρόντιζ-ε worry! (s.) (sc. 'about it')

ψόφ-ος a noise
ὦ O
ὡς how!

Vocabulary to be learnt
ἆρα ?
δεῦρο here, over here
ἐγώ I
καί also

σύ you (s.)
τίς; what? who?
ὦ O (addressing someone)

Vocabulary for Section One C

αἱ the
αἱ ὁλκάδες the merchant ships
ἀκού-ω I hear
ἀκού-ομεν we hear
ἄκου-ε listen! (s.)
ἀλλά but
βαίν-ετε you (pl.) are going
βλέπ-ετε look! (pl.)
γὰρ for
διὰ τί; why?
Δικαιόπολι Dikaiopolis
ἔγωγε I; I for my part
εἰσι(ν) (they) are
ἐλθ-έ come! (s.)
ἔλθ-ετε come! (pl.)

ἐστι(ν) (they) are
Ζηνόθεμι Sdenothemis
ἡμεῖς we
καλ-αί beautiful, fine
καλ-ά beautiful, fine
κατα-βαίν-ομεν we go down
κάτωθεν from below
λέγ-ε say! (s.)
μέν-ετε you (pl.) stay
μὴ don't
ὁρ-ῶ I see
ὁρ-ῶμεν (we) see
ὁρ-ᾶτε you (pl.) see
οὐκ not
ὁ ψόφ-ος the noise
πόθεν; from where?

ποῖ; where to?
Πόσειδον Poseidon (god of the sea)
σαφ-ῶς clearly
τὰ the
τὰ ἐμπόρι-α the markets
τὰς the
τὰς ὁλκάδας the merchant ships
τί μήν; so what?; of course
τὸν ψόφ-ον the noise
ὑμεῖς you (pl.)
φίλ-οι friends
φροντίζ-ετε worry! (pl.) (sc. 'about it')
ὡς how!

Vocabulary to be learnt
ἀλλά but
γάρ for
ἡμεῖς we

μή don't
οὐ, οὐκ, οὐχ no; not
ὡς how!

Vocabulary for Section One D

ἀκού-ω I hear
ἀληθῆ the truth
βλέπ-ε look! (s.)
βοηθ-εῖτε help! (pl.)

διὰ τί; why?
Δικαιόπολι Dikaiopolis
διώκ-ετε give chase! (pl.)
δύ-ει (he) is sinking

ἔγωγε I; I at least
ἐκ out of, from
ἐκ τοῦ πλοίου from the ship
ἐλθέ come! (s.)

ἐμαυτ-όν myself
ἐν τῇ δεξιᾷ in (his/your) right
  hand
ἔχ-ω (I) have/am holding
ἔχ-εις you (s.) have/are
  holding
ἔχ-ει (he) has/is holding
Ζεῦ Zeus
Ἡγέστρατ-ε Hegestratos
κατα-βαίν-ει (he) goes down
κατα-βαίν-ομεν we go down
κατα-βαίν-ουσι(ν) (they) go
  down
κατα-δύ-ει (he) is sinking
κάτω below
κάτωθεν from below
κυβερνῆτα captain
λαμβάν-ετε you (pl.)
  catch/seize
λέγ-εις you (s.) are saying

λέγ-ει (he) is telling
μέν ... δέ on one
  hand ... on the other
ναῦται sailors
ὁ ἄνθρωπ-ος the fellow
ὁ Δικαιόπολις Dikaiopolis
ὁ Ἡγέστρατ-ος Hegestratos
οἴμοι oh dear!
οἱ ναῦται the sailors, crew
ὁ κυβερνήτης the captain
ὁρ-ᾶτε you (pl.) see
ὁρ-ῶσι(ν) (they) see
οὐδέ and ... not
οὐδέν nothing
οὖν so, then, therefore
οὗτος hey, you!
ὁ ψόφ-ος the noise
πέλεκυς ⎫
πέλεκυν ⎬ an axe
ποι-ῶ (I) am doing

ποι-εῖς you (s.) are doing
ποι-εῖ (he) is making
ῥίπτ-ω I am throwing (going
  to throw)
ταν my dear chap
  (condescendingly)
τί; what?
τι something
τὸν ἄνθρωπ-ον the fellow
τὸν Ἡγέστρατ-ον
  Hegestratos
τὸν ψόφ-ον the noise
τὸ πλοῖ-ον the ship
ὑμεῖς you (pl.)
φεύγ-ω (I) am off
φίλ-ε friend
φρόντιζ-ε worry! (sc. 'about
  it')
ψόφ-ον οὐδένα any noise

Vocabulary to be learnt

ἀληθῆ the truth
ἔγωγε I; I at least/for my part
οὐδέν nothing

οὖν so, then, therefore
τί; what?
ὑμεῖς you (pl.)

Vocabulary for Section One E

ἄγε come on! (s.)
ἀνα-βαίν-ουσι (they) are
  coming up
ἄνω above
βλέπ-ει (he) looks
βοηθ-οῦσι (they) help
δή then; now
διώκ-ουσι(ν) (they)
  pursue/(give) chase
εἰς τὴν θάλατταν into the sea
ἐκ τοῦ πλοίου out of the ship
ἐν τῇ θαλάττῃ on the sea
ἐστί(ν) (it) is
Ζηνόθεμι Sdenothemis
ἤδη now; already
ἤδη γε yes, already
ἰδού look! (s.)

κάτωθεν from below
με me
μέν ... δέ on the one
  hand ... on the other
μέν-ει (he) stays/is waiting
μέν-ε stay! (s.)
ὁ Ζηνόθεμις Sdenothemis
ὁ Ἡγέστρατ-ος Hegestratos
οἱ ἄνδρες the men
οἴμοι oh dear!
οἱ ναῦται the sailors/crew
ὁ λέμβ-ος the life-boat
ὁρ-ῶ I see
ποῖ; where ... to?
ποι-εῖς you (s.) are doing
πρὸς τὸν Ζηνόθεμιν towards
  Sdenothemis

πρὸς τοὺς ναύτας towards the
  sailors
ῥίπτ-ε throw! (s.)
σεαυτ-όν yourself (s.)
σῷζ-ε save! (s.)
τῇ θαλάττῃ the sea
τὸν Ἡγέστρατ-ον
  Hegestratos
τοὺς the
  τοὺς ναύτας the sailors/crew
φεύγ-ω (I) am off
φεύγ-εις you (s.) are
  off/running away
φεύγ-ει (he) runs off
φεύγ-ε run away! be off! (s.)

Vocabulary to be learnt

μέν ... δέ on the one
hand ... on the other
ποῖ; where to?
σεαυτόν yourself (s.)

Vocabulary for Section One F

ἀπό from
ἀπὸ τοῦ πλοίου from the
  ship
ἀπο-θνῄσκ-ω I am dying
ἀπο-θνῄσκ-ομεν we are dying
ἀπο-θνῄσκ-ουσι(ν) (they) are
  dying
ἀπο-λύ-ει (he) lets go/releases
ἀπο-χωρ-εῖ (it) goes away
βοηθ-εῖτε help! (pl.)
Δικαιόπολι Dikaiopolis
ἑαυτ-ούς themselves
εἰς τὴν θάλατταν into the sea
εἰσι(ν) (they) are

ἐστι(ν) it is
Ζηνόθεμι Sdenothemis
ζητ-οῦσι(ν) they look for
Ἡγέστρατ-ε Hegestratos
κακ-οί bad
κακ-ῶς badly (tr. 'a bad
  death')
κυβερνῆτα captain
μέν-ουσι(ν) (they) wait
ναῦται sailors
ὁ Ἡγέστρατος Hegestratos
οἱ ἄνθρωπ-οι the fellows
οἴμοι alas! oh dear!
οἱ ναῦται the sailors/crew

ὁ κυβερνήτης the captain
ὁ λέμβ-ος the life-boat
ὁρ-ῶ I see
ὁρ-ᾷς you (s.) see
ὁρ-ῶσι(ν) (they) see
ποῦ; where?
ῥίπτ-ουσι(ν) (they) throw
τὴν φύγην their flight
τὸν λέμβ-ον the life-boat
τοὺς ἀνθρώπ-ους the fellows
φεύγ-ουσι(ν) they run away
φρόντιζ-ε worry! (s.) (sc.
  'about it')

Vocabulary to be learnt

οἴμοι alas! oh dear!
ποῦ; where?

Vocabulary for Section One G

ἀεί always
ἀκριβ-ῶς closely; in detail
ἀνα-βαίν-ει (he) comes up (on
  deck)
ἄνω above (on deck)
ἀπο-θνῄσκ-ομεν we are dying
ἀπο-χωρ-εῖ (it) goes away
βεβαία assured
διὰ τί; why?
Δικαιόπολι Dikaiopolis
ἐγγύς nearby
εἰς τὴν θάλατταν into the sea
εἰς τὸν λιμένα to the harbour
ἐκ τῆς θαλάττης out of the sea

ἐμ-όν mine
ἐν ἐμοί in my hands (lit. 'in
  me')
ἐν κινδύνῳ in danger
ἐσμέν we are
ἔστι(ν) (it) is
ἡ σωτηρία safety
ἡμᾶς us
θύ-ομεν we sacrifice
θυσίας sacrifices
καὶ δὴ καί and moreover
κακ-ῶς badly (tr. 'a bad
  death')
κατα-βαίν-ω (I) go down

κατα-βαίν-ει (he) goes down
κατα-δύν-ει (it) is sinking
μέν-ει (he) remains
νῦν now
ὁ Δικαιόπολις Dikaiopolis
ὁ κυβερνήτης the captain
ὁ λέμβ-ος the life-boat
ὁ λιμήν the harbour
περι-σκοπ-ῶ (I) look around
Πόσειδον Poseidon (god of the
  sea)
σιώπα be quiet! (s.)
σκοπ-εῖ (he) makes an
  examination, looks

σοι to you (s.)	σῶ-οι safe	τὸ πλοῖ-ον the ship
σῷζ-ε save! (s.)	σῶ-ον safe	τοὺς ἀνθρώπ-ους men
σῴζ-εις you (s.) save	τὸ ἔργ-ον the task	

Vocabulary to be learnt
διὰ τί; *why?*
νῦν *now*

O   Running grammar – preliminaries

Preliminaries

1 The aim of this running grammar is to describe, in terms as simple and practical as possible, the Greek language, so that students can understand the text and translate from Greek into English with the minimum difficulty. The Reference Grammar, at the end of this book (pp. 259–307), contains a slightly fuller picture of the language and presents morphology and syntax in summary form. The Language Surveys (pp. 308–34) examine in detail certain important features of the Greek language.

Warning: this running grammar is written to help students understand Greek and translate *from Greek into English*. Students will need more information from their teachers to translate English into Greek successfully, though help for the Greek–English exercises has been given very fully in the Greek–English vocabulary.

2 The early chapters will stress one essential difference between Greek and English – that is, that while in English the *order* in which the words occur is very important for determining the meaning of the sentence, in Greek the same function is expressed by the *shape* the words take. Consequently, words in a Greek sentence can come in a far greater variety of order than in English, according to what is being emphasised in the context.

3 Greek abounds in particles like δέ, δή, οὖν, γάρ, ἀλλά, etc. We have tried to give an English equivalent for each of these, but the resulting translation will often seem strained. This is because particles often indicate gesture, intonation, facial expression or attitude, which cannot necessarily be reproduced by a word-for-word translation. To get the particles right, you will often have to change your translation after the first effort (cf. Reference Grammar G).

Note
The hyphen which is used to split words up into their constituent parts (usually not more than two, though in theory one could use as many as five or six for certain words) is simply a device to indicate what part of the word stays fixed (we call

this part the 'stem') and what part changes (we call this part the 'ending'). You will find one or two slight inconsistencies in this terminology.

It should be stressed here that the positioning of the hyphen should not be taken to imply anything about the historical development of the language.

O Grammar for Section One A–G

Summary:
Pres. ind. act. -ω, -άω, -έω
Pres. imper. act. -ω, -άω, -έω
Def. art. ὁ ἡ τό (nom., acc.)
καλ-ός -ή -όν (ἡμέτερος) (nom., acc.)
ἄνθρωπος, ἔργον (nom., acc.)
Some preps.
μέν . . . δέ

Verbs
Present indicative active, βαίν-ω 'I go'

4 The forms of the pres. ind. act. are as follows:

Stem Ending	Meaning	Description
βαίν-ω	'I go/I am going'	*1st person singular (1st s.)*
βαίν-εις	'you go/you are going'	*2nd person singular (2nd s.)*
βαίν-ει	'he/she/it goes' (etc.)	*3rd person singular (3rd s.)*
βαίν-ομεν	'we go'	*1st person plural (1st pl.)*
βαίν-ετε	'you go'	*2nd person plural (2nd pl.)*
βαίν-ουσι(ν)	'they go'	*3rd person plural (3rd pl.)*

All uncontracted verbs ending in -ω follow this pattern. You have met ἀκούω, βλέπω, μένω, φεύγω, διώκω.

Note
This way of laying out a verb is called a 'conjugation'.

Present indicative active ('contracted'), ὁρά-ω 'I see', ποιέ-ω 'I do, make'

5 'Contracted' verbs are verbs of which the stem ends in a vowel (-α-, -ε- and, as we shall soon see, -ο-), e.g. ὁρά-ω, ποιέ-ω, δηλό-ω. The vowel coalesces with the vowel of the endings, with the result that the conjugation of contracted verbs looks different from that of uncontracted verbs; but the pattern on which they are originally based is identical.

Here are the contracted forms of ὁράω and ποιέω, with their earlier forms in parentheses after them, so that you can see the similarities:

1st s.	ὁρ-ῶ	(ὁρά-ω)	'I see'
2nd s.	ὁρ-ᾷς	(ὁρά-εις)	'you see'
3rd s.	ὁρ-ᾷ	(ὁρά-ει)	'he/she/it sees'
1st pl.	ὁρ-ῶμεν	(ὁρά-ομεν)	'we see'
2nd pl.	ὁρ-ᾶτε	(ὁρά-ετε)	'you see'
3rd pl.	ὁρ-ῶσι(ν)	(ὁρά-ουσι(ν))	'they see'
1st s.	ποι-ῶ	(ποιέ-ω)	'I do, make'
2nd s.	ποι-εῖς	(ποιέ-εις)	'you do'
3rd s.	ποι-εῖ	(ποιέ-ει)	'he/she/it does'
1st pl.	ποι-οῦμεν	(ποιέ-ομεν)	'we do'
2nd pl	ποι-εῖτε	(ποιέ-ετε)	'you do'
3rd pl.	ποι-οῦσι(ν)	(ποιέ-ουσι(ν))	'they do'

Of these types of verbs you have met ὁράω, ποιέω, σκοπέω, βοηθέω.

Notes

(i) English may use a pronoun to show who is doing the action (e.g. 'I', 'you', 'we', etc.). In Greek this is shown by the ending *of the verb, e.g.*

βαίν-<u>ω</u>   'I go'
βαίν-<u>ομεν</u> 'we go'

(ii) If the 3rd s. appears on its own with no stated subject, it means 'he, she, it – s', according to context. The same form is used when the subject is stated, e.g.

βαίνει *'he, she, it goes'*
ὁ ἄνθρωπος βαίνει *'the man goes'*

(iii) Note that Greek distinguishes between the s. and pl. forms of 'you'. Thus

βαίνεις *means 'you go' where one person is addressed*
βαίνετε *means 'you go' where more than one person is addressed*

Imperatives

6 The following forms, called imperatives, are used to express orders:

βαῖν-ε   'go!' *(s., addressed to one person)*
βαίν-ετε 'go!' *(pl., addressed to more than one person)*

Contract forms are slightly different:

ὅρ-α	(ὅρα-ε)	'see!' *(s.)*	ποί-ει	(ποίε-ε)	'do!, make!' *(s.)*
ὁρ-ᾶτε	(ὁρά-ετε)	'see!' *(pl.)*	ποι-εῖτε	(ποιέ-ετε)	'do!, make!' *(pl.)*

Notes

(i) You will notice that the plural order form is identical to that of the 2nd pl. of the indicative, i.e. βαίνετε *could mean 'go!' or 'you are going'. The context will tell you which is right.*

(ii) μή + *imperative means 'don't' e.g.* μὴ βαῖνε *'don't go!'*

(iii) Note the accent difference between ποίει *'do, act!', and* ποιεῖ *'he does, he acts'.*

Case

7 The technical term for the form which a noun takes when it is the subject of the sentence is the NOMINATIVE CASE; when it is the object of the sentence, the ACCUSATIVE CASE.

8 Consider the following sentence:

ὁ Ἡγέστρατος ὁρᾷ τὸν ἄνθρωπον 'Hegestratos sees the man'

As long as the words are in that form, it would make no odds what order the words occurred in; the sentence (apart from a slight difference of emphasis) would mean precisely the same – for Ἡγέστρατος is in the nominative case, indicating that he is subject of the sentence, and ἄνθρωπον is in the accusative case, indicating that it is object. And the definite articles also 'agree' with their nouns – ὁ (going with Hegestratos) is in the nominative, and τὸν (ἄνθρωπον) is in the accusative. If you wanted the sentence to mean 'the man sees Hegestratos', you would not need to alter the order of the words; but you would alter their case-forms, and make 'man' the subject (ὁ ἄνθρωπος) and 'Hegestratos' the object (τὸν Ἡγέστρατον):

τὸν Ἡγέστρατον ὁρᾷ ὁ ἄνθρωπος 'the man sees Hegestratos'

Note now the following sentence:

οἱ ἄνθρωποι ὁρῶσι τὸν Ἡγέστρατον 'the men see Hegestratos'

The verb here has changed its shape, because the subject of the sentence is no longer singular (ὁ ἄνθρωπος 'man'), but plural (οἱ ἄνθρωποι 'men') – so the verb must be plural too.

Finally, observe that, while word-order plays a very important role indeed for determining meaning in English, English words do also change their form to indicate different functions, e.g.

book (s.), book*s* (pl.)

I walk, he walk*s*

he/him; she/her; I/me.

'the cat lies down', 'where is the cat'*s* bowl?'

Note

There are in fact five cases for each Greek noun or adjective, and each case has a singular form and a plural form. (For the dual, see p. 239.) The cases are:

NOMINATIVE *(nom.)*
ACCUSATIVE *(acc.)*
GENITIVE *(gen.)*
DATIVE *(dat.)*
VOCATIVE *(voc.) (We shall comment only occasionally on this case.)*
We shall list all cases of nouns and adjectives, but for the moment you must concentrate on nom. *and* acc. *only and ensure that you know those forms.*

The definite article and adjectives

9 The forms of the def. art., which corresponds roughly to English 'the', are as follows:

ὁ ἡ τό *'the'*

s.					pl.			
nom.	*acc.*	*gen.*	*dat.*		*nom.*	*acc.*	*gen.*	*dat.*
ὁ	τόν	του	τῳ		οἱ	τούς	των	τοις
masculine (used with masculine nouns)								
ἡ	τήν	της	τῇ		αἱ	τάς	των	ταις
feminine (used with feminine nouns)								
τό	τό	του	τῳ		τά	τά	των	ταις
neuter (used with neuter nouns)								

There are three types of form, masculine (m.) forms, feminine (f.) forms and neuter (n.) forms, since Greek distinguishes three types of noun, m., f., and n. The distinction of m., f., and n. is one of 'gender'. The m., f. and n. genders do not simply correspond to 'male', 'female' and 'inanimate', e.g.

τὸ μειράκιον (n.) 'the boy'
ὁ ψόφος (m.) 'the noise'
ἡ θάλαττα (f.) 'the sea'

10 For the beginner, the definite article is very useful. For it *marks the case, and therefore the function* of the noun for you. When you find ὁ, ἡ, οἱ, αἱ, linked to a noun, you know it must be the subject; τόν, τήν, τούς, τάς linked to a noun indicate that it is the object (unless preceded by a preposition). You will already have observed the use of *linking devices* in the text to help you in this respect.

Thus you can define the function of the following nouns without knowing how they decline, simply because you know the function of the definite article:

τὴν‿πόλιν, τὸν‿βασιλέα, οἱ‿γέροντες, τὰς‿τριήρεις.

Note
In the early chapters, the def. art. will almost always come before its noun.

11 This rule of agreement applies to the relationship between all nouns and adjectives, and is very important. Masculine nouns will force the adjective to take its masculine form; feminine nouns will force it to adopt its feminine form; and neuter nouns, its neuter form.

12 You have already met the adjective καλός 'fine, beautiful'. Here it is in all its forms:

καλ-ός -ή -όν *'fine, beautiful'*

	s.				pl.			
	nom.	acc.	gen.	dat.	nom.	acc.	gen.	dat.
m.	καλ-ός	καλ-όν	καλ-οῦ	καλ-ῷ	καλ-οί	καλ-ούς	καλ-ῶν	καλ-οῖς
f.	καλ-ή	καλ-ήν	καλ-ῆς	καλ-ῇ	καλ-αί	καλ-άς	καλ-ῶν	καλ-αῖς
n.	καλ-όν	καλ-όν	καλ-οῦ	καλ-ῷ	καλ-ά	καλ-ά	καλ-ῶν	καλ-οῖς

Note
(i) Compare together the forms of the definite article and adjectives of the καλός type. You will see pleasing similarities between all their forms which means that learning one type lets you into the secret of a great many other types.
(ii) Adjectives of which the stem ends in ρ, ε, ι (e.g. ἡμέτερ-ος 'our(s)') decline like καλός, except that the feminine singular retains -α instead of -η all the way through, i.e.
    f. *ἡμετέρ-α* *ἡμετέρ-αν* *ἡμετέρ-ας* *ἡμετέρ-ᾳ*
(iii) Some adjectives of the καλός type keep the masculine endings even when describing feminine nouns. Such adjectives are dealt with at **141**.

Adverbs

13 These are undeclined forms, usually based on adjectives, nearly always formed by adding -ῶς or -έως to the adjective stem: e.g.

    καλός 'fine'   καλῶς 'finely'
    σαφής 'clear'   σαφῶς 'clearly'
    ἀκριβής 'accurate'   ἀκριβῶς 'accurately'
    βαθύς 'deep'   βαθέως 'deeply'

Cf. Language Survey (13) (iii), p. 329.

Nouns

14 Here is the full 'declension', as it is called, of all nouns like ἄνθρωπος, which is classified as TYPE 2A: almost all 2a nouns are MASCULINE.

ἄνθρωπ-ος, ὁ 'man, fellow' (2a)

s.

nom.	acc.	gen.	dat.	VOC.
ἄνθρωπ-ος	ἄνθρωπ-ον	ἀνθρώπ-ου	ἀνθρώπ-ῳ	αν θρω γ - ε

pl.

nom.	acc.	gen.	dat.
ἄνθρωπ-οι	ἀνθρώπ-ους	ἀνθρώπ-ων	ἀνθρώπ-οις

15 Here is the full declension of all nouns like ἔργον, classified as TYPE 2B and NEUTER

ἔργον, τό 'task, duty, job' (2b)

s.				pl.			
nom.	acc.	gen.	dat.	nom	acc.	gen.	dat.
ἔργ-ον	ἔργ-ον	ἔργ-ου	ἔργ-ῳ	ἔργ-α	ἔργ-α	ἔργ-ων	ἔργ-οις

Other 2b nouns you have met are νεώρι-ον, ἐμπόρι-ον.

> *Notes*
> *(i) Nom. and acc. are the same in s. and pl. of all neuter nouns. Only the context will tell you whether the word is to be taken as subject or object.*
> *(ii) Neuter nouns normally take a SINGULAR VERB, even when they are in the plural, e.g.*
>
> τὰ ἐμπόριά ἐστι καλά 'the markets are fine'
>
> *(iii) Compare the declension of these two nouns with the m. and n. forms of the adjectives like καλός and the def. art., and note the similarities.*
> *(iv) The vocative case is used when addressing people. The vocative s. of 2a nouns ends in -ε, e.g. ὦ ἄνθρωπε, τί ποιεῖς; 'Fellow, what are you doing?'*

Prepositions

16 Note that εἰς 'into' and πρός 'towards' take the acc. case. Note also that ἀπό 'away from', ἐκ 'out of, from' and ἐν 'in' take the genitive (ἀπο, ἐκ) and dative (ἐν) AND NO OTHER CASES. Consequently their meaning is fixed, and you need not worry for the moment about the form of the word which follows them. You will be dealing with genitives and datives later on.

quaerereὁράωx

Particles

17 One extremely important feature of the Greek language (and of Greek thought too) is the Greek love of drawing a contrast (even, at times, when there is not really one to be drawn). Such a contrast can be signalled by μέν 'on the one hand', which will usually be picked up by δέ 'on the other hand' later on. A smoother translation results if you translate with 'while' or 'but', e.g. not 'on the one hand he runs away, on the other hand the sailors pursue', but 'while he runs away, the sailors pursue' or '*he* runs away, but the sailors pursue'.

Vocabulary to be learnt with the grammar for Section One A–G

ἀκούω hear, listen
ἀναβαίνω (ἀναβα-)* go/come up
ἄνθρωπος, ὁ man; fellow (2a)
ἀπό (+gen.) from; away from
ἀποθνῄσκω (ἀποθαν-)* die
ἀποχωρέω go away, depart
βαίνω (βα-)* go/come, walk
βλέπω look (at)
βοηθέω run to help, help
διώκω pursue
εἰς (+acc.) to, into, onto
ἐκ (+gen.) out of
ἐλθέ come! (s.)

ἐν (+dat.) in; on; among
ἔχω (σχ-)* have; hold
θάλαττα, ἡ sea
κακός ή όν bad, evil, cowardly, lowly, mean
καλός ή όν fine, beautiful; good
καταβαίνω (καταβα-)* go/come down
κυβερνήτης, ὁ captain, helmsman
λέγω (εἰπ-)* say; speak; tell; mean
μένω (μειν-)* remain; wait for
ναύτης, ὁ sailor

ὁράω (ἰδ-)* see
πλέω (πλευσ-)* sail
πλοῖον, τό vessel; ship (2b)
ποιέω make; do
πρός (+acc.) to; towards
ῥίπτω throw
σῴζω save
σῶος α ον safe
σωτηρία, ἡ safety
φεύγω (φυγ-)* run off; flee
φίλος, ὁ friend (2a)
φροντίζω think; worry

* These parenthesised forms must be learnt with the word. They are very important stems of the verb (though different, as you can see, from the present), which will be introduced fully in later sections.

Exercises – notes

You should only do the exercises after the Text is read, the Vocabulary learnt, and the Grammar understood.

For ease of reference there are five divisions in the exercises:

(a) Words – vocabulary-building exercises, based on words you have already met. These are provided for Sections One–Ten only.

(b) Morphology⎱ practising forms and their manipulation in sentences.
(c) Syntax ⎰

(d) English into Greek – preceded in Sections One–Four by Greek–English patterns. English–Greek sentences appear from then on at convenient intervals. Each section has a passage of prose in addition. There is an English–Greek vocabulary at the end of the book; please use this wherever you find problems. It has been specially written to help with the exercises in this volume.

(e) Test exercises – these occur at the end of each section (twice in One and Six) and test grammar and vocabulary from the section just completed. They should be done as written exercises, without help from vocabulary or grammar, *after all other work on a section has been completed.*

No exercises are provided for the unadapted sections (Fourteen, Eighteen and Nineteen.)

Exercises for Section One A–G

(a) Words

1. From the words in the left-hand column (which you have met) deduce the meaning of those on the right:

βαίνω	ἐκβαίνω
διώκω	ἐκδιώκω
θάλαττα	θαλάττιος α ον
κυβερνήτης	κυβερνῶ
ναύτης	ναυτικός ή όν
ὁρῶ	εἰσορῶ
πλέω | πλοῖον	ὁ πλοῦς (=πλό -ος, contr.)
φεύγω	ἀποφεύγω

(b) Morphology

1. Translate each word, then give the plural form:
βαίν-εις, βλέπ-ω, ποι-εῖ, ὁρ-ᾷ, βοήθ-ει
2. Translate each word, then give the singular form:
φροντίζ-ετε, κατα-βαίν-ουσι, ἀνα-βαίν-ομεν, ὁρ-ᾶτε, ἀπο-χωρ-εῖτε
3. Fit the appropriate form of the definite article to the following nouns:
ἄνθρωπ-οι, ψόφ-ος, πλοῖ-α, λέμβ-ον (2a), νεώρι-ον (2b), ἀνθρώπ-ους
4. Put the adjective and noun into the correct form:
a. ὁ καλ- ἄνθρωπ-
b. τὰ καλ- νεώρι-
c. τὸ καλ- ἐμπόρι-
d. τοὺς καλ- ἀνθρώπ-
e. τὸν καλ- ἄνθρωπ-

(d) English into Greek

Translate these pairs of sentences:
1. ὁ Ζηνόθεμις βαίνει εἰς τὸ πλοῖον.
The man runs off towards the boat.

2. καλός ἐστιν ὁ Παρθενών.
   The ship is safe.
3. ἆρα οὐχ ὁρᾷς σὺ τὴν ἀκρόπολιν;
   Can you (s.) see the men too?
4. δεῦρο ἔλθετε καὶ βλέπετε.
   Come and help (pl.)! Chase the man! Don't run away!
5. οἱ ἄνθρωποι ἀναβαίνουσιν.
   The friends are waiting.

Test Exercise One A–G
Translate into English (n.b. underlined words are given in the vocabulary):

τὸ πλοῖον ἀποχωρεῖ μὲν ἀπὸ τῆς Εὐβοίας, πλεῖ δὲ πρὸς τὸν Πειραιᾶ. ὁ μὲν Ζηνόθεμις βλέπει πρὸς τὴν γῆν. ὁ δὲ Ἡγέστρατος κάτω μένει καὶ καταδύει τὸ πλοῖον. πέλεκυν γὰρ ἔχει ὁ ἄνθρωπος. ἄνω δέ εἰσιν ὁ κυβερνήτης καὶ ὁ Δικαιόπολις. βλέπουσι πρὸς τὴν γῆν καὶ ὁρῶσι τά τε νεώρια καὶ τὸν Παρθενῶνα. ἀλλὰ ἐξαίφνης ἀκούουσι τὸν ψόφον. ἔπειτα δὲ καταβαίνουσιν.

ΚΥΒΕΡΝΗΤΗΣ τίς ποιεῖ τὸν ψόφον; ἆρα ὁρᾷς, ὦ Δικαιόπολι;
ΔΙΚΑΙΟΠΟΛΙΣ ναί· ὁρῶ ἔγωγε· ὁ γὰρ Ἡγέστρατος τὸν ψόφον ποιεῖ.
         πέλεκυν γὰρ ἔχει ἐν τῇ δεξιᾷ.
ΚΥΒ.   μὴ μένετε, ὦ ναῦται, ἀλλὰ βοηθεῖτε καὶ διώκετε τὸν ἄνθρωπον.

ὁ μὲν Ἡγέστρατος φεύγει κάτωθεν, ὁ δὲ Ζηνόθεμις ἄνω μένει. οἱ μὲν ναῦται ἀναβαίνουσι κάτωθεν. οἱ δὲ ἄνθρωποι τοὺς ναύτας σαφῶς ὁρῶσι καὶ ῥίπτουσιν ἑαυτοὺς εἰς τὴν θάλατταν. εἰς τὴν μὲν θάλατταν φεύγουσιν οἱ ἄνθρωποι, ἐν δὲ τῇ θαλάττῃ ἀποθνῄσκουσιν.

Vocabulary (in order of occurrence in the text)

τὴν γῆν the land
κάτω below
καταδύω sink
πέλεκυν axe (acc.)
νεώριον, τό dockyard (2b)

ἐξαίφνης suddenly
ψόφος, ὁ noise (2a)
τῇ δεξιᾷ his right hand
κάτωθεν from below
ἑαυτούς themselves

Vocabulary for Section One H

ἀεί always
ἀκριβ-ῶς closely
δῆλόν ἐστι(ν) it is clear
διά (+acc.) because of

εἶ you (s.) are
ἐστι(ν) he/there/it is
ἐσμεν (we) are
εἰσι(ν) (they) are

ἐπί (+acc.) over
ἐρωτά-ω ask
ἡμᾶς us
ἡ ναῦς the ship

κοίλη ἐνὶ νηὶ in a hollow ship
κυβερνά-ω steer
κυβερνῆτα captain (voc.)
μέλαινα .black (nom.)
μῶρ-ος -α -ον stupid
ναῦτα sailor (voc.)
ναῦται sailors (voc.)
ναύτης τις a sailor (nom.)
νηὶ θοῇ a swift ship
νηὶ μελαίνῃ a black ship
νύξ night (nom.)

οἴνοπα πόντον the wine-faced
  sea (acc.)
ὁ ναύτης the sailor
ὁ Σωκράτης Socrates
οἶδα I know
οἶσθα you (s.) know
οἶδε(ν) (he) knows
ὁμηρίζ-ω quote Homer
ὅτι that
παίζ-ω (πρός +acc.) joke (at)
ῥαψῳδ-ός, ὁ rhapsode (2a)

ῥαψῳδ-ός τις a rhapsode
σαφ-ῶς clearly
σιωπά-ω be quiet
τᾶν my dear chap
  (condescendingly)
τὴν νύκτα the night/dark
τί τό what's this?
τὸν κυβερνήτην the captain
τὸν λιμένα the harbour
τοὺς μαθητάς the/his students
τῷ πλοίῳ the ship
ὥσπερ like

Vocabulary to be learnt

δῆλος η ον clear; obvious
ὅτι that
παίζω (πρός +acc.) play; joke
  (at)

ῥαψῳδός, ὁ rhapsode (2a)
σαφῶς clearly

Vocabulary for Section One I

ἀπαίδευτ-ος -ον an
  ignoramus
γιγνώσκ-ω know
διότι because
εἰμι I am
εἶ you (s.) are
ἐστί(ν) (he) is
ἐμ-ός -ή -όν my
ἔμπειρ-ος -ον experienced
ἔργ-ον, τό work, task (2b)
ἡ ναῦς the ship
ἤ or
θο-ός -ή -όν swift
κοῖλ-ος -η -ον hollow

μὰ Δία by Zeus
μέλαινα black (nom.)
μὲν οὖν no rather
μῶρ-ος -α -ον stupid
ναί yes
ναυτικ-ά, τά naval matters
  (2b)
οἶσθα you (s.) know
Ὅμηρ-ος, ὁ Homer (2a) (epic
  poet, author of the Iliad and
  Odyssey)
περὶ (+acc.)   about, with
  regard to
περὶ Ὁμήρου about Homer

πολεμικ-ός -ή -όν of war
πολλὰ many things (acc.)
πότερον . . . ἤ whether . . . or
πῶς how?
πῶς γὰρ οὔ; of course
στρατηγικ-ά, τά generalship
  (2b)
στρατηγικ-ός -ή -όν of a
  general
στρατιωτικ-ά, τά soldiering
  (2b)
τί δέ; what next?

Vocabulary to be learnt

γιγνώσκω (γνο-) know;
  perceive; resolve
ἔμπειρος ον skilled, experienced
ἔργον, τό task, job (2b)

μῶρος α ον stupid; foolish
περί (+acc.) about
πολλά many things (acc.)
ναί yes

Vocabulary for Section One J

ἀγαθ-ός -ή -όν good
ἀεί always
ἀκριβ-ῶς accurately

ἅμα at the same time
ἄριστ-ος -η -ον best
δήπου of course

εἶ you (s.) are
ἐστι(ν) (he/it) is
εἰσι(ν) (they) are

ἐμέ me
ἡ ναῦς the ship
ἡ ῥαψῳδική the rhapsode's skill
ἡ στρατηγική the general's skill
ἤ or
θο-ός -ή -όν swift
κοῖλ-ος -η -ον hollow
μάλιστα yes, indeed

μέλαινα black (nom.)
μέντοι yes indeed
μία τέχνη one and the same skill (nom.)
ναῦται sailors (voc.)
νὴ Δία by Zeus
οἱ Ἕλληνες the Greeks
οἶδε(ν) (he) knows
ὁ Σωκράτης Socrates
οὔκουν not . . . therefore

οὕτως thus, in this way
παῖδες children (nom.)
πότερον . . . ἤ whether . . . or
πῶς γὰρ οὔ; of course
στρατηγ-ός, ὁ general (2a)
Σωκράτε-ω play Socrates
τοὺς μαθητάς the/his students
τῶν Ἑλλήνων of the Greeks

Vocabulary to be learnt
ἀεί always
ἀκριβῶς accurately; closely
ἄριστος η ον best; very good
εἰμί be
Ἕλλην, ὁ Greek

ἤ or
ναῦς, ἡ ship
οἶδα know
πῶς γὰρ οὔ; of course
στρατηγός, ὁ general (2a)

O   Grammar for Section One H–J

Summary:
Pres. of εἰμί, οἶδα
N. pl. of adjs.
τε . . . καί

Verbs
Some irregular presents, εἰμί 'I am', οἶδα 'I know'

18 Note the verb 'to be' in the present:

εἰμί	'I am'	*1st s.*
εἶ	'you are'	*2nd s.*
ἐστί(ν)	'he/she/it is'	*3rd s.*
ἐσμέν	'we are'	*1st pl.*
ἐστέ	'you are'	*2nd pl.*
εἰσί(ν)	'they are'	*3rd pl.*

19 Note the verb 'to know' in the present:

οἶδα	'I know'	*1st s.*
οἶσθα	'you know'	*2nd s.*
οἶδε	'he/she/it/knows'	*3rd s.*
ἴσμεν	'we know'	*1st pl.*
ἴστε	'you know'	*2nd pl.*
ἴσασι(ν)	'they know'	*3rd pl.*

Notes

(i) *The verb 'to be' does not need to appear in a sentence if it can be assumed.* Cf. *English 'Let's pretend that the sea is red, the sky (is) green and the air (is) blue', and the very common* καλός *inscriptions on Greek pots, e.g.*

Μέμνων καλός *'Memnon (is) handsome'*

(ii) *In the sentence 'the Word was God', 'Word' is the subject, while 'God' is traditionally called the complement. In Greek, the complement does not normally have a definite article.*

(iii) *Complements always agree in case with the word with which they go; this is normally the nominative case.*

Nouns

20 πολλά means 'many things'. It is, in fact, the neuter plural of an adjective meaning 'much, many', and as neuter plural can take on the meaning 'many things'. In a similar way, στρατηγικός means 'of a general', but in the neuter plural with a def. art., τὰ στρατηγικά, it means 'a general's business', or 'generalship'. This use of the n. pl. of an adjective, especially when linked with the def. art., is very common, e.g.

τὰ ναυτικά 'naval matters'

τὰ στρατιωτικά 'military matters'

Particles

21 τε . . . τε and τε . . . καί link two words or phrases together ('both . . . and'), e.g.

ὅ τε Δικαιόπολις καὶ ὁ ῥαψῳδός 'Dikaiopolis and the rhapsode'

ὁρᾷ τε ὁ ἄνθρωπος καὶ φεύγει 'the man sees and runs'

Note the position of τε in these phrases.   O

Exercises for Section One H–J

(a) Words

1. From the words in the left-hand column deduce the meaning of those on the right:

ἀποχωρῶ	περιχωρῶ
βαίνω	περιβαίνω
δῆλος	δηλῶ
εἰμί	ἔνειμι
Ἕλλην	Ἑλληνικός ή όν
μένω	περιμένω
στρατηγός	στρατηγῶ

(b) Morphology

1. Translate each verb, then change to the singular or plural form as appropriate:

ἐστέ, γιγνώσκει, οἶσθα, ἐστί, ἴσασι, παῖζε, εἰμί, ἴσμεν

(c) Syntax

1. Translate these sentences:
   a. ὁ ῥαψῳδός ἐστιν Ἕλλην.
   b. ὁ Ἕλλην ἐστὶν ἄνθρωπος.
   c. στρατηγοὶ ἄριστοί εἰσιν οἱ ῥαψῳδοί.
   d. μῶρός ἐστιν ὁ ῥαψῳδός.
   e. κυβερνήτης ὁ ἄνθρωπος.

(d) English into Greek
Translate these pairs of sentences:

1. δῆλόν ἐστιν ὅτι ὁ Δικαιόπολις παίζει πρὸς τὸν ῥαψῳδόν.
   It is clear that the rhapsode knows many things.
2. ἔμπειρός εἰμι ἐγὼ περὶ πολλά.
   You are not experienced in the job.
3. οἱ ῥαψῳδοί εἰσι στρατηγοὶ ἄριστοι.
   The best general is a rhapsode.
4. ἆρ' οὐκ οἶσθα ὅτι ὁ ἄνθρωπος παίζει ἀεί;
   Doesn't he know that the rhapsode is speaking accurately?
5. ἔμπειρος μὲν οὐκ εἶ, μῶρος δέ.
   But I am not a fool; I know a lot.

Test Exercise One H–J
Translate into English:

τὸ μὲν οὖν πλοῖον πλεῖ πρὸς τὸν Πειραιᾶ. οἱ δὲ ναῦται οὐκ ἴσασι ποῦ ἐστι τὸ πλοῖον.
   ἐρωτῶσιν οὖν τὸν κυβερνήτην ποῦ ἐστιν. ὁ μὲν κυβερνήτης λέγει ὅτι ἐγγὺς τοῦ λιμένος ἐστὶ τὸ πλοῖον. ἐξαίφνης δὲ ὁ ῥαψῳδὸς ὁμηρίζει. καὶ δῆλόν ἐστιν ὅτι πολλὰ γιγνώσκει περὶ Ὁμήρου ὁ ἄνθρωπος. ὁ δὲ Δικαιόπολις παίζει πρὸς τὸν ῥαψῳδόν.

ΔΙΚΑΙΟΠΟΛΙΣ   ἆρα γιγνώσκεις τὰ ῥαψῳδικά, ὦ ῥαψῳδέ;
ΡΑΨΩΙΔΟΣ   πῶς δὲ οὔ; γιγνώσκω δὲ καὶ τὰ στρατηγικά.
ΔΙΚ.   τί λέγεις; ῥαψῳδὸς γὰρ εἶ καὶ οὐ στρατηγός.
ΡΑΨ.   ἆρα οὐκ οἶσθα ὅτι ὁ <u>ἀγαθὸς</u> ῥαψῳδός ἐστιν <u>ἅμα</u> καὶ στρατηγὸς ἀγαθός;

ΔΙΚ. οὐκ, ἀλλὰ οἶδα ὅτι σὺ μῶρος εἶ, ὦ ῥαψῳδέ. σὺ μὲν γὰρ ῥαψῳδὸς εἶ <u>τῶν Ἑλλήνων</u> ἄριστος καὶ ἔμπειρος περὶ τοῦ Ὁμήρου. περὶ δὲ τὰ στρατηγικὰ οὐκ ἔμπειρος εἶ, <u>οὐδὲ</u> οἶσθα οὐδὲν ἀκριβῶς.

Vocabulary

ἐγγὺς τοῦ λιμένος near the harbour
ἐξαίφνης suddenly
ὁμηρίζω recite Homer

ἀγαθός ή όν good
ἅμα at the same time
τῶν Ἑλλήνων of the Greeks
οὐδὲ and ... not

Section Two

Vocabulary for Section Two A

ἄγε come! (s.)
ἀλλήλ-ους one another (acc.)
βάρβαρ-ος, ὁ barbarian,
  Persian (2a)
βραδέ-ως slowly
γίγν-εται (it) happens
δή now, then (with
  imperative)
δια-λέγ-ονται (they) converse
δι-έρχ-εται (he) relates
ἐκεῖ there
ἔρχ-εται (it) is going
ἐρχ-όμεθα (we) are going
ἡδέ-ως gladly, with pleasure
ἤδη now
ἡμῖν to us
ἡσυχάζ-ω keep quiet

κάλλιστ-ος -η -ον very, most
  beautiful
λόγ-ος, ὁ story (2a)
μάλιστα yes, indeed; very
  well
μάχ-ονται (they) fight
Μηδικ-ά, τά the Persian Wars
  (2b)
Μῆδ-ος, ὁ Persian (2a)
ναῦτ-αι sailors
νῆσ-ος, ἡ island (2a)
οἱ Ἕλληνες the Greeks
οἱ ναῦτ-αι the sailors, crew
ὁπόσ-οι -αι -α how many?
οὐ γάρ; is he not?
παρά (+ acc.) past, along
περὶ Ὁμήρου about Homer

πίπτ-ω fall, die
ῥητορικ-ά, τά rhetoric (2b)
ῥητορικ-ός -ή -όν rhetorical
Σαλαμῖνα Salamis (acc.)
τὰ πράγματα events
τὰς Ἀθήν-ας Athens
τὴν ἡμετέρ-αν τόλμ-αν our
  courage
τὴν ναυμαχί-αν the naval
  battle
τὴν νίκ-ην the/our victory
τὴν Σαλαμῖνα Salamis
τίνα ἔργα what deeds (acc.)
τοῖς Μηδικοῖς the Persian
  Wars
τολμά-ω dare, undertake
τὸν Πειραιᾶ the Piraeus

Vocabulary to be learnt
ἡδέως with pleasure, sweetly
ἤδη by now, now, already
παρά (+ acc.) along, beside

Vocabulary for Section Two B

ἀγαθ-ός -ή -όν good
ἄειδ-ε sing! (s.)
Ἀθηναῖ-ος, ὁ Athenian (2a)

αἱ ἀπορί-αι the perplexities,
  distress
αἱ βο-αί the shouts

αἱ ἱκετεῖ-αι the supplications
αἱ νῆες the ships
αἱ τῶν Ἀθηναί-ων (the ships)
  of the Athenians

ἀπορέ-ω be at a loss, be perplexed
ἀφ-ικν-οῦνται (they) arrive
βάρβαρ-ος, ὁ Persian, barbarian (2a)
βέβαι-ος -α -ον secure
βραδέ-ως slowly
γίγν-εται (it) becomes
διά (+acc.) on account of
εἰσ-βαίν-ω embark
ἐλευθερ-οῦσι(ν) (they) set free
ἡ ἀπορί-α the perplexity, distress
ἡ ἀρετ-ή (the) courage, excellence
ἡ ἐλευθερί-α (the) freedom
ἡ στρατι-ά the army
ἡ τόλμ-α (the) courage
ἡ τῶν Ἑλλήνων (the courage) of the Greeks
Θε-ά goddess (voc.)
θύ-ω (make a) sacrifice
κίνδυν-ος, ὁ danger (2a)

μάχ-ονται (they) fight
μῆνιν οὐλομένην destructive wrath (acc.)
ναυτικ-όν, τό the navy (2b)
νικά-ω defeat, win
Ξέρξου θείου βασιλῆος of Xerxes, the god-like king
οἱ Ἕλληνες the Greeks
οἱ Πέρσ-αι the Persians
ὀλίγ-οι -αι -α few
ὅσ-οι -αι -α how many!
οὕτως thus, so
πίπτ-ω fall, die
πολλ-αί many (nom.)
πολλ-ή much (nom.)
πολ-ὺς much, great (nom.)
πολλὰ εὔχ-ονται they make many prayers
προσ-έρχ-εται (it) advances
προσ-έρχ-ονται (they) advance
τὰς θυσί-ας the sacrifices

τὰς ναῦς their ships
ταχέ-ως quickly
τέλος finally
τῇ ναυμαχί-ᾳ the naval battle
τὴν Ἑλλάδα Greece
τὴν πατρίδα the(ir) fatherland
τὴν πόλιν the city
τὴν τόλμ-αν their courage
τὴν ὕβριν the aggression
τοῖς θεοῖς to the gods
τὸ πλῆθος superior numbers
τῶν Ἀθηναί-ων of the Athenians
τῶν Ἑλλήνων of the Greeks
τῶν θε-ῶν of the gods
τῶν Περσ-ῶν of the Persians
τῶν στρατηγ-ῶν of their generals
ὑπὲρ τῆς ἐλευθερί-ας for freedom
φόβ-ος, ὁ fear (2a)
φοβ-οῦνται (they) fear

Vocabulary to be learnt

ἀγαθός ή όν good, noble, courageous
Ἀθηναῖος, ὁ Athenian (2a)
ἀπορέ-ω be at a loss; have no resources
βέβαιος α ον secure

βραδέως slowly
νικάω win, defeat
ὅσος η ον how great!
πίπτω (πεσ-) fall, die
τέλος in the end, finally

Vocabulary for Section Two C

ἀγών the contest (nom.)
αἱ νῆες the ships
ἀληθῶς truthfully
ἅμα at the same time
ἅμα ἕῳ at daybreak
αὖθις again
ἀφ-ικν-εῖται (it) arrives
βο-ή τις a shout
γίγν-εται there is, it becomes
γυναῖκας your wives (acc.)
δή then, now
ἐγγὺς Σαλαμῖνος near Salamis

ἐλευθερ-οῦτε free! (pl.)
Ἑλλήνων of the Greeks
ἐμ-ός -ή -όν my
ἔνθα καὶ ἔνθα this way and that
ἐν τοῖς βαρβάροις among the barbarians
ἐπειδή when
ζητέ-ω seek, look for
ἤδη now, already
ἡμῖν to us
ἡ σάλπιγξ trumpet

ἡσυχί-αν ἔχ-ω keep quiet
ἠχέ-ω echo
ἴσως perhaps
ἴτε come! (pl.)
κάλλιστ-ος -η -ον very fine, most lovely
καλόν τινα λόγον a fine tale
λόγ-ος, ὁ story, tale (2a)
μέντοι still, nonetheless
μοι to me
ναῦτ-αι sailors (voc.)
ναυτικ-όν, τό navy (2b)

νύξ night
οἱ Ἕλληνες the Greeks
οὐδὲν λέγ-ω speak nonsense
οὔκουν not . . . therefore
παῖδες children (voc.)
παῖδας your children (acc.)
πάππ-ος, ὁ grandfather (2a)
πατρίδ᾽ = πατρίδα fatherland
   (acc.)
πολλάκις often
πότερον . . . ἤ whether . . . or
Σαλαμῖνα Salamis (acc.)

Σαλαμινομάχ-ης a soldier at
   Salamis
σιωπά-ω be quiet
σκοπέ-ω look
τὰ ἀληθῆ the truth
τὰ πράγματα the events
τὰ περὶ . . . (the events)
   around
τὰ τῶν Ἑλλήνων (the fine
   deeds) of the Greeks
τὴν βο-ὴν the shout
τοῖς βαρβάροις the barbarians

τὸ ποίημα the poem
τῶν Ἑλλήνων of the Greeks
τῶν Περσ-ῶν of the Persians
τῶν πετρ-ῶν the rocks
ὑπὲρ πάντων for everything
φής you (s.) say
φόβ-ος, ὁ fear (2a)
ψευδῆ lies (acc.)
ψευδ-ῶς falsely
ὧδε as follows, thus
ὥσπερ like

Vocabulary to be learnt

ἅμα at the same time
αὖθις again,
βάρβαρος, ὁ barbarian,
   foreigner (2a)
ἐμός ή όν my, mine

ἡσυχάζω be quiet, keep quiet
κάλλιστος η ον most/very
   fine/beautiful/good
λόγος, ὁ story, tale (2a)
πότερον . . . ἤ whether . . . or

σιωπά-ω be silent
σκοπέ-ω look (at), consider
ψευδῶς falsely

Vocabulary for Section Two D

ἀκόσμ-ως in disorder
ἀλλήλοις to one another
ἀλλήλ-ους one another (acc.)
ἄλλ-ος -η -ο other, rest of
ἀνα-χωρέ-ω retreat
ἀτάκτ-ως out of rank
γίγν-ονται (they) become
δειν-ός -ή -όν terrible, dire
διὰ (+acc.) because of
ἐλεύθερ-ος -α -ον free
ἐξαίφνης suddenly, out of the
   blue
ἐπειδὴ when, since, because
ἐπ-έρχονται they advance
   against
ἐπὶ (+acc.) to, against,
   towards
ἐπι-πλέ-ω sail forward
   attack
ἔτι still
εὖ well
ἡ μεταβολ-ή the change
θε-ᾶται (he) watches, gazes at

θε-ός, ὁ god (2a)
κατὰ (+acc.) by, in,
   according to
κολάζ-ω punish
κόσμῳ in order
κυβερνήτα captain
λαμβάν-ω capture, take
μάλα very
μαχ-όμεθα (we) } fight
μάχ-ονται (they) } fight
Μηδικ-ά, τά the Persian Wars
   (2b)
Μῆδ-ος, ὁ Persian (2a)
μισέ-ω hate
μῖσος hatred (nom.)
ναυμαχί-αν a naval battle
   (acc.)
Ξέρξ-ης Xerxes (nom.)
ὁ βασιλεὺς the king
οἱ δὲ (with οἱ μὲν) others
οἱ μὲν (with οἱ δὲ) some
ὁμονοέ-ω be of one mind,
   agree

ὁμόνοι-α agreement (nom.)
ὁ Ξέρξης Xerxes
οὐκέτι no longer
οὕτως in this way
πολέμι-οι, οἱ the enemy (2a)
πόλεμ-ος, ὁ war (2a)
πολλ-ὴ much, great (nom.)
προσ-έρχονται (they)
   advance
τάξιν rank (acc.)
τὰς ναῦς the ships
ταχέ-ως quickly
τὴν ἀρετ-ὴν their courage
τὴν ναυμαχί-αν the naval
   battle
τὴν πόλιν the city
τὴν ὕβριν the aggression
τι a (nom.)
τοῖς Ἕλλησι the Greeks
τολμά-ω be daring
τότε then
τὸ φάσμα the phantom,
   apparition

τοὺς ναύτ-ας the sailors
τοὺς Πέρσ-ας the Persians
τῶν Περσ-ῶν of the Persians
τῶν πραγμάτων of/in things, affairs
φαίν-εται (it) appears

φάσμα τι γυναικεῖον a phantom in female form (nom. n.)
φεῦ alas!
φεῦ τοῦ πολέμου alas for the war!

φεῦ τῶν Ἑλλήνων alas for the Greeks!
φοβ-οῦμαι (I) fear
φοβ-εῖσθε be afraid of! (pl.)
ὥσπερ like, as

Vocabulary to be learnt

ἀναχωρέω retreat
διά (+acc.) because of
ἐλεύθερος α ον free
ἐπειδή when
ἐπί (+acc.) against, at, to

οὐκέτι no longer
οὕτω(ς) thus, so, in this way
πολέμιοι, οἱ the enemy (2a)
πολέμιος α ον hostile, enemy
πόλεμος, ὁ war (2a)

ταχέως quickly
τι a, something
τολμάω dare, be daring, undertake
ὥσπερ like, as

O   Grammar for Section Two

Summary:
Pres. ind. act. -όω
Pres. ind. and imper. mid. -ομαι, -άομαι, -έομαι
βοή, ἀπορία, τόλμα, ναύτης (nom., acc.)
Gen. pls. meaning 'of'
Uses of def. art.
More preps.

Verbs

Present indicative active of contracted verbs in ό-ω, δηλό-ω 'I show'

22 Here are the forms of the contracted verb δηλόω:

δηλ-ῶ	(δηλό-ω)	'I show' etc.
δηλ-οῖς	(δηλό-εις)	
δηλ-οῖ	(δηλό-ει)	
δηλ-οῦμεν	(δηλό-ομεν)	
δηλ-οῦτε	(δηλό-ετε)	
δηλ-οῦσι(ν)	(δηλό-ουσι(ν))	

Imperatives

δήλ-ου	(δήλο-ε)	'show!' (s.)
δηλ-οῦτε	(δηλό-ετε)	'show!' (pl.)

Present indicative middle verbs, contracted and uncontracted, ἔρχ-ομαι 'I go', φοβέ-ομαι 'I fear', θεά-ομαι 'I watch'

23 Most of the verbs you have met so far have ended in -ω in the 1st s. But there is a second set of verbal forms, called 'middle', which end in -ομαι. Of these you have met ἔρχομαι, γίγνομαι, μάχομαι, φοβέομαι, θεάομαι. Here are their conjugations in full:

ἔρχ-ομαι 'I go'	φοβ-οῦμαι (ἐ-ομαι) 'I fear'	θε-ῶμαι (ά-ομαι) 'I watch'
ἔρχ-ῃ (ει)	φοβ-ῇ (ἐ-ῃ)	θε-ᾷ (ά-ῃ)
ἔρχ-εται	φοβ-εῖται (ἐ-εται)	θε-ᾶται (ά-εται)
ἐρχ-όμεθα	φοβ-ούμεθα (ε-όμεθα)	θε-ώμεθα (α-όμεθα)
ἔρχ-εσθε	φοβ-εῖσθε (ἐ-εσθε)	θε-ᾶσθε (ά-εσθε)
ἔρχ-ονται	φοβ-οῦνται (ἐ-ονται)	θε-ῶνται (ά-ονται)

Imperative forms

ἔρχ-ου	'go!' (s.)	φοβ-οῦ (ἐ-ου)	'fear!'	θε-ῶ (ά-ου)	'watch!'
ἔρχ-εσθε	'go!' (pl.)	φοβ-εῖσθε (ἐ-εσθε)	'fear!'	θε-ᾶσθε (ά-εσθε)	'watch!'

Nouns

24 Here are four further noun types, categorised as types 1a, 1b, 1c, 1d, to add to the 2a and 2b types that you learnt in the last chapter. Note again the similarities between these type 1 nouns, and their resemblance to the feminine def. art. Types 1a, b, and c are FEMININE; 1d is MASCULINE.

βο-ή, ἡ 'shout' (1a)

s.

nom.	acc.	gen.	dat.
βο-ή	βο-ήν	βο-ῆς	βο-ῇ

pl.

nom.	acc.	gen.	dat.
βο-αί	βο-άς	βο-ῶν	βο-αῖς

ναύτ-ης, ὁ 'sailor' (1d)

s.

nom.	acc.	gen.	dat.
ναύτ-ης	ναύτ-ην	ναύτ-ου	ναύτ-ῃ

pl.

nom.	acc.	gen.	dat.
ναῦτ-αι	ναύτ-ας	ναυτ-ῶν	ναύτ-αις

ἀπορί-α, ἡ 'perplexity' (1b)

s.

nom.	acc.	gen.	dat.
ἀπορί-α	ἀπορί-αν	ἀπορί-ας	ἀπορί-ᾳ

pl.

nom.	acc.	gen.	dat.
ἀπορί-αι	ἀπορί-ας	ἀπορι-ῶν	ἀπορί-αις

τόλμ-α, ἡ 'daring' (1c)

s.   pl.

nom.	acc.	gen.	dat.	nom.	acc.	gen.	dat.
τόλμ-α	τόλμ-αν	τόλμ-ης	τόλμ-ῃ	τόλμ-αι	τόλμ-ας	τολμ-ῶν	τόλμ-αις

Note
1b *type nouns, like* ἀπορία, *keep the* α *all the way through the singular. They follow the same rule as already quoted for adjectives of which the stem ends in* ρ ε ι *(cf.* 12 *note). The final* α *may be* long *or* short; *the final* α *in the nom. and acc. s. of* 1c *nouns is* short.

Genitive case

25 All genitive plurals end in -ων, e.g. ἀνθρώπων, ἔργων, τῶν, καλῶν, ναυτῶν, etc. The genitive case has a wide range of functions, but is often equivalent to the English 'of' (it is this function you must learn at the moment), e.g.

τῶν ἀνθρώπων 'of the men'; τῶν ἔργων 'of the deeds'.

26 Note the order of the genitive in the following sentences:
τὸ πλοῖον τῶν ἀνθρώπων
τὸ τῶν ἀνθρώπων πλοῖον
τὸ πλοῖον τὸ τῶν ἀνθρώπων
τῶν ἀνθρώπων τὸ πλοῖον

The basic meaning of all these is 'the ship of the men, the men's ship'. Note especially the norm, which is τὸ τῶν ἀνθρώπων πλοῖον, e.g.

ὁρῶ τὸ τῶν ἀνθρώπων πλοῖον 'I am observing the men's ship' (in reply to the question 'What are you doing?'); but also note the very common:

τὸ πλοῖον ὁρῶ τὸ τῶν ἀνθρώπων 'it's the men's ship I see' (in reply to the question 'Whose ship do you see?').

27 Note also the use of the def. art. in the following phrases, especially its *position*:

τὰ περὶ Σαλαμῖνα πράγματα
τὰ πράγματα τὰ περὶ Σαλαμῖνα } 'events around Salamis'
τὰ περὶ Σαλαμῖνα

Likewise, consider:
οἱ ἐν Σαλαμῖνι 'the men in Salamis, those in Salamis'
αἱ ἐν τῷ Πειραιεῖ 'the women in the Piraeus'

This use of the def. art., to extend a phrase, is very common. It works in a similar way to the genitive usages outlined above.

Prepositions

28 Note παρά + acc. 'along, alongside'; and ἐπί + acc. 'at, onto, to', and διά + acc. 'because of'.

Vocabulary to be learnt with the grammar of Section Two

ἀπορία, ἡ perplexity; lack of provisions (1b)
βοή, ἡ shout (1a)
γίγνομαι (γεν-) become; be; be born; happen; arise
διέρχομαι (διελθ-) go through, relate
ἐλευθερία, ἡ freedom (1b)
ἐλευθερόω free, set free

ἐπέρχομαι (ἐπελθ-) go against, attack
ἔρχομαι (ἐλθ-) go, come
ἡσυχία, ἡ quiet, peace (1b)
θεά, ἡ goddess (1b)
μάχομαι (μαχεσ-) fight
ναυμαχία, ἡ naval battle (1b)
νίκη, ἡ victory, conquest (1a)

ὁμόνοια, ἡ agreement, harmony (1b)
προσέρχομαι (προσελθ-) advance, go/come towards
στρατιά, ἡ army (1b)
τόλμα, ἡ daring (1c)
φοβέομαι fear, be afraid (of)

○

Exercises for Section Two

(a) Words

1. Deduce the meaning of the words on the right from those on the left:

ἀληθῆ	ἡ ἀλήθεια
ἀκριβῶς	ἡ ἀκρίβεια
ἄνθρωπος, ὁ	ἡ ἄνθρωπος
βοή	βοῶ
ἔμπειρος	ἡ ἐμπειρία
ἔργον	ἐργάζομαι
ἡδέως	ἥδομαι, ἡ ἡδονή
κακός	ἡ κακία
μάχομαι	ὁ μαχητής, ἡ μάχη, ἄμαχος ον
μῶρος	ἡ μωρία
ναῦς/μάχομαι	ναυμαχῶ
νίκη/νικάω	ἀνίκητος ον
ποιέω	ὁ ποιητής
πόλεμος	ὁ πολεμήτης, πολεμῶ
σιωπάω	ἡ σιωπή
στρατιά	ὁ στρατός, στρατεύω, ὁ στρατιώτης
τολμάω	ὁ τολμητής, ἄτολμος ον, ἀτολμῶ
φίλος	φιλῶ, ἡ φιλία
φοβέομαι	ὁ φόβος
ψευδῶς	ψεύδομαι

(b) Morphology

1. Translate each verb, then change to singular or plural as appropriate:
διερχόμεθα, μάχεται, δηλοῦσι, φοβῇ, θεῶνται, δηλοῖς, θεᾶσθε, προσέρχεται, φοβοῦνται, δηλοῦμεν, φοβοῦμαι, γίγνονται, ἐπέρχῃ, φοβοῦ, μάχεσθε

2. Add the correct form of the definite article to these nouns:
ναύτης, τόλμαν, ναύτην, βοάς, νίκαι, ναῦται, στρατιάν, κυβερνήτας, νίκην, ἀπορία

3. Put in the correct form of adjective and noun:
ἡ καλλίστ- βο-   τὴν πολεμί- βο-
αἱ ἐμ- βο-   τὰς καλ- νίκ-
τὴν ἐμ- ἀπορί-

(c) Syntax

1. 'The Athenians' war' = ὁ πόλεμος ὁ τῶν Ἀθηναίων/ὁ τῶν Ἀθηναίων πόλεμος
Put together the following groups of words in the same patterns, and translate:

a. τὰ ἔργα + τῶν Περσῶν
b. ἡ στρατιά + τῶν βαρβάρων
c. ἡ βοή + ἐν τῷ λιμένι
d. οἱ ναῦται + ἐν τῷ πλοίῳ
e. τὸ πλοῖον + τῶν πολεμίων

(d) English into Greek

Translate these pairs of sentences:

1. ἡ ναῦς πρὸς τὴν ναυμαχίαν προσέρχεται.
The sailors converse with the rhapsode.

2. ὁ ἄριστος ῥαψῳδὸς ἀεὶ καλλίστους ποιεῖ τοὺς λόγους.
The captain relates with pleasure our sea-battle.

3. ἔπειτα μάχονται μὲν οἱ Ἀθηναῖοι, φοβοῦνται δὲ οἱ τῶν Περσῶν στρατηγοί.
Finally the Athenians are victorious, while the Athenians' enemies are falling.

4. μὴ ἀναχωρεῖτε, ὦ φίλοι, ἀλλὰ μάχεσθε.
Don't be afraid, sailors, but fight and become free.

5. ἴσμεν ὅτι προσέρχεται ἡ τῶν Ἑλλήνων στρατιά.
You (pl.) know that the Persians' generals are retreating.

Test Exercise Two
Translate into English

ἐπειδὴ οὖν προσέρχονται ἡ τῶν Περσῶν στρατιὰ καὶ τὸ <u>ναυτικόν</u>, οἱ
'Αθηναῖοι ταχέως εἰσβαίνουσιν εἰς τὰς ναῦς καὶ πρὸς τὴν Σαλαμῖνα
πλέουσιν. ἔπειτα δὲ οἵ τε 'Αθηναῖοι καὶ οἱ ἄλλοι Ἕλληνες ἡσυχάζουσι.
τέλος δὲ <u>ἀφικνεῖται</u> τὸ τῶν Περσῶν ναυτικόν, καὶ ἐπειδὴ <u>νὺξ</u> γίγνεται,
<u>ἔνθα καὶ ἔνθα</u> βραδέως πλέουσιν αἱ νῆες. καὶ ἐπειδὴ γίγνεται ἡ <u>ἡμέρα</u>, οἱ
μὲν Πέρσαι προσέρχονται ταχέως ἐπὶ ναυμαχίαν, οἱ δὲ Ἕλληνες
ἀποροῦσι καὶ φοβοῦνται. τέλος δὲ οὐκέτι φοβοῦνται, ἀλλὰ τολμῶσι καὶ
ἐπέρχονται ἐπὶ τοὺς βαρβάρους. μάχονται οὖν <u>εὐκόσμως</u> καὶ νικῶσι
τοὺς βαρβάρους. οἱ μὲν οὖν βάρβαροι φεύγουσι, φεύγει δὲ καὶ ὁ Ξέρξης.
οὕτως οὖν ἐλεύθεροι γίγνονται οἱ Ἕλληνες διὰ τὴν <u>ἀρετήν</u>.

Vocabulary

ναυτικόν, τό fleet, navy (2b)
ἀφικνέομαι arrive
νύξ night (nom.)
ἔνθα καὶ ἔνθα up and down

ἡμέρα, ἡ day (1b)
εὐκόσμως in good order
ἀρετή, ἡ courage (1a)

Section Three

Vocabulary for Section Three A

ἄγε come! (s.)
αἱ πολέμιαι νῆες the enemy
   ships
ἀφ-ικνέ-ομαι arrive, come
δεῖν-ός -ή -όν dire, terrible
δή then (with imper.)
δηλό-ω show, make clear
διότι because
ἐπι-στρέφ-ω turn round
ἐρωτά-ω ask
εὖ well
εὐθύς immediately

Ζεῦ Zeus
ἡ λαμπάς the torch
ἡμᾶς us
ἡ πόλις the city
ἰδού look! (s.)
κίνδυνός τις some danger
   (nom.)
κινδύνῳ danger
λαμπάδ-α a torch (acc.)
λαμπάδ-α τινά a torch (acc.)
νὴ τὸν Δί-α yes, by Zeus
νῆσ-ος, ἡ island (2a)

ὁπόθεν where from?
πόθεν from where?
πυρ-ά, τά fire-signal (2b)
Σαλαμῖνι Salamis
σπεύδ-ω hurry
τῇ νήσῳ the island
τὴν Σαλαμῖνα Salamis
τι δεινόν something terrible
τὸν λιμέν-α the harbour
φής you (s.) say
χωρέ-ω come, go

Vocabulary to be learnt
ἄγε come!
ἀφικνέομαι (ἀφικ-) arrive,
   come
δηλόω show, reveal

ἐρωτάω (ἐρ-) ask
ἰδού look! here! hey!
κίνδυνος, ὁ danger (2a)
νῆσος, ἡ island (2a)

πόθεν; from where?
πυρά, τά fire-signal (2b)
σπεύδω hurry
χωρέω go, come

Vocabulary for Section Three B

αὕτ-η this (with βο-ή) (nom.)
γεῖτον neighbour (voc.)
δεῖν-ός -ή -όν terrible
εἰπ-έ speak! tell (me)!
εἶτα then
ἐκεῖν-α, τά those (acc.)

ἐκεῖσε there, over there
ἐκ-φέρ-ω carry out
ἔξω outside
εὖ well
ἡ Σαλαμίς Salamis
θεά-ομαι watch, gaze at

θέ-ω run
θόρυβ-ος, ὁ din, hustle and
   bustle (2a)
καὶ δή yes (I am . . .)
κινδύνῳ danger
κόσμ-ος, ὁ order (2a)

μέγας ⎫ great (nom.)
μεγάλη ⎭
μετὰ ἐμοῦ with me
μοι to me
νύξ night
ὁ γείτων his neighbour
οἱ ἄνδρ-ες the men
οἴκαδε home(wards)
οἰκί-α, ἡ house (1b)
ὁ παῖς the slave
ὅπλ-α, τά weapons (2b)
οὐδαμοῦ nowhere
οὗτ-ος ὁ this (nom.)
οὗτ-ος this (with θόρυβος) (nom.)

πολλ-αί many (nom.)
πολλ-οὶ ἄνδρ-ες many men (nom.)
πολ-ὺς much, a lot of (nom.)
πορεύ-ομαι journey, come, go
Πρώταρχ-ος, ὁ Protarchos (2a) (an armed soldier on a trireme)
Πώλ-ος, ὁ Polos (2a) (a rower)
ταῖς ὁδοῖς the streets
ταῦτ-α τά these (acc.)
τὴν λαμπάδ-α the torch

τὴν ναῦν the ship
τῆς οἰκίας the house
τὸν λιμέν-α the harbour
τὸν τροπωτῆρ-α the/his oar-loop
τοῦ Πώλου Polos'
τοὺς ἄνδρ-ας the men
τρέχ-ω run
τῷ λιμένι the harbour
τῷ Πειραιεῖ the Piraeus
ὑπηρέσι-ον, τό cushion (2b)
φαίν-ομαι appear

Vocabulary to be learnt

δεινός ή όν terrible, dire, clever
εὖ well
θεάομαι watch, gaze at
θόρυβος, ὁ noise, din, hustle and bustle (2a)
οἰκία, ἡ house (1b)
οἴκαδε homewards
ὅπλα, τά weapons, arms (2b)
πορεύομαι march, journey, go
φαίνομαι (φαν-) appear, seem

Vocabulary for Section Three C

αἱ λαμπάδ-ες the torches
αἱ νῆ-ες the ships
ἀλλήλ-ους one another (acc.)
ἄλλ-ος -η -ο other, rest of
ἄλλ-ως otherwise
ἀπο-κρίν-ομαι answer
ἀπο-κτείν-ω kill
Ἀχαι-ός, ὁ Akhaian (2a) (Homer's word for 'Greek')
γὰρ δὴ really, I assure you
γεωργ-ός, ὁ farmer (2a)
γῆ, ἡ land (1a)
δια-λέγ-ομαι converse
ἐγγὺς τοῦ λιμένος near the harbour
εἰπ-έ speak! tell me!
ἐκεῖν-οι οἱ those (nom.)
ἐκεῖν-οι they, those men (nom.)

ἐκεῖν-ον τὸν ἄνδρ-α that man
ἐμπειρί-αν τινὰ some experience
ἐν τούτῳ meanwhile
ἐπειδὴ since, because
ἔτι still
Ζεῦ Zeus
θαλάττι-ος -α -ον sea, of the sea
καὶ δὴ καὶ and moreover
καὶ μὴν see!
κατά (+acc.) on, by
κρατέ-ω hold sway, power
κωλύ-ω prevent, stop
Λακεδαιμόνι-ος, ὁ Spartan (2a)
Λακεδαιμόνι-ος οὐδεὶς no Spartan
λαμβάν-ω take, capture

λόγ-ος, ὁ word (2a)
μανθάν-ω learn
μέγα great (nom.)
μελετά-ω practise
μελετ-ή, ἡ practice (1a)
μετὰ πολλῆς μελετῆς with much practice
μηδὲ and don't
μιμνήσκ-ομαι remember
μοι to me
μύρμηκ-ες ants (nom.)
ναυτικ-ός -ή -όν naval
ναυτικά, τά naval matters (2b)
ναυτικόν, τό navigation (2b)
ὁ ἀνήρ the man
οἱ ἄνδρ-ες the men
ὁ Περικλῆς Pericles
οὐδαμ-ῶς in no way, not at all

οὐδὲ and not
οὐδεμί-α ναῦς no ship (nom.)
οὐδεμί-αν ἐμπειρί-αν no experience (acc.)
οὐδέν-α any (acc.)
οὗτ-ος ὁ this
οὕτω = οὕτως
περὶ τοῦ πολέμου καὶ τῶν ναυτικῶν about the war and naval matters
πτώσσ-ω crouch, cower
ῥᾳδί-ως easily
Σαλαμῖνι Salamis
σε you (s.) (acc.)

συν-έρχ-ομαι assemble, come together, swarm
τᾶν my dear chap (condescending)
ταύτ-ην it, this (acc.)
ταύτ-ην τὴν this (acc.)
τέχν-η, ἡ skill (1a)
τῇ ἐκκλησίᾳ the Assembly of the people (where all political decisions were made)
τῇ νηί the ship
τίνες what? (nom.)
τις someone, one (nom.)
τὸν λιμέν-α the harbour

τὸ πλῆθος the number
τοῦ Περικλέους Pericles'
τοῦτ-ο this (acc.)
τοῦτ-ους these (with τοὺς Λακεδαιμονίους)
τριήραρχ-ος, ὁ trierarch (2a)
τῶν νεῶν of the ships
ὑμῶν of you
ὑφ᾽ Ἕκτορι at Hektor's mercy (Hektor: Trojan hero killed by Akhilleus)
φής you (s.) say
φησί (he) says
φόβ-ος, ὁ fear (2a)
χαλεπ-ῶς with difficulty

Vocabulary to be learnt

ἀλλήλους each other, one another (2a)
ἄλλος η ο other, the rest of
γῆ, ἡ land (1a)
ἐγγύς (+gen.) near, nearby
εἰπέ speak! tell me!
ἐπειδή when, since, because

κατά (+acc.) in, on, by, according to
λαμβάνω (λαβ-) take, capture
λόγος, ὁ word, speech; story, tale (2a)
μανθάνω (μαθ-) learn, understand

οὐδέ and not
Λακεδαιμόνιος, ὁ Spartan (2a)
τέχνη, ἡ skill, art, expertise (1a)
ναυτικός ή όν naval

Vocabulary for Section Three D

ἀ-δύνατ-ος -ον impossible
οἱ ἄνδρ-ες the men
βάλλε εἰς κόρακ-ας go to hell! (lit. 'to the crows')
βοά-ω shout (for)
γάρ που of course, no need to say
δεσπότ-ης, ὁ master (1d)
ἐκεῖν-α τὰ those (acc.)
ἐκεῖν-ον him (acc.)
ἐκεῖν-ος he (nom.)
ἐκεῖσε there
ἐμὲ me (acc.)
ἔνδον inside
ἔτι still
ζητέ-ω seek, look for
ἡμέτερ-ος -α -ον our
ἡ Σαλαμίς Salamis
ἥσυχ-ος -ον quiet, quietly

θέ-α, ἡ sight (1b)
θύρ-α, ἡ door (1b)
καθεύδ-ω sleep
καλέ-ω call, summon
κελευστ-ής, ὁ boatswain (1d)
κελευστ-ής τις a boatswain (he gave the time to the rowers)
κινδύνω danger
κόπτ-ω knock
μάλιστά γε yes, all right
με me (acc.)
μοι to me
οἴκοι at home
ὁ Κυδαθηναιεὺς the member of Kydathene deme (a district of Athens)
ὁ παῖς the slave
οὗτ-ος he, the latter (nom.)

οὕτως γε yes, he is
παῖ slave!
περὶ τούτου τοῦ κινδύνου about this danger
πολ-ύς much (nom.)
Σαλαμῖνι Salamis
σὲ you (acc. s.)
ταύτ-ην τὴν this (acc.)
ταχὺ quickly
τῇ νήσῳ the island
τῆς νεώς the ship
τίνα whom? (acc.)
τοῦτ-ο τὸ πρᾶγμα this business (nom.)
τρέχ-ω run
τριήραρχ-ος, ὁ trierarch (2a)
φέρ-ε come now!
φής you (s.) say, mean

Vocabulary to be learnt

βοάω shout (for)	καλέω call, summon
ἔτι still, yet	κελευστής, ὁ boatswain (1d)
ζητέω look for, seek	οἴκοι at home
θύρα, ἡ door (1b)	τρέχω (δραμ-) run
καθεύδω sleep	τριήραρχος, ὁ trierarch

Vocabulary for Section Three E

ἀπο-πλέ-ω sail off	κατα-κελεύ-ω give the time	τὰς ναῦς the ships
δή then, now	κελεύ-ω order, give orders	τὴν πατρίδ-α our fatherland
ἐκεῖν-ος the former (nom.)	πάλιν back, again	τοῖς θεοῖς to the gods
ἐμ-βαίν-ω embark	πολλάκις often	ὑπὲρ τῆς σωτηρίας for our
εὖ γε well done!	Πόσειδον Poseidon (sea god)	safety
εὐχ-ή, ἡ prayer (1a)	(voc.)	ὦναξ = ὦ ἄναξ O lord!
εὔχ-ομαι pray	σοι to you (s.)	ὦνδρες = ὦ ἄνδρ-ες men!
ἡμέτερ-ος -α -ον our	σπένδ-ω make a libation	ὠὸπ ὄπ in... out...in...out
θυσί-α, ἡ sacrifice (1b)	σπονδ-ή, ἡ libation (1a)	
θύ-ω sacrifice	σωτὴρ saviour (nom.)	

Vocabulary to be learnt

δή then, indeed	θυσία, ἡ a sacrifice (1b)
ἐμβαίνω (ἐμβα-) embark	θύω sacrifice
εὐχή, ἡ prayer (1a)	κελεύω order
εὔχομαι pray	σπένδω pour a libation
ἡμέτερος α ον our	σπονδή, ἡ a libation (1a)

○ Grammar for Section Three

Summary:
λιμήν, ναῦς, Ζεύς, οὗτος, ἐκεῖνος, ἐγώ, σύ, πολύς, μέγας (nom., acc.)
Negatives

Nouns

29 So far you have met nouns classified as types 1 or 2 (or 1st and 2nd declension). These nouns, and the adjectives like καλός, and the def. art. all showed very useful similarities, and their genders could for the most part be predicted.

Here is the most common type of type 3 noun, classified as 3a:

λιμήν(λιμεν-) 'harbour' (3a)

s.   pl.

nom.	acc.	gen.	dat.
λιμήν	λιμέν-α	λιμέν-ος	λιμέν-ι

nom.	acc.	gen.	dat.
λιμέν-ες	λιμέν-ας	λιμέν-ων	λιμέ-σι(ν)

Notes
(i) *The stem on which the noun is declined is* NOT THE SAME AS THE NOMINATIVE SINGULAR. *While patterns of stems will emerge over type 3 nouns, you will have to learn stems to start with, as you learn the noun. Thus you must learn* λιμήν (λιμεν-), ἀνήρ (ἀνδρ-), λαμπάς (λαμπαδ-), *so that you can spot the noun when it occurs in a form different from the nominative singular.*
(ii) *It is not always possible to predict the gender of type 3 nouns, and these must be learnt too. But again, you will find some patterns emerging as different type 3 nouns are met.*

30 Here are two irregular nouns:

ναῦς, ἡ 'ship'

s.   pl.

nom.	acc.	gen.	dat.
ναῦς	ναῦν	νεώς	νηί

nom.	acc.	gen.	dat.
νῆες	ναῦς	νεῶν	ναυσί(ν)

Ζεύς, ὁ 'Zeus'

s.

nom.	acc.	gen.	dat.
Ζεύς	Δία	Διός	Διί

Adjectives/pronouns
31 The Greek words for 'this' and 'that' can be used either as adjectives, when they will agree with a noun, or on their own, when they will mean 'this man', 'this woman', 'that thing' etc., depending on context.

Consider:

οὗτος ὁ ναύτης	'this sailor' or ὁ ναύτης οὗτος
ταῦτα τὰ ἔργα	'these deeds' or τὰ ἔργα ταῦτα
ἐκείνη ἡ βοή	'that shout' or ἡ βοὴ ἐκείνη
οὗτος ἀφικνεῖται	'this man is approaching'
αὗται τρέχουσιν	'these women are running'

n.b. the position of the article

32 οὗτος αὗτη τοῦτο *'this, this man/woman/thing, (s)he, it'*

οὗτος declines as follows:

s.   *pl.*

	nom.	acc.	gen.	dat.		nom.	acc.	gen.	dat.
m.	οὗτ-ος	τοῦτ-ον	τούτ-ου	τούτ-ῳ		οὗτ-οι	τούτ-ους	τούτ-ων	τούτ-οις
f.	αὕτ-η	ταύτ-ην	ταύτ-ης	ταύτ-ῃ		αὗτ-αι	ταύτ-ας	τούτ-ων	ταύτ-αις
n.	τοῦτ-ο	τοῦτ-ο	τούτ-ου	τούτ-ῳ		ταῦτ-α	ταῦτ-α	τούτ-ων	τούτ-οις

Notes

(i) Presence or absence of τ- at the front of the word follows the same pattern as the def. art.

(ii) α|η in the ending generates αυ in the stem; o|ω in the ending generates ου in the stem.

(iii) Note especially the neuter forms τοῦτο, ταῦτα.

33 ἐκεῖν-ος -η -ο *'that, that man/woman/thing, (s)he, it'*

ἐκεῖνος declines as follows:

s.   *pl.*

	nom.	acc.	gen.	dat.		nom.	acc.	gen.	dat.
m.	ἐκεῖν-ος	ἐκεῖν-ον	ἐκείν-ου	ἐκείν-ῳ		ἐκεῖν-οι	ἐκείν-ους	ἐκείν-ων	ἐκείν-οις
f.	ἐκείν-η	ἐκείν-ην	ἐκείν-ης	ἐκείν-ῃ		ἐκεῖν-αι	ἐκείν-ας	ἐκείν-ων	ἐκείν-αις
n.	ἐκεῖν-ο	ἐκεῖν-ο	ἐκείν-ου	ἐκείν-ῳ		ἐκεῖν-α	ἐκεῖν-α	ἐκείν-ων	ἐκείν-οις

Note

Both οὗτος *and* ἐκεῖνος *can occur in forms ending in -ι, e.g.* ἐκεινοσί, τουτονί *etc. This intensifies the pronouns, so that they mean 'this man* here*', 'that woman* there*', etc.*

34 ἐγώ 'I' (pl. 'we'), σύ 'you'

Learn the following pronouns, ἐγώ 'I' and σύ 'you'.

s.   pl.

nom.	acc.	gen.	dat.	nom.	acc.	gen.	dat.
ἐγώ	(ἐ)με	(ἐ)μου	(ἐ)μοι	ἡμεῖς	ἡμᾶς	ἡμῶν	ἡμῖν

σύ 'you'

s.   pl.

nom.	acc.	gen.	dat.	nom.	acc.	gen.	dat.
σύ	σέ	σοῦ	σοί	ὑμεῖς	ὑμᾶς	ὑμῶν	ὑμῖν

35 πολύς πολλ-ή πολύ (πολλ-) 'many, much'

πολύς (πολλ-) and μέγας (μεγαλ-) go just like καλός except for the four forms
underlined:

s.   pl.

	nom.	acc.	gen.	dat.	nom.	acc.	gen.	dat.
m.	πολ-ύς	πολ-ύν	πολλ-οῦ	πολλ-ῷ	πολλ-οί	πολλ-ούς	πολλ-ῶν	πολλ-οῖς
f.	πολλ-ή	πολλ-ήν	πολλ-ῆς	πολλῇ	πολλ-αί	πολλ-άς	πολλ-ῶν	πολλ-αῖς
n.	πολ-ύ	πολ-ύ	πολλ-οῦ	πολλ-ῷ	πολλ-ά	πολλ-ά	πολλ-ῶν	πολλ-οῖς

36 μέγας μεγάλ-η μέγα (μεγαλ-) 'great'

s.   pl.

	nom.	acc.	gen.	dat.	nom.	acc.	gen.	dat.
m.	μέγ-ας	μέγ-αν	μεγάλ-ου	μεγάλ-ῳ	μεγάλ-οι	μεγάλ-ους	μεγάλ-ων	μεγάλ-οις
f.	μεγάλ-η	μεγάλ-ην	μεγάλ-ης	μεγάλ-ῃ	μεγάλ-αι	μεγάλ-ας	μεγάλ-ων	μεγάλ-αις
n.	μέγ-α	μέγ-α	μεγάλ-ου	μεγάλ-ῳ	μεγάλ-α	μεγάλ-α	μεγάλ-ων	μεγάλ-οις

Idioms

37 (a) As we have already seen, Greek leaves out the verb 'to be' if it can be
assumed from the context. Likewise, other words can be left out if they are
understood easily from the context, e.g.

'Don't the Spartans practise?' οὔκ, ἀλλὰ ἡμεῖς κωλύομεν (understand
'them').

(b) Observe that what appears in Greek as an adjective may best be translated into English as an adverb, e.g. ἥσυχος καθεύδει ὁ δεσπότης 'the master sleeps peacefully'.

(c) Observe the way in which a Greek repeats a question which he has just been asked:

A. πόθεν ἡ λαμπάς;
B. ὁπόθεν; . . .

i.e. ὁ- is prefixed to the question word.

cf. A. τί ποιεῖς;
B. ὅ τι; οὐδὲν ποιῶ.

Negatives
38 (i) Two or more negatives with the simple negative (οὐ) *first* in the clause reinforce the negative, e.g.

οὐκ ἀφικνεῖται οὐδείς 'nobody comes'
οὐκ ἀφικνεῖται οὐδεὶς οὐδέποτε 'no one ever comes'

(ii) Where the simple negative *follows* a negative, they cancel each other out, οὐδεὶς οὐκ ἀφικνεῖται 'everyone comes' (i.e. 'nobody does not come')

Vocabulary to be learnt with the grammar

ἀνήρ (ἀνδρ-), ὁ man (3a)
γείτων (γειτον-), ὁ neighbour (3a)
ἐκεῖνος η ο that, (s)he, it
Ζεύς (Δι-), ὁ Zeus (3a)
λαμπάς (λαμπαδ-), ἡ torch (3a)

λιμήν (λιμεν-), ὁ harbour (3a)
μέγας μεγάλη μέγα (μεγαλ-) great, big
νύξ (νυκτ-), ἡ night (3a)
οὗτος αὕτη τοῦτο this, (s)he, it
παῖς (παιδ-), ὁ slave, child (3a)

πατρίς (πατριδ-), ἡ fatherland (3a)
πολύς πολλή πολύ (πολλ-) much, many
σωτήρ (σωτηρ-), ὁ saviour (3a)   O

Exercises for Section Three

(a) Words

1. Deduce the meanings of the words on the right from those on the left:

1. ἀνήρ   ἀνδρεῖος α ον
2. γῆ|ἔργον   ὁ γεωργός, γεωργέω
3. γιγνώσκω   ἀγνοέω
4. ἐκεῖσε   ἐκεῖ, ἐκεῖθεν
5. ἔμπειρος   ἄπειρος ον
6. θεάομαι   ἡ θέα, ὁ θεατής, τὸ θέατρον

7. θόρυβος   θορυβέω
8. ὁ κίνδυνος   κινδυνεύω, ἀκίνδυνος ον
9. μανθάνω   ὁ μαθητής
10. οἰκία   οἰκεῖος α ον
11. ὅπλα   ὁ ὁπλίτης
12. παῖς   ἀπαίδευτος, ἡ παιδεία, παιδεύω
13. φαίνομαι   φανερός ά όν

2. Group together the words in this list which seem to share common roots; translate the words:

οὕτως, βοηθέω, κελεύω, ὑμέτερος, σπένδω, ἐκεῖσε, ἔνδον, βοή, ἔμπειρος, εὔχομαι, ἡμεῖς, βοάω, ὑμεῖς, σπονδή, οὗτος, κελευστής, εὐχή, ἐκεῖνος, ἐμπειρία, ἡμέτερος, κατακελεύω, ἐν, θέω

(b) Morphology

1. Change nom. to acc.:
a. οὗτος ὁ ἀνήρ
b. ταῦτα τὰ ἔργα
c. αὕτη ἡ λαμπάς
d. αἱ βοαὶ αὗται
e. οὗτοι οἱ λιμένες

2. Change acc. to nom.:
a. τοῦτον τὸν γείτονα
b. ταύτας τὰς λαμπάδας
c. τὰ πυρὰ ταῦτα
d. τὴν πατρίδα ταύτην
e. τούτους τοὺς ἄνδρας

3. Insert the appropriate form of μέγας or πολύς:
a. (μέγας) τὸ ἔργον.
b. οἱ ἄνδρες (πολύς) ἐμπειρίαν ἔχουσιν εἰς τὰ ναυτικά.
c. ὁ κυβερνήτης πρὸς (μέγας) λιμένα κυβερνᾷ.
d. (πολύς) τὰ δεινά.

(c) Syntax

1. Translate the answers to exercises (b) 1–3 above.

(d) English into Greek

Translate these pairs of sentences:
1. ὁ οὖν κυβερνήτης πρὸς τὴν Σαλαμῖνα ταχέως βλέπει.
So the ship sails slowly towards that harbour.

2. μέγας μὲν γὰρ ὁ κίνδυνος ὁ τῶν Ἀθηναίων, πολὺς δὲ ὁ τῶν ἀνδρῶν
θόρυβος.
There is much din, a lot of shouting and many men appear.

3. ἆρ' οὐκ οἶσθα πότερον ἐκεῖνοι ναυταί εἰσιν ἢ οὔ;
I don't see whether that fellow is a general or not.

4. ὁ ἀγαθὸς κυβερνήτης οὐκ ἀκούει ταύτας τὰς βοάς.
That stupid rhapsode is afraid of these Spartans.

5. ἐκεῖνος μὲν γὰρ μῶρος περὶ πολλά, οὗτος δὲ περὶ οὐδέν.
They are experienced by land, but these by sea.

Test Exercise Three
Translate into English:
ἡ μὲν ναῦς πλεῖ παρὰ τὴν νῆσον, ὁ δὲ Δικαιόπολις λαμπάδα ὁρᾷ ἐν τῇ
νήσῳ. ὁ δὲ κυβερνήτης εὖ οἶδεν ὅτι οὐκ ἔστι λαμπάς, ἀλλὰ τὰ πυρά.
σπεύδει οὖν εἰς τὸν λιμένα· δηλοῖ γὰρ τὰ πυρὰ ὅτι οἱ πολέμιοι ἐπέρχονται
ἐπὶ τοὺς Ἀθηναίους. οἱ δὲ ἄνδρες οἱ ἐν τῷ λιμένι θεῶνται τὰ πυρὰ καὶ
οἴκαδε τρέχουσιν ἐπὶ τὰ ὅπλα. ἴσασι γὰρ ὅτι μέγας ὁ κίνδυνος. φόβος δὲ
μέγας λαμβάνει τὸν ῥαψῳδόν. φοβεῖται γὰρ τοὺς Λακεδαιμονίους. οἱ δὲ
ναῦται λέγουσιν ὅτι Ἀθηναῖοι μὲν κρατοῦσι κατὰ θάλατταν,
Λακεδαιμόνιοι δὲ κατὰ γῆν. καὶ Λακεδαιμόνιοι οὐ ῥᾳδίως μανθάνουσι
τὴν ναυτικὴν τέχνην. ἐπειδὴ οὖν τὸ πλοῖον ἀφικνεῖται εἰς τὸν λιμένα, ὁ
Δικαιόπολις καὶ ὁ ῥαψῳδὸς πορεύονται πρὸς τὰς ναῦς. καὶ δῆλόν ἐστιν
ὅτι αἱ νῆες αὗται ἐπέρχονται ἐπὶ ναυμαχίαν. οἱ μὲν γὰρ κελευσταὶ
ζητοῦσι τοὺς τριηράρχους. ἐκεῖνοι δὲ καθεύδουσιν ἥσυχοι. τέλος δὲ οἱ
τριήραρχοι οὗτοι ἀφικνοῦνται εἰς τὸν λιμένα καὶ ἐμβαίνουσιν. ἔπειτα
τὰς θυσίας θύουσι καὶ τὰς σπονδὰς σπένδουσι καὶ ἀνάγονται.

Vocabulary
ἀνάγομαι set sail, put out to
sea

PART TWO

Section Four

Vocabulary for Section Four A

ἀγρ-ός, ὁ field (pl. country) (2a)
αἰτί-α, ἡ reason, cause (1b)
αἴτι-ος -α -ον responsible
ἀστ-ός, ὁ townsman (2a)
γεωργ-ός, ὁ farmer (2a)
γυνή (γυναικ-), ἡ wife, woman (3a)
δ᾽=δέ
δαίμων (δαιμον-), ὁ god, daimon (3a)
δια-πέμπ-ομαι send across
δια-φθείρ-ω kill, destroy
εἰσ-κομίζ-ομαι bring in
ἐπι-γίγν-ομαι occur, follow
ἔτι καὶ νῦν even now
Εὔβοι-α, ἡ Euboia (1b)
ἡ πόλις city
ἦ που surely
Ἡράκλεις Herakles!
ἱερ-όν, τό sanctuary (2b)
κακο-δαίμων wretched, unlucky (nom.)
κακο-δαίμον-α wretched, unlucky (acc.)
κακό-δαιμον wretched, unlucky (nom.)
κακο-δαίμον-ες wretched, unlucky (nom.)
κακο-δαίμον-ας wretched,

unlucky (acc.)
κατα-λείπ-ω leave behind
κολάζ-ω punish
κρατέ-ω hold sway
μακρ-ός -ά -όν long
μάλιστα particularly
μετά (+acc.) after
μοι to me
νὴ (+acc.) by . . .!
νομίζ-ω think x (acc.) to be y (acc.)
νόσ-ος, ἡ plague (2a)
οἰκέ-ω dwell in, reside in
οἰκήσ-εις dwellings (nom.)
οἰκεῖ-ος, ὁ member of family (2a)
ὀλίγ-οι -αι -α few
ὀλοφύρ-ομαι lament, mourn for
ὄντ-α ⎫
ὄντ-ες ⎬ being (nom.)
ὄντ-ας ⎭ (acc.)
ὁ Περικλῆς Pericles
ὅσον πλῆθος what a lot! (nom.)
οὐκέτ᾽=οὐκέτι
οὖσ-α ⎫ (nom.)
οὖσ-αν ⎬ being (acc.)
οὖσ-ας ⎭ (acc.)

παιδί-ον, τό child (2b)
πείθ-ω persuade
Περικλέ-α Pericles (acc.)
πιθαν-ός -ή -όν persuasive
πλέ-ως -α -ων full
πόλ-ις a city (nom.)
πρόβατ-α, τά sheep (2b)
πρὸς τῶν θε-ῶν in the name of the gods
πρῶτον (μὲν) first
πυρ-ά, ἡ funeral pyre (1b)
ῥήτωρ (ῥητορ-), ὁ politician, orator (3a)
τὰ σκεύ-η equipment, furniture
τὰς οἰκήσ-εις the dwellings
τὰ τείχ-η the walls (of the city)
τὴν πόλ-ιν the city
τῇ πόλει the city
τινας some (acc.)
τὸ ἄστ-υ the city (of Athens)
τὸν Περικλέ-α Pericles
τὸ πλῆθος the people
τὸ πρᾶγμα the matter
τοσ-οῦτ-ον πλῆθος so great a number
υἱ-ός, ὁ son (2a)

ὑμέτερ-ος -α -ον your (where   φιλέ-ω love, be well disposed   ὤν being (nom.)
'you' = more than one)   to
φησὶ he says   χαλεπ-ός -ή -όν difficult

Vocabulary to be learnt

γεωργός, ὁ farmer (2a)   ἔτι καὶ νῦν even now, still now
γυνή (γυναικ-), ἡ woman,   κρατέω hold sway, power
wife (3a)   (over)
δαίμων (δαιμον-), ὁ god,   νή (+ acc.) by . . .!
daimon (3a)   ὀλίγος η ον small, few

Vocabulary for Section Four B

ἀδελφ-ός, ὁ brother (2a)
ἀλλ᾿ = ἀλλά
ἀ-νομί-α, ἡ lawlessness (1b)
ἆρ᾿ = ἆρα
ἀ-σέβει-α, ἡ disrespect
towards the gods, impiety
(1b)
ἀ-τιμάζ-ω hold in dishonour
᾿Αφροδίτ-η, ἡ Aphrodite (1a)
(goddess of love and sexual
pleasure)
βαρ-ὺς ⎫ (nom.)
βαρ-ὺν ⎬ heavy (acc.)
βί-ος, ὁ life (2a)
γέρων (γεροντ-), ὁ old man
(3a)
δ᾿ = δέ
δεσπότ-ης, ὁ master (1d)
δεῦρ᾿ = δεῦρο
δῆμ-ος, ὁ deme (2a) (local
districts into which Attica was
divided)
δια-φθείρ-ω kill
δοῦλ-ος, ὁ slave (2a)
ἐπ᾿ = ἐπί
ἐπὶ νεκροῖς on top of corpses
ἐπι-βάλλ-ω throw onto
εὐ-δαίμον-α fortunate (ruled
by a benevolent daimon)
(acc.)

εὐ-σεβέστατ-ος -η -ον most
respectful of the gods
(nom.)
εὐ-σεβοῦντες respecting the
gods (nom.)
εὔ-φρων well-disposed
ἐφ-ήμερ-ος -ον ephemeral,
short-lived
ἤ than
ἤ . . . ἤ either . . . or
ἡδον-ή, ἡ pleasure (1a)
θάπτ-ω bury
θαυμάζ-ω wonder
θε-ός, ὁ|ἡ god(-dess) (2a)
θνητ-ός -ή -όν mortal
κωλύ-ω prevent, stop
μάλιστα very much
μήτηρ (μητερ-), ἡ mother
(3a)
μιαρ-ός -ά -όν foul, polluted
μισέ-ω hate
μοι to me
νεανί-ας, ὁ young man (1d)
νεκρ-ός, ὁ corpse (2a)
νεκρ-όν τιν-α a corpse (acc.)
᾿νθρωπε = ἄνθρωπε
νόμ-ος, ὁ law, convention
(2a)
νόσ-ος, ἡ plague (2a)
νυν now then
ὄναρ a dream (nom.)

ὄντ-α ⎫ (acc.)
οὖσ-α ⎬ being (nom.)
οὖσ-ας ⎭ (acc.)
οὔτε . . . οὔτε neither . . . nor
οὗτος hey, you!
πατήρ (πατερ-), ὁ father (3a)
παύ-ομαι stop
παῦ-ε stop!
περὶ νόμων καὶ ὕβρεως about
laws and aggression
ποθέ-ω desire, long for
πολίτ-ης, ὁ citizen (1d)
πολὺ πλῆθος a great number
(nom.)
πρόβατ-α, τά sheep (2b)
πρὸς θε-ῶν in the name of the
gods!
πυρ-ά, ἡ funeral pyre (1b)
σέβ-ομαι show respect for
σκίας of a shadow
ταῖς οἰκίαις the houses
τῇ πόλει the city
τήμερον today
τὴν κόλασ-ιν punishment
τιμά-ω honour
τίν-ες; what? (nom.)
τὸ πρᾶγμα the matter
τοῖς ἱεροῖς the sanctuaries
τοὺς ἀ-σεβεῖς those who are
disrespectful of the gods
τοὺς εὐ-σεβεῖς those who
respect the gods

τρέπ-ομαι turn (oneself)
τύπτ-ω strike
υἱ-ός, ὁ son (2a)
φέρ-ω carry
φής you (s.) say

φόβ-ος, ὁ fear (2a)
ὦ τῆς ἀνομίας what
    lawlessness!
ὦ τῆς ἀσεβείας what
    irreverence!

ὦ τῆς ὕβρεως what aggressive
    behaviour!
ὤν being (nom.)

Vocabulary to be learnt

ἀτιμάζω dishonour, hold in
    dishonour
διαφθείρω (διαφθειρ-) destroy,
    kill
δεσπότης,, ὁ master (1d)
θεός, ὁ, ἡ god(-dess) (2a)

θνητός ή όν mortal
κωλύω prevent, stop
μάλιστα especially;
    particularly; yes
νεκρός, ὁ corpse (2a)
νόμος, ὁ law, convention (2a)

νόσος, ἡ plague, disease (2a)
πυρά, ἡ funeral pyre (1b)
τιμάω honour
τύπτω strike, hit
φέρω (ἐνεγκ-) carry, bear
φόβος, ὁ fear (2a)

O   Grammar for Section Four A–B

Summary:
πρᾶγμα, πλῆθος, πόλις, πρέσβυς, ἄστυ, εὔφρων, τίς, τις, οὐδείς, ὤν
(nom. acc.)

Nouns

39 Here are some more type 3 nouns, under the classifications 3b, c, e,
f. Note the genders which they tend to have – 3b, c and f are all NEUTER; 3e in -ις
are all FEMININE, in -υς all MASCULINE.

40 πρᾶγμα (πραγματ-), τό 'thing, matter' (3b)
s.

nom.	acc.	gen.	dat.
πρᾶγμα	πρᾶγμα	πράγματ-ος	πράγματ-ι

Plain
pl.

nom.	acc.	gen.	dat.
πράγματ-α	πράγματ-α	πραγμάτ-ων	πράγμα-σι(ν)

41 πλῆθ-ος, τό 'number, crowd, people' (3c) Πλῆθέα *(handwritten)*

s.				pl.			

nom.	acc.	gen.	dat.	nom.	acc.	gen.	dat.
πλῆθ-ος	πλῆθ-ος	πλῆθ-ους	πλῆθ-ει	πλήθ-η	πλήθ-η	πληθ-ῶν	πλήθε-σι(ν)

Plain (handwritten)

42 πόλ-ις, ἡ 'city–state' (3e) πόλι *(handwritten)*

s.				pl.			

nom.	acc.	gen.	dat.	nom.	acc.	gen.	dat.
πόλ-ις	πόλ-ιν	πόλ-εως	πόλ-ει	πόλ-εις	πόλ-εις	πολ-έων	πόλ-εσι(ν)

exc. (handwritten)

πρέσβ-υς, ὁ 'old man' (pl. 'ambassadors') (3e) πρέσβυ *(handwritten)*

s.				pl.			

nom.	acc.	gen.	dat.	nom.	acc.	gen.	dat.
πρέσβ-υς	πρέσβ-υν	πρέσβ-εως	πρέσβ-ει	*(then like πόλις)*			

exc. (handwritten)

43 ἄστ-υ, τό 'city' (of Athens) (3f) – Ν *(handwritten)*

s.				pl.			

nom.	acc.	gen.	dat.	nom.	acc.	gen.	dat.
ἄστ-υ	ἄστ-υ	ἄστ-εως	ἄστ-ει	ἄστ-η	ἄστ-η	ἀστ-έων	ἄστ-εσι(ν)

Plain (handwritten) Notes

(i) *Be careful not to confuse 3c types like* πλῆθος *with 2a types like* ἄνθρωπος.

(ii) *Note the appearance of* -ε- *in the ending of these nouns. (The* -ους *ending was once* -εος, *the* -η *ending once* -εα.)

(iii) *Some 3a nouns have an acc. s. in* -ιν, *e.g.* χάρις (χαριτ-) 'grace' *acc. s.* χάριν.

Adjectives/pronouns

44 There are a number of adjective types based on type 3 nouns, just as you have met καλός-type adjectives based on type 1/2 nouns. Note the similarity between the endings of these adjectives and of the type 3 nouns you have met so far (**29**):

εὔφρων εὖφρον (εὔφρον-) 'well-disposed'

s.

	nom.	acc.	gen.	dat.
m./f.	εὔφρων	εὔφρ-ον-α	εὔφρ-ον-ος	εὔφρ-ον-ι
n.	εὖφρον	εὖφρον	εὔφρ-ον-ος	εὔφρ-ον-ι

pl.

	nom.	acc.	gen.	dat.
m./f.	εὔφρ-ον-ες	εὔφρ-ον-ας	εὔφρ-όν-ων	εὔφρ-ο-σι(ν)
n.	εὔφρ-ον-α	εὔφρ-ον-α	εὔφρ-όν-ων	εὔφρ-ο-σι(ν)

45 In these adjectives, the same form describes both m. *and* f. nouns.

46 τις, τι (τιν-) 'a, a certain, some'

s.   pl.

	nom.	acc.	gen.	dat.
m./f.	τις	τιν-α	τιν-ος	τιν-ι
n.	τι	τι		

	nom.	acc.	gen.	dat.
m./f.	τιν-ες	τιν-ας	τιν-ων	τι-σι(ν)
n.	τιν-α	τιν-α		

τίς τί (τίν-) 'who? what? which?'

s.   pl.

	nom.	acc.	gen.	dat.
m./f.	τίς	τίν-α	τίν-ος	τίν-ι
n.	τί	τί		

	nom.	acc.	gen.	dat.
m./f.	τίν-ες	τίν-ας	τίν-ων	τί-σι(ν)
n.	τίν-α	τίν-α		

Notes
(i) *As above, the m./f. forms are identical.*
(ii) *Note the difference between* τίς *('who, which, what?') and the form* τις *('someone, a, a certain'). If* τις *is accented, the accent will fall on the last syllable, e.g.* τινά.

47 οὐδ-είς οὐδε-μία οὐδ-έν 'no, no one, nothing'

s.

	nom.	acc.	gen.	dat.
m.	οὐδ-είς	οὐδ-έν-α	οὐδ-εν-ός	οὐδ-εν-ί
f.	οὐδε-μί-α	οὐδε-μί-αν	οὐδε-μι-ᾶς	οὐδε-μι-ᾷ
n.	οὐδ-έν	οὐδ-έν	οὐδ-εν-ός	οὐδ-εν-ί

Notes

(i) Remember that both τίς, τις and οὐδείς, when on their own, stand as nouns ('who, someone, no one'); when describing a noun, as adjectives ('what person?', 'some woman', 'no boy').

(ii) οὐδείς is simply οὐδέ ('nor, not')+εἷς ('one). Observe that the feminine is -μία.

Participles

48 Here is the declension of 'being', the participle form of the verb 'to be':

ὤν οὖσα ὄν (ὀντ-) *'being'*

	s.				*pl.*			
	nom.	*acc.*	*gen.*	*dat.*	*nom.*	*acc.*	*gen.*	*dat.*
m.	ὤν	ὄντ-α	ὄντ-ος	ὄντ-ι	ὄντ-ες	ὄντ-ας	ὄντ-ων	οὐ-σι(ν)
f.	οὖσ-α	οὖσ-αν	οὔσ-ης	οὔσ-ῃ	οὖσ-αι	οὔσ-ας	οὐσ-ῶν	οὔσ-αις
n.	ὄν	ὄν	ὄντ-ος	ὄντ-ι	ὄντ-α	ὄντ-α	ὄντ-ων	οὐ-σι(ν)

Notes

*(i) The endings of the m./n. forms are like those of εὔφρων (**29**) but based on the stem οντ-; the f. declines as the 1c noun τόλμα (**24**). This 'mixed' declension has already been met in οὐδείς οὐδεμία οὐδέν (see **47**).*

*(ii) A number of verbs take a participle to complete their meaning. One such is φαίνομαι, 'I appear to . . ., I seem to . . .'. Thus φαίνομαι ὤν means 'I seem to be' – with the implication that you really are whatever it is you seem to be. Thus it comes to mean 'I am obviously . . .' (cf. **54**).*

(iii) Note the range of possible translations of ὤν, e.g. 'being', 'since being', 'although being', 'while being', 'as being', 'who/which is/are'.

Vocabulary to be learnt with the grammar

ἄστυ, τό *city (of Athens) (3f)*

κακοδαίμων κακόδαιμον (κακοδαιμον-) *unlucky, dogged by an evil daimon*

οἴκησις, ἡ *dwelling (3e)*

οὐδείς οὐδεμία οὐδέν (οὐδεν-) *no; no one, nothing*

πλῆθος, τό *number, crowd; the people (3c)*

πόλις, ἡ *city (state) (3e)*

πρᾶγμα (πραγματ-), τό *thing; matter; affair; (pl.) troubles (3b)*

σκεύη, τά *gear, furniture (3c)*

τάξις, ἡ *battle-array, order, rank (3e)*

τίς τί (τίν-) *who? what?*

τις τι (τιν-) *a, a certain; someone*

O

Exercises for Section Four A–B

(a) Words

1. Deduce the meaning of the words on the right from those on the left:

ἀπαίδευτος	ἡ παίδευσις, τὸ παίδευμα
ἀποθνῄσκω (ἀποθαν-) θνητός	ἀθάνατος ον, ὁ θάνατος
γίγνομαι (γεν-)	ἡ γένεσις
δηλόω	ἡ δήλωσις
ἐμβαίνω (ἐμβα-)	ἡ ἔμβασις
ἐρωτάω	τὸ ἐρώτημα
ζητέω	ἡ ζήτησις
θεάομαι	τὸ θέαμα
καλέω	ἡ κλῆσις
καλός	τὸ κάλλος
κρατέω	ἡ κρατία
μανθάνω	ἡ μάθησις, τὸ μάθημα
ποιέω	τὸ ποίημα, ἡ ποίησις
στρατηγός	τὸ στρατήγημα
στρατιά	τὸ στράτευμα
ταχέως	τὸ τάχος
τιμάω	ἡ τιμή, ἄτιμος ον
τολμάω	ἡ τόλμησις, τὸ τόλμημα
ψευδῶς	τὸ ψεῦδος

(b/c) Morphology and Syntax

1. Translate into Greek the italic phrases in the following sentences, using a part of ὤν οὖσα ὄν:

a. *Since I am unhappy*, I shall leave the city.
b. *We who are few* shall not defeat *you who are many*.
c. *As friends, ladies*, you do not quarrel.
d. *I, an Athenian and fortunate*, hate you, *Spartan that you are and hated by the gods*.
e. *Who are you* to threaten me?

(d) English into Greek

Translate these pairs of sentences:

1. ἐγὼ γὰρ θνητὸς ὢν οὐκ ἀτιμάζω τοὺς θεούς.
Since you are a farmer you know the laws.

2. ἐκείνους οὖν, ἐμπείρους ὄντας κατὰ γῆν, Ἀθηναῖοι νικῶσι κατὰ θάλατταν.
   As sailors we hold sway on the sea.
3. τὸ δ' ἄστυ καλὸν ὂν οὐ τιμῶ.
   I am not afraid of the number of corpses, though it is large.
4. ὁ δὲ στρατηγὸς οὗτος, ἄριστος ὤν, οὐ φοβεῖται τοὺς Λακεδαιμονίους πολεμίους ὄντας.
   My wife, who is unlucky, is afraid of the plague, which is evil.
5. οἱ γὰρ ἄνθρωποι, κακοδαίμονες ὄντες, τιμῶσι τοὺς τῶν θεῶν νόμους, ἀρίστους ὄντας.
   The people, since it is good, does not dishonour the gods, who are great.

Test Exercise Four A–B
Translate into English:

ΝΕΑΝΙΑΣ δεῦρ' ἐλθὲ καὶ εἰπέ. διὰ τί ὀλοφύρῃ, ὦ φίλε; ἆρα υἱόν τινα, κακοδαίμονα ὄντα, ὀλοφύρῃ, ἢ θυγατέρα ἢ γυναῖκα;

ΓΕΡΩΝ κακοδαίμων δὴ ὢν ἔγωγε, ὦ φίλε, τοῦτο ποιῶ. ὀλοφύρομαι γὰρ τόν τε υἱὸν τὸν οὐκέτ' ὄντα καὶ τὴν θυγατέρα τὴν ἤδη νεκρὸν οὖσαν.

ΝΕΑΝ. κακοδαίμων δὴ φαίνῃ ὤν. ἀλλὰ τί αἴτιόν ἐστιν; πῶς ἀποθνῄσκουσιν οἱ ἄνθρωποι;

ΓΕΡ. διὰ τὴν νόσον, ὦ φίλε, νεκροὶ ἐπὶ νεκροῖς πίπτουσι καὶ ἀποθνῄσκουσιν ἄνθρωποι κακοδαίμονες ὄντες.

ΝΕΑΝ. πολλὰ δὴ πράγματα ἔχομεν διὰ τὴν νόσον. ὁρῶ γὰρ ἔγωγε τὸ μὲν πλῆθος τῶν ἀνθρώπων κακόδαιμον ὄν, τὴν δὲ πόλιν πολλῇ ἐν ἀπορίᾳ οὖσαν, τοὺς δὲ ἀνθρώπους ἐφημέρους ὄντας καὶ κακοδαίμονας.

ΓΕΡ. μὴ οὖν ἀτίμαζε τοὺς θεοὺς μηδὲ ἀσέβει εἰς τὴν πόλιν, ἀλλὰ τόλμα καὶ τίμα τοὺς θεούς.

Vocabulary

ὀλοφύρομαι lament
υἱός, ὁ son (2a)
θυγάτηρ (θυγατερ-), ἡ daughter (3a)

ἐπὶ νεκροῖς on top of corpses
πράγματα, τά troubles (3b)
πολλῇ . . . ἀπορίᾳ much perplexity

ἐφήμερος ον short-lived
ἀσεβέω commit irreverent acts (on)

Vocabulary for Section Four C

ἀπ-άγ-ω lead away
ἅπαντες all (nom.)
ἀπο-φεύγ-ων escaping (nom.)

ἄ-τοπ-ος -ον strange
αὐτ-όν him (acc.)
αὐτ-ούς them (acc.)
δῆλ-ος clearly

διώκ-οντ-ες pursuing (nom.)
δοῦλ-ος, ὁ slave (2a)
δυσ-τυχής unfortunate (nom.)

ἐκείνῳ τῷ ἱερῷ that sanctuary
ἐξαίφνης suddenly
ἐφ' = ἐπί
ἔχ-ων having, wearing (nom.)
Ἡράκλει-ος -α -ον of Herakles
ἱερ-όν, τό sanctuary (2b)
ἱκετεί-α, ἡ supplication (1b)
ἱκέτ-ης, ὁ suppliant (1d)
ἴσως perhaps
καὶ μὴν look!
καίπερ although (-ing)
κῆρυξ (κηρυκ-), ὁ herald (3a)
λανθάν-ω escape the notice of x (acc.) in -ing
μὰ (+acc.) by . . .! (usually, 'no, by . . .!')
μοι to me

ξέν-ος, ὁ (or ξεῖν-ος, ὁ) stranger, foreigner (2a)
ὁδοι-πόρ-ος, ὁ traveller (2a)
οἱ ἔνδεκα the Eleven (a body of eleven magistrates responsible for the prisons and for summary justice)
ὀρθ-ῶς correctly
ὅσι-ος -α -ον sanctified
οὗτος hey, you!
ὁ φεύγ-ων the man running off
πάσχ-ω suffer, experience, undergo
ποτε ever
πρὸς Διός under Zeus' protection
προσ-τρέχ-οντ-α running towards (acc.)

Σάτυρ-ος, ὁ Satyros (2a)
τὸν φεύγ-οντ-α the man running off
τοὺς ἔνδεκα the Eleven
τρέπ-ομαι turn (oneself)
τρέχ-ων running (nom.)
τυγχάν-ω happen to be (–ing), be actually –ing
ὑπηρέτ-ης, ὁ public slave (1d)
φαίν-ομαι appear to be (–ing)
φεύγ-οντ-α } running off (acc.)
φεύγ-ων } (nom.)
φθάν-ω anticipate x (acc.) by –ing
χλαμύς (χλαμυδ-), ἡ short cloak, travelling cloak (3a)
ὦ τῆς ἀνομίας what lawlessness!

Vocabulary to be learnt

ἀνομία, ἡ lawlessness (1b)
ἀπάγω (ἀπαγαγ-) lead/take away
ἀποφεύγω (ἀποφυγ-) escape, run off

δοῦλος, ὁ slave (2a)
ἱερόν, τό sanctuary (2b)
ἱκέτης, ὁ suppliant (1d)
μά (+acc.) by . . .!
ξένος/ξεῖνος, ὁ foreigner, guest,

host (2a)
ὀρθός ή όν straight, correct, right

Vocabulary for Section Four D

ἀγορ-ά, ἡ agora, market-place (1b)
ἄ-δικ-ος -ον unjust
ἀπο-κόπτ-ω cut off
ἀπο-κτείν-ω kill
ἀπο-φαίν-ω make to appear
ἄρτι-ος -α -ον perfect
ἀ-σεβεῖς irreverent (nom.)
αὐτ-ὸν him (acc.)
ἀφ-έλκ-ω drag away
βασιλέ-α τὸν μέγαν the Great King (of Persia)
βίαι-ος -α -ον violent
βο-ῶν shouting (nom.)
δῆλ-ος clearly

δηλ-ῶν showing, making clear (nom.)
διδάσκαλ-ος, ὁ teacher (2a)
Δυσνομί-η, ἡ bad government (1a)
δυσ-τυχὴς unfortunate (nom.)
ἐγ-χειρ-ίδι-ον, τό dagger (2b)
εἰρήνη peace
ἐπὶ τοῦ βωμοῦ on the altar
ἐπι-καλέ-ομαι call upon (to witness)
ἐπι-καλ-ούμεν-ος calling upon (nom.)
εὔ-κοσμ-ος -ον in good order

εὐ-νομί-α/η, ἡ good government (1b-a)
εὐ-πορί-α/η, ἡ solution of difficulties; plenty (1b-a)
ἐφ' = ἐπί
ἦ που surely
ἱκέσι-ος -α -ον of suppliants (Zeus' title)
ἱκετεί-α, ἡ supplication (1b)
καθ-ίζ-ομαι sit down
καθ-ορά-ω look down upon, see clearly
καίπερ although
κῆρυξ (κηρυκ-), ὁ herald (3a)
λαμβάν-ομαι take hold of

μηδείς μηδεμί-α μηδέν no, no
  one
μισέ-ω hate
ναὶ τὼ σιώ by the two gods
  (*Castor and Pollux*) (*a typical*
  Spartan oath)
νέμεσ-ις, ἡ nemesis,
  retribution (3e)
ξένι-ος -α -ον of
  guests/strangers (*title of*
  Zeus)
ὀλοφυρ-όμεν-ος lamenting
  (for) (nom.)
ὅμως nevertheless
πάντ᾽ = πάντα
παρ-έχ-ω give, provide
πάσχ-ω experience, suffer
παύ-ομαι stop (–ing)
παῦ-ε stop! (s.) (–ing)

πλεῖστ-ος -η -ον very many
πόλει to the city
πορευ-όμεν-ος travelling
  (nom.)
πρέσβ-εις, οἱ ambassadors
  (3e)
πρεσβευτ-ής, ὁ ambassador
  (1d)
πρό-γον-ος, ὁ ancestor (2a)
Σάτυρ-ος, ὁ Satyros (2a)
τῇ πόλει the city
τὸν ἐπι-καλ-ούμεν-ον the one
  calling on (acc.)
τοῦ βωμοῦ the altar
τοὺς ἀ-σεβ-οῦντ-ας those
  who are being irreverent
τοὺς ἔχ-οντ-ας the ones who
  have
τοὺς τρεπ-ομέν-ους the ones
  turning

τοὺς φεύγ-οντ-ας the ones
  running off
τυγχάν-ω happen to be, be
  actually (–ing)
τῷ πολέμῳ (the) war
ὕβρ-ις, ἡ aggression (3e)
ὑπηρέτ-ης, ὁ public slave (1d)
ὑπὸ τῶν ᾿Αθηναί-ων at the
  hands of the Athenians
φαίν-ομαι appear to be (–ing)
φής you (s.) say
φιλ-ῶν being well-disposed
  to (nom.)
χείρ (χειρ-), ἡ hand (3a)
ὦ τῆς ἀνομίας what
  lawlessness!
ὦ τῆς ἀσεβείας what
  irreverence!

Vocabulary to be learnt

ἀποκτείνω (ἀποκτειν-) *kill*
ἀσέβεια, ἡ *irreverence to the*
  gods (1b)
αὐτόν ἥν ὁ *him, her, it, them*
ἀφέλκω (ἀφελκυσ-) *drag off*
βασιλεύς, ὁ *king (3g)*
βωμός, ὁ *altar (2a)*
ἐπικαλέομαι *call upon (to*
  witness)
κῆρυξ (κηρυκ-), ὁ *herald (3a)*
λανθάνω (λαθ-) *escape notice*
  of X (acc.) in –ing (part.)

μισέω *hate*
ὀλοφύρομαι *lament, mourn for*
πάσχω (παθ-) *suffer,*
  experience, undergo
παύομαι *stop*
πρεσβευτής, ὁ *ambassador (1d)*
πρέσβεις, οἱ *ambassadors (3e)*
τρέπομαι (τραπ-) *turn, turn in*
  flight
τυγχάνω (τυχ-) *happen to be*
  –ing, be actually –ing
  (+ nom. part.)

ὕβρις, ἡ *aggression, violence*
  (3e)
ὑπηρέτης, ὁ *servant, slave (1d)*
φαίνομαι (φαν-) *seem to be,*
  appear to be (+ part.)
φθάνω *anticipate X (acc.) in*
  –ing (nom. part.)
ὦ *what . . .! (+ gen.)*

○ Grammar for Section Four C–D

Summary:
Pres. part. act. and mid. (nom., acc.)
Vbs. taking parts.
βασιλεύς (nom., acc.)
Adjs. translated as advs.
Elision and crasis

Participles

49 As 'to be' gives us a participle-form 'being', so most verbs have a participle-form, e.g. to run – running; to stop – stopping. The participles are inflected like an adjective. Participles based on the present stem decline as follows:

50 *Present active participles* (uncontr.): τρέχ-ων -ουσα -ον *'running'*

	nom.	acc.	
m.	τρέχ-ων	τρέχ-οντ-α	
f.	τρέχ-ουσ-α	τρέχ-ουσ-αν	etc. as ὤν οὖσα ὄν **48**
n.	τρέχ-ον	τρέχ-ον	

Learn the nom., acc., s. and pl.

Note
These are formed by adding -ων -ουσα -ον to the present stem.

51 *Present middle participles* (uncontr.): παυόμεν-ος -η -ον *'stopping'*

	nom.	
m.	παυ-όμεν-ος	
f.	παυ-ομέν-η	etc. as καλ-ός -ή -όν **12**
n.	παυ-όμεν-ον	

Learn the nom., acc., s. and pl.

Note
The endings are the same as for καλός type adjectives. The -μεν- marks the middle participle.

52 Contract verbs have endings as follows in participle forms:

ὁράω: ὁρῶν ὁρῶσα ὁρῶν (ὁρωντ-) 'seeing' (= ὁρά-ων ὁρά-ουσα ὅρα-ον (ὁρα-οντ-))

ποιέω: ποιῶν ποιοῦσα ποιοῦν (ποιουντ-) 'doing' (=ποιέ-ων ποιέ-ουσα ποίε-ον (ποιε-οντ-))

δηλόω: δηλῶν δηλοῦσα δηλοῦν (δηλουντ-) 'showing' (= δηλό-ων δηλό-ουσα δηλό-ον (δηλο-οντ-))

θεάομαι: θεώμενος -η -ον 'watching' (=θεα-όμεν-ος -η -ον)

φοβέομαι: φοβούμενος -η -ον 'fearing' (= φοβε-όμεν-ος -η -ον)

Uses of the participle

53 A very common Greek usage is to join a participle with a definite article and use it as a noun: e.g.

τρέχων = 'running'
ὁ τρέχων = 'he who runs, the man who is running'
οἱ τρέχοντες = 'those who run, the men who are running, the running men'
αἱ τρέχουσαι = 'the running women, the women who run'

54 Note the following expressions which tend to include a participle:

τυγχάνω (φεύγων) 'I happen, chance to be, actually am (fleeing)'
λανθάνω (σε φεύγων) 'I escape the notice of (you, in fleeing)'
φθάνω (σε φεύγων) 'I anticipate (you, in fleeing), I flee before you (do)'
παύομαι (φεύγων) 'I stop (fleeing)'
δῆλός εἰμι (φεύγων) 'I am obviously (fleeing)'
καίπερ (φεύγων) 'although (fleeing)'

Cf. **48** (ii). Note that the participle will change to agree with the noun to which it refers, e.g. <u>αἱ γυναῖκες</u> τυγχάνουσι φεύγουσαι 'the women happen to be fleeing'.

Noun

55 Here is another noun-type, classified as 3g:

βασιλ-εύς, ὁ 'king' (3g)

s.   *pl.*

nom.	acc.	*gen.*	*dat.*	nom.	acc.	*gen.*	*dat.*
βασιλ-εύς	βασιλ-έα	βασιλ-έως	βασιλ-εῖ	βασιλ-ῆς (-εῖς)	βασιλ-έας	βασιλ-έων	βασιλ-εῦσι(ν)

Idiom

56 You have already met one adjective in Greek (ἥσυχος 'peaceful') which is best translated adverbially ('peacefully'; **37** (b)). Another one is δῆλος ('obvious, clear'), when used in the phrase δῆλός ἐστι + participle, i.e. 'he is *obviously* . . .'.

Elision and crasis

57 (1) Observe the following sentences and note the loss of vowels:
δεῦρ' ἐλθέ (= δεῦρο ἐλθέ)

βαρὺν δ' ὄντα φέρω (βαρὺν δὲ ὄντα φέρω)
ἆρ' οὐ σέβῃ τοὺς θεούς; (ἆρα οὐ . . .)
ἀποθνήσκουσι δ' οἱ ἄνθρωποι (ἀποθνήσκουσι δὲ οἱ . . .)

When a word ends in a short vowel, it may be dropped if the next word begins with a vowel. This is called 'elision'.

Observe what happens to the following words in elision:

ἀπὸ ἵππου→ἀφ' ἵππου
ἔστι ἡμέτερος→ἔσθ' ἡμέτερος
διὰ ἀσέβειαν→δι' ἀσέβειαν

Prefixes to verbs may be affected in the same way, e.g.

κατα-ὁράω→καθοράω
ἀπο-ὁράω→ἀφοράω

So with μετά (μετ', μεθ') and ἐπί (ἐπ', ἐφ') prefixing words beginning with vowels. τ becomes θ and π becomes φ before a rough breathing.

(2) Observe the loss of vowel in:

ὤνδρες (ὦ ἄνδρες) 'men'

This is called 'crasis'. It occurs when a vowel or diphthong at the end of a word contracts with one at the beginning of the next word. Consider further:

τἀγαθά (τὰ ἀγαθά) 'good things'
οὑπί (ὁ ἐπί) 'the one on . . .'
ἀνήρ (ὁ ἀνήρ) 'the man'

Revise

-ω and contr. vbs. pres. act. **4–5, 22**
Type 2 nouns (and 1/2 adjs.) **9–15**
οἶδα **18**   εἰμί **19**   O

Exercises for Section Four C–D

(a) Words *(on word-building, cf. Language Survey (13), p. 327)*:

1. Deduce the meaning of the words on the right from those on the left:

ἀσέβεια	τὸ σέβας
ἱερόν	ὁ ἱερεύς
ἱκέτης	ἱκετεύω
μισέω	τὸ μῖσος
ξένος	ἡ ξενία, ξενίζω
τυγχάνω|δυστυχής	ἡ τύχη
ὕβρις	ὑβρίζω

(b/c) Morphology and Syntax

1. Translate these sentences, completing the second sentence in each of
   the pairs by using a participle or combination of participle + definite
   article:
   e.g. τίς ἐπικαλεῖται ἡμᾶς; οἱ δοῦλοι ἀφέλκουσι (τὸν ἐπικαλούμενον).
   a. τίς τρέχει; οὐχ ὁρῶ ἔγωγε . . .
   b. τίνες ὀλοφύρονται; ποῦ εἰσιν . . .
   c. οἶδα τίς ἀποφεύγει. οὐ γὰρ λανθάνει ἐμὲ . . .
   d. τίνες φεύγουσιν; ἆρ' ὁρᾷς . . .
   e. ὁ ἀνὴρ ἀποτρέχει καὶ οὐ παύεται . . .
   f. αἱ γυναῖκες ἀεὶ φοβοῦνται. διὰ τί οὐ παύονται . . .

(d) English into Greek
Translate these pairs of sentences:
1. ἐγὼ δ' οὐχ ὁρῶ Λακεδαιμόνιον οὐδένα φεύγοντα.
   We see the men running.
2. ἆρα λανθάνει ὑμᾶς ὁ δεσπότης σκεύη ἔχων;
   Don't you (s.) see that the slave is dragging the suppliant away?
3. οἱ γὰρ πρέσβεις φθάνουσι τοὺς ὑπηρέτας ἀποφεύγοντες.
   The Spartan runs into the sanctuary before his pursuers.
4. ὁ δὲ κῆρυξ οὐ παύεται μισῶν τοὺς ξένους καὶ φοβούμενος.
   The stranger does not stop calling on us and shouting.
5. ἀλλὰ δῆλος εἶ ἱκέτης ὤν καὶ τυγχάνεις ὀλοφυρόμενος τὸ πρᾶγμα.
   The man is clearly an ambassador, and happens to be escaping.

Test Exercise Four C–D
Translate into English:
ξένος δέ τις τρέχων τυγχάνει εἰς τὸ Ἡράκλειον ἱερόν. καὶ δῆλός ἐστιν ὁ
ξένος δεινόν τι πάσχων, ἐπειδὴ ταχέως προσέρχονται ἄνδρες τινές,
διώκοντες αὐτόν. ὁ δὲ ξένος φθάνει τοὺς διώκοντας εἰς τὸ ἱερὸν φεύγων,
ἐγγὺς ὄν. ἀφικνοῦνται δὲ οἱ διώκοντες καὶ ἐρωτῶσι τὸν ῥαψῳδὸν ποῦ
τυγχάνει ὢν ὁ ξένος. δῆλον γάρ ἐστιν ὅτι ὁ ξένος οὐ λανθάνει τὸν
ῥαψῳδὸν ἀποφεύγων. ἐπειδὴ δὲ οἱ διώκοντες ὁρῶσιν αὐτὸν ἐν τῷ ἱερῷ
ὄντα, ἀπάγουσι, καίπερ βοῶντα καὶ τοὺς θεοὺς ἐπικαλούμενον. καὶ ὁ μὲν
ξένος οὐ παύεται ὀλοφυρόμενος καὶ δηλῶν τί πάσχει, ὁ δὲ ῥαψῳδὸς καὶ ὁ
Δικαιόπολις ἡσυχάζουσι, φοβούμενοι τοὺς ἕνδεκα.
   οὕτως οὖν ἥ τε ἀνομία καὶ ἡ ἀσέβεια γίγνονται ἐν <u>τῇ</u> τῶν Ἀθηναίων
<u>πόλει</u>.

Vocabulary
τῷ ἱερῷ the sanctuary
τῇ πόλει the city

Section Five

Vocabulary for Section Five A

ἄγρ-οικ-ος -ον from the country
ἄγρ-υπν-ος -ον sleepless
αἴτι-ος -α -ον responsible, to blame
ἀπορίᾳ perplexity
ἄστεως the city (of Athens)
ἀστικ-ός -ή -όν from the city
βαθύς deep (nom.)
βαθέ-ως deeply
βαρέα heavy (nom.)
βί-ος, ὁ life (2a)
γάμ-ος, ὁ marriage (2a)
δάκν-ω bite, worry
δαπάν-η, ἡ expense (1a)
δια-φθείρ-ω ruin
δι-ε-λέγ-ετο she used to converse (δια-λέγ-ομαι)
δι-έ-φθειρ-εν (it) was ruining (δια-φθείρ-ω)
δίκ-η, ἡ lawsuit (1a)
δίκ-ην λαμβάν-ω exact one's due
δίκ-ην ἐ-λάμβαν-ον they kept trying to exact their due
διότι because
ἐ-δίωκ-ον (they) kept on pursuing (διώκ-ω)
εἰσ-έ-φερ-ε(ν) (she) started to bring in/cause (εἰσ-φέρ-ω)
ἐ-κάθευδ-ον I was sleeping (καθεύδ-ω)

ἐ-λάμβαν-ε(ν) (she/he) used to take, kept taking (λαμβάν-ω)
ἐ-λοιδορ-ούμεθα we kept arguing (λοιδορέ-ομαι)
ἐ-μάνθαν-ε(ν) (he) used to learn (μανθάν-ω)
ἐξ = ἐκ
ἐ-παυ-όμεθα (we) used to stop (παύ-ομαι)
ἔ-σῳζ-ε(ν) (he) was saving (σῴζ-ω)
ἔ-φευγ-ον (I) was running away from (φεύγ-ω)
ἡδύς sweet (nom.)
ἤκουε (he) used to hear (ἀκούω)
ἦ I was
ἡμέρ-α, ἡ day (1b)
ἦν (she/it) was
ἰού alas!
ἱππο-μανής horse-mad (nom.)
ἵππ-ος, ὁ horse (2a)
καὶ γὰρ yes, certainly
καὶ δὴ καὶ and moreover
κεφαλ-ή, ἡ head (1a)
λοιδορέ-ομαι argue
νεανί-ας, ὁ young man (1d)
ὁ δυσ-τυχής the unlucky one

ὅλ-ος -η -ον (ὁ) all of
ὀνειρο-πολέ-ω dream (of)
ὅτε when
οὐδέποτε never
οὐδέπω not yet
οὑτοσί αὑτηί τουτοί this here (pointing)
ὀφείλ-ω owe
πατήρ (πατερ-), ὁ father (3a)
περὶ τοῦ παιδὸς about the child
περὶ τῶν ἵππ-ων about horses
πικρ-ός -ά -όν bitter
Στρεψιάδ-ης, ὁ Strepsiades (1d)
σχεδὸν nearly
τάλας unhappy me!
τοῖς ὀνείροις my dream
τότε then
υἱ-ός, ὁ son (2a)
ὕπν-ος, ὁ sleep (2a)
χθὲς yesterday
χρέ-α, τά debts (3c uncontr.)
χρῆμα (χρηματ-), τό thing; size; length (3b)
χρήματ-α, τά money (3b)
χρήστ-ης, ὁ creditor (1d)
χρόν-ος, ὁ time (2a)
ὠνειρο-πόλ-ει he used to dream of (ὀνειρο-πολέ-ω)
ὥσπερ ἔχεις just as you are

Vocabulary to be learnt

αἴτιος α ον *responsible (for),*
  guilty (of)
βαθύς *deep*
βαρύς *heavy*
βίος, ὁ *life, means, livelihood*
  (2a)
γάμος, ὁ *marriage (2a)*
διαλέγομαι *converse*
δίκη, ἡ *lawsuit; penalty; justice*
  (1a)

δίκην λαμβάνω (λαβ-) *exact*
  one's due; punish
  (παρά + gen.)
διότι *because*
δυστυχής *unlucky*
ἡδύς *sweet, pleasant*
εἰσφέρω (εἰσενεγκ-) *bring in,*
  carry in
ἵππος, ὁ *horse (2a)*
ὅλος η ον *whole of*

οὐδέπω|οὔπω *not yet*
ὀφείλω *owe*
πατήρ (πατ(ε)ρ-), ὁ *father*
  (3a)
σχεδόν *near, nearly; almost*
τότε *then*
υἱός, ὁ *son (2a)*
χρήματα, τά *money (3b)*

Vocabulary for Section Five B

ἅπτ-ω *light*
ἀργ-ός -ή -όν *lazy*
βαθεῖα *deep (nom.)*
γέρων (γεροντ-), ὁ *old man*
  (3a)
γνώμ-η, ἡ *plan (1a)*
ἐ-κόλαζ-ον *(they) used to*
  punish (κολάζ-ω)
ἔλαι-ον, τό *olive-oil (2b)*
ἐμαυτ-όν *myself*
ἔν-ειμι *be in*
ἐ-πείθ-οντο *they would obey*
  (πείθ-ομαι)
ἐ-φοβ-οῦντο *they were afraid*

of (φοβέ-ομαι)
ἦμεν *(we) were*
ἦσαν *(they) were*
ἰού *hurrah!*
καίπερ *although (+ part.)*
κακὰ ἐ-ποί-ουν *they would*
  treat badly (κακὰ ποιέ-ω)
κλαί-ω *weep, be punished*
κολάζ-ω *punish*
κόλασ-ις, ἡ *punishment (3e)*
λυχν-ός, ὁ *oil-lamp (2a)*
νεανί-ας, ὁ *young man (1d)*
νέ-ος-α-ον *young*
οἰκέτ-ης, ὁ *house-slave (1d)*

οἴμοι τῶν κακ-ῶν *alas for my*
  troubles!
ὅτε *when*
παύ-ω *stop x (acc.) –ing (acc.*
  part.)
πείθ-ομαι *obey*
τάλας *unhappy me!*
τῷ λυχνῷ *the oil-lamp*
φής *you (s.) say*
χρέ-α, τά *debts (3c uncontr.,*
  gen. pl. χρε-ῶν)
χρηστ-ός -ή -όν *good, fine*

Vocabulary to be learnt

ἅπτω *light; fasten, fix*
ἔνειμι *be in*
κακὰ ⎫ *ποιέω* *treat badly;*
κακῶς ⎭   *do harm to*
κολάζω *punish*
νεανίας, ὁ *young man (1d)*

νέος α ον *young*
οἰκέτης, ὁ *house-slave (1d)*
παύω *stop*
πείθομαι (πιθ-) *trust, obey*
  (+ dat.)
χρέα, τά *debts (3c uncontr.)*

φής *you (s.) say*
χρηστός ή όν *good, fine,*
  serviceable

○ Grammar for Section Five A–B

Summary:
Impf. ind. act. and mid.
Position of adj.

Verbs

Imperfect indicative active and middle ἔπαυον, ἐπαυόμην '*I was stopping*' *(and contracts)*

58 The forms of the imperfect indicative active are as follows:

παύ-ω		τιμ-άω	ποι-έω	δηλ-όω
ἔ-παυ-ον	'I was stopping, I stopped'	ἐ-τίμ-ων (a-ον)	ἐ-ποί-ουν (ε-ον)	ἐ-δήλ-ουν (ο-ον)
ἔ-παυ-ες	'you were stopping, you stopped'	ἐ-τίμ-ας (a-ες)	ἐ-ποί-εις (ε-ες)	ἐ-δήλ-ους (ο-ες)
ἔ-παυ-ε(ν)	'he/she/it was stopping', etc.	ἐ-τίμ-α (a-ε)	ἐ-ποί-ει (ε-ε)	ἐ-δήλ-ου (ο-ε)
ἐ-παύ-ομεν	'we were stopping'	ἐ-τιμ-ῶμεν (ά-ομεν)	ἐ-ποι-οῦμεν (έ-ομεν)	ἐ-δηλ-οῦμεν (ό-ομεν)
ἐ-παύ-ετε	'you were stopping'	ἐ-τιμ-ᾶτε (ά-ετε)	ἐ-ποι-εῖτε (έ-ετε)	ἐ-δηλ-οῦτε (ό-ετε)
ἔ-παυ-ον	'they were stopping'	ἐ-τίμ-ων (a-ον)	ἐ-ποί-ουν (ε-ον)	ἐ-δήλ-ουν (ο-ον)

59 The forms of the imperfect indicative middle are as follows:

παύ		τιμ	ποι	δηλ
ἐ-παυ-όμην	'I was stopping'	ἐ-τιμ-ώμην (a-όμην)	ἐ-ποι-ούμην (ε-όμην)	ἐ-δηλ-ούμην (ο-όμην)
ἐ-παύ-ου	'you were stopping' etc. as **58** above	ἐ-τιμ-ῶ (ά-ου)	ἐ-ποι-οῦ (έ-ου)	ἐ-δηλ-οῦ (ό-ου)
ἐ-παύ-ετο		ἐ-τιμ-ᾶτο (ά-ετο)	ἐ-ποι-εῖτο (έ-ετο)	ἐ-δηλ-οῦτο (ό-ετο)
ἐ-παυ-όμεθα		ἐ-τιμ-ώμεθα (a-όμεθα)	ἐ-ποι-ούμεθα (ε-όμεθα)	ἐ-δηλ-ούμεθα (ο-όμεθα)
ἐ-παύ-εσθε		ἐ-τιμ-ᾶσθε (ά-εσθε)	ἐ-ποι-εῖσθε (έ-εσθε)	ἐ-δηλ-οῦσθε (ό-εσθε)
ἐ-παύ-οντο		ἐ-τιμ-ῶντο (ά-οντο)	ἐ-ποι-οῦντο (έ-οντο)	ἐ-δηλ-οῦντο (ό-οντο)

Notes

(i) The distinguishing mark of a past indicative tense is the presence of the augment *(usually* ἐ-*) at the front of the verb, e.g.* ἔ-λεγον, ἔ-βαινον. *If the verb starts with a vowel, the vowel will lengthen, e.g.:*

οἰκέω→ᾤκουν '*I was living*'
ἀκούω→ἤκουον '*I was listening*'
ἔχω→εἶχον '*I had*'
ἐλευθερόω→ἠλευθέρουν '*I was freeing*'

Use the following chart to determine the augment on verbs beginning with vowels:

unaugmented vowel	augmented vowel
α|ε, ᾳ, αι, ει ⟷ η, ῃ	
ο, οι ⟶ ω, ῳ	
αυ|ευ ⟶ ηυ	
ε ⟶ ει|η	

(ii) The imperfect is based on the present *stem of the verb. Take the present stem and add an augment to the beginning and the appropriate personal endings.*

(iii) The augment is added to the base verb, not to any prefixes it may have acquired. Thus the imperfect of:

> διαβαίνω *is* δι-έ-βαινον
> εἰσβαίνω   εἰσ-έ-βαινον *etc.*

(iv) You have already seen how, in the imperfect, διαβαίνω *becomes* διέβαινον. *Observe how other prefixes to verbs react to the addition of an augment.*

κατα-βαίνω	κατ-έβαινον
ἀπο-βαίνω	ἀπ-έβαινον
ἐπι-βαίνω	ἐπ-έβαινον
μετα-βαίνω	μετ-έβαινον
ἐκ-βαίνω	ἐξ-έβαινον
ἐμ-βαίνω (= ἐν-βαίνω)	ἐν-έβαινον
ἐγ-καλῶ (= ἐν-καλῶ)	ἐν-εκάλουν
προ-βαίνω	προ-έβαινον (*or* προὔβαινον)

(v) The imperfect tense carries the meanings:

> 'I was –ing'   'I tried to –'
> 'I used to –'   'I began –ing, I kept on –ing'
> 'I continued –ing'

In other words, they denote an action continuing or going on in the past, as a process *rather than as a single event.*

(vi) Note the irregular imperfect of the verb 'to be':

> ἦ(ν)   *I was etc.*
> ἦσθα
> ἦν
> ἦμεν
> ἦτε (ἦστε)
> ἦσαν

Adjectives

60 Observe the subtle Greek use of the *position* of the adjective in relation to its noun + def. art. to indicate a slightly different meaning:

    (a) ὁ σοφὸς ἀνήρ 'the wise man'
    (b) ὁ ἀνὴρ ὁ σοφός 'the wise man'
BUT: (c) σοφὸς ὁ ἀνήρ 'the man is wise'
    (d) ὁ ἀνὴρ σοφός 'the man is wise'

This distinction applies to all cases of the noun, e.g.

    πολλὴν τὴν δαπανὴν εἰσέφερεν 'much the expense she caused'

i.e. 'the expense which she caused was much'; cf.

    πολλὴν δαπανὴν εἰσέφερεν 'she caused much expense'

When the adjective stands *outside* the def. art. + noun phrase and is not linked with it by a preceding def. art., it will carry this 'predicative' meaning (as in (c) and (d) above).

Exercises for Section Five A–B

(b/c) Morphology and Syntax

1. Translate each sentence, then change the verbs from the present to imperfect tense:

  a. καθεύδω ἐγώ, ἀλλ' ἔτι διώκουσί με οἱ ἄνδρες οὗτοι.

  b. τίς αἴτιός ἐστιν; ἡ γυνή. ἀεὶ γὰρ λαμβάνει τὸν υἱὸν καὶ διαλέγεται περὶ τῶν ἵππων.

  c. ὁ γάμος ὡς πικρός ἐστιν. ἀεὶ γὰρ πικρὸν ποιεῖ τὸν γάμον ἡ γυνή.

  d. νέοι ἐσμὲν καὶ κολάζομεν τοὺς οἰκέτας. οὕτως γὰρ χρηστοὶ γίγνονται οἱ οἰκέται.

  e. οὐ φοβοῦνται τοὺς δεσπότας οἱ δοῦλοι, οὐδὲ πείθονται.

2. Translate each verb, then change to singular or plural as appropriate (numbers in brackets indicate which person, where there is ambiguity):

  διελεγόμεθα, ἐθεώμεθα, εἰσέφερον (3), ὤφειλες, ἐνῆμεν, ἐθεᾶσθε, ἐπείθου, ἐφοβοῦντο, ἐπεκαλούμην, ἔπαυον (1), ἦν, ἐφοβοῦ, ἐθεᾶτο

(d) English into Greek

Translate into Greek:

1. I was sleeping deeply but my son did not stop shouting.

2. The father always punished his son.

3. Young men used to be good, and obey.
4. We used to give orders, but the slaves mistreated us.
5. We would shout and stop the slaves conversing.

Vocabulary for Section Five C

αἰτί-α, ἡ responsibility (1b)
ἀκούσ-ομαι I shall listen
  (ἀκού-ω)
αὔριον tomorrow
δια-νοέ-ομαι intend, have in
  mind
διά-νοι-α, ἡ plan (1b)
Διόνυσ-ος, ὁ Dionysos (2a)
  (god of nature, esp. wine)
ἤκου-ον ⎫
ἤκου-ες ⎭ imperfect of ἀκού-ω
ἱππι-ος -α -ον of horses,
  horsey
ἴσως perhaps
κελεύσ-ω I shall order
  (κελεύ-ω)
κελεύσ-εις you (s.) will order
  (κελεύ-ω)
λέξ-ω I shall tell (λέγ-ω)

μάτην in vain, to no purpose
μηδαμ-ῶς in no way, not at
  all
μοι to me
νυνί = νῦν
νῷ mind
οὐδέποτε never
οὐχί = οὐκ
πάνυ very
παύσ-ομαι I shall stop/cease
  (παύ-ομαι)
παυσ-όμεθα we shall stop,
  cease (παύ-ομαι)
παύσ-ω I shall stop (παύ-ω)
παύσ-ει (it) will stop (παύ-ω)
πείσ-ομαι I shall obey
  (πείθ-ομαι)
πείσ-ῃ you (s.) will obey
  (πείθ-ομαι)

ποιήσ-ω I shall do (ποιέ-ω)
ποιήσ-εις you will do
  (ποιέ-ω)
Ποσειδῶν (Ποσειδων-), ὁ
  Poseidon (3a)
πως somehow
σμικρ-ός -ά -όν small
σοι to you
σ-ός σ-ή σ-όν your
σώσ-ει (it) will save (σῴζ-ω)
Φειδιππίδ-ης, ὁ Pheidippides
  (1d)
Φειδιππίδι-ον dear little
  Pheidippides (2b)
φιλέ-ω love
φιλήσ-ω I shall love (φιλέ-ω)
φιλήσ-εις you (s.) will love
  (φιλέ-ω)

Vocabulary to be learnt

αἰτία, ἡ reason, cause,
  responsibility (1b)
διανοέομαι intend, plan
διάνοια, ἡ intention, plan (1b)
νοῦς, ὁ (νόος contr.) mind,
  sense (2a)

οὐδέποτε never
Ποσειδῶν (Ποσειδων-), ὁ
  Poseidon (god of sea) (3a)
  (voc. Πόσειδον; acc.
  Ποσειδῶ)

πως somehow
φιλέω love, kiss

Vocabulary for Section Five D

ἄ-δικ-ος -ον unjust
αἰβοῖ uggghh!
ἀκούσ-ομαι I shall listen
  (ἀκου-ω)
ἀκούσ-ῃ you (s.) will listen
  (ἀκού-ω)

ἀκριβεῖς exact, accurate (acc.)
ἄνθραξ (ἀνθρακ-), ὁ charcoal
  (3a)
ἀντί-δικ-ος, -ον adversary (in
  court) (2a)
ἀν-υπό-δητ-ος-ον unshod,

barefoot
ἀπο-βλέπ-ω gaze at, observe
  closely
αὔριον tomorrow
αὐτ-ὸς myself (nom.)

βοήσ-ομαι I shall shout
(βοά-ω)
βραδύς slow (nom.)
γε at least; yes, and
γενήσ-ομαι I shall become
(γίγν-ομαι)
γέρων (γεροντ-), ὁ old man
(3a)
γνώσ-ομαι I shall get to know
(γιγνώσκ-ω)
δέχ-ομαι receive
δῆτα then
δια-φθερ-εῖ (it) will get rid of
(δια-φθείρ-ω)
διδάσκ-ω teach
δίκαι-ος -α -ον just
διώξ-ω I shall chase (διώκ-ω)
δύο two (acc.)
εἰ (μή) if (not)
εἰσ-έρχ-ομαι enter
εἴσ-ειμι I shall enter
(εἰσ-έρχ-ομαι)
εἴσ-ει (you) (s.) will enter
(εἰσ-έρχ-ομαι)
εἴσ-εισι(ν) (he) will enter
(εἰσ-έρχ-ομαι)
εἴσ-ιμεν we will enter
(εἰσ-έρχ-ομαι)
εἰς κόρακας to hell! (lit. 'to the
crows')
ἐκ-βαλ-ῶ I shall throw out
(ἐκ-βάλλ-ω)
ἔνδον inside
ἐν-οικέ-ω live (in)
εὔξ-ομαι I shall offer prayers
(εὔχ-ομαι)

ἦ ἦ tut tut!
θύρι-ον, τό little door (2b)
ἵππι-ος -α -ον of horses,
horsey
καὶ δὴ καὶ and moreover
καλοί τε κἀγαθοί jolly good
chaps, real gentlemen
κόπτ-ω knock (on)
κόψ-ω I shall knock (on)
(κόπτ-ω)
λέξ-εις you (s.) will say
(λέγ-ω)
λήψ-ονται (they) will get
(λαμβάν-ω)
λόγ-ος, ὁ argument (2a)
μαθήσ-ομαι I shall learn
(μανθάν-ω)
μαθήσ-ονται they shall learn
(μανθάν-ω)
μαθητ-ής, ὁ student (1d)
μὴ not
μοι to me
νικήσ-ει (he) will win
(νικά-ω)
νικήσ-ουσι(ν) they will
defeat (νικά-ω)
νικη-φόρ-ος -ον victorious
νυν then
οἰκίδι-ον, τό little house (2b)
ὅμως nevertheless
ὄνομα (ὀνοματ-), τό name
(3b)
οὐδαμ-ῶς no way, not at all
οὔκουν not . . . therefore
οὐραν-ός, ὁ sky (2a)
οὔτε . . . οὔτε neither . . . nor

παρὰ τῶν μαθητῶν from the
students
παύσ-εται (he) will stop
(παύ-ομαι)
παυσ-όμεθα we shall cease
(παύ-ομαι)
παύσ-ω I shall stop (παύ-ω)
πείθ-ω persuade
πείσ-ομαι I shall obey
(πείθ-ομαι)
πείσ-ῃ you (s.) will obey
(πείθ-ομαι)
πνιγεύς, ὁ oven (3g)
ποιήσ-ω I shall do (ποιέ-ω)
ποιήσ-εις you (s.) will do
(ποιέ-ω)
πονηρ-ός -ά -όν wicked, nasty
σοφιστ-ής, ὁ sophist (1d)
σοφ-ός -ή -όν wise, clever
ταῖς δίκαις their lawsuits
τῆς οἰκίας the house
τήμερον today
τὸν Σωκράτη Socrates
φεύξ-ομαι I shall run off
(φεύγ-ω)
φιλο-σοφί-α, ἡ philosophy
(1b)
φροντιστήρι-ον, τό
think-tank, mental institute
(2b)
Χαιρεφῶν (Χαιρεφωντ-), ὁ
Khairephon (3a)
χρήστ-ης, ὁ creditor (1d)
ψυχ-ή, ἡ soul (1a)
ὡς that
ὠχρ-ός -ά -όν pale

Vocabulary to be learnt

ἄδικος ον unjust
αὔριον tomorrow
γε at least (denotes some sort of
reservation)
δέχομαι receive
διδάσκω teach
δίκαιος α ον just

εἰσέρχομαι (εἰσελθ-) enter
ἔνδον inside
καὶ δὴ καί moreover
κόπτω knock (on), cut
λόγος, ὁ argument; word,
speech; story, tale; reason (2a)
μαθητής, ὁ student (1d)

οὔτε . . . οὔτε neither . . . nor
πείθω persuade
σοφιστής, ὁ sophist, thinker
(1d)
σοφός ή όν wise, clever

○　Grammar for Section Five C–D

Summary:
Fut. ind. act. and mid.
Act./mid. distinction
Indef. words
Σωκράτης|τριήρης (nom., acc.)

Verbs
Future indicative active and middle παύσω, παύσομαι *'I shall stop'*

61 The forms of the future indicative active are as follows:

παύσ-ω　　　　　'I shall stop' *etc.*
παύσ-εις
παύσ-ει
παύσ-ομεν
παύσ-ετε
παύσ-ουσι(ν)

62 The forms of the future indicative middle are as follows:

παύσ-ομαι　　　'I shall stop'*etc.*
παύσ-ῃ (-ει)
παύσ-εται
παυσ-όμεθα
παύσ-εσθε
παύσ-ονται

Notes
(i) The distinguishing signs of the future are two:
(a) most commonly, the presence of some form of σ- *suffix at the end of the present stem,*
e.g.

παύω→παύσω　　'I shall stop'
εὔχομαι→εὔξομαι　'I shall pray'
κόπτω→κόψω　　'I shall knock'
πείθω→πείσω　　'I shall persuade'
Observe that κσ→ξ *and* πσ→ψ.

or (b) an -εω *suffix, after a stem different from that of the present, e.g.*

διαφθείρω→διαφθερῶ (-έω) *'I shall destroy'*
νομίζω→νομιῶ (-έω)　　　*'I shall think'*

This frequently applies to verbs whose stem ends in λ, μ, ν *or* ρ
(ii) The endings for the future active and middle are identical to those for the present.

(iii) Contr. vbs. lengthen the final vowel of the stem and add σ-, e.g.

ποιέω→ποιήσω 'I shall do'
δηλόω→δηλώσω 'I shall show'
τιμάω→τιμήσω 'I shall honour'

Notice that a lengthens to η, cf. τόλμα, τόλμης and ἀκούω, ἤκουον (but n.b. ρ ε ι at **12** *(ii) and* **24** *(note)).*

(iv) The meaning of the future is:
   'I will/shall –'
   'I am about to –'
   'I am going to –'

Some important futures

63 The following futures look irregular, but in fact fall into a pattern which you will soon come to recognise:

μανθάνω→μαθήσομαι 'I shall learn'
λαμβάνω→λήψομαι 'I shall take'
γιγνώσκω→γνώσομαι 'I shall get to know'
γίγνομαι→γενήσομαι 'I shall become'

N.b. the use of the middle forms in the future does not affect the meaning.

64 Ensure that you know the future of 'to be':

ἔσ-ομαι   'I shall be '*etc.*
ἔσ-η (-ει)
ἔσ-ται
ἐσ-όμεθα
ἔσ-εσθε
ἔσ-ονται

and the abnormal future εἶμι 'I shall go' (note accent and cf. εἰμί 'I am'):

εἶμι   'I shall go' *etc.*
εἶ
εἶσι
ἴμεν
ἴτε
ἴασι(ν)

Middles

65 So far, you have met verbs which have active forms, and verbs which have middle forms. But in this chapter, you have met verbs which display both types of form, e.g.

παύω 'I stop x'   παύομαι 'I stop myself'
πείθω 'I persuade'   πείθομαι 'I persuade myself, I trust, I believe in'

Very crudely, the difference can be described as follows: that in active verbs, the action moves out from the doer, but in middle verbs, it moves out from the doer and *back again* – i.e., in middle verbs, the doer's interest is involved. Consider the following examples:

$\phi\acute{\epsilon}\rho\omega$ 'I carry, bear' $\phi\acute{\epsilon}\rho o\mu a\iota$ 'I carry off for myself, win'

$\lambda\acute{\nu}\omega$ 'I release' $\lambda\acute{\nu}o\mu a\iota$ 'I release for myself, ransom'

Note
*This 'rule' only applies to verbs which display both active and middle forms in any one tense. It does not apply, for example, to **63** above, where the middle form of the future is the only form the verbs have. You will find quite a few verbs which have active present forms and middle future forms – but the meaning is not affected by the change because these will be the only forms they have, e.g.*

$\dot{a}\kappa o\acute{\nu}\omega$ *'I hear'* $\dot{a}\kappa o\acute{\nu}\sigma o\mu a\iota$ *'I shall hear'*

Indefinites/Interrogatives

66 You already know the distinction between $\tau\acute{\iota}s$ and $\tau\iota s$. The accented form means 'who?', the unaccented form means 'someone'. This distinction is carried across a wide range of Greek words, of which you have recently met $\pi\hat{\omega}s$ and $\pi\omega s$. The accented form means 'how?', the unaccented form means 'somehow'. These words are also connected with forms used in other contexts and built on different roots, characterised either by the absence of the initial π (hence $\dot{\omega}s$ 'how!' which you have already met), or by the presence of $\dot{o}$ before the consonant (to give in this case $\ddot{o}\pi\omega s$). Thus the complex of words $\pi\hat{\omega}s; \ddot{o}\pi\omega s, \pi\omega s, \dot{\omega}s$ all mean basically 'how', 'somehow', and Greek uses each in accordance with the context. Note the following chart:

Direct question	*Indirect question*	*Indefinite*	*Relative*
	'He asked where . . .' etc.	'Somewhere . . .'	'He goes where .
$\pi o\hat{\nu}$ 'where at?'	$\ddot{o}\pi o\nu$	$\pi o\nu$	$o\hat{\nu}, \ddot{o}\pi o\nu$
$\pi o\hat{\iota}$ 'to where?'	$\ddot{o}\pi o\iota$	$\pi o\iota$	$o\hat{\iota}, \ddot{o}\pi o\iota$
$\pi\acute{o}\theta\epsilon\nu$ 'from where?'	$\dot{o}\pi\acute{o}\theta\epsilon\nu$	$\pi o\theta\epsilon\nu$	$\ddot{o}\theta\epsilon\nu, \ddot{o}\pi o\theta\epsilon\nu$
$\pi\hat{\omega}s$ 'how?'	$\ddot{o}\pi\omega s$	$\pi\omega s$	$\dot{\omega}s, \ddot{o}\pi\omega s$
$\pi\acute{o}\tau\epsilon$ 'when?'	$\dot{o}\pi\acute{o}\tau\epsilon$	$\pi o\tau\epsilon$	$\ddot{o}\tau\epsilon, \dot{o}\pi\acute{o}\tau\epsilon$

N.b. The indefinite forms are all *enclitics* (see Reference Grammar A.3 (5)).

Noun

Here is the noun-type to be denoted 3d, like $\Sigma\omega\kappa\rho\acute{a}\tau\eta s$ (in the singular), and $\tau\rho\iota\acute{\eta}\rho\eta s$ (a trireme) in the plural:

67 Σωκράτης, ὁ 'Socrates' (3d)

s.

nom.	acc.	gen.	dat.
Σωκράτ-ης	Σωκράτ-η	Σωκράτ-ους	Σωκράτ-ει

pl.

nom.	acc.	gen.	dat.
τριήρ-εις	τριήρ-εις	τριήρ-ων	τριήρ-εσι(ν)

Notes

(i) *Words ending in -ης could be either like 1d ναύτης or 3d above.*

(ii) *The vocative form of 3d types is quite common: it is Σώκρατ-ες.* O

Exercises for Section Five C–D

(b/c) Morphology and Syntax

1. Translate these sentences, then change the verb(s) in each from the present to the future tense:

   a. ὁ πατὴρ κελεύει τὸν υἱόν.

   b. τί λέγεις, ὦ τᾶν;

   c. οὐ διδάσκομεν τοὺς διδασκάλους.

   d. οἱ ἄνδρες πολλὰ χρήματα δέχονται.

   e. οὐκ ἀκούομεν τοὺς λόγους.

   f. ἐγώ εἰμι σοφός, οὗτος δ' οὐ νικᾷ με.

   g. ὁ υἱὸς οὐ φιλεῖ τὸν πατέρα.

   h. ἡ διάνοια σῴζει ἡμᾶς.

   i. κόπτω τὴν θύραν καὶ βοῶ.

   j. τίς νικᾷ τὰς δίκας;

   k. οὐ παύονται μανθάνοντες οἱ μαθηταί.

   l. τίνες εἰσὶν οἱ σοφοί;

2. Translate each verb, then change to singular or plural as appropriate: παύσει, ἔσονται, ἀκουσόμεθα, διαφθερεῖς, εὔξεσθε

(d) English into Greek

Translate into Greek:

1. The young men will learn the unjust argument.

2. The good son will always love his father.
3. This horse will not stop running.
4. The student will go into the house.
5. The wise man will be just.

Vocabulary for Section Five E

ἄγρ-οικ-ος-ον from the
country
ἀ-μαθῆ ignorant (acc.)
ἀ-μαθής ignoramus (nom.)
ἄνοιγε open!
ἄξι-ος -α -ον worthy of
ἀπ-έ-κοψ-ας you (s.) cut off
(ἀπο-κόπτ-ω)
ἄρτι recently, just now
βάλλ' εἰς κόρακας go to hell!
δάκν-ω bite, worry
ἐ-βόησ-α I shouted (βοά-ω)
ἐ-βόησ-ας you (s.) shouted
(βοάω)
ἐ-βόησ-ε(ν) (he) shouted
(βοάω)
ἔ-θε-σαν they placed (τίθημι)
εἰς κόρακας to hell!
εἶτα then
ἐκ-βάλλ-ω throw out
ἐ-κέλευσ-α (I) gave the order
(κελεύ-ω)
ἐ-κέλευσ-ας you (s.) gave the
order (κελεύ-ω)
ἔ-κοψ-α (I) knocked at
(κόπτ-ω)
ἔ-κοψ-ε (he) knocked at
(κόπτ-ω)
ἔ-λυσ-αν they undid (λύ-ω)
ἐμβάς (ἐμβαδ-), ἡ slipper (3a)
ἐ-μέτρησ-αν they measured
(μετρέ-ω)
ἐ-παυσ-άμην I stopped
(παύ-ομαι)

ἐ-παύσ-ατο he stopped
(παύ-ομαι)
ἐπεί when
ἐ-πήδησ-ε(ν) (it) leapt
(πηδά-ω)
ἐ-ποίησ-ας (you) (s.) did
(ποιέ-ω)
ἐ-ποίησ-αν (they) did
(ποιέ-ω)
ἦ truly
ἥκ-ω I have come
Θαλ-ῆς, ὁ Thales (1d) (early
Greek scientist and inventor, a
by-word for cleverness)
θαυμάζ-ω wonder (at)
θέμις, ἡ right, lawful (lit. law
sanctioned by the gods) (3a)
θερμ-ός -ή -όν hot
καίπερ although (+part.)
κεφαλ-ή, ἡ head (1a)
κηρ-ός, ὁ wax (2a)
Κικυννόθεν from the deme
Kikynna
λύ-ω release, undo
μετρέ-ω measure (fut.
μετρήσω)
μοι to me
μόν-ος -η -ον alone
νῷ mind
ὁπόσους τοὺς ἑαυτῆς
πόδας how many of its
own foot lengths
οὗτος hey, you!

παιδί-ον, τό slave, slave dear
(2b)
πάλιν again
πηδά-ω leap
πήδημα (πηδηματ-), τό a
leap (3b)
πόδας see πούς
ποτε ever
πούς (ποδ-), ὁ foot (3a)
πρῶτον first
ῥᾳδί-ως easily
σοι to you
Σωκράτους Socrates'
τὴν ὀφρ-ῦν the eyebrow
τῆς σοφίας the cleverness!
τῆς ψύλλης of the flea
τί δέ; what next?
τί δῆτ' why then . . .?
τίθημι I place, put
τοῦ Ὀλυμπικοῦ στεφάνου the
Olympic crown
φροντίς (φροντιδ-), ἡ
thought (3a)
φροντιστήρι-ον, τό
think-tank, mental institute
(2b)
Χαιρεφῶντος Khairephon's
χωρί-ον, τό space, distance
(2b)
ψύλλ-α, ἡ flea (1c)
ψύλλης flea's
ψυχρ-ός -ά -όν cold
ὡς as

Vocabulary to be learnt

ἄγροικος ον *from the country,*
  boorish
βάλλ' εἰς κόρακας *go to hell!*
δάκνω (δακ-) *bite, worry*
ἐκβάλλω (ἐκβαλ-) *throw out*
ἐν νῷ ἔχω *intend, have in mind*

καίπερ *although (+part.)*
κεφαλή, ἡ *head (1a)*
λύω *release*
ὅτε *when*
πούς (ποδ-), ὁ *foot (3a)*
ῥᾴδιος α ον *easy*

ῥᾳδίως *easily*
φροντίς (φροντιδ-), ἡ *thought,*
  care, concern (3a)
ὡς *as*

Vocabulary for Section Five F

ἀ-δύνατ-ος -ον *impossible*
'Αθῆν-αι, αἱ *Athens (1a)*
ἀνα-μετρέ-ω *measure up*
ἄπ-ελθε *go away!*
ἄρα *then, in that case*
ἀστρο-νομέ-ω *observe the stars*
ἀστρο-νομί-α, ἡ *astronomy (1b)*
αὐτ-ός *Himself, the Master (nom.)*
βολβ-ός, ὁ *truffle (2a)*
γεωμετρί-α, ἡ *geometry (1b)*
γῆς *of the earth*
δῆμ-ος, ὁ *deme (2a)*
δικαστ-ής, ὁ *dikast, juror (1d)*

ἐ-βόησ-ας *you (s.) shouted (βοά-ω)*
ἐγγὺς ἡμῶν *near to us*
ἐ-θαύμασ-ας *you (s.) were amazed (θαυμάζ-ω)*
ἕνα *one (acc. m. of εἷς μία ἕν)*
ἐνταῦθα *here*
ἐπεί *since*
ἐπὶ τῆς κρεμάθρας *in the basket*
Εὔβοι-α, ἡ *Euboia (1b)*
'Ηράκλεις *Herakles!*
θαυμάζ-ω *be amazed*
θηρί-ον, τό *beast (2b)*
καθ-ίζομαι *sit down*
κατὰ γῆς *below the earth*

Λακεδαίμων (Λακεδαιμον-), ἡ
  Sparta (3a)
μοι *to me*
ὀλοφυρ-εῖσθ' = 2nd pl. fut.
  (contr.) of ὀλοφύρ-ομαι
ὅπου *where?*
οὐραν-ός, ὁ *sky (2a)*
πάνυ *very*
παπαῖ *good heavens!*
πείθ-ομαι *believe*
περί-οδ-ος, ἡ *map (2a)*
πόρρω *far*
πρωκτ-ός, ὁ *rump (2a)*
ταύτῃ *with this*
χρήσιμ-ος -η -ον *useful*

Vocabulary to be learnt

ἀδύνατος ον *impossible*
'Αθῆναι, αἱ *Athens (1a)*
δῆμος, ὁ *deme (2a)*
θαυμάζω *wonder at, be amazed at*

ὅπου *where? where*
οὐρανός, ὁ *sky, heavens (2a)*
πείθομαι (πιθ-) *believe, trust*

Grammar for Section Five E–F

Summary:
Wk. aor. ind. act. and mid.
ὀφρῦς (nom. acc.)

Verbs

Weak aorist indicative active and middle ἔπαυσα, ἐπαυσάμην '*I stopped*'

68 The forms of the weak aorist indicative active are as follows:

ἔ-παυσ-α   'I stopped' *etc.*
ἔ-παυσ-ας
ἔ-παυσ-ε(ν)
ἐ-παύσ-αμεν
ἐ-παύσ-ατε
ἔ-παυσ-αν

69 The forms of the weak aorist indicative middle are as follows:

ἐ-παυσ-άμην   'I stopped' *etc.*
ἐ-παύσ-ω
ἐ-παύσ-ατο
ἐ-παυσ-άμεθα
ἐ-παύσ-ασθε
ἐ-παύσ-αντο

Notes

(i) Note the presence of the augment, to denote the past tense (cf. **59** *(iii)).*

(ii) The distinguishing mark of the wk. aorist indicative is the augment, and a -(σ)a-suffix added to the stem (which is sometimes different from that of the present):

κόπτω→ἔκοψα   'I knocked'
διδάσκω→ἐδίδαξα   'I taught'
δέχομαι→ἐδεξάμην 'I received'

Note the stem change in μένω–ἔμεινα, διαφθείρω–διέφθειρα.

(iii) Contracted verbs lengthen the final vowel of their stem (cf. **62** *(iii)).*

ποιέω→ἐποίησα   'I did'
τιμάω→ἐτίμησα   'I honoured'
δηλόω→ἐδήλωσα 'I showed'

(iv) Aorist indicatives indicate that something has happened in the past without reference to the duration of time over which it occurred. They regard the action as a single event, not as a process (contrast imperfects at **59** *(iii)). Translate them as:*

'I –ed' (sometimes, also, 'I had –ed', sometimes 'I have –ed'.)

Noun

Here is the final noun-type, denoted 3h:

70 ὀφρ-ῦς, ἡ 'eyebrow' (3h)

s.				pl.			
nom.	*acc.*	*gen.*	*dat.*	*nom.*	*acc.*	*gen.*	*dat.*
ὀφρ-ῦς	ὀφρ-ῦν	ὀφρ-ύος	ὀφρ-ύι	ὀφρ-ύες	ὀφρ-ῦς	ὀφρ-ύων	ὀφρ-ύσι(ν)

Exercises for Section Five E–F

(b/c) Morphology and Syntax

1. Translate each sentence, then change the verb into the aorist:
   a. τίς κόπτει τὴν θύραν;
   b. τίς βιάζεται εἰς τὸ φροντιστήριον;
   c. ἀλλ' αὖθις κόπτω καὶ οὐ παύομαι κόπτων.
   d. λέξω σοί.
   e. τέλος δὲ τὰς ἐμβάδας λύσομεν.
   f. τί δῆτ' ἐκεῖνον τὸν Θαλῆν θαυμάζομεν;
2. Translate each sentence, then change the verb into the aorist:
   a. ἡ ψύλλα πηδᾷ ἐπὶ τὴν κεφαλὴν τὴν Σωκράτους.
   b. ἀλλὰ πῶς μετρήσεις, ὦ Χαιρέφων;
   c. τέλος δὲ μετροῦμεν τὸ χωρίον.
   d. ζητοῦσιν οὗτοι τὰ κατὰ γῆς καὶ οὐ παύονται ζητοῦντες.
   e. τί δηλοῖ τὸ πρᾶγμα, ὦ Σώκρατες;

(d) English into Greek

Translate into Greek:
1. The farmer gave a shout and a knock on the door.
2. Don't they know that you received this idea with pleasure?
3. The sophist did not persuade the clever young men.
4. The just man, though clever, was astounded at the unjust argument.
5. They stopped looking at the horses.

Vocabulary for Section Five G

ἀερο-βατέ-ω tread the air
ἀ-μαθής ignorant (nom.)
ἀνα-μετρέ-ω measure up
ἀπ-έρχ-ομαι depart
βιάζ-ομαι use force, force
  one's way
δρά-ω do
ἐ-γέν-ετο (it) became
  (γίγν-ομαι)
ἔ-δακ-ε (it) bit (δάκν-ω)
ἔ-θε-τε you (pl.) put (τίθημι)
εἶδ-ον (I) saw (ὁρά-ω)
εἶδ-ες (you) (s.) saw (ὁρά-ω)
εἶπ-ε (he) said (λέγ-ω)
εἶτα then, next
ἐ-λάβ-ετε you (pl.) took
  (λαμβάν-ω)
ἔ-λαθ-ες you (s.) escaped the
  notice of (λανθάν-ω)
ἔ-μαθ-ον (I) learnt
  (μανθάν-ω)
ἐμβάς (ἐμβαδ-), ἡ slipper (3a)
ἐξ-ευρίσκ-ω (ἐξευρ-) find
  out, discover
ἐξ-ηῦρ-ον (I) found out,
  discovered (ἐξ-ευρίσκ-ω)

ἐπὶ κρεμάθρας in a basket
ἐπὶ ταύτης τῆς κρεμάθρας in
  this basket
ἔ-σχ-ε(ν) (it) had (ἔχ-ω)
ἔ-τυχ-ε (it) happened to,
  actually was (τυγχάν-ω)
ἐφ-ήμερ-ος -ον lasting a day,
  creature of a day
ἦλθ-ον I came (ἔρχ-ομαι)
ἦλθ-ες (you) (s.) came
  (ἔρχ-ομαι)
ἥλι-ος, ὁ sun (2a)
ἦρ-ου you (s.) asked
  (ἐρωτά-ω)
θερμ-ός -ή -όν hot
κατὰ τί; for what?
κηρ-ός, ὁ wax (2a)
Κικυννόθεν from the deme
  Kikynna
κρεμάθρας a basket
μέμφ-ομαι blame, find fault
  with
μετέωρ-ος -ον in the air
μοι me
ὁπόσους τοὺς ἑαυτῆς
  πόδας how many of its
  own foot lengths

οὐδὲν λέγ-ω speak nonsense
οὐδέποτε never
ὀφρ-ῦς, ἡ eyebrow (3h)
περι-φρονέ-ω surround with
  thought,
  circumcontemplate
Περσικ-ός -ή -όν Persian
πηδά-ω leap
πρῶτον first
σ-ός σ-ή σ-όν your
Σωκρατίδι-ον dear Socrates
  (2b)
τῆς γῆς the earth
τί; why?
φροντιστήρι-ον, τό
  think-tank, mental institute
  (2b)
Χαιρεφῶντος of Khairephon
χωρί-ον, τό space, distance
  (2b)
ψύλλ-α, ἡ flea (1c)
ψυχρ-ός -ά -όν cold
ὡς that

Vocabulary to be learnt

ἀπέρχομαι (ἀπελθ-) depart, go
  away
βιάζομαι use force
εἶτα then, next
ἐξευρίσκω (ἐξευρ-) find out
ἥλιος, ὁ sun (2a)

πηδάω leap, jump
πόρρω far, far off
πρῶτος η ον first
πρῶτον first, at first
ὁπόσος η ον how many
Σωκράτης, ὁ Socrates (3d)

τί; why?
(τίθημι) θε- put, place
χωρίον, τό place, space, region
  (2b)

Vocabulary for Section Five H

ἀ-μαθής ignorant (nom.)
ἀ-μαθῆ ignorant (acc.)
ἀνα-τελ-εῖ (it) will rise (fut. of
  ἀνα-τέλλ-ω)

'Απόλλων ('Απολλων-),
  ὁ Apollo (3a) (acc.
  'Απόλλω)

γέρων (γεροντ-), ὁ old man
  (3a)
γνώμ-η, ἡ plan (1a)

δανείζ-ω lend (money)
δῆτα then; indeed
δρά-ω (δρασ-) do, act
ἐ-γεν-όμην I became
  (γίγν-ομαι)
ἐ-γέν-ου (you) (s.) became
  (γίγν-ομαι)
εἰ if
εἰ ἄρα whether, indeed
ἐκφροντίζ-ω think out
ἔ-λαθ-ον I escaped notice
  (λανθάν-ω)
ἐμαυτ-ὸν myself (acc.)
ἔ-παθ-ον I experienced,
  suffered (πάσχ-ω)
ἐπὶ τῆς κλίνης on the couch
ἕτερ-ος -α -ον the one (of 2)
ἦλθ-ον (I) came (ἔρχ-ομαι)
ἥττων ἧττον
  (ἥττον-) weaker, lesser

ἱππικ-ή, ἡ horse-fever (1a)
ἱππο-μανὴ horse-mad (acc.)
κατα-κλίνηθι lie down! (s.)
κλέπτω steal
κόρ-ις, ὁ bug (3e)
κρείττων κρεῖττον
  (κρειττον-) stronger,
  greater
λήσ-ω I shall escape notice
  (fut. of λανθάν-ω)
μὴ not
μήν (μην-), ὁ month (3a)
νυκτὶ at night
ὅπως; how?
ὅ τι; what?
οὗτος hey, you!
πάνυ at all
πέ-ος, τό penis (3c)

πότερ-ος -α -ον which (of
  two)?
προσ-αγορεύ-ω address
σεαυτοῦ your own
σελήν-η, ἡ moon (1a)
σιγά-ω be quiet
σ-ός σ-ή σ-όν your
Σωκρατίδι-ον dear Socrates
  (2b)
τῇ δεξιᾷ right hand
τήμερον today
ὑπο-χρέ-ως -ων in debt
φαρμακίς (φαρμακιδ-), ἡ
  witch, sorceress (3a)
φροντιστήρι-ον, τό
  think-tank, mental institute
  (2b)
χρήσιμ-ος -η -ον useful
χρήστ-ης, ὁ creditor (1d)

Vocabulary to be learnt

ἀμαθής ignorant
ἄρα then, in that case (inferring)
γέρων (γεροντ-), ὁ old man
  (3a)
γνώμη, ἡ mind, purpose,
  judgment, plan (1a)
δεξιός ά όν right
δεξιά, ἡ right hand (1b)
δῆτα then
δράω (δρασ-) do, act

εἰ if
ἐμαυτόν myself
ἕτερος α ον one (or the other) of
  two
ἥττων ἧττον (ἥττον-) lesser,
  weaker
κλέπτω steal
κρείττων κρεῖττον
  (κρειττον-) stronger, greater

οὗτος hey there! hey you!
πάνυ very (much); at all
πότερος α ον which (of two)
σελήνη, ἡ moon (1a)
σός σή σόν your (when 'you' are
  one person)
τήμερον today
χρήσιμος η ον useful, profitable

O   Grammar for Section Five G–H

Summary
Str. aor. ind. act. and mid., interrogatives

Verbs
Strong aorist indicative active and middle ἔλαβον ἐλαβόμην *'I took'*

71 The forms of the strong aorist indicative active are as follows:

ἔ-λαβ-ον   'I took' etc.
ἔ-λαβ-ες
ἔ-λαβ-ε(ν)

ἐ-λάβ-ομεν
ἐ-λάβ-ετε
ἔ-λαβ-ον

72 The forms of the strong aorist indicative middle are as follows:

ἐ-λαβ-όμην   'I took' *etc.*
ἐ-λάβ-ου
ἐ-λάβ-ετο
ἐ-λαβ-όμεθα
ἐ-λάβ-εσθε
ἐ-λάβ-οντο

Notes

(i) Verbs which take strong aorist forms nearly always undergo a more radical stem-change than weak aorists. These stem changes have to be learnt. Some you should already recognise from earlier learning vocabularies.

The most important and common verbs taking strong aorist forms are:

μανθάνω→ἔμαθον	'I learnt'	
λαμβάνω→ἔλαβον	'I took'	
τυγχάνω→ἔτυχον	'I happened'	
γίγνομαι→ἐγενόμην	'I became'	
εὑρίσκω→ηὗρον	'I found'	
ἔχω→ἔσχον	'I had'	
λέγω→εἶπον	'I said'	Note the use of a
ὁράω→εἶδον	'I saw'	completely different stem for
ἔρχομαι→ἦλθον	'I came/went'	the present and aorist
τρέχω→ἔδραμον	'I ran'	(cf. English 'go': 'went').

*(ii) The endings of the strong aorist forms are just the same as for the imperfects (see **58**, **59**). The difference lies in the change of stem, because the strong aorists have a stem of their own which is different from that of the present and imperfect. The imperfect adds endings to the present stem; the strong aorist adds endings to the strong aorist stem, e.g.*

μανθάνω impf. ἐ-μάνθαν-ον (μανθαν- is present stem)

μανθάνω aor. ἔ-μαθ-ον (μαθ- is strong aorist stem)

*(iii) The meaning of the strong aorist is just the same as the weak, i.e. 'I –ed' (see **69** (iv)). (On finding the lexicon form, cf. p. 335).*

Interrogatives

73 Observe that τί, which you have learnt to mean 'what?' can also, and very commonly, mean 'why?'. When τί does mean 'why?', it is in the accusative case and being used adverbially. Its literal meaning is 'in relation to what?' or 'in respect of what?' – in other words, 'why?'

Revise:
Pres. mid. **23**
Type 1 nouns **24**

Exercises for Section Five G–H

(b) Morphology

1. Form the aorist (1st s.) of these verbs and give the aorist stem:
   e.g. παύω   ἔπαυσα   παυσ(α)
   βιάζομαι
   κλέπτω
   θαυμάζω
   διδάσκω
   δέχομαι
   φιλέω
   πηδάω
   ποιέω
   δηλόω

2. Give the aorist (1st s.) of these verbs and give the aorist stem:
   e.g. τρέχω   ἔδραμον   δραμ-
   μανθάνω
   ἔρχομαι
   ἐξευρίσκω
   διαβάλλω

3. Give the meaning of each verb (unaugmented stem in brackets), then
   pair aorist with present from the list below:
   εἶδον (ἰδ-), εἶπον (εἰπ-), ἔλαθον (λαθ-), ηὗρον (εὑρ-), ἔμαθον (μαθ-),
   ἦλθον (ἐλθ-), ἐγενόμην (γεν-), ἔπαθον (παθ-)
   γίγνομαι, λέγω, πάσχω, λανθάνω, εὑρίσκω, ἔρχομαι, μανθάνω, ὁράω

(d) English into Greek
Translate into Greek:

1. The student said that he discovered how big the space was.
2. The farmer happened to be an ignoramus.
3. The old man departed.
4. The father became unjust.
5. I noticed that you were a bumpkin.

Exercises for Section Five

(a) Words

1. Deduce the meanings of the words in the right-hand columns from those in the left:

ἀδύνατος	ἡ δύναμις	δύναμαι	
αἴτιος/αἰτία	αἰτιάομαι		
βιάζομαι	βίαιος α ον	ἡ βία	
διδάσκω	ὁ διδάσκαλος	ἡ δίδαξις	διδακτικός ή όν
δίκη	δίκαιος ον	ὁ ἀντίδικος	ἄδικος ον
	ἀδικέω	ὁ δικαστής	δικάζω
δράω	τὸ δρᾶμα		
δυστυχής	δυστυχέω		
θαυμάζω	θαυμάσιος α ον	τὸ θαῦμα	θαυμαστός ή όν
ἱππομανής	μαίνομαι	ἡ μανία	
ἵππος	ἵππιος	ἡ ἱππική	ὁ ἱππεύς
κλέπτω	ὁ κλέπτης	ἡ κλοπή	
μανθάνω	μαθητής	ἀμαθής	μαθηματικός ή όν
νοῦς	διανοέομαι	διάνοια	νοέω ἐννοέω
οἰκέτης	οἰκίδιον	ἡ οἰκία	ἐνοικέω
	ὁ οἶκος	οἰκεῖος α ον	
σοφός	ἡ σοφία	σοφιστής	ἡ φιλοσοφία
	φιλέω		

2. Translate these pairs of words: what is the significance of the change from left to right?

γέρων	γερόντιον
θύρα	θυρίδιον
οἰκία	οἰκίδιον
παῖς	παιδίον
πατήρ	πατρίδιον
Σωκράτης	Σωκρατίδιον
Φειδιππίδης	Φειδιππίδιον

(b/c) Morphology and Syntax

1. Translate this passage (if you did not do Test Exercise Two); then change the tense of the verbs to imperfect or aorist as indicated:

ἐπειδὴ οὖν προσέρχονται (Aorist) ἡ τῶν Περσῶν στρατιὰ καὶ τὸ
ναυτικόν, οἱ Ἀθηναῖοι ταχέως εἰσβαίνουσιν (imperfect) εἰς τὰς ναῦς καὶ

πρὸς τὴν Σαλαμῖνα πλέουσιν (aorist). ἔπειτα δὲ οἵ τε Ἀθηναῖοι καὶ οἱ
ἄλλοι Ἕλληνες ἡσυχάζουσι (imperfect). τέλος δὲ ἀφικνεῖται (aorist) τὸ
τῶν Περσῶν ναυτικόν, καὶ ἐπειδὴ νὺξ γίγνεται (aorist), ἔνθα καὶ ἔνθα
βραδέως πλέουσιν (aorist) αἱ νῆες. καὶ ἐπειδὴ γίγνεται (aorist) ἡ ἡμέρα,
οἱ μὲν Πέρσαι προσέρχονται (aorist) ταχέως ἐπὶ ναυμαχίαν, οἱ δὲ
Ἕλληνες ἀποροῦσι (aorist) καὶ φοβοῦνται (imperfect). τέλος δὲ οὐκέτι
φοβοῦνται (imperfect), ἀλλὰ τολμῶσι (imperfect) καὶ ἐπέρχονται
(aorist) ἐπὶ τοὺς βαρβάρους. μάχονται (imperfect) οὖν εὐκόσμως καὶ
νικῶσι (aorist) τοὺς βαρβάρους. οἱ μὲν οὖν βάρβαροι φεύγουσι
(imperfect), φεύγει (aorist) δὲ καὶ ὁ Ξέρξης. οὕτως οὖν ἐλεύθεροι
γίγνονται (aorist) οἱ Ἕλληνες διὰ τὴν ἀρετήν.

Vocabulary

ἔνθα καὶ ἔνθα up and down	πλέω αορ. ἔπλευσα
ἡμέρα, ἡ day (1b)	ἀφικνέομαι αορ. ἀφικόμην
εὐκόσμως in good order	φεύγω αορ. ἔφυγον
ἀρετή, ἡ courage (1a)	

(d) English into Greek
Translate into Greek:
An old man and his son, a young man, were talking about money. The
youngster, as it happened, owed a lot of money. And because of this,
his creditors would not stop pursuing his father. The father did not
punish the son (for his mother stopped him), but conceived a clever
plan. When therefore the father managed to persuade his son, the boy
went obediently to the sophists and learnt a great deal. The sophists
always persuaded him, taught a lot of clever stuff and received a lot of
money. So the son learnt quickly the just and unjust arguments,
always winning his case. But when the youth came home, this plan did
not put a stop to his debts. The young man did not like his father (who
was a yokel), but hated him. So the boy never stopped mocking his
father. Finally, the old man threw him out.

Test Exercise Five
Translate into English:
νεανίας δέ τις ἔτυχε πολλὰ χρήματα ὀφείλων διὰ τὴν ἱππικήν. οὕτως οὖν
ὁ μὲν πατὴρ ἀεὶ τὰς δίκας τὰς τῶν χρηστῶν ἔφευγεν, οἱ δὲ χρῆσται
ἐδίωκον αὐτὸν καὶ οὐκ ἐπαύοντο δίκην λαμβάνοντες. διαλέγονται οὖν ὅ
τε πατὴρ καὶ ἡ μήτηρ.
ΠΑΤΗΡ σὺ δή, ὦ γύναι, φαίνῃ αἰτία οὖσα τῶν ἐμῶν κακῶν. τίς γὰρ

ἐλάμβανε τὸν υἱὸν καὶ περὶ ἵππων διελέγετο, εἰ μὴ σύ; τίς οὖν
ἱππομανῆ ἐποίησε τὸν υἱόν, εἰ μὴ σύ; τί νῦν ποιήσω ἐγώ; πῶς
παύσω τὰ χρέα;

ΜΗΤΗΡ σὺ δὴ αἴτιος εἶ, ὦ ἄνερ. ἀμαθῆ μὲν γὰρ καὶ ἄγροικον ὄντα σὲ οὐ
φιλεῖ ὁ νεανίας οὐδὲ πείθεται, ἐμὲ δὲ ἀστικὴν οὖσαν μάλιστα
φιλεῖ.

ἀλλὰ μὴ φρόντιζε. ἔχω γὰρ διάνοιάν τινα ἐγώ. πείσω καὶ
διδάξω τὸν υἱὸν ἔγωγε, πείθουσα δὲ παύσω ἐκ τῆς ἱππομανίας.

ἀλλὰ διδάσκουσα καὶ πείθουσα οὐκ ἐκώλυσε τὸν νεανίαν ἡ
μήτηρ, οὐδὲ ἐπαύετο ὁ υἱὸς ἱππομανὴς ὤν. τέλος δὲ ἦλθεν ὁ
νεανίας εἰς τὸ τῶν σοφιστῶν φροντιστήριον καὶ μαθητὴς
ἐγένετο. πολλὰ δὲ σοφὰ καὶ εἶδε καὶ ἤκουσε, πολλὰ δὲ ἐδίδαξαν
οἱ σοφισταί. ὅτε δὲ ἔμαθε τόν τε δίκαιον καὶ τὸν ἄδικον λόγον ὁ
υἱός, εἶπεν ὁ πατήρ.

ΠΑΤ. ἰοὺ ἰού. νῦν γὰρ οὐ λήψονται οὐκέτι οἱ χρῆσται τὰ χρήματα. ὁ
μὲν γὰρ υἱὸς νικήσει τὰς δίκας διὰ τὸν ἄδικον λόγον, τὸν
κρείττονα ὄντα, ἡμεῖς δὲ φευξόμεθα τοὺς χρήστας.

Vocabulary

ἱππικ-ή, ἡ horse-fever (1a)
μήτηρ (μητ(ε)ρ-), ἡ mother
    (3a)
χρήστης, ὁ creditor (1d)
ἱππομανῆ horse-mad (acc. s.
    m.)
ἀμαθῆ ignorant (acc. s. m.)

ἀστικός ή όν from the city
τῆς ἱππομανίας his
    horse-madness
ἱππομανής horse-mad (nom.
    s. m.)
ἰοὺ ἰού hurrah!

Section Six

Vocabulary for Section Six A

ἀλήθει-α, ἡ truth (1b)
ἀνάγκ-η, ἡ necessity (1a)
ἀνάγκ-η ἐστὶ it is obligatory
  for x (acc.) to – (inf.)
ἀπο-κρίν-ομαι
  (ἀποκριν-) answer
βούλ-ομαι wish, want
γὰρ δὴ I assure you; indeed
γάρ . . . που of course (no
  need to ask)
δεῖ it is necessary for x (acc.)
  to – (inf.)
Δελφ-οί, οἱ Delphi (2a) (site of
  Apollo's oracle)
Δελφοῖς Delphi
δια-βάλλ-ειν to slander
δια-βάλλ-ω (διαβαλ-) slander
δια-βολ-ή, ἡ a slander (1a)
διδάσκ-ειν to teach
δι-έ-βαλ-ον they slandered
  (aor. of διαβάλλ-ω)
δόξ-α, ἡ reputation (1c)
ἑαυτ-όν himself

εἰδέναι to know (οἶδα)
ἑταῖρ-ος, ὁ friend (2a)
ἤ than
ἤ-ει (he) went (impf. of
  ἔρχ-ομαι|εἶμι)
θορυβέ-ω make a din
ἰέναι to go (ἔρχ-ομαι|εἶμι)
ἴσως perhaps
καὶ μὴν moreover
λέγ-ειν to speak, say, tell
  (λέγ-ω)
λογίζ-ομαι reckon, consider
μαντεί-α, ἡ answer,
  pronouncement (1b)
μαντεύ-εσθαι to consult the
  oracle
μαντεύ-ομαι get from the
  oracle
μαρτυρέ-ω bear witness
μάρτυς (μαρτυρ-), ὁ witness
  (3a)
μέντοι however
νέου youth

παίζ-ειν to joke, to poke fun
  at (παίζ-ω)
πάντα everything (acc.)
παρὰ τῷ θεῷ in the god's
  presence
παρ-έχ-εσθαι to present
  (παρ-έχ-ομαι)
ποι-εῖν to do (ποιέ-ω)
ποτὲ once
Πυθί-α, ἡ the Pythian
  priestess (1b) (who sat on a
  tripod and delivered Apollo's
  oracle to the priest, who
  interpreted it)
σοφί-α, ἡ wisdom (1b)
σοφώτατ-ος -η -ον wisest
  (σοφ-ός)
σοφώτερ-ος -α -ον wiser
  (σοφ-ός)
σφοδρ-ός -ά -όν impetuous
φαν-οῦμαι I shall appear (fut.
  of φαίν-ομαι)

Vocabulary to be learnt

ἀλήθεια, ἡ truth (1b)
βούλομαι wish, want
διαβάλλω (διαβαλ-) slander
δόξα, ἡ reputation, opinion (1c)

ἑαυτόν himself
ἤ than
ἴσως perhaps
σοφία, ἡ wisdom (1b)

Vocabulary for Section Six B

αἰσχύν-ομαι be ashamed
ἀνάγκ-η ἐστί it is obligatory
   for x (acc.) to – (inf.)
ἀπ-ῆ-α I went off (impf. of
   ἀπ-έρχ-ομαι|ἄπειμι)
'Απόλλων ('Απολλων-), ὁ
   Apollo (3a) (acc.
   'Απόλλω)
ἀπορία perplexity
ἀποφαίν-ειν to reveal, to
   show (ἀπο-φαίν-ω)
αὐτῷ for him
γὰρ δή I am positive; really
γοῦν at any rate
δεῖ it is necessary for x (acc.)
   to – (inf.)
δοκέ-ω seem; consider oneself
   to – (+inf.)
εἰδέναι to know (οἶδα)
εἰδότ-ες knowing (nom.)
   (οἶδα)
εἰδ-ώς knowing (nom.)
   (οἶδα)
εἶναι to be (εἰμί)
ἐλέγχ-ειν to refute (ἐλέγχ-ω)

ἐν-θουσιασμ-ός, ὁ inspiration
   (2a)
ἐντεῦθεν from that point,
   from there
ἐπεί when
ἦ-α I went (impf. of
   ἔρχ-ομαι|εἶμι)
ζήτησ-ις, ἡ inquiry (3e)
θέμις lawful (lit. θέμις, ἡ law
   of the gods (3a))
θεό-μαντ-ις, ὁ prophet (3e)
καὶ γὰρ for really
κύων (κυν-), ὁ dog (3a)
λέγ-ειν to say, to tell (λέγ-ω)
λογίζ-ομαι reckon, consider
μαντεῖ-ον, τό oracle (2b)
μετά (+acc.) after
μωρότερ-ος -α -ον more
   stupid
νοέ-ω mean
ὅμως nevertheless
ὅ τι what
οὐ γὰρ δήπου . . . γε it can't
   be that . . .

οὑτωσὶ as follows
παρ-όντ-ες present (part. of
   πάρ-ειμι)
πειρά-ομαι try
ποίημα (ποιηματ-), τό poem
   (3b)
ποίησ-ις, ἡ poetry (3e)
ποιήτ-ης, ὁ poet (1d)
πολιτικ-ός -ή -όν concerned
   with the city
ποτε ever
σοφώτατ-ος -η -ον wisest
   (σοφ-ός)
σοφώτερ-ος -α -ον wiser
   (σοφ-ός)
χρησμ-ῳδ-ός, ὁ soothsayer
   (2a)
χρόν-ος, ὁ time (2a)
φύσ-ις, ἡ nature (3e)
ψεύδ-ομαι tell lies
ᾤμην I thought (οἶμαι)
ὡς that

Vocabulary to be learnt

ἀνάγκη ἐστί it is obligatory (for
   X (acc. or dat.)) to – (inf.)
ἀνάγκη, ἡ necessity (1a)
ἀποφαίνω reveal, show
γὰρ δή really; I assure you

δεῖ it is necessary for X (acc.)
   to – (inf.)
ἐντεῦθεν from then, from there
λογίζομαι reckon, calculate,
   consider

νοέω think, notice, mean, intend
πάρειμι be present, be at hand
ποιητής, ὁ poet (1d)
ποτε once, ever
ὡς that

Vocabulary for Section Six C

ἀπορ-εῖν to be at a loss
   (ἀπορέ-ω)
βαρεῖ-αι serious (nom.)
δια-βολ-ή, ἡ slander (1a)
δια-φθείρ-ω corrupt
δοκ-εῖν to seem (δοκέ-ω)
δοκέ-ω seem; consider oneself
   to –

εἰδέναι to know (οἶδα)
εἰδότ-ες knowing (nom.)
   (οἶδα)
εἰδότ-ων knowing (gen.)
   (οἶδα)
εἶναι to be (εἰμί)
ἐξ-ετάζ-ειν to question
   closely (ἐξ-ετάζ-ω)

ἐξ-ετάζ-ω question closely
ἐρωτ-ᾶν to ask (ἐρωτά-ω)
εὑρίσκ-ω find, discover
ἦ-α I went, came (impf. of
   ἔρχ-ομαι|εἶμι)
ᾔδ-η I knew (past of οἶδα)
ἥδ-ομαι enjoy
κατά-δηλ-ος -ον obvious

λέγ-ειν to say, tell (λέγ-ω)
μέντοι however, but
μετέωρ-α, τά things in the air
   (2b)
μή not
μιαρώτατ-ος -η -ον most
   abominable (person)
   (μιαρ-ός)
νομίζ-ειν to acknowledge
   (νομίζ-ω)
οἶμαι think
ὀργίζ-ομαι get angry
πάθ-ος, τό experience (3c)

πειρά-ομαι try
πλούσι-ος -α -ον rich
ποι-εῖν to make (ποιέ-ω)
πολλάκις often
πρεσβύτερ-ος, ὁ older man
   (2a)
σοφώτατ-ος -η -ον wisest
   (σοφ-ός)
σοφώτερ-ος -α -ον wiser
   (σοφ-ός)
σχολ-ή, ἡ leisure (1a)
ταυτησὶ τῆς ζητήσεως this
   inquiry

τοιοῦτος τοιαύτη τοιοῦτο(ν)
   ... καί the same sort of
   ... as
ὑβριστ-ής, ὁ bully (1d)
ὑπὸ γῆς beneath the earth
φιλό-σοφ-ος, ὁ philosopher
   (2a)
χειρο-τέχν-ης, ὁ craftsman
   (1d)
ᾤμην I thought (impf. of
   οἶμαι)

Vocabulary to be learnt

διαβολή, ἡ slander (1a)
διαφθείρω
   (διαφθειρ-) corrupt; kill;
   destroy
δοκέω seem; consider oneself
   to –

εἰδώς εἰδυῖα εἰδός
   (εἰδοτ-) knowing (part. of
   οἶδα)
εἶμι shall go; ἰέναι to go; ᾖα I
   went
ἐξετάζω question closely

εὑρίσκω (εὑρ-) find, come
   upon
μή not; don't! (with imper.)
οἶμαι think (impf. ᾤμην)
πειράομαι (πειρασ-) try, test
πολλάκις often

O   Grammar for Section Six A–C

Summary:
Pres. inf. act. and mid.
δεῖ
Comp. and sup. adjs.
ᾖα

Verbs

Present infinitive active and middle παύειν, παύεσθαι 'to stop'
74 Infinitives based on the present stem are formed as follows:
   Active infinitive: add -ειν to the present stem, e.g. παύ-ειν 'to stop'
   Middle infinitive: add -εσθαι to the present stem, e.g. παύ-εσθαι 'to stop'

   Notes
   (i) a-contracts have act. inf. in -ᾶν, mid. -ᾶσθαι (τιμᾶν, τιμᾶσθαι)
   ε-contracts have act. inf. in -εῖν, mid. -εῖσθαι (ποιεῖν, ποιεῖσθαι)
   o-contracts have act. inf. in -οῦν, mid. -οῦσθαι (δηλοῦν, δηλοῦσθαι)
(ii) Note the following infinitives:
   εἶναι   'to be'
   ἰέναι   'to go'
   εἰδέναι   'to know'

(iii) The negative with the infinitive is usually μή (cf. Language Survey (9)).

Some uses of the infinitive

75 Certain verbs take infinitive constructions, e.g.

βούλομαι   'I wish to' + inf.
δεῖ   'ought to, must' + inf.
ἀνάγκη ἐστί 'obligatory to' + inf.
δοκέω   'I seem to myself, I think that I' + inf.

Note

ἀνάγκη and δεῖ put the person who must into the accusative case, e.g.
δεῖ με ἰέναι   'I must go'
ἀνάγκη ἐστὶ τὸν θεὸν λέγειν 'the god is obliged to speak' (sometimes τῷ θεῷ)

Adjectives

76 Comparative and superlative adjectives of the καλός type are formed as follows:

σοφ-ός 'wise' σοφ-ώτερ-ος -α -ον 'wiser'   σοφ-ώτατ-ος -η -ον 'wisest'
δειν-ός 'clever' δειν-ότερ-ος -α -ον 'more clever' δειν-ότατ-ος -η -ον 'most clever'

Notes

(i) Comparatives also mean 'rather –', 'fairly –', 'quite –'; superlatives also mean 'most –', 'extremely –', 'very –'.
(ii) When two things are being compared, Greek uses ἤ = 'than', e.g.
ὁ ἀνήρ ἐστι σοφώτερος ἢ ὁ παῖς 'the man is wiser than the boy'. Note that the two things being compared are in the same case.
(iii) Difficult comparative forms are:

ἀγαθός, ἀμείνων, ἄριστος   'good', 'better', 'best'
κακός, κακίων, κάκιστος   'bad', 'worse', 'worst'   ⎫
καλός, καλλίων, κάλλιστος 'fine', 'finer', 'finest' ⎬ Comparatives decline
πολύς, πλείων, πλεῖστος   'much', 'more', 'most'   like εὔφρων 44
μέγας, μείζων, μέγιστος   'big', 'bigger', 'biggest' ⎭

Verbs

ᾖα 'I went'

77 εἶμι 'I shall go' has an irregular imperfect:

ᾖα   'I was going, I went' etc.
ᾔεισθα
ᾔει
ᾖμεν
ᾖτε
ᾖσαν

Exercises for Section Six A–C

(b/c) Morphology and Syntax

1. Change the following verbs into the infinitive form. Then, adding subjects where indicated, use them to complete the sentences. Translate the sentences:

   λέγω, διαβάλλω, δοκέω, ἀποφαίνω, διαλέγομαι, διαφθείρω, εὑρίσκω, εἶμι, εἰμί, οἶδα

   a. δεῖ (you) (pl.) τὴν ἀλήθειαν (tell), καὶ μή (slander) Σωκράτη.
   b. οὐ βουλόμεθα (to seem) ἄριστοι, ἀλλ᾽ (to be).
   c. οἱ σοφοὶ δοκοῦσί τι (know), οὐκ εἰδότες.
   d. ἀνάγκη ἦν (Socrates) (to go) πρὸς τοὺς σοφοὺς καὶ (to talk) περὶ σοφίας.
   e. Σωκράτης, ὡς ἐγὼ οἶμαι, οὐ πειρᾶται (to corrupt) τοὺς νέους.
   f. Σωκράτης ἐβούλετο (to discover) πότερον τὴν ἀλήθειαν λέγει ὁ ἐν Δελφοῖς θεὸς ἢ οὔ. καὶ πολλάκις ἐπειρᾶτο Σωκράτης (to show) τὸν θεὸν οὐ τἀληθῆ λέγοντα.

2. Pair up comparative forms with positive. Add the superlative where you can:

   ἀγαθός, βέβαιος, δεινός, κακός, καλός, μέγας, μῶρος, πολέμιος, πολύς, φίλος, χρήσιμος
   καλλίων, μείζων, φίλτερος, πολεμιώτερος, μωρότερος, δεινότερος, βεβαιότερος, ἀμείνων, χρησιμώτερος, πλείων, κακίων

(d) English into Greek

Translate into Greek:

1. I was obliged to go to the poets.
2. You must question me closely and consider carefully.
3. I am trying to discover how the poets show their wisdom.
4. You knew that you wanted to slander me.
5. From then on I appeared to be corrupting the young, although I knew nothing.

Vocabulary for Section Six D

ἀκούσ-ας upon hearing (nom. s. m.) (ἀκού-ω)
ἀλλὰ μὲν δή . . . γε but the fact is that . . .
ἀμαθεῖς ignorant (nom.)

ἀμφότερ-οι -αι -α both
ἀνδρεί-ως bravely
ἀπο-κρίν-ομαι answer (fut. ἀπο-κριν-οῦμαι)
ἀπο-κριν-άμεν-ος in answer,

answering (ἀπο-κρίν-ομαι)
ἀπορήσ-ας on being at a loss (nom. s. m.) (ἀπορέ-ω)
ἀρετ-ή, ἡ excellence, virtue (1a)

γὰρ δήπου of course
γε δή certainly
γελά-ω (γελασ-) laugh
γελάσ-ας on laughing, with a
    laugh (nom. s. m.)
    (γελά-ω)
Διονυσόδωρ-ος, ὁ
    Dionysodoros (2a)
εἶεν well, all right then!
ἐναντίον ἡμῶν in front of us
ἐνθάδε here
ἐρυθριά-ω blush
ἐρώτημα (ἐρωτηματ-), τό
    question (3b)
Εὐθύδημ-ος, ὁ Euthydemos
    (2a)

εὐθύς at once
ἔ-φην (I) said (φημί)
ἔ-φη (he) said (φημί)
ἕως while
ἥδ-ομαι enjoy
ἦν δ᾽ ἐγώ I said
ἦ δ᾽ ὅς he said
ἠρυθρίασ-εν see ἐρυθριά-ω
καὶ μὴν look here
κατα-λαμβάν-ω
    (κατα-λαβ-) come upon
Κλεινί-ας, ὁ Kleinias (1d)
Κρίτων (Κριτων-), ὁ Kriton
    (3a)

Λύκει-ον, τό Lykeion (2b) (a
    training ground, where young
    and old met)
μετ(ὰ) ἄλλων πολλῶν with
    many others
μηδέ and don't
νεανίσκ-ος, ὁ young man (2a)
προ-τρέπ-ω urge, impel
τούτῳ this interval
φιλοσοφί-α, ἡ philosophy
    (1b)
χθές yesterday

Vocabulary to be learnt

ἀνδρεῖος α ον brave, manly
ἀποκρίνομαι
    (ἀποκριν-) answer
ἀρετή, ἡ virtue, excellence (1a)

δήπου of course, surely
ἥδομαι enjoy, be pleased
ἦν δ᾽ ἐγώ I said
ἦ δ᾽ ὅς he said

νεανίσκος, ὁ young man (2a)
προτρέπω urge on, impel
φιλοσοφία, ἡ philosophy (1b)

Vocabulary for Section Six E

ἀμαθεῖς ignorant (nom.)
διδάσκαλ-ος, ὁ teacher (2a)
ἔ-φη (he) said (φημί)
ἦσ-μεν we knew (past of
    οἶδα)

Vocabulary to be learnt

διδάσκαλος, ὁ teacher (2a)
ὁμολογέω agree
οὐκοῦν therefore
οὔκουν not . . . therefore

ἦσ-τε you (pl.) knew (past of
    οἶδα)
μειράκι-ον, τό youth (2b)

πάνυ γε yes indeed
πω yet
ὡμο-λόγ-ει (he) agreed
    (ὁμο-λογέ-ω)

Vocabulary for Section Six F

ἀμαθεῖς ignorant (nom.)
ἀπορίᾳ perplexity
ἄρτι just now
γελάσ-αντ-ες laughing, with
    laughs (nom. pl. m.)
    (γελά-ω)
ἐκ-δεξ-άμεν-ος receiving in
    turn (ἐκ-δέχ-ομαι)

ἐκ-δέχ-ομαι take up, receive
    in turn
ἐμ-πίπτ-ω fall into
ἐνταῦθα at this point
ἐπ-αινέ-ω praise (aor.
    ἐπ-ήνεσ-α)

εὐθύς at once
ἔ-φη (he) said (φημί)
θορυβήσ-αντ-ες making a
    din, with a din (nom. pl.
    m.) (θορυβέ-ω)
καὶ δή let's suppose
σφαῖρ-α, ἡ ball (1b)

Vocabulary to be learnt

γελάω (γελασ-) laugh
ἐκδέχομαι receive in turn
ἐμπίπτω (ἐμπεσ-) fall into, on (+ἐν or εἰς)

ἐπαινέω (ἐπαινεσ-) praise
εὐθύς at once, straightaway
φημί|ἔφην I say/I said

O   Grammar for Section Six D–F

Summary:
Wk. aor. part. act. and mid.
Aspect
ἤδη, φημί, ἔφην

Participles

78 You have already met participles based on the *present* stem of verbs, e.g. βλέπων 'looking', τρέχων 'running' (**50**). Greek also has participles based on the *aorist* stem of verbs. To form the aorist stem take the *aorist indicative*, and discount (i) the augment, (ii) the personal endings, e.g.

ἔ-παυσ-α   aor. stem: παυσ-(α)
ἤ-κουσ-α   aor. stem: ἀκουσ-(α)
ἀπ-ε-κριν-άμην   aor. stem: ἀποκριν-(α)

To form the weak aorist participle, add endings as follows to the aorist stem:

Weak aorist participle active παύσας παύσασα παῦσαν (παυσαντ-)
'stopping'

s.

	nom.	acc.	gen.	dat.
m.	παύσ-ας	παύσ-αντ-α	παύσ-αντ-ος	παύσ-αντ-ι
f.	παύσ-ασ-α	παύσ-ασ-αν	παυσ-άσ-ης	παυσ-ά-σ-ῃ
n.	παῦσ-αν	παῦσ-αν	παύσ-αντ-ος	παύσ-αντ-ι

pl.

	nom.	acc.	gen.	dat.
m.	παύσ-αντ-ες	παύσ-αντ-ας	παυσ-άντ-ων	παύσ-ασι(ν)
f.	παύσ-ασ-αι	παυσ-άσ-ας	παυσ-ασ-ῶν	παυσ-άσ-αις
n.	παύσ-αντ-α	παύσ-αντ-α	παυσ-άντ-ων	παύσ-ασι(ν)

Note

For the endings (not the stem) of the active participles cf. εὔφρων (**45**) in the m., n., and τόλμα (**24**) for the f. Learn them as παύσας παύσασα παῦσαν (παυσαντ-).

79 *Weak aorist participle middle* παυσάμενος παυσαμένη παυσάμενον 'stopping'

	nom.	acc.	gen.	
m.	παυσ-άμεν-ος	παυσ-άμεν-ον	παυσ-αμέν-ου	
f.	παυσ-αμέν-η	παυσ-αμέν-ην	παυσ-αμέν-ης	*etc. just like* καλ-ός -ή -όν
n.	παυσ-άμεν-ον	παυσ-άμεν-ον	παυσ-αμέν-ου	

Learn the nom., acc., s. and pl.

Aspect

What is the difference in meaning between, say, παύων and παύσας, or between βλέπων and βλέψας? One vital thing to say is that the difference is NOT NECESSARILY ONE OF TIME. παύσας or βλέψας need not be translated 'having stopped', or 'having looked'. The difference is one of what is called ASPECT, and is the same as the difference that has already been shown to exist between the aorist and imperfect indicatives – i.e., the difference between regarding the action as a *process* (imperfect) and an *event* (aorist). A present participle regards the action as a *process* (and is therefore sometimes called 'imperfective'), while the aorist participle regards it simply as a single *event*. Thus it is possible to translate both βλέπων and βλέψας as 'looking'; in the former case, it would be understood that the look *went on*, in the latter that it simply took place. Indeed, there might be a case for translating an aorist participle by a NOUN to show that the idea of time is not necessarily involved, e.g. βλέψας πρὸς ἐμὲ ἠρυθρίασεν might best be translated 'with a glance at me, he blushed'. Alternatively, one might co-ordinate the sentence and write 'he looked at me and blushed'. Whatever else you do, it is essential that you pay close attention to actual Greek usage. At times the distinction between the two aspects may seem quite arbitrary to an English speaker. (On aspect in general, cf. Language Survey (3), p. 310.)

Two irregular verbs ᾔδη *'I knew'*, φημί *'I say'*
80 The past of οἶδα is as follows:
ᾔδη   'I knew' *etc.*
ᾔδησθα
ᾔδει
ᾖσμεν
ᾖστε
ᾖσαν (ᾔδεσαν)

81 φημί 'I say' inflects as follows in the present and imperfect (though note that the imperfect usually carries an aorist meaning 'I said'):

φημί   'I say' etc.   ἔφην   'I said' etc.
φής or φής   ἔφησθα or ἔφης
φησί   ἔφη
φαμέν   ἔφαμεν
φατέ   ἔφατε
φασί(ν)   ἔφασαν

Note

Do not use φημί *if you are translating English 'say that' into Greek. Use* λέγω ὅτι *for the moment. See further Reference Grammar K(i), p. 301.*

Exercises for Section Six D–F

(b/c) Morphology and Syntax

1. Translate into Greek the italic phrases, using either aorist or present participle to suit the sense:
   a. We sat silently, *all the time perplexed* as to his meaning.
   b. *With a glance* at me the teacher began to speak.
   c. The spectators *heard* his arguments and applauded.
   d. Dionysodoros replied *with laughter constantly in his voice.*
   e. The woman *picked up* the argument and replied.
   f. He happened to *say in answer.*

2. Form the aorist participles of these verbs:
   βλέπω   δέχομαι
   φροντίζω   βιάζομαι
   ῥίπτω   λογίζομαι
   σῴζω   μάχομαι (μαχεσ-)
   παύομαι   ἀποκρίνομαι (ἀποκριν-)

3. Form the aorist participles of these contracted verbs:
   ποιέω   ἐλευθερόω
   βοηθέω   τολμάω
   ἀπορέω   θεάομαι (θεασ-)

(d) English into Greek
Translate into Greek:

1. The teacher answered and said that the love of wisdom was a virtue.

2. Dionysodoros laughed and took up the argument.
3. The sophist, with a glance at me, agreed.
4. I praised them and said, 'Urge them on at once.'
5. Once in a state of perplexity, the student tried to escape.

Test Exercise Six A–F

Translate into English:

Kriton reports how he and Socrates discussed the nature of expertise and decided that an expert's opinion is more valuable than another man's.

(From Plato, *Kriton*)

'σὺ μέν, ὦ Σώκρατες', ἔφην ἐγώ, 'ἐξέταζε, ἐγὼ δ' ἀποκρινοῦμαι.'

'σκόπει οὖν', ἦ δ' ὃς ὁ Σωκράτης, 'καὶ εἴ τι ἔχεις ἀντιλέγειν, ἀντίλεγε, καὶ πείσομαι ἔγωγε.'

'καλῶς δοκεῖς λέγειν', ἦν δ' ἐγώ, 'ὡς ἐγὼ οἶμαι.'

'εἶεν', ἔφη, 'ἆρα ἀληθῆ λέγει ὁ φιλόσοφος ὁ λέγων ὅτι οὐ δεῖ ἡμᾶς ἐπαινεῖν πάσας τὰς δόξας τῶν ἀνθρώπων; τί φής; ἆρα ἀληθῆ δοκεῖ λέγειν, ταῦτα λέγων, ἢ οὔ; ἀποκρίνου.'

'ἀληθῆ', ἔφην.

'οὐκοῦν δεῖ ἡμᾶς τὰς μὲν ἀγαθὰς δόξας ἐπαινεῖν καὶ τιμᾶν, τὰς δὲ κακὰς μή;'

ὡμολόγουν.

'φέρε δή', ἔφη ὁ Σωκράτης, 'ἐπειδὴ ἡ νόσος ἐνέπιπτε καὶ διέφθειρε τὴν πόλιν, ποῖ ᾔεισθα σύ, πότερον πρὸς τοὺς φίλους, ἢ πρὸς τὸν ἰατρόν;'

'πρὸς τὸν ἰατρὸν ᾖα', ἦν δ' ἐγώ, 'ᾖσαν δὲ ἐνταῦθα καὶ οἱ φίλοι. ᾔδει γὰρ ὁ ἰατρὸς τὰ περὶ τῆς νόσου, ἐμπειρότερος ὢν ἢ οἱ ἄλλοι.'

'ἐμπειρότατος δὴ ἐφαίνετο ὢν ὁ ἰατρός', ἦ δ' ὃς ὁ Σωκράτης. 'ἔδει οὖν σὲ πρὸς τὸν ἰατρὸν ἰέναι, καὶ οὐδένα ἄλλον;'

'ἔδει', ἔφην ἐγώ.

'περὶ τῆς νόσου ἄρα οὐ δεῖ ἡμᾶς ἐπαινεῖν καὶ φοβεῖσθαι τὰς τῶν πολλῶν δόξας, ἀλλὰ τὴν τῶν ἰατρῶν, εἴ τις ἐμπειρότατος τυγχάνει ὤν; οὕτω φαμὲν ἢ οὔ;'

'φάμεν νὴ τὸν Δία', ἔφην.

Vocabulary

ἀντιλέγω object	ἰατρός, ὁ doctor (2a)
εἶεν well then	ἐνταῦθα here
πάσας all (acc. pl. f.)	φοβέομαι respect
φέρε come!	

Vocabulary for Section Six G

'Αμαζών ('Αμαζον-), ἡ
Amazon (3a)
ἀν-εἷλ-ον they took up (aor.
of ἀν-αιρέ-ω)
ἀν-ελ-όντ-ες on taking up
(nom. pl. m.)
(ἀναιρέ-ω|ἀν-εἷλ-ον)
ἄνεμ-ος, ὁ wind (2a)
ἀπ-ελθ-οῦσ-αι upon going
away (nom. pl. f.)
(ἀπ-έρχ-ομαι|ἀπ-ῆλθ-ον)
ἀπο-βᾶσ-αι upon
disembarking (nom. pl. f.)
(ἀπο-βαίν-ω|ἀπ-έ-βην)
ἀπο-πέμπ-ω send off
ἀφ-ικ-όμεν-αι arriving (nom.
pl. f.)
(ἀφ-ικνέ-ομαι|ἀφ-ικ-όμην)
ἀφ-ίκ-οντο they arrived (aor.
of ἀφ-ικνέ-ομαι)
γν-όντ-ες knowing, realising
(nom. pl. m.)
(γιγνώσκ-ω|ἔ-γνω-ν)
δι-αρπάζ-ω lay waste

Vocabulary to be learnt

ἀναιρέω (ἀνελ-) pick up
ἀποβαίνω (ἀποβα-) leave,
depart
ἕπομαι (ἑσπ-) follow

ἔ-γνω-σαν they recognised
(them) (aor. of γιγνώσκ-ω)
εἰσ-πεσ-όντ-ες attacking,
falling upon (nom. pl. m.)
(εἰσ-πίπτ-ω|εἰσ-έ-πεσ-ον)
ἐμ-πεσ-όντ-ες attacking,
falling upon (nom. pl. m.)
(ἐμ-πίπτ-ω|ἐν-έ-πεσ-ον)
ἐλθ-όντ-ες upon coming
(nom. pl. m.)
(ἔρχ-ομαι|ἦλθ-ον)
ἕπ-ομαι follow
ᾗπερ where
ηὗρ-ον they came upon (aor.
of εὑρίσκ-ω)
ἰδ-οῦσ-αι upon seeing (nom.
pl. f.) (ὁρά-ω|εἶδ-ον)
ἱππο-φόρβι-ον, τό herd of
horses (2b)
λαβ-όντ-ες upon taking
(nom. pl. m.)
(λαμβάν-ω|ἔ-λαβ-ον)
λαβ-οῦσ-αι upon taking
(nom. pl. f.)
(λαμβάν-ω|ἔ-λαβ-ον)

μάχη, ἡ fight, battle (1a)
μέντοι however, but
νομίζω think, acknowledge
φυλάττω guard

μαθ-οῦσ-αι upon
understanding (nom. pl. f.)
(μανθάν-ω|ἔ-μαθ-ον)
μέντοι however, but
νομίζ-ω think x (acc.) to be y
(acc.)
παιδο-ποιέ-ομαι beget
children
περι-οῦσ-ας surviving (part,
of περί-ειμι)
πλησίον nearby, near (+gen.)
Σκύθ-ης, ὁ Scythian (1d)
στρατοπεδεύ-ομαι make
camp
τῇ θαλάττῃ the sea
τῇ μάχῃ the battle
τῆς μάχης the battle
τρισὶ πλοίοις three ships
φυλάττ-ω guard
φωνή-ή, ἡ language, speech
(1a)

Vocabulary for Section Six H

ἀγαγ-οῦσ-αν bringing (acc. s.
f.) (ἄγ-ω|ἤγαγ-ον)
ἄγ-ω (ἀγαγ-) lead, bring
αἱ δὲ but they
'Αμαζών ('Αμαζον-), ἡ
Amazon (3a)
ἀπ-ελθ-ὼν going away (nom.
s. m.)
(ἀπ-έρχ-ομαι|ἀπ-ῆλθ-ον)

ἀπο-λαγχάν-ω
(ἀπο-λαχ-) obtain by lot
ἀπο-λαχ-όντ-ες upon
obtaining (nom. pl. m.)
(ἀπο-λαγχάν-ω|ἀπ-έ-λαχ-ον)
αὐτ-ὴν herself
αὐτ-ή she herself
αὐτ-οί they themselves
αὐτ-ὸς he himself

ἀφ-ικ-όμεν-οι upon arriving
(nom. pl. m.)
(ἀφ-ικνέ-ομαι|ἀφ-ικ-όμην)
γεν-όμεν-α, τά what had
happened, the happenings
(γίγν-ομαι|ἐ-γεν-όμην)
γυναικεῖ-ος -α -ον woman's
διὰ σημείου by means of
sign-language

δια-βάντ-ες crossing, once
across (nom. pl. m.)
(δια-βαίν-ω|δι-έ-βην)
δι-αρπάζ-ω lay waste
δυν-άμεθα (we) are able
δύο two (nom.)
ἐ-δύν-ατο she was able
(δύν-αμαι)
ἐ-δύν-αντο they were able
(δύν-αμαι)
εἰπ-οῦσ-αι saying (nom. pl.
f.) (λέγ-ω|εἰπ-ον)
ἐκεῖ there
ἐλθ-όντ-ας on going (acc. pl.
m.) (ἔρχ-ομαι|ἦλθ-ον)
ἐλθ-ών upon coming (nom. s.
m.) (ἔρχ-ομαι|ἦλθ-ον)
ἐξ-ανα-στ-άντ-ες upon
getting up and going off
(nom. pl. m.)
(ἐξ-αν-ίστα-μαι|ἐξ-αν-έ-στη-ν)
ἐξ-αν-ιστά-μεθα we get up
and go off
ἕξ-ομεν we shall have (fut. of
ἔχ-ω)
ἐπ-αν-ελθ-όντ-ας upon
returning (acc. pl. m.)
(ἐπ-αν-έρχ-ομαι|ἐπ-αν-ῆλθ-ον)

ἐπ-αν-έρχ-ομαι
(ἐπ-αν-ελθ-) return
ἐργάζ-ομαι perform, do
εὑρ-όντ-ες on finding (nom.
pl. m.) (εὑρίσκ-ω|ηὗρ-ον)
ἱππάζ-ομαι ride horses
κατα-λαβ-ὼν on coming
across (nom. s. m.)
(κατα-λαμβάν-ω|
κατ-έ-λαβ-ον)
κατα-λαμβάν-ω
(κατα-λαβ-) come across
κτῆμα (κτηματ-), τό
possession (3b)
λοιπ-ός -ή -όν other, rest of
μαθ-όντ-ες on learning
(nom. pl. m.)
(μανθάν-ω|ἔ-μαθ-ον)
μεθ' ἡμῶν with us
μέρ-ος, τό share, portion (3c)
μετὰ τῶν ὑμετέρων
γυναικῶν with your
women
μετά (+acc.) after
μόν-ος -η -ον alone

νόμ-ος, ὁ custom, usage (2a)
οἱ αὐτοὶ the same
οἰκέ-ω dwell in
ὁμοῦ together
πάλιν back, again
ποταμ-ός, ὁ river (2a)
σημαίν-ω give a sign
Σκύθ-ης, ὁ Scythian (1d)
συν-οικέ-ω live together
ταῖς ἁμάξαις their waggons
(Scythians were nomads)
Τάνα-ις, ὁ Tanais (3e)
τῇ ὑστεραίᾳ on the next day
τῆς γῆς ταύτης this land
τὸ αὐτ-ό the same
τοκ-ῆς, οἱ parents (3g)
τοξεύ-ω use bows and arrows
τούτῳ τῷ χώρῳ this land
ὑστεραί-α, ἡ next day (1b)
φωνέ-ω speak, converse
φων-ή, ἡ language (1a)
χρά-ομαι have intercourse
with
χῶρ-ος, ὁ place, region (2a)

Vocabulary to be learnt

ἄγω (ἀγαγ-) lead, bring
αὐτός ή ό self
διαβαίνω (διαβα-) cross
δύναμαι be able
δύο two
ἐπανέρχομαι
(ἐπανελθ-) return
καταλαμβάνω

(καταλαβ-) come across,
overtake
κτῆμα (κτηματ-), τό
possession (3b)
μετά (+acc.) after
ὁ αὐτός the same
οἰκέω dwell (in), live
πάλιν back, again

ποταμός, ὁ river (2a)
σημεῖον, τό sign, signal (2b)
ὑμέτερος a ον your
φωνέω speak, utter
φωνή, ἡ voice, language, speech
(1a)

O Grammar for Section Six G–H

Summary:
Str. aor. part. act. and mid.
αὐτός, ὁ αὐτός, αὐτόν.
δύναμαι

Participles

82 Verbs with weak aorists form their aorist participle on the weak aorist stem; verbs with strong aorists form it on the strong aorist stem, as follows:

83 *Strong aorist participle active* λαβών *'taking'*

s.

	nom.	acc.	gen.	dat.
m.	λαβ-ών	λαβ-όντ-α	λαβ-όντ-ος	λαβ-όντ-ι
f.	λαβ-οῦσ-α	λαβ-οῦσ-αν	λαβ-ούσ-ης	λαβ-ούσ-ῃ
n.	λαβ-όν	λαβ-όν	λαβ-όντ-ος	λαβ-όντ-ι

pl.

nom.	acc.	gen.	dat.
λαβ-όντ-ες	λαβ-όντ-ας	λαβ-όντ-ων	λαβ-οῦσι(ν)
λαβ-οῦσ-αι	λαβ-ούσ-ας	λαβ-ουσ-ῶν	λαβ-ούσ-αις
λαβ-όντ-α	λαβ-όντ-α	λαβ-όντ-ων	λαβ-οῦσι(ν)

84 *Strong aorist participle middle* λαβόμενος *'taking'*

	nom.	acc.	gen.	
m.	λαβ-όμεν-ος	λαβ-όμεν-ον	λαβ-ομέν-ου	
f.	λαβ-ομέν-η	λαβ-ομέν-ην	λαβ-ομέν-ης	*etc., like* καλ-ός -ή -όν
n.	λαβ-όμεν-ον	λαβ-όμεν-ον	λαβ-ομέν-ου	

Learn the nom., acc., s. and pl.

Note
The endings for these participles are exactly the same as for present participles (**50, 51**). (For a full survey of παύω, see Reference Grammar E.1, and cf. E.2.)

Adjectives/Pronouns

αὐτός, αὐτόν

85 The declension of αὐτός ('self', 'same'); αὐτόν ('him, her, it') is as follows:

	nom.	acc.	gen.	
m.	αὐτ-ός	αὐτ-όν	αὐτ-οῦ	
f.	αὐτ-ή	αὐτ-ήν	αὐτ-ῆς	*etc., just like* καλ-ός -ή -όν
n.	αὐτ-ό	αὐτ-ό	αὐτ-οῦ	

Learn the nom., acc., s. and pl.

86 It has a variety of meanings. As an adjective, it means 'self', e.g.

Σωκράτης αὐτός 'Socrates himself'

τὸν ἄνδρα αὐτόν 'the man himself' (acc.) (or αὐτὸν τὸν ἄνδρα)

87 It is used in the reflexive forms

ἐμαυτ-όν ░ού░ ░ῷ░ 'myself' pl. ἡμᾶς αὐτούς, etc.

σεαυτ-όν (or σαυτ-όν) ░ού░ ░ῷ░ 'yourself' pl. ὑμᾶς αὐτούς, etc.

ἑαυτ-όν (or αὐτ-όν) ░ού░ ░ῷ░ 'himself' pl. ἑαυτούς (or αὐτούς), etc.

Note

Reflexive forms are used when 'I' 'you' 'he' etc. refer to the same person as the subject of the clause. In indirect speech, they can refer to the subject of the main verb of the sentence, e.g. ἡ 'Αμαζὼν ἔπεισε τὸν ἄνδρα αὐτὴν λύειν '*The Amazon persuaded the man to release* her' *(i.e. the Amazon).*

88 Preceded by the definite article, it means 'same', e.g.

ὁ αὐτὸς νεανίας 'the same youth'

89 Used as a pronoun, but *never* in the nom., nor as first word of a clause, when it will always mean 'self', it means 'him', 'her', 'it', 'them', e.g.

εἶδεν αὐτοὺς τρέχοντας 'he saw them running'

ἔλαβον αὐτήν 'I caught her'   BUT

αὐτὸς εἶδον τὸν ἄνδρα 'I myself saw the man'

Verbs

90 Note the -α- dominated δύναμαι 'I am able, I can' and cf. ἀνίσταμαι

at **98**.

δύνα-μαι 'I am able' *etc.*

δύνα-σαι

δύνα-ται

δυνά-μεθα

δύνα-σθε

δύνα-νται

Revise:

Type 3 nouns **29–30, 40–3**

οὗτος **32**

ἐγώ|σύ **34**   O

Exercises for Section Six G–H

(b/c) Morphology and Syntax

1. Form the aorist indicative of these verbs, then construct the aorist participle.

94   A. Grammar, Vocabularies, Exercises

γίγνομαι, μανθάνω, ὁράω, ἀφικνέομαι, ἔρχομαι, λαμβάνω, εὑρίσκω, αἱρέω, πίπτω

2. Translate the following sentences, completing them with the aorist participle of the verbs indicated.

a. οἱ νεανίσκοι (ἀπέρχομαι) εἶπον ταῦτα πρὸς τοὺς λοιπούς.
b. αἱ 'Αμαζόνες (καταλαμβάνω) τοὺς νεανίας, διελέγοντο πρὸς αὐτούς.
c. ὁ νεανίας (ὁράω) τὴν 'Αμαζόνα, προσῆλθεν πρὸς αὐτήν.
d. οἱ Σκύθαι (εὑρίσκω) τὰς 'Αμαζόνας, πλησίον ἀφικνοῦνται.
e. οἱ νεανίσκοι, πλησίον (ἀφικνέομαι), ἐστρατοπεδεύσαντο.
f. οἱ Σκύθαι (ἀν-αιρέω) τοὺς νεκροὺς καὶ (μανθάνω) γυναῖκας οὔσας, ἐθαύμαζον.

3. In the following sentences, translate the italic words by the correct forms of αὐτός, αὐτόν, ὁ αὐτός.

a. We saw *them* approaching.
b. *The same man* did this too.
c. *She herself* brought another Amazon with her.
d. Did you see *the same* woman as I?
e. What does *he himself* think of it?
f. They all speak *about the same things*.
g. *I myself* do not enjoy sentences.
h. I saw *the young men themselves* behaving like this.
i. Women? We love *them*! Men? We hate *them*.

(d) English into Greek
Translate into Greek:
1. The men picked up the bodies of the women and went away.
2. Coming upon these women, the young men were amazed.
3. Once friends, the young men are able to converse with those women.
4. The women said these things and persuaded the young men.
5. After this the young men returned to their houses and took their possessions.

Exercises for Section Six

(a) Words *(on word-building, cf. Language Survey (13), pp. 327ff.)*
1. Deduce the meaning of the words in the right-hand columns from those in the left:

ἀνάγκη   ἀναγκαῖος α ον   ἀναγκάζω

γελάω	ὁ γέλως	γέλοιος α ον
διαβαίνω	ἡ διάβασις	
διαφθείρω	ἡ διαφθορά	
δύναμαι	δύνατος η ον	ἡ δύναμις
ἐπαινέω	ὁ ἔπαινος	
κτῆμα	κτάομαι	ἡ κτῆσις
λογίζομαι	ὁ λογισμός	
ὁμολογέω	ἡ ὁμολογία	
πειράομαι	ἡ πεῖρα	
φυλάττω	ὁ φύλαξ	ἡ φυλακή ἀφύλακτος ον

2. Group this pool of words into sets of cognate words. Give the meaning of each word:

μάχη, ἀληθής, διαβάλλω, σοφία, ἀποφαίνω, λόγος, ἡδέως, νέος, οἰκέω, φάσμα, δοκέω, νεανίας, διαβολή, μάχομαι, λογίζομαι, φαίνομαι, ἥδομαι, δόξα, σοφός, οἰκία, ἀλήθεια

(d) **English into Greek**
Translate into Greek:
When the Amazons had killed the Athenians, they came to the land of the Scythians. On arrival, they found horses and fought with the Scythians. The Scythians, defeating them and learning about them, wished to become friends. The young men therefore followed closely, but did not fight; and the Amazons, seeing this, kept quiet themselves. At last they became friends and lived together; but it was necessary for the young men and their wives to cross the river and inhabit another place. 'For', said the Amazons, 'we do not want to live in your land, since on arrival we fought you.'

Test Exercise Six
Translate into English:
Ἀμαζόνες τινές, εἰς τὴν τῶν Σκυθῶν γῆν ἀφικόμεναι καὶ ἀπὸ τῶν πλοίων ἀποβᾶσαι, εἰσπεσοῦσαι τὴν γῆν διήρπασαν. οἱ δὲ Σκύθαι, ἐν μάχῃ νικήσαντες αὐτάς, τοὺς νεκροὺς ἀνεῖλον καὶ μαθόντες γυναῖκας οὔσας, ἐβούλοντο ἐκ τῶν Ἀμαζόνων παιδοποιεῖσθαι. κελεύοντες οὖν τοὺς νεανίσκους μάχεσθαι μὲν μηδέποτε, πλησίον δὲ ἐλθόντας φίλους γίγνεσθαι, ἀπέπεμψαν αὐτοὺς πρὸς τὰς Ἀμαζόνας. αἱ δὲ Ἀμαζόνες, ἰδοῦσαι αὐτοὺς πλησίον μὲν ἑπομένους, μαχομένους δὲ οὐδέποτε, οὐκέτι ἐφρόντιζον αὐτῶν. ἔπειτα δὲ Σκύθης τις, καταλαβὼν Ἀμαζόνα τινὰ μόνην οὖσαν, καὶ φίλος γενόμενος, ἐκέλευε τοὺς ἄλλους ποιεῖν τὸ αὐτό,

καί, 'Αμαζόνας τινὰς εὑρόντας, φίλους γίγνεσθαι. ἐπείθοντο οὖν οἱ ἄλλοι, τέλος δὲ συνῴκουν οἵ τε Σκύθαι καὶ αἱ 'Αμαζόνες. ἀλλ' αἱ 'Αμαζόνες οὐκ ἐβούλοντο ἐπανιέναι εἰς τὸ τῶν Σκυθῶν πλῆθος. 'οὐ γὰρ δυνάμεθα', ἔφασαν, 'συνοικεῖν μετὰ τῶν γυναικῶν τῶν ὑμετέρων. οὐ γὰρ οἱ αὐτοὶ οἱ ἡμέτεροι νόμοι καὶ οἱ τῶν Σκυθῶν.' λαβόντες οὖν τὰ κτήματα καὶ διαβάντες τὸν ποταμόν, ηὗρον χωρίον τι πλησίον ὂν καὶ ᾤκησαν αὐτό.

Vocabulary

διαρπάζω lay waste
μηδέποτε never

PART THREE

Section Seven

Vocabulary for Section Seven A

ἀγορ-ά, ἡ market-place, agora (1b)

αἴτι-ος -α -ον responsible for

ἂν ἀκού-οιμι I would listen to

ἀν-ίστα-μαι get up and leave, emigrate

ἀπ-ιόντ-α going off (acc. s. m.) (part. of ἀπ-έρχ-ομαι|ἄπ-ειμι)

ἀ-πράγμων ἄ-πραγμον (ἀπραγμον-) free from trouble

ἀσπάζ-ομαι greet

βέλτιστ-ε my very good friend

βέλτιστ-ος -η -ον best

βελτίων βέλτιον (βελτιον-) better

διὰ τοῦ πλήθ-ους through the crowd

ἐκεῖσε (to) there

ἐκκλησί-α, ἡ assembly, ekklesia (1b)

ἐν τούτῳ meanwhile

ἐπὶ τῇ χειρί on his/your hand

ἑταῖρ-ος, ὁ friend, companion (2a)

Εὐελπίδ-ης, ὁ Euelpides (1d) ('Great hopes')

ἡγεμών (ἡγεμον-), ὁ leader (3a)

ἡγέ-ομαι lead

καθ-ορά-ω (κατ-ιδ-) see, notice

καν-οῦν, τό basket (2b ἑ-ον contr.) (holding sacrificial meal and knife)

κόραξ (κορακ-), ὁ crow (3a)

κύρι-ος -α -ον with power, sovereign

λαμβάν-ομαι (λαβ-) take hold of

λέγ-οιμι ἄν I will tell (you)

λέγ-οιτε ἄν won't you (pl.) please tell me?

μετ' αὐτ-οῦ with him

μετ' ἐκείν-ου τοῦ κόρακ-ος with that crow

μετὰ τοῦ ῥαψῳδ-οῦ with the rhapsode

μῶν surely not?

οἰκίζ-ω found (a city) (fut. οἰκιέ-ω)

ὄπισθεν behind

ὁ Στιλβωνίδ-ου Stilbonides' son

ὁ τοῦ Πολεμάρχ-ου Polemarkhos' son

Πεισ-έταιρ-ος, ὁ Peisetairos (2a) ('Persuasive-friend')

πέμπ-ω send

περι-μέν-ω wait around (fut. περι-μενέ-ω)

πολίτ-ης, ὁ citizen (1d)

προσ-δραμ-ὼν see προσ-τρέχ-ω

προσ-ιών approaching (nom. s. m.) (part. of προσ-έρχ-ομαι|πρόσ-ειμι)

προσ-τρέχ-ω (προσδραμ-) run towards

τῇ χειρί his hand

τῆς of the (s.)

τῆς βο-ῆς the shout (after αἴτιος)

τῆς βο-ῆς ἐκείν-ης that shout (after αἴτιος)

τῆς πατρίδ-ος our fatherland

τῆς τοῦ Δικαιοπόλ-εως (the hand) of Dikaiopolis

τῆς χειρ-ὸς the hand (after λαβ-όμενος)

τίν-ος ἀνθρώπ-ου; of which man? whose?

τόπ-ος, ὁ place (2a)

τοῦ of the (s.)

τοῦ ἐμ-οῦ ἱματί-ου my cloak (after λαμβάνῃ)

τοῦ Εὐελπίδ-ου of Euelpides

τοῦ ἱκέτ-ου of the suppliant

τοῦ ἱματί-ου his cloak (after
λαμβάν-εται)
τοῦ Πειραι-ῶς the Piraeus
τοῦ Πολεμάρχ-ου of

Polemarkhos
τῶν of the (pl.)
τῶν ἕνδεκα of the Eleven
ὑμ-ῶν ἕνεκα for your sake,

because of you
χαῖρ-ε hello! greetings!
ὡς (+acc) to

Vocabulary to be learnt

ἀγορά, ἡ market-place, agora
  (1b)
βελτίων βέλτιον
  (βελτιον-) better
βέλτιστος η ον best
ἐκεῖσε (to) there

ἐν τούτῳ meanwhile
ἡγεμών (ἡγεμον-), ὁ leader
  (3a)
ἡγέομαι lead (+dat.)
καθοράω (κατιδ-) see, look
  down on

πέμπω send
πολίτης, ὁ citizen (1d)
προστρέχω (προσδραμ-) run
  towards
χαῖρε hello! farewell!
χείρ (χειρ-), ἡ hand (3a)

Vocabulary for Section Seven B

ἀδικέ-ω do wrong
ᾄδ-ω sing
ἀν-ίστα-μαι get up and go,
  emigrate
ἀπ-ολ-οῦσι they will destroy
βαρέ-ως φέρ-ω find hard to
  bear, take badly
δῆμ-ος, ὁ the people (2a)
δικαστήρι-ον, τό law-court
  (2b)
δικαστ-ής, ὁ juror, dikast (1d)
εἰκότ-ως reasonably
ἐκκλησί-α, ἡ assembly,
  ekklesia (1b)
ἐπεὶ since
ἐπὶ τῶν δικ-ῶν on their
  lawsuits
ἐπὶ τῶν κραδ-ῶν on their
  branches
ἐρ-εῖς you (s.) will say
  (ἐρέ-ω, fut. of λέγ-ω)
ἕρπ-ω go along, take its
  course
εὐ-δαιμον-έστατ-ος -η -ον
  wealthiest, most blessed by

the gods (εὐ-δαίμων)
εὐ-δαιμον-έστερ-ος -α -ον
  more wealthy, more
  blessed (εὐ-δαίμων)
ἡγέ-ομαι consider x to be y
ἡμ-ῶν ἀν-αιτί-ων ὄντ-ων us,
  although we were innocent
  (after κατεψηφίσαντο)
κατα-ψηφίζ-ομαι condemn
κλαυθμ-ός, ὁ lamentation (2a)
μάρτυς (μαρτυρ-), ὁ witness
  (3a)
μέγιστ-ος -η -ον greatest
  (μέγας)
μείζων μεῖζον
  (μειζον-) greater (μέγας)
μῶν surely not?
οἰκτίρ-ω pity
πάθ-ος, τό experience (3c)
πανταχοῦ everywhere
περὶ τοῦ δικαστηρί-ου καὶ τῶν
  δικαστ-ῶν about the
  law-courts and the dikasts
πλέ-ως -α -ων full of
ποῖ-ος -α -ον; what? what sort of?

ῥήτωρ (ῥητορ-), ὁ politician,
  speaker (3a)
ταύτ-ης τῆς πόλ-εως than this
  city (after μείζων)
τέττιξ (τεττιγ-), ὁ cicada,
  grasshopper (3a)
τῆς ἀπορί-ας perplexity (after
  πλέως)
τῆς πόλ-εως the city (after
  ἐκ); of the city
τῆς τόλμ-ης the brazenness
  (after πλέα)
τί μήν; of course
τοι-οῦτ-ος τοι-αύτ-η
  τοι-οῦτ-ο(ν) like this, of
  this kind
ὑπὲρ σοῦ for you (s.)
φιλό-πολ-ις (φιλο-πολιδ-), ὁ,
  ἡ patriotic
χρόν-ος, ὁ time (2a)
ψευδο-μαρτυρί-α, ἡ
  false-witness, perjury (1b)

Vocabulary to be learnt

ἀδικέω be unjust, commit a
  crime, do wrong
ᾄδω|ἀείδω sing

ἀνίσταμαι (ἀναστα-) get up,
  emigrate
δικαστήριον, τό law-court (2b)

δικαστής, ὁ juror, dikast (1d)
δῆμος, ὁ people; deme (2a)

ἐκκλησία, ἡ assembly, ekklesia
(1b)
εὐδαίμων εὔδαιμον
(εὐδαιμον-) happy, rich,
blessed by the gods (comp.
εὐδαιμονέστερος a ον; sup.
εὐδαιμονέστατος η ον)

μέγιστος η ον greatest (sup. of
μέγας)
μείζων μεῖζον
(μειζον-) greater (comp. of
μέγας)
μῶν; surely not?
οἰκτίρω (οἰκτιρ-) pity

πάθος, τό experience, suffering
(3c)
πανταχοῦ everywhere
ῥήτωρ (ῥήτορ-) ὁ orator,
politician (3a)
χρόνος, ὁ time (2a)

Vocabulary for Section Seven C

ἀγρῷ the country
ἄγ-ω live in, be at
ἀλλ' οὖν however that may be
ἀνάγκῃ of necessity
ἂν βουλ-οίμην (I) would like
to
ἀνα-πείθ-ω bring over to
one's side
ἂν ποι-οίην (I) would do
ἀντὶ χειρόν-ων instead of
worse
ἄξι-ος -α -ον worth
ἀπ-ολ-εῖ (he) will destroy
ἀπορί-ας lack of provision;
perplexity (after πλέα)
ἀ-πράγμων ἄ-πραγμον
(ἀπραγμον-) free from
trouble
ἄρχ-ομαι begin (+inf.)
αὐτ-οῦ . . . πονηρ-οῦ
ὄντ-ος him . . . being
wicked (after
κατεψηφίσαντο)
ἀχν-ύμεν-ος -η -ον grieving
βελτί-ους better (nom./acc.)
γν-ούς knowing (nom. s. m.)
(γιγνώσκ-ω)
γούνασι lap (lit. 'knees')
δεξι-ός -ά -όν clever, handy
δικαιοσύν-η, ἡ justice, being
just (1a)
δῶρ-ον, τό gift (2b)
εἰκός it is likely
εἰρήν-η, ἡ peace (1a)

ἑορτ-ή, ἡ festival (1a)
ἐπεί since
ἐπὶ αὐχένι upon our neck
ἑτοῖμ-ος -η -ον ready (to)
(+inf.)
εὐ-δόκιμ-ος -ον well thought
of
ζυγ-ός, ὁ yoke (2a)
ἦ τοι indeed
ἡγέ-ομαι consider (x to be y)
ἡδον-ῆς pleasure (after πλέα)
Ἡράκλεις Herakles! (voc.)
καὶ . . . πέρ although
καίτοι nonetheless
κακὰ λέγ-ω speak ill of
καρτερέ-ω endure, put up
with
κατα-ψηφίζ-ομαι condemn
(x on charge of y)
κεῖται (they – ταῦτα) lie;
(it – ζυγὸς) lies
κλοπ-ή, ἡ theft (1a)
μόν-ος -η -ον alone
νε-ῶν of ships
νόσ-ου disease (after πλέως)
νυν then
οἶν-ου wine (after πλέα)
οἱ δὲ others
οἱ μὲν some
ὁ Περικλῆς Pericles
ὅ τι what
ὅτι because of
οὐδενὸς nothing (after ἄξιοι)
πάντ-ων of all

παρασκευ-ῆς equipping (after
πλέως)
περὶ εἰρήν-ης about peace
Περικλῆς Pericles (nom.)
πλέ-ως -α -ων full of
ποιέ-ομαι make
πλήν except
πλούτ-ου riches, wealth (after
πλέα)
σίτ-ου food (after πλέα)
σπεύδ-οιμι ἂν I would hurry
σπονδ-αί, αἱ truce, treaty (1a)
συγγεν-ής, ὁ relation (3d)
τὰ βελτί-ω the better things
(acc.)
τᾶν my dear chap
(condescendingly)
τέτλαμεν we endure
τῇ ἐκκλησίᾳ the assembly
τῇ νηὶ the ship
τῆς πατρίδ-ος my fatherland
τῆς πόλ-εως of the city
τὸν Περικλέ-α Pericles
τόπ-ος, ὁ place (2a)
τῷ δήμ-ῳ the people
ὑγιεί-ας health (after πλέα)
φέρε come! (s.)
φιλό-πολις patriotic (nom.)
φιλό-σοφ-ος, ὁ philosopher
(2a)
χαλεπ-ός -ή -όν difficult, hard
χείρ-ους worse (nom.)
χείρων χεῖρον
(χειρον-) worse

Vocabulary to be learnt

ἄγω (ἀγαγ-) *live in, be at;*
lead, bring
ἄξιος α ον *worth, worthy of*
(+gen.)
ἀπολέω *I shall kill, destroy*
δεξιός ά όν *clever; right-hand*
διά (+gen.) *through*
ἐγγύς (+gen.) *near*
εἰρήνη, ἡ *peace (1a)*
εἰρήνην ἄγω *live in/be at peace*
ἐναντίον (+gen.) *opposite, in*
front of
ἐπεί *since*
ἐπί (+gen.) *on*

ἕτοιμος η ον *ready (to) (+inf.)*
ἡγέομαι *think, consider; lead*
(+dat.)
ἡδονή, ἡ *pleasure (1a)*
Ἡρακλῆς, ὁ *Herakles (3d*
uncontr.)
λαμβάνομαι *take hold of*
(+gen.)
μετά (+gen.) *with*
μόνος η ον *alone*
νυν *then (cf. νῦν now)*
ὁ μέν . . . ὁ δέ *one . . . another*
περί (+gen.) *about*
πλέως α ων *full of (+gen.)*
(as if α-ος α-α α-ον contr.)

ποιέομαι *make*
σπονδαί, αἱ *treaty, truce (1a)*
σῖτος, ὁ *food (2a) (pl. σῖτα, τά*
2b)
συγγενής, ὁ *relation (3d)*
τᾶν *my dear chap*
(condescendingly)
ὑπέρ (+gen.) *for, on behalf of*
ὑπό (+gen.) *by, at the hands of*
φιλόσοφος, ὁ *philosopher (2a)*
χαλεπός ή όν *difficult, hard*
χείρων χεῖρον (χειρον-) *worse*

○ Grammar for Section Seven

Summary:
Gen. (all types), and usages
Irr. comp., and contr. comp.
Pres. opt. act. and mid.
ἄν + opt.
ἀνίσταμαι, ἀπολέω, τί + part., ἰέναι, ἰών, Περικλῆς

Nouns/adjectives

Genitives

91 The forms of the genitive singular and plural across the range of noun and adjective types you have met are as follows:

s.				pl.			
nom.	*acc.*	*gen.*	*dat.*	*nom.*	*acc.*	*gen.*	*dat.*
1a	βο-ή, ἡ	βο-ήν	βο-ῆς	βο-ῇ	βο-αί	βο-άς	βο-ῶν	βο-αῖς
1b	ἀπορί-α, ἡ	ἀπορί-αν	ἀπορί-ας	ἀπορί-ᾳ	ἀπορί-αι	ἀπορί-ας	ἀπορι-ῶν	ἀπορί-αις
1c	τόλμ-α, ἡ	τόλμ-αν	τόλμ-ης	τόλμ-ῃ	τόλμ-αι	τόλμ-ας	τολμ-ῶν	τόλμ-αις
1d	ναύτ-ης, ὁ	ναύτ-ην	ναύτ-ου	ναύτ-ῃ				
	νεανί-ας, ὁ	νεανί-αν	νεανί-ου	νεανί-ᾳ	ναῦτ-αι	ναύτ-ας	ναυτ-ῶν	ναύτ-αις
2a	ἄνθρωπ-ος, ὁ	ἄνθρωπ-ον	ἀνθρώπ-ου	ἀνθρώπ-ῳ	ἄνθρωπ-οι	ἀνθρώπ-ους	ἀνθρώπ-ων	ἀνθρώπ-οις
2b	ἔργ-ον, τό	ἔργ-ον	ἔργ-ου	ἔργ-ῳ	ἔργ-α	ἔργ-α	ἔργ-ων	ἔργ-οις
3a	λιμήν, ὁ	λιμέν-α	λιμέν-ος	λιμέν-ι	λιμέν-ες	λιμέν-ας	λιμέν-ων	λιμέ-σι(ν)

b	πρᾶγμα, τό	πρᾶγμα	πράγματ-ος	πράγματ-ι	πράγματ-α	πράγματ-α	πραγμάτ-ων	πράγμα-σι(ν)
c	πλῆθ-ος, τό	πλῆθ-ος	πλήθ-ους	πλήθ-ει	πλήθ-η	πλήθ-η	πληθ-ῶν	πλήθ-εσι(ν)
d	τριήρ-ης, ἡ	τριήρ-η	τριήρ-ους	τριήρ-ει	τριήρ-εις	τριήρ-εις	τριήρ-ων	τριήρ-εσι(ν)
e	πόλ-ις, ἡ / πρέσβ-υς, ὁ	πόλ-ιν / πρέσβ-υν	πόλ-εως	πόλ-ει	πόλ-εις	πόλ-εις	πόλ-εων	πόλ-εσι(ν)
f	ἄστ-υ, τό	ἄστ-υ	ἄστ-εως	ἄστ-ει	ἄστ-η	ἄατ-η	ἄστ-εων	ἄατ-εσι(ν)
g	βασιλ-εύς, ὁ	βασιλ-έα	βασιλ-έως	βασιλ-εῖ	βασιλ-ῆς / βασιλ-εῖς	βασιλ-έας	βασιλ-έων	βασιλ-εῦσι(ν)
h	ὀφρύ-ς, ἡ	ὀφρῦ-ν	ὀφρύ-ος	ὀφρύ-ι	ὀφρύ-ες	ὀφρῦ-ς	ὀφρύ-ων	ὀφρύ-σι(ν)

Irregular nouns

ναῦς, ἡ	ναῦν	νεώς	νῆί	νῆες	ναῦς	νεῶν	ναυσί(ν)
γραῦς, ἡ	γραῦν	γραός	γραί	γρᾶες	γραῦς	γραῶν	γραυσί(ν)
Ζεύς, ὁ	Δία	Διός	Διί				

Personal pronouns

| ἐγώ | (ἐ)μέ | (ἐ)μοῦ | (ἐ)μοί | ἡμεῖς | ἡμᾶς | ἡμῶν | ἡμῖν |
| σύ | σέ | σοῦ | σοί | ὑμεῖς | ὑμᾶς | ὑμῶν | ὑμῖν |

Adjectives

m.	καλ-ός	καλ-όν	καλ-οῦ	καλ-ῷ	καλ-οί	καλ-ούς	καλ-ῶν	καλ-οῖς
f.	καλ-ή	καλ-ήν	καλ-ῆς	καλή	καλ-αί	καλ-άς	καλ-ῶν	καλ-αῖς
n.	καλ-όν	καλ-όν	καλ-οῦ	καλ-ῷ	καλ-ά	καλ-ά	καλ-ῶν	καλ-οῖς
m.	ἡμέτερ-ος	ἡμέτερ-ον	ἡμετέρ-ου	ἡμετέρ-ῳ	ἡμέτερ-οι	ἡμετέρ-ους	ἡμετέρ-ων	ἡμετέρ-οις
f.	ἡμετέρα	ἡμετέρ-αν	ἡμετέρ-ας	ἡμετέρ-ᾳ	ἡμέτερ-αι	ἡμετέρ-ας	ἡμετέρ-ων	ἡμετέρ-αις
n.	ἡμέτερ-ον	ἡμέτερ-ον	ἡμετέρ-ου	ἡμετέρ-ῳ	ἡμέτερ-α	ἡμέτερ-α	ἡμετέρ-ων	ἡμετέρ-οις
m.	οὗτ-ος	τοῦτ-ον	τούτ-ου	τούτ-ῳ	οὗτ-οι	τούτ-ους	τούτ-ων	τούτ-οις
f.	αὗτ-η	ταύτ-ην	ταύτ-ης	ταύτ-ῃ	αὗτ-αι	ταύτ-ας	τούτ-ων	ταύτ-αις
n.	τοῦτ-ο	τοῦτ-ο	τούτ-ου	τούτ-ῳ	ταῦτ-α	ταῦτ-α	τούτ-ων	τούτ-οις
m.	ἐκεῖν-ος	ἐκεῖν-ον	ἐκείν-ου	ἐκείν-ῳ	ἐκεῖν-οι	ἐκείν-ους	ἐκείν-ων	ἐκείν-οις
f.	ἐκείν-η	ἐκείν-ην	ἐκείν-ης	ἐκείν-ῃ	ἐκεῖν-αι	ἐκείν-ας	ἐκείν-ων	ἐκείν-αις
n.	ἐκεῖν-ο	ἐκεῖν-ο	ἐκείν-ου	ἐκείν-ῳ	ἐκεῖν-α	ἐκεῖν-α	ἐκείν-ων	ἐκείν-οις
m.	αὐτ-ός	αὐτ-όν	αὐτ-οῦ	αὐτῷ	αὐτ-οί	αὐτ-ούς	αὐτ-ῶν	αὐτ-οῖς
f.	αὐτ-ή	αὐτ-ήν	αὐτ-ῆς	αὐτ-ῇ	αὐτ-αί	αὐτ-άς	αὐτ-ῶν	αὐτ-αῖς
n.	αὐτ-ό	αὐτό	αὐτ-οῦ	αὐτ-ῷ	αὐτ-ά	αὐτ-ά	αὐτ-ῶν	αὐτ-οῖς
m.	πολ-ύς	πολ-ύν	πολλ-οῦ	πολλ-ῷ	πολλ-οί	πολλ-ούς	πολλ-ῶν	πολλ-οῖς
f.	πολλ-ή	πολλ-ήν	πολλ-ῆς	πολλ-ῇ	πολλ-αί	πολλ-άς	πολλ-ῶν	πολλ-αῖς
n.	πολ-ύ	πολύ	πολλ-οῦ	πολλ-ῷ	πολλ-ά	πολλ-ά	πολλ-ῶν	πολλ-οῖς
m./f.	εὔφρων	εὔφρον-α	εὔφρον-ος	εὔφρον-ι	εὔφρον-ες	εὔφρον-ας	εὐφρόν-ων	εὔφρο-σι(ν)
n.	εὔφρον	εὔφρον	εὔφρον-ος	εὔφρον-ι	εὔφρον-α	εὔφρον-α	εὐφρόν-ων	εὔφρο-σι(ν)
m./f.	τις	τιν-α	τιν-ος	τιν-ι	τιν-ες	τιν-ας	τιν-ων	τι-σι(ν)
n.	τι	τι	τιν-ος	τιν-ι	τιν-α	τιν-α	τιν-ων	τι-σι(ν)
m.	οὐδ-είς	οὐδ-ένα	οὐδ-ενός	οὐδ-ενί				
f.	οὐδε-μία	οὐδε-μίαν	οὐδε-μιᾶς	οὐδε-μιᾷ				
n.	οὐδ-έν	οὐδ-έν	οὐδ-ενός	οὐδ-ενί				

m.	ὤν	ὄντ-α	ὄντ-ος	ὄντ-ι	ὄντ-ες	ὄντ-ας	ὄντ-ων	οὖ-σι(ν)
f.	οὖσ-α	οὖσ-αν	οὖσ-ης	οὖσ-η	οὖσ-αι	οὖσ-ας	οὖσ-ῶν	οὖσ-αις
n.	ὄν	ὄν	ὄντ-ος	ὄντ-ι	ὄντ-α	ὄντ-α	ὄντ-ων	οὖ-σι(ν)
m.	παύσ-ας	παύσ-αντα	παύσ-αντος	παύσ-αντι	παύσ-αντες	παύσ-αντας	παυσ-άντων	παύσ-ασι(ν)
f.	παύσ-ασα	παύσ-ασαν	παυσ-άσης	παυσ-άση	παυσ-άσαι	παυσ-άσας	παυσ-ασῶν	παυσ-άσαις
n.	παύσ-αν	παύσ-αν	παύσ-αντος	παύσ-αντι	παύσ-αντα	παύσ-αντα	παυσ-άντων	παύσ-ασι(ν)

Notes

(i) Genitive plurals all end in -ων.

(ii) Genitive singulars of type 3 nouns/adjectives all originally ended in some form of -ος. Later contractions and changes created forms in -ους and -εως.

(iii) Watch the changing patterns of α|η in 1st declension nouns (cf. 24) and note the gen. s. of ναύτης: ναύτου.

Uses of the genitive

92 The most common uses of the genitive are as follows:

(i) to correspond to English phrases introduced by 'of' in such senses as:

(a) possession, e.g. ἡ τοῦ Δικαιοπόλεως οἰκία 'the house of Dikaiopolis'

(b) description, e.g. τὸ τῶν πολιτῶν πλῆθος 'the crowd of citizens, the citizen crowd'

(c) source or origin, e.g. οἱ λόγοι οἱ τοῦ ἀνθρώπου 'the words of the fellow', and ἡ τῶν Ἕνδεκα ἀνομία 'the lawlessness of the Eleven'

(d) a part, e.g. ὀλίγοι τῶν ἀνθρώπων 'few of the men'

(ii) with certain adjectives, e.g.

ἄξιος   'worthy of'

αἴτιος   'responsible for'

πλέως   'full of'

(iii) with certain prepositions, e.g.

ἀπό   'away from'

ἐκ   'out of, from'

μετά   'in company with'

διά   'through'

ἕνεκα   'for the sake of' (comes AFTER the noun)

περί   'concerning, about' (and cf. Reference Grammar F, p. 290)

(iv) with certain verbs, e.g.

ἀκούω   'I hear' (a person)

λαμβάνομαι   'I seize, take hold of'

καταδικάζω   'I condemn'

(v) to express comparison. So far you have met comparisons of the type described in 76, i.e. done with ἤ='than'. Greek can also express comparison without ἤ by putting the thing compared in the genitive, e.g. Σωκράτης σοφώτερός ἐστι τούτου τοῦ ἀνθρώπου 'Socrates is wiser than this fellow' (as opposed to the method described in **76,** which gives: Σωκράτης σοφώτερός ἐστιν ἢ οὗτος ὁ ἀνήρ).

Note
Revise **26.** *and see Language Surveys (10), (11).*

Further comparative forms

93 Note the following irregular comparatives and superlatives:
ἀγαθός βελτίων βέλτιστος 'good', 'better', 'best'
μέγας μείζων μέγιστος 'great', 'greater', 'greatest'
Cf. **76,** and note the alternative comparison of ἀγαθός.

Note
Comparative forms in -(ι)ων may form the acc. s. m./f., the nom. pl. and the acc. pl. from an alternative stem without the -ν-, where the vowel of the stem and that of the ending contract, e.g.
βελτίο(ν)α→βελτίω *(acc. s., m./f.; nom./acc. pl. n.)*
βελτίο(ν)ες→βελτίους *(nom. pl. m./f.)*
βελτίο(ν)ας→βελτίους *(acc. pl. m./f.)*

94 Observe also that adjectives ending in -ων like κακοδαίμων have comparatives and superlatives in
-ονέστερ-ος -α -ον (comparative)
-ονέστατ-ος -η -ον (superlative)
e.g.
εὐδαιμονέστερος 'more lucky'
εὐδαιμονέστατος 'most lucky, very lucky'

Verbs

Present optative active and middle παύοιμι, παυοίμην

95 The forms of the present optative, active and middle, for non-contracted verbs are as follows:

Active	*Middle*
παύ-οιμι	παυ-οίμην
παύ-οις	παύ-οιο
παύ-οι	παύ-οιτο
παύ-οιμεν	παυ-οίμεθα
παύ-οιτε	παύ-οισθε
παύ-οιεν	παύ-οιντο

Note
Look for a present stem with an -οι- in it.

Present optative of contract verbs

96 The forms for contracted verbs in the *active* are as follows. Note that the forms arise from contracting the vowel with the endings -οίην, -οίης, -οίη in the singular.

a-contracts τιμ-ῴην	ε-contracts ποι-οίην	o-contracts δηλ-οίην
τιμ-ῴην (-α-οίην)	ποι-οίην (-ε-οίην)	δηλ-οίην (-ο-οίην)
τιμ-ῴης (-α-οίης)	ποι-οίης (-ε-οίης)	δηλ-οίης (-ο-οίης)
τιμ-ῴη (-α-οίη)	ποι-οίη (-ε-οίη)	δηλ-οίη (-ο-οίη)
τιμ-ῷμεν (-ά-οιμεν)	ποι-οῖμεν (-έ-οιμεν)	δηλ-οῖμεν (-ό-οιμεν)
τιμ-ῷτε (-ά-οιτε)	ποι-οῖτε (-έ-οιτε)	δηλ-οῖτε (-ό-οιτε)
τιμ-ῷεν (-ά-οιεν)	ποι-οῖεν (-έ-οιεν)	δηλ-οῖεν (-ό-οιεν)

Middle forms contract with the middle endings as in **95,** e.g. τιμ-ῴμην, ποι-οίμην, δηλ-οίμην (see also p. 280 (ii)).

ἄν and optative

97 The optative forms are used with the particle ἄν to express a 'polite' request or agreement. Sometimes 'polite' requests are difficult to distinguish from a straight request. The best translations involve using the English forms 'would', 'would like to', 'can', or the simple future 'will', e.g.

λέγοις ἄν μοι; 'Would you tell me? Would you like to/can you/will you tell me?'

λέγοιμι ἄν 'I would/would like to/can/will tell you'.

Two verbs to watch for

98 Note ἀνίσταμαι 'I get up and go, I am leaving, emigrating', the stem of which is dominated by -α- in the present:

ἀνίστα-μαι   'I leave' etc.
ἀνίστα-σαι
ἀνίστα-ται
ἀνιστά-μεθα
ἀνίστα-σθε
ἀνίστα-νται

Infinitive: ἀνίστασθαι 'to leave'
Participle: ἀνιστά-μεν-ος -η -ον 'leaving'
Cf. δύνα-μαι 'I am able' (**90**)

99 Note ἀπολέω 'I shall destroy, ruin, kill'. Bear in mind the ἀπολ- stem for future reference.

A common Greek construction

100 Note the Greek love of τί + participle, and the variety of possible translations it takes:

τί βουλόμενος τοῦτο ποιεῖς; (lit.) 'Wanting what do you do this?', i.e. 'What do you want when you do this? What do you have in mind in doing this? What is your motive for doing this?'

τί παθὼν τοῦτο λέγεις; (lit.) 'Suffering what do you say this?', i.e. 'What did you suffer to make you say this?'

Note also that πάσχω basically means 'I have something done to me', so that a perfectly good translation would also be 'What made you say this?'

101 Revise εἶμι 'I shall go' (**64**), and remember the infinitive form ἰέναι 'to go', and the participle form ἰών 'going' *(ἰών ἰοῦσα ἰόν (ἰοντ-)).* These forms are not used in a future sense (cf. **74** (ii)).

Nouns

102 Uncontracted 3d type nouns decline as follows:

Περικλῆς, ὁ 'Pericles' *(3d)*

nom.	*acc.*	*gen.*	*dat.*
Περικλῆς (= Περικλέ-ης)	Περικλέα	Περικλέους	Περικλεῖ

These are restricted to proper names. Cf. also Ἡρακλῆς, but contrast the contracted Σωκράτης at **67**. *(For full noun survey, see Reference Grammar B, p. 270.)*

Revise:

Pres. parts. **48–54** Reference Grammar I
Def. art. Language Survey (12)   O

Exercises for Section Seven

(a) Words

1. Deduce the meaning of the words on the right from those on the left:

ἀδικέω	τὸ ἀδίκημα
ἀνίσταμαι	ἡ ἀνάστασις
ἄξιος	ἀξιόλογος ον
δῆμος|κρατέω	ἡ δημοκρατία

ἡγεμών	ἡ ἡγεμονία	
κρατέω	κράτιστος	
πέμπω	ἡ πομπή	
πολίτης	ἡ πολιτεία	πολιτεύω πολιτικός ή όν
χαλεπός	χαλεπαίνω	
χείρ	ἐπιχειρέω	

(b/c) Morphology and Syntax

1. Translate the whole passage into English, putting the bracketed words into the genitive case:

A. ἀλλὰ τίς αἴτιός ἐστι (οὗτος ὁ πόλεμος) καὶ (αὕτη ἡ ἀπορία);

B. οἱ ῥήτορες, εὖ οἶδ' ὅτι, αἴτιοι (τοῦτο τὸ πρᾶγμα). ἡ γὰρ πόλις πλέα (θόρυβος) καὶ (βοή) διὰ τόν τε πόλεμον καὶ τὴν (οἱ ῥήτορες) τόλμαν. τίς γὰρ οὐκ οἶδε περὶ (ἡ τόλμα) (αὐτούς);

A. ἀλλ' οὐκ αἰτίους (ταῦτα τὰ πράγματα) ἡγοῦμαι τοὺς ῥήτορας ἔγωγε, ἀλλὰ βελτίστους (ἄνθρωποι). ἀεὶ γὰρ μάχονται περὶ (τὸ πλῆθος) καὶ (ἡ πόλις), ὡς φασὶν αὐτοί.

B. ναί. ἀλλὰ ψευδῆ λέγουσι. κακὸν γὰρ τὸ (οὗτοι οἱ ἄνδρες) πλῆθος καὶ οὐδεὶς χείρων (ῥήτωρ). οἱ γὰρ ῥήτορες λαμβάνονται (ἡ ἐκκλησία) καὶ (τὸ δικαστήριον).

2. Convert these verbs into the polite form (optative + ἄν) and translate:

(a) μένεις   (e) ἀποκρίνῃ
(b) λέγω   (f) κελεύεις
(c) βουλόμεθα   (g) παύομαι
(d) πείθεσθε   (h) φέρομεν

3. Translate these sentences and contrast the use of the preposition in each pair:

a (i). ὁ ξένος ἐπὶ τοῦ βωμοῦ καθίζεται.
(ii). ἡ ναῦς ἐπὶ τοὺς πολεμίους ἐπέρχεται.
b (i). εἶμι αὔριον εἰς τὴν ἀγορὰν μετὰ τῶν φίλων.
(ii). μετὰ δὲ ταῦτα ἐπάνειμι εἰς τὴν οἰκίαν.
c (i). τὸ πλοῖον πλεῖ παρὰ τὴν νῆσον.
(ii). ὁ σοφιστὴς πολλὰ χρήματα δέχεται παρὰ τῶν μαθητῶν.
d (i). ὁ παῖς προσέδραμε πρὸς ἡμᾶς, βιαζόμενος διὰ τοῦ πλήθους.
(ii). ἡ ἐμὴ γυνὴ φοβεῖται τὸ ἄστυ διὰ τὴν νόσον.

4. Compare Dionysodoros unfavourably with Euthydemos using the words listed below and these formulae:

$$\left.\begin{array}{l}\text{Διονυσόδωρος κακίων}\\ \text{χείρων}\end{array}\right\} \ \text{ἐστί}(\nu) \ \left\{\begin{array}{l}\text{Εὐθυδήμου}\\ \text{ἢ Εὐθύδημος}\end{array}\right.$$

καλός, μέγας, κακοδαίμων, εὔφρων, ἀγαθός, μῶρος, σοφός

(d) English into Greek

1. Translate into Greek:
   1. The man's slave goes up to the rhapsode and grabs his hand.
   2. Who is responsible for those shouts, which are very loud?
   3. You are a sophist and worth nothing.
   4. Why are the politicians richer than the people of the city? Tell me!
   5. We suffered many bad experiences, but fought against the Persians for freedom.

2. Translate into Greek:

DIKAIOPOLIS Look! I see a slave running towards us. Whose slave are you?

SLAVE As it happens I am slave of Euelpides, your friend.

DIK. Would you please say what you want, and for what reason you ran to me?

SLAVE I will. For I must, as Euelpides ordered, ask you to wait.

DIK. Then I shall wait. Hullo, Euelpides and Peisetairos. Why are you leaving the city? Where are you off to?

PEISETAIROS We have to go away to a new and more useful city.

Test Exercise Seven

παῖς τις, διὰ τοῦ τῶν πολιτῶν πλήθους ἰών, προσέδραμε πρὸς τὸν
Δικαιόπολιν καί, λαβόμενος τῆς χειρός, μένειν ἐκέλευεν. ἔπειτα οἱ τὸν
παῖδα πέμψαντες, ὅ τε Εὐελπίδης καὶ ὁ Πεισέταιρος, φίλοι ὄντες τοῦ
Δικαιοπόλεως προσελθόντες ἠσπάζοντο Δικαιόπολιν. ὁ δὲ Δικαιόπολις
οὐκ εἰδὼς τί βουλόμενοι ἐκ τοῦ ἄστεως ἀπέρχονται, ἤρετο ποῖ ἀπιέναι
διανοοῦνται καὶ τίνος ἕνεκα. ἐκεῖνοι δὲ ἀπεκρίναντο ὅτι δεῖ αὐτοὺς
Νεφελοκοκκυγίαν ζητεῖν, εὑρόντας δὲ οἰκεῖν. Δικαιόπολις δὲ
εὐδαιμονεστάτας ἡγεῖτο τὰς ᾿Αθήνας καὶ βελτίω τῶν ᾿Αθηνῶν οὐδεμίαν
πόλιν. πρῶτον μὲν οὖν μανθάνειν οὐκ ἐδύνατο τίνος ἕνεκα ἀνίστανται,
ἔπειτα ἀκούσας τὰ περὶ τῶν δικαστῶν καὶ τοῦ δικαστηρίου καὶ τῶν
ῥητόρων, ὡμολόγησεν. οἱ μὲν γὰρ δικασταὶ ἐφαίνοντο ἀδικοῦντες τοὺς
ἀγαθούς, οἱ δὲ ῥήτορες (ὡς ἔδοξαν) ἔτυχον διαφθείροντες τὸν δῆμον καὶ
οὐκ οἰκτίροντες. οἱ μὲν οὖν φίλοι οἱ Δικαιοπόλεως ἀπῇσαν. αὐτὸς δέ,
βαρέως φέρων τὰ τῆς τε πόλεως καὶ τοῦ δήμου καὶ βελτίστην ἡγούμενος
τὴν εἰρήνην, διενοεῖτο σπονδὰς ποιεῖσθαι ἐν τῇ ἐκκλησίᾳ. ἀλλ᾿ ὁ
ῥαψῳδός, ἀμαθεῖς ἡγούμενος τοὺς ἄνδρας καὶ μώρους, αὐτὸς οὐκ
ἐβούλετο μετιέναι μετ᾿ αὐτοῦ, ἀλλ᾿ ἀπῆλθε μόνος.

Vocabulary

Νεφελοκοκκυγία, ἡ   ἀμαθεῖς ignorant (acc. pl. m.)   μετιέναι inf. of
  Cloud-cuckoo land (1b)   μετέρχομαι accompany

Section Eight

Vocabulary for Section Eight A

ἀλλήλ-οις to each other
βο-ῇ a shout (after χρῶμαι)
δρᾶμα (δραμετ-), τό drama,
    play (3b)
δυσ-τυχεῖ unlucky (goes with
    κακοδαίμονι ἀνθρώπῳ ὄντι)
ἐμ-πεσ-εῖται it will befall
    (fut. of ἐμ-πίπτ-ω)
ἐμπρόσθεν (+ gen.) in front
    of, before
θεατ-ής, ὁ spectator, member
    of the audience (1d)

θηρί-ον, τό beast (2b)
καὶ δή well, all right; look
κακο-δαίμον-ι ἀνθρώπ-ῳ
    ὄντ-ι unlucky/ill-favoured
    man that you are
κατα-λέγ-ω
    (κατ-ειπ-) recount, tell
μοι to me
Ξανθί-ας, ὁ Xanthias (1d)
οἷ-ος -α -ον what sort of
πολλ-οῖς οὖσιν being many
    (goes with τοῖς θεατ-αῖς)

σοι to you (s.); you (after
    ἐμ-πεσ-εῖται)
σοῦ ἕνεκα for your sake
Σωσί-ας, ὁ Sosias (1d)
τίν-ι to whom? (s.)
τοῖς to/with/by the
τοῖς θεατ-αῖς to the audience
τῷ to/with/by the
τῷ πλήθ-ει to the crowd
χρά-ομαι use, employ

Vocabulary to be learnt
δρᾶμα (δραμετ-), τό play,
    drama (3b)
θεατ-ής, ὁ spectator, member of
    audience (1d)

Vocabulary for Section Eight B

ἄνω above, up there
ἀπορί-ᾳ perplexity
ἀρχ-ή, ἡ beginning (1a)
ἔ-γνω he realised
    (γιγνώσκ-ω|ἔ-γνω-ν)
ἡμ-ῖν to us
ἡμ-ῖν ἐρωτ-ῶσιν to us asking

ἥσυχ-ος -ον quiet(ly)
κατα-πύγων κατά-πυγον
    (καταπυγον-) homosexual,
    queer
κελεύ-οντ-ι him ordering
    (after ἐπιθόμεθα)
κύων (κυν-), ὁ dog (3a)

μοι ἐρ-ομέν-ῳ to me asking
ὄνομα (ὀνομετ-), τό name
    (3b)
οὐ μὴν ἀλλά nonetheless
πονηρ-ός -ά -όν wicked, bad
ταύτ-ῃ τῇ νόσ-ῳ to this
    disease

τῇ in/with/by the
τῇ πόλ-ει the city
τοι-οῦτ-ος τοι-αύτ-η
  τοι-οῦτ-ο(ν) of such a
  kind, like this
τῷ ἀνδρ-ὶ to the man

τῷ δεσπότ-ῃ to the master
τῷ πατρ-ὶ to the father
φέρε come!
φιλο- love
φιλο-θύτ-ης, ὁ lover of
  sacrifices (1d)

φιλό-κυβ-ος -ον lover of dice,
  gambler
φιλό-ξεν-ος -ον loving
  strangers, hospitable
Φιλόξεν-ος, ὁ Philoxenos (2a)
  (a noted homosexual)

Vocabulary to be learnt

ἄνω up, above
ἥσυχος ον quiet, peaceful
ὄνομα (ὀνοματ-), τό name
  (3b)
πονηρός ά όν wicked, wretched

τοιοῦτος τοιαύτη
  τοιοῦτο(ν) of this kind, of
  such a kind
φέρε come!

Vocabulary for Section Eight C

ἀνα-πείθ-ω persuade,
  convince
ἀπορί-ᾳ perplexity
αὐλ-ή, ἡ courtyard (1a)
αὐτ-ῷ ... ἀνα-πείθ-οντ-ι him
  ... trying to persuade (him)
  (after ἐπείθετο)
αὐτῷ τῷ τυμπάν-ῳ drum and
  all
βαρέ-ως φέρ-ω take hard,
  find hard to bear
Βδελυ-κλέων (Βδελυκλεων-),
  ὁ Bdelykleon (3a) ('Loather
  of Kleon')
γράφ-ω write
Δῆμ-ος, ὁ Demos (2a) (a
  notably handsome young man)
δικάζ-ω be a juror, decide a
  case
ἐγ-κλεί-ω shut in
ἐξ-έρχ-ομαι go out
ἐπεί when
ἐραστ-ής, ὁ lover (1d)

ἡλιάστ-ης, ὁ juror in the
  Eliaia court (1d)
θύρ-ᾳ τιν-ὶ a door
θυράζε out of doors
καθ-ίζ-ομαι sit down
καίτοι furthermore
κῆμ-ος, ὁ funnel (2a) (through
  which the voting pebble goes
  into the voting urn)
κορυβαντίζ-ω introduce into
  the Korybantic rites (a
  mystery religion involving
  wildness of all kinds, and the
  beating of drums)
ὀνειρο-πολέ-ω dream
παρα-γράφ-ω write alongside
πλησίον nearby
πολλ-οῖς τε οὖσι καὶ
  μεγάλ-οις being many and
  large (goes with τούτ-οις
  τοῖς μόχλ-οις)
τῆς ἡμέρ-ας during the day
τῆς νυκτ-ὸς during the night

τοιόσδε τοιάδε τοιόνδε like
  this, as follows
τούτ-οις τοῖς δικτύ-οις with
  these nets
τούτ-οις τοῖς μόχλ-οις with
  these bars
τῷ γέροντ-ι to the old man
τῷ δικαστηρί-ῳ the
  law-court
τῷ πατρ-ὶ his father (after
  ἐμ-πεσ-οῦσ-α)
τῷ σῷ υἱ-ῷ your son (after
  πείσ-ῃ)
τῷ υἱ-ῷ τούτ-ῳ to this son
  here
ὑμ-ῖν ... οὖσι to you (pl.)
  being
φιλ-ηλιάστ-ης, ὁ lover of
  being a juror in the court of
  the Eliaia (1d)
Φιλο-κλέων (Φιλοκλεων-), ὁ
  Philokleon (3a) ('Lover of
  Kleon')

Vocabulary to be learnt

ἀναπείθω persuade over to one's
  side
βαρέως φέρω take badly, find
  hard to bear

δικάζω be a juror; make a
  judgment
ἐξέρχομαι (ἐξελθ-) go out;
  come out

ἐπεί when; since
καθίζομαι sit down
καθίζω sit down
πλησίον nearby, (+gen.) near

Vocabulary for Section Eight D

ἄναξ (ἀνακτ-), ὁ lord (3a)
βο-ῇ a shout (after χρῆται)
ἐμ-οὶ to me
ἔμ-οιγε to me at least
ἐνταῦθα (from) here
ἐν-τυγχάν-ω (ἐν-τυχ-) meet, chance upon
ἔργ-ῳ in fact, indeed (i.e. actually)
ἡμ-ῖν to us
ἡμ-ῖν καθεύδ-ουσιν us sleeping (after ἐντυχὼν)
ἱπν-ός, ὁ oven (2a)
κάπν-η, ἡ chimney (1a)

καπν-ῷ . . . ἐξ-ιόντ-ι smoke coming out (after ὅμοι-ος)
καπν-ός, ὁ smoke (2a)
λόγ-ῳ in word (i.e. supposedly)
μηχαν-ή, ἡ device, scheme (1a)
μοι to me
ὅμοι-ος -α -ον like
ὀπ-ή, ἡ hole (1a)
ὅ τι; what?
οὐδεν-ὶ no one (after ὁμοιότερος)
πολλ-ῇ σπουδ-ῇ with much urgency (i.e. very urgently)

σοί to you (s.)
τάλας wretched (me)
τέγ-ος, τό roof (3c)
τίσι; to whom? (pl.)
τοῖς δούλ-οις to the slaves
τόλμ-η brazenness (after χρῆται)
τῷ Φιλο-κλέων-ι Philokleon (after ὁμοιότερος)
Φιλο-κλέων-ι Philokleon (after ὅμοιος)
χρά-ομαι use, employ (3rd s. χρῆται)
ψοφέ-ω make a noise

Vocabulary to be learnt

ἄναξ (ἀνακτ-), ὁ prince, lord, king (3a)
ἐνταῦθα here, at this point

μέλας μέλαινα μέλαν (μελαν-) black
τάλας τάλαινα τάλαν (ταλαν-) wretched, unhappy

Vocabulary for Section Eight E

ἄμεινον better
ἄνοιγε open!
ἀπο-δραμ-ὼν see ἀπο-τρέχ-ω
ἀπο-τρέχ-ω (ἀπο-δραμ-) run away
'Απο-δρασ-ιππ-ίδης, ὁ the son of Runawayhorse (1d) (comic name)
αὐτ-οῖς τοῖς κανθηλί-οις pack-saddle and all
βῶλι-ον, τό clod of earth (2b)
δίκτυ-ον, τό net (2b)
δυν-αίμην I would be able (opt. of δύν-αμαι)
ἐγ-κλείσ-ασι . . . ἡμ-ῖν to us shutting (him) in

ἐγ-κλεί-ω shut in
ἐκ-φεύγ-ω (ἐκ-φυγ-) escape
ἔμοι-γε to me
ἐξ-άγ-ω bring out, lead out
ἡμίον-ος, ὁ mule (2a)
'Ιθακήσι-ος, ὁ (an) Ithakan (2a)
κάτω below, underneath
λήσ-ει he will escape notice (fut. of λανθάν-ω)
λίθ-ος, ὁ stone (2a)
μηκέτι no longer
μιαρ-ός -ά -όν foul
μοι me (after ἐνέπεσε); my (after ἐστι)
νου-μηνί-α, ἡ first of the month (1b) (market-day)

'Οδυσσ-εύς, ὁ Odysseus (3g)
ὅμοι-ος -α -ον like
ὅτι because
Οὖ-τις No-man
πάντ-ων of all
παρα-σκευάζ-ομαι devise, prepare
ποδαπός from which country?
πράγματα παρ-έχ-ω cause problems (fut. παρ-έξ-ω)
πωλέ-ω sell
σοί to you (s.)
σοῦ shoo!
σπουδ-ῇ πάσ-ῃ with all urgency (i.e. most urgently)

στέν-ω groan
στρουθ-ός, ὁ sparrow (2a)
ταῖς χερσὶ with your hands
τῇ ἀγορ-ᾷ the market-place
τῷ δικτύ-ῳ with the net

τῷ 'Οδυσσ-εῖ Odysseus (*after*
ὁμοιότατος)
ὑφ-έλκ-ω drag from beneath
φθήσ-εται he will anticipate
(fut. of φθάν-ω)

φύλαξιν οὖσι (to us) being
guards (*goes with*
ἐγκλείσασι . . . ἡμῖν)
ὠθέ-ω push

Vocabulary to be learnt

ἀμείνων ἄμεινον
  (ἀμεινον-) better
ἀποτρέχω (ἀποδραμ-) run
  away
ἐγκλείω shut in, lock in
ἐκφεύγω (ἐκφυγ-) escape
ἐξάγω (ἐξαγαγ-) lead/bring
  out

ἡμίονος, ὁ mule (2a)
μηκέτι no longer
μιαρός ά όν foul, polluted
ὅμοιος α ον like, similar to
  (+dat.)
παρέχω (παρασχ-) give to,
  provide

πράγματα παρέχω cause
  trouble
πωλέω sell
στένω groan
χράομαι use, employ (+dat.)

○ Grammar for Section Eight A–E

Summary:
Dat. (all types), and usages
ἐρωτάω, λανθάνω

Nouns/adjectives

Datives

103 The forms of the dative singular and plural across the range of noun and adjective types you have met are as follows:

s.

pl.

	nom.	acc.	gen.	dat.		nom.	acc.	gen.	dat.
a	βο-ή, ἡ	βο-ήν	βο-ῆς	βο-ῇ		βο-αί	βο-άς	βο-ῶν	βο-αῖς
b	ἀπορί-α, ἡ	ἀπορί-αν	ἀπορί-ας	ἀπορ-ίᾳ		ἀπορί-αι	ἀπορί-ας	ἀπορι-ῶν	ἀπορί-αις
c	τόλμ-α, ἡ	τόλμ-αν	τόλμ-ης	τόλμ-ῃ		τόλμ-αι	τόλμ-ας	τόλμ-ῶν	τόλμ-αις
d	ναύτ-ης, ὁ	ναύτ-ην	ναύτ-ου	ναύτ-ῃ ⎫		ναύτ-αι	ναύτ-ας	ναυτ-ῶν	ναύτ-αις
	νεανί-ας, ὁ	νεανί-αν	νεανί-ου	νεανί-ᾳ ⎭					
a	ἄνθρωπ-ος, ὁ	ἄνθρωπ-ον	ἀνθρώπ-ου	ἀνθρώπ-ῳ		ἄνθρωπ-οι	ἀνθρώπ-ους	ἀνθρώπ-ων	ἀνθρώπ-οις
b	ἔργ-ον, τό	ἔργ-ον	ἔργ-ου	ἔργ-ῳ		ἔργ-α	ἔργ-α	ἔργ-ων	ἔργ-οις
b	λιμήν, ὁ	λιμέν-α	λιμέν-ος	λιμέν-ι		λιμέν-ες	λιμέν-ας	λιμέν-ων	λιμέ-σι(ν)
c	πρᾶγμα, τό	πρᾶγμα	πράγματ-ος	πράγματ-ι		πράγματ-α	πράγματ-α	πραγμάτ-ων	πράγμα-σι(ν)
c	πλῆθ-ος, τό	πλῆθ-ος	πλήθ-ους	πλήθ-ει		πλήθ-η	πλήθ-η	πληθ-ῶν	πλήθ-εσι(ν)
d	τριήρ-ης, ἡ	τριήρ-η	τριήρ-ους	τριήρ-ει		τριήρ-εις	τριήρ-εις	τριήρ-ων	τριήρ-εσι(ν)

	s.					pl.		
	nom.	*acc.*	*gen.*	*dat.*	*nom.*	*acc.*	*gen.*	*dat.*
3e	πόλ-ις, ἡ πρέσβ-υς, ὁ	πόλ-ιν πρέσβ-υν }	πόλ-εως	πόλ-ει	πόλ-εις	πόλ-εις	πόλ-εων	πόλ-εσι(ν)
3f	ἄστ-υ, τό	ἄστ-υ	ἄστ-εως	ἄστ-ει	ἄστ-η	ἄστ-η	ἄστ-εων	ἄστ-εσι(ν)
3g	βασιλ-εύς, ὁ	βασιλ-έα	βασιλ-έως	βασιλ-εῖ	βασιλ-ῆς } βασιλ-εῖς	βασιλ-έας	βασιλ-έων	βασιλ-εῦσι(ν
3h	ὀφρῦ-ς, ἡ	ὀφρῦ-ν	ὀφρύ-ος	ὀφρύ-ι	ὀφρύ-ες	ὀφρῦ-ς	ὀφρύ-ων	ὀφρύ-σι(ν)

Irregular nouns

ναῦς, ἡ	ναῦν	νεώς	νηί	νῆες	ναῦς	νεῶν	ναυσί(ν)
γραῦς, ἡ	γραῦν	γραός	γραί	γρᾶες	γραῦς	γραῶν	γραυσί(ν)
Ζεύς, ὁ	Δία	Διός	Διί				

Personal pronouns

ἐγώ	(ἐ)μέ	(ἐ)μοῦ	(ἐ)μοί	ἡμεῖς	ἡμᾶς	ἡμῶν	ἡμῖν
σύ	σέ	σοῦ	σοί	ὑμεῖς	ὑμᾶς	ὑμῶν	ὑμῖν

Adjectives

{ m.	καλ-ός	καλ-όν	καλ-οῦ	καλ-ῷ	καλ-οί	καλ-ούς	καλ-ῶν	καλ-οῖς
{ f.	καλ-ή	καλ-ήν	καλ-ῆς	καλ-ῇ	καλ-αί	καλ-άς	καλ-ῶν	καλ-αῖς
{ n.	καλ-όν	καλ-όν	καλ-οῦ	καλῷ	καλ-ά	καλ-ά	καλ-ῶν	καλ-οῖς
{ m.	ἡμέτερ-ος	ἡμέτερ-ον	ἡμετέρ-ου	ἡμετέρ-ῳ	ἡμέτερ-οι	ἡμετέρ-ους	ἡμετέρ-ων	ἡμετέρ-οις
{ f.	ἡμετέρα	ἡμετέρ-αν	ἡμετέρ-ας	ἡμετέρ-ᾳ	ἡμέτερ-αι	ἡμέτερ-ας	ἡμετέρ-ων	ἡμετέρ-αις
{ n.	ἡμέτερ-ον	ἡμέτερ-ον	ἡμετέρ-ου	ἡμετέρ-ῳ	ἡμέτερ-α	ἡμέτερ-α	ἡμετέρ-ων	ἡμετέρ-οις
{ m.	οὗτ-ος	ταῦτ-ον	τούτ-ου	τούτ-ῳ	οὗτ-οι	τούτ-ους	τούτ-ων	τούτ-οις
{ f.	αὕτ-η	ταύτ-ην	ταύτ-ης	ταύτ-ῃ	αὗτ-αι	ταύτ-ας	τούτ-ων	ταύτ-αις
{ n.	τοῦτ-ο	ταῦτ-α	τούτ-ου	τούτ-ῳ	ταῦτ-α	ταῦτ-α	τούτ-ων	τούτ-οις
{ m.	ἐκεῖν-ος	ἐκεῖν-ον	ἐκείν-ου	ἐκείν-ῳ	ἐκεῖν-οι	ἐκείν-ους	ἐκείν-ων	ἐκείν-οις
{ f.	ἐκείν-η	ἐκείν-ην	ἐκείν-ης	ἐκείν-ῃ	ἐκεῖν-αι	ἐκείν-ας	ἐκείν-ων	ἐκείν-αις
{ n.	ἐκεῖν-ο	ἐκεῖν-ο	ἐκείν-ου	ἐκείν-ῳ	ἐκεῖν-α	ἐκεῖν-α	ἐκείν-ων	ἐκείν-οις
{ m.	αὐτ-ός	αὐτ-όν	αὐτ-οῦ	αὐτῷ	αὐτ-οί	αὐτ-ούς	αὐτ-ῶν	αὐτ-οῖς
{ f.	αὐτ-ή	αὐτ-ήν	αὐτ-ῆς	αὐτ-ῇ	αὐτ-αί	αὐτ-άς	αὐτ-ῶν	αὐτ-αῖς
{ n.	αὐτ-ό	αὐτ-ό	αὐτ-οῦ	αὐτ-ῷ	αὐτ-ά	αὐτ-ά	αὐτ-ῶν	αὐτ-οῖς
{ m.	πολ-ύς	πολ-ύν	πολλ-οῦ	πολλ-ῷ	πολλ-οί	πολλ-ούς	πολλ-ῶν	πολλ-οῖς
{ f.	πολλ-ή	πολλ-ήν	πολλ-ῆς	πολλ-ῇ	πολλ-αί	πολλ-άς	πολλ-ῶν	πολλ-αῖς
{ n.	πολ-ύ	πολ-ύ	πολλ-οῦ	πολλ-ῷ	πολλ-ά	πολλ-ά	πολλ-ῶν	πολλ-οῖς
{ m./f. εὔφρων	εὔφρον-α	εὔφραν-ος	εὔφρον-ι	εὔφρον-ες	εὔφρον-ας	εὐφρόν-ων	εὔφρο-σι(ν)
{ n. εὔφραν	εὔφρον	εὔφραν-ος	εὔφρον-ι	εὔφρον-α	εὔφρον-α	εὐφρόν-ων	εὔφρο-σι(ν)
{ m./f. τις	τιν-α	τιν-ος	τιν-ι	τιν-ες	τιν-ας	τιν-ων	τι-σι(ν)
{ n. τι	τι	τιν-ος	τιν-ι	τιν-α	τιν-α	τιν-ων	τι-σι(ν)
{ m.	οὐδ-είς	οὐδ-ένα	οὐδ-ενός	οὐδ-ενί				
{ f.	οὐδε-μία	οὐδε-μίαν	οὐδε-μιᾶς	οὐδε-μιᾷ				
{ n.	οὐδ-έν	οὐδ-έν	οὐδ-ενός	οὐδ-ενί				

s.				pl.			
nom.	*acc.*	*gen.*	dat.	*nom.*	*acc.*	*gen.*	dat.

	nom.	*acc.*	*gen.*	dat.	*nom.*	*acc.*	*gen.*	dat.
m.	ὤν	ὄντ-α	ὄντ-ος	ὄντ-ι	ὄντ-ες	ὄντ-ας	ὄντ-ων	οὖ-σι(ν)
f.	οὖσ-α	οὖσ-αν	οὔσ-ης	οὔσ-η	οὖσ-αι	οὔσ-ας	οὐσ-ῶν	οὔσ-αις
n.	ὄν	ὄν	ὄντ-ος	ὄντ-ι	ὄντ-α	ὄντ-α	ὄντ-ων	οὖ-σι(ν)
m.	παύσ-ας	παύσ-αντα	παύσ-αντος	παύσ-αντι	παύσ-αντες	παύσ-αντας	παυσ-άντων	παύσ-ασι(ν)
f.	παύσ-ασα	παύσ-ασαν	παύσ-άσης	παυσ-άσῃ	παύσ-ασαι	παυσ-άσας	παυσ-ασῶν	παυσ-άσαις
n.	παῦσ-αν	παῦσ-αν	παύσ-αντος	παύσ-αντι	παύσ-αντα	παύσ-αντα	παυσ-άντων	παύσ-ασι(ν)

Notes
(i) Dative singulars all end in -ι (*whether subscript or not*).
(ii) Dative plurals all end in -ις or -σι(ν). (*But note* ἡμῖν, ὑμῖν.)
(iii) Type 3 stems in -οντ- have dat. pl. in -ουσι (*e.g. participles like* παύ-ων *with stem* παυοντ- *and dat. pl.* παύουσι). Those in -αντ- have dat. pl. in -ασι.
(iv) Type 3's with single consonant at the end of the stem either drop it in the dat. pl. (λιμήν, *stem* λιμεν-, *dat. pl.* λιμέσι) *or let it coalesce* (φύλαξ, *stem* φυλακ-, *dat. pl.* φύλαξι (=φύλακ-σι)).

Uses of the dative

104 The most common uses of the dative are as follows:
(i) to express English indirect object phrases introduced by 'to', e.g.
τοῦτό μοι παρέχει 'he offers this *to me*'
λέγε τοῖς θεάταις 'speak *to the spectators*'
(ii) to express the idea of possession with the verb 'to be', e.g.
ἔστι μοι πατήρ (lit.) 'there is *to me* a father', i.e. 'I have a father'
(iii) to show the means by which something is achieved, usually expressed by the English 'by' or 'by means of' or 'with', e.g.
φυλάττομεν τὸν γέροντα τοῖς δικτύοις 'we guard the old man *with the nets*'
(iv) to show the way in which something is done (rather like an adverb), usually expressed by the English 'with' again, e.g.
πολλῇ σπουδῇ 'with much enthusiasm, enthusiastically'
(v) Note the two expressions:
(a) αὐτοῖς τοῖς κανθηλίοις 'baggage and all'
(b) λόγῳ μέν . . . ἔργῳ δέ . . . 'in word . . . but in fact', i.e.
outwardly something appears to be the case, but the reality is very different.
(vi) Certain verbs take the dative, e.g.
χράομαι   'I use, have to do with'
πείθομαι   'I obey, trust in'
ἐμπίπτω   'I fall on, attack'

ἐντυγχάνω 'I meet with'
ἕπομαι 'I follow'
δοκεῖ μοι 'it seems to me'
(vii) Certain adjectives take the dative, e.g.
 ὅμοιος 'resembling, like (to)'
(viii) With prepositions, e.g.
 ἐν 'in'
 ἐπί 'on, for the purpose of'
 παρά 'with, near'
 πρός 'near, in addition to'
 σύν 'with the help of'
(cf. *Reference Grammar F, p. 290, and Language Surveys (10), (11)*).

Time phrases

In *time* phrases, the *accusative* case expresses time throughout, or during which
something happens (English 'for'), e.g.
 καθεύδει ὅλην τὴν ἡμέραν 'he sleeps for the whole day'
The *genitive* case expresses time within which something happens (English 'in
the course of', or simply 'in'), e.g.
 τῆς νυκτὸς κρίνει 'he judges in the night, in the course of the night'
The *dative* case expresses the point of time at which something happens
(English 'at, on'), e.g.
 τῇ ὑστεραίᾳ ἀπῆλθεν 'he left on the next day'

Note
A visual representation may help:
the accusative case ('during') may be considered   as a line   ———
the dative case ('point at which')   as a dot •
the genitive case   as a circle O *(the action is taking
place somewhere within the circle but one doesn't know where.)*

Verbs

More optatives, ἐρωτάω, λανθάνω

105 You have already seen how -a- dominates certain verbs in the
indicative, e.g. δύναμαι **90** and ἀνίσταμαι **98**. It continues to dominate in the
optative, e.g. δυναίμην, δύναιο, δύναιτο etc. (cf. **95**).

106 Note the past of ἐρωτάω 'I ask' is ἠρόμην 'I asked' (stem ἐρ-). Distinguish
this stem from ἐρ-έω 'I shall say' (future of λέγω).

107 The principal parts of λανθάνω are
λανθάνω 'I escape the notice of'
λήσ-ω (fut.) 'I shall escape the notice of'
ἔ-λαθ-ον (aor.) 'I escaped the notice of' ○

Exercises for Section Eight A–E

(b/c) Morphology and Syntax

1. Give the dative singular and plural of the following nouns:
   ἄνθρωπος, βοή, ἀπορία, ἀνήρ, γυνή, πόλις, βασιλεύς, γέρων, ναύτης

2. Translate the sentences, then change underlined dative singulars into plurals or vice-versa, as appropriate:

   a. ἔστι πατήρ μοι, πάνυ πονηρὸς ὤν.
   b. μέγα κακόν σοι ἐμπεσεῖται, κακοδαίμονι ὄντι.
   c. λόγῳ μὲν ἐν τῇ πόλει οὐδεὶς ἀμείνων ἐστὶ τοῦ πατρός, ἔργῳ δὲ οὐδεὶς χείρων.
   d. λέγε τῷ θεατῇ τὸν τοῦ δράματος λόγον πάσῃ προθυμίᾳ.
   e. βοαῖς χρώμεθα μεγάλαις.
   f. ἐν τοῖς πλοίοις ἔτυχον ὄντες οἱ ναῦται.
   g. τοῖς κελεύουσι δεῖ ἡμᾶς πείθεσθαι.
   h. τί τὸ ὄνομα τῷ βασιλεῖ;
   i. διὰ τί πειρᾶσθε ἀναπείθειν ἐμὲ τούτῳ τῷ λόγῳ;
   j. τῇ δ' ὑστεραίᾳ ὁ υἱὸς ἐδίωξε τὸν πατέρα πάλιν εἰς τὴν οἰκίαν τοῖς μεγάλοις δικτύοις.

(d) English into Greek
Translate into Greek:

1. This spectator's name is Philoxenos.
2. He is speaking to you and to the spectators.
3. They will find sitting in the court hard to bear.
4. I shut my father in by using many slaves.
5. The politicians persuaded the people with fine words.

Vocabulary for Section Eight F

ἀλεκτρυών (ἀλεκτρυον-), ὁ cockerel (3a)
ἀναγκάζ-ω force, compel
ἀνα-μέν-ω hold on, wait around

ἀν-ίστασο get up! (s.)
(ἀν-ίστα-μαι)
ἀτάρ but
γεν-έσθαι to become
(γίγν-ομαι/ἐ-γεν-όμην)

δειν-ὸς καθεύδειν clever at sleeping
δειν-ὸς φαγ-εῖν clever at eating
δι' ὀλίγου after a short while

δικάσ-αι to give a judgment (δικάζ-ω)

δυνήσ-ομαι I will be able (fut. of δύν-αμαι)

δυνήσ-η you (s.) will be able (fut. of δύν-αμαι)

ἐά-ω (ἐασ-) allow

ἐγείρ-ω wake up

ἔδ-ομαι I shall eat (fut. of ἐσθί-ω)

ἐθέλ-ω wish, want (to)

ἐκ-φέρ-ω (ἐξ-ενεγκ-) carry out

ἐνεγκ-εῖν to bring (φέρ-α|ἤνεγκ-ον)

ἐνθάδε here

ἔξ-εστι it is possible (for x (dat.) to –)

ἐξ-ευρ-εῖν to discover (ἐξ-ευρίσκ-ω|ἐξ-ηῦρ-ον)

ἐξ-ήνεγκ-ας you (s.) brought out (aor. of ἐκ-φέρ-ω)

ἐξ-οίσ-ω I shall bring out (fut. of ἐκ-φέρ-ω)

ἐσθί-ω (φαγ-) eat

ἥκ-ω come

ἰού hurrah!

κατά-σκοπ-ος, ὁ scout, spy, inspector (2a)

κατήγορος, ὁ prosecutor (2a)

λαβ-εῖν to exact (λαμβάν-ω|ἔ-λαβ-ον)

μακρ-ός -ά -όν long

μισθ-ός, ὁ pay (2a)

μόγις with difficulty

οἷ-ός τ' εἰμί be able (to) (+ inf.)

ὅμως nevertheless, however

ὁπόθεν from where

ὅ τι; what?

οὔπω = οὐδέπω not yet

παρά (+gen.) from

πάντ-α everything (acc.)

πάσ-η προθυμί-ᾳ with all eagerness (i.e. most eagerly)

παύσ-ασθαι to stop; to cease from (+ gen.) (παύ-ομαι)

πιθ-έσθαι to obey (πείθ-ομαι|ἐ-πιθ-όμην)

ποιῆσ-αι to act on (ποιέ-ω)

πῦρ (πυρ-), τό fire, brazier (3b)

τίν-ι τρόπ-ῳ how? in what way? (τρόπ-ος, ὁ way (2a))

φακ-ῆ, ἡ lentil-soup (1a)

χρή it is necessary (for x (acc.) to –)

Vocabulary to be learnt

ἀναμένω (ἀναμειν-) wait, hold on

ἀτάρ but

δεινός ή όν clever at (+inf.); dire, terrible

ἐάω (ἐασ-) allow

ἐκφέρω (ἐξενεγκ-) carry out; (often: carry out for burial)

ἐνθάδε here

ἔξεστι it is possible (for X (dat.) to – (inf.))

ἐσθίω (φαγ-) eat (fut. ἔδομαι)

ὅμως nevertheless, however

ὅ τι; what? (in reply to τί;)

χρή it is necessary (for X (acc.) to – (inf.))

Vocabulary for Section Eight G

ἀκούσ-ατε listen! pay attention! (pl.) (ἀκού-ω)

ἄκουσ-ον listen! pay attention! (s.) (ἀκού-ω)

ἀμίς (ἀμιδ-), ἡ chamber-pot (3a)

ἄνευ (+gen.) without

ἄπ-ιθι go away! (s.) (ἀπ-έρχ-ομαι|ἄπ-ειμι)

ἀρέσκ-ει it pleases (+dat.)

ἄρχ-ομαι begin (+ part.)

ἔασ-ον leave me be! (s.) (ἐά-ω)

ἐκ-τρέχ-ω run out

ἐνεγκ-έ fetch! (φέρ-ω|ἤνεγκ-ον)

ἐξ-ένεγκ-ατε fetch out! (pl.) (ἐκ-φέρ-ω|ἐξ-ήνεγκ-α)

εὔξ-ασθε pray! (pl.) (εὔχ-ομαι)

θέ-σθαι to cast (τίθεμαι|ἐ-θέ-μην)

ἴθι come! (s.) (ἔρχ-ομαι|εἶμι)

ἴσθι know! (s.) (οἶδα)

κάδ-ος, ὁ voting-urn (2a)

κάδ-ων ἕνεκα because of the urns

καὶ δὴ well, all right (you have my attention)

καλῶς γε fine!

κατηγορέ-ω accuse, prosecute

κλεψύδρ-α, ἡ water-clock (1b)

κυμβί-ον, τό cup (2b)

λέξ-ον out with it! (λέγ-ω)

μηδαμ-ῶς in no way

πάντ-α everything; all (nom.)

πάντ-ες all (nom. pl. m.)

πᾶσι to all (dat. pl. m.)

παῦσ-αι stop! (s.) (παύ-ομαι)

πίθ-εσθε obey! (pl.) (πείθ-ομαι|ἐ-πιθ-όμην)

πιθ-οῦ obey! (s.) (πείθ-ομαι|ἐ-πιθ-όμην)

πλήν (+gen.) except

πῦρ (πυρ-), τό fire (3b)

ψῆφ-ος, ἡ vote (2a) (lit. voting-pebble)

Vocabulary to be learnt

ἄρχομαι *begin (+ inf. or part.)*   πάρειμι *be present*
ἐκτρέχω (ἐκδραμ-) *run out*   πᾶς πᾶσα πᾶν (παντ-) *all*
ἕνεκα (+gen.)   *because, for the*   ὁ πᾶς *the whole of*
    sake of (usually placed after   πλήν (+gen.) *except*
    the noun)   πῦρ (πυρ-), τό *fire (3b)*

○ Grammar for Section Eight F–G

Summary:
Aor. inf. act. and mid.
Aor. imper. act. and mid. (inc. εἰμί, εἶμι, οἶδα)
φέρω, ἔξεστι, δεῖνος, πᾶς
Verbs

Aorist infinitives, active and middle: παῦσαι, παύσασθαι *'to stop'*,
λαβεῖν, λαβέσθαι *'to take'*

108 You have already met present infinitives (infinitives based on the present
stem). Greek also has infinitives based on the aorist stems (weak and strong).
Their forms are as follows:

    Weak aorist active: παῦσ-αι *'to stop'*
    Weak aorist middle: παύσ-ασθαι *'to stop'*

    Note
    Take the weak aorist stem and for active verbs add -αι, *for middle verbs add*
-ασθαι. *Note the dominance of the -(σ)α- ending in the stem again (cf. aorist indicatives*
at **68** *and* **69***).*

    Strong aorist active: λαβ-εῖν *'to take'*
    Strong aorist middle: λαβ-έσθαι *'to take'*

    Note
    Take the strong aorist stem (without augment) and for active verbs add -εῖν,
for middle verbs add -έσθαι. *Observe that the endings (except for accent) are just the*
same as the endings for the present infinitives active and middle, BUT THE STEM IS
DIFFERENT. (Cf. present infinitives at **74** *and strong aorist participles at* **82–4***.)*

    Aspect in the infinitive

    109 The difference in meaning between present and aorist infinitives is
not one of time, but one of aspect (cf. on participles at **79** (iii)). Both παύειν and
παῦσαι mean 'to stop', but the present infinitive carries the idea of process with

it ('keep on stopping'), the aorist looks at the action as a simple event. But this distinction is often a very fine one and 'rules' as such are very difficult to make. It is far better to observe closely actual Greek usage.

Aorist imperatives, active and middle: παῦσον, παῦσαι 'stop!' λαβέ, λαβοῦ 'take!'

110 You have already met present imperatives (see **6**), which are based on the present stem. There are also imperatives based on the aorist stem. Their forms are as follows:

Weak aorist imperatives active: *s.*   παῦσ-ον   'stop!'
                 pl.   παύσ-ατε   'stop!'
Weak aorist imperatives middle: *s.*   παῦσ-αι   'stop!'
                 pl.   παύσ-ασθε   'stop!'

Note
Again observe the dominance of -(σ)α- in the aorist stem. Note particularly carefully the singular imperative form in -(σ)-ον.

Strong aorist imperatives active: *s.*   λαβ-έ   'take!'
                 pl.   λάβ-ετε   'take!'
Strong aorist imperatives middle: *s.*   λαβ-οῦ   'take!'
                 pl.   λάβ-εσθε   'take!'

Note
*As with strong aorist participles (**82–4**) and strong aorist infinitives (**108**), the endings of the strong aorist imperatives are identical to those for present imperatives, but based on the aorist stem.*

Observe that you have been meeting some strong aorist imperatives all through the course in the forms:

ἐλθέ 'come!'   (ἦλθον)
εἰπέ 'say!'   (εἶπον)
ἰδού 'look!'   (εἶδον, middle)

Aspect in the imperative

111 Again, the distinction between present and aorist imperatives is one not of time but of aspect (cf. **109** and **79** (iii));* equally, it is sometimes very difficult indeed to tell the difference between the two, or to decide exactly why a writer used this, rather than that, imperative at any one time (Aristophanes seems to use φέρε and ἔνεγκε 'bring!' quite indiscriminately). The distinction, when it can be made, is between an instruction to do something and keep on doing it (present imperative), and one to do something, but just once (aorist imperative).

* Besides, how could one have a *past* imperative?!

Note

It is natural that certain verbs have, by their very nature, a tendency to lean towards one aspect or the other. Thus, for example, λαμβάνω 'I take' tends to use the aorist forms of participle, infinitive and imperative, because 'taking' is the sort of thing that occurs once or at once and does not involve a long-drawn-out process. On the other hand, a verb like ζητέω 'seek', which naturally implies a process, tends to appear in the present forms of participle, infinitive and imperative.

Four imperatives

112 Note the imperative forms of εἰμί 'I am', εἶμι 'I shall go', οἶδα 'I know':

	εἰμί	εἶμι	οἶδα
s.	ἴσθι 'be!'	ἴθι 'go!'	ἴσθι 'know!'
pl.	ἔστε 'be!'	ἴτε 'go!'	ἴστε 'know!'

N.b. the imperative forms of ἀνίσταμαι: ἀνίστασο   'get up!'

ἀνίστασθε   'get up!'

φέρ-ω

113 Observe the irregular verb φέρω:

φέρ-ω 'I bear, carry, put up with'

οἴσ-ω fut. 'I shall bear'

ἤνεγκ-ον (ἐνεγκ-) or ἤνεγκ-α (aor.) 'I bore, carried'

ἔξεστι + infinitive 'be permitted to' and δεινός + infinitive 'clever at'

114 You have already met δεῖ (=χρή), which means 'must, ought' and takes an accusative and infinitive (**75**).

ἔξεστι 'it is permitted, it is possible' works in the same way, except that it takes a *dative* (not accusative) of the person, e.g. ἔξεστι τῷ ἀνθρώπῳ ἐξελθεῖν 'the man is permitted/allowed to go out, the man may go out'.

115 Note also δεινός + inf. = 'clever at –ing', e.g. δεινὸς λέγειν 'clever at speaking'.

Adjectives

πᾶς πᾶσα πᾶν (παντ-) 'all, every'

116 Observe that πᾶς goes exactly like an aorist participle of the παύσας type (see **78**), i.e.

πᾶς   (παντ-)   m.

πᾶσα   f.

πᾶν   (παντ-)   n.   O

Exercises for Section Eight F–G

(b/c) Morphology and Syntax

1. Write down the aorist of these verbs. Then construct the aorist infinitive:

παύομαι	φέρω	ὁράω
ἀκούω	γίγνομαι	πείθομαι
ποιέω	μανθάνω	πίπτω
ἀδικέω	λαμβάνω	
λέγω	ἀφικνέομαι	

2. Translate these imperatives. Give in brackets the person and aspect (i.e. s./pl., pres./aor.):

μάθετε, λέγε, εἰπέ, φεύγετε, ζήτει, ὅρα, δήλωσον, ἴσθι, μείνατε, γενοῦ, ἀφίκεσθε, ἔνεγκε, ἴτε, φοβεῖσθε, πιθοῦ, εὕρετε, παύσατε, ἰδού, παῦσαι

3. Put the verb in brackets into the present or aorist infinitive as requested, and translate the sentences:

a. βούλομαι (δικάζω) (aorist) ἐν τῇ οἰκίᾳ, ἀλλ᾽ ὁ υἱὸς οὐκ ἐᾷ με (δικάζω) (present) ἐνθάδε.

b. δεῖ ἡμᾶς πάντας (ἔξειμι) (present) εἰς τὴν ἀγοράν.

c. τί χρή σε (ποιέω) (aorist);

d. ἔξεστι Φιλοκλέωνι (κατηγορέω) (present).

e. ὁ υἱὸς οὐκ εἴασε τὸν πατέρα (εἶμι) (aorist) εἰς τὸ δικαστήριον.

f. πῶς πείσω σε, ὦ πάτερ, (ἀκούω) (aorist) πάντων τῶν λόγων;

g. διὰ τί οὐ βούλῃ (ἐκφέρω) (aorist) Φιλοκλέωνα, ὦ ἡμίονε;

h. δεῖ σε δικαστὴν (γίγνομαι) (aorist) ἐν τῇ οἰκίᾳ.

i. χρὴ αὐτοὺς (μανθάνω) (aorist) τοὺς τοῦ δράματος λόγους.

j. βούλεταὶ αὐτὸς (λαμβάνω) (present) πάντα τὸν μισθὸν παρὰ τοῦ υἱοῦ.

k. οὐκ ἐάσω αὐτὸν (ἀφικνέομαι) (present) εἰς τὸ δικαστήριον.

l. ἔξεστί μοι ἐνθάδε καὶ (λαμβάνω) (aorist) πάντα τὸν μισθὸν καὶ (ἐσθίω) (aorist).

(d) English into Greek
Translate into Greek:

1. Father, you must stay here and give judgments.
2. It will be possible for you all to sell your mules.
3. Everything is here except the fire.
4. Bring out the torches, slaves!
5. 'Out with it, what were you looking for when you ran out?' 'What? Everything.'

Vocabulary for Section Eight H

ἀγαθ-ός -ή -όν good (at)
(+inf.)
Αἴξων-εύς, ὁ man from the
deme Aixone (3g)
αἱρέ-ω (ἑλ-) convict
αἰτέ-ω ask (for)
ἀκού-ω listen (to) (+gen.)
ἀμφότερ-οι -αι -α both
ἀνα-βάς going up
(ἀνα-βαίν-ω|ἀν-έ-βην)
ἀνα-βῆν-αι to go up
(ἀνα-βαίν-ω|ἀν-έ-βην)
ἀν-έ-βη (he) went up
(ἀνα-βαίν-ω|ἀν-έ-βην)
ἀν-αίτι-ος -ον innocent
ἅπας ἅπασ-α ἅπαν
(ἁπαντ-) all
ἀπο-λογέ-ομαι make speech
for the defence
ἀπο-λογήσ-εσθαι to make the
defence speech
αὖ αὖ woof! woof!
αὖ again, moreover
γραφ-ή, ἡ indictment, charge
(1a)
γράφ-ομαι indict x (acc.) for
y (gen.)
δικανικ-ά, τά court affairs,
legal matters (2b)
διώκ-ω prosecute
ἐθέλ-ω wish, want (to)

εἰσ-ίτω let him come in!
(εἰσ-έρχ-ομαι|εἴσ-ειμι)
εἰσ-καλέ-ω call in, summon
ἐλ-εῖν ⎰
ἔλ-ετε ⎱ see αἱρέ-ω
ἐλπίζ-ω hope, expect (to)
ἐξ-απατήσ-ειν to deceive
(ἐξ-απατά-ω)
ἔξω outside
ἐπ-ίστα-μαι know how (to)
(+inf.)
εὖ γε well done! hurrah!
ἡλιάστ-ης, ὁ juror in the
Eliaia court (1d)
θέ-σθαι to cast
(τίθε-μαι|ἐ-θέ-μην)
καὶ δή and indeed
καὶ μήν and look ...
κατά-βηθι get down! (s.)
(κατα-βαίν-ω|κατ-έ-βην)
κατ-εσθί-ω (κατα-φαγ-) eat
up
κατηγορέ-ω prosecute, make
a prosecution speech
κατηγορί-α, ἡ prosecution
(1b)
κηρύττ-ω announce
κλέπτ-ης, ὁ thief (1d)
κλοπ-ή, ἡ theft (1a)
Κυδαθηναι-εύς, ὁ man from
the deme Kydathene (3g)

κυμβί-ον, τό cup (2b)
κύων (κυν-), ὁ dog (3a)
Λάβης (Λαβητ-), ὁ Labes
(3a) ('Grabber')
μάρτυς (μαρτυρ-), ὁ witness
(3a)
μέλλ-ω be about (to)
μέρ-ος, τό share (3c)
μονο-φαγ-ίστατ-ος most
selfish (lit. 'alone') eater
πολὺ much
προ-κατα-γιγνώσκ-ω prejudge
πρός (+gen.) in the name of
προσ-ιόντων let them come
forward!
(προσ-έρχ-ομαι|πρόσ-ειμι)
προσ-ίτω let him come
forward
(προσ-έρχ-ομαι|πρόσ-ειμι)
σιγά-ω be quiet
σπευδ-έτω let him hurry!
(σπεύδ-ω)
τυρό-κνηστις (τυροκνηστιδ-),
ἡ cheese-grater (3a)
τυρ-ός, ὁ cheese (2a)
φακ-ῆ, ἡ lentil-soup (1a)
φανερ-ός -ά -όν clear, obvious
φεύγ-ω be a defendant
χυτρ-ά, ἡ cooking-pot
ψῆφ-ος, ἡ vote (2a) (lit.
'voting-pebble')

Vocabulary to be learnt

ἀκούω hear, listen to (+gen. of
person/thing)
ἀπολογέομαι defend oneself,
make a speech in one's own
defence
γραφή, ἡ indictment, charge,
case (1a)
γράφομαι indict, charge
γραφὴν γράφομαι indict X
(acc.) on charge of Y (gen.)

διώκω prosecute, pursue
ἐθέλω wish, want (to)
κατηγορέω prosecute X (gen.)
on a charge of Y (acc.)
κατηγορία, ἡ speech for the
prosecution (1b)
κύων (κυν-), ὁ dog (3a)
μάρτυς (μαρτυρ-), ὁ witness
(3a)
μέρος, τό share, part (3c)

πολύ (adv.) much
πρός (+gen.) in the name of,
under the protection of
φεύγω (φυγ-) be a defendant,
be on trial; flee
ψῆφος, ἡ vote, voting-pebble
(2a)

Vocabulary for Section Eight I

αἰβοῖ yuk! arghh!
αἱρέ-ω (ἑλ-) convict
αἰτέ-ω ask
ἀμφότερ-οι -αι -α both
ἀνά-βηθι go up! (s.)
(ἀνα-βαίν-ω|ἀν-έ-βην)
ἀντι-βολέ-ω beg, plead
(with)
ἀπο-λογί-α, ἡ defence speech
(1b)
ἀπο-λύ-ω acquit
ἀπο-λύσ-ατε pl. as if to a whole
jury
ἄρχ-ομαι begin (+gen.)
αὖ again, further
δαιμόνι-ε my good fellow
δακρύ-ω weep
ἑλ-εῖν }
ἑλ-όντ-α } see αἱρέ-ω
ἐλπίζ-ω hope, expect
ἐξ-απατά-ω deceive
ἐπ-ίστα-μαι know (how to)
(+inf.)
θάνατ-ος, ὁ death (2a)
καίτοι and yet

κατα-βάντ-ος getting down
(gen. s. m.)
(κατα-βαίν-ω|κατ-έ-βην)
κατά-βηθι get down! (s.)
(κατα-βαίν-ω|κατ-έ-βην)
κατα-βῆναι to get down
(κατα-βαίν-ω|κατ-έ-βην)
κατα-βήσ-ομαι I shall get
down
(κατα-βαίν-ω|κατ-έ-βην)
κατα-δικάζ-ω convict, find
guilty (+gen.)
κατα-κνά-ω grate
κατ-εσθί-ω eat up
κιθαρίζ-ω play the kithara
(i.e. be educated)
κλέπτ-ης, ὁ thief (1d)
λύκ-ος, ὁ wolf (2a)
μέγα loudly
μὲν οὖν no, rather
μηδεὶς μηδεμί-α μηδέν
(μηδεν-) no
νυνὶ = νῦν
ὅδε ἤδε τόδε this
οἰκτίρ-ατε pl. as if to a whole
jury

οἶός τ' εἰμί be able (to)
ὄφελ-ος, τό use (3c)
παιδί-ον, τό puppy (2b)
παρά (+gen.) from
περι-βαίν-ω surround
πονηρ-ός -ά -όν poor,
wretched
πρόβατ-α, τά sheep (2b)
σιτί-α, τά provisions, food
(2b)
συγγνώμ-ην ἔχ-ω forgive
τόδε see ὅδε
τοσ-οῦτ-ος, τοσ-αύτ-η
τοσ-οῦτ-ο(ν) so great
τυγχάν-ω (τυχ-) chance on,
happen upon, hit upon
(+gen.)
τυρό-κνηστις (τυροκνηστιδ-),
ἡ cheese-grater (3a)
ὑφ-αιρέ-ομαι (ὑφ-ελ-) steal,
take by stealth for oneself
ὑφ-αιρήσ-εσθαι to steal
(ὑφ-αιρέ-ομαι)
ψεύδ-ομαι lie

Vocabulary to be learnt

αἱρέω (ἑλ-) take, capture,
convict
αἰτέω ask (for)
ἀμφότεροι αι α both
ἀπολογία, ἡ speech in one's
own defence (1b)
ἄρχομαι begin (+gen.); begin
to (+part. or inf.)

αὖ again, moreover
ἐλπίζω hope, expect (+fut.
inf.)
θάνατος, ὁ death (2a)
καταδικάζω condemn, convict
(X (gen.) on charge of Y
(acc.))
κλέπτης, ὁ thief (1d)

παιδίον, τό child; slave (2b)
παρά (+gen.) from
τυγχάνω (τυχ-) hit, chance on,
happen on, be subject to
(+gen.); happen (to), be
actually (+part.)
ὑφαιρέομαι (ὑφελ-) steal, take
for oneself by stealth

Vocabulary for Section Eight J

ἀγωνίζ-ομαι contest
ἄκων ἄκουσ-α ἆκον
(ἀκοντ-) unwilling(ly)
ἀπο-δακρύ-ω burst into tears

ἀπο-λύ-ω acquit
ἀπο-φεύγ-ω (ἀποφυγ-) be
acquitted
βαδίζ-ω walk

δαιμόνι-ε my dear fellow
δηλώσ-ειν to reveal (δηλό-ω)
ἑκών ἑκοῦσ-α ἑκόν
(ἑκοντ-) willing(ly)

ἐξ-απατά-ω deceive
ἐπ-αίρ-ω raise up, lift
ἐπ-ίστα-μαι know (how to)
   (+inf.)
εὖ γε hurrah!
θὲ-ς put! (s.) (τίθη-μι|-θε-)
θε-ὶς putting (nom. s. m.)
   (τίθη-μι|-θε-)
κάδ-ος, ὁ voting-urn (2a)
κατ-εσθί-ω eat up
κιθαρίζ-ω play the kithara
   (i.e. be educated)

μέλλ-ω be about to
ὅδε ἥδε τόδε this (here)
ὄντ-ως really
ὅτι because
πατρίδιον daddy dear (2b)
πείσ-ομαι I shall suffer (fut. of
   πάσχ-ω)
περι-άγ-ω lead round
περί-πατ-ος, ὁ walkabout
   (2a)
πολυ-τίμητ-ος -ον
   much-honoured

πρότερ-ος -α -ον first (of
   two), former
συγγνώμ-ην ἔχ-ω forgive
   (+dat.)
τῇδε this way
τήνδε see ὅδε
ὕδωρ (ὑδατ-), τό water (3b)
ὕστερ-ος -α -ον last (of two),
   further
φακ-ῆ, ἡ lentil-soup (1a)
φέρε . . . περιάγω come . . . let
   me take you round

Vocabulary to be learnt

ἀπολύω acquit, release
ἐξαπατάω deceive, trick
ἐπίσταμαι know how to
   (+inf.); understand

μέλλω be about to (+fut. inf.);
   intend; hesitate (+pres. inf.)
ὅδε ἥδε τόδε this
ὅτι because

συγγνώμην ἔχω forgive,
   pardon (+dat.)
ὕστερος α ον later, last (of two)
ὕστερον later, further

○ Grammar for Section Eight H–J

Summary:
3rd person imper. pres./aor., act. and mid.
Fut. inf. and usages
ἀκούω, αἱρέω, τίθημι, ἐπίσταμαι, βαίνω, πάσχω (principal parts)

Verbs

Third person imperatives, present and aorist, active and middle

117 As well as having second person imperatives, which you have
already met (**110** and **6**), Greek has third person imperative forms, which mean
'let him –', 'let them –'. Here are the imperative forms of παύω in full, with the
third person imperatives taking their place beside the second persons:

118 *Present imperatives*

Active: 2nd s.	παῦ-ε	*Middle:* 2nd s.	παύ-ου
3rd s.	παυ-έτω 'let him stop'	3rd s.	παυ-έσθω
2nd pl.	παύ-ετε	2nd pl.	παύ-εσθε
3rd pl.	παυ-όντων 'let them stop'	3rd pl.	παυ-έσθων

119 *Aorist imperatives (weak)*

Active: 2nd s. παῦσ-ον	*Middle: 2nd s.* παῦσ-αι	
3rd s. παυσ-άτω 'let him stop'	*3rd s.* παυσ-άσθω	
2nd pl. παύσ-ατε	*2nd pl.* παύσ-ασθε	
3rd pl. παυσ-άντων 'let them stop'	*3rd pl.* παυσ-άσθων	

120 *Aorist imperatives (strong)* (λαμβάνω, λαμβάνομαι)

Active: 2nd s. λαβ-έ	*Middle: 2nd s.* λαβ-οῦ
3rd s. λαβ-έτω 'let him take'	*3rd s.* λαβ-έσθω
2nd pl. λάβ-ετε	*2nd pl.* λάβ-εσθε
3rd pl. λαβ-όντων 'let them take'	*3rd pl.* λαβ-έσθων

Notes

(i) Note again the similarity of endings between aorist (strong) and present forms of the third person imperative.

(ii) Third person imperatives are fairly rare, but note that the present plural form (in -οντων) and the aorist plural form (in -σαντων) could be mistaken for present and aorist participles in the genitive plural! The presence of a stated subject in the nominative and/or lack of any other possible finite verb-form will tell you that the third person imperative is being used, e.g.

ἀπελθόντων οἱ ᾿Αθηναῖοι 'let the Athenians depart!'
διωκόντων τὸν ἄνδρα 'let them pursue the man!' BUT
ἀκούω τῶν λεγόντων 'I hear the men talking'

(iii) Note the full imperatives of εἰμί 'I am', εἶμι 'I shall go', οἶδα 'I know':

εἰμί	εἶμι	οἶδα
2nd s. ἴσθι 'be!'	ἴθι 'go!'	ἴσθι 'know!'
3rd s. ἔστω 'let him be!' etc.	ἴτω 'let him go!' etc.	ἴστω 'let him know!' etc.
2nd pl. ἔστε	ἴτε	ἴστε
3rd pl. ἔστων	ἰόντων	ἴστων

Future infinitives active and middle: παύσειν, παύσεσθαι 'to be about to stop'

121 Here are the forms of the future infinitives active and middle:

Active: παύσ-ειν   'to be about to stop'
Middle: παύσ-εσθαι 'to be about to stop'

Notes

(i) Future infinitives bear the meaning 'to be about to, to be going to'.

(ii) They are formed by taking the future stem and adding -ειν or -εσθαι as appropriate (endings the same as for present infinitives. Cf. **74**).

Uses of the future infinitive

122 One common use of the future infinitive is with verbs that offer some future hope, intention or promise, for example:

ἐλπίζω 'I hope/expect to . . .' e.g. ἐλπίζω νικήσειν 'I hope/expect to win'

μέλλω 'I am about to . . ., I am on the point of . . .' e.g. ἔμελλε παύσεσθαι 'he was about to stop'

ὑπισχνέομαι 'I promise to . . .' e.g. ὑπισχνεῖται λήψεσθαι 'he promises to take'

Five verbs to follow

123 Note the principal parts of αἱρέω ('I take, capture; condemn'), αἱρέομαι ('I take for myself; I choose'):

αἱρέ-ω 'I take'	αἱρέ-ομαι 'I choose'
αἱρήσ-ω (fut.) 'I shall take'	αἱρήσ-ομαι (fut.) 'I shall choose'
εἷλ-ον (ἑλ-) (aor.) 'I took'	εἱλ-όμην (aor.) 'I chose'

124 τίθημι 'I put, place' (middle τίθεμαι) has a present stem in τιθε- and an aorist stem in θε-. It will be dealt with in full later on (together with other -μι verbs), but for the moment note:

θές
θοῦ } aor. imperatives active
                            middle } 'place! put!'

θεῖναι
θέσθαι } aor. infinitives active
                            middle } 'to put, to place'

125 Revise δύναμαι and ἀνίσταμαι (90 and 98) and note that ἐπίσταμαι 'I know' conjugates in the same way.

Note

ἐπίσταμαι *followed by an infinitive means* 'know how to', *e.g.* ἐπίσταμαι κιθαρίζειν '*I know how to play the cithara*'.

126 Principal parts of βαίνω 'I go' are:

βαίν-ω 'I go'
βήσ-ομαι (fut.) 'I shall go'
ἔ-βη-ν (βα-, βη-) (aor.) 'I went'

ἔβη-ν is what is called a 'root' aorist: it simply adds personal endings onto the root ἔβη- without any intervening vowels, i.e.

ἔ-βη-ν
ἔ-βη-ς
ἔ-βη
ἔ-βη-μεν
ἔ-βη-τε
ἔ-βη-σαν

Infinitive: βῆναι
Participle: βάς, βᾶσα, βάν (βαντ-)

127 Principal parts of πάσχω 'I suffer, experience, have something happen to me' are:
πάσχ-ω 'I suffer'
πείσ-ομαι (fut.) 'I shall suffer'
ἔ-παθ-ον (παθ-) (aor.) 'I suffered'
Note here that the principal parts of πείθω 'I persuade' are:
πείθ-ω 'I persuade'
πείσ-ω (fut.) 'I shall persuade'
ἔ-πεισ-α (aor.) 'I persuaded'
The middle form of πείθω is πείθομαι, which means 'I trust, believe in', the future of which will be πείσομαι 'I shall trust, believe in' – exactly the same form as the future of πάσχω. Only the context will tell you whether πείσομαι means 'I shall believe in' or 'I shall experience'.

128 ἀκούω 'I hear' takes a genitive of the person heard, e.g.
ἀκούω τοὺς λόγους 'I hear the speeches', but
ἀκούω σοῦ λέγοντος 'I hear you speaking'.

Revise:
Impf. tense **58–9**
Fut. tense **61–4**
Aor. tense **68–9, 71–2**   O

Exercises for Section Eight H–J

(b/c) Morphology and Syntax
1. Sort this list into present, aorist and future infinitives:
πλεῖν, φροντιεῖν, βοηθῆσαι, διώξειν, ἀποχωρεῖν, ἔσεσθαι, μαχέσασθαι, μαθήσεσθαι, ἀφικέσθαι, σπεύδειν, ὀλοφυρεῖσθαι, κρατῆσαι, ποιήσειν, ὀφείλειν, παύσεσθαι, δέξεσθαι, βιάσασθαι, λήσειν

2. Give the aorist imperative, infinitive and participle of these verbs:
δέχομαι, δράω, ἔρχομαι, γίγνομαι, κωλύω, ἐπαινέω, βάλλω, παύω

3. Give meaning of verb and part shown in right-hand column. Then pair up the right column with left:

αἱρέω	λήσειν
ἀποθνῄσκω	λάβετε
βάλλω	ἑλεῖν
γίγνομαι	ἰδών
εἰμί	λαθών
εἶμι	ἐλθέ
ἔρχομαι	λήψεσθαι
ἐρωτάω	ἀπέθανε
ἐσθίω	γενήσεσθαι
εὑρίσκω	ἐρόμενος
ἔχω	μαθόντες
λαμβάνω	γένεσθε
λανθάνω	δραμεῖν
μανθάνω	οἴσουσα
οἶδα	τυχούσῃ
ὁράω	ἐνέγκατε
πίπτω	εἶναι
τρέχω	ἰόντος
τυγχάνω	ᾔδεσαν
φέρω	ᾔεισθα
	βαλεῖν
	εἰδότες
	εὑρήσειν
	πεσόντι
	σχές
	πεσουμένῳ
	ἔδεσθαι
	ἕξειν

(Cf. list of important stems in Language Survey (13), p. 332.)

(d) English into Greek

Translate into Greek:

1. Let the dogs come in!
2. Let the thief steal this dog's share!
3. I expect the defendants will make a good defence speech.
4. This juror is going to condemn the dog to death.
5. Let the prosecutor begin the prosecution!

Exercises for Section Eight

(a) Words

1. Deduce the meaning of the words on the right from those on the left:

αἱρέω	καθαιρέω
γράφομαι	τὸ γράμμα
ἐλπίζω	ἡ ἐλπίς
ἐπίσταμαι	ἡ ἐπιστήμη
μάρτυς	ἡ μαρτυρία, μαρτυρέω
ὄνομα	ὀνομάζω
πονηρός	ἡ πονηρία

(d) English into Greek

1. Translate into Greek:

A young man had an old man for a father. The young man's name was Bdelykleon, the old man's Philokleon. The old man, it happened, had a terrible disease – he never stopped wanting to judge in the law-courts. The young man tried to persuade him not to judge, but the old man would not obey him, for all his persuasion. Finally, the young man locked him in the house. The old man was in despair and tried to escape, using all sorts of arguments. But he was not able to escape without being seen by the slaves, who guarded the house.

2. Translate into Greek:

BDELYKLEON Once and for all, father, listen and obey me. I shall not allow you to leave the house and judge in the courtroom.

PHILOKLEON Why aren't I allowed to? I expect you to tell me everything.

BDEL. Because you are the wickedest man in the city.

PHIL. Well, what am I allowed to do? What do you intend to do?

BDEL. I shall allow you to pass judgment here in the house. Would you like that?

PHIL. Yes, I would. Tell me quickly, what must I do?

BDEL. Wait here. I shall fetch out the legal equipment.
(Fetches gear; sets up the court)
Let the advocate come forward! Let the trial begin! Where is the prosecutor? Come here, dog, and prosecute. Get up and speak. Tell us who has made the charge and for what reason. Father, I hope you will pay attention.

PHIL. Don't worry. Come on, dog, speak up!

Test Exercise Eight
Translate into English:
Philokleon laments his luck to the passing jurors, and prays to Zeus and Lykos to change his appearance, so that he will be able to escape; the jurors send for help to rescue him.
(From Aristophanes, *Wasps*)

ΦΙΛΟΚΛΕΩΝ ἴτε, πάντες φίλοι, ἴτε. ἀκούω γὰρ ὑμῶν ᾀδόντων, ἀλλ' οὐχ οἷός τ'
  εἰμὶ ᾄδειν ἐγώ. τί ποιήσω; οὗτοι γάρ με φυλάττουσιν, καίπερ
  βουλόμενον μεθ' ὑμῶν ἐλθεῖν πρὸς τὸ δικαστήριον καὶ κακόν τι ποιῆσαι.
  ἀλλ' ὦ Ζεῦ, παῦσαι πράγματά μοι παρέχων καὶ φίλος γενοῦ καὶ οἴκτιρον
  τὸ πάθος. σῶσόν με, ὦ Ζεῦ. ἤ με ποίησον <u>κάπνον</u> ἐξαίφνης, ἤ δῆτα <u>λίθον</u>
  με ποίησον, ἐφ' οὗ τὰς ψήφους ἀριθμοῦσιν. τόλμησον, ἄναξ, σῶσαί με.
ΔΙΚΑΣΤΑΙ τίς γάρ ἐστιν ὁ ἐγκλείων σε; λέξον, αἰτοῦμέν σε.
ΦΙΛ.   ὁ ἐμὸς υἱός, εὖ ἴστε. ἀλλὰ μὴ βοᾶτε. καὶ γὰρ τυγχάνει οὑτοσὶ <u>πρόσθεν</u>
  καθεύδων.
ΔΙΚ.   τίνος ἕνεκα οὐκ ἔξεστί σοι μεθ' ἡμῶν συνελθόντι ἀκοῦσαι τῶν τε
  κατηγορούντων καὶ τῶν ἀπολογουμένων;
ΦΙΛ.   ὁ υἱὸς οὐκ ἐᾷ με, ὦνδρες, δικάζειν οὐδὲ δρᾶν οὐδὲν κακόν. ἀλλὰ ζητεῖτε
  <u>μηχανήν</u> τινα, αἰτῶ ὑμᾶς. μέλλω γὰρ ἐγὼ τήμερον ἀκούσεσθαι τῶν τε
  διωκόντων καὶ τῶν φευγόντων.
ΔΙΚ.   οὐκ ἂν δυναίμεθα, ὦ φίλε, σῶσαί σε. φυλάττουσι γάρ σε οἱ <u>οἰκεῖοι</u>
  πάντες, καὶ οὐκ ἔξεστί σοι φυγεῖν.
ΦΙΛ.   χρὴ οὖν με εὔξασθαι τοῖς θεοῖς, ἐλπίζοντα φεύξεσθαι. ἀκουόντων οὖν οἱ
  θεοί, καὶ βοηθούντων. ὦ Λύκε δέσποτα, γείτων <u>ἥρως</u> – σὺ γὰρ φιλεῖς τὸ
  δικαστήριον – οἴκτιρον καὶ σῶσόν με ἐν ἀπορίᾳ <u>ὄντα</u>.
ΔΙΚ.   (*addressing slaves who are leading them*)
  καὶ ὑμεῖς, ὦ παῖδες, τρέχετε καὶ βοᾶτε καὶ Κλέωνι ταῦτ' <u>ἀγγέλλετε</u> καὶ
  κελεύετε αὐτὸν <u>ἥκειν</u>. ὁ γὰρ Βδελυκλέων λέγει ὅτι χρὴ μὴ δικάζειν
  δίκας. ἴτω οὖν Κλέων καὶ σωτὴρ γενέσθω τῷ γέροντι.

Vocabulary

καπνός, ὁ smoke (2a)
λίθος, ὁ stone (2a)
ἐφ' οὗ on which
ἀριθμέω count
πρόσθεν in front
μηχανή, ἡ device (1a)

οἰκεῖος, ὁ family member (2a)
ἥρως, ὁ hero (*his shrine was
  next to the lawcourts*)
ἀγγέλλω tell
ἥκω come

Section Nine

Vocabulary for Section Nine A

ἃ what, which (acc. pl. n.)
ἀναγκάζ-ω compel
ἄνευ (+gen.) without
ἂν ἴδ-οιμι I would (like to) see
(ὁρά-ω|εἶδ-ον)
ἂν ποιήσ-αιμι I will do
(ποιέ-ω)
ἅπας ἅπασ-α ἅπαν
(ἁπαντ-) all, the whole
ἀπ-έχ-ομαι refrain from
(+gen.)
ἀφροδίσι-α, τά sex (2b)
βαδίζ-ω walk
γέν-ος, τό race, kind (3c)
δαί then
δακρύ-ω weep
δοκ-εῖ it seems a good idea (to
x (dat.) to y (inf.))
ἐθελήσ-αιμι ἂν I would (like
to) (ἐθέλ-ω)
εἴπερ if indeed, if really (-περ
strengthens the word to which
it is attached)

ἕρπ-ω go along, take its
course
ἥ who (nom. s. f.)
κατα-λύ-ω bring to an end
Κλεονίκ-η, ἡ Kleonike (1a)
Λάκαιν-α, ἡ Spartan woman
(1c)
Λυσι-στράτ-η, ἡ Lysistrata
(1a) ('Destroyer of the
army')
μᾶλλον . . . ἤ rather than
μέλλ-ω intend
μηχαν-ή, ἡ plan, scheme (1a)
Μυρρίν-η, ἡ Myrrhine (1a)
ναὶ τὼ σιώ (Spartan dialect) by
the Two Gods! (Castor and
Pollux)
ὅ what, which (acc. s. n.)
οἵ who (nom. pl. m.)
οὐδαμ-ῶς not at all, in no way
οὓς which, who (acc. pl. m.)
ὀψ-όμεθα we shall see (fut. of
ὁρά-ω)

παγ-κατάπυγον totally
lascivious
παρ-έρχ-ομαι
(παρ-ελθ-) come forward
ποιήσ-ειας ἂν will you (s.) do
(ποιέ-ω)
ποιήσ-ειε ἂν will (he) do
(ποιέ-ω)
συμ-ψηφισ-αίμην ἂν I will
vote with (+dat.)
(συμ-ψηφί-ομαι)
συμ-ψηφίσ-αιο ἂν will you
(s.) vote with
(συμ-ψηφίζ-ομαι) (+dat.)
συν-δοκ-εῖ it seems a good
idea to x (dat.) also
σώσ-αιμεν ἂν we might save
(σώζ-ω)
τοι then
τοίνυν so, then
φίλτατ-ος -η -ον most dear
(φίλ-ος)
χἡμῖν = καὶ ἡμῖν

Vocabulary to be learnt
ἀπέχομαι refrain, keep away
(from) (+gen.)
ἅπας ἅπασα ἅπαν
(ἁπαντ-) all, the whole

βαδίζω walk, go (fut.
βαδιέομαι)
δοκεῖ it seems a good idea to X
(dat.) to do Y (inf.); X (dat.)
decides to do Y (inf.)

καταλύω bring to an end; finish
μηχανή, ἡ device, plan (1a)
οὐδαμῶς in no way, not at all

Vocabulary for Section Nine B

ἀκρόπολ-ις, ἡ acropolis (3e)
ἀναγκάζ-ω compel
ἀπο-πέμπ-ω send away,
 dismiss
ἀργύρι-ον, τό silver (2b)
 (deposited in the Parthenon;
 these were reserves built up
 from the silver mines at
 Laurion)
ἄρτι just now, recently
ἅς who (acc. pl. f.) (after ἔδει)
γν-οῦσ-α recognising (nom.
 s. f.) (γιγνώσκ-ω|ἔ-γνω-ν)
γνῶ-ναι to recognise
 (γιγνώσκ-ω|ἔ-γνω-ν)
γραῦς (γρα-), ἡ old woman
 (3a)
δῶρ-ον, τό gift, bribe (2b)
ἔ-γνω-ν (I) recognised
 (γιγνώσκ-ω|ἔ-γνω-ν)

ἔ-γνω-ς you (s.) recognised
 (γιγνώσκ-ω|ἔ-γνω-ν)
ἔ-γνω (she) recognised
 (γιγνώσκ-ω|ἔ-γνω-ν)
ἐξαίφνης suddenly
ἥ which (nom. s. f.)
ἥν which (acc. s. f.)
ἰού oh!
καὶ μὴν look!
Κινησί-ας, ὁ Kinesias (1d)
 (comic name implying sexual
 prowess)
Λακεδαίμων (Λακεδαιμον-),
 ἡ Sparta (3a)
Λαμπιτώ, ἡ Lampito (voc.
 Λαμπιτοῖ)
ὅ which (acc. s. n.)
ὁδ-ός, ἡ road (2a)
οἵ who (nom. pl. m.)
οἰμώζ-ω cry οἴμοι

ὅς who (nom. s. m.)
οὗ whose (gen. s. m.)
παρά (+dat.) with, at, beside
παρα-μέν-ω remain beside
παρα-σκευάζ-ομαι prepare
προσ-αγορεύ-ω address
συν-εξ-απατήσ-αιμ' ἄν I will
 join with x (dat.) in
 deceiving
 (συν-εξ-απατά-ω)
συν-οικέ-ω live (with)
 (+dat.)
τριήρ-ης, ἡ trireme (3d)
τίν-ι τρόπ-ῳ how? in what
 way?
φέρ-ω lead
ᾧ with whom (dat. s. m.)
ὧν whose (gen. pl. f.)
ὡς (+acc.) to

Vocabulary to be learnt

ἀναγκάζω force, compel
ἄρτι just now, recently
γραῦς (γρα-), ἡ old woman (3
 irr.) (acc. s. γραῦν; acc. pl.
 γραῦς)
δῶρον, τό gift, bribe (2b)

ἐξαίφνης suddenly
παρά (+dat.) with, beside, in
 the presence of
συνοικέω live with, live
 together

Vocabulary for Section Nine C

ἄ-λουτ-ος -ον unwashed
ἄν διδ-οίην I would like to
 give (δίδω-μι|δο-)
γοῦν at any rate
δαιμονί-α my dear lady
διὰ στόμα on her lips
διδό-ναι to give
 (δίδω-μι|δο-)
δίδω-μι I give, offer
δώσ-ω I shall give
 (δίδω-μι|δο-)

δώσ-εις you (s.) will give
 (δίδω-μι|δο-)
δώσ-ουσι they will grant
 (δίδω-μι|δο-)
ἔ-δο-σαν they granted
 (δίδω-μι|δο-)
δό-τε grant! (pl.)
 (δίδω-μι|δο-)
δυσ-τυχ-ῆ unlucky (acc. s.
 m.)
εἶεν very well

ἐκ-καλέ-ω call out
ἐκποδών out of the way
εὖ γε hurrah! good!
ἥ who (nom. s. f.)
θεράπων (θεραποντ-), ὁ slave,
 servant (3a)
καὶ μὴν look!
καλ-ῶ I shall call (fut. of
 καλέ-ω; ἐ-ω contr.)
μαμμί-α, ἡ mummy (1b)
μῆλ-ον, τό apple (2b)

Μυρρινίδιον Myrrhine baby
ὅ which (acc. s. n.); which
  (nom. s. n.)
οἷ-ος -α -ον what sort of a!
οἷς to whom (dat. pl. m.)
ὅπερ what indeed, the very
  thing which (acc. s. n.)
ὅς who (nom. s. m.)
Παιονίδ-ης, ὁ of the deme
  Paionis (1d) (comic name
  implying sexual prowess)

προσ-αγορεύ-ω address
σπασμ-ός, ὁ discomfort (2a)
σπουδ-ή, ἡ haste (1a)
τεῖχ-ος, τό wall (of a city) (3c)
τὸ τεκ-εῖν to be a mother,
  motherhood
  (τίκτ-ω|ἔ-τεκ-ον)
ὑπ-ακού-ω obey, listen to
  (+dat.)

φίλτατ-ος -η -ον dearest
  (φίλ-ος)
φύλαξ (φυλακ-), ὁ, ἡ guard
  (3a)
ᾧ with/to whom (dat. s. m.)
ὡς since, because

Vocabulary to be learnt

οἷος α ον what a! what sort of a!
προσαγορεύω address, speak to
σπουδή, ἡ haste, zeal,
  seriousness (1a)
τεῖχος, τό wall (of a city) (3c)

φίλτατος η ον most dear
  (φίλος)
φύλαξ (φυλακ-), ὁ, ἡ guard
  (3a)

Vocabulary for Section Nine D

ἀ-μελ-εῖ uncaring (dat. s. m.)
ἀ-μελέστερ-ος -α -ον more
  uncaring (ἀ-μελ-ής)
ἀ-μελ-ῆ uncaring (acc. s. m.)
ἂν δράσ-ειε (he) might do
  (δρά-ω)
βαδι-οῦμαι I shall walk (fut.
  of βαδίζ-ω; έ-ω contr.)
βαδι-ῇ you (s.) will walk (fut.
  of βαδίζ-ω; έ-ω contr.)
γλυκ-εῖ-α sweet (nom. s. f.)
γλυκ-ὺ sweet (nom. s. n.)
γλυκ-ὺν sweet (acc. s. m.)
γλυκ-ύς sweet (nom. s. m.)
δυσ-τυχέστερ-ος -α -ον more
  unlucky (δυσ-τυχ-ής)

ἐκποδών out of the way
εὐ-τυχί-α, ἡ good luck (1b)
θεράπων (θεραποντ-), ὁ
  servant, slave (3a)
καὶ δὴ there!
καίτοι and yet
κατα-γέλαστ-ος
  -ον laughable, silly
κατα-κλίν-ομαι lie down
κλινίδι-ον, τό little couch (2b)
Μαν-ῆς, ὁ Manes (voc.
  Μαν-ῆ) (1d)
μέμφ-ομαι criticise (+dat.)
μηδαμ-ῶς not at all

μήτηρ (μητ(ε)ρ-), ἡ mother
  (3a)
ὅς who (nom. s. m.)
παύ-ομαι cease from (+gen.)
προσ-άγ-ω bring (to) (+dat.)
πρότερον before, first
πύλ-η, ἡ gate (1a)
τέκν-ον, τό child (2b)
τοι then
φέρε . . . φιλήσω come . . . let
  me kiss
φίλημα (φιλημματ-), τό kiss
  (3b)
χαμαί on the ground

Vocabulary to be learnt

καίτοι and yet
κατακλίνομαι lie down
μέμφομαι blame, criticise, find
  fault with (+acc. or dat.)
μηδαμῶς not at all, in no way

μήτηρ (μητ(ε)ρ-), ἡ mother
  (3a)
παύομαι cease from (+gen.)
τοι then (inference)

Vocabulary for Section Nine E

ἀλείφ-ομαι anoint (oneself)
ἀμέλει of course
ἀνα-πηδά-ω jump up
ἀπ-ολ-οίμην may I die
(ἀπ-όλλ-υμαι|ἀπ-ολ-)
ἀπ-όλ-οιτο may he die
(ἀπ-όλλ-υμαι|ἀπ-ολ-)
Ἄρτεμις, ἡ Artemis (3a) (acc.
Ἄρτεμιν) (goddess of hunting
and chastity)
βινέ-ω make love (to)
(colloquial)
γοῦν at any rate
δαιμονί-α my dear lady
δέ-ομαι need, ask for (+gen.)
δια-τριβ-ή, ἡ delay (1a)
δός grant! (s.) (δίδω-μι|δο-)
δυσ-τυχέστατ-ος -η -ον most
unlucky (δυσ-τυχ-ής)
δώσ-ω I shall give
(δίδω-μι|δο-)
ἔ-δωκ-ας you (s.) gave
(δίδω-μι|δο-)

ἐκ-δύ-ομαι undress
ἔ-λιπ-ον see λείπ-ω
ἡδ-ύ sweet, pleasant (nom. s.
n.)
καὶ δή there!
κάκιστα most badly (tr. 'an
awful death')
κατα-κλίν-ηθι lie down! (s.)
κλινίδι-ον, τό small couch
(2b)
κυνέ-ω (κυσ-) kiss
λείπ-ω (λιπ-) leave
λύ-ομαι undo (one's own)
μηδείς μηδεμί-α μηδέν
(μηδέν-) no one, nothing
μυρίζ-ω anoint with myrrh
(fut. μυριέ-ω)
μύρ-ον, τό myrrh (2b)
Μυρρινίδιον Myrrhine,
darling
ὅ what, which (acc. s. n.)
ὄζ-ω smell of (+gen.)
ὅσ-ων of all the things which

(gen. pl. n.) (lit. 'as many
as')
ὅσ-τις he who (nom. s. m.)
ποῖ-ος -α -ον; what sort of?
προσ-κεφάλαι-ον, τό pillow
(2b)
προ-τείν-ω stretch forth
Ῥόδι-ος -α -ον from Rhodes
σισύρ-α, ἡ blanket (1b)
στρόφι-ον, τό sash (2b)
ταχὺ quickly
ὑπο-λύ-ομαι undo one's shoes
φιλέ-ω kiss
φυλάττ-ομαι μή take care not
(to)
ψηφίζ-ομαι vote (fut.
ψηφιέ-ομαι)
ψίαθ-ος, ἡ mattress (2a)
ὧν which (gen. pl. f.)

Vocabulary to be learnt

ἀμελής ές uncaring
γλυκύς εῖα ύ sweet
γοῦν at any rate
δέομαι need, ask, beg (+gen.)
δίδωμι (δο-) give, grant
ἐκδύομαι undress

μηδείς μηδεμία μηδέν
(μηδέν-) no, no one
ὅς ἥ ὅ who, what, which
ὅσπερ ἥπερ ὅπερ who/which
indeed
ὅστις ἥτις ὅ τι who(ever),

what(ever)
ποῖος α ον; what sort of?
ψηφίζομαι vote (fut.
ψηφιέομαι)

○ Grammar for Section Nine

Summary:
Aor. opt. act. and mid.
δίδωμι, γιγνώσκω, ἀμελής, γλυκύς
Rel.

Verbs

Aorist optatives, active and middle: παύσαιμι, παυσαίμην; λάβοιμι, λαβοίμην

129 You have already met present optatives (**95–7**). Here are the forms of the aorist optatives, based on the aorist stems:

Active (weak)	*Middle (weak)*
παύσ-αιμι	παυσ-αίμην
παύσ-ειας (-αις)	παύσ-αιο
παύσ-ειε (-αι)	παύσ-αιτο
παύσ-αιμεν	παυσ-αίμεθα
παύσ-αιτε	παύσ-αισθε
παύσ-ειαν (-αιεν)	παύσ-αιντο

Notes

(i) Look for the aorist stem + αι or ει.

(ii) Note the alternative forms of the 2nd and 3rd s. and 3rd pl. of the weak active. (On optative in general, cf. Language Survey (4) p. 312.)

Active (strong)	*Middle (strong)*
λάβ-οιμι	λαβ-οίμην
λάβ-οις	λάβ-οιο
λάβ-οι	λάβ-οιτο
λάβ-οιμεν	λαβ-οίμεθα
λάβ-οιτε	λάβ-οισθε
λάβ-οιεν	λάβ-οιντο

Notes

(i) Observe yet again that the endings of the strong aorist optative are identical to those for the present. Look out for aorist stem + οι.

(ii) As you will hardly need informing by now, there is no difference of time between present and aorist optative: the difference is one of aspect, if there is a difference at all which is really noticeable in translation.

130 Note the phrase ἀπολοίμην (sometimes just ὀλοίμην) to express a wish – 'may I die! damn me!' (cf. the stem ἀπολ- noted at **99**). This use of the optative *without* ἄν to express a wish for the future will be fully introduced later on.

δίδωμι *'I give'*

131 You have already made a brief acquaintance with one -μι verb, τίθημι, (see **124**), and noted its stems τιθε-, θε-. Here now, in full, is the conjugation of δίδωμι. It will give you the key to *all* -μι verbs, as you will see.

Present indicative active	*Participle*	*Infinitive*	*Imperative*	*Optative*
Stem: διδο-				
δίδω-μι	διδο-ύς	διδό-ναι	δίδο-υ	διδο-ίην
δίδω-ς	διδο-ῦσα		διδό-τω	διδο-ίης
δίδω-σι(ν)	διδό-ν		δίδο-τε	διδο-ίη
δίδο-μεν	(διδοντ-)		διδό-ντων	διδο-ῖμεν
δίδο-τε				διδο-ῖτε
διδό-ασι(ν)				διδο-ῖεν

Present indicative middle	*Participle*	*Infinitive*	*Imperative*	*Optative*
δίδο-μαι	διδό-μεν-ος	δίδο-σθαι	δίδο-σο	διδο-ίμην
δίδο-σαι	-η		διδό-σθω	διδο-ῖο
δίδο-ται	-ον		δίδο-σθε	διδο-ῖτο
διδό-μεθα			διδό-σθων	διδο-ίμεθα
δίδο-σθε				διδο-ῖσθε
δίδο-νται				διδο-ῖντο

Imperfect indicative active

Stem: διδο-

ἐ-δίδο-υν
ἐ-δίδο-υς
ἐ-δίδο-υ
ἐ-δίδο-μεν
ἐ-δίδο-τε
ἐ-δίδο-σαν

Imperfect indicative middle

ἐ-διδό-μην
ἐ-δίδο-σο
ἐ-δίδο-το
ἐ-διδό-μεθα
ἐ-δίδο-σθε
ἐ-δίδο-ντο

Aorist indicative active	*Participle*	*Infinitive*	*Imperative*	*Optative*
Stem: δο-				
ἔ-δω-κα	δο-ύς	δο-ῦναι	δό-ς	δο-ίην
ἔ-δω-κας	δο-ῦσα		δό-τω	δο-ίης
ἔ-δω-κε	δό-ν		δό-τε	δο-ίη

ἔ-δο-μεν   (δοντ-)   δό-ντων   δο-ῖμεν
ἔ-δο-τε   δο-ῖτε
ἔ-δο-σαν (ἔ-δω-καν)   δο-ῖεν

Aorist indicative middle	Participle	Infinitive	Imperative	Optative
ἐ-δό-μην	δό-μεν-ος	δό-σθαι	δο-ῦ	δο-ίμην
ἔ-δο-υ	-η		δό-σθω	δο-ῖο
ἔ-δο-το	-ον		δό-σθε	δο-ῖτο
ἐ-δό-μεθα			δό-σθων	δο-ίμεθα
ἔ-δο-σθε				δο-ῖσθε
ἔ-δο-ντο				δο-ῖντο

Future active

δώσ-ω

(etc., like παύσ-ω)

Future middle

δώσ-ομαι

(etc., like παύσ-ομαι)

Notes

(i) Given that one keeps a firm grip on the stems (διδο-, δο-), there is very little here that is difficult to recognise. The most remarkable feature is the aorist inflection with its change from ἔ-δω-κα, -κας, -κε to ἔ-δο-μεν, -τε, -σαν in the plural.

(ii) τίθημι 'I place, put' follows exactly the same pattern. For διδο-, δο- write τιθε-, θε- and note that

(a) διδω- δω- corresponds to τιθη- θη-

(b) διδου- δου- corresponds to τιθει- θει- (but note the impf. ἐτίθην), and you have the forms of τίθημι. In summary form, they are:

	Indicative	Participle	Infinitive	Imperative	Optative
Present (active) (stem τιθε-):	τίθη-μι	τιθε-ίς	τιθέ-ναι	τίθε-ι	τιθε-ίην
Present (middle):	τίθε-μαι	τιθέ-μενος	τίθε-σθαι	τίθε-σο	τιθε-ίμη
Imperfect (active):	ἐ-τίθη-ν				
Imperfect (middle):	ἐ-τιθέ-μην				
Aorist (active) (stem θε-):	ἔ-θη-κα	θε-ίς	θε-ῖναι	θέ-ς	θε-ίην
Aorist (middle):	ἐ-θέ-μην	θέ-μενος	θέ-σθαι	θ-οῦ	θε-ίμην
Future (active):	θήσ-ω (regular)				
Future (middle):	θήσ-ομαι (regular)				

(On -μι verbs in general, see Language Survey (7).)

Another 'root' verb

132 The aorist of γιγνώσκω 'I know, perceive, resolve' is as follows:

ἔ-γνω-ν I knew
ἔ-γνω-ς
ἔ-γνω
ἔ-γνω-μεν
ἔ-γνω-τε
ἔ-γνω-σαν

Infinitive: γνῶ-ναι to know
Participle: γνούς, γνοῦσα, γνόν (γνοντ-) 'knowing'
It is another 'root' aorist, like βαίνω, ἔβη-ν (cf. **126**).

Note
ἔγνων *can also be translated 'I made up my mind, I was convinced'.*

Adjectives

ἀμελής, γλυκύς

133 The declension of adjective-types like ἀμελής and γλυκύς is as follows:

ἀμελ-ής -ές 'uncaring'

s.				pl.			
nom.	*acc.*	*gen.*	*dat.*	*nom.*	*acc.*	*gen.*	*dat.*
m./f. ἀμελ-ής	ἀμελ-ῆ	ἀμελ-οῦς	ἀμελ-εῖ	ἀμελ-εῖς	ἀμελ-εῖς	ἀμελ-ῶν	ἀμελ-έσι(ν)
n. ἀμελ-ές	ἀμελ-ές	ἀμελ-οῦς	ἀμελ-εῖ	ἀμελ-ῆ	ἀμελ-ῆ	ἀμελ-ῶν	ἀμελ-έσι(ν)

γλυκύς -εῖα -ύ 'sweet'

s.			
nom.	*acc.*	*gen.*	*dat.*
m. γλυκ-ύς	γλυκ-ύν	γλυκ-έος	γλυκ-εῖ
f. γλυκ-εῖ-α	γλυκ-εῖ-αν	γλυκ-εί-ας	γλυκ-εί-ᾳ
n. γλυκ-ύ	γλυκ-ύ	γλυκ-έος	γλυκ-εῖ

pl.			
nom.	*acc.*	*gen.*	*dat.*
m. γλυκ-εῖς	γλυκ-εῖς	γλυκ-έων	γλυκ-έσι(ν)
f. γλυκ-εῖ-αι	γλυκ-εί-ας	γλυκ-ει-ῶν	γλυκ-εί-αις
n. γλυκ-έα	γλυκ-έα	γλυκ-έων	γλυκ-έσι(ν)

Notes
(i) Observe that, while ἀμελής has the same forms for the m. and f. (cf. εὔφρων 45), γλυκύς types are of mixed declension – the m. and n. declining like type 3 nouns, the f. declining like a 1st declension noun ἀπορία. (Cf. participles 48 and 50.) (ii) The dominant vowel in the stem of both of these types of adjective is -ε-. Compare their declension with noun-types 3c, d, e and f (41–3, 67) (For comparison, and summary of all adjectives, see Reference Grammar C 1–3, pp. 271 ff.) (iii) υἱός 'son' can decline like 2a nouns, but it can also decline like the m. form of γλυκύς (except for the acc. s.), i.e. υἱός, υἱόν, υἱέος, υἱεῖ, υἱεῖς, υἱεῖς, υἱέων, υἱέσι(ν).

Nouns

The relative pronoun ὅς ἥ ὅ 'who, which, what'

134 The relative pronoun declines as follows:

	s.				*pl.*			
	nom.	*acc.*	*gen.*	*dat.*	*nom.*	*acc.*	*gen.*	*dat.*
m.	ὅς	ὅν	οὗ	ᾧ	οἵ	οὕς	ὧν	οἷς
f.	ἥ	ἥν	ἧς	ᾗ	αἵ	ἅς	ὧν	αἷς
n.	ὅ	ὅ	οὗ	ᾧ	ἅ	ἅ	ὧν	οἷς

Notes
(i) The relative declines, for the most part, exactly like the definite article without the τ-.
(ii) Note that, in places where the forms of the relative correspond with the definite article, the relative is accented, e.g. ἥ οἵ αἵ.
135 The relative pronoun means:
nom.: who, which, what
acc.: who, whom, which, what
gen.: of whom, of which, whose
dat.: to, for, by, with which/whom
Consider the following phrases:
ἡ γυνὴ ἥ οὐ φιλεῖ τὸν ἄνδρα 'the woman *who does not love her husband*'
ὁ παῖς ὅν φιλῶ 'the boy *whom I like*'
ἡ γυνὴ ἧς τὸν ἄνδρα μισῶ 'the woman *whose husband I hate*'
οἱ παῖδες οἷς δίδωμι τὰ μῆλα 'the boys *to whom I give the apples*'
ἡ οἰκία εἰς ἥν ἔρχομαι 'the house *to which I go*'
αἱ γυναῖκες μεθ' ὧν πορεύομαι 'the women *with whom I travel*'
ἡ οἰκία ἐν ᾗ οἰκῶ 'the house *in which I live*'
Observe that the relative agrees with the word which it picks up (the technical

term for the word it picks up is 'antecedent': thus the antecedent of the first phrase is 'woman', of the second phrase 'boy', etc.) in *gender* and *number* (singular or plural); but its case is entirely determined by the function it fulfils in the relative clause – as you can see from the examples given.

Notes

(i) Sometimes the antecedent is suppressed. In that case, the relative will mean 'the man who', 'the woman who', 'the thing which', depending on its gender, e.g.

ἃ ἐθέλεις, ἔχεις *'what you want, you have' (i.e.* 'the things *which you want . . .')*

ὃν οἱ θεοὶ φιλοῦσι ἀποθνῄσκει νέος *'whom the gods love, dies young' (i.e.* 'he *whom . . .')*

As you can see from the above examples, Greek works rather like English in this respect.

(ii) If the antecedent is in the genitive or dative case, the Greek relative is sometimes attracted into that case, irrespective of the function it should have in the relative clause, e.g.

περὶ τῶν ἀνδρῶν ὧν γιγνώσκω *'concerning the men whom I recognise' (We would expect:* περὶ τῶν ἀνδρῶν οὓς γιγνώσκω, *since 'whom' is the object of 'recognise'; but the relative is attracted into the case of its antecedent* ἀνδρῶν *and becomes* ὧν *instead of* οὓς.)

136 The relative pronoun does have a number of other forms, though its meaning is only slightly altered thereby:

ὅσπερ (ὅσ-περ) 'the very one who'

ὅστις (ὅς-τις) 'anyone who'. This declines as follows:

	s.				*pl.*			
	nom.	*acc.*	*gen.*	*dat.*	*nom.*	*acc.*	*gen.*	*dat.*
m.	ὅστις	ὅντινα	οὗτινος	ᾧτινι	οἵτινες	οὕστινας	ὧντινων	οἷστισι(ν)
f.	ἥτις	ἥντινα	ἧστινος	ᾗτινι	αἵτινες	ἅστινας	ὧντινων	αἷστισι(ν)
n.	ὅτι	ὅτι	οὗτινος	ᾧτινι	ἅτινα	ἅτινα	ὧντινων	οἷστισι(ν)

Notes

(i) This is simply a compound of ὅς *and* τις, *each separately declined. Sometimes the two words appear as one (e.g. as declined above), at other times they are kept separate, e.g.* ὅς τις, ὅ τι *etc.*

(ii) The following variant forms are allowed:

gen.: ὅτου *for* οὗτινος; ὅτων *for* ὧντινων

dat.: ὅτῳ *for* ᾧτινι; ὅτοις *for* οἷστισι

nom./acc. pl. ἅττα *for* ἅτινα

(iii) ὅστις *can be used to introduce indirect questions (cf.* **66,** *and check the list of relative usages there).*

O

Revise

Pres. inf. **74–5**

Aor. parts. **78–9, 82–4**

φημί **81**

αὐτός **85–9**

Exercises for Section Nine

(a) Words *(cf. Language Survey (13), pp. 327 ff.)*

1. Deduce the meaning of the words in the right-hand columns from those in the left:

ἀμελής	μέλει		
δίδωμι	ἀποδίδωμι	ἡ δόσις	ἡ ἀντίδοσις
δῶρον	ἡ δωρέα	δωρέω	
μηχανή	μηχανάομαι		
σπουδή	σπουδάζω	σπουδαῖος α ον	
συνοικέω	ἡ συνοίκησις		
τεῖχος	τειχίζω		

(b/c) Morphology and Syntax

1. Translate each sentence, then convert present optatives to aorist:
a. προσαγορεύοις ἂν ἐμέ.
b. ἡδέως ἂν παυοίμην τοῦ πολέμου.
c. ἐθέλοιμεν ἂν σπονδὰς ποιεῖσθαι πολλῇ σπουδῇ.
d. οὐκ ἂν ποιοίην ταῦτα, ὦ μῆτερ.
e. ὁρῴην ἂν ἐγὼ τὴν πόλιν.

2. Translate each sentence then substitute the correct part of δίδωμι for παρέχω:
a. ἆρα παρέξεις μοι ὃ ἔχεις;
b. παρεῖχε τὰ χρήματα τῇ γυναικί.
c. τί οὐκ ἐθέλεις παρέχειν μοι ἃ δέομαι;
d. τί παρέχεις μοι τοῦτο τὸ μῆλον, ὦ Μυρρίνη;
e. ἐξαίφνης παρασχὼν τὰ χρήματα ἃ ἐδεῖτο ἡ γυνή, ἀπῆλθεν ὁ ἄνθρωπος.

3. Translate each of the following pairs of sentences. Then join them together into one sentence, following these patterns:
   (a) Λυσιστράτη γυνὴ Ἀθηναία ἐστί· Λυσιστράτη λέγει.
   = Λυσιστράτη, ἣ γυνὴ Ἀθηναία ἐστί, λέγει.
   (b) τίνες εἰσὶν οὗτοι; τίνες διώκουσι τὸν ἄνδρα;
   = τίνες εἰσὶν οὗτοι, οἳ διώκουσι τὸν ἄνδρα;

a. Κινησίας ἐστὶν ἀνὴρ Μυρρίνης. Κινησίας βαδίζει πρὸς τὴν ἀκρόπολιν.
b. αἱ γυναῖκές εἰσιν ἐν τῇ ἀκροπόλει. αἱ γυναῖκες βοῶσιν.
c. οἱ ἄνδρες τὰς μάχας μάχονται. οἱ ἄνδρες οὐκ ἐθέλουσιν οὐδαμῶς τὸν πόλεμον καταλῦσαι.
d. τί ἐστι τοῦτο; τί ἐθέλεις λέγειν;
e. αἱ γυναῖκες ἐθέλουσιν ἀκούειν τοὺς λόγους. τοὺς λόγους λέγει Λυσιστράτη.
f. αἱ γρᾶες ἔχουσι τὴν ἀκρόπολιν. ἐγὼ τὰς γραῦς ἰδεῖν δύναμαι.
g. ποῦ ἐστι Κινησίας; Μυρρίνη ἐστὶν ἡ γυνὴ αὐτοῦ.
h. ποῦ αἱ γρᾶες; τὸ ἔργον ἐστὶν αὐτῶν φυλάττειν τὰ χρήματα.
i. ἆρα γιγνώσκεις τὸν ἄνδρα; ὁ ἀνὴρ προσέρχεται.
j. δεῖ ἡμᾶς εἰρήνην ἄγειν. ἡ εἰρήνη αἰτία ἐστὶ πολλῶν καλῶν.

(d) English into Greek

1. Translate into Greek:
   1. Will the women refrain from the bribes which the men will give them?
   2. These guards are uncaring and guard with no zeal.
   3. The old women are making a plan by which they will capture the walls.
   4. It seems a good idea to us women to bring the war to an end.
   5. Won't anyone force the men to stop fighting?

2. Translate into Greek (words in italics are given in the vocabulary):

LYSISTRATA We must stop the war and make a truce. We will persuade the men, whose duty it is to fight, to do what we want.

WOMAN I should like to. But how is it possible for us, who are women, to do this? Say what you have in mind.

LYS. Would you do what I order?

WOMEN We would, by Zeus

LYS. The plan I have in mind happens to be difficult. Listen then to the words I speak, and obey. We must all refrain from *sex*!

MYRRHINE I will not do it!

KLEONIKE Neither will I!

LYS. Is there anyone who will do what I order?

LAMPITO We must bring peace and stop the men who fight the wars. I will *vote with* you.

LYS. Dear Lampito! Give me your hand.

LAMP. Here, I give it.

LYS. Go then to *Sparta* and persuade the Spartans.

LAMP. I will go at once.

Vocabulary

sex ἀφροδίσια, τά (2b)
vote with συμψηφίζομαι
  (+dat.)
Sparta Λακεδαίμων
  (Λακεδαιμον-), ἡ (3a)

Test Exercise Nine

Translate into English:

A Spartan envoy arrives. After he has explained how things stand in Sparta, he and his Athenian counterpart agree to come to terms with Lysistrata. Lysistrata states the conditions on which a return to work might be agreed.
(From Aristophanes, *Lysistrata*)

ΛΑΚΕΔΑΙΜΟΝΙΟΣ ποῦ ἡ τῶν Ἀθηναίων βουλή; ἐθελήσαιμι ἂν ἀγγεῖλαι νέον τι.

ΑΘΗΝΑΙΟΣ σὺ δὲ τίς εἶ ὃς δεῦρο βαίνεις πρὸς τὸ τεῖχος, πολλῇ σπουδῇ βαδίζων;

ΛΑΚ.   κῆρυξ ἐγώ, ναὶ τὼ σιώ, καὶ ἔβην ἄρτι ἀπὸ Σπάρτης περὶ εἰρήνης.

ΑΘ.   τί δ' ἐστί σοι τόδε, ὃ ἔχεις ἐν ταῖς χερσί;

ΛΑΚ.   σκυτάλα Λακαινικά.

ΑΘ.   εὖ οἶδ' ὃ λέγεις. ἀλλὰ τί γίγνεται ἐν Λακεδαιμόνι; εἴποις ἄν.

ΛΑΚ.   εἴποιμι ἂν ἡδέως. κακὸν γάρ τι μέγα ἐνέπεσεν ἡμῖν· αἰτία δὲ Λαμπιτώ, ἢ ἐξ Ἀθηνῶν ἀναβᾶσα ἔπεισε τὰς γυναῖκας ἀπέχεσθαι τῶν ἀφροδισίων.

ΑΘ.   καὶ πῶς ἔχετε; κακῶς πάσχετε, ἐξ ὧν λέγεις.

ΛΑΚ.   κακῶς παθὼν τυγχάνω, ναὶ τὼ σιώ. δεῖ οὖν ἡμᾶς, πειθομένους ταῖς γυναιξί, σπονδὰς ποιήσασθαι, ἃς κελεύσουσιν αὐταί, καὶ καταλῦσαι τὸν πόλεμον.

ΑΘ.   τί οὐ καλοῦμεν δῆτα τὴν Λυσιστράτην, ἢ ποιήσαιτ' ἂν ἡμῖν σπονδὰς μόνη; ἐπάθομεν γὰρ καὶ ἡμεῖς τοῦτο τὸ κακόν.

ΛΑΚ.   ναὶ τὼ σιώ. τίς ἂν εἴποι ποῦ ἐστιν ἡ Λυσιστράτη;

ΑΘ.   ἀλλ' ἡμᾶς οὐ δεῖ καλεῖν αὐτήν· αὐτὴ γάρ, ἀκούσασα ἃ ἐλεγόμεν, ἥδε βᾶσα τυγχάνει.

ΛΥΣΙΣΤΡΑΤΗ ἴτε, ἄνδρες. τῶν λόγων ἀκούετε ὧν λέγω. ἐγὼ γυνὴ μέν εἰμι, νοῦς δ' ἔνεστί μοι. τί νῦν οὕτως μάχεσθε καὶ οὐ παύεσθε τῆς μοχθηρίας ὑμεῖς, οἷς οἱ αὐτοί εἰσι βωμοὶ καὶ αἱ αὐταὶ θυσίαι; τί νῦν Ἕλληνας ἄνδρας καὶ πόλεις ἀπόλλυτε, οἷς ἀντὶ τούτων ἔξεστιν εἰρήνην ἰδεῖν, φίλοις τ' οὖσι καὶ συμμάχοις;

ΛΑΚ. ΚΑΙ ΑΘ.   καίτοι οὐδὲν ἄλλο δῶρον δεόμεθα ἢ βινεῖν δύνασθαι.

ΛΥΣ.   ἄπαντες οὖν σπονδὰς ποιησάμενοι καταλύσατε τὸν πόλεμον. κἄπειτα τὴν αὑτοῦ γυναῖκα λαβὼν ἀπίτω ἕκαστος.

Vocabulary

βουλή, ἡ Council of Five
  Hundred (1a)
ναὶ τὼ σιώ by the Two Gods*
σκυτάλα Λακαινικά a Spartan
  code-staff**
ἀφροδίσια, τά sex (2b)
ἀγγέλλω announce (aor.
  ἤγγειλα)
μοχθηρία, ἡ nastiness (1b)
ἀπόλλυμι destroy
ἀντί (+gen.) instead of
σύμμαχος, ὁ ally (2a)
βινέω make love *(colloquial)*
ἕκαστος η ον each

* The two gods – Castor and Pollux.
** The message was written on a leather strip wrapped round the pole and when removed
was unintelligible; the recipient would have a similar staff for use in decoding.

Section Ten

Vocabulary for Section Ten A

ἀγορεύ-ω speak
ἀγρ-ός, ὁ country (2a)
ἀ-θάνατ-ος -ον immortal
Ἀμφί-θε-ος, ὁ Amphitheos
 (2a) (comic name; 'god on
 both sides')
ἀπαγόντων . . . αὐτῶν them
 leading (him) off
ἀπο-βλέπ-ω look out
ἐντός (+gen.) inside
ἐρῆμ-ος -ον empty, deserted
εὔ-νους -ουν well-disposed
ἐφ-όδι-α, τά
 travelling-expenses,
 journey-money (2b)
ἥκ-ω come
θορυβέ-ω clamour, raise a
 clamour

κάθαρμα (καθαρματ-), τό
 purified place (3b)
κάτω down
κηρύττ-ω proclaim, herald,
 announce
κύρι-ος -α -ον sovereign, with
 power
μένοντος Ἀμφιθέου
 Amphitheos remaining ·
ὅπως how, that
ὀργίζ-ομαι become/be made
 angry
ὄψε late
παρελθόντων πάντων all
 coming forward
παρ-έρχ-ομαι|πάρ-ειμι
 (παρελθ-) come forward

Πνύξ (Πυκν-), ἡ Pnyx (3a)
 (meeting-place of the ekklesia)
ποθέ-ω desire
πρόσθεν in front
πρύταν-ις, ὁ prytanis (3e)
 (current administrative officer
 of the βουλή)
σιγά-ω be quiet
σχοινί-ον, τό rope (2b) (this
 was stained with red dye, and
 swept up and down the agora
 by slaves to drive the citizens
 into the ekklesia)
τοξότ-ης, ὁ archer (1d)
 (Scythian archers in Athens
 were public slaves used for a
 variety of policing duties)
χρηματίζ-ω do business

Vocabulary to be learnt

ἀγορεύω speak (in assembly),
 proclaim
ἀγρός, ὁ field, country(side)
 (2a)
ἀθάνατος ον immortal
ἀποβλέπω look steadfastly at
 (and away from everything
 else)
ἥκω come

θορυβέω make a disturbance,
 din
κάτω below
κηρύττω announce, proclaim
ὅπως how? (answer to πῶς;),
 how (indir. q.)
παρέρχομαι (παρελθ-) come
 forward, pass by, go by

πρύτανις, ὁ prytanis (3e)
 (member of the βουλή
 committee currently in
 charge of public affairs)
σιγάω be quiet

Vocabulary for Section Ten B

ἄ-γραφ-ος -ον unwritten
ἀδικ-ούμεθα we are being
  wronged (ἀδικέ-ω)
ἀδικ-ουμέν-οις being
  wronged (ἀδικέ-ω)
ἄκων ἄκουσ-α ἆκον
  (ἀκοντ-) unwilling(ly)
ἀναγκάζ-εται he is forced
  (ἀναγκάζ-ω)
ἀναγκαζ-όμεν-ον being
  forced (ἀναγκάζ-ω)
ἀναγκάζ-ονται they are
  (being) forced
  (ἀναγκάζ-ω)
ἄνευ (+gen.) without
ἀπ-ολλύ-μεθα we are being
  ruined (ἀπ-όλλυ-μι|ἀπολ-)
ἀπ-ολλύ-μεν-οι being ruined
  (ἀπ-όλλυ-μι)
ἀπ-όλ-οιντο may they perish!
  (ἀπ-όλλυ-μαι|ἀπολ-)
ἄρχ-εται (it) is ruled (ἄρχ-ω)
ἄρχ-ω rule
ἀτεχν-ῶς really, utterly
γεγραμμέν-ος -η -ον written
δια-φθειρ-όμεν-ος being
  corrupted (δια-φθείρ-ω)
δραχμ-ή, ἡ drachma (1a)
εἶεν all right then
ἐκ-δικάζ-ω make judgment

ἐμ-βάλλ-ω bump into
  (+dat.)
ἐξ-απατ-ᾶσθαι to be deceived
  (ἐξ-απατά-ω)
ἐξ-απατ-ώμεθα we are
  (being) deceived
  (ἐξ-απατά-ω)
ἐξ-απατ-ώμεν-ος being
  deceived (ἐξ-απατά-ω)
ἐξ-ίστα-μαι get out of the
  way
ἔστω let it be; so be it
εὐ-δαιμονέ-ω be happy
εὔ-νους -ουν well-disposed
ἐφ-όδι-α, τά travelling
  expenses (2b)
θέσ-ις, ἡ making (3e)
θωπευ-όμεν-ος being
  flattered (θωπεύ-ω)
θωπευ-εσθαι to be flattered
  (θωπεύ-ω)
θωπεύ-ω flatter
ἱερ-ά, τά sacrifices (2b)
κάκιστα most horribly
μέγεθ-ος, τό great size (3c)
μήτε . . . μήτε neither . . . nor
νεώρι-ον, τό dockyard (2b)
ὁδοι-πόρ-ος, ὁ traveller (2a)
ὁδ-ός, ἡ road (2a)
οἷς what (after πείθ-ομαι)

ὅσ-οι -αι -α as many as
ὀκτώ eight
ὄλ-οιντο may they die
  (ὄλλυ-μαι|ὀλ-)
πείθ-εσθαι to be persuaded
  (πείθ-ω)
πειθ-όμεν-ος being persuaded
  (πείθ-ω)
πείθ-ονται they are (being)
  persuaded (πείθ-ω)
πολεμέ-ω make war
πόρ-ος, ὁ ways of raising,
  provision (2a)
πρεσβεύ-ομαι deal with
  ambassadors
συμ-βουλεύ-ω give advice
σύμ-μαχ-ος, ὁ ally (2a)
τιμ-ᾶται (he) is (being)
  honoured (τιμά-ω)
τριήρ-ης, ἡ trireme (3d)
τοῦ Δικαιοπόλεως
  δόντος Dikaiopolis giving
τῶν ἄλλων πολεμούντων the
  others making war
χρηματίζ-ω do business
φαίη he might say (with ἄν)
  (opt. of φημί)
φιλέ-ω be accustomed, used
  to

Vocabulary to be learnt

ἄκων ἄκουσα ἆκον
  (ἀκοντ-) unwilling(ly)
ἀπόλλυμι (ἀπολεσ-,
  ἀπολ-) kill, ruin, destroy;
  (in pass.) be killed etc. (aor.
  ἀπωλόμην)
ἄνευ (+gen.) without
δραχμή, ἡ drachma (1a) (coin;

pay for two days'
  attendance at the ekklesia)
εἶεν very well then!
εὔνους ουν well-disposed
μήτε . . . μήτε neither . . . nor
ὁδοιπόρος, ὁ traveller (2a)
ὁδός, ἡ road, way (2a)
ὄλλυμι (ὀλεσ-, ὀλ-) destroy,

kill; (in pass.) be killed, die,
  perish (aor. ὠλόμην)
ὅσος η ον as much as (pl. as
  many as)
πολεμέω make war
τριήρης, ἡ trireme (3d)
φιλέω be used to; love; kiss
χρηματίζω do business

Vocabulary for Section Ten C

αἰβοῖ yuk!

αἱρέ-ομαι choose

αἰσθάν-ομαι
(αἰσθ-) perceive, notice

ἀμβροσί-α, ἡ ambrosia (1b)

ἀρέσκ-ω please (+dat.)

Ἀχαρν-εύς, ὁ member of the
deme Akharnai (3g) (in
central Attica, in the path of
Spartan attacks)

γεῦμα (γευματ-), τό taste,
sample (3b)

γεύ-ομαι taste

δεκέτ-ης -ες for ten years

Δικαιοπόλεως . . . εἰπόντος
Dikaiopolis saying

Διονύσι-α, τά festival of
Dionysus (2b)

δόντος Ἀμφιθέου Amphitheos
giving

ἥδιστα most pleasurably
(ἡδ-ύς)

λαβόντων αὐτῶν them taking

Λακεδαιμονίων . . . ὀλεσάντων
the Spartans destroying

Λακεδαίμων (Λακεδαιμον-),
ἡ Sparta (3a)

λίθ-ος, ὁ stone (2a)

Μαραθωνο-μάχ-ης, ὁ fighter
at the battle of Marathon
(which took place in 490) (1d)

μήπω not yet

νέκταρ (νεκταρ-), τό nectar
(3b)

ὄζ-ω smell of (+gen.)

ὀξ-ύτατ-α most sharply
(ὀξ-ύς)

παρα-σκευ-ή, ἡ preparation,
equipping (1a)

πεντέτ-ης -ες for five years

τρία three (n. of τρεῖς)

τριακοντούτ-ης -ες for thirty
years

χαίρειν πολλὰ
κελεύων bidding a long
farewell to

Vocabulary to be learnt

αἱρέομαι (ἑλ-) choose

αἰσθάνομαι (αἰσθ-) perceive,
notice

ἀρέσκω please (+dat.)

ἄρχομαι be ruled

ἄρχω rule (+gen.)

γεῦμα (γευματ-), τό taste,
sample (3b)

γεύομαι taste

ἥδιστος η ον most pleasant
(sup. of ἡδύς)

λίθος, ὁ stone (2a)

ὁ δέ and/but he

οἱ δέ and/but they

ὀξύς εῖα ύ sharp; bitter; shrill

παρασκευή, ἡ preparation,
equipping; force (1a)

τρεῖς τρία three

Grammar for Section Ten

Summary:
Pres., impf. pass.
Gen. abs.
Comp. adv. and two-termination adjs.
Opt. of φημί

Verbs
Present and imperfect passive
137 So far you have met and learnt verbs which are *active* in voice and verbs which are *middle* in voice. The distinction has usually been one of form (active verbs in -ω or -μι, middle verbs in -μαι), though occasionally the

meaning has been radically altered by the conversion of an active verb into a middle, e.g.

πείθω 'I persuade'
πείθομαι 'I believe in, trust'

We now come to the third and final voice – the PASSIVE. This does have a specific meaning, which cannot be ignored. It signifies that the subject of the sentence is *having something done to it*, e.g. 'the slave is being beaten', 'the soldiers were cut down', 'I shall be defeated.'

THE FORMS OF THE PASSIVE IN THE PRESENT AND IMPERFECT INDICATIVE, PARTI-CIPLE, INFINITIVE, IMPERATIVE, OPTATIVE (and all) ARE IDENTICAL TO THE FORMS FOR THE *MIDDLE*. So you have no new learning to do; but you must now be alert to the possibility that what you are used to as a middle form might be passive – and therefore carry a different meaning.

138 Consequently, to take an extreme example, πείθομαι could mean 'I trust', but it could equally be the passive form of πείθω and mean 'I am being persuaded'. Likewise, παύομαι could mean 'I stop myself' or 'I am being stopped'. In practice, of course, the context will make it clear which meaning is required. To help you get used to the new meaning, passive forms will always be accompanied by ὑπό + genitive = ('by' a person), or by a dative ('by' a thing, or 'with' a thing), e.g.

πείθεται ὑπὸ ἐμοῦ 'he is being persuaded by me'
ἐπαύοντο ὑπὸ τῶν ἀνδρῶν 'they were being stopped by the men'
φυλαττόμεθα τοῖς δικτύοις* 'we are being guarded by nets'
ἐβαλλόμην τοῖς λίθοις 'I was being pelted with stones'

Genitive absolute

139 When a noun + participle stand together in the GENITIVE, they must often be translated by a clause beginning with 'when', 'as', 'since', 'after', 'because', as best suits the context, e.g.

κελεύοντος τοῦ κήρυκος, τί μένεις; (lit. 'the herald ordering, why do you wait?') 'why wait when the herald orders?'
τῶν ἀνδρῶν φυγόντων, ἐπανῆλθον. (lit. 'the men fleeing, I returned') 'when the men fled, I returned'

Adverbs

Comparative and superlative adverbs

140 The comparative adverb is the accusative singular neuter of the comp. adj., e.g.

* Observe that φυλαττόμεθα τὰ δίκτυα means 'we are guarding ourselves against the nets', or 'we are watching out for the nets'.

σοφώτερος 'more wise'→σόφωτερον 'more wisely'
κακίων 'worse'→κάκιον 'in a worse way, worse'
The superlative adverb is the acc. n. pl. of the superlative adjective, e.g.
σοφώτατος 'most, very wise'→σοφώτατα 'most, very wisely'

Note

Irregular adverbs μᾶλλον 'more, rather (more)'
μάλιστα 'much, very much, a great deal'

Adjectives

Two-termination adjectives

141 You have already met some types of adjective that decline the same in the m. and f. (e.g. κακοδαίμων). There are a number of adjectives like this of the καλός type as well, which do not decline -η -ην etc. in the f., but, like the masculine, -ος -ον, etc. These are called two-termination adjectives because they have only two sets of endings – one for m./f., one for n. You have already met one of these, ἐρῆμος 'deserted', which has occurred in the sentence ἐρῆμος ἡ Πνύξ 'the Pnyx is deserted'. One would have expected ἐρήμη, but the adjective is two-termination, using the same form for m. and f.

Most two-termination adjectives are *compounds*, e.g.

ἄ-δικ-ος -ον 'unjust'
ἀ-θάνατ-ος -ον 'immortal'
εὐ-δόκιμ-ος -ον 'of good reputation'
ἀ-δύνατ-ος -ον 'impossible'

but there are a number of other adjectives which are two-termination without being compounds as such, e.g.

βάρβαρ-ος -ον 'barbarian, foreign'

Verb

Optative of φημί

142 Note the optative of φημί 'I say'

φα-ίην
φα-ίης
φα-ίη
φα-ῖμεν
φα-ῖτε
φα-ῖεν

Revise:

Gen. case **91–2** Pres. opt. **95–7**

Exercises for Section Ten

(a) Words

1. Deduce the meaning of the words on the right from those on the left:

αἰσθάνομαι   ἡ αἴσθησις
ἄκων   ἑκών
πρύτανις   τὸ πρυτανεῖον

(b/c) Morphology and Syntax

1. Translate each sentence, then, making the necessary changes in nouns and verbs, change from active to passive:

a. τιμᾷ τοὺς χρηστούς ὁ δῆμος.

b. ἀναγκάζει ἡμᾶς σπονδὰς ποιεῖσθαι ἡ Λυσιστράτη.

c. ἀδικοῦσιν οἱ ῥήτορες τὴν πόλιν.

d. ἐξαπατᾷ ὁ ῥήτωρ τὸν δῆμον.

e. θωπεύομεν τὴν ἐκκλησίαν τοῖς λόγοις.

f. πείθετε τοὺς πολίτας εἰρήνην ἄγειν.

g. τὰ δῶρα ἔπειθε τὸν δῆμον.

h. οἱ λόγοι τῶν ῥητόρων ἠδίκουν τὴν ἐκκλησίαν.

i. τὰ τείχη ἐφύλαττε τὴν πόλιν.

j. αἱ μηχαναὶ τῶν γυναικῶν ἠνάγκαζον τοὺς ἄνδρας σπονδὰς ποιεῖσθαι.

2. Translate each pair of sentences, then join them into one, using the genitive absolute construction:

a. ἀπῆλθον οἱ ἄνδρες. ἡμεῖς δὲ πρὸς τὴν πόλιν ἐπορευόμεθα.

b. ἔδωκέ μοι τὸ ἀργύριον ἡ γυνή. ἐγὼ δ' ἀπῆλθον.

c. ὁ θεὸς μένει. οἱ δ' Ἀθηναῖοι οὐ βούλονται ἀκούειν.

d. οἱ ἄλλοι πολεμοῦσιν. ἐγὼ δ' οὐ πολεμήσω.

e. ἡ πόλις ἀδικεῖται ὑπὸ τῶν ῥητόρων. οἱ δ' Ἀθηναῖοι οὐδὲν φροντίζουσιν.

f. ἡ ἐκκλησία περὶ τοῦ πολέμου ἐχρημάτιζεν. ὁ δὲ Δικαιόπολις οὐδὲν ἐφρόντιζεν.

g. ἡ ἐκκλησία ὑπ' οὐδενὸς ἄρχεται. ὁ δὲ δῆμος ποιεῖ ἃ ἐθέλει.

h. οἱ Ἀχαρνεῖς λίθους ἔλαβον. ἐγὼ δ' ἔφευγον.

i. ὁ μὲν Ἀμφίθεος ἔδωκε τὰς σπονδάς. Δικαιόπολις δ' ἐδέξατο.

j. ὁ μὲν κῆρυξ ἐκήρυξεν. ὁ δὲ θεὸς ἐσίγησεν.

(d) English into Greek

Translate into Greek:

1. The herald was making his announcement while the prytanes came into the assembly.

2. The people were being persuaded to make war by the politicians, while the farmers gazed out into the countryside.
3. The politicians are said to be well-disposed towards the city.
4. The Spartans are destroying our land while we are being deceived by the politicians.
5. The assembly is ruled by no one.

2. Translate into Greek:
Here are the prytanes! Now they have come, you can be sure that the politicians will come forward, wishing to speak. We farmers will keep quiet, looking out into the country, forced against our will to hear the words spoken by them. But they will not tell the truth. They always say that the city is ruled by itself and is beloved of all the politicians. But they are well-disposed only to themselves. The city is being destroyed by them; but no one will move business about that, or about peace. The whole thing is not at all to my liking.

Test Exercise Ten
Translate into English:
Dikaiopolis defends his action in getting a peace treaty for himself with the Spartans. He gives his own version of the causes of the Peloponnesian War.
(From Aristophanes, *Akharnians*)

ΔΙΚΑΙΟΠΟΛΙΣ μὴ θορυβεῖτε, ὦνδρες οἱ θεώμενοι, εἰ πτωχὸς ὢν ἥκω ἐγὼ καὶ ἐν
Ἀθηναίοις λέγων ἄρχομαι περὶ τῆς πόλεως, κωμῳδίαν ποιῶν. τὸ γὰρ
δίκαιον οἶδε καὶ κωμῳδία. ἐγὼ δὲ λέξω δεινὰ μέν, δίκαια δέ. οὐ γάρ με
νῦν γε διαβαλεῖ Κλέων ὅτι, ξένων παρόντων, ὑπ᾽ ἐμοῦ κακῶς λέγεται ἡ
πόλις. αὐτοὶ γάρ ἐσμεν, κοὔπω ξένοι πάρεισιν. ἐγὼ δὲ μισῶ μὲν
Λακεδαιμονίους σφόδρα. ἀπόλοιντο αὐτοὶ καὶ οἱ παῖδες καὶ αἱ γυναῖκες.
ὑπ᾽ αὐτῶν γὰρ ἡ ἀμπελία μου κόπτεται, ἡμεῖς δ᾽ ἐν τῇ πόλει
ἐγκλειόμεθα ἄκοντες, τῇ δὲ νόσῳ ἀπολλύμεθα, εἰς δὲ τοὺς ἀγροὺς ἀεὶ
ἀποβλέπομεν. ἀτάρ, (ὑμεῖς γὰρ οἱ παρόντες φίλοι) πῶς αἴτιοι
Λακεδαιμόνιοι τούτων κακῶν; ἡμῶν γὰρ ἄνδρες (οὐχὶ τὴν πόλιν λέγω,
μέμνησθε τοῦθ᾽, ὅτι οὐχὶ τὴν πόλιν λέγω) αἴτιοι, μάλιστα δὲ Περικλῆς
Οὐλύμπιος, ὃς ἐτίθει νόμον ὡς χρὴ Μεγαρέας μήτε γῇ μήτ᾽ ἐν ἀγορᾷ,
μήτ᾽ ἐν θαλάττῃ μήτ᾽ ἐν ἠπείρῳ μένειν. τῶν δὲ Μεγαρέων καὶ τῶν
Λακεδαιμονίων δεομένων πολλάκις καὶ αἰτούντων ἡμᾶς ἀφέλεσθαι τὸ
ψήφισμα, οὐκ ἠθέλομεν· οὐ γὰρ ἤρεσκε τῷ Περικλεῖ.
    αὕτη ἡ ἀρχὴ τοῦ πολέμου.

Vocabulary

πτωχός, ὁ beggar (2a)
*(Dikaiopolis has borrowed
some rags from Euripides to
gain sympathy)*
κωμῳδία, ἡ comedy (1b)
αὐτοί alone, by ourselves

σφόδρα very much
ἀμπελία, ἡ vineyard (1b)
ἀτάρ but
μέμνησθε remember
Οὐλύμπιος the Olympian
τίθημι pass (of a law)

ἤπειρος, ἡ mainland (2a)
ἀφαιρέομαι
  (ἀφελ-) withdraw
ψήφισμα, τό decree (3b)
ἀρχή, ἡ cause (1a)

PART FOUR

Section Eleven

Vocabulary for Section Eleven A

Note: from now on, prefixes in compounds will not be hyphenated, and new forms will be glossed as a whole, without hyphens.

ἄλλος ... ἄλλον one ... another

ἄπειρ-ος -ον inexperienced in (+gen.)

Ἀπολλόδωρ-ος, ὁ Apollodoros (2a) (prosecuting in the case)

ἀσπάζ-ομαι greet, welcome

διατρίβ-ω pass time, be

δικανικ-ός -ή -όν judicial

ἐντεύξεσθαι fut. inf. of ἐντυγχάνω

ἐντυγχάν-ω meet (+dat.)

ἕτερος ... ἕτερον one ... another (of two)

Εὐεργίδ-ης, ὁ Euergides (1d) (a dikast)

ἱμάτι-ον, τό cloak (2b)

Κωμί-ας, ὁ Komias (1d) (a dikast)

λαμπρ-ός -ά -όν famous, notorious

μηδέ ... μηδέ neither ... nor

Νέαιρ-α, ἡ Neaira (1b) (defendant in the case)

νὴ καὶ σύ γε and you, too

οὗ where (at)

ὄχλ-ος, ὁ crowd (2a)

Στρυμόδωρ-ος, ὁ Strymodoros (2a) (a young dikast)

τύχ-η, ἡ fortune, piece of luck (1a)

χρῆμα (χρηματ-), τό astonishing size, amount (3b)

ὠθέ-ω push, shove

Vocabulary to be learnt

ἄλλος ... ἄλλον one ... another

ἀσπάζομαι greet, welcome

δικανικός ή όν judicial

ἐντυγχάνω (ἐντυχ-) meet with, come upon (dat.)

ἕτερος ... ἕτερον one ... another (of two)

ἱμάτιον, τό cloak (2b)

μηδέ ... μηδέ neither ... nor

τύχη, ἡ chance, fortune (good or bad) (1a)

ὠθέω push, shove

Vocabulary for Section Eleven B

ἀγωνίζ-ομαι go to law

ἀποδίδω-μι (ἀποδο-) pledge, give back

βῆμα (βηματ-), τό stand, podium (3b)

διαφέρ-ω make a difference

εἰκός rightly, reasonably

εἴτε ... εἴτε whether ... or

ἑκάτερ-ος -α -ον each (of two)

εὐεργετέ-ω benefit
εὔνοι-α, ἡ good will (1b)
ἔφυ-ν be, be naturally (from
  φύ-ομαι)
ἐχθρ-α, ἡ hostility, enmity
  (1b)
καὶ μήν what's more
κατά (+acc.) in accordance
  with
κατήγορ-ος, ὁ prosecutor,
  accuser (2a)

κοιν-ός -ή -όν common,
  undivided
κύρι-ος -α -ον valid
ξενί-α, ἡ alien status (1b)
ὅπως see to it that (+fut.
  ind.)
ὅρκ-ος, ὁ oath (2a)
πολυπράγμων
  πολύπραγμον meddling
προκαταγιγνώσκ-ω
  (προκαταγνο-) pre-judge

προσέχ-ω τὸν νοῦν pay
  attention
τιμωρέ-ομαι revenge oneself
  on
ὑπάρχ-ω begin, start (+gen.)
φιλόπολις patriotic, loyal
φύσ-ις, ἡ nature (3e)
φύ-ομαι grow (see ἔφυν)
χρέμπτ-ομαι clear one's
  throat

Vocabulary to be learnt

διαφέρ-ω make a difference;
  differ from (+gen.); be
  superior to (+gen.)
εἴτε... εἴτε whether... or
ἑκάτερος a ον both (of two)

εὔνοια, ἡ good will (1b)
καὶ μήν what's more; look!
κατά (+acc.) according to;
  down; throughout; in relation
  to

κατήγορος, ὁ prosecutor (2a)
ὅρκος, ὁ oath (2a)
προσέχω τὸν νοῦν pay attention
  to (+dat.)

Vocabulary for Section Eleven C

ἀγών (ἀγων-), ὁ trial, contest
  (3a)
ἀγωνίζ-ομαι go to law, fight
ἀδικηθείς harmed, wronged
  (nom. s. m.) (ἀδικέ-ω)
ἀδικηθέντες harmed,
  wronged (nom. pl. m.)
  (ἀδικέ-ω)
ἀναστάντες standing up
  (nom. pl. m.)
  (ἀνίσταμαι|ἀναστα-)
ἀντίδικ-ος, ὁ contestant (2a)
ἀρχ-ή, ἡ start (1a)
διατελέ-ω finish
ἔοικε it seems
ἔσχατ-ος -η -ον furthest,
  worst
εὖ ποιέ-ω do good to, treat
  well
ἐχθρ-α, ἡ hostility (1b)

ἐχθρ-ός, ὁ an enemy (2a)
ἠδικήθη (he) was harmed,
  wronged (ἀδικέ-ω)
ἠδικήθην I was harmed,
  wronged (ἀδικέ-ω)
θυγάτηρ (θυγατ(ε)ρ-), ἡ
  daughter (3a)
καθίστη-μι (καταστησ-) set
  up, put, place (x in y
  position)
καὶ γὰρ in fact
καταστάς being put (nom. s.
  m.)
(καθίσταμαι|καταστα-)
κατέστην I was placed
(καθίσταμαι|καταστα-)
κατέστη he was placed
(καθίσταμαι|καταστα-)
κατέστημεν we were placed
(καθίσταμαι|καταστα-)

κατέστησε (he) placed
  (καθίστημι|καταστησ-)
μεγάλα very much, greatly
ὅπως see to it that (+fut.
  ind.)
οὐ μόνον... ἀλλὰ καί not
  only... but also
πενί-α, ἡ poverty (1b)
πιστεύ-ω trust (+dat.)
προδιηγέ-ομαι give a
  preliminary outline of
πώποτε ever, yet
Στέφαν-ος, ὁ Stephanos (2a)
  (who lived with Neaira in
  Athens)
τιμωρέ-ομαι take revenge on
τιμωρί-α, ἡ revenge (1b)
ὑπάρχ-ω begin (+gen.)

Vocabulary to be learnt

ἀγών (ἀγων-), ὁ contest, trial
  (3a)
ἀγωνίζομαι contest, go to law

ἀντίδικος, ὁ contestant in
  lawsuit (2a)
ἀρχή, ἡ beginning, start (1a)

εὖ ποιέω treat well, do good to
ἔχθρα, ἡ enmity, hostility (1b)
ἐχθρός, ὁ enemy (2a)

ἐχθρός ά όν hostile, enemy
θωπεύω flatter
καὶ γάρ in fact; yes, certainly

οὐ μόνον . . . ἀλλὰ καί not
only . . . but also
πιστεύω trust (+dat.)

τιμωρέομαι take revenge on
τιμωρία, ἡ revenge, vengeance
(1b)
ὑπάρχω begin (+gen.)

Vocabulary for Section Eleven D

ἀδικηθείς wronged, harmed
(nom. s. m.) (ἀδικέω)
αἰσχύν-η, ἡ sense of shame,
humiliation (1a)
ἀλλότρι-ος -α -ον alien
ἄνανδρ-ος -ον cowardly,
feeble
ἀσεβέ-ω εἰς commit sacrilege
upon
ἄτιμ-ος -ον deprived of all
rights
ἀφαιρέ-ομαι take x (acc.)
from γ (acc.), claim
βουλευτ-ής, ὁ member of
βουλή (1d)
γράφ-ω propose
δημότ-ης, ὁ member of
deme, demesman (1d)
ἐγγυά-ω give in marriage
εἰσάγ-ω (εἰσαγαγ-) introduce
ἐκτίν-ω (ἐκτεισ-) pay (a fine)
ἐλάττων (ἐλαττον-) less,
smaller (comp. of ὀλίγος)
ἔνδει-α, ἡ poverty (1b)
ἐξελέγχ-ω convict, expose
ἐπείσθησαν (they) were
persuaded (πείθω)

ἐπιδείκνυ-μι
(ἐπιδειξ-) demonstrate,
prove
ἔσχατ-ος -η -ον worst, most
severe
ἑταίρ-α, ἡ whore, prostitute
(1b)
ἠδικήθην I was wronged,
harmed (ἀδικέω)
θυγάτηρ (θυγατ(ε)ρ-), ἡ
daughter (3a)
καταστάς
(κατασταντ-) placed, put,
made
(καθίσταμαι|καταστα-)
καταστήσας
(καταστησαντ-) placing,
putting, making
(καθίστημι|καταστησ-)
καταστήσεσθαι to be put
(καθίσταμαι|καταστα-)
καταφρονέ-ω despise, hold in
contempt (+gen.)
οἰκεῖ-ος ὁ relative (2a)
οἷός τ' εἰμί be able to (+inf.)
ὀνειδίζ-ω rebuke, reproach
(+dat.)

παρά (+acc.) against
παρακαλέ-ω encourage, urge
παρανόμων as illegal
πενί-α, ἡ poverty (1b)
προίξ (προικ-), ἡ dowry (3a)
πρότερον previously, first
συμφορ-ά, ἡ chance,
misfortune, disaster (1b)
τιμά-ω fine (+dat.)
τίμημα (τιμηματ-), τό a fine
(3b)
τοσ-οῦτος -αύτη -οῦτο(ν) so
great
ὑβρίζ-ω εἰς act violently
against
φάσκ-ω allege
φράτηρ (φρατερ-), ὁ member
of a phratry (3a) (a phratry is
a group of families: as such it
fulfilled various religious and
social functions)
ψευδ-ής -ές false, lying
ψήφισμα (ψηφισματ-), τό
decree (3b)
χάριν οἶδα be grateful to
(+dat.)

Vocabulary to be learnt

ἀσεβέω εἰς commit sacrilege
upon
ἀλλότριος α ον someone else's,
alien
ἄτιμος ον deprived of citizen
rights

ἀφαιρέομαι (ἀφελ-) take X
(acc.) from Y (acc.), claim
εἰσάγω (εἰσαγαγ-) introduce
ἔσχατος η ον worst, furthest,
last
θυγάτηρ (θυγατ(ε)ρ-). ἡ

daughter (3a)
καθίστημι (καταστησα-) set
up, make, place, put X (acc.)
in (εἰς) Y
καθίσταμαι (καταστα-) be
placed, be put, be made

οἷός τ' εἰμί *be able to (+ inf.)*
παρά *(+ acc.) against; to;*
compared with; except; along,
beside
πενία, ἡ *poverty (1b)*
πρότερος α ον *first (of two),*
previous

πρότερον *(adv.) previously*
τιμάω *fine (+ dat.)*
τίμημα *(τιμηματ-), τό a fine*
(3b)
τοσοῦτος αὕτη οὗτο(ν) *so*
great

ψευδής ές *false, lying*
ψήφισμα *(ψηφισματ-),*
τό *decree (3b)*

○ Grammar for Section Eleven A–D

Summary:
Aor. pass.
ἵστημι, καθίστημι

Verbs

Aorist passive ἐπαύ[σ]θην '*I was stopped*'

143 The forms of the aorist passive are as follows:

Indicative		*Participle*
ἐ-παύσθ-ην	'I was stopped' *etc.*	παυσθ-είς -εῖσα -έν *(εντ-)* 'stopped'
ἐ-παύσθ-ης		
ἐ-παύσθ-η		
ἐ-παύσθ-ημεν		
ἐ-παύσθ-ητε		
ἐ-παύσθ-ησαν		

Notes

(i) The aorist passive means 'I was –ed', regarded simply as an event, not a process (cf. the imperfect passive, which regards the action as a process – 'I was being –ed').

(ii) Note the augment, to show the past tense, and the stem/endings in -θη-. Not all verbs have the θ in the aorist passive, but the -η- will give the clue, e.g. γράφω→ἐγράφ-η-ν.

(iii) Note that the form of the aorist passive is impossible to predict, though it is usually easy to recognise (the θ-η gives the clue), e.g. παύω→ἐπαύθην *or* ἐπαύσθην; κελεύω→ἐκελεύσθην; κωλύω→ἐκωλύθην.

(iv) Note the change of the final consonant of the stem before -θ in:

πέμπ-ω *(*ἐπέμπ-θην*)→*ἐπέμφ-θην
διώκω *(*ἐδιώκ-θην*)→*ἐδιώχ-θην
φυλάττω *(uncontr. aor.* ἐφυλακ-σα*)→*ἐφυλάχ-θην

For verbs which use the aorist passive form, but are active *in meanings, see* **206.**

(v) Note the aor. pass. of δίδωμι: ἐ-δόθ-ην.

ἵστημι 'I set up'

144 You have already met ἀνίσταμαι 'I get (myself) up and go' **98**: here now are the details of the verb of which it is a compound.

Remember two things:

(a) the basic meaning is 'I am in the act of setting something up';

(b) (i) one set of forms, the active ones, carry the meaning 'I am setting something up', and will always have an object in the accusative so that you know what it is that the person is setting up;

(ii) another set of forms, called 'quasi-passive', mean 'I am in the act of setting myself up', i.e. 'I am in the act of standing', and need no object;

(iii) the last set of forms, called 'middle', mean 'I am setting x up for myself'. A number of these middle forms are the same as the quasi-passive.

Here are the principal forms and meanings of ἵστημι divided according to meaning:

(a) Active (taking a direct object)

Present indicative	Participle	Infinitive	Imperative	Optative
'I am setting x up': *present stem* ἱστα-				
ἵστη-μι	ἱστά-s	ἱστά-ναι	ἵστ-η	ἱστα-ίην
ἵστη-s	ἱστᾶ-σα		ἱστά-τω	ἱστα-ίης
ἵστη-σι(ν)	ἱστά-ν		ἵστα-τε	ἱστα-ίη
ἵστα-μεν	(ἱσταντ-)		ἱστά-ντων	ἱστα-ῖμεν
ἵστα-τε				ἱστα-ῖτε
ἱστᾶ-σι(ν)				ἱστα-ῖεν

Imperfect indicative

'I was setting x up'

ἵστη-ν
ἵστη-s
ἵστη
ἵστα-μεν
ἵστα-τε
ἵστα-σαν

Aorist indicative	Participle	Infinitive	Imperative	Optative
'I (did) set x up': *aorist stem* στησ(α)-				
ἔ-στησ-α	στήσ-αs -ασα -αν	στῆσ-αι	στῆσ-ον	στήσ-αιμι
(etc., like ἔπαυσα)				

Future indicative

'I will set x up'

στήσ-ω

(etc., like παύσ-ω*)*

> *Notes*
>
> *(i)* Note similarities with δίδωμι – τίθημι *(see* **131** *and Notes). The present stem is* ἱστα-, ἱστη-, *and that controls the shape of all present and imperfect forms: where* διδο-/δίδω- *occur, observe now* ἱστα-/ἱστη-. *The future and aorist stem is* στησ-, *and gives absolutely regular weak aorist and future forms.*

(b) Quasi-passive (taking no direct object)

Present indicative	Participle	Infinitive	Imperative	Optative
'I am in the act of standing up': *present stem* ἱστα-				
ἵστα-μαι	ἱστά-μεν-ος	ἵστα-σθαι	ἵστα-σο	ἱστα-ίμην
ἵστα-σαι	-η		ἱστά-σθω	ἱστα-ῖο
ἵστα-ται	-ον		ἵστα-σθε	ἱστα-ῖτο
ἱστά-μεθα			ἱστά-σθων	ἱστα-ίμεθα
ἵστα-σθε				ἱστα-ῖσθε
ἵστα-νται				ἱστα-ῖντο

Imperfect indicative

'I was in the act of standing up'

ἱστά-μην
ἵστα-σο
ἵστα-το
ἱστά-μεθα
ἵστα-σθε
ἵστα-ντο

Aorist indicative	Participle	Infinitive	Imperative	Optative
'I did stand up, I stood up': *aorist stem* στη-/στα-				
ἔ-στη-ν	στά-ς	στῆ-ναι	στῆ-θι	στα-ίην
ἔ-στη-ς	στᾶ-σα		στή-τω	στα-ίης
ἔ-στη	στά-ν		στῆ-τε	στα-ίη
ἔ-στη-μεν	(σταντ-)		στά-ντων	στα-ῖμεν
ἔ-στη-τε				στα-ῖτε
ἔ-στη-σαν				στα-ῖεν

Future indicative
'I shall stand up'
στήσ-ομαι
(etc., like παύσ-ομαι*)*

(c) Middle (taking a direct object)

Forms are the same in the present and imperfect as for the quasi-passive. Note the middle aorist: 'I set up x for myself'.

Aorist indicative
ἐ-στησ-άμην
ἐ-στήσ-ω
ἐ-στήσ-ατο
ἐ-στησ-άμεθα
ἐ-στήσ-ασθε
ἐ-στήσ-αντο

Cf. the aorist indicative active.

Notes

(i) This is all absolutely predictable in the present, imperfect and future – the forms are the regular middle forms based on the active. The single oddity is the aorist ἔστην *(*στα-, στη-*) (cf. the root aorist* ἔβη-ν *126).*

(ii) Interestingly, you are not yet in a position to be able to say in Greek 'I am standing.' You can say 'I am in the process of standing', but not actually 'here I stand'. To say that, you will have to use the (as yet unmet) perfect tense in the form which means 'I have set myself up' – and consequently am standing.

(iii) If you note nothing else, hold on to the vital difference in form and meaning between the aorists (since you will tend to meet these most of all in reading):

ἔστησα *(*στησ-*) 'I did set (someone) up' (needing an object)*
ἔστην *(*στα-, στη-*) 'I stood' (no object needed)*

(iv) The 'true' aorist passive is ἐ-στάθ-ην *'I was set up'.*

145 The most important compound of ἵστημι is καθίστημι. In its *active* forms (καθίστημι, καθίστην, κατέστησα, καταστήσω) it means 'I put someone in (usually εἰς) a certain position'; in its middle forms (καθίσταμαι, καθιστάμην, κατέστην, καταστήσομαι), it means 'I am put into a certain position', or 'I am elected, I am made, I *become*', e.g.:

κατέστην εἰς πενίαν 'I was placed in poverty, I became poor'
κατέστησε ἡμᾶς εἰς ἀπορίαν 'he placed us in despair, he made us despair, he reduced us to despair'

Exercises for Section Eleven A–D

(b/c) Morphology and Syntax

1. Translate the passage, choosing the form of the verb which fits the context:

'Απολλόδωρος ἐμὲ ἠδίκησε μεγάλα καὶ (κατέστη/κατέστησεν) ἡμᾶς πάντας εἰς πολλὴν ἀπορίαν. μάρτυρας γὰρ ψευδεῖς (ἀναστὰς/ ἀναστήσας) ἐν τῷ δικαστηρίῳ εἷλεν ἐμὲ καὶ τίμημα ᾔτησε μέγα. ἐγὼ οὖν ὀφείλων τὸ τίμημα τῇ πόλει καὶ εἰς ἀτιμίαν (καταστὰς/ καταστήσας), ἐκ τῆς πόλεως (ἐξανέστησα/ἐξανέστην)· ἔπειτα δέ, ἐκ τῆς πατρίδος (ἀναστὰς/ἀναστήσας) εἰς Μέγαρα ἀπῆλθον, οὗ εἰς πενίαν (καταστὰς/καταστήσας) ἔμενον δύο ἔτη.

2. Translate each sentence, then change present tense to aorist:

a. ἡ γὰρ ἐμὴ θυγάτηρ εἰς πενίαν καθίσταται διὰ ταύτην τὴν δίκην.

b. 'Αθηναῖοι οὖν ἀνίστασιν ἐκ τῆς Αἰγίνης τοὺς Αἰγινήτας.

c. ὑμεῖς δέ, ὦ ἄνδρες δικασταί, καθίστατε εἰς πολλὴν ἀπορίαν τὰς ἐμὰς θυγατέρας καταδικάσαντες ἐμοῦ.

d. ὁ δὲ κατήγορος οὑτοσὶ ἀνίσταται ἐν τῷ δικαστηρίῳ καὶ τὸν φεύγοντα εἰς φόβον καθίστησιν.

3. Translate these aorist passives, then pair with their present forms:

ἐκλήθησαν, ἐλήφθη, ἠπορήθην, κατεδικάσθητε, ἐξηλέγχθης (convict), ἐξεδόθημεν (give in marriage), ὑβρίσθη (do violence to), διηλλάχθησαν (be reconciled to), ἐγράφην, ὠργίσθητε (be made angry), ἐλέχθη, ἐβιάσθημεν, κατηγορήθη, ἀπελύθης, ἀπεπέμφθησαν (send away), ἐξηπατήθης, ἐπείσθην

πείθω, λέγω, καλέω, λαμβάνω, βιάζομαι, ἐκδίδωμι, ὀργίζομαι, ὑβρίζω, ἐξαπατάω, ἀποπέμπω, ἐξελέγχω, διαλλάττομαι, γράφομαι, κατηγορέω, ἀπορέω, ἀπολύω, καταδικάζω

4. Translate these sentences, then change the aorist passive verbs, with their subjects if necessary, to singular or plural as appropriate:

a. οἱ μὲν γὰρ δικασταὶ ὑπὸ τῆς ἀπολογίας οὐκ ἐπείσθησαν, ἐγὼ δὲ κατεδικάσθην.

b. ἀλλὰ μὴν οὐ διαφέρει μοι εἰ οὐκ ἀπελύθης, ἀλλὰ κατεδικάσθης.

c. καὶ γὰρ οὗτος ὁ λόγος ἐλέχθη ὑπὸ τοῦ ἀντιδίκου.

d. ὑμεῖς δὲ ἠδικήθητε ὑπὸ τούτου μεγάλα.

5. Translate these sentences, filling in the correct form of the aorist passive participle:

a. ἐγὼ εὔνοιαν ἔχω εἰς τὸν ἄνδρα τὸν ὑπὸ Στεφάνου ἀδικηθ– .

b. ἡμεῖς δὲ πεισθ– ὑπὸ τοῦ ἀντιδίκου δίκην ἐλάβομεν.

c. τῆς δὲ γυναικὸς ἐξαπατηθ– ὑπὸ τοῦ ἀτίμου κατεφρόνησεν ὁ ἀνήρ.

d. βιασθ– δ᾽ ἐμοῦ εἰσάγειν τὸ παιδίον εἰς τοὺς φράτερας, ἡ θυγάτηρ εἰς ἔχθραν κατέστη.

e. ἐμοὶ δὲ ἀτίμῳ ὄντι καὶ ἀπορηθ– οἱ φίλοι ἐβοήθησαν.

f. τοῖς δὲ γερούσι τοῖς ὑπὸ Κλέωνος ἐξαπατηθ– πολλὰς δραχμὰς ἔδομεν.

(d) English into Greek
Translate into Greek:
1. Apollodoros was grievously wronged by Stephanos and Neaira.
2. A big fine was asked for by Stephanos.
3. Apollodoros faced the prospect of getting into terrible trouble.
4. Stephanos put Apollodoros in great danger.
5. Apollodoros was persuaded to take vengeance against Stephanos.

Vocabulary for Section Eleven E

αἰσχύν-ομαι feel shame, be ashamed
ἀνέκδοτ-ος -ον unmarried
ἄρχ-ω begin (+gen.)
ἀτιμί-α, ἡ loss of rights (1b)
γαμέ-ω marry

εἰκός right(ly)
ἐκδίδω-μι (ἐκδο-) give in marriage
καταφρονέ-ω despise (+gen.)
πᾶς τις everyone
προίξ (προικ-), ἡ dowry (3a)

σπουδάζ-ω be concerned
σπουδαῖ-ος -α -ον important, serious
τεκμήρι-ον, τό evidence (2b)

Vocabulary to be learnt
αἰσχύνομαι be ashamed, feel shame
ἄρχω begin (+gen.); rule (+gen.)
ἀτιμία, ἡ loss of citizen rights (1b)

εἰκός likely, probable, reasonable, fair
καταφρονέω despise, look down on (+gen.)

σπουδάζω be concerned, serious; do seriously
σπουδαῖος α ον important, serious

O   Grammar for Section Eleven E

Summary:
Acc. (nom.) and inf.

Accusative and infinitives

146 You have already met words which take an infinitive (e.g. βούλομαι ἰέναι 'I wish to go') and words which can take an accusative and infinitive (e.g. δεῖ με ἰέναι 'I must go'; βούλομαί σε ἰέναι 'I want you to go'). Here are some more, but of a different type. They all introduce some sort of *indirect speech* (i.e. words, thoughts, feelings etc. not directly quoted, but *reported* as taking place), and it is this indirect speech which goes into the accusative and infinitive:

οἴομαι   'I think that . . .' (but not necessarily very strongly)
φημί   'I say that . . .'
νομίζω   'I consider that . . .'
ἡγοῦμαι 'I think that . . .' (of a firmly held opinion)
φάσκω   'I allege that . . .'

147 The subject of the 'that' clause appears in the ACCUSATIVE, and the verb in the INFINITIVE. Remember to start your translation with the word 'that', e.g.

νομίζω σε μῶρον εἶναι 'I consider *that* you are foolish' (cf. English 'I consider you to be foolish')

ἔφη Νέαιραν καταφρονεῖν τῶν θεῶν 'he said *that* Neaira despised the gods'

148 Observe that the tense of the infinitive tells you what was actually said. If the speaker said originally 'we will knock', this becomes ἔφη ἡμᾶς κόψειν 'he said that we would knock' (*future* infinitive).

149 If the subject of the 'that' clause is the same as that of the main verb, it will either not appear, or else will appear as a *nominative*, e.g.

ἔφην ἀφίξεσθαι 'I said that I would come'
ἔφην ἐκεῖνον ἀφίξεσθαι 'I said that he would come'
ἡγεῖτο αὐτὸς σοφὸς εἶναι 'he considered that he was himself wise'
ἡγεῖτο αὐτὸν σοφὸν εἶναι 'he considered that he (i.e. *someone else*) was wise'   ○

Exercises for Section Eleven E

(b/c) Morphology and Syntax

1. Translate each statement, then, using the verbs given, turn them into indirect statements. How is the translation altered if you use the past form of the verb?

   1. ὁ κατήγορος σπουδαιότατός ἐστιν ἀνθρώπων. (φημί/ἔφην)
   2. ἐγὼ εἰς μέγαν κίνδυνον κατέστην. (φησί/ἔφη)
   3. ἀεὶ λέγουσί τι δεινὸν οἱ ἀντίδικοι. (ἡγοῦμαι/ἡγούμην)
   4. ὁ Στέφανος εἰσήγαγεν εἰς τοὺς φράτερας τοὺς ἀλλοτρίους παῖδας. (φασί/ἔφασαν)
   5. ἡ Νέαιρα οὐκ αἰσχύνεται καταφρονοῦσα τῶν νόμων. (τίς οὐκ ἂν οἴοιτο;/τίς οὐκ οἴεται;)
   6. ἐβουλόμεθα τότε τιμωρεῖσθαι τοὺς ἐχθρούς. (φαμέν/ἔφαμεν)

Vocabulary for Section Eleven F

'Αθήναζε to Athens
ἀστ-ή, ἡ female citizen (1a)
ἀστ-ός, ὁ male citizen (2a)
ἔθηκεν he put down
   (τίθημι|θε-)
ἐλήφθησαν aor. pass. of
   λαμβάνω
ἑορτ-ή, ἡ festival (1a)
ἐπιδείκνυ-μι
   (ἐπιδειξ-) show, prove
ἐραστ-ής, ὁ lover (1d)
ἐργάζ-ομαι work, earn a
   living
ἑταίρ-α, ἡ whore, prostitute
   (1b)

ἦθε-ος, ὁ bachelor (2a)
καταθεῖναι to put down
   (κατατίθημι|καταθε-)
Κόρινθ-ος, ἡ Corinth (2a)
Λυσί-ας, ὁ Lysias (1d) (lover of
   Metaneira)
Μετάνειρ-α, ἡ Metaneira (1a)
   (slave of Nikarete)
μικρ-ός -ά -όν small
μυέ-ω initiate
μυστήρι-α, τά the Mysteries
   (2b)
Νικαρέτ-η, ἡ Nikarete (1a)
   (slave-owner)
παιδοποιέ-ομαι have children

συνέρχ-ομαι (συνελθ-) come
   together
σῶμα (σωματ-), τό body (3b)
τεκμήρι-ον, τό evidence,
   proof (2b)
τιθέναι to be putting down
   (τίθημι)
τοίνυν well now (resuming a
   narrative)
τρέφ-ω rear, raise
φανερ-ός -ά -όν clear, obvious
Φιλόστρατ-ος, ὁ Philostratos
   (2a) (Lysias' friend)
ὡς (+acc.) to (the house of),
   with

Vocabulary to be learnt

'Αθήναζε to Athens
ἀστή, ἡ female citizen (1a)
ἀστός, ὁ male citizen (2a)
ἑταίρα, ἡ whore, prostitute (1b)
ἑταῖρος, ὁ (male) companion
   (2a)

(σ)μικρός ά όν small, short,
   little
παιδοποιέομαι have children
συνέρχομαι (συνελθ-) come
   together
τεκμήριον, τό evidence, proof
   (2b)

τίθημι (θε-) put, place, make
φανερός ά όν clear, obvious
ὡς (+acc.) towards, to the
   house of

Grammar for Section Eleven F

Summary:
τίθημι

Verbs

τίθημι 'I place, put'

150 You have already been alerted to the similarities between τίθημι
'I put, place' and δίδωμι (see **131** (ii)). Here are the forms in full:

Present indicative active	Participle	Infinitive	Imperative	Optative
Stem: τιθε-				
τίθη-μι	τιθε-ίς	τιθέ-ναι	τίθε-ι	τιθε-ίην
τίθη-s	τιθε-ῖσα		τιθέ-τω	τιθε-ίης

	Participle	Infinitive	Imperative	Optative
τίθη-σι(ν)	τιθέ-ν		τίθε-τε	τιθε-ίη
τίθε-μεν	(τιθεντ-)		τιθέ-ντων	τιθε-ῖμεν
τίθε-τε				τιθε-ῖτε
τιθέ-ασι(ν)				τιθε-ῖεν

Present indicative middle/
passive

τίθε-μαι	τιθέ-μεν-ος	τίθε-σθαι	τίθε-σο	τιθε-ίμην
τίθε-σαι	-η		τιθέ-σθω	τιθε-ῖο
τίθε-ται	-ον		τίθε-σθε	τιθε-ῖτο
τιθέ-μεθα			τιθέ-σθων	τιθε-ίμεθα
τίθε-σθε				τιθε-ῖσθε
τίθε-νται				τιθε-ῖντο

Imperfect indicative active

ἐ-τίθη-ν
ἐ-τίθε-ις
ἐ-τίθε-ι
ἐ-τίθε-μεν
ἐ-τίθε-τε
ἐ-τίθε-σαν

Imperfect indicative middle/
passive

ἐ-τιθέ-μην
ἐ-τίθε-σο
ἐ-τίθε-το
ἐ-τιθέ-μεθα
ἐ-τίθε-σθε
ἐ-τίθε-ντο

Aorist indicative active
Stem: θε-

ἔ-θη-κα	θε-ίς	θε-ῖναι	θέ-ς	θε-ίην
ἔ-θη-κας	θε-ῖσα		θέ-τω	θε-ίης
ἔ-θη-κε	θέ-ν		θέ-τε	θε-ίη
ἔ-θε-μεν	(θεντ-)		θέ-ντων	θε-ῖμεν
ἔ-θε-τε				θε-ῖτε
ἔ-θε-σαν (ἔ-θη-καν)				θε-ῖεν

Aorist indicative middle	Participle	Infinitive	Imperative	Optative
ἐ-θέ-μην	θέ-μεν-ος	θέ-σθαι	θο-οῦ	θε-ίμην
ἔ-θ-ου	-η		θέ-σθω	θε-ῖο
ἔ-θε-το	-ον		θέ-σθε	θε-ῖτο
ἐ-θέ-μεθα			θέ-σθων	θε-ίμεθα
ἔ-θε-σθε				θε-ῖσθε
ἔ-θε-ντο				θε-ῖντο

Aorist indicative passive

Stem: τεθ-

ἐ-τέθ-ην	τεθ-είς	τεθ-ῆναι	τέθ-ητι	τεθ-είην
ἐ-τέθ-ης				
ἐ-τέθ-η				
ἐ-τέθ-ημεν				
ἐ-τέθ-ητε				
ἐ-τέθ-ησαν				

(All quite regular, like ἐ-παύσθ-ην)

Future indicative active

θήσ-ω
(etc., like παύσ-ω)

Future indicative middle

θήσ-ομαι
(etc., like παύσ-ομαι)

Notes

(i) Remember the stems τιθε-, θε-.
(ii) Note the aorist active ἔθηκα (cf. ἔδωκα).
(iii) Remember that κεῖμαι 'lie' can also mean 'be placed, be made' and as such is often used as the passive of τίθημι.
(iv) Observe the morphology of verbs ending in -υμι, e.g. δείκν-υμι. These tend to have fut. and aor. stems in -ξ-, and as such are quite regular (e.g. fut. δείξω aor. ἔδειξα). They follow the δίδω-μι\τίθη-μι pattern in the present and imperfect (except for the optative, cf. διδο-ίην 131), e.g.

Present active:	Participle	Infinitive	Imperative	Optative
δείκνυ-μι	δείκνυ-ς -σα -ν	δεικνύ-ναι	δείκνυ	δεικνύ-οιμι
δείκνυ-ς				
δείκνυ-σι(ν) etc.				

Present middle: Participle   Infinitive   Imperative   Optative
δείκνυ-μαι etc.   δεικνύ-μενος -η -ον δείκνυ-σθαι δείκνυ-σο δεικνυ-οίμην
Imperfect active:
ἐδείκνυ-ν
ἐδείκν-υς
ἔδεικ-υ etc.
Imperfect middle:
ἐδεικνύ-μην etc.

○

Exercises for Section Eleven F

(b/c) Morphology and Syntax

1. Translate the following sentences, then change the tense or aspect of the verbs as indicated:

a. ὑπὲρ δὲ τῆς Μετανείρας ὁ σοφιστὴς πολλὰς δραχμὰς τίθησιν (aor.).

b. τιθέντος (aor.) δὲ τοῦ σοφιστοῦ τὰ χρήματα ὑπὲρ Μετανείρας, ἡ Νικαρέτη οὐκ ἐδίδου (pres.) αὐτῇ οὐδέν, ἀλλὰ καθίστη (aor.) εἰς ἀπορίαν τὴν παῖδα.

c. ἔπειτα δέ, τῆς παιδὸς εἰς ἀπορίαν καταστάσης (pres.), ἔδοξε τῷ σοφιστῇ τιθέναι (aor.) πολλὰς δραχμὰς εἰς τὰ μυστήρια.

d. 'ἐγὼ δέ', ἔφη, 'οὕτω ποιῶν τὰ χρήματα ταῦτα ὑπὲρ Μετανείρας θήσω (aor.) αὐτῆς.'

e. ἐλθὼν δ' Ἀθήναζε ὁ Λυσίας καὶ πολλὰς δραχμὰς θείς (pres.), καθίστησι (aor.) τὴν Νικαρέτην καὶ Μετάνειραν ὡς Φιλόστρατον.

(d) English into Greek
Translate into Greek:

1. Stephanos will say that Apollodoros began their enmity.
2. Apollodoros said that he wanted to avenge himself on Stephanos.
3. Apollodoros will say that he did not wrong Stephanos.
4. Many men put down a lot of money on Neaira's account.
5. Apollodoros says that Stephanos is living with a slave as his wife.

Vocabulary for Section Eleven G

ἄν (+opt.) 'would'
ἄν (+impf.) 'would'
ἅπαξ once

ἄρχων (ἀρχοντ-), ὁ archon (3a)
διακρίν-ω determine, judge

εἰ (+opt.) 'if ... were to'
εἰ (+impf.) 'if ... were –ing'
εἰδείην optative of οἶδα

εἴθε (+opt.) I wish that! would that!

ἔοικε it seems (reasonable)

ἐπικαλύπτ-ω conceal, hide

ἐπιλανθάν-ομαι (ἐπιλαθ-) forget (+gen.)

Ἱππί-ας, ὁ Hippias (1d) *(a sophist)*

καταλέγ-ω recite, list

μαρτυρί-α, ἡ evidence, witness (1b)

μέντἄν = μέντοι ἄν

μνεί-α, ἡ mention (1b)

μνημονεύ-ω remember

ὅπως (+ fut. ind.) see to it that

πένης (πενητ-), ὁ poor man (3a)

πεντήκοντα fifty

πλούσι-ος -α -ον rich, wealthy

Σόλων (Σολων-), ὁ Solon (3a) *(famous statesman)*

συγγίγν-ομαι (συγγεν-) be with (+dat.)

φύσ-ις, ἡ nature (3e)

Vocabulary to be learnt

ἄν *(use of, in conditionals, see Grammar 151–2)*

εἴθε (+opt.) I wish that! would that!

ἐπιλανθάνομαι (ἐπιλαθ-) forget (+gen.)

καταλέγω (κατειπ-) recite, list

μαρτυρία, ἡ evidence, witness (1b)

μνεία, ἡ mention (1b)

μνημονεύω remember

ὅπως (+fut. ind.) see to it that

πένης (πενητ-), ὁ poor man (3a) *(or adj. poor)*

πλούσιος α ον rich, wealthy

συγγίγνομαι (συγγεν-) be with, have intercourse with (+dat.)

O   Grammar for Section Eleven G

Summary:

Fut. remote, pres. unfulf. cond.

Wishes for fut.

ὅπως+fut. ind.

Opt. εἰμί, εἶμι, οἶδα

Conditional sentences (with ἄν)

151 So far, you have met ἄν+optative in the sense 'would you . . ., would you like to . . .', expressing a polite request or agreement (cf. **95** and **129**).

If however you find ἄν+optative linked with (usually preceded by) εἰ ('if')+optative, the sentence will express something like: 'If x *were to happen*, y *would result*', e.g.

εἰ με πείθοις|πείσειας, λέγοιμι|εἴποιμι ἄν σοι 'if you were to persuade me, I would tell you'

εἰ φεύγοιεν|φύγοιεν, διώκοιμεν|διώξαιμεν ἄν 'if they were to flee, we would pursue'

Note

The difference in meaning between present and aorist optative will, as usual, be one not of time but of aspect.

This construction is called a 'future remote or improbable condition'.

152 If, however, you replace the optatives in the above sentences with *imperfect indicatives*, the meaning will now be altered to the formula: 'If x *were the case now*, Y *would now be resulting*', e.g.

    εἴ με ἔπειθες, ἔλεγον ἄν 'if you persuaded (were persuading) me, I would tell (be telling)'

    εἰ ἔφευγον, ἐδιώκομεν ἄν 'if they were fleeing, we would be pursuing'

In other words, the action is being referred not to the future, but to the present.

Note

    (i) This construction is called a 'present unfulfilled condition'.

(ii) The negative in the 'if' clause is μή. Observe that μή, where one might expect οὐ, gives a conditional 'colouring' to utterances which do not appear to be conditions, e.g. πῶς ἂν τιθεῖτό τις τὴν ψῆφον, μὴ μνημονεύσας τοὺς λόγους; 'How can one vote, not remembering (i.e. if one does not remember) the speeches?' Watch out for μή with this force in participle and relative clauses.

Wishes for the future

    153 You have already met ἀπολοίμην 'may I be killed', expressing a wish for the future (cf. **130**). Such wishes are more often expressed by εἴθε or εἰ γάρ+optative (although the plain optative is found), e.g.

    εἰ γάρ|εἴθε γενοίμην|γιγνοίμην σοφώτερος 'Would that I were to become more clever!'

Note

Wishes for the past are often expressed by (εἰ γάρ|εἴθε) ὤφελον+infinitive, e.g. (εἰ γάρ|εἴθε) ὠφέλομεν ἐλθεῖν 'Would that we had gone!' Note also that ἄν is NOT used in wishes. (Cf. Language Survey (4), p. 312.)

ὅπως +future indicative 'see to it that . . .'
154 This means 'see to it that . . .', e.g.

    ὅπως σώφρων ἔσει 'see to it that you are sensible'

    ὅπως μὴ παύσῃ 'see to it that you do not stop'

Verbs

Three optatives

155 See to it that you do not forget the following optatives:

εἰμί 'I am'	οἶδα 'I know'	εἶμι 'I go'
εἴην	εἰδείην	ἴοιμι
εἴης	εἰδείης	ἴοις

εἴη	εἰδείη	ἴοι
εἶμεν	εἰδεῖμεν	ἴοιμεν
εἶτε	εἰδεῖτε	ἴοιτε
εἶεν	εἰδεῖεν	ἴοιεν

Exercises for Section Eleven G

(b/c) Morphology and Syntax

1. Translate the following statements; then change them into wishes for the future (make a free choice of construction and aspect of the verb).

 a. βούλομαι δικαστὴς καθίστασθαι καὶ τίθεσθαι τὴν ψῆφον.

 b. ἐθέλω σοφιστὴς γενέσθαι.

 c. βούλομαι σὲ εἰς ἐμὲ χρήματα θεῖναι.

 d. οὐκ ἐθέλω ἀπολέσθαι.

 e. βούλομαι ὑμᾶς εἰδέναι ταῦτα.

 f. ἐθέλω σοφιστὴν ποιεῖν τὸν παῖδα.

 g. βούλομαι αὐτὸν μνημονεῦσαι τὴν μαρτυρίαν.

 h. ἐθέλω αὐτοὺς ἐπιλαθέσθαι τούτων τῶν λόγων.

 i. βούλομαι πλούσιος εἶναι.

 j. ἐθέλω τοὺς οἰκείους εἶναι πλουσίους.

2. Translate each pair of statements (omitting εἰ), then link them by making them future remote conditions or present unfulfilled conditions (see Grammar 151–2).

 a. (εἰ) τιμῶ τίμημα μέγα|δίκην λαμβάνει ὁ ἀντίδικος.

 b. (εἰ) οἱ δικασταὶ πείθονται ὑπὸ τοῦ κατηγόρου|τοῦ φεύγοντος καταδικάζουσιν.

 c. (εἰ) ὑπάρχετε τῆς ἔχθρας|τὰ τεκμήριά ἐστι φανερά.

 d. (εἰ) μνείαν ποιεῖς τῶν ἀστῶν|οὐκ ἐπιλανθάνεται ὁ κατήγορος.

 e. (εἰ) οἱ ἀστοὶ ἐξ ἑταιρῶν παιδοποιοῦνται|ἴσμεν σαφῶς.

 f. (εἰ μὴ) οἱ πλούσιοι ταῖς ἑταίραις συγγίγνονται|τοὺς πένητας ἀσπάζονται ἐκεῖναι.

3. Translate these commands. Turn each into an exhortation using ὅπως or ὅπως μή + fut. ind.

 a. πρόσεχε τὸν νοῦν καὶ ἄκουε.

 b. μὴ θωπεύετε τοὺς δικαστάς.

 c. μὴ ἐπιλανθάνου τῶν λόγων.

 d. κάτειπε τὸν τοῦ δράματος λόγον.

 e. μνημόνευε τοὺς λόγους.

f. μὴ παιδοποιεῖσθε ἐκ τῶν ἑταιρῶν.

g. εὖ τίθει τὸ πρᾶγμα.

h. μὴ καταφρόνει τοῦ ἑταίρου.

Vocabulary for Section Eleven H

ἀγαπά-ω love
ἀποδιδράσκ-ω run off
ἀργύρι-ον, τό silver, money (2b)
ἀσελγῶς disgracefully
δεῖπν-ον, τό dinner-party (2b)
διατρίβ-ω spend time
διηγέ-ομαι reveal, describe, explain
διοίκησ-ις, ἡ management (3e)
ἐπί (+dat.) for the purpose of
ἐπιδημέ-ω come into town, live
ἐπιθυμέ-ω desire (+gen.)
ἔτ-ος, τό year (3c)

εὐπορί-α, ἡ resources (1b)
θεράπαιν-α, ἡ slave girl (1c)
Θρᾶττ-α, ἡ Thratta (1c) (one of Neaira's slaves)
ἱκαν-ός -ή -όν sufficient
κατάγ-ομαι lodge
κατατίθη-μι (καταθε-) pay
Κοκκαλίν-η, ἡ Kokkaline (1a) (slave of Neaira)
κωμάζ-ω revel
Μέγαρ-α, τά Megara (2b) (a town on the isthmus)
οἴχ-ομαι go
ὀλίγωρ-ος -ον contemptuous
ὀργίζ-ομαι grow angry with (+dat.)

πανταχοῖ everywhere
προΐστα-μαι make x (acc.) sponsor of y (gen.)
προπηλακίζ-ω treat like dirt, insult
σοβαρ-ός -ά -όν pompous
συσκευάζ-ομαι gather up, collect
τοίνυν well then (resuming argument)
τρόπ-ος, ὁ manner, way (2a)
Φρυνίων (Φρυνιων-), ὁ Phrynion (3a) (owner of Neaira)
χρυσί-ον, τό gold (trinkets or money) (2b)

Vocabulary to be learnt

ἀργύριον, τό silver, money (2b)
διατρίβω pass time, waste time
ὀργίζομαι grow angry with (+dat.)

τοίνυν well then (resuming and pushing argument on further)
τρόπος, ὁ way, manner (2a)

Vocabulary for Section Eleven I

ἀδικηθήσεσθαι 'would be harmed' (ἀδικέω)
'Αθήνησι at Athens
ἅπτ-ομαι touch (+gen.)
'Αρίστων ('Αριστων-), ὁ Ariston (3a) (Neaira's son)
ἀτέλει-α, ἡ exemption, immunity (ἐξ ἀτελείας = free) (1b)
ἅψεσθαι fut. inf. of ἅπτομαι

δυοῖν two (sc. 'reasons')
Δωρόθε-ος, ὁ Dorotheos (2a) (Athenian householder)
εἰσαχθήσεσθαι 'would be introduced' (εἰσάγω)
'Ελευσίνι-ος -α -ον of Eleusis
ἐλπ-ίς (ἐλπιδ-), ἡ hope (3a)
ἐξ-=fut. stem of ἔχω
ἐπιδημέ-ω be in town
ἐργάζ-ομαι work

'Ερμ-ῆς, ὁ Hermes (1d)
θρεψ-=fut./aor. stem of τρέφω
κατατίθη-μι (καταθε-) pay
κατεγγυά-ω compel x (acc.) to give securities
Κλεινόμαχ-ος, ὁ Kleinomakhos (2a) (Athenian householder)
κομπάζ-ω boast

κόρ-η, ἡ girl, maiden (1a)
Μέγαρ-α, τά Megara (2b)
μεταξύ (+gen.) between
οἰκίδι-ον, τό house, small
house (2b)
παραλαμβάν-ω
(παραλαβ-) take
πολέμαρχ-ος, ὁ Polemarch
(2a) (state official)
Πρόξεν-ος, ὁ Proxenos (2a)
(son of Neaira)

πρός (+dat.) before
πρόσοδ-ος, ἡ income (2a)
πυνθάν-ομαι (πυθ-) learn,
hear, discover
συκοφαντί-α, ἡ informing
(1b)
τρέφ-ω (θρεψ-) maintain,
keep
Φανώ, ἡ Phano (Neaira's
daughter)

φράτηρ (φρατερ-), ὁ member
of phratry (3a) (a group of
families, with certain religious
and social functions)
ψιθυριστ-ής ὁ whisperer (1d)
ὡς (+fut. part.) in order to
ὡς ἄξων in order to take
ὡς ἕξων in order to have
ὡς ἐργασομένην αὐτὴν καὶ
θρέψουσαν in order for her
to work and maintain

Vocabulary to be learnt

'Αθήνησι(ν) at Athens
ἐλπίς (ἐλπιδ-), ἡ hope,
expectation (3a)
ἐπιδημέω come to town, be in
town

ἐργάζομαι work, perform
κατατίθημι (καταθε-) put
down, pay, perform
οἰκίδιον, τό small house (2b)

παραλαμβάνω
(παραλαβ-) take, receive
from

◯ Grammar for Section Eleven H–I

Summary:
Acc. and part.
Fut. pass.

Accusative and participle

156 You have already met verbs which take an accusative and infinitive construction (see **146–9**). Some verbs, however, prefer an accusative and participle to express their 'that' clauses, e.g.

οἶδα   'I know that . . .'
πυνθάνομαι   'I learn by inquiry that . . ., hear'
μανθάνω   'I learn that . . .'
γιγνώσκω   'I recognise that . . .'

Precisely the same principles apply to these clauses as to those already described in **146–9**. If the 'that' clause has a subject different from the main verb, the subject and its participle will go into the accusative; if subjects are the same, there will be no accusative and the participle will go into the *nominative*. The tense of the participle will point to the tense of what was originally said. Consider:

οἶδα σοφὸς ὤν   'I know I am wise'
οἶδα σε μῶρον ὄντα   'I know you are foolish'

ἐμάθομεν φεύγοντας αὐτούς 'we learnt that they were fleeing'
ἐπύθοντο ἡμᾶς παυσαμένους 'they heard that we had stopped'
(On indirect speech in general, see Reference Grammar K, p. 301.)

Verbs

Future passive παυσθήσομαι *'I shall be stopped'*

157 The forms of the future passive indicative are as follows:

παυσθ-ήσ-ομαι   'I shall be stopped'
παυσθ-ήσ-ει(η)
παυσθ-ήσ-εται
παυσθ-ησ-όμεθα
παυσθ-ήσ-εσθε
παυσθ-ήσ-ονται
Infinitive: παυσθ-ήσ-εσθαι

Notes

(i) Once you have the appropriate stem, these endings are entirely regular, being like the endings for the present middle/passive.

(ii) The stem is always based upon the stem of the aorist *passive, less* augment *plus* σ. *Thus:*

ἐπαύσθην→παυσθήσ-ομαι
ἠδικήθην→ἀδικηθήσ-ομαι   N.B. *loss of augment*
εἰσήχθην→εἰσαχθήσ-ομαι

Look for the -θη- *of the aorist passive followed by a* -σ-, *the give-away clue to the future, and translate 'will/shall be –ed' (cf. aor. pass.* **143***).*

Revise
Dat. case **103–4,** Language Survey (10)–(11)   ○

Exercises for Section Eleven I

(b/c) Morphology and syntax

1. Translate these future passives. Then pair each with its present form:
   εἰσαχθήσομαι, ἐξελεγχθησόμεθα (convict), ἀναγκασθήσει,
   ὀργισθήσεται, ζημιωθήσεσθαι (fine), ἀδικηθήσονται
   ἀναγκάζω, εἰσάγω, ἀδικέω, ἐξελέγχω, ὀργίζομαι, ζημιόω

2. Translate each statement, then, using the present tense verbs given,
   turn them into indirect statements. What difference does the use of the
   past introductory verb make to your translation?

a. ἡ γυνὴ ἀδικηθήσεται ὑπ' οὐδενός. *(φαμέν/ἔφαμεν)*

b. οἱ τῆς ἑταίρας παῖδες πολῖται γενήσονται. *(οἴεται/ᾤετο)*

c. ἀφίξονται Στέφανος καὶ Νέαιρα ἐκ τῶν Μεγάρων Ἀθήναζε.
(ἡγεῖται/ἡγήσατο)

d. ἀναγκασθήσομαι παρὰ Φρυνίωνος τὴν Νέαιραν ἀφαιρεῖσθαι.
(φησίν/ἔφη)

3. Translate each statement, then, using present tense verbs given, turn
into indirect statements. What difference does the use of the past
introductory verb make to your translation?

a. ὁ Φρυνίων ἠδικήθη ὑπ' ἐμοῦ καὶ ὠργίσθη ἐμοί. *(οἶδα/ᾔδη)*

b. ἡ Νέαιρα ἐπεδήμει καὶ ἦλθεν ὡς Στέφανον. *(ὁρᾷ/εἶδεν)*

c. ἠδικήθημεν ὑπὸ τοῦ κατηγόρου καὶ κατεδικάσθημεν ὑπὸ τῶν δικαστῶν.
(αἰσθάνονται/ᾔσθοντο)

d. ἠδικήσατε τὴν πόλιν καὶ τῶν νόμων κατεφρονεῖτε καὶ ἠσεβεῖτε εἰς τοὺς
θεούς. *(γιγνώσκετε/ἔγνωτε)*

e. ἑταίρα εἶ καὶ παιδοποιεῖ ἐξ ἀστῶν. *(οἶσθα/ᾔδεισθα)*

(d) English into Greek

1. Sentences
Translate into Greek:
   1. If only I could remember the arguments of the prosecutor!
   2. If I were a sophist, I would be remembering these arguments.
   3. If I could remember the evidence, I would cast my vote justly.
   4. Phrynion knew that Neaira was in town and had the money.
   5. Stephanos says that Neaira will be wronged by nobody.

2. Prose
Translate into Greek:
Apollodoros, wronged and put into a dangerous position by Stephanos, is contesting this suit. For the laws do not allow a citizen to live
with a prostitute as his wife. Apollodoros says that he will give clear
evidence that Stephanos is doing this very thing. If Stephanos were
doing this, it would clearly be a very serious matter. Consequently, I
hope that Apollodoros will win the suit. If he were to win it, it would
be a good thing for the city.

Test Exercise Eleven
Translate into English:
*The prosecutor describes how the man Timarkhos, on trial for immoral
behaviour, left Antikles to live with the slave Pittalakos. Timarkhos soon
deserted Pittalakos to live with Hegesandros.*
(From Aiskhines *Timarkhos*, 53–62)

ἀλλὰ τὰ μετὰ ταῦτα ἐρῶ. ὅπως ἀκούσεσθε, ὦ ἄνδρες δικασταί. ὡς γὰρ
ἀπηλλάγη παρὰ τοῦ Ἀντικλέους Τίμαρχος οὑτοσί, διημέρευεν ἐν τῷ
κυβείῳ. τῶν δὲ κυβευτῶν ἐστί τις Πιττάλακος, οἰκέτης τῆς πόλεως.
οὗτος ἰδὼν Τίμαρχον ἐν τῷ κυβείῳ ἀνέλαβεν αὐτὸν καὶ ἔσχε παρ᾽ ἑαυτῷ.
καὶ τὰς ὕβρεις ἃς ἐγὼ οἶδα σαφῶς γενομένας ὑπὸ τοῦ ἀνθρώπου
τούτου εἰς Τίμαρχον, ἐγὼ μὰ τὸν Δία τὸν Ὀλύμπιον οὐκ ἂν τολμήσαιμι
πρὸς ὑμᾶς εἰπεῖν. νὴ Δία, κάκιστ᾽ ἀπολοίμην εἰ μνείαν ποιοῦμαι τῶν
τοιούτων. ἐγὼ γάρ, εἰ ἐν ὑμῖν εἴποιμι ἃ οὑτοσὶ ἔπραξεν, οὐκ ἂν δυναίμην
ἔτι ζῆν.

ἐν δὲ τούτῳ καταπλεῖ δεῦρο ἐξ Ἑλλησπόντου Ἡγήσανδρος, οὗ τὸν
τρόπον ἄδικον ὄντα καὶ ὀλίγωρον ὑμεῖς ἴστε κάλλιον ἢ ἐγώ. εἰσφοιτῶν δ᾽
οὗτος ὡς τὸν Πιττάλακον συγκυβευτὴν ὄντα, καὶ Τίμαρχον ἐκεῖ πρῶτον
ἰδών, ἐβούλετο ὡς αὐτὸν ἀναλαβεῖν. καὶ γὰρ ἡγήσατο αὐτὸν ἐγγὺς εἶναι
τῆς αὐτοῦ φύσεως.

*The jilted Pittalakos, trying to get Timarkhos back, is beaten up for his pains
and next day takes refuge at an altar, where Timarkhos appeases him.*

ὡς δ᾽ ἀπηλλάγη μὲν παρὰ τοῦ Πιτταλάκου, ἀνελήφθη δὲ ὑπὸ
Ἡγησάνδρου, ὠργίσθη ὁ Πιττάλακος, γνοὺς τοσοῦτον ἀργύριον μάτην
ὑπὲρ Τιμάρχου καταθείς, καὶ ἐφοίτα ἐπὶ τὴν οἰκίαν τὴν Ἡγησάνδρου
πολλάκις. ὅτε δ᾽ αὐτῷ ὠργίζοντο φοιτῶντι Ἡγήσανδρος καὶ Τίμαρχος,
εἰσπηδήσαντες νύκτωρ εἰς τὴν οἰκίαν οὗ ᾤκει ὁ Πιττάλακος, πρῶτον
μὲν συνέτριβον τὰ σκεύη, τέλος δὲ αὐτὸν τὸν Πιττάλακον ἔτυπτον πολὺν
χρόνον. τῇ δ᾽ ὑστεραίᾳ, ὀργισθεὶς τῷ πράγματι ὁ Πιττάλακος ἔρχεται
γυμνὸς εἰς τὴν ἀγορὰν καὶ καθίζει ἐπὶ τὸν βωμὸν τὸν τῆς μητρὸς τῶν
θεῶν. ὄχλου δὲ συνδραμόντος, ὅ τε Ἡγήσανδρος καὶ ὁ Τίμαρχος
τρέχουσι πρὸς τὸν βωμὸν καὶ περιστάντες ἐδέοντο τοῦ Πιτταλάκου
ἀναστῆναι, φάσκοντες τὸ ὅλον πρᾶγμα παροινίαν γενέσθαι. καὶ αὐτὸς ὁ
Τίμαρχος ἔφασκε πάντα πραχθήσεσθαι ὑφ᾽ αὑτοῦ, τοῦ Πιτταλάκου
ἀναστάντος. τέλος πείθουσιν αὐτὸν ἀναστῆναι ἀπὸ τοῦ βωμοῦ.

Vocabulary

ἀπηλλάγη aor. pass. of	μάτην to no purpose
ἀπαλλάττω release	φοιτάω *cf.* εἰσφοιτάω
διημερεύω spend one's days	νύκτωρ at night
κυβεῖον, τό casino,	συντρίβω smash up
gambling-den (2b)	ὑστεραία, ἡ next day (1b)
κυβευτής, ὁ gambler (1d)	γυμνός ή όν naked
ζῆν inf. of ζάω live	ὄχλος, ὁ crowd (2a)
ὀλίγωρος ον disdainful	φάσκω assert
εἰσφοιτάω go into	παροινία, ἡ drunken
συγκυβευτής *cf.* κυβευτής	behaviour (1b)
φύσις, ἡ nature (3e)	

Section Twelve

Vocabulary for Section Twelve A

Αἰγιλ-εύς, ὁ of the deme Aigileia (3g)

ἀκολασί-α, ἡ extravagance (1b)

ἄν (+aor. indic.) 'would have . . .'

ἀναιρέ-ομαι (ἀνελ-) take away

ἀπέδρα 3rd s. aor. of ἀποδιδράσκω

ἀποδιδράσκ-ω (ἀποδρα-) run off

ἀποδίδω-μι (ἀποδο-) return, give back

ἀποπέμπ-ω send away, divorce

ἀφίστα-μαι give up any claim to (+gen.)

γαμέ-ω (γημ-) marry

γνήσι-ος -α -ον legitimate

διαλλάττ-ομαι πρός be reconciled with

ἐγγυά-ω engage, promise

εἰ (+aor. ind.) 'if . . . had —ed . . .'

ἐκβάλλ-ω (ἐκβαλ-) divorce

ἐκδίδω-μι (ἐκδο-) give in marriage

ἐκπίπτ-ω (ἐκπεσ-) be divorced

ἐνιαυτ-ός, ὁ year (2a)

ἐξαπατηθῆναι 'had been deceived' (ἐξαπατάω)

ἐξεδόθη aor. pass. of ἐκδίδωμι

ἐξελέγχ-ω convict

ἐπιδείκνυ-μι (ἐπιδειξ-) show, demonstrate

ἐργάτ-ης, ὁ working man (1d)

ζημί-α, ἡ penalty (1b)

ἠπίστατο impf. of ἐπίσταμαι know how to (+inf.)

καὶ δή and really, and as a matter of fact

καταμαρτυρέ-ω give evidence against (+gen.)

κατεγγυά-ω demand securities from

κινδυνεύ-ω run a risk of (+inf.)

κόρ-η, ἡ maiden, girl (1a)

κόσμι-ος -α -ον well-behaved

κυέ-ω be pregnant

λαγχάν-ω (λαχ-) bring (suit) against (+dat.)

Μέγαρα, τά Megara (2b)

μν-ᾶ, ἡ mina (=60 drachmas) (1b)

περιπίπτ-ω (περιπεσ-) meet with (+dat.)

πολέμαρχ-ος, ὁ the Polemarch (2a) (magistrate dealing with lawsuits involving aliens)

πρίν before (+inf.)

προίξ (προικ-), ἡ dowry (3a)

πρός (+dat.) before

πυνθάν-ομαι (πυθ-) learn, hear

Στρυβήλ-η, ἡ Strybele (1a) (Phano's former name)

συλλέγ-ομαι make, collect

τριάκοντα thirty (indecl.)

ὑβρίζ-ω treat disgracefully

ὑβρισθῆναι 'had been treated disgracefully' (aor. pass. inf. of ὑβρίζω)

Φανοῦς Phano (gen. s.) (see List of Proper Names for full declension)

Φανώ Phano (acc. s.) (see List of Proper Names for full declension)

Φράστωρ (Φραστορ-), ὁ Phrastor (3a) (Phano's husband)

φύσ-ις, ἡ nature, temperament (3e)

Vocabulary to be learnt

ἀποδίδωμι (ἀποδο-) give
back, return
ἀποπέμπω send away, divorce
ἀφίσταμαι
(ἀποστα-) relinquish claim
to; revolt from
ἐγγυάω engage, promise
ἐκβάλλω (ἐκβαλ-) throw out;
divorce
ἐκδίδωμι (ἐκδο-) give in
marriage

ἐκπίπτω (ἐκπεσ-) be thrown
out, divorced
ἐξελέγχω convict, refute,
expose
ζημία, ἡ fine (1b)
ἠπιστάμην impf. of
ἐπίσταμαι know how to
(+inf.)
καὶ δή and really; as a matter of
fact; let us suppose; there!
look!

κατεγγυάω demand securities
from (+acc.)
κόρη, ἡ maiden, girl (1a)
μνᾶ, ἡ mina (60 drachmas) (1b)
προίξ (προικ-), ἡ dowry (3a)
ὑβρίζω treat violently,
disgracefully
φύσις, ἡ nature, temperament,
character (3e)

Vocabulary for Section Twelve B

ἄν (+aor. ind.) 'would
have ...'
ἀναλαμβάν-ω take back
ἀνθρώπιν-ος -η -ον human,
mortal
ἄπαις (ἀπαιδ-) childless
ἀπέθανεν aor. of ἀποθνῃσκω
(ἀποθαν-) die
ἀσθενέ-ω fall ill
γεννήτ-ης, ὁ member of genos
(a smaller grouping of families
within the phratry) (1d)
γνήσι-ος -α -ον legitimate
διατίθε-μαι be put in x (adv.)
state
διαφορ-ά, ἡ disagreement,
differences (1b)
εἰ (+aor. ind.) 'if ... had
–ed'
ἐκπέμπ-ω divorce

ἐοικ-ώς (ἐοικοτ-) reasonable
ἐπιμελέ-ομαι take care of
(+gen.)
ἐπισκοπέ-ομαι visit
ἐρῆμος -ον lacking in (+gen.)
ἔτεκε see τίκτω
ἔχ-ω (+adv.) be (in x
condition)
θεραπεύ-ω look after
κάμν-ω be ill
κυέ-ω be pregnant
λογισμ-ός, ὁ calculation (2a)
μῖσ-ος, τό hatred (3c)
οἰκεῖ-ος, ὁ relative (2a)
ὀργ-ή, ἡ anger (1a)
παλαι-ός -ά -όν of old
παροῦσα being with (+dat.)
(part. of πάρειμι)
περιγίγν-ομαι survive
πονηρῶς poorly

πρίν before (+inf.)
προθύμως readily, actively
πρόσφορ-ος -ον useful for
(+dat.)
τίκτ-ω (τεκ-) bear
τῶν θεραπευσόντων 'of those
who would look after him'
ὑγιαίν-ω be healthy, well
ὑπισχνέ-ομαι
(ὑποσχ-) promise (to)
(+fut. inf.)
φράτηρ (φρατερ-), ὁ member
of phratry (family group)
(3a)
ψυχαγωγέ-ω win over
ὡς (+fut. part.) in order to
ὡς θεραπεύσουσαι καὶ ...
ἐπιμελησόμεναι 'to look
after and take care of'
(nom. pl. f.)

Vocabulary to be learnt

ἀναλαμβάνω (ἀναλαβ-) take
back, take up
ἄπαις (ἀπαιδ-) childless
ἐκπέμπω send out, divorce
ἐπιμελέομαι care for (+gen.)
ἐρῆμος ον empty, deserted;
devoid of (+gen.)
ἔχω (+adv.) be (in X
condition)

λογισμός, ὁ calculation (2a)
μῖσος, τό hatred (3c)
οἰκεῖος, ὁ relative (2a)
οἰκεῖος α ον related, domestic,
family
ὀργή, ἡ anger (1a)
παλαιός ά όν ancient, old, of old
πρίν (+inf.) before

πρόθυμος -ον ready, eager,
willing, active
φράτηρ (φρατερ-), ὁ member
of a phratry (a group of
families with certain
religious and social
functions) (3a)
ὡς (+fut. part.) in order to

O   Grammar for Section Twelve A–B

Summary:
Aor. inf. pass.
Fut. part.
ὡς +fut. part.
πρίν+inf.

Verbs

Aorist infinitive passive παυσθῆναι *'to be stopped'*

158 The form of the aorist passive infinitive is as follows:
παυσθῆ-ναι 'to be stopped'

Note
The formation depends on the aorist passive stem+(η)ναι. Cf.
ἠδικήθην – ἀδικηθῆναι
ἐγράφην – γραφῆναι.
Cf. aor. pass. at **143.**

Future participle active, middle, passive: παύσων *'about to stop' etc.*

159 The forms of the future participles are as follows:

Active:	παύσ-ων -ουσα -ον (-οντ-)	'about to stop'
Middle:	παυσ-όμεν-ος -η -ον	'about to stop'
Passive:	παυσθη-σόμεν-ος -η -ον	'about to be stopped'

Notes
(i) The meanings of the future participle are 'about to . . ., on the point of . . ., intending to . . .'.
(ii) The future active and middle are based on the future stem, to which present participle endings (active or middle) are added.
The future passive participle, like the infinitive and indicative (see **157***), is based on the future passive stem, e.g.*
παύω – (ἐπαύσθην)→παυσθήσομαι→παυσθησόμενος

ὡς +future participle 'in order to'

160 Observe the use of ὡς +future participle to denote *purpose* (lit. 'as on the point of –') 'with the intention of –, in order to –'. As you have already met in accusative and infinitive/participle constructions (**146, 156**), if the subject of the ὡς clause is the same as the main verb, the participle will go into the nominative; if different, into the accusative, e.g.

ἦλθον ὡς ἄξων Νέαιραν 'I came with the intention of taking Neaira'

Note

From now on, the Greek practice of changing the subject in certain clauses to the accusative if it is different from the subject of the main verb (or leaving it in the nominative (or not quoting it at all) if it is the same) will be referred to as 'Change of subject in the accusative'.

πρίν **'before'**

161 πρίν means 'before' and takes an infinitive, e.g. πρὶν ἀπελθεῖν 'before departing'. The tense of the infinitive has no temporal, only aspectual, force. Change of subject in the accusative, e.g.

πρὶν ἀπελθεῖν εὔξαντο 'before they left, they prayed'
ἀφικόμην πρὶν Νέαιραν Ἀθήναζε ἐλθεῖν 'I arrived before Neaira went to Athens'

○

Exercises for Section Twelve B

(b/c) Morphology and Syntax

1. Pick out from the following list the future participles. Give their 1st s. pres. ind. form and its meaning:

ἐκβαλοῦντι, λαβούσης, ἐντευξομένη, εἰσαχθησόμενος, θωπεύσαντος, ὑπαρξάσας, καταστήσοντι, παρέξοντες, τιμῶσα, ἐκδώσοντα, ἀδικηθεῖσι, ἐρῶν, θησόντων, καταφρονοῦντες, ἀφαιρησόμενος, ἀγωνισαμέναις, γνωσομένην, ὀλέσασι, λήσουσαν, ἑλόν, ἐσόμενον, ἀναγκασθησομένῳ, ἐπιδειξουσῶν, πευσομένων, γραψαμένῳ, ἀποθανουμένῃ, παραληψομένῃ, ἐργασαμένους, ἐκπεσούμενοι, ἐκπέμποντι

2. Pick out from this list aorist passive infs. Give their pres. ind. form. What verbs do the other infs. in the list belong to?

εἶναι, πεισθῆναι, ἐκπεμφθῆναι, εἰδέναι, ἀποδιδόναι, ἐξαπατηθῆναι, θεῖναι, ἐξελεγχθῆναι, δεικνύναι, ἀπολλύναι, ὑβρισθῆναι, ἐκβληθῆναι, ἀποδοῦναι, ἀφιστάναι, διατεθῆναι, τιθέναι

3. Translate these sentences, changing the form of the bracketed word to fut. part., to complete the sense:

a. ἦλθον ἐκεῖνοι ἐπὶ τὴν οἰκίαν τὴν Στεφάνου ὡς (ἄγω) τὴν Νέαιραν.
b. ἀπῆλθον αἱ γυναῖκες Ἀθήναζε ὡς (διατρίβω) ἐν τῇ Στεφάνου οἰκίᾳ καὶ (ἐργάζομαι).

c. βαδίζω οὖν πρὸς αὐτὸν ὡς (λέγω) ἀληθῆ καὶ (ἀκούω) ψευδῆ.

d. εἰσῆλθεν εἰς τὸ δικαστήριον ὁ ἀνὴρ ὡς (ἀπολογέομαι) καὶ (ἀπολύομαι).

4. Translate the introductory statement and each of the bracketed sentences; then change the bracketed sentences into πρίν+inf. clauses, dependent upon the introductory statement. Translate your answers:

a. ὁ Στέφανος εἰσήγαγεν εἰς τὸ δικαστήριον τὸν Φράστορα

   (i) (ὁ Φράστωρ ἐγράψατο γραφήν)

   (ii) (τὸ τῆς Φανοῦς παιδίον ἐγένετο)

   (iii) (τὸ παιδίον ἀνελήφθη ὑπὸ Φράστορος)

   (iv) (ἔγνω ὅτι ἐξελεγχθήσεται ἀδικῶν)

b. ὁ Φράστωρ ἀνείλετο τὴν γραφὴν

   (i) (εἰσῆλθεν εἰς τὸ δικαστήριον)

   (ii) (ἐξέπεμπε τὴν Φανώ)

   (iii) (ὑπισχνεῖται ἀναλήψεσθαι τὸ παιδίον)

   (iv) (ἐλέχθησαν οὗτοι οἱ λόγοι ὑπὸ τῆς Νεαίρας)

Vocabulary for Section Twelve C

ἀδελφ-ή, ἡ sister (1a)
ἄν (+aor. ind.) 'would have'
ἀποψηφίζ-ομαι vote against, reject (+gen.)
ἀσθένει-α, ἡ illness (1b)
ἀσθενέ-ω be ill
Βρύτιδ-ες, οἱ the Brytidai (3a) (name of genos to which Phrastor belonged)
γεννήτ-ης, ὁ member of genos (1d)
γέν-ος, τό genos (a smaller group of families within the phratry) (3c)
γνήσι-ος -α -ον legitimate
Δίφιλ-ος, ὁ Diphilos (2a) (the brother of Phrastor's new wife)

ἐγγράφ-ω enlist, register
ἐγγυητ-ός -ή -όν legally married
εἰ (+aor. ind.) 'if . . . had –ed'
ἐκ-ών -οῦσα -όν willing(ly)
ἐπιδείκνυ-μι (ἐπιδειξ-) show, prove
ἦ μήν indeed, truly
θεραπεύ-ω tend, look after
ἱερ-ά, τά sacrifices (2b)
κατά (+gen.) by, in name of
λαγχάν-ω (λαχ-) bring (suit) against (+dat.)
λείπ-ω (λιπ-) leave, abandon
Μελιτ-εύς, ὁ of the deme Melite (3g)

νοσέ-ω be sick
ὄμνυ-μι (ὀμοσ-) swear
περιφαν-ής -ές very evident
πράττ-ω (πραξ-) do
προκαλέ-ομαι challenge
Σάτυρ-ος, ὁ Satyros (2a) (father of Phrastor's new wife)
τέλει-ος -α -ον perfect, unblemished
τό+inf.=noun
τὸ ἄπαις εἶναι childlessness
τὸ ἀσθενεῖν illness
τὸ θεραπεύειν care, looking after
τὸ μισεῖν hating, hatred
τὸ νοσεῖν being sick, illness
ὡς τάχιστα as soon as

Vocabulary to be learnt

ἀσθένεια, ἡ illness, weakness (1b)
ἀσθενέω be ill, fall ill
γεννήτης, ὁ member of genos (1d)
γένος, τό genos (smaller groupings of families

within the phratry) (3c)
γνήσιος α ον legitimate, genuine
ἐγγράφω enrol, enlist, register
ἑκών οὖσα όν willing(ly)
ἐπιδείκνυμι (ἐπιδειξ-) prove, show, demonstrate
θεραπεύω look after, tend

λαγχάνω (δίκην) (λαχ-) bring (suit) against, obtain by lot, run as candidate for office
λείπω (λιπ-) leave, abandon
νοσέω be sick
ὄμνυμι (ὀμοσ-) swear

O   Grammar for Section Twelve C

Summary:
Past unfulf. cond.

Conditional sentences with ἄν

162 You have already met 'future remote conditions' (**151**) and 'present unfulfilled conditions' (**152**), the former indicated by an optative in both clauses, the latter by an imperfect in both clauses, and both showing ἄν in the main clause.

Past unfulfilled conditions show an AORIST INDICATIVE in both clauses, with ἄν in the main clause, and take the form 'If x *had –,* y *would have resulted'* e.g.

εἰ ἡμᾶς ἔπεισας, ἠκούσαμεν ἄν 'if you had persuaded us, we would have listened'.

Notes
(i) That completes unfulfilled conditions. Note that one can have mixed conditions, e.g. 'If I had done this, I would now be happy', and in these cases Greek follows the individual rules for each clause separately – in this case, the 'if' clause would be aorist, the main clause imperfect.

(ii) Where no ἄν appears, translate normally, without using 'would', 'should', etc., e.g.
εἰ σοφός εἰμι ἐγώ, σὺ μῶρος εἶ 'if I am wise, you are foolish'
(On conditionals in general, Reference Grammar O; and Language Survey (6).)

O

Exercises for Section Twelve C

1. Translate each pair of statements (omitting εἰ), then link the two statements by making them into past conditions with ἄν:

a. *(εἰ) ἄπαις ἀποθνῄσκει Φράστωρ|οἱ οἰκεῖοι λαμβάνουσι τὰ αὐτοῦ*

b. *(εἰ) ἀστῆς θυγάτηρ ἐστὶ Φανώ|οὐκ ὀργίζεται Στέφανος*

c. *(εἰ) οἶδε Φανὼ Νεαίρας οὖσαν θυγατέρα ὁ Φράστωρ|ἐκβάλλει ὡς τάχιστα αὐτήν*

d. *(εἰ) Φανὼ ξένης θυγάτηρ καλεῖται|Φράστωρ οὐκ ἐξαπατᾶται*

e. *(εἰ) οὐ λαγχάνει Στέφανος τὴν δίκην ταύτην|οὐ γράφεται Φράστωρ αὐτὸν γραφήν*

Vocabulary for Section Twelve D

ἀποψηφίζ-ομαι reject, vote
against (+gen.)
γαμέ-ω (γημ-) marry
ἐπιδεικνύ-ω = ἐπιδείκνυ-μι
καταμαρτυρέ-ω give
evidence against (+gen.)

μαρτυρέ-ω give evidence,
bear witness
περιφαν-ής -ές very clear
πρᾶξ-ις, ἡ deed, action, fact
(3e)
τό + inf. = noun

τὸ ἄπαις εἶναι childlessness
τὸ ἀποψηφίζεσθαι rejection
τὸ μὴ ἐθέλειν|ἐθελῆσαι not
wanting, refusal

Vocabulary to be learnt
ἀποψηφίζομαι reject (+gen.)
γαμέω (γημ-) marry
καταμαρτυρέω give evidence
against (+gen.)

μαρτυρέω give evidence, bear
witness
περιφανής ές very clear

O   Grammar for Section Twelve D

Summary:
τό + inf.

Infinitives as nouns

163 τό + infinitive fulfils the function of a noun, e.g.
τὸ φιλεῖν, or τὸ φιλῆσαι   'loving, love'
τὸ μισεῖν   'hatred, hating'
They are used exactly as nouns are in Greek, e.g.
διὰ τὸ μισεῖν   'because of his hatred'
τῷ μὴ ἀδικεῖν   'by not committing a crime'
τοῦ ἀπολογεῖσθαι ἕνεκα   'for the sake of his defence'
τὸ πλούσιον εἶναι   'wealth'

164 Observe that, since the infinitive is a *verb*-form, it can have a subject; and the change of subject in the accusative rule applies, e.g.
Νέαιρα ἀπῆλθε διὰ τὸ κακοδαίμων εἶναι 'Neaira left because she was unlucky'
Νέαιρα ἀπῆλθε διὰ τὸ Φράστορα μισεῖν αὐτήν 'Neaira left because Phrastor hated her'

Note

Pay attention, as far as is possible, to the aspectual sense of the verb. Thus τὸ φιλεῖν *means 'loving' (permanently), while* τὸ φιλῆσαι *means demonstrating* φιλία *by an act, e.g. 'kissing'. By using the article with the infinitive, it was possible to indicate differences of aspect which nouns could not indicate.*   O

Exercises for Section Twelve D

(b/c) Morphology and Syntax

1. Translate each sentence, then convert the underlined words or clauses into expressions using τό, τοῦ, τῷ +inf.:

a. <u>κακόν ἐστιν ἡ ἀσθενεία</u>

b. Φράστωρ ἀνέλαβε τὸ παιδίον <u>διὰ τὴν νόσον</u> καὶ <u>τὸ μῖσος τὸ πρὸς τοὺς οἰκείους</u> καὶ τὴν ἀπαιδίαν.

c. Στέφανος δῆλος ἦν ἀδικῶν, <u>διότι οὐκ ὤμοσεν.</u>

d. φανερόν ἐστι τὸ παιδίον ξένης ὄν, <u>διότι οἱ γεννῆται ἀπεψηφίσαντο αὐτοῦ καὶ οὐκ ἐνέγραψαν εἰς τὸ γένος.</u>

e. οἱ δὲ γεννῆται ἐβιάσθησαν ἀποψηφίσασθαι τοῦ παιδίου, <u>διότι ᾔδεσαν αὐτὸν οὐ γνήσιον ὄντα.</u>

f. <u>ἀγαθόν ἐστιν ἡ θεραπεία.</u>

g. καὶ μνείαν ἐποιήσατο τούτων, <u>ὅτι ἠσθένει</u> καὶ <u>εἰς ἀπορίαν κατέστη</u> καὶ <u>ὅτι ὑπὸ Νεαίρας ἐθεραπεύετο.</u>

h. <u>μέγα γὰρ κακόν ἐστιν ἡ ἀσέβεια.</u>

i. ἠναγκάσθην εἰσελθεῖν <u>βιαζόμενος.</u>

(d) English into Greek
Translate into Greek:

1. Stephanos went to Phrastor, intending to promise him Phano in marriage.

2. Phrastor married Phano before he knew she was Neaira's daughter.

3. If Phano had not looked after Phrastor, he would not have taken back the child.

4. Phrastor took back Phano's child because of his being ill and because of Phano's looking after him.

5. If the child had been legitimate, Phrastor would have sworn the oath.

Vocabulary for Section Twelve E

ἅγι-ος -α -ον holy
ἄκυρ-ος -ον invalid
ἀναίδει -α, ἡ shamelessness (1b)
ἄπειρ-ος -ον inexperienced in (+gen.)

ἀπόρρητ-ος -ον forbidden
ἄρρητ-ος -ον secret, mysterious
ἀρχ-ή, ἡ office, position (1a)
ἀσεβ-ής -ές unholy, impious
βασιλ-εύς, ὁ basileus archon

(3g) (state officer, in charge of certain important religious rites)
βασιλεύ-ω be basileus
δεδήλωκ-α I have shown (δηλό-ω)

διηγέ-ομαι explain
Διόνυσ-ος, ὁ Dionysos (2a)
(*god of nature, especially of wine*)
ἔθ-ος, τό manner, habits (3c)
ἐμφαν-ής -ές open
εὐγεν-ής -ές well-born, aristocratic
εὐλάβει-α, ἡ respect (1b)
Θεογέν-ης, ὁ Theogenes (3d)
(*Phano's husband for a short while*)

ἱερ-ά, τά rites, sacrifice (2b)
καταπεφρόνηκ-ε(ν) he has despised (καταφρονέω)
λαγχάν-ω (λαχ-) run as (candidate for office)
μετέχ-ω take part in (+gen.)
οἷ (to) where
ὁποῖ-ος -α -ον of what sort
ὅτου=οὗτινος (ὅστις)
πάρεδρ-ος, ὁ assistant (2a)
πάτρι-α, τά ancestral rites (2b)

πεποίηκ-ε(ν) (she) has done (ποιέω)
πρᾶξ-ις, ἡ fact, action (3e)
πράττ-ω (πραξ-) do, act
προσήκ-ει it is fitting, right (for, +dat.)
τέθυκ-ε(ν) (she) has sacrificed (θύω)
φάσκ-ω allege, claim

Vocabulary to be learnt

ἄπειρος ον inexperienced in (+gen.)
ἀρχή, ἡ position, office; start; rule (1a)
ἀσεβής ές unholy
βασιλεύς, ὁ king, king archon (3g)

βασιλεύω be king, be king archon
ἐμφανής ές open, obvious
ἔθος, τό manner, habit (3c)
ἱερά, τά rites, sacrifices (2b)
οἷ (to) where

ὁποῖος α ον of what kind
πρᾶξις, ἡ fact, action (3e)
πράττω (πραξ-) do, perform, fare

○ # Grammar for Section Twelve E

Summary:
Perf. ind. act.

Verbs

The perfect indicative active πέπαυκα '*I have stopped*'

165 The forms of the perfect indicative active are as follows:
πέπαυκ-α   'I have stopped'
πέπαυκ-ας
πέπαυκ-ε(ν)
πεπαύκ-αμεν
πεπαύκ-ατε
πεπαύκ-ασι(ν)

Notes
(i) *At an early stage of the language, the perfect meant '*I am in the position of having –ed*', i.e. there is a strong* present *force to it, e.g.*
τέθνηκα (θνῄσκω) '*I am dead*' cf. ὄλωλα (*perfect of* ὄλλυμι) *meaning '*I am done for, ruined*'*
ἕστηκα (ἵσταμαι) '*I am standing*' (cf. **144** (ii))

In Classical Greek, it also acquired the meaning 'I have –ed' (a meaning often associated, though not exclusively, with the -κα suffix). Sometimes the same perfect form can have both forces. It is important to bear the early meaning in mind.
*(ii) The mark of the perfect is the reduplicated stem. This is in fact a feature you have already met with the -μι verbs (e.g. δο, διδο; θε, τιθε), so it is not wholly new. This reduplication is maintained throughout all the forms (participle, infinitive, etc.) and is not dropped as, for example, the augment is for non-indicative forms of the aorist. Verbs reduplicate after prefixes (cf. on augments **59** note (iv)).*
(iii) Observe the following patterns of reduplication:
  (a) normal:
      παύω – πέπαυκα   *'I have stopped'*
      λύω – λέλυκα   *'I have released'*
  (b) θ, φ, χ reduplicate with τ, π, κ, e.g.
      θύω – τέθυκα   *'I have sacrificed'*
      φαίνω – πέφηνα   *'I have revealed'*
      χαίρω – κεχάρηκα *'I have rejoiced'*
(iv) Note the perfect of δίδωμι→δέδωκα 'I have given', of τίθημι→τέθηκα 'I have placed', and of δείκνυμι→δέδειχα 'I have shown'. Their forms in the perfect are entirely regular.   ○

Exercises for Section Twelve E

(b/c) Morphology and Syntax

1. Write down the perfect reduplication of the following verbs, going no further than the first three letters (e.g. for θύω, write τεθ-: do *not* count prefixes):

   τιμάω, θωπεύω, μαρτυρέω, γίγνομαι, φαίνομαι, πυνθάνομαι,
   ἐπιδημέω, ἐπιδείκνυμι, καλέω, τίθημι, πείθω, ἐκβάλλω, γράφω,
   ἐκπέμπω, πράττω, βιάζομαι, λείπω, λύω, νικάω, χράομαι, φύω, γαμέω

2. Translate and give the 1st s. pres. ind. act. form of each of these regular perfects (consulting the Greek–English vocabulary where necessary). Change singulars to plural and vice-versa:

   λελύκασι, μεμαρτυρήκατε, νενίκηκε, τετιμήκαμεν, ἐπιδεδήμηκας,
   γέγραφα, βεβοήκατε, κεκέλευκε, πεπράχαμεν, πεφίληκα, κεχώρηκας,
   πεφροντίκασι

Vocabulary for Section Twelve F

ἀκακί-α, ἡ innocence (1b)
ἄκακ-ος -ον innocent
ἄνθρωπ-ος, ἡ woman (2a)
ἀντιβολέ-ω entreat
ἀπελαύν-ω exclude, reject
Ἀρεοπαγίτ-ης, ὁ member of
  the Areopagos council (1d)
Ἄρε-ος πάγ-ος, ὁ Areopagos
  hill (2a) (where the council
  met)
ἄρρητ-ος -ον secret,
  mysterious
ἄρχων (ἀρχοντ-), ὁ archon (3a)
βουλ-ή, ἡ council (1a)

διοικέ-ω administer
ἐλεέ-ω pity
ἐννέα nine (indecl.)
ἐξαπατηθείη he was deceived
  (ἐξαπατάω)
ἐπέχ-ω (ἐπισχ-) hold off
ζημιό-ω fine
ἱκετεύ-ω beg
κηδεύ-ω ally oneself by
  marriage to (+dat.)
κρίν-ω judge, accuse
πάρεδρ-ος, ὁ assistant (2a)
πρόνοιαν ποιέ-ομαι show
  concern

πυνθάν-ομαι (πυθ-) learn,
  hear, discover
συνέδρι-ον, τό council board
  (2b)
ὑπισχνέ-ομαι
  (ὑποσχ-) promise
φαίν-ομαι (+inf.) seem
  to – (but not in fact to –)
χαλεπῶς φέρ-ω be angry,
  displeased
ψεύδ-ομαι lie

Vocabulary to be learnt

ἄνθρωπος, ἡ woman (2a)
ἄρχων (ἀρχοντ-), ὁ archon
  (3a)
βουλή, ἡ council (1a)
διοικέω administer, run

ἱκετεύω beg, supplicate
κρίνω (κριν-) judge, decide
πυνθάνομαι (πυθ-) learn, hear
  by inquiry

φαίνομαι (+inf.) seem
  to – (but not in fact to –)
χαλεπῶς φέρω be angry at,
  displeased with
ψεύδομαι lie, tell lies

O   Grammar for Section Twelve F

Summary:
Aor. opt. pass.
Opt. in indir. sp.
Fut. opt.

Verbs

The aorist optative passive παυσθείην

166 The forms of the aorist passive optative are as follows:

παυσθ-είην
παυσθ-είης
παυσθ-είη
παυσθ-εῖμεν
παυσθ-εῖτε
παυσθ-εῖεν

Note
Look for these by the presence of the aorist passive stem in -θ- with the endings dominated by -ει-.

Use of the optative in indirect speech

167 Indirect speech which uses the indicative after (for example) ὅτι 'that' can use the *optative* in place of the indicative *(without altering the meaning at all)* when the verb introducing the indirect speech is imperfect or aorist. The optative will adopt the same tense as the indicative and will, like the indicative, indicate what the speaker himself actually said, e.g.

Indicative: ἔλεξεν ὅτι ἐπαύσατο	'he said that he had stopped'
Optative: ἔλεξεν ὅτι παύσαιτο	
Indicative: ἤδη ὅτι παύσεται	'I knew that he would stop'
Optative: ἤδη ὅτι παύσοιτο	

Note
From now on we will use the term 'secondary sequence' to mean that the main verb *of the sentence is* imperfect or aorist, *and the term 'primary sequence' to mean that the* main verb of the sentence is *present, future or perfect. (Cf. also Reference Grammar K, p. 301.)*

Future optative παύσοιμι, παυσοίμην

168 The forms of the future optative are, in the active and middle, the same as for the present, but based on the future stem, e.g.

Active: παύσ-οιμι, παύσ-οις, *etc.* } Cf. **95**
Middle: παυσ-οίμην, παύσ-οιο, *etc.*

For the passive, they are like the present middle but based on the future passive stem, i.e.

Passive: παυσθησ-οίμην, παυσθήσ-οιο, *etc.*

Note
The future optative is used only in indirect speech as indicated in **167**. *Distinguish carefully* παύοιμι *(pres.),* παύσοιμι *(fut.) and* παύσαιμι *(aor.).* ○

Exercises for Section Twelve F

(b/c) Morphology and Syntax
1. Translate these sentences, then change the subordinate verbs from indicative to optative:
   a. οἱ δικασταὶ ἤροντο ὅ τι ἔπραξεν ὁ Στέφανος καὶ ὁποία ἦν ἡ ἀσέβεια ἡ τῆς Νεαίρας καὶ ὅπως τὴν πόλιν ἠδίκησεν.

b. οὐ γὰρ ᾔδει ὁ Θεογένης ὅτου θυγάτηρ ἐστὶ οὐδὲ ὅτι ἠργάζετο τῷ σώματι.

c. Θεογένης εἶπεν ὅτι οὐκ ᾔδει ὁποῖοι ἦσαν οἱ τῆς Φανοῦς τρόποι καὶ ὅτι ἐπείσθη ὑπὸ Στεφάνου ποιεῖν τοῦτο.

d. ἡ βουλὴ χαλεπῶς ἔφερεν τὸ πρᾶγμα, ὅτι Φανὼ ἐξεδόθη τῷ Φράστορι καὶ ὡς τὰ ἱερὰ ὑπὲρ τῆς πόλεως ἐπράχθη ὑπὸ ξένης.

e. ἆρ' οὐκ ἤκουες ὡς εἰς τὸ δικαστήριον εἰσήλθομεν καὶ ὡς ἐκεῖνοι οἱ ἄνδρες κατεδικάσθησαν καὶ ἅττα ἐλέχθη ἐν τῇ κατηγορίᾳ;

Vocabulary

ἅττα = ἅτινα

2. Translate the following questions, then turn them into indirect questions, using ἠρόμην as the introductory verb, and altering direct question words to indirect (see 66 and 136), and indicative verbs to optative e.g:
τί ἔπραξεν ὁ Στέφανος; = ἠρόμην ὅ τι πράξειεν ὁ Στέφανος.

a. τίς ταῦτα ἐποίησεν;
b. πῶς ἔπραξεν οἱ ἄρχοντες;
c. τίς ἦν ἡ γυνὴ ἡ Θεογένους;
d. ποία γυνὴ ἦν ἡ Φανώ;
e. πόθεν ἐξέβαλε τὴν γυναῖκα ὁ Θεογένης;

Vocabulary for Section Twelve G

αἰσχρ-ός -ά -όν base, shameful
ἀποφαίνωσι (they) display (ἀποφαίνω)
γεγένημαι I have become, been (γίγνομαι)
διαπράττ-ομαι do
διαπεπραγμένον having done (διαπράττομαι)
διαπεπρᾶχθαι to have done (διαπράττομαι)
εἰκότως reasonably
εὐεργεσί-α, ἡ good service, public service (1b)
καθεστῶτα having been made (καθίσταμαι)

καταπεφρονηκέναι to have despised (καταφρονέω)
λειτουργέ-ω perform (a state duty)
λειτουργί-α, ἡ a state duty (1b)
λελειτουργηκέναι to have performed (λειτουργέω)
νενικηκέναι to have won (νικάω)
οἳ ἄν who(ever)
πολιτεί-α, ἡ state, constitution (1b)
πεπολίτευμαι I have governed (πολιτεύομαι)

πολιτεύ-ομαι govern
πρόγον-ος, ὁ forebear, ancestor (2a)
συμφορ-ά, ἡ disaster (1b)
σφέτερ-ος -α -ον their own
τετριηραρχηκότα having served as trierarch (τριηραρχέω)
τριηραρχέ-ω serve as trierarch
φάσκ-ω allege
φιλότιμ-ος -ον ambitious
χορηγ-ός, ὁ chorus-financier (2a) (a duty which the state imposed on the rich)

Vocabulary to be learnt

αἰσχρός ά όν base, shameful;
ugly (of people) (comp.
αἰσχίων; sup. αἴσχιστος)
διαπράττομαι (διαπραξ-) do,

act, perform
εἰκότως reasonably, rightly
πολιτεία, ἡ state, constitution
(1b)

πολιτεύομαι be a citizen
πρόγονος, ὁ forebear, ancestor
(2a)
φάσκω allege, claim, assert

Vocabulary for Section Twelve H

ἁμαρτάν-ω make a mistake
ἀπόλωλεν he is done for
(ἀπόλλυμι)
γεγενημένην having been
(γίγνομαι)
εἴληφε he has taken
(λαμβάνω)
εἴρηται (it) has been spoken
(λέγω)
εἰσηγμένος having been

introduced (εἰσάγω)
ἰσχυρ-ός -ά -όν strong,
powerful
καταμεμαρτύρηται he has had
evidence brought against
him (καταμαρτυρέω)
κέχρηται he has used
(χράομαι)
παλλακ-ή, ἡ kept slave,
concubine (1a)

πέπρακται (it) has been done
(πράττω)
πεφύκασιν (they) are born to
(φύομαι) (+inf.)
πεφυκυῖαν born (acc. s. f.)
(φύομαι)
φαίν-ω reveal, declare
φύ-ω bear; mid., grow
(ἔφυν=I am naturally)
ὥστε so that; and so

Vocabulary to be learnt

ἁμαρτάνω (ἁμαρτ-) err; do
wrong, make a mistake
ἀπόλωλα (perf. of
ἀπόλλυμαι) I am lost
γεγένημαι (perf. of γίγνομαι) I
have been

ἰσχυρός ά όν strong, powerful
εἴρημαι (perf. of λέγω) I have
been said
καθέστηκα (perf. pass. of
καθίσταμαι) I have been
made, put

εἴληφα (perf. of λαμβάνω) I
have taken
φύω bear; mid., grow; aor. mid.
ἔφυν, perf. πέφυκα be
naturally
φαίνω reveal, declare, indict

Vocabulary for Section Twelve I

ἀκηκόατε you have heard
(ἀκούω)
δίκην δίδωμι (δο-) pay
penalty, be punished
εἴργασται he has done
(ἐργάζομαι)
ἐλάττων (ἐλαττον-) smaller
εὐσεβέ-ω act righteously
ἠδικηκότας having
committed crimes against
(acc. pl. m.)

ἠδικημένοι having been
injured (nom. pl. m.)
(ἀδικέω)
ἠσεβηκέναι to have been
impious (ἀσεβέω)
ἠσεβηκότων having been
impious (gen. pl. m.)
(ἀσεβέω)
ἠσεβηκυῖαν having been
impious (acc. s. f.)
(ἀσεβέω)

καταπεφρονηκέναι to have
despised (καταφρονέω)
μᾶλλον ἤ rather than, more
than
πεφυκότας inclined by nature
(acc. pl. m.) (φύομαι)
τιμωρίαν ποιέ-ομαι take
revenge on (+gen.)
ὑβρισμένοι having been
violently treated (nom. pl.
m.) (ὑβρίζω)

Vocabulary to be learnt

ἀκήκοα *(perf. of ἀκούω) I have heard*

δίκην δίδωμι *(δο-) be punished, pay penalty*

ἐλάττων *(ἐλαττον-) smaller, less, fewer*

εὐσεβέω *act righteously*

μᾶλλον ἤ *rather than; more than*

○ Grammar for Section Twelve G–I

Summary:
Perf. ind. mid./pass.
Perf. inf., part.
Irr. perf.

Verbs

Perfect indicative middle and passive πέπαυμαι *'I have stopped, been stopped'*

169 The forms of the perfect indicative middle and passive are as follows:

πέπαυ-μαι   'I have stopped' *or* 'I have been stopped'
πέπαυ-σαι
πέπαυ-ται
πεπαύ-μεθα
πέπαυ-σθε
πέπαυ-νται (or πεπαυ- μέν-οι -αι εἰσίν)

Notes
(i) Since the middle and passive forms are the same, we shall distinguish passive meaning to start with by the use of ὑπό 'by' or a dative of instrument, 'by, with'.
(ii) There is an alternative third person plural form to -νται- that is, -μένοι εἰσί(ν) (i.e. perfect participle + εἰμί).
(iii) Note that, after a perfect, 'by a person' can be expressed by the DATIVE, e.g. πάνθ' ἡμῖν πεποίηται 'everything has been done by us'.

Perfect infinitives and participles

170 The forms of the perfect infinitives and participles are as follows:

Infinitives

Active: πεπαυκ-έναι 'to have stopped'
Middle/Passive: πεπαῦ-σθαι 'to have stopped/been stopped'

Note
Look for a perfect reduplicated stem + -έναι or -σθαι.

Participles

Active: πεπαυκ-ώς -υῖα -ός (-οτ-) 'having stopped'
Middle/Passive: πεπαυ-μέν-ος -η -ον (n.b. accent) 'having stopped,
                 having been stopped'

Notes
(i) The active participle is of mixed declension, with the m. and n. declining
like *3a* nouns on the stem -οτ- and the *f*. declining like *1b* nouns.
(ii) The middle/passive declines like καλός.

Regular and irregular perfects

171 Note the following perfect forms and changes involved:

(a) Regular changes

ἀσεβέω→ἠσέβηκα   'I have acted impiously'
ἀδικέω→ἠδίκηκα   'I have done wrong'
ὑβρίζω→ὕβρικα   'I have acted aggressively'
ἀγγέλλω→ἤγγελκα   'I have announced'
ζητέω→ἐζήτηκα   'I have sought'
στερέω →ἐστέρηκα   'I have deprived'
ῥίπτω→ἔρριφα   'I have hurled'

(b) Irregular changes

ἔρχομαι→ἐλήλυθα 'I have come'
λαμβάνω→εἴληφα   'I have taken'
λέγω→εἴρηκα   'I have said' (from stem ἐρ – cf. **106**)
φέρω→ἐνήνοχα   'I have carried, endured'
πάσχω→πέπονθα   'I have suffered'
ἵσταμαι→ἔστηκα   'I stand' (participle ἐστ-ώς 'standing,
                 established')

(*Cf. Language Survey (8), p. 318.*)

Note
Cf. perfect ἔστηκα and aorists ἔθηκα, ἔδωκα.

Revise:
Aor. opt. **129** Reference Grammar N
δίδωμι **131**
ἀμελής/γλυκύς **133**
Rels. **134–6**   O

Exercises for Section Twelve I

(b/c) Morphology and Syntax

1. Translate the sentences, then change singular verbs to plural and vice-versa:
   a. εὖ πεπολίτευσαι.
   b. ἠδικήμεθα μεγάλα ὑπὸ Στεφάνου.
   c. οὗτοι οἱ λόγοι ὑπὸ τῆς Νεαίρας εἴρηνται.
   d. τεκμηρίῳ φανερῷ κέχρησθε, ὦ ἄνδρες.
   e. ἐγὼ αὐτὸς καταμεμαρτύρημαι ὑπ' ἐμαυτοῦ.
   f. ἐκεῖνοι δὲ οἱ ἄνδρες ταῦτα διαπεπραγμένοι εἰσίν.
   g. ὁ Φανοῦς παῖς εἴσηκται ὑπὸ Στεφάνου εἰς τοὺς φράτερας.
   h. οὗτοι αἴτιοι γεγενημένοι εἰσὶ πολλῶν κακῶν ἐν τῇ πόλει.
   i. μεγάλα, ὦνδρες, ὕβρισθε καὶ ἠδίκησθε.
   j. τοῦτο δ' εἴργασται ὁ κατήγορος.

2. Use (a) οἶδα (b) φάσκω to change the above sentences into indirect statements using nom./acc. + part. with οἶδα and nom./acc. + inf. with φάσκω (use verbs in 1st s.).

3. Do the same as in 2 with the following sentences:
   a. (ἴσμεν/φαμέν) Στέφανος οὐδέποτε δίκην δέδωκεν.
   b. (εὖ οἶδα/φημί) Φανὼ ξένη πέφυκεν.
   c. (ᾔδεισθα/ἔφασκες) ἡ Νέαιρα ἠσέβηκεν εἰς τοὺς θεούς.
   d. (ἴστε/φατέ) δικασταὶ καθεστήκατε.
   e. (οἶσθα/φῄς) ὡς τὴν αὑτοῦ θυγατέρα τὴν Φανὼ ἐκδέδωκεν ὁ Στέφανος.

(d) English into Greek

1. Sentences
   Translate into Greek:
   1. I have shown that Phano has made sacrifices on behalf of the city.
   2. The council asked what sort of wife the king archon had married.
   3. Theogenes said that he had been deceived by Stephanos.
   4. Stephanos has governed well and performed many noble deeds.
   5. We all know that nothing noble has ever been said or done by Stephanos.

2. Prose
   Translate into Greek:
   Once Phano was proved to be Neaira's daughter, Phrastor divorced her. She, divorced, waited for a short time, intending that Phrastor

should take back her child. And, not long afterwards, Phrastor fell ill. And, because he hated his family and did not want them to get his property, he took back the child before he recovered, not wishing to die childless. Clearly, Phrastor would never have taken back the child had he not fallen ill; for when he recovered, he married a legitimate wife, according to the laws.

Test Exercise Twelve

Translate into English:

Menekles put away his wife, since he could not give her children. But, being childless and aging, he wished to adopt a son. He opted for one of his ex-wife's two brothers. The adopted brother here describes how Menekles made this choice.

(From Isaios, *Menekles*, 10–13, 46–7)

μετὰ δὲ ταῦτα ἐσκόπει ὁ Μενεκλῆς ὅπως μὴ ἔσοιτο ἄπαις, ἀλλ᾽ ἔσοιτο αὐτῷ παῖς, ὅς τις θεραπεύσοι αὐτὸν πρὶν ἀποθανεῖν καὶ τελευτήσαντα θάψοι καὶ εἰς τὸν ἔπειτα χρόνον τὰ νομιζόμενα αὐτῷ ποιήσοι.

ἐπειδὴ οὖν ηὕρισκεν οὐδένα ἄλλον οἰκειότερον ἡμῶν ὄνθ᾽ ἑαυτῷ, λόγους πρὸς ἡμᾶς ἐποιεῖτο, καὶ 'ἡ τύχη', ἔφη, 'οὐκ εἴασε ἐκ τῆς ἀδελφῆς τῆς ὑμετέρας παῖδας ἐμαυτῷ γενέσθαι. οὐ μὴν ἀλλ᾽ ἐκ ταύτης τῆς οἰκίας ἐπαιδοποιησάμην ἄν, εἰ οἷός τ᾽ ἦ. ὑμῶν οὖν βούλομαι τὸν ἕτερον ποιήσασθαι υἱόν.' καὶ ὁ ἀδελφὸς ἐμὸς ἀκούσας ταῦτα ἐπήνεσέ τε τοὺς λόγους αὐτοῦ καὶ εἶπεν ὅτι ὁ Μενεκλῆς διὰ τό τε γέρων εἶναι καὶ τὸ ἐρῆμος εἶναι δέοιτο ἐμοῦ ὡς θεραπεύσοντος αὐτόν. 'ἐγὼ μὲν γάρ', ἔφη, 'ἀεὶ ἀποδημῶ, ὡς σὺ οἶσθα· ὁ δὲ ἀδελφὸς οὑτοσί', ἐμὲ λέγων, 'ὃς ἀεὶ ἐπιδημεῖ, τῶν τε σῶν ἐπιμελήσεται καὶ τῶν ἐμῶν. τοῦτον οὖν ποίησαι υἱόν.' καὶ ὁ Μενεκλῆς καλῶς ἔφη αὐτὸν λέγειν, καὶ οὕτως ἐποιεῖτό με.

The brother, who claims to have looked after Menekles from then until his death, ends his case with a plea to the jurors not to allow his opponent, who is challenging his right to Menekles' property, to take away his estate and leave Menekles without heirs.

ὁ δ᾽ ἀντίδικος οὗτος νυνὶ ἄκληρον μὲν ἐμὲ ποιεῖν, ἄπαιδα δὲ τὸν τελευτήσαντα καὶ ἀνώνυμον βούλεται καταστῆσαι. μὴ οὖν, ὦ ἄνδρες, πεισθέντες ὑπὸ τούτου ἀφαιρεῖσθέ μου τὸ ὄνομα. ἀλλ᾽ ἐπειδὴ τὸ πρᾶγμα εἰς ὑμᾶς ἀφῖκται καὶ ὑμεῖς κύριοι γεγένησθε, βοηθήσατε καὶ ἡμῖν καὶ ἐκείνῳ τῷ ἐν Ἅιδου ὄντι, καὶ μεμνημένοι τοῦ νόμου καὶ τοῦ ὅρκου ὃν ὀμωμόκατε καὶ τῶν εἰρημένων ὑπὲρ τοῦ πράγματος, τὰ δίκαια κατὰ τοὺς νόμους ψηφίσασθε.

Vocabulary

τελευτάω die
θάπτω bury
νομιζόμενα, τά customary
   rites (2b)
ἀδελφή, ἡ sister (1a)

ἀδελφός, ὁ brother (2a)
ἀποδημέω go abroad
ἄκληρος ον disinherited
ἀνώνυμος ον nameless
κύριος α ον responsible (for

making the decision)
ἐν ῞Αιδου in Hades
μεμνημένος perf. part. of
   μιμνήσκομαι
ὀμώμοκα perf. of ὄμνυμι

Section Thirteen

Vocabulary for Section Thirteen A

ἀδίκημα (ἀδικηματ-), τό
crime (3b)
ἀμέλει-α, ἡ indifference (1b)
ἀτιμώρητ-ος -ον unavenged
γραφῆναι aor. inf. pass. of
γράφω
ἐάν if
ἐγνωσμένην known
(γιγνώσκω)
εἴργασται she has worked
(ἐργάζομαι)

ἐλήλυθεν she has gone
(ἔρχομαι)
Ἑλλάς (Ἑλλαδ-), ἡ Greece
(3a)
ἐπί (+dat.) for the purpose of
καθ᾽ ἡμέρας daily, day by day
καταλείπ-ω
(καταλιπ-) bequeath,
leave by right
κολάσητε you punish
(κολάζω)

κύρι-ος -α -ον able,
empowered
μισθ-ός, ὁ pay (2a)
ὀλίγωρ-ος -ον contemptuous
πέπυσθε you have learnt
(πυνθάνομαι)
πολῖτις (πολιτιδ-), ἡ female
citizen (3a: but acc. s.
πολῖτιν)
πορνεύ-ομαι prostitute
oneself
σῶμα (σωματ-), τό body,
person (3b)

Vocabulary to be learnt

ἀδίκημα (ἀδικηματ-), τό *crime*
(3b)
ἐλήλυθα *perf. of* ἔρχομαι *I*
have come
Ἑλλάς (Ἑλλαδ-), ἡ *Greece (3a)*

ἐπί (+dat.) *for the purpose of,*
at, near
ἡμέρα, ἡ *day (1b)*
καταλείπω (καταλιπ-) *leave*
behind, bequeath

κύριος α ον *able, with power,*
by right, sovereign
μισθός, ὁ *pay (2a)*
σῶμα (σωματ-), τό *body,*
person (3b)

Vocabulary for Section Thirteen B

ἄδει-α, ἡ freedom,
carte-blanche (1b)
ἀνόητ-ος -ον foolish,
thoughtless
ἀποψηφίζ-ομαι acquit
(+gen.)

ἄρρητ-ος -ον secret,
mysterious
βούλωνται they wish
(βούλομαι)
διηγέ-ομαι explain, go
through

Διόνυσ-ος, ὁ Dionysos (2a)
(god of nature, and especially
of wine)
ἕκαστ-ος -η -ον each
εἴπητε you say (εἶπον)
ἐπειδὰν when (ever)

ἐπιμελ-ής -ές careful
ἔρηται she asks (ἠρόμην)
καταξιό-ω think it right
μετέχ-ω share in (+gen.)
μνημονικῶς indelibly

Vocabulary to be learnt

ἀποψηφίζομαι acquit (+gen.);
reject (+gen.)
διηγέομαι explain, relate, go
through

ὀλίγωρ-ος -ον contemptuous
ὁμογνώμων (ὁμογνωμον-) in
agreement with, content
with, acquiescent in
(+dat.)

ἕκαστος η ον each
ἐπιμελής ές careful
μετέχω share in (+gen.)
ὀλίγωρος ον contemptuous

ὁμοίως equally with (+dat.)
πύθωνται they learn
(ἐπυθόμην)
σώφρων (σωφρον-) sensible,
law-abiding
ὅ τι ἂν whatever

Vocabulary for Section Thirteen C

ἄκυρ-ος -ον invalid
ἀποψηφισώμεθα we acquit
(ἀποψηφίζομαι)
βούλωνται they wish
(βούλομαι)
γε δήπου of course
ἐὰν if

ἐλέγχ-ω refute, argue against
ἐπειδὰν when (ever)
λέγῃ (he) speaks (λέγω)
μέλει x (dat.) is concerned
about y (gen.)
οἷς ἂν with whomever
ὅ τι ἂν whatever

οὗ ἂν of whomever
πολῖτ-ις (πολιτιδ-), ἡ female
citizen (3a)
πόρν-η, ἡ prostitute (1a)
συνεπαίν-ω join in praising
τύχωσιν they happen upon
(ἔτυχον)

Vocabulary to be learnt

ἄκυρος ον invalid
ἐάν if (ever)
ἐλέγχω refute, argue against
ἐπειδάν when(ever)

μέλει X (dat.) is concerned
about Y (gen.)
πολῖτις (πολιτιδ-), ἡ female
citizen (3a: but acc. s.
πολῖτιν)

Vocabulary for Section Thirteen D

ἀνέκδοτ-ος -ον unmarried
ἀξίωμα (ἀξιωματ-), τό
reputation (3b)
ἀποδιδῷ (it) gives
(ἀποδίδωμι)
ἀπολυθῇ (she) is acquitted
(ἀπολύω)
ἀπορηθῇ (she) is in dire straits
(ἀπορέω)
βούληται (he) wishes
(βούλομαι)

βούλωνται they wish
(βούλομαι)
γαμῶσιν (they) marry
(γαμέω)
διακρίν-ω differentiate
between
δύνηται he is able (δύναμαι)
δυνώμεθα we are able
(δύναμαι)
ἐργασί-α, ἡ function, work
(1b)

ἥντινα ἂν whomever
ἱκαν-ός -ή -όν adequate,
sufficient
καθεστήκῃ he is placed
(καθέστηκα)
κάλλιον better
μέτρι-ος -α -ον reasonable,
acceptable
νομοθέτ-ης, ὁ lawgiver (1d)
ὄψ-ις, ἡ face, looks (3e)

παιδοποιῶνται (they) have children (παιδοποιέομαι)
παντελῶς completely, outright

πόρν-η, ἡ prostitute (1a)
σκοπέω ὅπως see to it that (+fut. ind.)
τελετ-ή, ἡ rite (1a)

τιμ-ή, ἡ privilege, honour (1a)
τρέφ-ω rear, raise
ὡς ἂν in whatever way

Vocabulary to be learnt

διακρίνω decide, judge between
ἱκανός ή όν sufficient, able
παντελῶς completely, outright
πόρνη, ἡ prostitute (1a)

τιμή, ἡ honour, privilege, right (1a)
τρέφω (θρεψ-) rear, raise, feed, nourish

Vocabulary for Section Thirteen E

ἀποβλέπητε you gaze at (ἀποβλέπω)
ἀσελγ-ής -ές disgusting
γένησθε you are (ἐγενόμην)
ἔλεγχ-ος, ὁ examination, refutation

ἐπί (+gen.) on, concerned with
ἐπιμέλει-α, ἡ care, concern (1b)
ἦτε you are (εἰμί)
ὀμωμόκατε you have sworn (ὄμνυμι)

ὅταν when (ever)
συγγίγν-ομαι (συγγεν-) have intercourse with (+dat.)
σωφροσύν-η, ἡ discipline, sense of right and wrong (1a)

Vocabulary to be learnt

ἔλεγχος, ὁ examination, refutation (2a)
ἐπιμέλεια, ἡ care, concern (1b)
ὅταν whenever

Vocabulary for Section Thirteen F

ἀπολυθῇ (she) is acquitted (ἀπολύω)
ἀσπάζωνται (they) greet (ἀσπάζομαι)
ἕδρ-α, ἡ seat (1b)
ἔοικε it seems, it is reasonable
ἔρωνται (they) ask (ἠρόμην/ἐρωτάω)

θώμεθα we cast (τίθημι/θε-)
ἴω I go (subj. of εἶμι)
καταδικασθῇ (she) is condemned (καταδικάζω)
κύκλ-ος, ὁ circle (2a)
λέγῃ (he) says (λέγω)
περιέλκ-ω drag round
προθυμέ-ομαι be eager,

willing
στόμα (στοματ-), τό mouth (3b)
τριώβολ-ον, τό three obols (dikast's pay) (2b)
φλυαρέ-ω talk nonsense

Vocabulary to be learnt

ἔοικε it seems, it is reasonable, it resembles (+dat.)

O   Grammar for Section Thirteen

Summary:
Subj.
Indef. with ἄν

Verbs

The subjunctive

172 The forms of almost all subjunctives in all aspects depend upon the following endings attached to the appropriate stems:

Active (and aorist passive)   *Middle and passive*

stem + -ω   stem + -ωμαι
  -ῃς   -ῃ
  -ῃ   -ηται
  -ωμεν   -ωμεθα
  -ητε   -ησθε
  -ωσι(ν)   -ωνται

Consider the following subjunctives:

Present active   *Present middle/passive*

παύ-ω -ῃς -ῃ *etc.*   παύ-ωμαι *etc.*

Aorist active   *Aorist middle*

παύσ-ω, παύσ-ῃς *etc.*   παύσ-ωμαι *etc.*

Aorist passive

παυσθ-ῶ, παυσθ-ῇς *etc.*

Perfect active   *Perfect middle/passive*

πεπαύκ-ω, πεπαύκ-ῃς *etc.*   πεπαυμένος ὦ, πεπαυμένος ᾖς *etc.*
or: πεπαυκὼς ὦ
πεπαυκὼς ᾖς *etc.*

Notes
(i) While the subjunctive does have a special meaning when used on its own, you will not be meeting this usage for some time. For the moment, translate the subjunctive as if it were indicative.
(ii) The difference between present and aorist subjunctives is aspectual, not temporal.

Contr. subjunctives, εἰμί *and* εἶμι
Active

ποιέ-ω		τιμά-ω		δηλό-ω	
ποι-ῶ	(έ-ω)	τιμ-ῶ	(ά-ω)	δηλ-ῶ	(ό-ω)
ποι-ῇς	(έ-ῃς)	τιμ-ᾷς	(ά-ῃς)	δηλ-οῖς	(ό-ῃς)
ποι-ῇ	(έ-ῃ)	τιμ-ᾷ	(ά-ῃ)	δηλ-οῖ	(ό-ῃ)
ποι-ῶμεν	(έ-ωμεν)	τιμ-ῶμεν	(ά-ωμεν)	δηλ-ῶμεν	(ό-ωμεν)
ποι-ῆτε	(έ-ητε)	τιμ-ᾶτε	(ά-ητε)	δηλ-ῶτε	(ό-ητε)
ποι-ῶσι(ν)	(έ-ωσι)	τιμ-ῶσι(ν)	(ά-ωσι)	δηλ-ῶσι(ν)	(ό-ωσι)

Middle/Passive

ποιέ-ομαι		τιμά-ομαι		δηλό-ομαι	
ποι-ῶμαι	(έ-ωμαι)	τιμ-ῶμαι	(ά-ωμαι)	δηλ-ῶμαι	(ό-ωμαι)
ποι-ῇ	(έ-ῃ)	τιμ-ᾷ	(ά-ῃ)	δηλ-οῖ	(ό-ῃ)
ποι-ῆται	(έ-ηται)	τιμ-ᾶται	(ά-ηται)	δηλ-ῶται	(ό-ηται)
ποι-ώμεθα	(ε-ώμεθα)	τιμ-ώμεθα	(α-ώμεθα)	δηλ-ώμεθα	(ο-ώμεθα)
ποι-ῆσθε	(έ-ησθε)	τιμ-ᾶσθε	(ά-ησθε)	δηλ-ῶσθε	(ό-ησθε)
ποι-ῶνται	(έ-ωνται)	τιμ-ῶνται	(ά-ωνται)	δηλ-ῶνται	(ό-ωνται)

173 Note the subjunctives of εἰμί '*I am*' and εἶμι '*I shall go*'

ὦ	ἴω
ᾖς	ἴῃς
ᾖ	ἴῃ
ὦμεν	ἴωμεν
ἦτε	ἴητε
ὦσι(ν)	ἴωσι(ν)

Subjunctive of δίδωμι

174 A very few verbs keep the -ω- *all the way through* the conjugation of the subjunctive, e.g. δίδωμι.

Present active	*Present middle/passive*
διδῶ	διδῶμαι
διδῶς	διδῷ
διδῷ	διδῶται
διδῶμεν	διδώμεθα
διδῶτε	διδῶσθε
διδῶσι(ν)	διδῶνται

Aorist active   *Aorist middle*

δῶ, δῷς, δῷ etc.   δῶμαι, δῷ, δῶται etc.

Cf. ἔγνων (132), with aor. subj. γνῶ, γνῷς, γνῷ etc.

ἄν again

175 So far, the force of ἄν in a sentence has been to impart the idea of English 'would' in a variety of what were called 'unfulfilled conditions'. In these cases, ἄν took the optative or indicative.

ἄν attached to a conjunction or relative, followed by a subjunctive, makes a statement 'indefinite' in application – a force best brought out by the English 'ever', e.g.

ὅστις ἂν τοῦτο ποιῇ|ποιήσῃ . . . 'whoever does this . . .'

τρόπῳ ᾧ ἂν βούλωνται   'in whatever way they will'

ὅταν ἔλθωσι|ἴωσι   'whenever they go'

176 Note that ἄν need not be translated by 'ever' when it refers specifically to the future (especially when the main verb is future), e.g.

ἐὰν ποιῶμεν|ποιήσωμεν τοῦτο, παύσομεν τοὺς πολεμίους 'if we do this, we shall stop the enemy'

ἐὰν οἴκαδε ἐπανίῃ|ἐπανέλθῃ, ὄψεται τὴν γυναῖκα 'if he returns home, he will see his wife'

Note

ἄν combines with conjunctions as follows:

εἰ+ἄν=ἐάν, ἤν *and sometimes* ἄν

ὅτε+ἄν=ὅταν

ἐπειδή+ἄν=ἐπειδάν

Revise

Pres. and impf. pass. **137–8**

Gen. abs. **139**   O

Exercises for Section Thirteen

(b/c) Morphology and Syntax

1. Translate these sentences, changing the verbs underlined into the subjunctive requested to make the Greek grammatical:

   a. ὅ τι ἂν μαρτυροῦσι (pres.) καὶ <u>λέγουσιν</u> (pres.) οἱ μάρτυρες, ἀεὶ ἐπιμελῶς διακρίνομεν.

b. ἐπειδὰν λέγει (pres.) καὶ <u>πείθει</u> (pres.) ἡμᾶς ὁ κατήγορος, καταδικάζομεν.

c. ἐπειδὰν ἢ ἀστός τις <u>ἀγωνίζεται</u> (aor.) ἢ οἱ γεννῆται <u>ἀποψηφίζονται</u> (aor.) παιδίου ἐκ ξένης τινὸς γενομένου, οἱ νόμοι σῴζονται.

d. ὃς ἂν <u>μὴ καταδικάζεται</u> (aor.), ἀλλ' <u>ἀπολύεται</u> (aor.) ὑπὸ τῶν δικαστῶν, τοῦτον ἀναίτιον εἶναι οἰόμεθα.

e. ἐὰν εἰς ἀτιμίαν <u>καθίσταται</u> (aor.) πονηρός τις, πάντες οἱ πολῖται ἥδονται.

f. ὅταν βούλει (pres.) λέγειν τι δεινὸν καὶ <u>δηλοῖς</u> (pres.) τἀληθῆ, ἀεὶ τιμωρήσονται σὲ οἱ ἐχθροί.

g. ὃ ἂν δίκαιον <u>ἡγεῖσθε</u> (pres.) καὶ <u>τιμᾶτε</u> (pres.), τοῦτο τὸ τίμημα, ὦ δικασταί, ὁ καταδικασθεὶς ὀφείλει τῇ πόλει.

h. ᾗτινι ἂν ὁ πατὴρ προῖκα <u>μὴ δίδωσι</u> (aor.), ταύτῃ ἱκανὴν τὴν προῖκα παρέχει ὁ νόμος.

i. ἐὰν ἐπιμελῶς <u>προσέχετε</u> (aor.) τὸν νοῦν πρὸς τὴν κατηγορίαν καὶ <u>προθυμεῖσθε</u> (pres.), <u>καταψηφιεῖσθε</u> τῆς Νεαίρας.

j. ἐπειδὰν <u>εἰσέρχῃ</u> (pres.) εἰς τὴν οἰκίαν καὶ <u>ἐντυγχάνει</u> (aor.) σοι ἡ γυνή, ὅπως θωπεύσεις αὐτήν.

(d) **English into Greek**

1. Sentences
   Translate into Greek:

   1. When the dikasts go home, their wives greet them.
   2. When a woman gets hold of money, she becomes difficult.
   3. If you pay attention to the defence speech, you will acquit the defendant.
   4. When prosecutors speak, they always say the same thing.
   5. If you are loved by your daughters, they will give you whatever you want.

2. Prose
   Translate into Greek:

   When Stephanos makes his defence speech, what will he say? Obviously he will claim that he has been a good governor and has performed many noble deeds. And yet we all know that nothing noble or good has ever been done by him. Or have you ever heard of any such thing at all? You have not; for neither he nor his forefathers are naturally inclined to piety, but to impiety.

Test Exercise Thirteen

Translate into English:

In Lokris, because of a singular method of treating the legislator, only one new law has been passed in a very long time. The story involves a one-eyed man's search for justice.

(From Demosthenes, *Timokrates*, 139–41)

βούλομαι δ' ὑμῖν διηγήσασθαι ὡς ἐν Λοκροῖς <u>νομοθετοῦσι</u>. ἐκεῖ γὰρ οἴονται τοὺς πολίτας δεῖν τοῖς <u>πάλαι κειμένοις</u> νόμοις χρῆσθαι καὶ τὰ πάτρια φυλάττειν. <u>ὥστε</u> ἐάν τις βούληται νόμον <u>καινὸν</u> τιθέναι, ἐν <u>βρόχῳ</u> τὸν <u>τράχηλον</u> ἔχων νομοθετεῖ. καὶ ἐὰν μὲν δόξῃ καλὸς καὶ χρήσιμος εἶναι ὁ νόμος, <u>ζῇ</u> ὁ τιθεὶς καὶ ἀπέρχεται. εἰ δὲ μή, τέθνηκεν <u>ἐπισπασθέντος</u> τοῦ βρόχου. καὶ γάρ τοι καινοὺς μὲν οὐ τολμῶσι τιθέναι νόμους, τοῖς δὲ πάλαι κειμένοις ἀκριβῶς χρῶνται. ἐν πολλοῖς δὲ πάνυ <u>ἔτεσιν</u> <u>εἷς</u> λέγεται νόμος καινὸς τεθῆναι. νόμος μὲν γὰρ ἐν Λοκροῖς κεῖται ὅτι, ἐάν τις <u>ὀφθαλμὸν</u> ἐκκόψῃ, δεῖ τὸν ἐκκόψαντα παρασχεῖν τὸν ἑαυτοῦ ὀφθαλμὸν <u>ἀντεκκόψαι</u>. ἐχθρὸς δέ τις λέγεται ἀπειλῆσαι ἐχθρῷ ὃς ἕνα ὀφθαλμὸν ἔτυχεν ἔχων, ὅτι ἐκκόψοι τοῦτον τὸν ἕνα ὀφθαλμόν. γενομένης δὲ ταύτης τῆς ἀπειλῆς, χαλεπῶς ἐνεγκὼν ὁ <u>ἑτερόφθαλμος</u>, καὶ ἡγούμενος <u>ἀβίωτον</u> εἶναι τὸν βίον ἑαυτῷ τοῦτο παθόντι, λέγεται τολμῆσαι νόμον τοιόνδε εἰσενεγκεῖν· ἐάν τις ἑτεροφθάλμου τινὸς τὸν ὀφθαλμὸν ἐκκόψῃ, δεήσει αὐτὸν <u>ἀμφὼ</u> τοὺς ὀφθαλμοὺς ἀντεκκόψαι παρασχεῖν. οὕτω γὰρ τὸ αὐτὸ πάθος <u>ἀμφότεροι</u> πάθοιεν ἄν. καὶ τοῦτον μόνον λέγονται Λοκροὶ θέσθαι τὸν νόμον ἐν πλέον ἢ <u>διακοσίοις</u> ἔτεσιν.

Vocabulary

νομοθετέω frame laws
πάλαι long ago
κεῖμαι be established
ὥστε and so
καινός ή όν new
βρόχος, ὁ noose (2a)
τράχηλος, ὁ neck (2a)

ζάω live
ἐπισπασθέντος aor. part. pass.
  of ἐπισπάω draw tight
ἔτος, τό year (3c)
ὀφθαλμός, ὁ eye (2a)
ἀντεκκόπτω knock out in
  return

ἀπειλέω threaten (+dat.)
εἷς (ἑν-) one
ἑτερόφθαλμος, ὁ one-eyed
  man (2a)
ἀβίωτος ον unlivable
ἄμφω both
διακόσιοι αι α two hundred

Section Fourteen

Vocabulary for Section Fourteen A

αἰτέ-ομαι beg, ask
ἄλοχ-ος, ἡ wife (2a)
ἀσκέ-ομαι adorn oneself
ἄωρ-ος -ον untimely, before
    time
γενναῖ-ος -α -ον noble, fine
δέσποιν-α, ἡ mistress (1c)
δόμ-οι, οἱ house, home; (with
    κέδριν-ος) chest, box (2a)
ἐκ . . . ἐλοῦσα taking out from
ἐκπίμπλη-μι
    (ἐκπλησ-) complete
ἐναντιό-ομαι deny, disagree
ἐνδείκνυ-μαι
    (ἐνδειξ-) declare oneself as
    (+part.)
ἔσθης (ἐσθητ-), ἡ clothes (3a)
'Εστί-α, ἡ household hearth
    (1b)
εὐκλε-ής -ές glorious, of
    good reputation
εὐπρεπ-ής -ές becoming,
    proper
ἦσθεθ'=ἦσθετο (aor. of
    αἰσθάνομαι)
θανεῖν . . . παῖδας 'that my

children (do not) die'
θέλουσα=ἐθέλουσα
θεράπαιν-α, ἡ female servant
    (of Alkestis) (1c)
θνῄσκ-ω (θαν-) die
ἵστα-μαι (στα-) stand
ἴστω γυνή 'let the woman
    know (that she)'
κατά (+gen.) beneath
καταθνῄσκ-ω die away (fut.
    καταθανοῦμαι)
κατεύχ-ομαι pray earnestly
κατθανουμένη see καταθνῄσκω
κέδριν-ος -η -ον of cedar
κλύ-ω hear
κόσμ-ος, ὁ decoration (2a)
λευκ-ός -ή -όν white
λού-ω wash
μακρῷ by far
ὀρφανεύ-ω look after as
    orphans
πανύστατ-ος -η -ον for the
    very last time
πατρῷ-ος -α -ον father's,
    ancestral
πόσ-ις, ὁ husband (3e)

ποτάμι -ος -α -ον from a river
πρόσθεν (+gen.) in front of
προσπίτν-ω=προσπίπτ-ω fall
    upon, embrace
προτιμά-ω hold in honour
συζεύγνυ-μι (συζευξ-) join in
    marriage
τέκν-ον, τό child (2b)
τεκοῦσα, ἡ mother (τίκτω
    (τεκ-) bear)
τερπν-ός -ή -όν joyful,
    pleasant
ὕδωρ (ὑδατ-), τό water (3b)
ὑπερβεβλημένην 'who
    surpasses' (sc. Alkestis)
    (ὑπερβάλλομαι)
ὑπερθνῄσκ-ω (ὑπερθαν-) die
    for another
ὑπό (+dat.) under
χθών (χθον-), ἡ earth (3a)
χορ-ός, ὁ chorus (of
    townsmen) (2a)
χρώς (χρωτ-), ὁ skin, flesh
    (3a) (acc. χρόα)

Vocabulary to be learnt

γενναῖος α ον noble, fine
δέσποινα, ἡ mistress (1c)
δόμοι, οἱ house, home (2a)

εὐπρεπής ές seemly, proper,
    becoming
θνῄσκω (θαν-) die

ἵστημι|ἵσταμαι set up, stand,
    raise
κατά (+gen.) below

καταθνήσκω (καταθαν-) die
away
κλύω hear
κόσμος, ὁ decoration,
ornament; order; universe (2a)
μακρός ά όν large, big, long

πανύστατος η ον for the very
last time
πατρῷος α ον of one's father,
ancestral
πόσις, ὁ husband, spouse (3e)
προσπίτνω fall upon, embrace

τέκνον, τό child (2b)
τίκτω (τεκ-) bear, give birth to
ὕδωρ (ὑδατ-), τό water (3b)
ὑπό (+dat.) under, beneath
χρώς (χρωτ-), ὁ flesh, skin
(acc. χρόα) (3a)

Vocabulary for Section Fourteen B

Ἄδμητ-ος, ὁ Admetos (2a)
ἄκλαυτ-ος -ον unweeping
ἀστένακτ-ος -ον without
lamentation
δακρύ-ω weep
ἐσπίπτ-ω (ἐσπεσ-) fall into,
on
ἐκστέφ-ω garland, crown
ἔνθα there
εὐειδ-ής -ές graceful, pleasant
εὐτυχ-ής -ές fortunate

ἐχθαίρ-ω hate
θάλαμ-ος, ὁ bedroom (2a)
κἀξέστεψε = καὶ ἐξέστεψε
κἄπειτα = καὶ ἔπειτα
κατά (+acc.) throughout
κορεύματ-α, τά maidenhood
(3b)
κεκτήσεται (she) will have
gained (κτάομαι)
λέκτρ-ον, τό bed (2b)
λέχ-ος, τό bed (3c)

μεθίστη-μι change, alter
ὀκνέ-ω shrink from (+inf.)
παρθένει-ος -α -ον maiden,
virgin
προδίδω-μι (προδο-) betray
προσεύχ-ομαι address in
prayer
σώφρων (σωφρον-) modest,
chaste
τοὐπιόν = τὸ ἐπιόν (pres. part.
n. of ἐπέρχομαι)

Vocabulary to be learnt

δακρύω weep
εἰσπίπτω (εἰσπεσ-) fall into,
on
ἔνθα there

εὐτυχής ές fortunate, lucky
θάλαμος, ὁ bedchamber (2a)
κτάομαι acquire, get, gain
προδίδωμι (προδο-) betray

σώφρων (σωφρον-) modest,
chaste, discreet, sensible,
law-abiding, prudent,
disciplined, temperate

Vocabulary for Section Fourteen C

ἀγκάλ-η, ἡ arm (1a)
ἄθλι-ος -α -ον pathetic,
miserable
ἄκοιτ-ις, ἡ wife (3e)
ἄλγ-ος, τό pain, agony (3c)
ἄλλοτ' ἄλλον now one, now
the other
ἀμήχαν-ος -ον hopeless,
impossible
αὐγ-ή, ἡ ray (1a)
βάρ-ος, τό weight, burden
(3c)

δάκρυ-ον, τό tear (2b)
δέμνι-ον, τό bed, bedding
(usu. pl.) (2b)
δεύ-ω wet, bedew, besprinkle
ἐμπνέ-ω breathe
ἐξηρτημέν-ος clinging to
(+gen.)
ἐπεστράφη she turned back
(ἐπιστρέφω)
ἐσθλ-ός -ή -όν noble, fine
ἦ που no doubt
κἄρριψεν = καὶ ἔρριψεν

κλαί-ω weep
κοίτ-η, ἡ bed (1a)
κόρ-ος, ὁ sufficiency, enough,
fill (2a)
κυνέ-ω kiss
λελήσεται he will have
forgotten (λανθάνομαι)
λίσσ-ομαι beg
μαραίν-ομαι die away (pass.)
οἶκ-ος, ὁ household (often
pl.) (2a)
οὔποτε never

οὔτις *(οὐτιν-)* no one
ὀφθαλμότεγκτ-ος -ον welling
   from the eyes
παρειμέν-ος -η -ον exhausted
πέπλ-ος, ὁ robe (2a)
πλημμυρίς *(πλημμυριδ-)*, ἡ
   flood (3a)
προνωπ-ής -ές forward,
   headlong

προσλέγ-ω
  (προσειπ-) address (aor.
  pass. προσερρήθην)
προτείν-ω stretch out
σμικρ-ός -ά -όν = μικρός
στέγ-αι, αἱ house (1c)
στείχ-ω go
στενάζ-ω weep, lament
στερέ-ω deprive of (+gen.)

σφέ he (= Admetos)
τἀμήχανα = τὰ ἀμήχανα
τἄν = τοι ἄν 'truly, he would
  have . . .'
τοισίδ' = τοῖσδε
φθίν-ω die, waste away
χειρός *i.e.* on Admetos' hand
χεροῖν 'in both hands' (dual
  form)

Vocabulary to be learnt

ἄθλιος α ον *pathetic, miserable,*
  wretched
βάρος, τό *weight, burden (3c)*
δάκρυον, τό *tear (2b)*
ἐσθλός ή όν *noble, fine, good*
κλαίω *weep*

οἶκος, ὁ *household, house (2a)*
οὔποτε *never*
οὔτις *no one*
προσλέγω *address*
στείχω *go, come*

O   Grammar for Section Fourteen

Summary:
Fut. perf.
Tragic usages and iambic trimeters

Verbs

The future perfect

177 There is only one form of the future perfect. This is the middle/
passive form, as follows:

Indicative: πεπαύ-σομαι   'I shall have stopped (been stopped)' etc.
            πεπαύ-σῃ
            πεπαύ-σεται
            πεπαυ-σόμεθα
            πεπαύ-σεσθε
            πεπαύ-σονται
Infinitive: πεπαύ-σεσθαι
Participle: πεπαυ-σόμενος
Optative: πεπαυ-σοίμην

Notes

(i) This is a rare form: many verbs do not appear in this form, and most prefer
either *the passive meaning (most usual)* or *the middle meaning.*

Look for a perfect middle/passive stem (no -κ-, but reduplication), with future middle endings i.e. -σομαι -ση -σεται etc. e.g.

λελύσομαι   (λύω)   'I shall have been released'
             (λύομαι) 'I shall have ransomed'
πεπράξεται   (πράσσω) 'it will have been done'
πεπαύσομαι   (παύομαι) 'I shall have ceased'

As usual the middle verbs will carry an active meaning:

κεκτήσομαι   (κτάομαι) 'I shall have obtained'

(ii) In meaning, particularly in poetry, it can be used as an emphatic future, e.g.

κεκτήσεται 'she will possess'
φράζε καὶ πεπράξεται 'speak, and it shall be done'

(iii) The active 'I shall have −ed' is supplied by the perfect active participle and the future of the verb 'to be' e.g.

λελυκότες ἐσόμεθα 'we shall have released'

The passive may also be formed with the passive participle:

λελυμένος ἔσομαι (=λελύσομαι) 'I shall have been released'

Tragic usages
178 Note the following tragic usages:
(i) Observe the elision or crasis displayed by the following phrases:
l. 25   κἄπειτα (καὶ ἔπειτα)
l. 16   τἀμά (τὰ ἐμά)
l. 38   κἄρριψεν (καὶ ἔρριψεν)
l. 47   τἂν (τοι ἄν)
l. 9   ᾔσθεθ' ἡμέραν (ᾔσθετο ἡμέραν)

Verse displays far more features of this type than prose, though doubtless crasis and elision occurred in spoken language, even if they were not indicated in writing.

(ii) Note the prefixes to:
l. 1   καταθνῄσκω
l. 13   κατεύχομαι
l. 22   προσεύχομαι
l. 45   προσλέγω

The basic meaning of the word is retained, but the prefix shades its meaning differently. This subtlety is one you should try to take into account when translating.

(iii) Word order in verse can be far more flexible than in prose; again, utterances can be far more oblique and tightly packed with meaning. Since this is a matter of the individual author's style, only wide reading in an author will accustom you to his particular quirks.

Note particularly the splitting of preposition from its verb ('tmesis'):

l. 11 ἐκ⌐δ᾽⌐ἑλοῦσα κεδρίνων δόμων 'taking from the cedar box'

(iv) Observe the use of the poetic forms (e.g. τοῖσι for τοῖς in τοισίδε κακοῖς, l. 49), and the figurative use of words, e.g.

l. 11 δόμων, usually 'house', here = 'chest, box'

Tragic verse metre

179 English verse can be described in terms of the number of 'beats' to a line, and sometimes in terms of rhyme as well, e.g.

> 'As I was going up the stair
> I met a man who wasn't there.
> He wasn't there again today.
> I wish, I wish he'd stay away.'

There are four 'beats' to each line, and the lines rhyme AA, BB.

Greek verse does *not* rhyme; nor is it to be described in terms of 'beats', but in terms of the *value (long or short) of each and every syllable which makes up the line*. EVERY SYLLABLE COUNTS IN GREEK VERSE. (On determining long and short syllables, see **228**.)

The commonest metre of Greek tragedy is the IAMBIC TRIMETER (nearly all the dialogue of Greek tragedy is written in iambic trimeters). A trimeter is composed of three 'metra'. An iambic 'metron' is ⏑ – ⏑ – (i.e. doubtful syllable, called 'anceps', which can be either long or short, + long–short–long syllables). (Sometimes it is helpful to speak of iambic 'feet', i.e. ⏑ – or – –.)

Thus an iambic trimeter looks like:

$$\underline{\smile} - \smile - \mid \underline{\smile} - \smile - \mid \underline{\smile} - \smile -$$

One might express it 'blank tum-ti-tum, blank tum-ti-tum, blank tum-ti-tum'.

In some Greek metres (and the iambic trimeter is among them) one long syllable can be replaced by two short syllables. This 'resolution' of one long into two shorts is more common in some authors than others, and in some parts of the line than others.

Here are five lines of the passage from *Alkestis* scanned, i.e. with the longs and shorts marked and the line split up into metra:

$$\overline{} \quad - \smile - \quad - \quad - \quad \smile - \smile - \smile -$$
πως δ᾽ οὐκ ἀρισ|τη; τις δ᾽ ἐναν|τιωσεται;

$$\smile - \smile - \quad - - \smile - \quad \smile - \smile -$$
τι χρη γενεσ|θαι την ὑπερ|βεβλημενην

$$\smile - \smile - \quad - \quad - - \smile - \smile -$$
γυναικα; πως | δ᾽ ἀν μαλλον ἐν|δειξαιτο τις

$$\overset{\cup\ -\quad\cup\ -\ -\quad-\ \cup\ -\quad\cup\ -\ \cup\ -}{\pi\text{οσιν } \pi\text{ροτι}|\mu\omega\sigma' \; \mathring{\eta} \; \theta\epsilon\lambda\text{ου}|\sigma' \; \mathring{\upsilon}\pi\epsilon\rho\theta\alpha\nu\epsilon\iota\nu;}$$

$$\overset{-\quad-\ \cup\quad-\quad-\ -\quad\cup\ -\quad\cup\ -\quad\cup-}{\kappa\alpha\iota\ \tau\alpha\upsilon\tau\alpha\ \mu\epsilon\nu\ |\ \delta\eta\ \pi\alpha\sigma'\ \mathring{\epsilon}\pi\iota\sigma|\tau\alpha\tau\alpha\iota\ \pi\text{ολις}.}$$

Note
The last syllable counts LONG for the purpose of scansion, whatever its composition.

Revise
Aor. and fut. pass. **143, 157** Language Survey (2)
ἵστημι **144** Language Survey (7)
τίθημι **150**
Acc.+inf./part. **146–9, 156** Reference Grammar K, p. 301.

PART FIVE

Section Fifteen

Vocabulary for Section Fifteen A

ἀθυμῶς ἔχ-ω be gloomy, disheartened

ἀπελευθέρ-α, ἡ freedwoman (1b)

Ἀπολλόδωρ-ος, ὁ Apollodoros (2a) (*friend of Aristarkhos*)

Ἀρίσταρχ-ος, ὁ Aristarkhos (2a) (*whose story is told*)

Ἀρίστων, ὁ Ariston (3a) (*father of Aristarkhos*)

διεξέρχ-ομαι (διεξελθ-) tell, go through in detail

διεπέπρακτο (he) had done (διαπράττομαι)

ἐνθυμέ-ομαι take to heart

ἐξηγητ-ής, ὁ Adviser (1d)

ἔξω (+gen.) outside

ἔοικ-α seem

ἐπεποιήκει he had done (ποιέω)

ἐπεπόνθη I had suffered (πάσχω)

εὐθύς (+gen.) straight towards

ἠδικήκει (he) had wronged (ἀδικέω)

Θεόφημ-ος, ὁ Theophemos (2a) (*enemy of Aristarkhos and responsible for the death of a freedwoman*)

Ἰλισ-ός, ὁ River Ilisos (2a)

κάθαρσ-ις, ἡ purification (3e)

πύλ-η, ἡ gate (1a)

συμφορ-ά, ἡ disaster, occurrence (1b)

συντυγχάν-ω (συντυχ-) meet with (+dat.)

ταφ-ή, ἡ burial (1a)

ὑβριστ-ής, ὁ violent, criminal character (1d)

ὑπό (+acc.) up under, along under

φονεύ-ω kill, murder

χωρί-ον, τό farm (2b)

Vocabulary to be learnt

ἀπελεύθερος, ὁ freedman (2a)

ἀπελευθέρα, ἡ freedwoman (1b)

διεξέρχομαι (διεξελθ-) go through, relate

ἔξω (+gen.) outside

ἔοικα seem, resemble

εὐθύς (+gen.) straight towards

πύλη, ἡ gate (1a)

συμφορά, ἡ disaster, mishap, occurrence (1b)

συντυγχάνω (συντυχ-) meet with (+dat.)

ὑβριστής, ὁ violent, criminal person (1d)

ὑπό (+acc.) under, along under, up under

χωρίον, τό farm; place, space, region (2b)

Vocabulary for Section Fifteen B

ἀθυμέ-ω be gloomy, disheartened, downhearted

ἀθυμητέον (you) should be gloomy

ἀκο-ή, ἡ hearing (1a)

ἀλλ' οὖν well, anyway;

however that might be

ἀποκρύπτ-ω conceal, hide

βραχ-ύς -εῖα -ύ brief, short

γεγενημένα, τά events
διηγητέον I (dat.) must
   tell/relate
διπλ-οῦς -ῆ -οῦν double
εἴσομαι fut. of οἶδα
ἐπέχ-ω (ἐπισχ-) hold on,
   hold back
ἐπιεικῶς pretty, fairly
ἐπιθυμέ-ω desire
ἐπιτήδει-ος -α -ον suitable
ἵνα (+subj.) in order that
κάθη-μαι be seated

Μέγαράδε to Megara
μή (+aor. subj.) don't
παντῶς in every way, wholly
πάνυ μὲν οὖν certainly
περίπατ-ος, ὁ walk, stroll (2a)
πνῖγ-ος, τό midday heat,
   stifling heat (3c)
προθυμέ-ομαι be eager, ready
προθυμητέον (you) should be
   ready (for action)
προσήκ-ων -ουσα -ον fitting
   for (+dat.)

σκέπτ-ομαι consider
σκεπτέον we (dat.) must
   consider
συμβουλεύ-ομαι debate with,
   take counsel with
σχολ-ή, ἡ leisure (1a)
φοβέ-ομαι μή I am afraid
   that/lest (+subj.)
χάρις (χαριτ-), ἡ thanks (3a)
χάριν οἶδα feel grateful to
   (+dat.)
ὥστε so that, and so

Vocabulary to be learnt

ἀθυμέω be downhearted,
   gloomy
ἀκοή, ἡ hearing (1a)
ἀλλ' οὖν well anyway; however
   that may be
βραχύς εῖα ύ short, brief
γεγενημένα, τά events,
   occurrences (2b)
ἐπέχω (ἐπισχ-) hold on,

   restrain, check
ἐπιθυμέω desire, yearn for
   (+gen.)
ἐπιτήδειος α ον suitable, useful
   for
κάθημαι be seated
μή (+aor. subj.) don't
πάνυ μὲν οὖν certainly, of course
προθυμέομαι be ready, eager

σκέπτομαι examine, look
   carefully at
σχολή, ἡ leisure (1a)
φοβέομαι μή fear that/lest
   (+subj.)
χάριν οἶδα be grateful to
   (+dat.)
χάρις (χαριτ-), ἡ thanks, grace
   (3a)

O   Grammar for Section Fifteen A–B

Summary:
Plup.
μή+aor. subj.
φοβοῦμαι μή
-τέος verb-forms

Verbs

Pluperfects (very rare) ἐπεπαύκη, ἐπεπαύμην *'I had stopped, been stopped'*

180 The forms of the pluperfect are as follows:

Active		Middle/Passive	
ἐπεπαύκ-η	'I had stopped'	ἐπεπαύ-μην	'I had (been) stopped'
ἐπεπαύκ-ης		ἐπέπαυ-σο	
ἐπεπαύκ-ει		ἐπέπαυ-το	
ἐπεπαύκ-εμεν		ἐπεπαύ-μεθα	
ἐπεπαύκ-ετε		ἐπέπαυ-σθε	
ἐπεπαύκ-εσαν		ἐπέπαυ-ντο	

Notes

(i) *The pluperfect means 'I had –'. It is very rare.*

(ii) *Spot the pluperfect by the presence of the augment before the reduplication. In other words, the pluperfect pushes the perfect one step further back in time (cf. present, and augmented aorist/imperfect).*

Imperatives

181 You have already met μή+present imperative to mean 'don't', e.g. μὴ ἄκουε 'don't listen'. (Cf. **6**.)

μή+aorist subjunctive also means 'don't'. The phrase has an aoristic aspect and it may imply 'don't do it just this once', e.g.

μὴ ἀκούσῃς 'don't listen' (s.)
μὴ ἔλθητε 'don't go' (pl.)

Verbs of fearing

182 φοβοῦμαι means

(i) 'I fear, am afraid of' (+object)
(ii) 'I am afraid to' (+infinitive)
(iii) 'I am afraid that/lest'. In this sense it takes μή+subjunctive if the fear refers to the future; otherwise, the natural tense of the indicative, e.g.

φοβοῦμαι μὴ ἔλθῃ 'I am afraid that he will come'
φοβοῦμαι μὴ ἦλθεν 'I am afraid that he came'

Verb-forms in -τέος

183 These forms are based upon the verb-stem e.g.

ἀθυμέω→ἀθυμητέος 'to be disheartened'
πράττω→πρακτέος 'to be done'
πείθω→πειστέος 'to be persuaded'

Observe particularly οἰστέος (φέρω) 'to be carried'
ἰτέος (εἶμι) 'to be journeyed'

These carry the idea of necessity, i.e. that something *must* take place or be done. They are used in two ways:

(i) as straight adjectives, meaning 'to be –ed', e.g. πειστέοι οἱ ἄνθρωποί εἰσιν 'the men are to be persuaded, must be persuaded'.

(ii) in the form -τέον [ἐστί] as if=δεῖ+infinitive. The subject can go into the accusative or dative; the -τέον form remains (usually) quite unchanged (if there is a change, it will be to the neuter plural, -τέα), e.g.

ἡμῖν }
ἡμᾶς } ποιητέον [ἐστι] ταῦτα   'we must do this' *(δεῖ ἡμᾶς ποιεῖν ταῦτα)*

γραπτέον ἦν τὴν ἐπιστολὴν { αὐτοῖς / αὐτούς }   'they had to write the letter' *(ἔδει αὐτοὺς τὴν ἐπιστολὴν γράψαι)* ○

A. Grammar, Vocabularies, Exercises

Exercises for Section Fifteen A–B

(b/c) Morphology and Syntax

1. Translate these commands, then change into negative commands using μή + aorist subjunctive:
   a. κωλύσατε τὸν ἄνδρα.
   b. τιμωρήσασθε τοὺς φίλους.
   c. καταφρόνησον τῶν θεῶν.
   d. θοῦ τὴν ψῆφον.
   e. ἐπιλάθεσθε τούτου τοῦ πράγματος.
   f. κάτειπε τὸν τῆς ἀπολογίας λόγον.
   g. μνημονεύσατε πάντας τοὺς λόγους.
   h. παράλαβε νεανίσκους.
   i. ἐπίσχες.
   j. ἐπιθυμήσατε.
   k. ἀθύμησον.

2. Translate the following sentences:
   a. φοβούμεθα μὴ ταῦτ᾽ ἀκούσας ἀθυμήυῃ ὁ ἀνήρ.
   b. δεινῶς ἀθυμῶ μὴ οὐ ποιῇ τοῦτο ὁ ἑταῖρος.
   c. ὅρα μὴ ψευδῆ λέγῃς πρὸς τοὺς δικαστὰς περὶ τῶν γεγενημένων.
   d. φοβοῦμαι μὴ τοὺς ἄνδρας οὐκ ἔσωσεν ὁ Δημοσθένης.

3. Translate these statements, then using the pool of -τέος verb-forms, convert them as follows:
   e.g. δεῖ ἐμὲ ποιεῖν ταῦτα→ἐμοὶ|ἐμὲ ποιητέον ταῦτα or ταῦτα ποιητέα μοι.
   a. δεῖ ἡμᾶς ἀκριβῶς σκοπεῖσθαι περὶ ταῦτα.
   b. δεῖ σὲ ἰέναι οἴκαδε.
   c. δεῖ αὐτοὺς βοηθεῖν.
   d. δεῖ τὸν ἄνδρα φέρειν τὴν συμφοράν.
   e. δεῖ ὑμᾶς πολεμεῖν.
   f. δεῖ οἴκαδε πέμπειν σέ.
   σκεπτέος, οἰστέος, ἰτέος, πολεμητέος, βοηθητέος, πεμπτέος

Vocabulary for Section Fifteen C

ἀποστέλλ-ω send out
ἄφθον-ος -ον unlimited
βοήθει-α, ἡ rescue operation
(1b)

γράφ-ω propose (a decree)
δέον it being necessary (δεῖ)
διὰ τάχους with all speed

ἐξέρχ-ομαι end, finish
ἐξόν it being possible (ἔξεστι)

ἵνα (+subj./opt.) in order
    that, to
κομίζ-ομαι collect
νεώρι-ον, τό dockyard (2b)
ὅθεν from where
ὀθόνι-ον, τό sail-cloth (2b)
παραδίδω-μι (παραδο-) hand
    over
παρασκευάζ-ω equip,
    prepare
Πειραι-εύς, ὁ Piraeus (3g)

πρίασθαι to buy (aor. inf. of
    ὠνέομαι)
πρός (+dat.) in addition to
προστάττ-ω
    (προσταξ-) instruct, order
σκεύ-η, τά ship's gear (pl.)
    (3c)
στάσ-ις, ἡ revolution (3e)
στυππεῖ-ον, τό tow, coarse
    flax (2b)
σύμμαχ-ος, ὁ ally (2a)

σχοινί-ον, τό rope (2b)
τριηραρχέ-ω serve as
    trierarch
ὑπάρχ-ω be in supply
Χαιρέδημ-ος, ὁ Khairedemos
    (2a) (*proposer of a decree about
    ship's gear in 357*)
ὡς τάχιστα as quickly as
    possible
ὥστε consequently, so that,
    and so

Vocabulary to be learnt

βοήθεια, ἡ help, rescue
    operation (1b)
γράφω propose (a decree); write
δέον it being necessary
ἐξόν it being permitted, possible
ὅθεν from where

παραδίδωμι (παραδο-) hand
    over
παρασκευάζω prepare, equip
πρός (+dat.) in addition to, near
σκευή, τά ship's gear; gear,
    furniture (3c)

σύμμαχος, ὁ ally (2a)
τριηραρχέω serve as trierarch
ὠνέομαι (πρια-) buy
ὡς(+sup.) as – as possible
ὥστε so that, with the result
    that, consequently

O   Grammar for Section Fifteen C

Summary:
Acc. abs.
ὡς + sup.

Accusative absolute δέον 'it being necessary', ἐξόν 'it being permitted'

184 δέον, ἐξόν (neuter accusative participle) are the forms adopted by δεῖ, ἔξεστι when they are being used absolutely (cf. **139**), e.g.

δέον ἡμᾶς ἐλθεῖν, ἴωμεν 'it being necessary for us to go, let us go' (or 'since we must go . . .')

ἐξὸν ἡμῖν ἐλθεῖν, ἐμείναμεν 'it being permitted for us to go, we remained' (or 'although we could go . . .')

ὡς + superlative

185 Note the use of ὡς + superlative to mean 'as – as possible', e.g.

ὡς τάχιστα 'as fast as possible'
ὡς μάλιστα 'as much as can be'   O

Exercise for Section Fifteen C

(b/c) Morphology and Syntax

1. Translate the following pairs of statements, then join into one sentence by the use of acc. absolute:

a. δεῖ τὸν ὀφείλοντα τῇ πόλει τὰ σκεύη παραδιδόναι τῷ τριηραρχήσοντι| ἐγὼ ὡς τὸν Θεόφημον προσῆλθον.

b. εἶτα οὐκ ἔξεστί μοι τὴν τριήρη παρασκευάζειν|προσῆλθον πρὸς τὴν βουλήν.

c. ἔδει ἡμᾶς παρασκευάζειν ὡς τάχιστα τὰς ναῦς|γράφει Χαιρέδημος ψήφισμα.

d. οὐκ ἐξῆν ἐν τῷ Πειραιεῖ οὐδὲν πρίασθαι ὧν ἔδει|οἱ τριήραρχοι οὐκ ἐδύναντο παρασκευάζειν τὰς ναῦς.

Vocabulary for Section Fifteen D

ἀδελφ-ός, ὁ brother (2a)
ἄλλοθεν from elsewhere
ἀπαιτέ-ω demand x (acc.) from y (acc.)
ἄπειμι be absent
ἀρχ-ή, ἡ board of officials (1a)
διαλείπ-ω (διαλιπ-) leave

Εὐεργ-ος, ὁ Euergos (2a) (Theophemos' brother)
ἵνα (+opt.) in order that, to
κακὰ λέγ-ω curse, insult (+acc.)
κοιν-ός -ή -όν common, shared
κομίζ-ομαι collect

ὁπόταν whenever
οὗ where (at)
οὐσί-α, ἡ property (1b)
πλεῖστ-ος -η -ον very many, most (sup. of πολύς)
φράζ-ω mention, talk
χωρίς separately, apart

Vocabulary to be learnt

ἀδελφός, ὁ brother (2a)
ἀπαιτέω demand X (acc.) from Y (acc.)
ἄπειμι be absent
διαλείπω (διαλιπ-) leave
ἵνα (+subj., opt.) in order to, that

κοινός ή όν common, shared
κομίζομαι collect
ὁπόταν whenever
οὗ where (at)
οὐσία, ἡ property, wealth (1b)
πλεῖστος η ον very much, most (sup. of πολύς)

φράζω utter, mention, talk
χωρίς apart; separately; (prep.) apart/separately from (+gen.)

O Grammar for Section Fifteen D

Summary:
ἵνα+subj./opt.

ἵνα 'in order that'

186 When followed by a subjunctive (in primary sequence – see note to **167**), or by an optative (in secondary sequence), ἵνα means 'in order that, in order to, to, so that', e.g.

ἔρχεται ἵνα   πείθῃ ⎫
               πείσῃ ⎬   τοὺς ἄνδρας 'he is coming to persuade the men'

ἦλθεν ἵνα   πείθοι ⎫
             πείσειε ⎬   τοὺς ἄνδρας 'he came to persuade the men'

Notes
(i) ὅπως and ὡς can be used instead of ἵνα in such clauses.
*(ii) Cf. ὡς +future participle (**160**).*   O

Exercise for Section Fifteen D

(d) English into Greek
Translate into Greek:
1. Don't be downhearted, my friend.
2. Are you afraid that you will suffer again at the hands of these rogues?
3. Although Theophemos is obliged to hand over the gear, I cannot force him to do this.
4. I shall go to the council, so that they may draft a decree.
5. I went to a friend's house, to find out where Theophemos lived.

Vocabulary for Section Fifteen E

ἀκολουθέ-ω follow,
  accompany
δείκνυ-μι (δειξ-) show
διάγραμμα (διαγραμματ-), τό
  register (3b)

ἐνέχυρ-ον, τό security, pledge
  (2b)
μετέρχ-ομαι (μετελθ-) send
  for

ὁπότε when
  (+opt. = whenever)
ὑπακού-ω reply, answer

Vocabulary to be learnt
δείκνυμι (δειξ-) *show*
ὁπότε *when*
  (+opt. =whenever)
ὑπακούω *reply, answer; obey*
  (+dat.)

O   Grammar for Section Fifteen E

Summary:
Indef. in sec. seq.

'Indefinites' in secondary sequence

187 You have already met ἄν+subjunctive to denote the idea 'ever', e.g. ὁπόταν 'whenever', ἐάν 'if ever', ὅστις ἄν 'whoever' (cf. **175, 176**).

In secondary sequence, however, the idea of 'ever' is expressed not by ἄν+subjunctive, but by the plain *optative*, with *no* ἄν at all, e.g.

ὁπότε ἔλθοι|ἴοι   'whenever he came'
ὅστις τοῦτο ποιοίη|ποιήσειε   'whoever did this'

So whenever you meet a word like ὁπότε, ἐπεί, ὅς(τις), consider translating with 'ever' if the verb is optative.

188 Do not confuse the above construction with the use of the optative in secondary sequence in indirect speech. In **187** the optative is being used in a sub-clause, prefaced by, e.g., 'when(ever)', 'who(ever)' etc. An optative in indirect speech will be used in place of the indicative for a *main* verb, and will not alter the meaning at all, e.g.

ἔλεξεν ὅτι πείθοι   'he said that he was persuading'
ᾔδει ὅτι πείσειε   'he knew that he had persuaded'
ᾔδει ὅτι πείσοι   'he knew that he would persuade'

189 Revise the forms of the future optative as laid out at **168**.   O

Exercise for Section Fifteen E

(b/c) Morphology and Syntax

1. Translate the following sentences, then change from primary to past sequence or vice-versa (remember to change both introductory and subordinate verbs):

   a. ἐβουλόμην κομίζεσθαι τὰ σκεύη, ἵνα τὴν τριήρη παρασκευάζοιμι.

   b. φοβοῦμαι μὴ Εὔεργος οὐ δείξῃ (*use opt.*) τὸ πρᾶγμα τῷ Θεοφήμῳ.

   c. ἐκέλευον τὸν παῖδα καλέσαι τοὺς πολίτας, ἵνα μάρτυρές μοι εἶεν τῶν λεχθέντων.

   d. οὐ παύομαι ἑπόμενος, ἵνα τὰ γεγενημένα μάθω.

2. Translate the following pairs of sentences:

   a. (i) ὅτε εἰσέλθοι, ἑώρα καθιζομένην τὴν γυναῖκα.

(ii) ὅτε εἰσῆλθεν, εἶδε τὴν γυναῖκα ἐπὶ τοῦ βωμοῦ καθιζομένην.

b. (i) ἠρόμην τὸν παῖδα, ὅπου εἴη ὁ δεσπότης.

(ii) ἐκέλευον τὴν ἄνθρωπον μετελθεῖν τὸν δεσπότην, ὅπου εἴη.

c. (i) ἤδη ἐπεπύσμην ἐγώ, ὅτι τύχοι γεγαμηκώς.

(ii) ὁ δεσπότης ἐκέλευεν αὐτὸν ἀποδιδόναι τῇ πόλει, ὅ τι τύχοι ἔχων.

d. (i) ὁ παῖς ἐκάλεσεν ἐκ τῆς ὁδοῦ πάντας τοὺς πολίτας, οὓς εἶδεν, ὡς μαρτυρήσοντας.

(ii) ἐκελεύσθη ὁ παῖς καλέσαι ἐκ τῆς ὁδοῦ πολίτας ὡς μαρτυρήσοντας, εἴ τινας ἴδοι.

e. (i) ἡμῖν ἔδοξεν χρῆναι ἕκαστον λόγον περὶ Ἔρωτος εἰπεῖν ὡς δύναιτο κάλλιστον. (Plato abridged)

(ii) Λύσανδρος δὲ ἀφικόμενος εἰς Αἴγιναν ἀπέδωκε τὴν πόλιν Αἰγινήταις, ὅσους ἐδύνατο πλείστους αὐτῶν ἀθροίσας. (Xenophon)

Vocabulary

χρῆναι inf. of χρή
ἀθροίζω collect, gather

Vocabulary for Section Fifteen F

ἀγανακτέ-ω be angry
ἁλίσκ-ομαι ((ἐ)αλ-) be convicted, caught (aor. ἑάλων)
ἁλῶναι to be convicted (ἁλίσκομαι)
ἁλώσεται he will be convicted (ἁλίσκομαι)
ἀμύν-ομαι defend oneself
ἀνεῳγμένη open (perf. part. pass. of ἀνοίγνυμι)
ἀπόστολ-ος, ὁ sailing, mission (2a)
ἀφῆ-κα I released (ἀφίημι)
βουλευτ-ής, ὁ member of council (1d)
γεγαμηκὼς εἴη he was married (perf. opt. of γαμέω)

διάκει-μαι be in x (adv.) state
διακωλύ-ω prevent
ἑάλω see ἁλίσκομαι
εἴκοσι twenty (indecl.)
εἰσαγγέλλ-ω (εἰσαγγειλ-) impeach
ἐνέχυρ-ον, τό security, pledge (2b)
ἐπεπόνθη I had suffered (πάσχω)
ἐπεπύσμην I had ascertained (πυνθάνομαι)
ἐπί (+dat.) at, on
ἐπιεικ-ής -ές fair, moderate
ἐπιμαρτύρ-ομαι call as witnesses
ζημιό-ω fine, punish
κρίσ-ις, ἡ judgment (3e)
μετέρχ-ομαι (μετελθ-) send for

μέτρι-ος -α -ον reasonable, fair
παί-ω strike
πεντακόσι-οι -αι -α five hundred
πέντε five
πεπονθὼς ἦ 'I had suffered' (πάσχω)
πληγ-ή, ἡ blow (1a)
πύξ with the fist
στόμα (στοματ-), τό mouth (3b)
συγκόπτ-ω hit, strike (aor. pass. συνεκόπ-ην)
συγχωρέ-ω agree with, to (+dat.)

Vocabulary to be learnt

ἁλίσκομαι (ἁλ-) be caught, convicted (aor. ἑάλων)

βουλευτής, ὁ member of council (1d)

διακωλύω prevent

εἴκοσι twenty

εἰσαγγέλλω (εἰσαγγειλ-) impeach

ἐνέχυρον, τό security, pledge (2b)

ἐπί (+dat.) at, on; for the purpose of

ζημιόω fine, penalise, punish

κρίσις, ἡ judgment, dispute, trial, decision (3e)

μετέρχομαι (μετελθ-) send for, chase after

μέτριος α ον fair, moderate, reasonable

στόμα (στοματ-), τό mouth (3b)

συγχωρέω agree with, to (+dat.); yield to

O   Grammar for Section Fifteen F

Summary:
Perf. opt.
ἁλίσκομαι

Verbs

Perfect optatives πεπαύκοιμι, πεπαυμένος εἴην

190 The forms of the perfect optatives are as follows:

Active

πεπαύκ-οιμι *or* πεπαυκὼς εἴην
   -οις   πεπαυκὼς εἴης
   -οι etc. πεπαυκὼς εἴη etc.

Middle/passive

πεπαυμένος εἴην
πεπαυμένος εἴης
πεπαυμένος εἴη etc.

ἁλίσκομαι

191 Note the principal parts of ἁλίσκομαι 'be captured, found guilty':

ἁλίσκομαι   'I am captured'
ἁλώσομαι (fut.)   'I will be captured'
ἑάλω-ν (ἁλ-) (aor.)   'I was captured' (root aorist, cf. **126, 132**)

ἑάλων keeps its ω all the way through the indicative and subjunctive (cf. ἔγνων, **132**), and has

Participle: ἁλούς (cf. γνούς)
Infinitive: ἁλῶναι (cf. γνῶναι)
Optative: ἁλοίην (cf. γνοίην)
Subjunctive: ἁλῶ, ἁλῷς, ἁλῷ etc. (cf. γνῶ).

Revise

Conditions with ἄν **151–2, 162,** Reference Grammar O p. 305, Language Survey (6)

τό + inf. **163–4** Reference Grammar J

Perf. **165–6, 169–71** Language Survey (8)   ○

Vocabulary for Section Fifteen G

ἀθυμί-α, ἡ lack of spirit, depression (1b)

ἀλλὰ μήν . . . γε but naturally

ἀναπαύ-ομαι rest, take a breather

διάκει-μαι be in x (adv.) condition

διατελέ-ω finish, complete

εἰσαγγελί-α, ἡ impeachment (1b)

ἐκεῖ there

ἐπιεικ-ής -ές fair, moderate

ἕως ἄν (+subj.) until

ἤπι-ος -α -ον mild

Ἥρ-α, ἡ Hera *(1b) (wife of Zeus)*

ἴωμεν let us go

καθιζώμεθα let us sit

καταγωγ-ή, ἡ place, spot (1a)

κατέχ-ω restrain, hold

μένωμεν let us stay

παυώμεθα let us stop

περιπατέ-ω walk, stroll

πλάταν-ος, ἡ plane-tree (2a)

πλέον (any) more

πνεῦμα (πνευματ-), τό breeze (3a)

πνῖγ-ος, τό stifling heat (3c)

πο-ά, ἡ grass (1c)

προάγ-ω lead on

σκι-ά, ἡ shade (1b)

σκόπωμεν let us survey, consider

συλλέγ-ω gather, collect

τεκμαίρ-ομαι conclude, infer

τί μήν; of course (so what follows?)

ὑψηλ-ός -ή -όν high, tall

Vocabulary to be learnt

ἀθυμία, ἡ *lack of spirit, depression (1b)*

διάκειμαι *be in X (adv.) state, mood*

εἰσαγγελία, ἡ *impeachment (1b)*

ἐκεῖ *there*

ἐπιεικής ές *fair, reasonable, moderate*

ἕως ἄν (+subj.) *until*

πλέον *more (adv.)*

προάγω *lead on*

συλλέγω *collect, gather*

τεκμαίρομαι *conclude, infer*

○   # Grammar for Section Fifteen G

Summary:

1st person orders

ἕως ἄν

Subjunctive orders 'let us'

192 The subjunctive, used on its own in the 1st person plural, means 'let us', e.g. μένωμεν 'let us wait', πυθώμεθα 'let us inquire'.

ἕως 'until'

193 ἕως ἄν means 'until such time as', and the verb goes into the subjunctive. The implication behind this sense of 'until' is that the time of the event awaited in the 'until' clause is viewed as being not entirely certain, or as lying in the indefinite future (cf. on indefinite use of ἄν, **175–6**), e.g. μένωμεν ἕως ἂν ἐπανέλθῃ ὁ δεσπότης 'let us wait till such time as the master returns' (whenever *that* may be).   O

Vocabulary for Section Fifteen H

αἰκεί-α, ἡ assault (1b)
ἀκολουθέ-ω follow
ἀναίτι-ος -ον innocent
ἀντί (+gen.) instead of
ἀπολαμβάν-ω (ἀπολαβ-) take
αὐτίκα at once, directly
ἐνθυμέ-ομαι take to heart

ἥκιστα least of all, not
καταδίκ-η, ἡ fine (1a)
κηδεστ-ής, ὁ cousin (1d)
μάλα virtually, quite, very
Μνησίβουλ-ος, ὁ Mnesiboulos
   (2a) (*Theophemos' cousin*)
τράπεζ-α, ἡ bank (1c)

ὑπισχνέ-ομαι
   (ὑποσχ-) promise (to)
   (+fut. inf.)
φοβέ-ομαι μή fear that/lest
   (+opt.)

Vocabulary to be learnt

ἀναίτιος ον innocent
ἀντί (+gen.) instead of, for
ἀπολαμβάνω (ἀπολαβ-) take
ἐνθυμέομαι take to heart, be
   angry at

ἥκιστα least of all, no, not
καταδίκη, ἡ fine (1a)
μάλα very, quite, virtually (cf.
   μᾶλλον, μάλιστα)
ὑπισχνέομαι

(ὑποσχ-) promise (to)
(+fut. inf.)
φοβέομαι μή fear that/lest
(+opt.)

O   # Grammar for Section Fifteen H

Summary
φοβοῦμαι μή+opt.

φοβοῦμαι again

194 You have already met φοβοῦμαι μή+subjunctive to mean 'fear that something will/may happen'. When the verb of fearing is in secondary sequence, the μή clause will take the optative, e.g.
ἐφοβεῖτο μὴ οὐκ ἀφίκοιτο ἡ στρατιά 'he was afraid the army might not come'

Note
You have now met three constructions in which the verbs are in the subjunc-tive *in primary* sequence, *and* optative *in secondary sequence, i.e.* ἵνα (**186**), *indefinites* (**187**) *and here with verbs of fearing. You should bear this principle in mind, but be aware that Greek usage in this respect is very flexible and you will find the* subjunctive *used in places where you would expect the optative.*   O

Exercises for Section Fifteen F–H

English into Greek

1. Sentences

Translate into Greek:

1. The decree demanded that the trierarchs get back the gear in whatever way was most easy for them.
2. Whenever the trierarchs came across someone not handing over the gear, they went back to the council.
3. Let us stop travelling and sit down.
4. We shall stay here until we feel better.
5. Before returning home, let us sit down over there until the sun becomes more tolerable.

2. Prose

Translate into Greek:

Since it was impossible to get the gear, the city was in great danger. So the council had to do something, so that we might equip a rescue-force of triremes as soon as possible. I had gone to Theophemos' house, but he was not in. I was afraid that he would not hand over the gear. So Khairedemos drafted a decree. And the trierarchs, whenever they came across someone who would not give back the gear, showed him the decree.

Test Exercise Fifteen

Translate into English:

Apollodoros claims that the defendant Polykles would not take over a trireme from him, although he had been appointed as its joint-trierarch for the next year, and that he himself served several months overtime with the boat as a consequence. Apollodoros relates what happened when he tackled Polykles the first time in Thasos.

(From Demosthenes, *Polykles*, 29–37)

ἐπειδὴ οὗτος ἀφίκετο εἰς Θάσον, παραλαβὼν ἐγὼ μάρτυρας τῶν τε πολιτῶν ὡς ἐδυνάμην πλείστους καὶ τοὺς ἐπιβάτας, προσέρχομαι αὐτῷ ἐν Θάσῳ ἐν τῇ ἀγορᾷ, καὶ ἐκέλευον αὐτὸν τήν τε ναῦν παραλαμβάνειν παρ' ἐμοῦ ὡς διάδοχον ὄντα, καὶ τοῦ ἐπιτετριηραρχημένου χρόνου ἀποδιδόναι μοι τὰ ἀναλώματα. λογίσασθαι δ' ἤθελον αὐτῷ καθ' ἕκαστον, ἕως μοι μάρτυρες παρῆσαν τῶν ἀνηλωμένων, ἵνα, εἴ τι ἀντιλέγοι, εὐθὺς ἐξελέγχοιμι. ἐγέγραπτο γὰρ ὑπ' ἐμοῦ ἀκριβῶς τὰ

ἀναλώματα. προκαλουμένου δέ μου ταῦτα, ἀπεκρίνατό μοι Πολυκλῆς
ὅτι οὐδὲν αὐτῷ μέλοι ὧν λέγοιμι.
Apollodoros gets no further on the next occasion either. Returning from a
voyage ordered by the general Timomakhos to Thasos, he decides to go direct
to the top and have the general there when he tries to hand over the vessel
formally to Polykles for the second time.

καταλαμβάνω οὖν καὶ Πολυκλέα ἐκεῖ καὶ τοὺς τριηράρχους καὶ τοὺς
διαδόχους καὶ ἄλλους τινὰς τῶν πολιτῶν, καὶ εἰσελθὼν εὐθὺς ἐναντίον
τοῦ στρατηγοῦ λόγους πρὸς αὐτὸν ἐποιούμην, καὶ ἐκέλευον αὐτὸν τήν τε
ναῦν παραλαμβάνειν παρ' ἐμοῦ, καὶ τοῦ ἐπιτετριηραρχημένου χρόνου
ἀποδιδόναι μοι τὰ ἀναλώματα. ταῦτα δέ μου προκαλουμένου αὐτόν, 'τίς
ἂν δύναιτ'', ἔφη, 'τὴν σὴν <u>μανίαν</u> καὶ <u>πολυτέλειαν</u> <u>ὑπομεῖναι</u>, ὃς σκεύη
<u>ἴδια</u> μόνος ἔχεις τῶν τριηράρχων καὶ ἀργύριον πολὺ δίδως τοῖς ναύταις;
κακῶν γὰρ διδάσκαλος γέγονας ἐν τῷ <u>στρατεύματι</u>, διαφθείρας τοὺς
ναύτας καὶ τοὺς ἐπιβάτας, δέον σε <u>τὰ αὐτὰ</u> ποιεῖν τοῖς ἄλλοις
τριηράρχοις.' λέγοντος δὲ αὐτοῦ ταῦτα, ἀπεκρινάμην αὐτῷ, 'περὶ μὲν
τῶν ναυτῶν καὶ τῶν ἐπιβατῶν, εἰ φῂς ὑπ' ἐμοῦ αὐτοὺς διεφθάρθαι,
παραλαβὼν τὴν τριήρη αὐτὸς σαυτῷ <u>κατασκεύασαι</u> καὶ ναύτας καὶ
ἐπιβάτας, οἵτινές σοι μηδὲν ἀργύριον λαβόντες <u>συμπλεύσονται</u>. τὴν δὲ
ναῦν παράλαβε· οὐ γὰρ ἔτι μοι <u>προσήκει</u> τριηραρχεῖν.' λέγοντος δέ μου
ταῦτα, ἀποκρίνεταί μοι ὅτι ὁ <u>συντριήραρχος</u> αὐτῷ οὐχ ἥκοι ἐπὶ τὴν ναῦν·
'οὔκουν παραλήψομαι μόνος τὴν τριήρη.'

Vocabulary

ἐπιβάτης, ὁ marine (1d)
διάδοχος, ὁ successor (2a)
ἐπιτριηραρχέω serve (as
  trierarch) over one's time
ἀνάλωμα (ἀναλωματ-), τό
  expense (3b)
ἕως (+indic.) while
ἀνηλωμένος perf. part. pass.
  of ἀναλίσκω spend

ἀντιλέγω object
προκαλέομαι challenge
μανία, ἡ madness (1b)
πολυτέλεια, ἡ extravagance
  (1b)
ὑπομένω (ὑπομειν-) endure
ἴδιος α ον private
στράτευμα (στρατευματ-), τό
  army (3b)

ὁ αὐτός (+dat.) the same as
κατασκευάζομαι provide
συμπλέω (fut.
  συμπλεύσομαι) sail with
προσήκει it is the business of
  (dat.)
συντριήραρχος, ὁ
  joint-trierarch (2a)

Section Sixteen

Vocabulary for Section Sixteen A

ἀκόλουθ-ος -ον accompanying (+dat.)
ἀναγκαῖ-ος -α -ον necessary
ἀποφέρ-ω carry back, return
ἀριστά-ω have breakfast
ἁρπάζ-ω seize, plunder
ᾄσσ-ω dart, dash
αὐλ-ή, ἡ courtyard (1a)
ἀφείθη she was let go (aor. pass. of ἀφίημι)
ἀφειμένη let go, released (perf. pass. of ἀφίημι)
ἀφῆκε (he) let go (aor. of ἀφίημι)
γεωργέ-ω farm
διαιτά-ομαι live
διάκον-ος, ὁ servant (2a)
διαφεύγ-ω (διαφυγ-) get away from
ἐκ-βάλλ-ω (ἐκβαλ-) break open

ἐκτίν-ω (ἐκτεισ-) pay
ἐκφορέ-ω carry off
ἐπεισέρχ-ομαι (ἐπεισελθ-) invade
ἕως (+opt.) until
ᾖξαν see ᾄσσω
θεράπαιν-α, ἡ servant (1c)
ἱππόδρομ-ος, ὁ race-course, downs (2a)
κῆπ-ος, ὁ garden (2a)
κλεί-ω close
κραυγ-ή, ἡ shouting, tumult (1a)
μαλακ-ός -ή -όν soft-fleeced
μειράκι-ον, τό youth (2b)
ἐκ μειρακίου from a young boy
οἴχ-ομαι be off, be gone
ὁρμά-ομαι charge

οὗπερ where
πεντήκοντα fifty
πιστ-ός -ή -όν trustworthy, reliable
ποιμαίν-ω tend
ποιμήν (ποιμεν-), ὁ shepherd (3a)
ποίμν-η, ἡ flock of sheep (1a)
πρεσβύτερ-ος -α -ον older, rather old
πρόβατ-ον, τό sheep (2b)
πρός (+dat.) near; in addition
πύργ-ος, ὁ tower (2a)   [to
τίτθ-η, ἡ nurse (1a)
ὑδρί-α, ἡ hydria, large vessel (1b)
ὑπόλοιπ-ος -ον remaining, left over
φέρ-ω lead
χαλκ-οῦς -ῆ -οῦν bronze

Vocabulary to be learnt

ἀναγκαῖος α ον *necessary*
ἀποφέρω (ἀπενεγκ-) *carry back*
αὐλή, ἡ *courtyard (1a)*
ἀφίημι (ἀφε-) *release, let go*
διαφεύγω (διαφυγ-) *get away, flee*
ἐκβάλλω (ἐκβαλ-) *break open; throw out*

ἐπεισέρχομαι (ἐπεισελθ-) *attack*
ἕως (+opt.) *until*
θεράπαινα, ἡ *maidservant (1c)*
κλείω *close, shut*
ὁρμάομαι *charge, set off, make a move*
οὗπερ *where*
πιστός ή όν *faithful,*

trustworthy, reliable
ποιμήν (ποιμεν-), ὁ *shepherd (3a)*
πρεσβύτερος α ον *older, rather old*
πρός (+dat.) *near; in addition to*
φέρω (ἐνεγκ-) *lead*
χαλκοῦς ῆ οῦν *bronze*

O   Grammar for Section Sixteen A

Summary:
ἕως +opt.
(ἀφ)ἵημι

ἕως 'until'

195 In secondary sequence ἕως when it means 'until such time as' takes the optative (cf. **193**). E.g.,

ἐμένομεν ἕως ἔλθοι 'we waited until he should come'

Verb

(ἀφ)ἵημι 'release, let go, shoot'

196 You have already met -μι verbs δίδωμι (**131**), τίθημι (**150**), ἵστημι (**144**), and have seen how their forms are related. ἵημι is no exception, and follows most closely the pattern of τίθημι. ἀφίημι, the common compound, is used here.

Present indicative active

Stem: ἀφιε-

	Participle	Infinitive	Imperative	Optative	Subjunctive
ἀφίη-μι	ἀφιε-ίς	ἀφιέ-ναι	ἀφίε-ι	ἀφιε-ίην	ἀφι-ῶ
ἀφίη-ς	ἀφιε-ῖσα		ἀφιέ-τω	ἀφιε-ίης	ἀφι-ῇς
ἀφίη-σι(ν)	ἀφιέ-ν		ἀφιέ-τε	ἀφιε-ίη	ἀφι-ῇ
ἀφίε-μεν	(ἀφιεντ-)		ἀφιέ-ντων	ἀφιε-ῖμεν	ἀφι-ῶμεν
ἀφίε-τε				ἀφιε-ῖτε	ἀφι-ῆτε
ἀφι-ᾶσι(ν)				ἀφιε-ῖεν	ἀφι-ῶσι(ν)

Present indicative middle/passive

	Participle	Infinitive	Imperative	Optative	Subjunctive
ἀφίε-μαι	ἀφιέ-μεν-ος	ἀφίε-σθαι	ἀφίε-σο	ἀφιε-ίμην	ἀφι-ῶμαι
ἀφίε-σαι	-η		ἀφιέ-σθω	ἀφιε-ῖο	ἀφι-ῇ
ἀφίε-ται	-ον		ἀφιέ-σθε	ἀφιε-ῖτο	ἀφι-ῆται
ἀφιέ-μεθα			ἀφιέ-σθων	ἀφιε-ίμεθα	ἀφι-ώμεθα
ἀφίε-σθε				ἀφιε-ῖσθε	ἀφι-ῆσθε
ἀφίε-νται				ἀφιε-ῖντο	ἀφι-ῶνται

Imperfect indicative
active

ἀφίη-ν
ἀφίε-ις
ἀφίε-ι
ἀφίε-μεν
ἀφίε-τε
ἀφίε-σαν

Imperfect indicative
middle/passive

ἀφιέ-μην
ἀφίε-σο
ἀφίε-το
ἀφιέ-μεθα
ἀφίε-σθε
ἀφίε-ντο

Aorist indicative
active

	Participle	Infinitive	Imperative	Optative	Subjunctive

Stem: ἀφε- (note augmented form is ἀφη- or ἀφει-)

ἀφῆ-κα	ἀφε-ίς	ἀφε-ῖναι	ἄφε-ς	ἀφε-ίην	ἀφ-ῶ
ἀφῆ-κας	ἀφε-ῖσα		ἀφέ-τω	ἀφε-ίης	ἀφ-ῇς
ἀφῆ-κε	ἀφέ-ν		ἄφε-τε	ἀφε-ίη	ἀφ-ῇ
ἀφεῖ-μεν	(ἀφεντ-)		ἀφέ-ντων	ἀφε-ῖμεν	ἀφ-ῶμεν
ἀφεῖ-τε				ἀφε-ῖτε	ἀφ-ῆτε
ἀφεῖ-σαν (ἀφῆ-καν)				ἀφε-ῖεν	ἀφ-ῶσι(ν)

Aorist indicative
middle

	Participle	Infinitive	Imperative	Optative	Subjunctive
ἀφεί-μην	ἀφέ-μεν-ος	ἀφέ-σθαι	ἀφ-οῦ	ἀφε-ίμην	ἀφ-ῶμαι
ἀφεῖ-σο	-η		ἀφέ-σθω	ἀφε-ῖο	ἀφ-ῇ
ἀφεῖ-το	-ον		ἄφε-σθε	ἀφε-ῖτο	ἀφ-ῆται
ἀφεί-μεθα			ἀφέ-σθων	ἀφε-ίμεθα	ἀφ-ώμεθα
ἀφεῖ-σθε				ἀφε-ῖσθε	ἀφ-ῆσθε
ἀφεῖ-ντο				ἀφε-ῖντο	ἀφ-ῶνται

Aorist indicative
  passive   *Participle   Infinitive   Imperative Optative   Subjunctive*

Stem: ἀφεθ-
ἀφείθ-ην   ἀφεθ-είς   ἀφεθ-ῆναι ἀφέθ-ητι   ἀφεθ-είην ἀφεθ-ῶ
ἀφείθ-ης
ἀφείθ-η
ἀφείθ-ημεν
ἀφείθ-ητε
ἀφείθ-ησαν

Future indicative active
ἀφήσ-ω (regular, like παύσ-ω)

Future indicative middle
ἀφήσ-ομαι (regular, like παύσ-ομαι)

Future indicative passive
ἀφεθ-ή-σομαι (regular, like παυσθ-ήσ-ομαι)

Perfect indicative active
ἀφεῖκ-α (regular, like πέπαυκ-α)

Perfect indicative middle/passive
ἀφεῖ-μαι (regular, like πέπαυ-μαι)

Notes
(i) *Common compounds of* ἵημι *are* συνίημι '*understand*' *and* μεθίημι '*let go of*'.
(ii) *Main stems of* ἵημι *are* ἱε-, ἑ- *or* εἱ-. *For* τιθε- *in the present and imperfect forms of* τίθημι, *you will find* ἱε- *in* ἵημι. *For* θε- *in the aorist, you will find* ἑ-; *but remember that for augmented forms, you will find the* ἐθε- *of* τίθημι *replaced by* ἡ- *or* εἱ-, *e.g.* ἔθηκα–ἧκα, ἐθέμην–εἵμην.
(iii) *On* -μι *verbs in general, see Language Survey (7).*

Exercise for Section Sixteen A

(b/c) Morphology and Syntax
1. Translate these sentences. Say what each of the other choices of verb would mean:
  a. ἡ θεράπαινα ὑπὸ τοῦ πατρὸς τοῦ ἐμοῦ ἀφεῖται ἐλευθέρα.
  (ἀφείθη/ἀφεθήσεται/ἀφίεται/ἀφίετο)

b. ὁ δὲ πατὴρ ὁ ἐμὸς ἀφῆκε τὴν θεράπαιναν.
  (ἀφίησι/ἀφεῖκε/ἀφίει/ἀφήσει)
c. ἡ γὰρ θεράπαινα, ἀφειμένη ἐλευθέρα ὑπὸ τοῦ πατρός, συνῴκησεν ἀνδρὶ
  ἀφειμένῳ καὶ ἐκείνῳ ὑπὸ τοῦ δεσπότου.
  (ἀφεθεῖσα/ἀφεθέντι:ἀφιεμένη/ἀφιεμένῳ:ἀφεθησομένη/ἀφεθησομένῳ)
d. τοὺς γὰρ δούλους τοὺς ἐν ἐκείνῃ τῇ ναυμαχίᾳ ναυμαχήσαντας ἀφεῖσαν οἱ
  Ἀθηναῖοι.
  (ἀφείκασι/ἀφίασιν/ἀφήσουσιν/ἀφίεσαν)

Vocabulary for Section Sixteen B

Ἀγνόφιλ-ος, ὁ Hagnophilos
  (2a) (a friend of Aristarkhos)
ἄγχ-ω throttle, strangle
ἄλλως τε καί especially
ἀμυχ-ή, ἡ scratching, tearing
  (1a)
Ἀνθεμίων (Ἀνθεμιων-), ὁ
  Anthemion (3a) (a
  neighbour of Aristarkhos)
ἀπαγγέλλ-ω announce,
  report
ἀπαγορεύ-ω (ἀπειπ-) forbid
ἀπαντά-ω meet (+dat.)
ἀπεῖπε see ἀπαγορεύ-ω
ἀποστρέφ-ω twist back
βραχίων (βραχιον-), ὁ arm
  (3a)
διατίθη-μι (διαθε-) dispose
ἕλκ-ω drag
ἐντίθη-μι (ἐνθε-) insert, put in

Ἑρμογέν-ης, ὁ Hermogenes
  (3d)
ἑώρα impf. of ὁράω (3rd s.)
ἕως (+ind.) until
ἠκηκόει plup. of ἀκούω (3rd
  s.)
θεράπων (θεραπον-), ὁ
  servant (3a)
καρπ-ός, ὁ wrist (2a)
κεῖ-μαι lie
κόλπ-ος, ὁ bosom, lap (2a)
κραυγ-ή, ἡ shout, cry (1a)
κυμβί-ον, τό cup (2b)
λοιπ-ός -ή -όν left, remaining
οἴχ-ομαι go, depart
παραγίγν-ομαι (παραγεν-) be
  present, turn up
παράκει-μαι lie beside
  (+dat.)

παριόντας part. of
  παρέρχομαι, pass by
πελι-ός -ά -όν bruised
πεντήκοντα fifty
πίν-ω (πι-) drink
πορθέ-ω ransack
πρίν ἄν (+subj.) until
πρίν (+opt.) until
πρόβατ-ον, τό sheep (2b)
προσκαλέ-ω summon (aor.
  part. pass. προσκληθείς)
στῆθ-ος, τό chest (3c)
τέγ-ος, τό roof (3c)
τιμά-ω value, reckon
τίτθ-η, ἡ nurse (1a)
τράπεζ-α, ἡ bank (1c)
τράχηλ-ος, ὁ throat (2a)
ὕφαιμ-ος -ον bloody

Vocabulary to be learnt

ἀπαγγέλλω
  (ἀπαγγειλ-) announce,
  report
ἀπαγορεύω (ἀπειπ-) forbid
διατίθημι (διαθε-) dispose, put
  X in Y (adv.) state
ἐντίθημι (ἐνθε-) place in, put
  in
θεράπων (θεραπον-), ὁ

  servant (3a)
κεῖμαι lie, be placed, be made
λοιπός ἡ όν left, remaining
οἴχομαι be off, depart
παραγίγνομαι (παραγεν-) be
  present, turn up at (+dat.)
παράκειμαι lie beside, be placed
  beside (+dat.)
πεντήκοντα fifty

πίνω (πι-) drink
πρίν ἄν (+subj.) until
πρίν (+opt.) until
πρόβατον, τό sheep (2b)
προσκαλέω summon, call (aor.
  part. pass. προσκληθείς)
τιμάω value, reckon; honour
τίτθη, ἡ nurse (1a)
τράπεζα, ἡ bank; table (1c)

O   Grammar for Section Sixteen B

Summary:
ἕως+ind.
πρὶν ἄν+subj., πρίν+opt.
διατίθημι, διάκειμαι

ἕως 'while, until'

197 You have already met ἕως meaning 'until' (**193, 195**), and it has been explained that, when it takes a subjunctive+ἄν or an optative, there is uncertainty or indefiniteness about the time of the 'until' clause. When it takes the *indicative*, it means either 'until' (and the action of the 'until' is *known* to be completed), *or* 'while'. Only the context will tell you which is correct, e.g.

ἐβόησε ἕως ἐκέλευον παύσασθαι 'he shouted, until I told him to stop'

μένωμεν ἕως ἔξεστιν 'let us wait while it is possible'

πρίν 'until'

198 You have already met πρίν+infinitive, when it means 'before' (**161**). When πρίν is followed by ἄν+subjunctive (primary sequence) or optative (secondary sequence – cf. **194** note), it means 'until'; and, like ἕως, it can also be followed by the indicative, when it will still mean 'until' but the action of the 'until' clause will have been completed, e.g.

οὐκ ἀπῆλθον πρὶν ἔδειξα τὴν ὁδόν 'they did not leave till I showed them the road'

οὐ χρή με ἀπελθεῖν πρὶν ἂν ἴδω τὴν γυναῖκα 'I must not go till I see my wife'

Note
You will find that, as with ἕως, ἄν sometimes drops out of the construction with the subjunctive, especially in poetry. (In general, see Language Survey (6), p. 315, and Reference Grammar L, p. 303.)

Verb
διατίθημι|διάκειμαι 'treat, be treated'

199 διατίθημι means 'I dispose, I treat' someone in a certain way; to express its passive form Greek normally uses διάκειμαι 'I am treated, disposed' in a certain way (cf. **150** note (iii)).

The main parts of κεῖμαι are:

Present: κεῖ-μαι, (part.) κείμενος, (inf.) κεῖσθαι, (imper.) κεῖσο!
Imperfect: ἐ-κεί-μην
Future: κείσ-ομαι

○

Exercise for Section Sixteen B

(b/c) Morphology and Syntax

1. Translate the following sentences:
   a. αἱ μὲν θεράπαιναι ἔμειναν ἐν τῷ πυργῷ ἕως ἀπῆλθον οἱ ἄνδρες.
   b. ἡ δὲ γυνὴ ᾔτει τὸν Θεόφημον μὴ λαβεῖν τὰ σκεύη πρὶν ἐπανίοι ὁ ἀνήρ.
   c. 'ἀλλὰ μὴ αἴτει μηδὲ τοῦτο', ἦ δ' ὃς ὁ γείτων. 'ὑβρισταὶ γὰρ ὄντες οἱ ἄνδρες οὗτοι οὐ παύσονται ἁρπάζοντες τὴν οἰκίαν πρὶν ἂν ἀφαίρωνται πάντα.'
   d. ἐγὼ δ' ἦν ἐν Πειραιεῖ, ἕως ἡ οἰκία ἡ ἐμὴ ἐπορθεῖτο, καὶ οὐκ ἀπῆα οἴκαδε πρὶν ἀπηγγέλθη μοι ἐκεῖσε τὰ γεγενημένα.
   e. πρὶν ἐξελθεῖν ἐκ τῆς οἰκίας, εἰρήκη τῇ γυναικὶ ὡς τὸ ἀργύριον κέοιτο ἐπὶ τῇ τραπέζῃ.

2. Complete these sentences by inserting the correct word from the brackets. Then translate:
   a. ἡ γραῦς κακῶς (ἔκειτο/διέκειτο) διὰ τὸ συγκοπῆναι.
   b. Θεόφημος καὶ Εὔεργος οὕτω (ἔθεσαν/διέθεσαν) τὴν γραῦν ὥστε ὕφαιμοι ἐγένοντο οἱ βραχίονες.
   c. ἡ γυνὴ εἶπε τῷ Θεοφήμῳ ὅτι τὸ ἀργύριον (διάκειται/κεῖται) ἐπὶ τῇ τραπέζῃ.
   d. ἡ γραῦς (ἐνέθηκεν/διέθηκεν) εἰς τὸν κόλπον τὸ κυμβίον ὃ (παρέκειτο/διέκειτο) αὐτῇ.

Vocabulary for Section Sixteen C

ἄγγελ-ος, ὁ messenger (2a)
ἀκολουθέ-ω follow, accompany
ἀνδράποδ-ον, τό slave (2b)
ἀπόκρισ-ις, ἡ reply (3e)
ἁρπάζ-ω seize, plunder
αὐτίκα at once
δέκα ten

διαμαρτύρ-ομαι beg earnestly
διατριβ-ή, ἡ delay (1a)
δίκ-η, ἡ fine (1a)
ἐδυνήθην aor. of δύναμαι
ἐκτίν-ω (ἐκτεισ-) pay
ἐκφορέ-ω carry off
ἐμποιέ-ω engender, cause
ἕωθεν at dawn

ἰατρ-ός, ὁ doctor (2a)
κακά . . . πολλὰ λέγω curse vehemently
καταφέρ-ω carry down
κατηνέχθη aor. pass. of καταφέρω
κινδυνεύ-ω be in danger, run a risk

λιθοκόπ-ος, ὁ stone-mason (2a)

μνῆμα (μνηματ-), τό memorial, monument (3b)

μόλις scarcely, reluctantly

ὀβολ-ός, ὁ obol (2a) *(one-sixth of a drachma)*

Πειραι-εύς, ὁ Piraeus (3g)

πλεονεκτέ-ω be greedy

πλησί-ος -α -ον nearby

προτεραῖ-ος -α -ον previous, of previous day

τῇ προτεραίᾳ on the previous day

πύργ-ος, ὁ tower (2a)

συγκόπτ-ω beat up (aor. pass. συνεκόπην)

σφόδρα very much, exceedingly

τριακόσι-οι -αι -α three

hundred

ὑπόλοιπ-ος -ον remaining, left

ὑστεραῖ-ος -α -ον next, of next day

τῇ ὑστεραίᾳ on the next day

χίλι-οι -αι -α thousand

χρεί-α, ἡ need, necessity (2b)

ψυχ-ή, ἡ life, soul (1a)

Vocabulary to be learnt

ἄγγελος, ὁ messenger (2a)

ἀκολουθέω follow, accompany

ἀπόκρισις, ἡ reply, answer (3e)

ἁρπάζω seize, plunder, snatch

δέκα ten

διατριβή, ἡ delay; pastime; discussion; way of life (1a)

δίκη, ἡ fine; case; justice (1a)

ἐκτίνω (ἐκτεισ-) pay

ἐκφορέω carry off

καταφέρω (κατενεγκ-) carry down

κινδυνεύω be in danger, run risk, be likely to

πλησίος α ον nearby

προτεραῖος α ον previous, of previous day

πύργος, ὁ tower (2a)

συγκόπτω beat up, strike (aor. pass. συνεκόπην)

σφόδρα very much, exceedingly

ὑπόλοιπος ον remaining

ὑστεραῖος α ον next day

χίλιοι αι α thousand

ψυχή, ἡ soul, life (1a)

◯ Grammar for Section Sixteen C

Summary:
ὥστε + ind./inf.
Numerals

οὕτως . . . ὥστε 'so . . . that'

200 You have already met ὥστε at the start of a sentence, meaning 'consequently, as a result'. It can also introduce a clause on its own, when it means 'so as to' (and will be followed by an infinitive – change of subject in the accusative rule), or 'so that' (when it will be followed by an indicative), e.g.

μηχανὴν εὑρίσκουσιν ὥστε ἐκφυγεῖν 'they find a plan so as to escape' (or 'an escape-plan') (but do they escape?)

μηχανὴν ηὗρον ὥστε ἐξέφυγον 'they found a plan so that they escaped'

201 Frequently, ὥστε is preceded by οὕτω(ς) 'so' (or by words such as τοσοῦτος 'so great', τοιοῦτος 'of such a sort', τόσος 'so many'), to form what is called a 'result' or 'consecutive' clause, of the form 'so . . . that'. The ὥστε clause will still take an indicative or infinitive, e.g.

οὕτως ἀνόητός ἐστιν ὥστε ἐλπίζει ἐκφεύξεσθαι 'he is so foolish that he hopes to escape'

οὕτως ἀνόητός ἐστιν ὥστε ἐλπίζειν ἐκφεύξεσθαι 'he is so foolish as to hope to escape' (but does he actually hope to escape?)
(On infinitives in general, see Reference Grammar J, p. 299.)
202 There is sometimes a very fine distinction between the force of the clauses taking an infinitive or an indicative, and it is often not possible to make as clear a distinction as we have done.

Numerals

203	Cardinals	Ordinals	Adverbs
	('one, two' *etc.*)	('first, second' *etc.*)	('once, twice' *etc.*)
I	εἷς μία ἕν	πρῶτ-ος -η -ον	ἅπαξ
2	δύο	δεύτερ-ος -α -ον	δίς
3	τρεῖς τρία	τρίτ-ος -η -ον	τρίς
4	τέτταρες τέτταρα	τέταρτ-ος (etc.)	τετράκις
5	πέντε	πέμπτος	πεντάκις
6	ἕξ	ἕκτος	ἑξάκις
7	ἑπτά	ἕβδομος	ἑπτάκις
8	ὀκτώ	ὄγδοος	ὀκτάκις
9	ἐννέα	ἔνατος	ἐνάκις
10	δέκα	δέκατος	δεκάκις
11	ἕνδεκα	ἑνδέκατος	ἑνδεκάκις
12	δώδεκα	δωδέκατος	δωδεκάκις
13	τρεῖς καὶ δέκα	τρίτος καὶ δέκατος	τρισκαιδεκάκις
14	τέτταρες καὶ δέκα	τέταρτος καὶ δέκατος	τετταρακαιδεκάκις
15	πεντεκαίδεκα	πέμπτος καὶ δέκατος	πεντεκαιδεκάκις
16	ἑκκαίδεκα	ἕκτος καὶ δέκατος	ἑκκαιδεκάκις
17	ἑπτακαίδεκα	ἕβδομος καὶ δέκατος	ἑπτακαιδεκάκις
18	ὀκτωκαίδεκα	ὄγδοος καὶ δέκατος	ὀκτωκαιδεκάκις
19	ἐννεακαίδεκα	ἔνατος καὶ δέκατος	ἐννεακαιδεκάκις
20	εἴκοσι(ν)	εἰκοστός	εἰκοσάκις
30–90	-κοντα	-κοστός	-κοντάκις
100	ἑκατόν	ἑκατοστός	ἑκατοντάκις
200–900	-κόσιοι-αι -α	-κοσιοστός	-κοσιάκις
1,000	χίλιοι-αι -α	χιλιοστός	χιλιάκις
10,000	μύριοι-αι -α	μυριοστός	μυριάκις

Notes
(i) All ordinals, and cardinals in the 100's and above, decline in full like καλ-ός -ή -όν, *or* ἡμέτερ-ος -α -ον.

The declension of 'one', 'two', 'three', 'four'

εἷς 'one'   δύο 'two'

	nom.	acc.	gen.	dat.
m.	εἷς	ἕνα	ἑνός	ἑνί
f.	μία	μίαν	μιᾶς	μιᾷ
n.	ἕν	ἕν	ἑνός	ἑνί

	nom.	acc.	gen.	dat.
m./f./n.	δύο	δύο	δυοῖν	δυοῖν

τρεῖς 'three'   τέτταρες 'four'

m./f.	τρεῖς	τρεῖς	τριῶν	τρισί(ν)
n.	τρία	τρία	τριῶν	τρισί(ν)

m./f.	τέτταρες	τέτταρας	τεττάρων	τέτταρσι(ν)
n.	τέτταρα	τέτταρα	τεττάρων	τέτταρσι(ν)

Exercise for Sixteen C

(b/c) Morphology and Syntax

1. Translate these sentences, then convert indicative to infinitive in the ὥστε clauses and translate the new versions:

a. οὕτω πονηροὶ ἦσαν οἱ ἄνδρες ἐκεῖνοι ὥστε ἔτυπτον τὴν γυναῖκα καὶ ἀφείλοντο ἀπ' αὐτῆς τὸ κυμβίον.

b. ἀλλ' οὕτω αἰσχροὶ ἦσαν ἐκεῖνοι ὥστε οὐκ ᾐσχύνοντο εἰς τὴν γυναῖκα εἰσιόντες.

c. πᾶν ποιοῦσιν ὥστε δίκην οὐ διδόασιν.

d. εἰς τοῦτο ἀσεβείας ἦλθεν ὁ ἄνθρωπος ὥστε εἰσελθὼν εἰς τὸ ἱερὸν ἱκέτην ἀφείλκυσεν ἀπὸ τοῦ βωμοῦ.

Vocabulary for Section Sixteen D

αἰσχυνθῆναι aor. inf. of αἰσχύνομαι
ἄλλη in some other way
ἀσέλγει-α, ἡ disreputable behaviour (1b)
αὐτίκα at once
ἀφοσιό-ομαι purify oneself
ἐβουλήθη aor. of βούλομαι
ἐδυνήθην aor. of δύναμαι
εἰ μή τι ἄλλο if nothing else

εἰς τοῦτο (gen.) ἔρχομαι reach such a pitch of . . .
ἐμνήσθην aor. of μιμνήσκομαι
ἐν γένει σοι related to you
ἐξηγητ-ής, ὁ Adviser (1d)
ἕκτ-ος -η -ον sixth
ἐπαγγέλλ-ω (ἐπαγγειλ-) order
ἔτ-ος, τό year (3c)
εὐλαβέ-ομαι μή take care not to (+subj.)

εὐλαβήθητι aor. imper. s. of εὐλαβέομαι
ἐφάνησαν aor. of φαίνομαι
ἰατρ-ός, ὁ doctor (2a)
κυμβί-ον, τό cup (2b)
μιμνήσκ-ομαι remember
ὀνομαστί by name
ὁρμηθῆναι aor. of ὁρμάομαι
παραινέ-ω advise

πῇ in any way
προαγορεύ-ω make a public
  denunciation against
  (+dat.)

πρῴ early
ῥᾷστα most easily (sup. adv.
  of ῥᾴδιος)
τελευτά-ω die

φέρ-ω (ἐνεγκ-) bear, endure
φόν-ος, ὁ murder (2a)
χθές yesterday
ὡρμήθησαν aor. of ὁρμάομαι

Vocabulary to be learnt

αὐτίκα *at once*
ἐπαγγέλλω (ἐπαγγειλ-) *order*
ἔτος, τό *year (3c)*
ἰατρός, ὁ *doctor (2a)*

μιμνήσκομαι
  (μνησθ-) *remember,*
  mention
ῥᾷστος η ον *very easy*
τελευτάω *die, end, finish*

φέρω (ἐνεγκ-) *bear, endure;*
  lead; carry
φόνος, ὁ *murder (2a)*
χθές *yesterday*

○ Grammar for Section Sixteen D

Summary:
Aor. pass. imper.
Mids. with pass. forms in aor.

Verbs

Aorist passive imperatives (and others) παύσθητι *'be stopped!'*

204 The forms of the aorist passive imperative are as follows:

2nd s.	παύσθ-ητι 'be stopped!' (and -ηθι, e.g. κατακλίνηθι 'lie down!')
3rd s.	-ήτω 'may he be stopped!' etc.
2nd pl.	-ητε
3rd pl.	-έντων

205 Observe the similarities with the active imperative of the root aorists:

	ἔγνων		ἔβην		ἔστην	
2nd s.	γνῶ-θι	'know!'	βῆ-θι	'go!'	στῆ-θι	'stand!'
3rd s.	γνώ-τω		βή-τω		στή-τω	
2nd pl.	γνῶ-τε		βῆ-τε		στῆ-τε	
3rd pl.	γνό-ντων		βά-ντων		στά-ντων	

Learn the imperative of φημί 'I say':

φά-θι   'say!' etc.
φά-τω
φά-τε
φά-ντων

Revise aorist imperatives as a whole (**110–12**).

Middles which adopt aorist passive forms

206 Many middles become passive in FORM (not in meaning) in the aorist. Check the following list:

βούλομαι→ἐβουλήθην	'I wished'
δύναμαι→ἐδυνήθην	'I was able'
δέομαι→ἐδεήθην	'I begged'
ἐπίσταμαι→ἠπιστήθην	'I knew'
ἥδομαι→ἥσθην	'I found pleasure in'
μιμνήσκομαι→ἐμνήσθην	'I remembered'
διαλέγομαι→διελέχθην	'I conversed'
οἴομαι→ᾠήθην	'I thought'
φοβέομαι→ἐφοβήθην	'I feared'
χαίρω→ἐχάρην	'I rejoiced'
ὀργίζομαι→ὠργίσθην	'I grew angry'

Revise

Subj. morphology **172–4** Language Survey (5)   O

Vocabulary for Section Sixteen E

ἄλλως otherwise
ἀνόητ-ος -ον foolish
βουλεύ-ομαι discuss
ἕωθεν daybreak
κοινῇ together, in common
ὅτι χρῶμαι ἐμαυτῷ; what I
    am to do with myself?

πλανά-ομαι wander, roam
    about
ποῖ τράπωμαι; where am I to
    turn?
συμβουλεύ-ομαι discuss with
    (+dat.)
συμπροθυμέ-ομαι share

enthusiasm of (+dat.)
τί γένωμαι; what will become
    of me?
τί δρῶμεν; what are we to do?
τί ποιήσω; what am I to do?
ὕει it is raining

Vocabulary to be learnt

ἄλλως otherwise; in vain
ἀνόητος ον foolish
βουλεύομαι discuss, take advice
συμβουλεύομαι discuss with

(+dat.)
συμπροθυμέομαι share
    enthusiasm of (+dat.)

O   Grammar for Section Sixteen E

Summary:
Dels.
χράομαι
Correlatives

'What am I to do?'

207 A question-word followed by a subjunctive (nearly always in the first person) turns the question into an appeal, best translated into English by the form 'What *am I to/are we to* –?', e.g.

ποῖ τράπωμαι;   'Where am I to turn?'
τί γένωμαι;   'What is to become of me?'
τί τις λέγῃ;   'What is one to say?' (where 'one' really = 'I')

This is called the 'deliberative' subjunctive.

208 This construction sometimes appears after βούλομαι, e.g.

βούλῃ εἴπω τοῦτο;   'Do you wish me to say this?' (lit. 'that I
                      should say this')
βούλῃ ποιήσω τοῦτο; 'Do you wish that I should do this?'

(N.b. ποιήσω is 1st person aor. subj., NOT future!)

(Cf. in general Reference Grammar Q, R, p. 306.)

Verbs

χράομαι *'I use, have to do with'*

209 This word means basically 'I use' or 'I have to do with'. It is used quite often in deliberatives to mean 'what am I to do with . . .?' e.g.

τί χρῶμαι ἐμαυτῷ;   'What am I to do with myself?'

Correlatives

210 You have already met the sentence:

οὐ γὰρ τούτους οὕτως μισῶ ὡς ἐμαυτὸν φιλῶ 'I do not hate these as (so) much as I like myself'

Note the parallel of οὕτως 'as/so much' with ὡς 'as'. In the same way, Greek parallels such words as τοιοῦτος 'of such a sort' with οἷος 'as'; τοσοῦτος 'so great' with ὅσος 'as', e.g.

οὐκ ἐστί μοι τοιαύτη ἐπιστολὴ οἵα (ἐστί) σοι 'I do not have a letter of the sort that you have'

οὐκ ἔλεγε τοσούτους λόγους ὅσους σὺ (ἔλεγες) 'he did not speak as many words (make as many speeches) as you' ○

Exercises for Section Sixteen

(d) English into Greek

1. Sentences
Translate into Greek:
1. The maidservants did not wait until they were caught.

2. They didn't stop carrying furniture out of the house until they had grabbed everything.
3. They were taking off my son, until a neighbour told them that he was the child of a citizen, and not a slave.
4. I was angry that the rogues had put my nurse into such poor condition that she was actually in danger of her life.
5. They were disdainful enough to enter my house and carry out my furniture.

2. Prose
Translate into Greek:
My wife got angry and said, 'Do not seize this furniture. Have you not already got fifty sheep? Wait for a while; you must not go off till my husband returns.' They took no notice of my wife's words, but took everything and left. A messenger came to the Piraeus to tell me what had happened. When I heard the news, I risked being angry enough to strike Theophemos myself. But I went to him the next day and ordered him to follow me to the bank, to collect the money which was deposited.

Text Exercise Sixteen
Translate into English:
Socrates and Phaidros are taking a walk at midday, when most people take a snooze. Socrates tells the story of the cicadas and their close connection with the Muses to explain his reasons for feeling that philosophic discussion should be the order of the day.
(From Plato, *Phaidros* 258e–259d)

ΣΩΚΡΑΤΗΣ διαλεγώμεθα οὖν, ὦ φίλε Φαῖδρε· σχολὴ μὲν δή, ὡς ἔοικε.
καὶ ἅμα μοι δοκοῦσιν οἱ τέττιγες ἡμᾶς καθορᾶν, ᾄδοντες καὶ ἀλλήλοις
διαλεγόμενοι. εἰ οὖν ἴδοιεν καὶ ἡμᾶς ὥσπερ τοὺς πολλοὺς ἐν μεσημβρίᾳ
μὴ διαλεγομένους, ἀλλὰ καθεύδοντας καὶ κηλουμένους ὑφ᾽ αὑτῶν δι᾽
ἀργίαν τῆς διανοίας, δικαίως ἂν καταγελῷεν, ἡγούμενοι δούλους τινὰς
ὥσπερ πρόβατα περὶ τὴν κρήνην εὕδειν. ἐὰν δὲ ὁρῶσιν ἡμᾶς
διαλεγομένους καὶ ἀκηλήτους παραπλέοντάς σφας ὥσπερ Σειρῆνας,
τάχ᾽ ἂν δοῖεν ἡμῖν ἡσθέντες ἐκεῖνο τὸ δῶρον, ὃ παρὰ θεῶν ἔχουσιν
ἀνθρώποις διδόναι.
ΦΑΙΔΡΟΣ τί τὸ δῶρον; μὴ ἀποκρύψῃς. ἀνήκοος γάρ, ὡς ἔοικε, τυγχάνω ὤν.
ΣΩΚ.   τί δρῶ; δῆλον ὅτι ἐμὲ δεῖ σοι λέγειν· πρέπον γὰρ φιλόμουσον καλεῖσθαι
σέ, φοβοῦμαι μὴ ἄμουσος εἶναι δόκῃς, τῶν τοιούτων ἀνήκοος ὤν.
λέγεται δ᾽ ὥς ποτ᾽ ἦσαν οἱ τέττιγες ἄνθρωποι, πρὶν τὰς Μούσας

γεγονέναι. γενομένων δὲ Μουσῶν καὶ φανείσης <u>ᾠδῆς</u> οὕτως ἄρα τινὲς τῶν τότε ἀνθρώπων <u>ἐξεπλάγησαν</u> ὑφ' ἡδονῆς ἀκούοντες, ὥστε ᾄδοντες <u>ἠμέλησαν</u> σίτων τε καὶ <u>ποτῶν</u>, καὶ ἔλαθον αὑτοὺς τελευτήσαντες. καὶ ἐκ τούτων τῶν ἀνθρώπων τὸ τῶν τεττίγων γένος μετ' ἐκεῖνο φύεται, δῶρον τοῦτο παρὰ Μουσῶν λαβόν, μηδὲν <u>τροφῆς</u> δεῖσθαι, ἀλλ' ἄσιτόν τε καὶ ἄποτον ὂν ᾄδειν, ἕως ἂν τελευτήσῃ, καὶ μετὰ ταῦτα ἐλθὸν παρὰ Μουσὰς ἀπαγγέλλειν, τίς τῶν ἀνθρώπων τὰς Μούσας τιμᾷ. πολλῶν δὴ οὖν ἕνεκα λεκτέον τι καὶ οὐ καθευδητέον ἐν τῇ μεσημβρίᾳ.

ΦΑΙΔ. λεκτέον γὰρ οὖν.

Vocabulary

τέττιξ (τεττιγ-), ὁ cicada (3a)
μεσημβρία, ἡ midday (1a)
κηλέω bewitch
ἀργία, ἡ laziness (1b)
κρήνη, ἡ fountain (1a)
ἀκήλητος ον uncharmed
παραπλέω cf. πλέω

σφας them
ἀποκρύπτω conceal
ἀνήκοος ον unaware (of)
 (+gen.)
πρέπει it is fitting
γεγονέναι perf. inf. of
 γίγνομαι

ᾠδή, ἡ song, singing (1a)
ἐξεπλάγησαν aor. pass. of
 ἐκπλήττω astound
ἀμελέω neglect (+gen.)
ποτά, τά drink (2b)
τροφή, ἡ nourishment (1a)

Section Seventeen

Vocabulary for Section Seventeen A

ἀϊστό-ω destroy
ἀμπίσχ-ω surround, clothe
ἄοπλ-ος -ον unarmed
ἀσθεν-ής -ές weak
αὐξάν-ω (αὐξ-) make grow, increase
γένεσ-ις, ἡ birth (3e)
δύναμ-ις, ἡ power, faculty (3e)
εἱμαρμέν-ος -η -ον allotted
ἔνδον (+gen.) inside, within
ἐπανισό-ω put on a par, make equal
'Επιμηθ-εύς, ὁ Epimetheus (3g) ('Aftersight')

ἐπισκοπέ-ομαι (ἐπισκεψ-) review
εὐλάβει-α, ἡ care (1b)
ἰσχ-ύς, ἡ strength (3h)
κατάγει-ος -ον under the earth
κεράννυ-μι mix
κοσμέ-ω equip
μέγεθ-ος, τό size (3c)
μηχανά-ομαι contrive, devise
μίγνυ-μι (μιξ-) mix
νέμ-ω (νειμ-) allot, distribute, assign
ὁπλίζ-ω arm
παραιτέ-ομαι beg

πρέπει it is fitting, suitable
Προμηθ-εύς, ὁ Prometheus (3g) ('Foresight')
προσάπτ-ω attach, give
προστάττ-ω (προσταξ-) order (+dat.)
πτην-ός -ή -όν winged
σμικρότης (σμικροτητ-), ἡ smallness (3a)
τάχ-ος, τό speed (3c)
τυπέ-ω fashion, shape
τῶν of those things
φυγ-ή, ἡ flight (1a)
φῶς (φωτ-), τό light (3b)

Vocabulary to be learnt
ἀσθενής ές weak, ill
γένεσις, ἡ birth (3e)
δύναμις, ἡ power, ability, faculty (3e)
ἐπισκοπέομαι (ἐπισκεψ-) review
μηχανάομαι devise, contrive
νέμω (νειμ-) distribute, allot, assign
παραιτέομαι beg

προστάττω (προσταξ-) order (+dat.)
τάχος, τό speed (3c)
φυγή, ἡ flight (1a)

Vocabulary for Section Seventeen B

ἀλληλοφθορί-α, ἡ mutual destruction (1b)
ἀμύν-ω keep off, withstand
ἀμφιέννυ-μι dress, clothe
ἀναλίσκ-ω kill, consume
ἄναιμ-ος -ον bloodless
αὐτοφυ-ής -ές natural
βορ-ά, ἡ food, meat (1b)
βοτάν-η, ἡ grass (1a)

δένδρ-ον, τό tree (2b)
δέρμα (δερματ-), τό skin (3b)
διαφυγ-ή, ἡ means of escape from (1a)
δυνατ-ός -ή -όν able (sc. 'to withstand')
ἐκπορίζω supply
ἐπαρκέ-ω provide enough (of)
ἔστι . . . οἷς 'to some'
εὐμάρει-α, ἡ comfort (1b)
εὐν-ή, ἡ bed (1a)
ζῷ-ον, τό animal (2b)

θρίξ (τριχ-), ἡ hair (3a) (dat. pl. θριξί)
ἱκαν-ός -ή -όν sufficient (+inf. 'to')
καρπ-ός, ὁ fruit (2a)
καῦμα (καυματ-), τό heat (3b)
οἰκεῖ-ος -α -ον personal
ὀλιγογονί-α, ἡ production of few young (1b)
ὁπλ-ή, ἡ hoof (1a)
ὅπως (+opt.) = ἵνα (+opt.)
πολυγονί-α, ἡ fertility (1b)

πορίζ-ω provide, offer
προσάπτ-ω give, attach to (+dat.)
πυκν-ός -ή -όν thick
ῥίζ-α, ἡ root (1c)
στερε-ός -ά -όν hard
στρωμν-ή, ἡ bedding (1a)
τοὐντεῦθεν = τὸ ἐντεῦθεν next
τροφ-ή, ἡ food (1a)
ὑπάρχ-ω serve as, be
ὑποδέ-ω shoe
χειμών (χειμων-), ὁ winter, storm (3a)
ὥρα, ἡ season (1b)

Vocabulary to be learnt

ἀμύνω keep off, withstand
ἀναλίσκω (ἀναλωσ-) spend; use; kill
δένδρον, τό tree (2b)
δέρμα (δερματ-), τό skin (3b)
διαφυγή, ἡ flight, means of escape (1a)
δυνατός ή όν able, possible

ἐκπορίζω supply, provide
ζῷον, τό animal, creature, living thing (2b)
ἱκανός ή όν sufficient, capable, able (+inf.)
ὅπως = ἵνα (+subj./opt.) in order to
πορίζω provide, offer

προσάπτω give, attach to (+dat.)
στρωμνή, ἡ bedding (1a)
τροφή, ἡ food, nourishment (1a)
χειμών (χειμων-), ὁ winter, storm (3a)

Vocabulary for Section Seventeen C

Ἀθην-ᾶ, ἡ Athene (1b)
ἀκόσμητ-ος -ον unprovided for
ἀκρόπολ-ις, ἡ acropolis (3e)
ἄλογ-ος -ον speechless
τὰ ἄλογα brute beasts
ἀμήχαν-ος -ον impracticable, impossible
ἀμήχανον ἦν it was impossible to (inf.)
ἀνυπόδητ-ος -ον unshod
ἄοπλ-ος -ον unarmed
ἄστρωτ-ος -ον without a bed
ἅτε in that, since, seeing that (+part.)
γυμν-ός -ή -όν naked
δὴ οὖν but
δίκη μετέρχεται a charge of x (gen.) is brought against γ (acc.)

δωρέ-ω bestow, give as a gift
ἐγχωρεῖ it is permitted for x (dat.)
εἱμαρμέν-ος -η -ον allotted, appointed
ἐμμελῶς ἔχ-ω be well off for (+gen.)
ἔμπυρ-ος -ον of fire
ἔντεχν-ος -ον artistic
εὐπορί-α, ἡ abundance, means (1b)
ἐφιλοτεχνείτην the two of them practised their skills
ᾗπερ as
Ἥφαιστ-ος, ὁ Hephaistos (2a) (god of fire)
καταναλίσκ-ω (καταναλωσ-) spend lavishly
κλοπ-ή, ἡ theft (1a)

κτητ-ός -ή -όν possessed
νομ-ή, ἡ distribution (1a)
οἴκημα (οἰκηματ-), τό dwelling (3b)
ὅ τι χρήσαιτο what he should make of it
πολιτικ-ός -ή -όν political
πρός (adv.) in addition
σύν (+dat.) with, with the help of
σχόμεν-ος -η -ον being in (+dat.) (aor. mid. of ἔχω)
ταύτῃ in this way
τῳ = τινι
φοβερ-ός -ά -όν terrible, awe-inspiring
φυλακ-ή, ἡ sentinel, guard (1a)
φῶς (φωτ-), τό light (3b)

Vocabulary to be learnt

ἀκόσμητος ον *unprovided for*
ἀκρόπολις, ἡ *acropolis, citadel (3e)*
ἄλογος ον *speechless, without reason*
ἀμήχανος ον *impossible, impracticable*
ἄοπλος ον *unarmed*

δωρέω *bestow, give as a gift*
εἱμαρμένος η ον *allotted, appointed*
εὐπορία, ἡ *abundance, means (1b)*
κλοπή, ἡ *theft (1a)*
νόμη, ἡ *distribution (1a)*
οἴκημα (οἰκηματ-), τό

dwelling (3b)
πολιτικός ἡ όν *political*
πρός *(adv.) in addition*
σύν *with, together with (+ dat.)*
φοβερός ά όν *terrible, frightening*
φυλακή, ἡ *sentinel, guard (1a)*
φῶς (φωτ-), τό *light (3b)*

Vocabulary for Section Seventeen D

ἄγαλμα (ἀγαλματ-), τό image, statue (3b)
ἀθροίζω *gather, collect*
ἅτε *since, seeing that (+part.)*
βοηθ-ός, ὁ *helper, assistant (2a)*
δημιουργικ-ός -ή -όν *technical*
διαρθρό-ομαι *articulate (i.e. invent)*
ἐνδε-ής -ές *insufficient, lacking*

lacking
ἐπιχειρέ-ω *undertake, set to work*
ἔσθης (ἐσθητ-), ἡ *clothes (3a)*
θεῖ-ος -α -ον *divine*
θηρί-ον, τό *beast (2b)*
ἱδρύ-ομαι *erect*
κτίζ-ω *found*
μοῖρ-α, ἡ *portion (1b)*
μόνον *alone among (+gen.)*

πανταχῇ *in every respect*
παρασκευασμένος *perf. part. pass. of* παρασκευάζω *prepare, equip*
πολεμικ-ός -ή -όν *military, martial*
σκεδάννυ-μι *scatter*
σποράδην *scattered, in groups*
συγγένει-α, ἡ *kinship (1b)*
ὑπόδεσ-ις, ἡ *shoe (3e)*

Vocabulary to be learnt

ἄγαλμα (ἀγαλματ-), τό *image, statue (3b)*
ἀθροίζω *gather, collect*
ἅτε *since, seeing that (+part.)*

ἐπιχειρέω *undertake, set to work (+inf.)*
ἔσθης (ἐσθητ-), ἡ *clothing (3a)*
θεῖος α ον *divine*

θηρίον, τό *beast (2b)*
πολεμικός ἡ όν *military, of war, martial*
συγγένεια, ἡ *kinship (1b)*

Vocabulary for Section Seventeen E

αἰδ-ώς (-ῶ -οῦς -οῖ), ἡ *respect for others*
ἀνέχ-ομαι *put up with (+gen.)*
δείδ-ω (δεισ-) *fear*
δεσμ-ός, ὁ *bond (2a)*
δημιουργικ-ός -ή -όν *technical*
δημιουργ-ός, ὁ *expert (2a)*
δικαιοσύν-η, ἡ *justice (1a)*
εἷς μία ἕν (ἑν-) *one*
ἐκτός (+gen.) *outside*

ἰατρικ-ός -ή -όν *medical*
ἰδιώτ-ης, ὁ *layman, private citizen (1d)*
ἰέναι *(to) be conducted, (to) go along*
κτείν-ω *kill*
μέτεστι x (dat.) *has a share in* y (gen.)
περί (+dat.) *about*
προσήκει *it is fitting for (+dat.)*

συμβουλ-ή, ἡ *discussion, advice (1a)*
συναγωγ-ός -όν *uniting, unifying*
σωφροσύν-η, ἡ *moderation, good sense (1a)*
τεκτονικ-ός -ή -όν *architectural*
φιλία, ἡ *friendship (1b)*
ὧδε *thus, so*

Vocabulary to be learnt

αἰδώς, ἡ respect for others (acc.
αἰδῶ; gen. αἰδοῦς; dat. αἰδοῖ)
ἀνέχομαι put up with
(+gen.)
δεσμός, ὁ bond (2a)
δημιουργικός ή όν technical, of
a workman
δημιουργός, ὁ craftsman,
workman, expert (2a)

δικαιοσύνη, ἡ justice (1a)
εἷς μία ἕν (ἑν-) one
ἰατρικός ή όν medical, of
healing
ἰδιώτης, ὁ layman, private
citizen (1d)
κτείνω (κτειν-) kill
περί (+dat.) about

προσήκει it is fitting (for)
(+dat.)
συμβουλή, ἡ discussion,
recommendation (1a)
σωφροσύνη, ἡ moderation,
good sense (1a)
φιλία, ἡ friendship (1b)
ὧδε thus, as follows

○ Grammar for Section Seventeen

Summary:
Dels. in sec. seq.
ἅτε + part.
Duals

Deliberatives again

211 When a deliberative question is reported in indirect speech (e.g. 'he wondered what he was to do') the question will be followed by the *optative* in secondary sequence, e.g.

(direct) τίνα μηχανὴν εὕρω; 'What device am I to find?'
(indirect) ἠπόρει ἥντινα μηχανὴν εὕροι 'he did not know what device to find'

ἅτε + participle 'because, as'

212 Translate ἅτε by 'as' or 'because', and make the participle an indicative, e.g.

ἅτε οὐ πάνυ τι σοφὸς ὤν . . . (lit. 'because (as) not being too smart')
'because he was not too smart'

(On participles in general, see Reference Grammar I, p. 298.)

Duals

213 When a verb has two people or things as its subject, or when a noun or adjective represents two people or things, the words can adopt a special form known as the dual.

Verbs

Verbs are restricted to duals in the 2nd and 3rd person plural only.

Watch out for the following endings attached to the stem + vowel-ending of the part in use:

	Active	*Middle/passive*
2nd	-τον	-σθον
3rd	-τον *(primary)*	-σθον *(primary)*
	-την *(secondary)*	-σθην *(secondary)*

e.g. παύσετον 'you two/they both will stop'

ἐπαυσάτην 'they both stopped'

παύσαιτον 'you two stop' (aor. optative active)

παυσαίσθην 'they both stop themselves' (aor. optative middle)

Note

The dual forms of εἰμί are:

ἔστον *(ind.)*

ἦτον *(subj.)*

εἶτον *(opt.)*

Nouns/adjectives

Watch out for endings in accordance with the following chart:

	Nominative/accusative		*Genitive/dative*
Types 1/2	-ω	Types	-οιν
	-ᾱ	1/2/3	-αιν
Types 3	-ε		
	-ει		

e.g. τὼ σοφὼ ἀνθρώπω 'the two wise men'

ἐν ταῖν ὁδοῖν 'in the two roads'

Definite article in the dual

	nom./acc	gen./dat.
m.	τώ	τοῖν
f.	τά (τώ)	ταῖν (τοῖν)
n.	τώ	τοῖν

Revise

μή + aor. subj./subj. orders **181, 192** Reference Grammar Q Negatives, Language Survey (9)

Indefs. (prim./past seq.) **175–6, 187** Reference Grammar L, Language Survey (6)

Opt. in indir. sp. **167, 188** Reference Grammar K   O

PART SIX

Section Eighteen

Vocabulary for Section Eighteen A

ἄγ-ομαι bring in marriage
αἰχμ-ή, ἡ point of a spear (1a)
ἀκόντι-ον, τό javelin (2b)
ἀληθείη = ἀλήθεια
ἀνδρεών (ἀνδρεων-), ὁ men's apartment (3a)
ἀπολέει = ἀπολεῖ (fut. of ἀπόλλυμι)
Ἄτ-υς, ὁ Atys (3e) (Croesus' healthy son)
βάλλ-ω (βαλ-) hit, strike (aor. pass. ἐβλήθην)
βληθέντα aor. part. pass. of βάλλω
διέφθαρτο he was disabled (plup. pass. of διαφθείρω)
δοράτι-ον, τό spear (2b)
ἐκκομίζ-ω carry out
ἐξεγείρ-ομαι wake up (aor. ἐξηγέρθην)
ἐπείτε when
εὕδ-ω sleep

ἐφίστα-μαι (ἐπιστα-) stand near (+dat.)
ἐωθώς (ἐωθοτ-) accustomed to (+inf.)
ἑωυτόν = ἑαυτόν
ἑωυτῷ = ἑαυτῷ
ἧλιξ (ἡλικ-), ὁ comrade, companion (3a)
κατά (+acc.) in relation to, concerning
καταρρωδέ-ω fear
κρέμα-μαι hang over (+dat.)
Κροῖσ-ος, ὁ Croesus (2a) (king of Lydia)
κωφ-ός -ή -όν deaf and dumb
λόγον δίδω-μι take counsel with (+dat.)
Λυδ-οί, οἱ the Lydians (2a) (Croesus' people)
μιν him, her (acc.) (goes with (i) βληθέντα l. 3; (ii) ἐωθότα l. 5)
νέμεσ-ις, ἡ retribution (3e)

οἱ to him, her (dat.) (goes with εὕδοντι)
ὄλβι-ος -α -ον happy, blest
ὄνειρ-ος, ὁ dream (2a)
οὐδαμῇ (to) nowhere
οὔνομα = ὄνομα
οὔτερος = ὁ ἔτερος
πρῆγμα = πρᾶγμα
σημαίν-ω tell, announce, point out
σιδηρέ-ος -η -ον iron, metal
Σόλων (Σολων-), ὁ Solon (3a) (Athenian lawgiver)
στρατηγέ-ω lead (as commander) (+gen.)
συννέ-ω pile up
τὰ πάντα in all respects
τοῖσι = οἷς which (relative)
τῶν = ὧν of whom (relative)
χρέωνται = χρῶνται
ὧν = οὖν
ὡς εἰκάσαι to make a reasonable guess

Vocabulary to be learnt

διεφθάρ-μην I was disabled, ruined (plup. pass. of διαφθείρω)
μιν him, her (acc.) (enclitic)
οἱ to him, her (dat.) (enclitic)
ὄνειρος, ὁ dream (2a)

Vocabulary for Section Eighteen B

ἀδελφεόν=ἀδελφόν
Ἄδρηστ-ος, ὁ Adrastos (2a)
  ('Unable to escape')
ἀέκων=ἄκων
ἀμείβ-ομαι answer, reply
ἀμηχανέ-ω be in need of
  (+gen.)
ἀπικνέεται=ἀφικνεῖται
βασιλήϊ-ος -η -ον of the king,
  royal
γενε-ή, ἡ birth (1a)
γένεος=γένους (gen. s. of
  γέν-ος, τό family (3c))
Γορδί-ας, ὁ Gordias (gen. s.
  Γορδιέω) (1d)
ἐγένεο=ἐγένου
ἐδέετο=ἐδεῖτο
ἔκγον-ος, ὁ son (2a)
ἐμεωυτοῦ=ἐμαυτοῦ
ἐν ἡμετέρου in our house
ἔνθα where (relative)
ἐξελαύν-ω drive out (perf.

part. pass. ἐξεληλαμέν-ος -η
  -ον)
ἐπείτε when
ἐπικυρέ-ω receive, partake of
  (+gen.)
ἐπίστι-ος -ον suppliant
ἐπιχώρι-ος -η -ον of the land,
  native
ἑών=ὤν
καθαίρ-ω (καθηρ-) cleanse,
  purify
καθαρ-ός -ή -όν pure, clean
καθάρσι-ον, τό purification
  (2b)
κάθαρσ-ις, ἡ purification (3e)
κερδαίν-ω profit (fut.
  κερδανέω)
κόθεν=πόθεν
κουφ-ός -ή -όν light
Λυδοῖσι=Λυδοῖς
Μίδ-ας, ὁ Midas (gen. s.
  Μιδέω) (1d)

νομίζ-ομαι be accustomed
τὰ νομιζόμενα the
  customary things (2b)
οἰκί-α, τά palace (2b)
ὁκόθεν=ὁπόθεν from where
ὀνομάζ-ω name, call
παραπλήσι-ος -η -ον similar
Σάρδι-ες, αἱ Sardis (Croesus'
  capital)
στερέ-ω deprive of (+gen.)
  (perf. part. pass.
ἐστερημέν-ος -η -ον)
συμφορή=συμφορᾶ
συμφορήν=συμφοράν
τοῖσι=τοῖς
φονεύ-ω kill, murder
Φρυγι-ή, ἡ Phrygia (1a)
Φρύξ (Φρυγ-), ὁ Phrygian
  (3a)
χεῖρας in respect of his hands
χρῆμα (χρημᾰτ-), τό thing
  (3b)

Vocabulary to be learnt

ἀέκων=ἄκων
ἐμεωυτόν=ἐμαυτόν
ἐν (+gen.) in the house of
ἑών=ὤν
ἑωυτόν=ἑαυτόν
ἐπείτε when, since

Dropping of aspirates in some
  verb compounds, e.g.
ἀφικνέομαι=ἀπικνέομαι
νομίζομαι be accustomed
ὁπόθεν (ὁκόθεν) from where
οὔνομα=ὄνομα

στερέω deprive of (+gen.)
  (perf. part. pass.
ἐστερημένος)
τοῖσι=τοῖς
χρῆμα (χρημᾰτ-), τό thing
  (3b)

Vocabulary for Section Eighteen C

ἀμείβ-ομαι reply
ἀναφαίν-ομαι
  (ἀναφαν-) appear
γίνεται=γίγνεται
δίαιτ-α, ἡ dwelling (1c)
διακελεύ-ομαι exhort, direct
  (+dat.)
διαφθείρεσκε=διέφθειρε (the

-εσκ- suffix implies
  continuation, repetition)
ἐξαιρέ-ω (ἐξελ-) remove
ἔπ-ος, τό word (3c) (uncontr.
  pl. ἔπεα)
ἔργ-ον, τό result of work (i.e.
  tilled field) (2b)
ἰοῦσι dat. pl. m. of ἰών (part.

of ἔρχομαι)
κυνηγέσι-ον, τό dog-pack
  (2b)
λογάς (λογαδ-), ὁ picked,
  chosen (man) (3a)
Μύσι-ος -η -ον in Mysia
Μυσ-ός, ὁ a Mysian (2a)

νεηνί-ης, ὁ = νεανίας
νεόγαμ-ος -ον newly married
Ὄλυμπ-ος, ὁ Mt Olympos (2a)
ὄρεος = ὄρους (gen. s. of ὄρος, τό mountain (3c))
ποιέεσκον = ἐποίουν (the -εσκ- suffix implies continuation, repetition)

προθυμεόμενοι = προθυμούμενοι
πρός (+gen.) at the hands of
προσδέ-ομαι beg x (gen.) for y (acc.)
σευ = σου
συμπέμπ-ω send with (+dat.)
συνεξαιρέ-ω (συνεξελ-) join x (dat.) in destroying

σφι to them (dat.)
ὑὸς χρῆμα μέγα|μέγιστον huge monster of a boar
ὗς, ὁ boar (3h)
χώρ-η, ἡ country (1a)
ὦν = οὖν
ὡς ἄν (+subj.) so that, in order that

Vocabulary to be learnt

γίνομαι = γίγνομαι
ἔπος, τό word (3c) (uncontr. pl. ἔπεα)
νεηνίης = νεανίας
συμπέμπω send with (+dat.)

χώρη, ἡ land (1a)
ὦν = οὖν so, therefore
Note uncontracted -ε- in ὄρεος (= ὄρους), προθυμεόμενοι (προθυμούμενοι) etc.

Note η for a in, e.g., χώρη (= χώρα), συμφορή (συμφορά) etc.

Vocabulary for Section Eighteen D

ἄγρ-η, ἡ hunt (1a)
αἰχμ-ή, ἡ spear-point (1a)
ἀμείβ-ομαι reply, answer
ἀποκληΐ-ω shut x (acc.) off from y (gen.)
ἀποχρέ-ομαι be content with (+dat.)
ἄχαρις ἄχαρι (ἀχαριτ-) disagreeable
δειλί-η, ἡ cowardice
διακλέπτ-ω steal (i.e. snatch from the jaws of death)
ἐνύπνι-ον, τό dream (2b)
ἐπί (+gen.) in the time of
ἔστι τῇ it is the case that
εὐδοκιμέ-ω win a glorious reputation
ἐφίστα-μαι (ἐπιστα-) stand by (+dat.)
ζό-η, ἡ life (1a)
θήρ-η, ἡ hunt (1a)

κοῖος = ποῖος
κοτε = ποτε
κως = πως
μεθ-|μετ-ίημι allow; let go
μεταγιγνώσκ-ω change one's mind
μοῦνος = μόνος
νεόγαμ-ος -ον newly wed
ὀδούς (ὀδοντ-), ὁ tusk (3a)
οἶκε = ἔοικε resemble, be like (+dat.)
ὅκως = ὅπως
ὀλιγοχρόνι-ος -ον short-lived
ὄμμα (ὀμματ-), τό eye (3b)
ὄνειρ-ον, τό dream (2b)
ὄψ-ις, ἡ sight, vision (3e)
παραλαμβάν-ω undertake
παρορά-ω (παριδ-) notice x (acc.) in y (dat.)
πολιήτῃσι = πολίταις
πρός (+acc.) with a mind to

σέο/σευ = σοῦ
σιδηρέ-ος -η -ον metal, iron
σφι to them (dat.)
τὰ = ἃ what (relative)
τέοισι = τίσι with what (goes with ὄμμασι)
τευ = τινος
τὴν = ἣν which (relative)
το (l. 9) this
τοι = σοι
τῶν = ὧν what (relative)
ὕπν-ος, ὁ sleep (2a)
ὗς, ὁ boar (3h)
φοβέαι = φοβῇ
φοιτέ-ω go
φοιτέοντας (understand, e.g., ἄνδρας, i.e. 'that men should go . . .')
φυλακὴν ἔχω take care
χρῆν past of χρή

Vocabulary to be learnt

αἰχμή, ἡ spear-point (1a)
ἀμείβομαι answer, reply to (+acc.)

ἐπί (+gen.) in the time of
μετ-|μεθίημι (μεθε-) allow; let go

οἶκε = ἔοικε resemble, be like (+dat.)
ὄψις, ἡ vision, sight (3e)

παραλαμβάνω (παραλαβ-)
  undertake; take from
παροράω (παριδ-) notice
σέο/σευ=σοῦ
σιδηρέος η ον iron, metal
σφι to them (dat.)
τευ=τινος

τοι=σοι
ὕπνος, ὁ sleep (2a)
ὗς, ὁ boar (3h)
Note κ for π in e.g. κοτε (ποτε),
  κοῖος (ποῖος), κως (πως),
  ὁκόθεν (ὁπόθεν) etc.
Note the declension of σφεῖς

'they':
Attic: σφεῖς σφᾶς σφῶν
  σφίσι(ν)
Ionic: σφεῖς σφέας σφέων
  σφί(ν) (σφέα n.)

Vocabulary for Section Eighteen E

ἄγρ-η, ἡ hunt (1a)
ἄεθλ-ον, τό contest (2b)
ἄλλως in other circumstances
ἀπήμων ἄπημον
  (ἀπημον-) unharmed
ἀπολαμπρύν-ομαι distinguish
  oneself in (-έαι=-ει|ῃ 2nd s.
  pres. (possibly fut. here))
ἀπονοστέ-ω return
ἄχαρις ἄχαρι
  (ἀχαριτ-) unpleasant
δαπάν-η, ἡ expense, money
  (1a)
δήλησ-ις, ἡ harm (3e)
διακελεύ-ομαι exhort, direct
  (-έαι=-ει|ῃ 2nd s. pres.)
εἵνεκεν=ἕνεκα
εἶπας=εἶπων (wk. aorist is
  εἶπα 'I said')
ἐμεῦ=ἐμοῦ

ἔνθα where (relative)
ἐπὶ δήλησι bent on mischief
εὖ πρήσσω=εὖ πράττω
ἤια=ᾖα (past of ἔρχομαι|εἶμι)
ἴσχ-ω hold back, restrain
καθαίρ-ω cleanse, purify
κακοῦργ-ος -ον evil
κεχρημένον 'for one who has
  met'
κλώψ (κλωπ-), ὁ thief (3a)
μεταπέμπ-ομαι send for
οἰκί-α, τά palace (2a)
οἰκός=εἰκός likely
ὁμῆλιξ (ὁμηλικ-), ὁ
  companion (3a)
ὀνειδίζ-ω blame x (acc.) on y
  (dat.)
πάρα=πάρεστι it is in one's
  power, possible

πλήσσ-ω strike (perf. part.
  pass. πεπληγμένος)
πολλαχῇ for many reasons
προποιέ-ω do first, do before
προσδοκά-ω expect
προσέτι besides
ῥώμ-η, ἡ strength (1a)
τοιόσδε τοιήδε τοιόνδε like
  this
ὑπάρχ-ω be, be sufficient
ὑποδέκ-ομαι welcome,
  entertain (=ὑποδέχ-ομαι)
φανέωσι=φανῶσι (3rd pl. aor.
  subj. of φαίνομαι)
Φρύξ (Φρυγ-), ὁ Phrygian
  (2a)
χαρίζ-ομαι oblige (+dat.)
χρεόν ἐστι=χρή
χρηίζ-ω desire

Vocabulary to be learnt

ἄγρη, ἡ hunt (1a)
εὖ πράττω fare well, be
  prosperous
πάρα, πάρεστι it is possible for
  X (dat.)
τοιόσδε τοιήδε τοιόνδε of this
  kind

ὑπάρχω be, be sufficient; begin
  (+gen.)
ὑποδέχομαι welcome, entertain
χαρίζομαι oblige; please; be
  dear to (+dat.)
Note that -εαι is used for -ει or -ῃ
  in the 2nd s. middle, mostly of

ε contr. verbs only, but
  occasionally of other verbs as
  well, e.g. διακελεύεαι,
  ἀπολαμπρυνέαι (where the ε
  may indicate the future tense).

Vocabulary for Section Eighteen F

ἀγγέλλ-ω announce, report
  (fut. ἀγγελέω)
ἀκοντίζ-ω throw javelin at

ἁμαρτάν-ω miss (+gen.)
ἀπολωλεκώς perf. part. of
  ἀπόλλυμι

βάλλ-ω (βαλ-) hit (aor. pass.
  ἐβλήθην)
βαρυσύμφορ-ος -ον accursed

βιώσιμ-ος -ον worth living
βόσκ-ω nurture, feed
γέγονα irr. perf. of γίγνομαι
  (part. γεγονώς or γεγώς)
Γορδί-ας, ὁ Gordias (1d)
  (gen. Γορδιέ-ω)
δεινολογέ-ομαι grieve
εἰ μὴ ὅσον except in as far as
εἶς = εἶ you are
ἐκπίμπλη-μι (ἐκπλησ-) fulfil
ἔνθα where (tr. 'at this point')
ἐξαρτύ-ω equip
ἐξεργάζ-ομαι do a deed
  (ἐξεργάσαο = ἐξηργάσω,
  2nd s. aor.)
ἐπὶ ἐκείνῃ 'in addition to that
  (previous tragedy)'
ἐπικατασφάζ-ω slay x (acc.)
  over γ (dat.)
ἐπίστι-ος -ον (sc. 'Zeus, god')
  of the hearth
ἑσακοντίζ-ω hurl a javelin at
ἑταιρήϊ-ος (sc. 'Zeus, god') of
  friendship

ἤδεε = ἤδει (past of οἶδα)
ἤισαν = ἦσαν (past of
  ἔρχομαι|εἶμι)
θάπτ-ω bury
θέ-ω run
καθαίρ-ω purify, cleanse
καθάρσι-ος -ον (sc. 'Zeus,
  god') of purification
κατοικτίρ-ω pity
κου = που
κύκλ-ος, ὁ circle (2a)
λογάς (λογαδ-), ὁ selected
μαρτύρ-ομαι invoke
Μίδ-ας, ὁ Midas (1d) (gen.
  Μιδέ-ω)
μόρ-ος, ὁ fate (2a)
οἰκήϊ-ος -η -ον personal
οἰκί-α, τά palace (2b)
οἰκός = εἰκός
Ὄλυμπ-ος, ὁ Olympos (2a)
ὀνομάζ-ω name
ὄπισθε behind
ὄρ-ος, τό mountain (3c)
πάλαι long ago

πεπονθώς perf. part. of
  πάσχω
περιημεκτέ-ω be grieved at
  (+ dat.)
περιίστα-μαι
  (περιστα-) stand round
πρό (+ gen.) in front of
προσημαίν-ω prophesy
προτείν-ω stretch out
Σάρδι-ες, αἱ Sardis (Croesus'
  capital)
σῆμα (σηματ-), τό mound
  (3b) (marking a grave)
σημαίν-ω tell
συγγιγνώσκ-ομαι
  acknowledge
συνταράσσ-ω overwhelm
τὸν δὲ 'and on Zeus as
  ἑταιρήϊος, because . . .'
τὸν μὲν 'and on Zeus as
  ἐπίστιος, because . . .'
τύμβ-ος, ὁ grave (2a)
φήμ-η, ἡ prophecy (1a)
φον-εύς, ὁ murderer (3g)

Vocabulary to be learnt
ἀγγέλλω (ἀγγειλ-; fut.
  ἀγγελέω) report, announce
ἁμαρτάν-ω (ἁμαρτ-) miss;
  make a mistake
βάλλω (βαλ-) hit (aor. pass.
  ἐβλήθην)
γέγον-α irr. perf. of γίγνομαι
  (part. γεγον-ώς or γεγ-ώς)

ἔνθα where, there
θέω run
καθαίρω (καθηρ-) purify,
  cleanse
μαρτύρομαι invoke, call to
  witness
οἰκία, τά palace (2b)
οἰκός = εἰκός

ὄρ-ος, τό mountain (3c)
πάλαι long ago
κου = που
πρό (+ gen.) before, in front of
προτείνω stretch out
σημαίνω tell, signal

O Grammar for Section Eighteen

Summary:
Herodotus' dialect
Acc. of respect
οὐ φημί

The main features of Herodotus' Ionic dialect
214 Herodotus may have η where Attic has ā (especially after ρ, ε, ι),
e.g. πρῆγμα (Attic πρᾶγμα).
Give the Attic form for νεηνίης, συμφορή

215 Herodotus uses σσ for Attic ττ, e.g. θάλασσα (Attic θάλαττα).
   Give the Attic form for πρήσσω, φυλάσσω.

216 Herodotus can have
   ει for ε e.g. ξεῖνος (Attic ξένος)
   ου for ο e.g. οὔνομα (Attic ὄνομα)
   ηι for ει e.g. ἑταιρήϊος (Attic ἑταιρεῖος)
   Give the Attic form for μοῦνος, εἵνεκα.

217 Herodotus may not contract ε verbs, nor nouns with ε in the stem, e.g.
   φιλέω   (Attic φιλῶ)
   ποιέειν   (Attic ποιεῖν)
   ἐδέετο   (Attic ἐδεῖτο)
   ὄρεος   (Attic ὄρους)
   σεο   (Attic σου)
   N.b. εο can change to ευ, giving e.g.
   σευ (for σεο, Attic σου)
   μευ (for Attic μου)
   ποιεύμενα (for ποιεόμενα, Attic ποιούμενα)
   Give the Attic form for ἐγένεο, καλεόμενος, ἀπολέει, ποιεῦμεν.

218 Herodotus uses -εω for the gen. s. of 1d nouns (e.g. νεηνίεω, not νεηνίου),
and -έων for the gen. pl. of all type 1 nouns, e.g. θυρέων, not θυρῶν.
   Give the Attic form for Περσέων.

219 Herodotus uses -σι in the dat. pl. of type 1/2 adjectives and nouns, e.g.
   τούτοισι (Attic τούτοις)
   τοῖσι (Attic τοῖς)
   Give the Attic form for ταύταισι, χρηστοῖσι.

220 Except for ὅς, Herodotus uses the form of the definite article in place of the
relative, e.g. παῖς τὸν φυλάσσεις (Attic παῖς ὃν φυλάττεις).

221 Herodotus often omits aspiration in composition (i.e. words with prefixes,
etc.), e.g.
   ἀπικνέομαι   (Attic ἀφικνέομαι)
   μετίημι   (Attic μεθίημι)

222 Note the following important Herodotean forms:

Herodotus		Attic
ὦν	'therefore'	οὖν
ἐών	'being'	ὤν
ἑωυτόν	'himself'	ἑαυτόν
ἐμεωυτόν	'myself'	ἐμαυτόν
κοῖος (ὁκοῖος)	'of what sort'	ποῖος
κότε (ὁκότε)	'when'	πότε

κῶς (ὁκῶς)	'how'	πῶς
μιν	'him, her' (acc.)	no comparable Attic form
οἱ	'to him, to her' (dat.)	very rare in Attic

Note

It should be stressed that these are general rules, applying to most cases; that some of them illustrate simply alternative forms; and that the 'rules' are in fact far more complex than they are made to seem here (which is why you will be able to spot what look like inconsistencies).

Accusative of respect

223 You have already met τί in the sense 'why?', when it was explained (**73**) that the literal meaning in this context was 'in respect of what?' This use of the accusative to mean 'in respect of' is very common, especially after adjectives, and should be carefully looked for, e.g.

οὐ καθαρὸς χεῖρας 'not pure in respect of his hands' (i.e. 'with impure hands')

διεφθαρμένος τὴν ἀκοήν 'disabled in respect of his hearing' (i.e. 'deaf')

This construction is very common in poetry, and Homer is full of examples, e.g.

πόδας ὠκὺς Ἀχιλλεύς 'Achilles, swift in respect of his feet' (i.e. 'swift-footed')

οὐ φημί

224 Observe that this means 'I deny that . . .', i.e. 'I say that x is NOT the case' (cf. Latin 'nego'). It does not mean 'I do not say that . . .', e.g.;

Κροῖσος οὐκ ἔφη τὸν παῖδα συμπέμψειν 'Croesus said that he would not send his son' 'C. denied that he would send his son'

Revise

ἕως (all uses) **193, 195, 197** Reference Grammar L
πρίν (all uses) **161, 198**
ὥστε **200–2** Reference Grammar J ○

PART SEVEN

Section Nineteen

Vocabulary for Section Nineteen A

ἄγῃσι=ἄγῃ (3rd s. pres. subj.)
ἄγ-ομαι lead in marriage
'Ἀθήν-η, ἡ Athene (1a)
αἴγλ-η, ἡ light, radiance (1a)
αἰεί=ἀεί
αἴθρ-η, ἡ clear sky (1a)
ἀκηδ-ής -ές uncared for
ἅμα (+dat.) at the same time
  as
ἅμαξ-α, ἡ wagon (1c)
ἄνεμ-ος, ὁ wind (2a)
ἀνέφελ-ος -ον unclouded
ἀπό . . . εἰμί be distant from
  (+gen.)
ἄρα straightaway, then
ἀρημέν-ος -η -ον overcome
ἀριστ-εύς, ὁ nobleman (3g)
ἀσφαλ-ής -ές safe, secure
αὐτάρ but
βῆ=ἔβη
γείνατο=ἐγείνατο
γείν-ομαι (γειν-) bear
γλαυκῶπις (γλαυκωπιδ-), ἡ
  grey-eyed
δέμνι-α, τά bed (2b)
δεύ-ω besprinkle, bedew
δήν for a long time
διεπέφραδε aor. of
  διαφράζω speak to
δῖ-ος -α -ον godlike

Δύμας (Δυμαντ-), ὁ Dymas
  (3a)
ἕδ-ος, τό seat (3c)
ἐεισάμεν-ος -η -ον likening x
  (acc.) to γ (dat.)
ἔην=ἦν
εἰδόμεν-ος -η -ον making
  oneself like (+dat.)
εἵματα, τά clothes (3b)
ἔμμεναι=εἶναι
ἐνί=ἐν
ἔννυ-μαι put on
ἐντύν-ομαι get oneself ready
  (ἐντυνέαι=2nd s. subj.)
ἐπιδέδρομεν (it) is spread over
  (perf. of ἐπιτρέχω)
ἐπιπίλνα-μαι come near
ἐπισεύ-ομαι hurry to (+acc.)
ἐποτρύν-ω urge, persuade
ἐς=εἰς
ἔσσεαι=ἔσει (2nd s. fut. of
  εἰμί)
ἐφοπλίζ-ω get ready
ζώστρ-ον, τό belt, girdle (2b)
ἠέ=ἤ
ἦμαρ (ἤματ-), τό day (3b)
ἠῶθι πρό before dawn
ἠώς, ἡ dawn (dat. ἠοῖ)
θυμ-ός, ὁ heart, soul (2a)
ἵνα (+ind.) where, when

ἴομεν=ἴωμεν
καθεῦδε=ἐκάθευδε
κάλλιον (understand ἐστί) it is
  better
κάματ-ος, ὁ weariness (2a)
κε=ἄν
κεχάριστο 3rd s. perf. of
  χαρίζομαι
κλυτ-ός -ή -όν famous
κούρ-η, ἡ maiden (1a)
λευκ-ός -ή -όν white
μάκαρ (μακαρ-), ὁ blessed
μεθήμων μέθημον
  (μεθημον-) lax, careless
μνά-ομαι woo, court
μῦθ-ος, ὁ word (2a)
Ναυσικά-α, ἡ Nausikaa (1b)
  (daughter of Alkinoos, king of
  the Phaiakians)
ναυσικλειτ-ός -ή -όν famous
  for ships
νυ=νυν
'Ὀδυσσ-εύς, ὁ Odysseus (3g)
ὅθι where; in which place
ὄμβρ-ος, ὁ shower, rain (2a)
ὁμηλικί-η of same age as
  (+dat.)
Οὔλυμπόνδε to Olympos
ὄφρα=ἵνα (+subj.) in order
  to

παρθέν-ος, ἡ maiden,
  unwedded girl (2a)
πέπλ-ος, ὁ robe, mantle (2a)
πετάννυ-μι spread out (perf.
  pass. πέπταμαι)
πλυν-ός, ὁ washing place (2a)
πλύν-ω wash (fut. πλυνέω)
πνοι-ή, ἡ breath (1a)
ποδέσσι(ν)=ποσί(ν) on foot
  (πούς)
πόληος=πόλεως
πολλόν far, a long way
πολύτλας long-suffering

πότνια lady (nom. s. f.)
πρός . . . εἶπεν addressed x
  (acc.) to y (acc.)
πρόσφημι speak to
ῥῆγ-ος, τό rug, blanket (3c)
σιγαλό-εις -εσσα -εν
  (σιγαλοεντ-) shining
στῆ=ἔστη
συνέριθ-ος, ἡ fellow-worker,
  companion (2a)
τά=αὐτά 'things'
τέρπ-ομαι enjoy oneself
τῇ=αὐτῇ (i.e. Dymas'

daughter)
τινάσσ-ω shake
τοι 'let me tell you/look here'
τοῖσι . . . οἵ=αὐτοῖς . . . οἵ 'for
  those . . . who'
τῷ=αὐτῷ
ὑπέρ (+gen.) above
Φαίηκες, οἱ Phaiakians (3a)
φαινομένηφι=φαινομένη
φάτ-ις, ἡ reputation (3e)
χαίρ-ω rejoice
χιών (χιον-), ἡ snow (3a)
ὡς thus, so

Vocabulary to be learnt

αἰεί=ἀεί
ἄρα straightaway
ἀσφαλής ἐς safe, secure
δέμνια, τά bed, bedding (2b)
κε (κεν) (enclitic)=ἄν

κούρη=κόρη, ἡ daughter, girl
  (1a)
χαίρω rejoice
ὡς thus, so

Vocabulary for Section Nineteen B

ἀγαυ-ός -ή -όν noble
ἄγ-ομαι bring for oneself
ἄγχι close
αἰδ-ομαι feel reticence about
  (+inf.)
ἁλιπόρφυρ-ος -ον purple
'Αλκίνο-ος, ὁ Alkinoos (2a)
  (king of the Phaiakians,
  Nausikaa's father)
ἀμφίπολ-ος, ἡ servant,
  handmaiden (2a)
ἀπήν-η, ἡ wagon (1a)
ἀποθαυμάζ-ω wonder at
ἀραρυῖαν fitted (acc. s. f. perf.
  part. of ἀραρίσκω)
ἄφαρ at once
γεγάασιν 3rd pl. perf. of
  γίγνομαι
διά (+acc.) through
δμώς (δμω-), ὁ slave (3a)
  (dat. pl. δμώεσσιν)
δώματ-α, τά house, palace
  (3b)

ἐγείρ-ω rouse
ἔγειρε=ἤγειρε
εἵματ-α, τά clothes (3b)
ἐνί=ἐν
ἐξονομαίν-ω (ἐξονομην-)
  mention
ἔοικε it is right for (+dat.)
ἐόντα l. 31 take with σοι l. 31
ἐόντας l. 22 understand 'parents'
ἔρχευ=ἔρχου
ἐς=εἰς
ἐσχάρ-η, ἡ hearth (1a)
εὔθρον-ος -ον lovely,
  fair-throned
εὔκυκλ-ος -ον with fine
  wheels
εὔπεπλ-ος -ον fair-robed
ἐφοπλίζ-ω get ready (fut.
  ἐφοπλίσσω)
ἔχοντα l. 32 take with σοι l. 31
ἤΐθε-ος, ὁ bachelor (2a)
ἠλάκατ-α, τά wool (on the
  distaff) (2b)

ἧμαι be seated (ἧστο 3rd s.
  past)
ἡ μέν i.e. her mother
ἠώς, ἡ dawn
θαλέθ-ω thrive
θαλερ-ός -ή -όν fruitful
θύραζε to the outside, out
ἵμεναι=ἰέναι
ἵνα (+ind.) where
καθαρ-ός -ή -όν clean
κάλεον=ἐκάλουν
κέλ-ομαι command (+dat.)
  (ἐκέκλετο 3rd s. aor.)
κιγχάν-ω (κιχησ-) meet
κλειτ-ός -ή -όν famous
κλυτ-ός -ή -όν splendid,
  lovely
μέγαρ-α, τά house, palace
  (2b)
μέμηλεν perf. of μέλει
μετά (+acc.) among
  (+dat.) among, in company
  with

μῦθ-ος, ὁ word (2a)
νεόπλυτ-ος -ον newly washed
ξύμβλητο=ξυνέβλητο (3rd s.
aor. mid. of
ξυμβάλλομαι meet
(+dat.))
ὀπυί-ω be married
πάππας, ὁ father (voc.
πάππα)

πέντε five
πλύν-ω wash (fut. πλυνέω)
προσέειπε=προσεῖπε spoke
to
ῥερυπωμέν-ος -η -ον dirty
στρωφά-ω twist, spin
τέκ-ος, τό child (3c uncontr.)
τοκ-εύς, ὁ parent (3g)
τῷ=αὐτῷ (i.e. father)

ὑπερτερί-η, ἡ covering,
canopy (1a)
ὑψηλ-ός -ή -όν high
φθον-έω begrudge (+gen.)
φρήν (φρεν-), ἡ heart, mind
(3a)
χορός, ὁ dance (2a)
χρώς, ὁ body, flesh (dat. χροΐ)

Vocabulary to be learnt

ἄγομαι (ἀγαγ-) bring (for
oneself), lead, marry
εἵματα, τά clothes (3b)
ἔοικε it is right for (+dat.)
ἐνί=ἐν
ἐς=εἰς
ἐφοπλίζω equip, get ready (fut.

ἐφοπλίσσω)
ἠώς, ἡ dawn (=Attic ἕως)
(acc. ἠῶ; gen. ἠοῦς; dat. ἠοῖ)
μετά (+dat.) among, in
company with
μῦθος, ὁ word, story (2a)

πλύνω wash (fut. πλυνέω)
προσεῖπον (προσέειπον) spoke
X (acc.) to Y (acc.)
Lack of augment on past tenses
e.g. στῆ=ἔστη,
κάλεον=ἐκάλουν etc.

Vocabulary for Section Nineteen C

ἄγρι-ος -η -ον wild
αἰπειν-ός -ή -όν steep
ἀμφέρχ-ομαι (aor.
ἀμφήλυθ-ον) surround
(+acc.)
ἀμφίπολ-ος, ἡ handmaiden
(2a)
αὐδή-εις -εσσα -εν
(αὐδηεντ-) speaking with
human voices
αὖτε again, on the contrary,
this time
ἀϋτ-ή, ἡ cry, shriek (1a)
ἀΰ-ω scream
βασίλει-α, ἡ princess (1b)
βροτ-ός, ὁ mortal (2a)
γαῖ-α, ἡ (1c)=γῆ
γλαυκῶπις (γλαυκωπιδ-), ἡ
grey-eyed
δίν-η, ἡ eddy (1a)
δῖ-ος -α -ον god-like

ἐγείρ-ομαι (aor.
ἐγρό-μην) wake up
ἐγών=ἐγώ
ἕζ-ομαι sit
ἐμβάλλ-ω (ἐμβαλ-) throw in
(+dat.)
εὐῶπις (εὐωπιδ-), ἡ beautiful
ζεύγνυ-μι (ζευξ-) yoke
ἦ= ? (dir. or indir.)
ἦ ... ἦε double question
ἠδέ and
θεουδ-ής -ές god-fearing
θῆλ-υς -εια -υ female
θυμ-ός, ὁ heart (2a)
ἱκάν-ω come
κάρην-ον, τό peak (2b)
μετά (+acc.) to
νέ-ομαι return
νοέ-ω plan
νό-ος, ὁ=νοῦς, ὁ
νυ=νυν

νύμφ-η, ἡ nymph (1a)
οἴκόνδε home, homewards
ὁρμαίν-ω debate, consider
πειρήσομαι let me try (aor.
subj. of πειράομαι)
πηγ-ή, ἡ source (1a)
πίσε-α, τά meadows (3c
uncontr.)
ποιή-εις -εσσα -εν
(ποιηεντ-) grassy
που somewhere, anywhere
(enclitic)
πτύσσ-ω (πτυξ-) fold
ῥα=ἄρα
σφαῖρ-α, ἡ ball (1b)
σχεδόν (+gen.) near
τέων=τίνων
φιλόξειν-ος -ον loving
strangers, hospitable
φρήν (φρεν-), ἡ mind (3a)
ὥς=ἵνα (+subj./opt.) in
order that

Vocabulary to be learnt

ἀμφέρχομαι surround (+acc.)
   (aor. ἀμφήλυθον)
ἀμφίπολος, ἡ handmaiden (2a)
γλαυκῶπις (γλαυκωπιδ-), ἡ
   grey-eyed (used of Athene)
δῖος α ον godlike
θυμός, ὁ heart, anger (2a)

νοέω plan, devise; notice
νυ=νυν (enclitic)
φρήν (φρεν-), ἡ heart, mind
   (3a)
ὡς (+subj./opt.)=ἵνα in order
   to/that

Vocabulary for Section Nineteen D

ἀγρότερ-ος -η -ον wild
ἄη-μι blow upon (of wind)
ἀλκί strength, prowess (dat.)
ἄλλυδις (ἄλλη) in different
   directions
ἅλμ-η, ἡ brine (1a)
ἄντα face to face
ἀποσταδά at a distance
αὐτάρ but, now
αὔτως simply
γαστήρ (γαστερ-), ἡ stomach,
   hunger (3a)
γοῦν-α, τά knees (2b)
   (take γούνων after λαβών
   'taking hold of')
γυῖ-α, τά limbs (2b)
γυμν-ός -ή -όν naked
δαί-ομαι blaze
δέ-ος, τό fear (3c)
δοάσσατο it seemed to x (dat.)
ἕ=αὐτόν
ἐκ . . . εἵλετο (aor. of
   ἐξαιρέομαι) remove from
   (+gen.)
ἔλαφ-ος, ἡ hind (2a)
εὐπλόκαμ-ος -ον with pretty
   hair
εὐῶπις (εὐωπιδ-), ἡ beautiful
ἔχ-ομαι (σχ-) hold one's

ground
ἤ . . . ἠέ either . . . or
ἤ . . . ἤ whether . . . or
ἠιών (ἠιον-), ἡ shore, strand
   (3a)
θάμν-ος, ὁ bush (2a)
θάρσ-ος, τό courage, boldness
   (3c)
ἱκάν-ω come to, come upon
ἵμεν=ἰέναι
κακό-ω disfigure
κέλ-ομαι order
κερδαλέ-ος -η -ον cunning
κέρδιον more profitable
κλάζ-ω break
λίσσ-ομαι beseech
μειλίχι-ος -η -ον winning,
   soothing
μερμηρίζ-ω consider, debate
μετέρχ-ομαι attack (+dat.,
   or+μετά+acc.)
μήδε-α, τά genitals (3c
   uncontr.)
μῆλ-ον, τό sheep (2b)
μίγνυ-μαι meet with (+dat.)
   (fut. μίξομαι)
ὄιεσσιν dat. pl. of ὄις
οἶ-ος -η -ον alone
ὄις, ὁ, ἡ sheep

ὀρεσίτροφ-ος -ον
   mountain-bred
ὄσσε both eyes (nom.)
παχ-ύς -εῖα -ύ thick, clenched
πειρά-ω test (+gen.)
πεποιθώς trusting in (+dat.)
   (perf. part. of πείθ-ω)
περ=καίπερ
περί (+dat.) around, about
προέχ-ω jut out
πτόρθ-ος, ὁ branch (2a)
πυκιν-ός -ή -όν dense,
   thick-foliaged
ῥύ-ομαι protect, hide
σμερδαλέ-ος -η -ον frightful,
   terrible
τῇ=αὐτῇ
τρέ-ω tremble, flee
ὕλ-η, ἡ bush, tree (1a)
ὑποδύ-ομαι emerge from
   (+gen.)
ὕ-ω rain (upon)
φρονέ-ω consider
φύλλ-ον, τό leaf (2b)
φώς (φωτ-), ὁ mortal (3a)
χολό-ομαι be angry with
   (+dat.)
χρείω, ἡ need
χρώς, ὁ flesh, body (dat. χροΐ)

Vocabulary to be learnt

γοῦνα, τά knees (2b)
   (sometimes γούνατα (3b))
ἱκάνω come, come to/upon
   (+acc.)

ἵμεν=ἰέναι
λίσσομαι beseech
ὁ ἥ τό he, she, it
φρονέω think, consider

χρώς, ὁ flesh (Attic χρωτ- 3a)
   (Ionic/Epic acc. χρόα; gen.
   χροός; dat. χροΐ)

Vocabulary for Section Nineteen E

ἄγα-μαι admire, look at in
awe
ἄγχιστα most closely
αἰέν=ἀεί
αἰνῶς terribly
ἄλγ-ος, τό source of grief (3c
uncontr.) (understand 'these
things are . . .')
ἀμφιβάλλ-ομαι
(ἀμφιβαλ-) put on
ἄνασσ-α, ἡ princess (1c)
ἀνέρχ-ομαι (ἀνηλυθ-) come
up
ἅπτ-ομαι touch (+gen.)
ἄρειον better
Ἄρτεμις (Ἀρτεμιδ-), ἡ
Artemis (3a) (goddess of
hunting and chastity)
βρίθ-ω load down
βροτ-ός, ὁ mortal (2a)
γαῖ-α, ἡ (1c)=γῆ
γουνό-ομαι beseech
δείδια I fear
Δῆλ-ος, ἡ Delos (2a) (island
birthplace and sanctuary of
Apollo)
δήν for a long time
δόρυ (δορατ-), τό piece of
wood, shaft (3b)
δυσμεν-ής, ὁ enemy
ἔεδν-α, τά bridal gifts (2b)
ἐεικοστ-ός -ή -όν twentieth
εἶδ-ος, τό looks, appearance
(3c)
εἴλυμα, τό wrapping (3b)
εἵνεκα=ἕνεκα
ἐίσκ-ω liken x (acc.) to y
(dat.) in z (acc.)
εἰσοιχνέ-ω enter
εἰσορά-ω behold, look upon
ἐκ l. 26 goes with γαίης
ἐλεαίρ-ω show mercy
ἔξοχον (+gen.) above, more
than

ἔρν-ος, τό young stem (3c)
ἐσσι=εἶ you (s.) are
εὐμενέτ-ης, ὁ friend (1d)
εὐρ-ύς -εῖα -ύ broad, wide
εὐφροσύν-η, ἡ pleasure (1a)
ἔχες=εἶχες
ἔχητον 'the two of them
keep' (3rd dual)
ἤ or
ἠδέ and
ἦμαρ (ἤματ-), τό day (3b)
θάλ-ος, τό budding branch
(3c)
θύελλ-α, ἡ storm (1c)
ἰαίν-ω warm
ἱκνέ-ομαι (ἱκ-) come to
κάββαλε=κατέβαλε
κασίγνητ-ος, ὁ brother (2a)
καταβάλλ-ω (καταβαλ-) cast
down
κεῖν-ος=ἐκεῖν-ος
κεῖσε=ἐκεῖσε
κήδε-α, τά troubles (3c
uncontr.)
κῆρ (κηρ-), τό heart (3a)
κλύ-ω be respected
κραιπν-ός -ή -όν swift
κῦμα (κυματ-), τό wave (3b)
λα-ός, ὁ people (2a)
λεύσσ-ω see (take λευσσόντων
with σφισι)
μάκαρ (μακαρ-) blessed
(μακάρτατ-ος -η -ον is the
sup.)
μέγεθ-ος, τό size (3c)
μενοινά-ω desire
μογέ-ω suffer
ναιετά-ω dwell
νόημα (νοηματ-), τό thought
(3b)
οἰκόνδε home, homewards
οἶνοψ (οἰνοπ-) wine-faced
(wine-dark)
οἴ-ω think

ὁμοφρονέ-ω be in agreement,
compatible
ὁμοφρονέοντε nom. part.
dual
ὁμοφροσύν-η, ἡ compatibility
(1a)
ὀπάζ-ω grant
ὀφθαλμ-ός, ὁ eye (2a)
ὄφρα=ἵνα (+subj.) in order
that
πάροιθεν before then
πένθ-ος, τό grief (3c)
περί (+dat.) in
πόντ-ος, ὁ sea (2a)
πότνι-α lady (nom. s. f.)
που somewhere, anywhere
(enclitic)
πω yet (enclitic)
ῥάκ-ος, τό tattered garment
(3c)
σέβας, τό respect (3c)
σεῖο=σοῦ
σπεῖρ-ον, τό garment (2b)
σφισι=σφι
τέθηπα be astonished (perf.)
(past ἐτεθήπεα)
τελέ-ω complete, bring to
pass (fut. τελέ-ω)
τῇδε here
τοι=οἱ
τοῖ-ος=τοιοῦτος
τόσσ-ος -η -ον as many (take
with ὅσος 'as many as')
τοῦ=τούτου (gen. of
comparison)
τόφρα for so long
τρισμάκαρ (τρισμακαρ-)
thrice-blessed
φοῖνιξ (φοινικ-), ὁ, ἡ
date-palm
φορέ-ω carry
φυ-ή, ἡ stature (1a)
χάρμα (χαρματ-), τό source
of joy (3b)

χθιζ-ός -ή -όν yesterday's (tr.
  'yesterday')
χθών (χθον-), ἡ earth (3a)
χορ-ός, ὁ dance (2a)

Ὠγυγί-η, ἡ Ogygia (1a)
  (island of Kalypso)
ὡς δ' αὔτως in the same way

Vocabulary to be learnt

ἄνασσα, ἡ princess, queen (1c)
ἅπτομαι touch (+gen.)
βροτός, ὁ mortal (2a)
γαῖα, ἡ=γῆ
εἰσοράω (εἰσιδ-) behold, look
  at
ἐσσι=εἶ you (s.) are

ἤ or
ἦμαρ (ἡματ-), τό day (3b)
ἱκνέομαι (ἱκ-) come to, arrive
  at
κεῖνος=ἐκεῖνος
μέγεθος, τό size (3c)
οἰκόνδε home, homewards

ὀφθαλμός, ὁ eye (2a)
περί (+dat.) in, on
που somewhere, anywhere
  (enclitic)
πω yet (enclitic)
τοί=οἵ (relative)
χορός, ὁ dance; chorus (2a)

Vocabulary for Section Nineteen F

ἀλά-ομαι wander
Ἀλκινόοιο=Ἀλκινόου
ἄμμι=ἡμῖν
ἀνέμοιο=ἀνέμου
ἄνεμος, ὁ wind (2a)
ἀντιά-ω meet, encounter
ἀντίον in reply
ἀπάνευθε far away
αὐδά-ω speak, say
ἄφρων ἄφρον (ἀφρον-)
  stupid, thoughtless
βί-η, ἡ dominion (1a)
βρῶσ-ις, ἡ meat, food (3e)
γένηται (l. 29) '(he) will ever
  be' (subj. in general
  statement)
δεύ-ομαι lack (+gen.) (fut.
  δευήσομαι)
δηϊοτής (δηϊοτητ-), ἡ
  slaughter (3a)
διερ-ός -ά -όν living
δόσ-ις, ἡ gift, giving (3e)

δυσμεν-ής -ές hostile
δύστην-ος -ον wretched
ἐθέλῃσιν=ἐθέλῃ (3rd s. pres.
  subj.)
ἐκ (l. 25) governs τοῦ
ἔμμεναι=εἶναι
ἔμπης doubtless, at any rate
ἐπέοικε it befits, it is right for
  (+dat.)
ἐπί . . . ἔστ' is, is found
ἐπιμίσγ-ομαι have to do with
  (+dat.)
εὐπλόκαμ-ος -ον with pretty
  hair
ἔχ-ομαι (ἐκ) depend (on)
ἦ (l. 26) she spoke
ἦ μή surely you don't
ἠδέ and
κάρτ-ος, τό power (3c)
κομέ-ω look after, care for
λα-ός, ὁ people, inhabitant
  (2a)

λευκώλεν-ος -ον white-armed
λού-ω wash
μεγαλήτωρ (μεγαλητορ-)
  great-hearted
ὄλβ-ος, ὁ happiness, wealth
  (2a)
πολύκλυστ-ος -ον
  loud-roaring
πόντ-ος, ὁ sea (2a)
πόσε; (to) where?
πόσ-ις, ἡ drink (3e)
πρός (+gen.) under the
  protection of
πτωχ-ός, ὁ beggar (2a)
σκέπας, τό cover, shelter (sc.
  'from')
ταλαπείρι-ος -ον weary
τετλάμεν to endure (perf. inf.
  of τλάω)
φώς (φωτ-), ὁ mortal, man
  (3a)

Vocabulary to be learnt

ἄνεμος, ὁ wind (2a)
ἔμμεναι=εἶναι
εὐπλόκαμος ον with pretty hair

ἠδέ and
λαός, ὁ people, inhabitant (2a)
λούω wash (mid. wash oneself)

πόντος, ὁ sea (2a)
φώς (φωτ-), ὁ man, mortal
  (3a)

Vocabulary for Section Nineteen G

ἀδμής (ἀδμητ-), ἡ unwed
ἀεικέλι-ος -η -ον wretched
ἀέκητι against the will of
  (+gen.)
αἴ γάρ=εἰ γάρ
αἰδέ-ομαι feel shame at
  (+inf.)
ἀλείφ-ω anoint
ἅλμ-η, ἡ brine (1a)
ἀλοιφ-ή, ἡ ointment (1a)
ἅλς (ἁλ-), ὁ sea (3a)
ἀμπέχ-ω cover, lie thick
  upon
ἀμφί round about (adv.)
ἀμφί . . . ἕννυμαι put on (aor.
  ἑσσάμην)
ἀνδάν-ω (ἁδ-) please (+dat.)
ἄνθ-ος, τό flower (3c)
ἄντην face to face, in front of
  (sc. 'you')
ἀντίθε-ος -η -ον god-like
ἀπάνευθεν afar off
ἄπαστ-ος -ον not having
  tasted (+gen.)
ἀπό . . . ἐστίν has been absent
  (from+gen.)
ἀπολούσομαι 1st s. aor. subj.
  of ἀπολού-ομαι wash off
  oneself
ἀπόπροθεν far off
ἄργυρ-ος, ὁ silver (2a)
ἁρπαλέως greedily
ἀτρυγέτοιο=ἀτρυγέτου
ἀτρύγετ-ος -ον unharvested
αὐτάρ then, but
αὐτόθι here
βρῶσ-ις, ἡ meat, food (3e)
γυμνό-ομαι strip
δέατο he seemed
δέδαεν 3rd s. perf. of
  δι-δά-σκω

δηρόν for a long time
ἐδητύς, ἡ food (3h)
ἕζ-ομαι sit
ἐκγεγαυῖα born of (+gen.)
  (nom. s. f.)
ἔλαι-ον, τό olive oil (2b)
ἐπιμίσγ-ομαι meet with
  (+dat.)
εὐρ-ύς -εῖα -ύ broad
ἦ indeed
ἦεν=ἦν
ἤνωγον they ordered
ἦσθε=ἤσθιε (he) ate
ἦ τοι then indeed
θηέ-ομαι look at admiringly
θίς (θιν-), ὁ shore (3a)
ἴδρις skilful, cunning (nom.)
ἴσαν=ἦσαν they went
κάδ=κατά
κάδ (=κατά) . . . ἕζ-ω to
  seat (aor. εἷσα)
κάλλ-ος, τό beauty (3c)
κάρη (καρητ-), τό head (3b)
καταχεύ-ω pour down x
  (acc.) on y (dat.) over z
  (acc.)
κί-ω go
κόμ-η, ἡ hair (1a)
λευκώλεν-ος -ον white-armed
λήκυθ-ος, ἡ oil-jar (2a)
λίπα richly
λοέσσατο 3rd s. aor. mid. of
  λούω
λοέσσομαι fut. mid. of λούω
μεγαλήτωρ (μεγαλητορ-)
  great-hearted
μετανδά-ω say (to)
μετέρχ-ομαι (μετελθ-) go
  among (+dat.)
μίμν-ω=μένω
ναιετά-ω dwell, live

νίζ-ομαι wash x (acc.) from y
  (acc.)
νῶτ-ον, τό back (2b)
Ὄλυμπ-ος, ὁ Olympus (2a)
οὖλ-ος -η -ον thick, bushy
ὄφρα=ἵνα (+subj.) in order
  that
Πάλλας (Παλλαδ-), ἡ Pallas
  (3a)
παντοῖ-ος -η -ον of all kinds
πάρ=παρά beside (adv.)
παρθέν-ος, ἡ maiden (2a)
πάσσων -ον
  (πασσον-) broader
περιχεύ-ομαι inlay, gild x
  (acc.) on y (dat.)
πολύτλας ὁ long-enduring
πόρε (she) provided, gave
  (3rd s. of ἔπορον)
πόσ-ις, ἡ drink (3e)
πρόσθεν previously
ῥο-ή, ἡ stream, current (1a)
σκέπας, τό cover, shelter
σμήχ-ω wipe
στίλβ-ω shine
τελεί-ω complete
ὑακίνθιν-ος -η -ον of a wild
  hyacinth
ὑγρ-ός -ή -όν moist
φᾶρ-ος, τό cloak (3c)
χαρί-εις -εσσα -εν
  (χαριεντ-) graceful
χιτών (χιτων-), ὁ tunic (3a)
χνό-ος, ὁ scum, scurf (2a)
χρί-ομαι anoint oneself
χρυσέ-ος -η -ον golden
ὤμοϊιν 'from my two
  shoulders' (gen. dual of
  ὦμος)
ὦμ-ος, ὁ shoulder (2a)

Vocabulary to be learnt

ἀπάνευθεν *afar off*
αὐδάω *speak, say*
αὐτάρ *then, but*
εὐρύς εἶα ύ *broad, wide*
κάδ=κατά
κατά (+gen.) *down from, against; below*
κάρη (καρητ-), τό=κάρα

(κρατ- (3b); Attic) *head*
μεταυδάω *speak to*
μετέρχομαι (μετελθ-) *go among (+dat.); attack (+dat. or μετά); send for (+dat. or μετά); send for*
ὄφρα=ἵνα+subj./ opt. *in order to/that*
πάρ=παρά

παρθένος, ἡ *maiden (2a)*
πρόσθεν (+gen.) *previously, before*
χρυσέος η ον *golden (Attic χρυσοῦς ῆ οὖν)*
ὦμος, ὁ *shoulder (2a)*
Genitive s. of type 2 nouns (-οιο for -ου)·

O   Grammar for Section Nineteen

Summary:
Homeric dialect, syntax and respelling
Homeric hexameters
Verse quantity

Some vital features of Homeric dialect and syntax

225 The Reference Grammar (A.4) contains a fuller list of features of Homeric dialect. Meanwhile, note the following highly characteristic features:

(i) lack of augment – βάλον=ἔβαλον; ἔμβαλε=ἐνέβαλε;

(ii) dative plurals in -σι, -εσσι e.g. δώροισι, πόδεσσι;

(iii) dative plural ταῖς appears as τῆς, τῆσι; so all type 1a b c nouns (e.g. θύρῃσι);

(iv) genitive singular in -οιο – δώροιο; and in -αο, -εω, in place of -ου of 1d types;

(v) infinitives in -μεν, -μεναι, -εναι (ἔμεν, ἔμμεν, ἔμεναι, ἔμμεναι=εἶναι; ἵμεν(αι)=ἰέναι; ἀκουέμεναι=ἀκούειν);

(vi) use of οἱ to mean 'to him, her', and τοι meaning 'to you' (2nd s.);

(vii) definite articles οἱ, αἱ appear also as τοί, ταί;

(viii) presence of η where Attic has α or ε, e.g. χώρη=χώρα; βασιλῆας=βασιλέας;

(ix) use of definite article to mean 'he', 'she', 'it', 'they';

(x) 'tmesis', i.e. the splitting of the prefix of a verb from the verb with which it is (in Attic) normally joined, e.g. πρὸς μῦθον ἔειπεν=μῦθον προσέειπεν 'he addressed a word';

(xi) κεν (κε, κ') is used in place of ἄν.

Note

It should be stressed that the above list does not represent a series of hard-and-fast rules, which will always apply; the examples given are the most important alternative *forms that Homer uses. (Cf. Reference Grammar A.4, p. 267.)*

Homeric hexameters

226 A hexameter is made up of six feet, each foot being either a *dactyl* or a *spondee*.

A dactyl scans: $-\cup\cup$ (long–short–short, 'tum-ti-ti')

A spondee scans: $--$ (long–long, 'tum-tum').

In Homer, the FIRST FOUR FEET can be either dactyl or spondee;

the FIFTH FOOT is usually a DACTYL;

the SIXTH FOOT is always a SPONDEE if we assume a final syllable is always treated as long.

Thus a Homeric hexameter looks like:

1	2	3	4	5	6
$-\cup\cup$	$-\cup\cup$	$-\cup\cup$	$-\cup\cup$	$-\cup\cup$	$--$
or	or	or	or		
$--$	$--$	$--$	$--$	$(--)$	

Notes

There are a number of peculiar features of Homeric scansion, of which the three most important are as follows:

(i) 'correption' – that is, that a naturally long vowel/diphthong at the end of a word becomes short *if the next word begins with a vowel, e.g.*

$\cup--$

καὶ ἡμῖν

(ii) the influence of 'digamma' (ϝ) on the scansion. By classical times, digamma as a letter had dropped out of the alphabet, but its influence was felt so strongly that in Homer the scansion reacted to it as if it were still there. It was originally pronounced like English 'w'. E.g.

$-\cup\cup\ --\ -\cup\cup\ ---\cup\cup--$

τῷ οἱ ἐ|πεκλώ|σαντο θε|οὶ οἶ|κόνδε νέ|εσθαι '*him the gods fated to return home*'

The rule of correption makes οἱ *short before* ἐπεκλώσαντο, *but why then is not* τῷ *short before* οἱ, *and* θεοί *short before* οἶκόνδε? *The answer is that* οἱ *was once* ϝοι *and* οἶκόνδε *was once* ϝοῖκόνδε. *Consequently the words do not really start with a vowel and the rule of correption cannot apply.*

(iii) effects of metre on the language:

The pattern of the dactyl–spondee rhythm of the Homeric hexameter imposes certain limitations and makes some words unusable. Homer gets round this by a number of devices:

(i) *words which are naturally long–short–long are scanned long–long–long, e.g.*
‾ ◡‾   ‾ ‾‾
ἱστιη *is scanned* ἱστιη.

(ii) *words which are naturally short–short–short have the first element lengthened, e.g.*

◡ ◡ ◡ ◡   ‾ ◡ ◡ ◡
ἀκαματος – ἀκαματος *'unwearied'*

◡ ◡ ◡   ‾ ◡ ◡
ἀνερα – ἀνερα *'man' (acc.)*

(iii) *by the use of alternative forms, e.g. dative in -εσσι rather than -εσι e.g.* ◡‾◡ ἐπεσσι ◡ ◡ ◡ *or* ἐπεσι, *etc.*

Finally, observe that in some cases one is given a choice whether to scan dactyl or spondee, e.g.

‾ ‾ ‾ ‾   ‾◡◡ ‾ ‾
'Αργει|φοντης *or* 'Αργεϊφοντης *'slayer of Argos' (epithet for Hermes)*

Here are the first five lines of the Homer extract scanned:

‾ ◡ ◡   ‾ ◡ ◡ ‾ ◡◡ ‾ ‾   ‾◡ ◡ ‾ ‾
ὡς ὁ με|ν ἐνθα κα|θευδε πο|λυτλας | διος 'Ο|δυσσευς,

‾ ◡ ◡   ‾ ◡ ◡ ‾ ‾   ‾◡◡   ‾ ◡ ‾ ‾
ὑπνῳ | και καμα|τῳ ἀ|ρημενο|ς. αὐταρ 'Α|θηνη

‾ ‾   ‾ ‾ ‾   ◡ ◡   ‾ ◡ ◡ ‾ ‾
βη ρ' ἐς | Φαιη|κων ἀν|δρων δη|μον τε πο|λιν τε

‾ ◡◡   ‾ ‾   ‾ ◡◡‾   ◡◡   ◡◡   ‾ ‾
ἠ δ' ἀνε|μου ὡς | πνοιη ἐ|πεσσυτο | δεμνια | κουρης

‾ ◡ ◡ ‾   ◡ ◡ ‾   ‾   ‾   ‾◡ ◡‾ ‾
στη δ' ἀρ' ὑ|περ κεφα|λης, και | μιν προς | μυθον ἐ|ειπεν

Homeric respelling

227 The text of Homer as we have it is based on a third-century Hellenistic edition. We do not know what earlier texts would have been like, but it does appear that some modernisation of the text took place. This has sometimes produced artificial forms in the text, such as εἵως for what must have been ἦος.

Greek metre

228 Greek verse is made up of regular sequences of syllables, *each* of which counts as long or short for the purpose of the metre. *Every* syllable counts. In order therefore to determine what any metre is, we must decide the quantity of each syllable – whether long or short. The quantity of the syllable is determined by the vowel(s) and consonant(s) which make it up.

Basic rules

Syllables containing η, ω and diphthongs, and ᾱ, ῑ, ῡ (these last three have to be known, or adduced from context) are always LONG in verse, no matter what. (N.b. the note on Homeric correption at **226** (i).)

Syllables containing ε, o and ᾰ, ῐ, ῠ are always SHORT in verse, UNLESS they are followed by two consonants (including ζ (σδ), ξ (κs) and ψ (πs))when, for the purpose of the scansion, they will *count as* long. There is one major exception to this rule – any combination of π τ κ φ θ χ β δ γ+λ μ ν ρ need not necessarily make the preceding syllable long for scansion purposes. Thus, πατρός can scan – ∪ or ∪ ∪.

Notes

(i) Ignore word-division for the purpose of scansion. Thus the o of ἄνθρωπός τις *scans* LONG, *because it is followed by two consonants,* στ.

(ii) Watch out for elision of short vowels at the end of a word (cf. **57, 178**). *This should not cause problems since your texts will usually elide out such vowels for you anyway.*

(iii) This is a highly simplified account of a complex subject. Its main weakness is to confuse vowels which are pronounced *long or short, with syllables which* count *as (but were certainly not pronounced as) long or short for metrical purposes. Consider* ἔρχονται. *The first two vowels are short by pronunciation, and would certainly have been pronounced short in all circumstances. But for the purpose of scansion, they count as long, because they are followed by two consonants.*

B *REFERENCE GRAMMAR*

O   A.1 Preliminaries

Some definitions

(i) *Aspect*

This refers to the way in which a *verb*-form suggests that the reader should look at the action under consideration. The clearest example of aspect can perhaps be best seen in Greek's use of the imperfect and aorist to refer to action in the past: the imperfect suggests that the action should be viewed as continuing, as a process, the aorist suggests that it simply took place as an event. Participles, infinitives, imperatives, optatives and subjunctives are virtually always differentiated in their present and aorist forms by *aspect*, not by time (necessarily). Their present forms suggest that the action should be viewed as continuing; their aorist forms suggest that the action should be viewed as simply happening.

(ii) *Change of subject in the accusative*

In clauses which take a verb in the infinitive or participle, the subject is placed in the *accusative* if it is different from that of the main verb, e.g.

οἶδα σε μῶρον ὄντα '*I* know that *you* are foolish'

ἐνομίζομεν τοὺς Ἕλληνας παῖδας εἶναι '*we* used to consider that *the Greeks* were children'

(iii) *Sequence*

'Primary sequence' means that the main verb is present, future or perfect; 'secondary sequence' means that the main verb is aorist, imperfect or pluperfect. Sequence plays an important part in determining whether the subjunctive or optative is to be used in certain constructions.

O   A.2 The Greek alphabet

Before the fourth century there were many forms of the Greek alphabet in use in different cities. After 403 Athens and eventually most other cities adopted the so-called Ionic form of the alphabet, which is the one in use today.

One important letter which does not appear in the Ionic alphabet is the digamma (ϝ). This was originally the sixth letter of the alphabet (cf. English fF), and had the value of English 'w'. The Attic and Ionic dialects lost the sound at prehistoric date, and consequently the letter was not used in their alphabets. Other dialects maintained the sound, and the letter continued in use in these dialects down to the adoption of the Ionic alphabet in the fourth century. After this, traces of digamma are found, sometimes represented by Greek β, e.g. a Hellenistic text writes ῥίζα 'root' in Sapphic dialect as βρίσδα, using the β to represent the digamma which Sappho used (ϝρισδα).

The importance of the digamma lies in the fact that Homeric scansion may react to it as if it were still there. Thus one would expect, for example, ἐνὶ οἴκῳ in Homer to elide into ἐν οἴκῳ; but no, for it was originally ϝοῖκος, starting with a consonant. (See further notes on Homeric metre in the Running Grammar **226**.)

Alphabet and pronunciation

Greek capital	Greek minuscule	English transcription used in this course*	Pronunciation (recommended)	Phonetic transcription**
A	α (alpha)	a	English 'cup' (Italian 'amare')	[a]
(when long)	ā		English 'calm' (Italian 'amare')	[a:]
	ᾳ		as ā (more correctly, with -ι at the end)	[a:i]
	αι		English 'high'	[ai]
	αυ		English 'how'	[au]
	ᾱυ		as αυ (with first element long)	[a:u]
B	β (beta)	b	as English 'b'	[b]
Γ	γ (gamma)	g	English 'got'; before κ, χ, γ, as 'ink' or 'song'	[g; ŋ]
Δ	δ (delta)	d	French 'd' (with tongue on teeth, not gums)	[d]
E	ε (epsilon)	e	English 'pet'	[e]
	ει		English 'fiancée' (German 'Beet')	[e:]
	ευ		Cockney 'belt' (Italian 'eulogia')	[eu]

Greek capital	Greek minuscule	English transcription used in this course*	Pronunciation (recommended)	Phonetic transcription**
Z	ζ (zeta)	sd	English 'wisdom'	[zd]
H	η (eta)	e	English 'hairy' (French 'tête')	[ɛ:]
	ῃ		as η (more correctly, with -ι at the end)	[ɛ:i]
	ηυ		as ευ (with first element long)	[ɛ:u]
Θ	θ (theta)	th	English 'top' (emphatically pronounced; later, as in 'thin')	[th]
I	ι (iota)	i	English 'bit' (French 'vitesse')	[i]
(when long)	ῑ		English 'bead'	[i:]
K	κ (kappa)	k	English 'skin'	[k]
Λ	λ (lambda)	l	English 'left'	[l]
M	μ (mu)	m	English 'man'	[m]
N	ν (nu)	n	English 'net'	[n]
Ξ	ξ (xi)	x	English 'box'	[ks]
O	o (omicron)	o	English 'pot' (or German 'Gott')	[o]
	οι		English 'boy'	[oi]
	ου		English 'too'	[u:]
Π	π (pi)	p	English 'spin'	[p]
P	ρ (rho)	r	Scottish 'rolled' r	[r]
Σ	σ, ς (sigma)	s	English 'sing', 'lesson'	[s]
T	τ (tau)	t	t (with tongue on teeth, not gums)	[t]
Y	υ (upsilon)	u, y	u, as in French 'lune' (German 'Müller')	[y]
(when long)	ῡ		u, as in French 'ruse' (German Mühle')	[y:]
	υι		close to French 'huit'	[yi]
Φ	φ (phi)	ph	English 'pot' (emphatically pronounced; later, as in 'fear')	[ph]
X	χ (khi)	kh	English 'cat' (emphatically pronounced; later, as in 'loch')	[kh]
Ψ	ψ (psi)	ps	English 'lapse'	[ps]
Ω	ω (omega)	o	English 'saw'	[ɔ:]
	ῳ		As ω (more correctly, with -ι at the end)	[ɔ:i]

* See also notes on p. 332.
** IPA system, in which : adds length; th, ph, kh mean aspirated t, p, k.

Notes

(i) *Most Greek texts use two forms of minuscule sigma:* ς *at the end of the word,* σ *elsewhere (e.g.* ὅσος). *Some Greek texts print a 'lunate' sigma,* c, *which is used in all positions (e.g.* ὅcoc).

(ii) *For the principles of transcription of names from Greek into English, see Notes to the Text, p. xv.*

Use the following poem by the fifth-century poet Kallias to memorise the alphabet:

ά   β   γ   δ   ε
ἔστ' ἄλφα, βῆτα, γάμμα, δέλτα καὶ τὸ εἶ,

ζ   η   θ   ι   κ   λ   μ
ζῆτα, ἦτα, θῆτα, ἰῶτα, κάππα, λάβδα, μῦ,

ν   ξ   ο   π   ρ   σ,ς   τ   υ
νῦ, ξεῖ, τὸ οὖ, πεῖ, ῥῶ, τὸ σῖγμα, ταῦ, τὸ ὖ

φ   χ   ψ   ω
φεῖ, χεῖ τε καὶ ψεῖ καὶ τελευταῖον τὸ ὦ.

Notes
(i) ζ, ξ, and ψ indicate a double consonant:
    ζ is written for σδ
    ξ is written for κς
    ψ is written for πς
(ii) Vowels do not always indicate a distinction of length (or quantity):
    ε, o always indicate a short vowel
    η, ω always indicate a long vowel
    a, ι, υ are used for both long and short vowels.
(iii) All double consonants are given their full value in pronunciation, e.g.
    ππ is pronounced as in 'hip-pocket'
    ττ is pronounced as in 'rat-trap'
    σσ is pronounced as in 'disservice'
    λλ is pronounced as in 'wholly' (cf. 'holy').
The exception is γγ, which is pronounced as in 'finger' (and so too γκ (as in 'ink'), γξ (as in 'lynx') and γχ (as in 'ink-horn')).
(iv) Words beginning with a vowel show a 'breathing' mark over the first (sometimes the second) letter, either ' or ', e.g.
    ὄρος ('oros')
    ὅρος ('horos')
The 'rough' breathing, ', denotes the presence of 'h'.
The 'smooth' breathing, ', is merely a convention to denote the absence of 'h'.
Note that all words beginning with ρ take a rough breathing, e.g. ῥήτωρ ('rhetor'). This may have indicated a special pronunciation.
(v) You will already have noticed that Greek words have accent marks, i.e. ' (acute), ` (grave), ˆ (circumflex). These denote the musical pitch at which the accented syllable was pronounced – high pitch ('), low pitch (`), high pitch falling to low (ˆ: originally written as a combination of acute+grave, ˆ). This accent is only found on long vowels,

and diphthongs). *There is no reason why you should not attempt to 'pitch' the accent, but you will find it fairly difficult to do without constant care and attention. English speakers naturally 'stress' syllables. If you cannot 'pitch', then you must 'stress' the accented syllable, even though this may obscure the accent which is being used (whether ´, ` or ˆ). Learn the word with its accent* as part of its pronunciation. *That is why the accent is there.*

For a fuller, though by no means complete, account of Greek methods of accentuation, see the Reference Grammar A.3.

(vi) There are four punctuation marks in Greek, though we have used some English ones in places to ease reading. The four Greek marks are:

. *full stop, as in English*
, *comma, as in English*
· *colon or semi-colon (note that* · *is placed slightly* above *the line)*
; *question-mark (?)*

(vii) Now the truth must be told that a fifth-century Greek would hardly have recognised a single one of all these conventions you have just learnt. *Fifth-century Greeks wrote in* CAPITAL LETTERS, *with* NOGAPSBETWEENWORDS, *with* NO ACCENTS, *with* NO SMOOTH BREATHINGS *and virtually* NO PUNCTUATION.* *All these conventions sprang up later, some very much later indeed. Modern Greek continues to use most of them.*

(viii) Greeks generally liked their language to run smoothly, and to achieve this they regularly ran words together, or modified their endings (as we do too, e.g. 'isn't' for 'is not', 'we're' for 'we are', 'Tom 'n' Jerry' for 'Tom and Jerry'). We shall not do this until Section Four, but in the meantime, notice the changes that the Greek for 'no(t)' undergoes in response to its environment:

* *Consequently the act of reading for an ancient Greek must have required a high level of intelligence and concentration, especially since the endings of the words are so crucial for meaning. It is bad enough in English: here is a translated extract from Plato's* Republic:

FARLESSIAGREESOWECANTHAVEHOMERSAYING
OFTHEGODSANDAFITOFHELPLESSLAUGHTER
SEIZEDTHEHAPPYGODSASTHEYWATCHEDHEPHAESTUS
BUSTLINGUPANDDOWNTHEHALLYOURARGUMENT
WOULDNTALLOWTHATCALLITMYARGUMENTIFYOU
LIKEHEREPLIEDINANYEVENTWECANTALLOWIT
ANDSURELYWEMUSTVALUETRUTHFULNESSHIGHLY,
and so on.
The Greek looked roughly as follows:
ΠΟΛΥΜΕΝΤΟΙΗΔΗΟΣΟΥΚΟΥΝΗΟΜΗΡΟΥΟΥΔΕΤΑ
ΤΟΙΑΥΤΑΑΠΟΔΕΞΟΜΕΘΑΠΕΡΙΘΕΩΝΑΣΒΕΣΤΟΣ
ΔΑΡΕΝΩΡΤΟΓΕΛΩΣΜΑΚΑΡΕΣΣΙΘΕΟΙΣΙΝΗΩΣΙΔΟΝ
ΗΗΦΑΙΣΤΟΝΔΙΑΔΩΜΑΤΑΠΟΙΠΝΥΟΝΤΑΟΥΚΑΠΟΔΕΚ
ΤΕΟΝΚΑΤΑΤΟΝΣΟΝΛΟΓΟΝΕΙΣΥΕΦΗΒΟΥΛΕΙΕΜΟΝΤΙ
ΘΕΝΑΙΟΥΓΑΡΟΥΝΑΠΟΔΕΚΤΕΟΝΑΛΛΑΜΗΝΚΑΙΑΛΗΘΕΙΑΝ
ΓΕΠΕΡΙΠΟΛΛΟΥΠΟΙΗΤΕΟΝ . . .

Δικαιόπολις οὐ βαίνει πρός . . .   '*Dikaiopolis does not go to . . .*'
Δικαιόπολις οὐκ ἔστιν ἐν . . .   '*Dikaiopolis is not in . . .*'
Δικαιόπολις οὐχ ὁρᾷ τόν . . .   '*Dikaiopolis does not see the . . .*'
Greek uses οὐ *before a consonant*
    οὐκ *before a vowel with no '*h*' sound ('unaspirated')*
    οὐχ *before a vowel with an '*h*' sound ('aspirated')*
Observe also that -ν *is used at the end of some words to smooth over 'hiatus' (the awkward transition between two vowels, one ending a word and the next beginning a word), e.g.*
    βαίνουσι πρός . . .   '*they go towards . . .*'
    βαίνουσιν εἰς . . .   '*they go into . . .*'

○   A.3 Accentuation

General remarks

1. Accent-marks were invented about the third century. Their purpose was to indicate the musical pitch of the syllable on which the accent was placed.
2. There are three accents:
    the acute   ′ (high pitch)
    the grave   ` (low pitch, or perhaps a *falling* of the voice)
    the circumflex ^ (high pitch falling to low)
3. Most Greek words have their own accent, which has to be learnt with the word. Observe the differing accents on:
    ἄνθρωπος, πλοῖον, βοή, οἰκία.

In NOUNS and ADJECTIVES, the accent is persistent – that is, it nearly always stays where it occurs in its dictionary form unless forced to move or change by the rules of accent which follow. You must *learn* where the accent falls *when you learn the word*.

In VERBS, accentuation is almost entirely predictable: a basic grasp of the rules of accentuation will give you almost complete mastery over all verb accents.

The position of the accent

If a word has an accent, it will fall on one of the last three syllables. The following diagram shows you where it is possible for accents to fall:

Third-last	Second-last	Last
syllable	syllable	syllable
(antepenultimate)	(penultimate)	(ultimate)

N.b. each of these accents has a technical name, by which you may find it denoted:

	Third-last	*Second-last*	*Last*
Acute:	´ proparoxytone	´ paroxytone	´ oxytone
Grave:			` barytone
Circumflex:		ˆ properispomenon	ˆ perispomenon

(i) The acute ´

This can fall on any of the last three syllables. If the last syllable has a long vowel or diphthong, the accent can only fall on the last two, e.g. ἄνθρωπος, ἀνθρώπου.

If the acute falls on the last syllable, it will become grave when followed by another word in the same sentence (unless a comma intervenes, or the following word is an enclitic, q.v.), e.g.

πόθεν ἡ βοή; ἡ βοὴ τοῦ ἀνθρώπου . . .

(ii) The circumflex ˆ

This can only fall on the last two syllables; it can only stand on a long vowel or a diphthong.

If the last syllable is LONG, a circumflex cannot stand on the second last, e.g. οὗτος, αὕτη.

(iii) The grave `

This can only stand on the last syllable, and will only do so when the word is followed directly by another word in the same sentence which is not an enclitic (see (i) above). Observe the change of accent on the last syllable in:

καλὴ ἡ γυνή. ἡ γυνὴ βαίνει. ἡ γυνὴ καλή.

Enclitics

Not all words have an accent of their own. Those which do not are distinguished into two types:

(i) Proclitics

These are accentually linked to the word which follows them, and only show an accent when the word which follows is an enclitic. The commonest proclitics are ὁ, ἡ, οἱ, αἱ, ἐν, εἰς, οὐ, εἰ.

(ii) Enclitics

These are accentually linked to the preceding word, and sometimes change the accentuation of the preceding word. The principal enclitics are: τε, τις ('a certain', and all indefinite words, e.g. που 'somewhere'), unemphatic με, μου, μοι, σε, σου, σοι, εἰμί ('I am') and φημί ('I say') in the PRESENT INDICATIVE (though not the 2nd s.), γε.

Note
An enclitic cannot stand first in a clause. Observe that there are other words which cannot stand first in a clause, but these are not necessarily enclitics, e.g. γάρ, δέ, οὖν.

(a) Acute on the last remains acute if the following word is enclitic, e.g.
    ἀνὴρ βαίνει, ἀνήρ τις βαίνει.
(b) If the preceding word has an acute on the third last syllable, or a circumflex on the second last, that word will take *as well as its normal accent* an acute on its last syllable, e.g.
    ἄνθρωπός τις
    πλοῖόν τι
(c) If the preceding word has a circumflex on the last syllable, the enclitic simply loses any accent, e.g. οὖν ἐστι
(d) Strings of enclitics will throw accents back onto each other, e.g.
    ἄνθρωπός τίς ποτέ μοι ἔλεγε . . . 'a certain man once said to me . . .'
(do not confuse τίς here with τίς;='who, what?')
(e) Forms of τις with two syllables will accent the *last* if they follow a paroxytone word, e.g.
    πρὸς οἰκίαν τινά 'to a certain house'
(τινά cannot throw its accent back onto οἰκίαν because οἰκίαν does not have an acute on the third-last or a circumflex on the second-last. Note that the accent on τίς; falls on the *first* syllable in all its forms, e.g.
    πρὸς τίνα οἰκίαν βαίνεις; 'to what house are you going?')

Some general hints
(a) Nouns, pronouns, adjectives
    (i) For the purposes of accentuation (NOT METRE), -οι and -αι of nom. pl. count SHORT at the end of these words. Thus ἄνθρωποι, διάνοιαι.
    (ii) Words of 1st and 2nd declension with an acute on the last syllable of nom. s. take circumflex in the genitives and datives, e.g. ἀγαθός – ἀγαθοῦ ἀγαθῷ ἀγαθῆς ἀγαθῇ ἀγαθῶν ἀγαθοῖς ἀγαθαῖς.
    (iii) ALL 1st declension nouns have a circumflex on the -ῶν of the genitive plural (*no matter where* the accent was originally), e.g. νίκη gen. pl. νικῶν; so with 3rd declension nouns in -ος (σκευῶν), if contracted (cf. σκευέων).
    (iv) Note especially πόλεως, πόλεων, breaking the rule of 4 (i).
    (v) Monosyllables of the 3rd declension are accented on the final syllable of

the genitive and dative; e.g. πούς; gen. s. ποδός; dat. s. ποδί; gen. pl. ποδῶν; dat. pl. ποσί.

(vi) Noms. and accs. accented on the final syllable are acute, unless contracted; e.g. ὁ Παρθενών but ὁ Περικλῆς (Περικλέ-ης).

(b) Verbs

(i) The accent normally goes back as far as it can, and is nearly always acute (but see under contracted verbs later on).

(ii) For the purposes of accentuation (NOT METRE), -αι counts SHORT (except in the optative, in which both -αι and -οι count long), e.g.

ἀποκρίνεται, λύεσθαι but νομίζοι

(iii) If the infinitive ends in -ναι, the infinitive will be accented on the second last (acute or circumflex), and its nom. s. m. participle on the last syllable:

λελυκέναι – λελυκώς (gen. m./n. λελυκότος)
διδόναι – διδούς (f. διδοῦσα; gen. m./n. διδόντος)
λυθῆναι – λυθείς (f. λυθεῖσα; gen. m./n. λυθέντος)

(iv) Strong aorists accent on the last syllable in infinitive and participle active, e.g.

φυγεῖν, φυγών (contrast φεύγειν, φεύγων of the present)

(v) For contracted verbs, examine the *uncontracted* form and determine where the accent would come on that. If an accented syllable is involved in the contraction, the accent will be circumflex on the resulting contraction, if the rule under 4 (ii) does not apply. If 4 (ii) does apply, the accent will be acute. e.g.

ποιέ-ει – ποιεῖ
ἐποίε-ε – ἐποίει
ὁρα-οίην – ὁρῴην

O   A.4 Homeric dialect – the main features

Nouns

First declension	*Second declension*	*Third declension*
Types 1a b c (f.)	*Gen. s.*: ends in -οιο as well as -ου, e.g. πεδίοιο and πεδίου.	*Acc. s.*: ends in -ιν as well as -ιδα, e.g. γλαυκῶπιν and γλαυκώπιδα.
Nom. s: ends in η, even after ρ, ε, ι e.g. χώρη, not χώρα.	*Gen. + dat. dual:* ends in -οιϊν, so ἵπποιϊν, not ἵπποιν.	Endings in -ηα correspond to -εᾱ, e.g. βασιλῆα = βασιλέα.
Some nouns end in ᾰ.	*Dat. pl.*: ends in -οισι and -οις, e.g. φύλλοισι and φύλλοις.	*Gen. s.*: endings in -ηος and -ιος correspond to -εως, e.g. βασιλῆος = βασιλέως;
Gen. pl.: usually ends in -αων, -εων, e.g. νυμφάων, not νυμφῶν.		
Dat. pl.: nearly always ends		

First declension
Types 1a b c (f.)
in -ῃσι(ν), or -ῃs, e.g.
πύλῃσιν = πύλαις.

Type 1d (m.)
Nom. s.: may end in ᾱ, not
-ης, e.g. ἱππότᾱ, not
ἱππότης.
Gen. s.: ends in -ao, -εω,
not ου, e.g. Ἀτρείδαο, not
Ἀτρείδου.

Pronouns
ἐγώ, σύ 'I', 'you'
Gen. s.: ἐμεῖο, ἐμέο, ἐμεῦ,
μευ, ἐμέθεν. So with
σύ – σεῖο, σέο, etc.

ἡμεῖς, ὑμεῖς 'we', 'you'
Acc.: ἡμέας, ἄμμε.
Gen.: ἡμείων, ἡμέων.
Dat.: ἄμμι(ν). So with
ὑμεῖς.

Second declension

ἕ 'him'
Gen.: εἷο, ἕο, εὗ, ἕθεν.
Dat.: ἑοῖ, οἷ.

σφε 'them'
Acc.: σφε, σφέας, σφας.
Gen.: σφείων, σφέων.
Dat.: σφι, σφισί.

Third declension

πόλιος = πόλεως.
Acc. pl.: endings in -ηας
correspond to -εας, e.g.
βασιλῆας = βασιλέας.
Gen. pl.: endings in -ηων
correspond to -εων, e.g.
βασιλήων = βασιλέων.
Dat. pl.: ends in -εσσι and
-σι, e.g. πόδεσσι, ἔπεσσι.

τίς 'who, what, which'
Is declined:
τίς
τίνα
τέο|τεῦ
τέῳ
Gen. pl.: τέων.

ὁ ἡ τό 'he, she, it' or 'the'
Nom. pl.: οἱ, αἱ, or τοί, ταί.
Dat. pl.: τοῖς, τοῖσι, τῆς,
τῇσι as well as ταῖς.

Note
(i) *Observe the Homeric alternation between* -σ- *and* -σσ- *(which can be metrically useful), e.g.* τόσος→τόσσος, μέσος→μέσσος, ποσί→ποσσί.
(ii) *The termination* -φι *(*-οφι*) may be used for the dat. s. and pl. of nouns and adjectives (and sometimes the gen. s. and pl. too), e.g.*
βιῆφι *'by force',* δακρύοφιν *'with tears',* ὀρέσφιν *'in the mountains'.*

Verbs
Person endings
-ν for -σαν, e.g. ἔσταν for ἔστησαν in 3rd pl. act.
3rd pl. mid./pass. often ends in -αται, -ατο, e.g. ἥατο = ἥντο.

Tenses
Future: generally uncontracted, e.g. ἐρέω (ἐρῶ), τελέω (τελέσω).
Present/Imperfect: sometimes reinforced by a form in -σκ- implying repetition, e.g.
φύγεσκον *'they kept on running away'.*

Aorist/Imperfect: in both the augment may be missing e.g. βάλον *(ἔβαλον)*: observe the necessary adjustments in compounds, e.g. ἔμβαλε *(ἐνέβαλε)*.

Moods

Subjunctive:
(i) appears with a short vowel, e.g. ἴομεν=ἴωμεν
(ii) has 2nd s. mid. in -ηαι, -εαι
(iii) has 3rd s. act. in -σι, e.g. φορέῃσι=φορῇ
(iv) is used in place of the future; and can be used in general remarks.

Infinitive

It appears with the endings -μεν, -μεναι, -ναι for -ειν, -ναι e.g. δόμεναι=δοῦναι; ἴμεν=ἰέναι; ἔμεν, ἔμμεν, ἔμμεναι=εἶναι; ἀκουέμεν(αι)= ἀκούειν.

Contracted verbs

In contracted verbs, where Attic has -ω-, we can find -οω-, -ωω- in place of -αο-, e.g. ὁρόωντες for Attic ὁρῶντες.
Similarly, where Attic would contract αε to α, and αει to ᾳ, Homeric Greek can show αα, αᾳ.

Adverbs

Note the way the following suffixes are used to create adverbs:
-δε 'whither', as in πόλεμόνδε 'to the war' N.b. -δε *here is attached to the acc.; in all the rest, the suffix is attached to stem.*
-δον 'how', as in κλαγγηδόν 'with cries'
-θεν 'whence', as in ὑψόθεν 'from above'
-θι 'where', as in ὑψόθι 'on high'
Cf. Language Survey (13) (iii).

Particles

Note particularly the use and force of the following particles:
ἄρα *(ἄρ, ῥά)*   'so, next' (showing transition)
δή   'indeed' (emphasising)
ἦ   'surely' (emphasising)
περ   'just, even' (emphasising)
τε   'and' (or to show a general remark)
τοι   'I tell you' (assertion) (But it may also=σοι,
            'to you, for you'.)
Cf. Reference Grammar G.

B. Nouns

Here is a summary chart of the noun-types which have been met:

	s. nom.	acc.	gen.	dat.	pl. nom.	acc.	gen.	dat.
1a	βο-ή, ἡ	βο-ήν	βο-ῆς	βο-ῇ	βο-αί	βο-ᾱ̄ς	βο-ῶν	βο-αῖς
1b	ἀπορί-ᾱ, ἡ	ἀπορί-ᾱν	ἀπορί-ᾱ̄ς	ἀπορί-ᾳ	ἀπορί-αι	ἀπορίᾱς	ἀπορι-ῶν	ἀπορί-αις
1c	τόλμ-α, ἡ	τόλμ-αν	τόλμ-ης	τόλμ-ῃ	τόλμ-αι	τόλμ-ᾱς	τολμ-ῶν	τόλμ-αις
1d	ναύτ-ης, ὁ	ναύτ-ην	ναύτ-ου }	ναύτ-ῃ }	ναῦτ-αι	ναύτ-ᾱς	ναυτ-ῶν	ναύτ-αις
	νεανί-ᾱς, ὁ	νεανί-ᾱν }		νεανί-ᾳ }				
2a	ἄνθρωπ-ος, ὁ	ἄνθρωπ-ον	ἀνθρώπ-ου	ἀνθρώπ-ῳ	ἄνθρωπ-οι	ἀνθρώπ-ους	ἀνθρώπ-ων	ἀνθρώπ-οις
2b	ἔργ-ον, τό	ἔργ-ον	ἔργ-ου	ἔργ-ῳ	ἔργ-α	ἔργ-α	ἔργ-ων	ἔργ-οις
3a	λιμήν, ὁ	λιμέν-α	λιμέν-ος	λιμέν-ι	λιμέν-ες	λιμέν-ας	λιμέν-ων	λιμέ-σι(ν)
3b	πρᾶγμα, τό	πρᾶγμα	πράγματ-ος	πράγματ-ι	πράγματ-α	πράγματ-α	πραγμάτ-ων	πράγμα-σι(
3c	πλῆθ-ος, τό	πλῆθ-ος	πλήθ-ους	πλήθ-ει	πλήθ-η	πλήθ-η	πληθ-ῶν	πλήθ-εσι(ν
3d	τριήρ-ης, ἡ	τριήρ-η	τριήρ-ους	τριήρ-ει	τριήρ-εις	τριήρ-εις	τριήρ-ων	τριήρ-εσι(ν
3e	πόλ-ις, ἡ	πόλ-ιν }	πόλ-εως	πόλ-ει	πόλ-εις	πόλ-εις	πόλ-εων	πόλ-εσι(ν)
	πρέσβ-υς, ὁ	πρέσβ-υν }						
3f	ἄστ-υ, τό	ἄστ-υ	ἄστ-εως	ἄστ-ει	ἄστ-η	ἄστ-η	ἄστ-εων	ἄστ-εσι(ν)
3g	βασιλ-εύς, ὁ	βασιλ-έᾱ	βασιλ-έως	βασιλ-εῖ	βασιλ-εῖς } βασιλ-ῆς }	βασιλ-έᾱς	βασιλ-έων	βασιλ-εῦσι
3h	ὀφρῦ-ς, ἡ	ὀφρῦ-ν	ὀφρύ-ος	ὀφρύ-ι	ὀφρύ-ες	ὀφρῦ-ς	ὀφρύ-ων	ὀφρύ-σι(ν)

Note

A number of nouns are contracted, e.g. πλοῦς 'voyage', contracted from πλόος, νοῦς 'mind' contracted from νόος, ὀστοῦν 'bone' contracted from ὀστέον. For contract rules see Reference Grammar E.2 note (ii).

Irregular nouns

	s. nom.	acc.	gen.	dat.	pl. nom.	acc.	gen.	dat.
	ναῦς, ἡ	ναῦν	νεώς	νηί	νῆες	ναῦς	νεῶν	ναυσί(ν)
	γραῦς, ἡ	γραῦν	γρᾱός	γρᾱί	γρᾶες	γραῦς	γραῶν	γραυσί(ν)
	Ζεύς, ὁ	Δία	Διός	Διί				

Personal pronouns

ἐγώ (ἐ)μέ (ἐ)μοῦ (ἐ)μοί ἡμεῖς ἡμᾶς ἡμῶν ἡμῖν

σύ σέ σοῦ σοί ὑμεῖς ὑμᾶς ὑμῶν ὑμῖν

Vocatives

The form of the vocative is the same as the nominative in most instances in the singular and all instances in the plural. Forms of the vocative different from the nominative are:

1d ναῦτα, νεανίᾱ
2a ἄνθρωπε
3d Σώκρατες, Περίκλεις
3e πόλι, πρέσβυ
3g βασιλεῦ
3h ὀφρύ

Note

Observe the shortening in the following vocatives:
λέων (λεοντ-)→λέον
ἐλπίς (ἐλπιδ-)→ἐλπί
σωτήρ (σωτηρ-)→σῶτερ
δαίμων (δαιμον-)→δαῖμον
ἀνήρ (ἀνδρ-)→ἄνερ

On morphology, see *Language Survey (10); on noun-formation see Language Survey (13) (i); on use of cases, see Index and Language Survey (11).*

C.1 Adjectives/pronouns

Here is a summary of all the adjective/pronoun types you have met, including participles:

| | s. | | | | pl. | | | |
	nom.	acc.	gen.	dat.	nom.	acc.	gen.	dat.
m.	καλ-ός	καλ-όν	καλ-οῦ	καλ-ῷ	καλ-οί	καλ-ούς	καλ-ῶν	καλ-οῖς
f.	καλ-ή	καλ-ήν	καλ-ῆς	καλ-ῇ	καλ-αί	καλ-άς	καλ-ῶν	καλ-αῖς
n.	καλ-όν	καλ-όν	καλ-οῦ	καλ-ῷ	καλ-ά	καλ-ά	καλ-ῶν	καλ-οῖς
m.	ἡμέτερ-ος	ἡμέτερ-ον	ἡμετέρ-ου	ἡμετέρ-ῳ	ἡμέτερ-οι	ἡμέτερ-ους	ἡμετέρ-ων	ἡμέτερ-οις
f.	ἡμετέρᾱ	ἡμετέρ-ᾱν	ἡμετέρ-ᾱς	ἡμετέρ-ᾳ	ἡμέτερ-αι	ἡμετέρ-ᾱς	ἡμετέρ-ων	ἡμέτερ-αις
n.	ἡμέτερ-ον	ἡμέτερ-ον	ἡμετέρ-ου	ἡμετέρ-ῳ	ἡμέτερ-α	ἡμέτερ-α	ἡμετέρ-ων	ἡμέτερ-οις

	s.				pl.			
	nom.	*acc.*	*gen.*	*dat.*	*nom.*	*acc.*	*gen.*	*dat.*
m.	οὗτ-ος	τοῦτ-ον	τούτ-ου	τούτ-ῳ	οὗτ-οι	τούτ-ους	τούτ-ων	τούτ-οις
f.	αὕτ-η	ταύτ-ην	ταύτ-ης	ταύτ-ῃ	αὗτ-αι	ταύτ-ᾱς	τούτ-ων	ταύτ-αις
n.	τοῦτ-ο	τοῦτ-ο	τούτ-ου	τούτ-ῳ	ταῦτ-α	ταῦτ-α	τούτ-ων	τούτ-οις
m.	ἐκεῖν-ος	ἐκεῖν-ον	ἐκείν-ου	ἐκείν-ῳ	ἐκεῖν-οι	ἐκείν-ους	ἐκείν-ων	ἐκείν-οις
f.	ἐκείν-η	ἐκείν-ην	ἐκείν-ης	ἐκείν-ῃ	ἐκεῖν-αι	ἐκείν-ᾱς	ἐκείν-ων	ἐκείν-αις
n.	ἐκεῖν-ο	ἐκεῖν-ο	ἐκείν-ου	ἐκείν-ῳ	ἐκεῖν-α	ἐκεῖν-α	ἐκείν-ων	ἐκείν-οις
m.	αὐτ-ός	αὐτ-όν	αὐτ-οῦ	αὐτῷ	αὐτ-οί	αὐτ-ούς	αὐτ-ῶν	αὐτ-οῖς
f.	αὐτ-ή	αὐτ-ήν	αὐτ-ῆς	αὐτ-ῇ	αὐτ-αί	αὐτ-ᾱς	αὐτ-ῶν	αὐτ-αῖς
n.	αὐτ-ό	αὐτ-ό	αὐτ-οῦ	αὐτ-ῷ	αὐτ-ά	αὐτ-ά	αὐτ-ῶν	αὐτ-οῖς
m.	πολ-ύς	πολ-ύν	πολλ-οῦ	πολλ-ῷ	πολλ-οί	πολλ-ούς	πολλ-ῶν	πολλ-οῖς
f.	πολλ-ή	πολλ-ήν	πολλ-ῆς	πολλ-ῇ	πολλ-αί	πολλ-ᾱς	πολλ-ῶν	πολλ-αῖς
n.	πολ-ύ	πολ-ύ	πολλ-οῦ	πολλ-ῷ	πολλ-ά	πολλ-ά	πολλ-ῶν	πολλ-οῖς
m./f.	εὔφρων	εὔφρον-α	εὔφρον-ος	εὔφρον-ι	εὔφρον-ες	εὔφρον-ας	εὐφρόν-ων	εὔφρο-σι(ν)
n.	εὔφρον	εὔφρον	εὔφρον-ος	εὔφρον-ι	εὔφρον-α	εὔφρον-α	εὐφρόν-ων	εὔφρο-σι(ν)
m./f.	τις	τιν-α	τιν-ος	τιν-ι	τιν-ες	τιν-ας	τιν-ων	τι-σι(ν)
n.	τι	τι	τιν-ος	τιν-ι	τιν-α	τιν-α	τιν-ων	τι-σι(ν)
m.	οὐδ-είς	οὐδ-έν-α	οὐδ-εν-ός	οὐδ-εν-ί				
f.	οὐδε-μί-α	οὐδε-μί-αν	οὐδε-μί-ᾱς	οὐδε-μί-ᾳ				
n.	οὐδ-έν	οὐδ-έν	οὐδ-εν-ός	οὐδ-εν-ί				
m.	ὤν	ὄντ-α	ὄντ-ος	ὄντ-ι	ὄντ-ες	ὄντ-ας	ὄντ-ων	οὐ-σι(ν)
f.	οὖσ-α	οὖσ-αν	οὔσ-ης	οὔσ-ῃ	οὖσ-αι	οὔσ-ᾱς	οὐσ-ῶν	οὔσ-αις
n.	ὄν	ὄν	ὄντ-ος	ὄντ-ι	ὄντ-α	ὄντ-α	ὄντ-ων	οὐ-σι(ν)
m.	παύσ-ᾱς	-αντ-α	-αντ-ος	-αντ-ι	-αντ-ες	-αντ-ας	-άντ-ων	-ᾱ-σι(ν)
f.	παύσ-ᾱσ-α	-ᾱσ-αν	-άσ-ης	-άσ-ῃ	-ᾱσ-αι	-άσ-ᾱς	-ασ-ῶν	-άσ-αις
n.	παῦσ-αν	-αν	-αντ-ος	-αντ-ι	-αντ-α	-αντ-α	-άντ-ων	-ᾱ-σι(ν)
m.	παυσθ-είς	-έντ-α	-έντ-ος	-έντ-ι	-έντ-ες	-έντ-ας	-έντ-ων	-εῖ-σι(ν)
f.	παυσθ-εῖσ-α	-εῖσ-αν	-είσ-ης	-είσ-ῃ	-εῖσ-αι	-είσ-ᾱς	-εισ-ῶν	-είσ-αις
n.	παυσθ-έν	-έν	-έντ-ος	-έντ-ι	-έντ-α	-έντ-α	-έντ-ων	-εῖ-σι(ν)
m.	πεπαυκ-ώς	-ότ-α	-ότ-ος	ότ-ι	-ότ-ες	-ότ-ας	-ότ-ων	-ό-σι(ν)
f.	πεπαυκ-υῖ-α	-υῖ-αν	-υί-ᾱς	-υί-ᾳ	-υῖ-αι	-υί-ᾱς	-υι-ῶν	-υί-αις
n.	πεπαυκ-ός	-ός	-ότ-ος	-ότ-ι	-ότ-α	-ότ-α	-ότ-ων	-ό-σι(ν)
m./f.	ἀμελ-ής	ἀμελ-ῆ	ἀμελ-οῦς	ἀμελ-εῖ	ἀμελ-εῖς	ἀμελ-εῖς	ἀμελ-ῶν	ἀμελ-έσι(ν)
n.	ἀμελ-ές	ἀμελ-ές	ἀμελ-οῦς	ἀμελ-εῖ	ἀμελῆ	ἀμελ-ῆ	ἀμελ-ῶν	ἀμελ-έσι(ν)
m.	γλυκ-ύς	γλυκ-ύν	γλυκ-έος	γλυκ-εῖ	γλυκ-εῖς	γλυκ-εῖς	γλυκ-έων	γλυκ-έσι(ν)
f.	γλυκ-εῖ-α	γλυκ-εῖ-αν	γλυκ-εί-ᾱς	γλυκ-εί-ᾳ	γλυκ-εῖ-αι	γλυκ-εί-ᾱς	γλυκ-ει-ῶν	γλυκ-εί-αις
n.	γλυκ-ύ	γλυκ-ύ	γλυκ-έος	γλυκ-εῖ	γλυκ-έα	γλυκ-έα	γλυκ-έων	γλυκ-έσι(ν)

Cf. Language Survey (13) (iii).

Note

A number of adjectives are contracted e.g. χρυσοῦς χρυσῆ χρυσοῦν 'of gold' are the contracted forms of χρυσέος χρυσέα χρυσέον. Cf. χαλκοῦς 'of bronze', ἀργυροῦς 'of silver'.

Among o-contract adjectives is διπλοῦς διπλῆ διπλοῦν 'double', contracted from διπλόος διπλόη διπλόον.

For contract rules see Reference Grammar E.2 note (ii)

O   C.2 Comparison of adjectives

Most comparatives end in -τερ-ος -α -ον (some irregulars end in (ι)ων).
Most superlatives end in -τατ-ος -η -ον (some irregulars end in (ι)στος).

Regular comparative forms

δεινός	'clever'	δεινότερος	δεινότατος
σοφός	'wise'	σοφώτερος	σοφώτατος
γλυκύς	'sweet'	γλυκύτερος	γλυκύτατος
ἀμελής	'careless'	ἀμελέστερος	ἀμελέστατος
εὔφρων	'pleasant'	εὐφρονέστερος	εὐφρονέστατος

Irregular comparative forms

ἀγαθός	'good'	ἀμείνων	ἄριστος
		βελτῑων	βέλτιστος
αἰσχρός	'disgraceful'	αἰσχῑων	αἴσχιστος
ἡδύς	'sweet'	ἡδῑων	ἥδιστος
κακός	'bad'	κακῑων	κάκιστος
		χείρων	χείριστος
καλός	'fine'	καλλῑων	κάλλιστος
μέγας	'great'	μείζων	μέγιστος
ὀλίγος	'little, few'	ἐλάττων	ἐλάχιστος
πολύς	'much'	πλείων	πλεῖστος
ῥᾴδιος	'easy'	ῥᾴων	ῥᾷστος
ταχύς	'swift'	θάττων	τάχιστος

Observe that comparatives basically mean 'more –, –er', but can also mean 'quite –, fairly –, rather –'.

Superlatives basically mean '–est, most –, very –, extremely –'.

Construction with comparatives

When two things are being compared (using English 'than'), Greek either:

(i) uses ἤ = 'than', and puts the two things being compared in the same case, e.g. Σωκράτης σοφώτερός ἐστιν ἢ Κρίτων 'Socrates is wiser than Kriton'; or (ii) puts the thing compared into the genitive (no ἤ), e.g. Σωκράτης σοφώτερός ἐστι Κρίτωνος 'Socrates is wiser than Kriton'.

Notes
(i) Comparatives in -ων decline like εὔφρων.
(ii) Comparatives declining like εὔφρων can drop the final ν and contract in the nominative and accusative, e.g.

βελτῑο(ν)α   → βελτῑω

βελτῑο(ν)-ες ⎫
            ⎬ → βελτῑους
         -ας ⎭

○   C.3 Noun/adjective endings – a summary

The following chart summarises the endings of the noun and adjective types you have met:

		s.				pl.			
		nom.	*acc.*	*gen.*	*dat.*	*nom.*	*acc.*	*gen.*	*dat.*
Type 1 nouns	*f.*	-η|-α		-ης|-ας					
(and adj. like	*(a, b, c)*								
καλή, ἡμετέρα,			-ην|-αν		-η|-ᾳ	-αι	-ᾱς	-ῶν	-αις
οὖσα)*									
	m.	-ης|-ας		-ου					
	(d)								
Type 2 nouns	*m.*	-ος				-οι	-ους		
(and adj. like	*(a)*		-ον	-ου	-ῳ			-ων	-οις
καλός, ἡμέτερος)*					—				
(and adj. like	*n.*	-ον				-α	-α		
καλόν, ἡμέτερον)*	*(b)*								
Type 3 nouns m./f.	*(a)*		-α	-ος		-ες	-ας		
(and adj. like	*(d)*	-ης	-η	-ους	-(ε)ι	-εις	-εις	-(ε)ων	-(α|ε)ο
κακοδαίμων,*	*(e)*	-ις|-υς	-ιν|-υν	-εως|-εος					
ἀληθής, γλυκύς)*	*(g)*	-ευς	-εα	(adj.)		-ης	-εας		-ευσι
	(h)	-υς	-υν	-υος	-υι	-υς	-υς	-υων	-υσι

		s.				pl.			
		nom.	acc.	gen.	dat.	nom.	acc.	gen.	dat.
Type 3 nouns n. and adj. like κακόδαιμον, ἀληθές, γλυκύ)	(b)	-α|-ον|-αν (adj.)	-α|-ον|-αν (adj.)	-ος		-α	-α		
	(c)	-ος|-ες (adj.)	-ος|-ες (adj.)	-ους	-(ε)ι	-η	-η	-(ε)ων	-(α|ε)σι
	(f)	-υ	-υ	-εως|-εος (adj.)		-εα	-εα		

Cf. Language Survey (10).

O   D. Adverbs

Most adverbs are formed by the addition of -ως to the stem of the adjective, e.g.

σοφός	'wise'	σοφ-ῶς	'wisely'
βαθ-ύς (βαθε-)	'deep'	βαθέ-ως	'deeply'
σώφρων (σωφρον-)	'sensible'	σωφρόν-ως	'sensibly'

Comparative and superlative adverbs are formed by using the neuter singular comparative of the adjective (for comparative adverbs) and the neuter plural superlative of the adjective (for superlative adverbs), e.g.

σοφῶς	'wisely'	σοφώτερον	'more wisely'	σοφώτατα	'most wisely'
κακῶς	'badly'	κάκιον	'worse, more evilly'	κάκιστα	'very evilly'
ταχέως	'quickly'	θᾶττον	'more quickly'	τάχιστα	'very quickly'

Note:

εὖ	'well'	ἄμεινον	'more well, better'	ἄριστα	'best'
μάλα	'much'	μᾶλλον	'rather, more'	μάλιστα	'very much'

Cf. Language Survey (13) (iii).

O   E.1 The verb – synopsis

Here is a complete picture of παύω|παύομαι in all forms:

resent active (stem παυ-) 'I stop'

	Indicative	Infinitive	Participle	Imperative	Optative	Subjunctive
s.	παύ-ω	παύ-ειν	παύ-ων			
d s.	παύ-εις		παύ-ουσ-α		παύ-οιμι	παύ-ω
s.	παύ-ει		παύ-ον	παῦ-ε	παύ-οις	παύ-ῃς
pl.	παύ-ομεν		(παυοντ-)	παυ-έτω	παύ-οι	παύ-ῃ
d pl.	παύ-ετε				παύ-οιμεν	παύ-ωμεν
pl.	παύ-ουσι(ν)			παύ-ετε	παύ-οιτε	παύ-ητε
			παυ-όντων	παύ-οιεν	παύ-ωσι(ν)	

Present middle and passive (stem παυ-) 'I stop (myself), am stopped'

	Indicative	Infinitive	Participle	Imperative	Optative	Subjunctive
1st s.	παύ-ομαι	παύ-εσθαι	παυ-όμεν-ος		παυ-οίμην	παύ-ωμαι
2nd s.	παύ-ει(ῃ)		-η	παύ-ου	παύ-οιο	παύ-ῃ
3rd s.	παύ-εται		-ον	παυ-έσθω	παύ-οιτο	παύ-ηται
1st pl.	παυ-όμεθα				παυ-οίμεθα	παυ-ώμεθα
2nd pl.	παύ-εσθε			παύ-εσθε	παύ-οισθε	παύ-ησθε
3rd pl.	παύ-ονται			παυ-έσθων	παύ-οιντο	παύ-ωνται

Imperfect active (stem παυ-) 'I was stopping'

1st s.	ἔ-παυ-ον
2nd s.	ἔ-παυ-ες
3rd s.	ἔ-παυ-ε(ν)
1st pl.	ἐ-παύ-ομεν
2nd pl.	ἐ-παύ-ετε
3rd pl.	ἔ-παυ-ον

Imperfect middle and passive (stem παυ-) 'I was stopping (myself), was stopped'

1st s.	ἐ-παυ-όμην
2nd s.	ἐ-παύ-ου
3rd s.	ἐ-παύ-ετο
1st pl.	ἐ-παυ-όμεθα
2nd pl.	ἐ-παύ-εσθε
3rd pl.	ἐ-παύ-οντο

Aorist active (stem παυσ-(α)), 'I stopped'

	Indicative	Infinitive	Participle	Imperative	Optative	Subjunctive
1st s.	ἔ-παυσ-α	παῦσ-αι	παύσ-ᾱς		παύσ-αιμι	παύσ-ω
2nd s.	ἔ-παυσ-ας		παύσ-ᾱσ-α	παῦσ-ον	παύσ-ειας (-αις)	παύσ-ῃς
3rd s.	ἔ-παυσ-ε(ν)		παῦσ-αν	παυσ-άτω	παύσ-ειε(ν) (-αι)	παύσ-ῃ
1st pl.	ἐ-παύσ-αμεν		(παυσαντ-)		παύσ-αιμεν	παύσ-ωμεν
2nd pl.	ἐ-παύσ-ατε			παύσ-ατε	παύσ-αιτε	παύσ-ητε
3rd pl.	ἔ-παυσ-αν			παυσ-άντων	παύσ-ειαν (-αιεν)	παύσ-ωσι(ν)

Aorist middle (stem παυσ-(α)) 'I stopped myself'

	Indicative	Infinitive	Participle	Imperative	Optative	Subjunctive
1st s.	ἐ-παυσ-άμην	παύσ-ασθαι	παυσ-άμεν-ος		παυσ-αίμην	παύσ-ωμαι
2nd s.	ἐ-παύσ-ω		-η	παῦσ-αι	παύσ-αιο	παύσ-ῃ
3rd s.	ἐ-παύσ-ατο		-ον	παυσ-άσθω	παύσ-αιτο	παύσ-ηται
1st pl.	ἐ-παυσ-άμεθα				παυσ-αίμεθα	παυσ-ώμεθα
2nd pl.	ἐ-παύσ-ασθε			παύσ-ασθε	παύσ-αισθε	παύσ-ησθε
3rd pl.	ἐ-παύσ-αντο			παυσ-άσθων	παύσ-αιντο	παύσ-ωνται

Aorist passive (stem παυσθ-) 'I was stopped'

	Indicative	Infinitive	Participle	Imperative	Optative	Subjunctive
s.	ἐ-παύσθ-ην	παυσθ-ῆναι	παυσθ-είς		παυσθ-είην	παυσθ-ῶ
d s.	ἐπαύσθ-ης		παυσθ-εῖσ-α	παύσθ-ητι	παυσθ-είης	παυσθ-ῇς
d s.	ἐ-παύσθ-η		παυσθ-έν	παυσθ-ήτω	παυσθ-είη	παυσθ-ῇ
pl.	ἐ-παύσθ-ημεν		(παυσθεντ-)		παυσθ-εῖμεν	παυσθ-ῶμεν
d pl.	ἐ-παύσθ-ητε			παύσθ-ητε	παυσθ-εῖτε	παυσθ-ῆτε
d pl.	ἐ-παύσθ-ησαν			παυσθ-έντων	παυσθ-εῖεν	παυσθ-ῶσι(ν)

Future active (stem παυσ-) 'I shall stop'

s.	παύσ-ω	παύσ-ειν	παύσ-ων		παύσ-οιμι
d s.	παύσ-εις				

etc., exactly like the present active, on the stem παυσ-

Future middle (stem παυσ-) 'I shall stop (myself)'

s.	παύσ-ομαι	παύσ-εσθαι	παυσ-όμεν-ος		παυσ-οίμην
d s.	παύσ-ει (or -ῃ)				

etc., exactly like the present middle, on the stem παυσ-

Future passive (stem παυσθη(σ)- based on aorist passive) 'I shall be stopped'

s.	παυσθήσ-ομαι	παυσθήσ-εσθαι	παυσθησ-όμεν-ος		παυσθησ-οίμην
d s.	παυσθήσ-ῃ				

etc., exactly like the present middle/passive on the stem παυσθησ-

Perfect active (stem πεπαυκ-) 'I have stopped'

st s.	πέπαυκ-α	πεπαυκ-έναι	πεπαυκ-ώς		πεπαύκ-οιμι	πεπαύκ-ω
nd s.	πέπαυκ-ας		πεπαυκ-υῖ-α	πέπαυκ-ε*	πεπαύκ-οις	πεπαύκ-ῃς
rd s.	πέπαυκ-ε(ν)		πεπαυκ-ός	πεπαυκ-έτω	πεπαύκ-οι	πεπαύκ-ῃ
st pl.	πεπαύκ-αμεν		(πεπαυκοτ-)		πεπαύκ-οιμεν	πεπαύκ-ωμεν
nd pl.	πεπαύκ-ατε			πεπαύκ-ετε	πεπαύκ-οιτε	πεπαύκ-ητε
rd pl.	πεπαύκ-ᾱσι(ν)			πεπαυκ-έτωσαν	πεπαύκ-οιεν	πεπαύκ-ωσι(ν)

* Only in verbs where the perfect has a present meaning (very rare).

Perfect middle/passive (stem πεπαυ-) 'I have stopped myself), have been stopped'

t s.	πέπαυ-μαι	πεπαῦ-σθαι	πεπαυ-μέν-ος		πεπαυμένος εἴην	πεπαυμένος ὦ
d s.	πέπαυ-σαι		-η	πέπαυ-σο	εἴης	ᾖς
rd s.	πέπαυ-ται		-ον	πεπαύ-σθω	εἴη	ᾖ
st pl.	πεπαύ-μεθα				πεπαυμένοι εἶμεν	πεπαυμένοι ὦμεν
nd pl.	πέπαυ-σθε			πέπαυ-σθε	εἶτε	ἦτε
rd pl.	πέπαυ-νται			πεπαύ-σθων	εἶεν	ὦσι(ν)
	(πεπαυμένοι εἰσί)					

Future perfect middle/passive (stem πεπαυ-) 'I shall have stopped (myself), been stopped'

	Indicative	Infinitive	Participle	Imperative	Optative	Subjunctive
1st s.	πεπαύ-σομαι	πεπαύ-σεσθαι	πεπαυ-σόμεν-ος		πεπαυ-σοίμην	
2nd s.	πεπαύ-σει (or -ῃ)		-η			
3rd s.	πεπαύ-σεται		-ον			
1st pl.	πεπαυ-σόμεθα					
2nd pl.	πεπαύ-σεσθε					
3rd pl.	πεπαύ-σονται					

Pluperfect active (stem ἐπεπαυκ-) 'I had stopped'

1st s.	ἐ-πεπαύκ-η (-ειν)
2nd s.	ἐ-πεπαύκ-ης (-εις)
3rd s.	ἐ-πεπαύκ-ει(ν)
1st pl.	ἐ-πεπαύκ-εμεν
2nd pl.	ἐ-πεπαύκ-ετε
3rd pl.	ἐ-πεπαύκ-εσαν

Pluperfect middle/passive (stem ἐπεπαυ-) 'I had stopped (myself), had been stopped'

1st s.	ἐ-πεπαύ-μην
2nd s.	ἐ-πέπαυ-σο
3rd s.	ἐ-πέπαυ-το
1st pl.	ἐ-πεπαύ-μεθα
2nd pl.	ἐ-πέπαυ-σθε
3rd pl.	ἐ-πέπαυ-ντο

⭕ E.2 Verb summary chart (uncontracted, weak aorist)

Indicative forms (temporal)

In general, these forms point to the *time* at which the action happened.

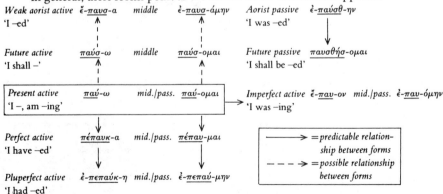

Non-indicative forms (aspectual)

In general, these forms point to the *aspect* of the action (see Reference Grammar A1 (i)).

The endings are added to the appropriate *unaugmented* stem of the verb.

Infinitive:

Present, Future	active	-ειν
	middle/passive	-εσθαι
Aorist	active	-αι
	middle	-ασθαι
	passive	-ῆναι
Perfect	active	-έναι
	middle/passive	-σθαι

Participle:

Present, Future	active	-ων -ουσα -ον (-οντ-)
	middle/passive	-όμεν-ος -η -ον
Aorist	active	-ᾱς -ᾱσα -αν (-αντ-)
	middle	-άμεν-ος -η -ον
	passive	-είς -εῖσα -έν (-εντ-)
Perfect	active	-ώς -υῖα -ός (-οτ-)
	middle/passive	-μέν-ος -η -ον

Imperative:

Present	active	-ε -έτω -ετε -όντων
	middle/passive	-ου -έσθω -εσθε -έσθων
Aorist	active	-ον -άτω -ατε -άντων
	middle	-αι -άσθω- -ασθε -άσθων
	passive	-ητι -ήτω -ητε -έντων

Optative:

Present, Future, Perfect active	$\left\{\begin{array}{ccc} \text{-οιμι -οις -οι} \\ \text{or} \quad \text{or} \quad \text{or} \\ \text{-οίην -οίης -οίη} \end{array}\right\}$ -οιμεν -οιτε -οιεν
Present, Future, Perfect middle/passive	-οίμην -οιο -οιτο -οίμεθα -οισθε -οιντο
Aorist active	-αιμι -ειας (αις) -ειε(αι) -αιμεν -αιτε -ειαν (-αιεν)
middle	-αίμην -αιο -αιτο -αίμεθα -αισθε -αιντο
passive	-είην -είης -είη -εῖμεν -εῖτε -εῖεν

Subjunctive:

Active (and Aorist -ω -ῃς -ῃ -ωμεν -ητε -ωσι(ν)
passive)
Middle/passive -ωμαι -ῃ -ηται -ώμεθα -ησθε -ωνται

In general, see Language Survey (3).

Notes
(i) Strong aorists, in their active and middle forms, have
(a) INDICATIVE ENDINGS like the IMPERFECT
(b) ALL OTHER ENDINGS like the PRESENT, e.g.:

Aorist indicative active	*Aorist indicative middle*
ἔ-λαβ-ον	ἐ-λαβ-όμην
ἔ-λαβ-ες	ἐ-λάβ-ου
ἔ-λαβ-ε	ἐ-λάβ-ετο
ἐ-λάβ-ομεν	ἐ-λαβ-όμεθα
ἐ-λάβ-ετε	ἐ-λάβ-εσθε
ἔ-λαβ-ον	ἐ-λάβ-οντο

Infinitive:	λαβ-εῖν	λαβ-έσθαι
Participle:	λαβ-ών	λαβ-όμενος
Imperative:	λαβ-έ	λαβ-οῦ
Optative:	λάβ-οιμι	λαβ-οίμην
Subjunctive:	λάβ-ω	λάβ-ωμαι

N.b. *the aor. pass.* ἐλήφθ-ην *is regular in endings.*
(ii) Contracted verbs form different endings, owing to the contraction of their final vowel
with the ending. Rules of contraction are, in summary form:

→a	ε	ει	ι	η	ῃ	ο	ου	οι	ω	ῳ
a	α	α	ᾳ	αι	α	ᾳ	ω	ω	ῳ	ω	ῳ
ε	η	ει	ει	ει	η	ῃ	ου	ου	οι	ω	ῳ
ο	ω	ου	οι	οι	ω	οι	ου	ου	οι	ω	ῳ

The first vowel is in the LEFT-HAND column, the second in the TOP ROW: read
off the resultant contraction where they intersect, e.g. α+ι=αι.
(iii) It is only in indirect speech that participles, infinitives and optatives can take on a
specifically temporal function. In all other cases, their function is aspectual – i.e. they
give a particular view about the way in which the action is taking place, not when it is
taking place.
(iv) For -μι verbs, see Running Grammar: δίδωμι **131**; τίθημι **150**; ἵστημι **144**;
ἀφίημι **196**; *Reference Grammar E.3 and Language Survey (7).*

○   E.3 Irregular verbs

εἰμί 'I am'

Present

	Indicative	Infinitive	Participle	Imperative	Optative	Subjunctive
1st s.	εἰμί	εἶναι	ὤν		εἴην	ὦ
2nd s.	εἶ		οὖσ-α	ἴσθι	εἴης	ᾖς
3rd s.	ἐστί(ν)		ὄν	ἔστω	εἴη	ᾖ
1st pl.	ἐσμέν		(ὀντ-)		εἶμεν	ὦμεν
2nd pl.	ἐστέ			ἔστε	εἶτε	ἦτε
3rd pl.	εἰσί(ν)			ὄντων	εἶεν	ὦσι(ν)

Imperfect 'I was'

1st s.	ἦ(ν)
2nd s.	ἦσθα
3rd s.	ἦν
1st pl.	ἦμεν
2nd pl.	ἦτε
3rd pl.	ἦσαν

Future 'I shall be'

1st s.	ἔσομαι	ἐσ-εσθαι	ἐσ-όμεν-ος		ἐσ-οίμην
2nd s.	ἔσει		-η		ἔσ-οιο etc.
3rd s.	ἔσται		-ον		
1st pl.	ἐσόμεθα				
2nd pl.	ἔσεσθε				
3rd pl.	ἔσονται				

εἶμι 'I shall go'

	Future Indicative	Present Infinitive	Participle	Imperative	Optative	Subjunctive
1st s.	εἶμι	ἰέναι 'to go'	ἰών 'going'		ἴοιμι	ἴω
2nd s.	εἶ		ἰοῦσ-α	ἴθι	ἴοις	ἴῃς
3rd s.	εἶσι(ν)		ἰόν	ἴτω	ἴοι	ἴῃ
1st pl.	ἴμεν		(ἰοντ-)		ἴοιμεν	ἴωμεν
2nd pl.	ἴτε			ἴτε	ἴοιτε	ἴητε
3rd pl.	ἴᾱσι(ν)			ἰόντων	ἴοιεν	ἴωσι(ν)

Imperfect 'I went'

1st s. ᾖα (ᾔειν)
2nd s. ᾔεισθα (ᾔεις)
3rd s. ᾔει(ν)
1st pl. ᾖμεν
2nd pl. ᾖτε
3rd pl. ᾖσαν (ᾔεσαν)

οἶδα 'I know'

	Present Indicative	Infinitive	Participle	Imperative	Optative	Subjunctive
1st s.	οἶδα	εἰδέναι	εἰδ-ώς		εἰδείην	εἰδῶ
2nd s.	οἶσθα		-υῖ-α	ἴσθι	εἰδείης	εἰδῇς
3rd s.	οἶδε		-ός	ἴστω	εἰδείη etc.	εἰδῇ etc.
1st pl.	ἴσμεν		(εἰδοτ-)			
2nd pl.	ἴστε			ἴστε		
3rd pl.	ἴσᾱσι(ν)			ἴστων		

Past 'I knew'

1st s. ᾔδη (ᾔδειν)
2nd s. ᾔδησθα (ᾔδεις)
3rd s. ᾔδει(ν)
1st pl. ᾖσμεν
2nd pl. ᾖστε
3rd pl. ᾖσαν

Future 'I shall know'

1st s.   εἴσομαι *or* εἰδήσω
2nd s.   εἴσει *etc.* εἰδήσεις *etc.*

φημί 'I say'

Present

Indicative	Infinitive	Participle	Imperative	Optative	Subjunctive
1st s. φημί	φάναι	φάσκ-ων		φαίην	φῶ
2nd s. φής		-ουσ-α φαθί		φαίης	φῇς
3rd s. φησί(ν)		-ον φάτω		φαίη *etc.*	φῇ *etc.*
1st pl. φαμέν		(φασκοντ-)			
2nd pl. φατέ			φάτε		
3rd pl. φᾶσί(ν)			φάντων		

Note

The form φάς, φᾶσα, φάν (φαντ-) for participle is found: also φάμενος -η -ον often in Homer. Both have the same meaning as φάσκων.

Imperfect 'I said'

1st s.   ἔφην
2nd s.   ἔφησθα *or* ἔφης
3rd s.   ἔφη
1st pl. ἔφαμεν
2nd pl. ἔφατε
3rd pl. ἔφασαν

Note

In Homer middle forms often occur, e.g. ἔφατο for ἔφη.

Aorist 'I said'

1st s.   ἔφησ-α
2nd s.   ἔφησ-ας *etc. (regular)*

Future 'I shall say'

1st s.   φήσ-ω
2nd s.   φήσ-εις *etc. (regular)*

O   E.4 Important principal parts

The following list gives the main principal parts of verbs learnt in the first half of the Course which may be said to be difficult. A few other verbs are also included for reference, and should be learnt as well.

Verb	Main stem (no aug.)	Future	Aorist	Perfect	Aorist passive
ἀγγέλλ-ω 'announce'	ἀγγειλ-	ἀγγελέ-ω	ἤγγειλ-α	ἤγγελκ-α	ἠγγέλθ-ην
ἄγ-ω 'lead'	ἀγαγ-	ἄξ-ω	ἤγαγ-ον	ἦχ-α	ἤχθ-ην
ᾄδω (ἀείδ-ω) 'sing'	ᾀσ-/ἀεισ-	ᾄσ-ομαι	ᾖσ-α		ᾔσθ-ην
αἰνέ-ω 'praise'	αἰνεσ-	αἰνέσ-ω	ᾔνεσ-α	ᾔνεκ-α	ᾐνέθ-ην
αἱρέ-ω 'take' (mid. 'choose')	ἑλ-	αἱρήσ-ω	εἷλ-ον	ᾕρηκ-α	ᾑρέθ-ην
αἴρ-ω (ἀείρ-ω) 'lift, remove'	ἀρ-/ἀειρ-	ἀρέ-ω	ἦρ-α	ἦρκ-α	ἤρθ-ην
αἰσθάν-ομαι 'perceive'	αἰσθ-	αἰσθήσ-ομαι	ᾐσθ-όμην	ᾔσθη-μαι	
αἰσχύν-ω 'disgrace' (pass. 'be ashamed')	αἰσχυν-(θ)-	αἰσχυνέ-ω αἰσχυνέ-ομαι (pass.)	ᾔσχυν-α		ᾐσχύνθ-ην
ἀκού-ω 'hear'	ἀκουσ-	ἀκούσ-ομαι	ἤκουσ-α	ἀκήκο-α	ἠκούσθ-ην
ἁλίσκ-ομαι 'be caught'	ἁλ-	ἁλώσ-ομαι	ἑάλω-ν	ἑάλωκ-α	
ἀλλάττ-ω 'change, exchange'	ἀλλαξ-	ἀλλάξ-ω	ἤλλαξ-α	ἤλλαχ-α	ἠλλάχθ-ην } ἠλλάγ-ην }
ἁμαρτάν-ω 'err, miss'	ἁμαρτ-	ἁμαρτήσ-ομαι	ἥμαρτ-ον	ἡμάρτηκ-α	ἡμαρτήθ-ην
ἀμύν-ω 'ward off' (mid. 'defend oneself')	ἀμυν-	ἀμυνέ-ω	ἤμυν-α		
ἀναλίσκ-ω 'spend'	ἀναλωσ-	ἀναλώσ-ω	ἀνάλωσ-α } ἀνήλωσ-α }	ἀνάλωκ-α } ἀνήλωκ-α }	ἀναλώθ-ην } ἀνηλώθ-ην }
ἀνέχ-ομαι 'put up with'	ἀνασχ-	ἀνέξ-ομαι	ἠνεσχ-όμην		
ἀνοίγνυ-μι 'open'	ἀνοιξ-	ἀνοίξ-ω	ἀνέῳξ-α	ἀνέῳγ-μαι (pass.)	ἀνεῴχθ-ην
ἅπτ-ω 'fasten, light' (mid. 'touch')	ἁψ-/ἁφθ-	ἅψ-ω	ἧψ-α	ἧμ-μαι (mid., pass.)	ἥφθ-ην
ἀρέσκ-ω 'please'	ἀρεσ-(θ)-	ἀρέσ-ω	ἤρεσ-α		ἠρέσθ-ην
ἁρπάζ-ω 'seize'	ἁρπασ-	ἁρπάσ-ω	ἥρπασ-α	ἥρπηκ-α	ἡρπάσθ-ην

Verb	Main stem (no aug.)	Future	Aorist	Perfect	Aorist passive
ἄρχ-ω 'rule: begin' (usu. mid.)	ἀρχ-|ἀρξ-	ἄρξ-ω	ἦρξ-α	ἦργ-μαι (mid.)	ἤρχθ-ην
ἀφικνέ-ομαι 'arrive'	ἀφικ-	ἀφίξ-ομαι	ἀφικ-όμην	ἀφῖγ-μαι	
βαίν-ω 'go'	βη-|βα-	βήσ-ομαι	ἔβη-ν	βέβηκ-α	
βάλλ-ω 'throw, pelt'	βαλ-|βληθ-	βαλέ-ω	ἔβαλ-ον	βέβληκ-α	ἐβλήθ-ην
βλάπτ-ω 'harm'	βλάψ-|βλαβ-	βλάψ-ω	ἔβλαψ-α	βέβλαφ-α	{ ἐβλάβ-ην / ἐβλάφθ-ην
βούλ-ομαι 'wish'	βουλ-|βουληθ-	βουλήσ-ομαι		βεβούλη-μαι	ἐβουλήθ-ην 'I wished'
γαμέ-ω 'marry'	γημ-	γαμέ-ω	ἔγημ-α	γεγάμηκ-α	
γελά-ω 'laugh'	γελασ-	γελάσ-ομαι	ἐγέλασ-α		ἐγελάσθ-ην
γίγν-ομαι 'become'	γεν-	γενήσ-ομαι	ἐγεν-όμην	γεγένη-μαι } γέγον-α	
γιγνώσκ-ω 'recognise'	γνο-|γνω-	γνώσ-ομαι	ἔγνω-ν	ἔγνωκ-α	ἐγνώσθ-ην
γράφ-ω 'write'	γραψ-	γράψ-ω	ἔγραψ-α	γέγραφ-α	ἐγράφ-ην
δάκν-ω 'bite'	δακ-|δηχθ-	δήξ-ομαι	ἔδακ-ον	δέδηγ-μαι (pass.)	ἐδήχθ-ην
δέδοικ-α 'fear'	δεισ-|δεδοικ-|δειδ-	δείσ-ομαι	ἔδεισ-α		
δείκνυ-μι 'show'	δειξ-	δείξ-ω	ἔδειξ-α	δέδειχ-α	ἐδείχθ-ην
δέχ-ομαι 'receive'	δεξ-|δεγ-	δέξ-ομαι	ἐδεξ-άμην	δέδεγ-μαι	ἐδέχθ-ην
δέ-ω 'want, need' (mid. 'ask'; δεῖ 'it is necessary')	δεησ-	δεήσ-ω	ἐδέησ-α	δεδέηκ-α	ἐδεήθ-ην (mid.)
διδάσκ-ω 'teach'	διδαξ-	διδάξ-ω	ἐδίδαξ-α	δεδίδαχ-α	ἐδιδάχθ-ην
δίδω-μι 'give'	διδο-|δο-	δώσ-ω	ἔδω-κα ἐδό-μην (mid.)	δέδωκ-α	ἐδόθ-ην
δρά-ω 'do, act'	δρασ-	δράσ-ω	ἔδρασ-α	δέδρακ-α	ἐδράσθ-ην
δύνα-μαι 'be able'	δυνα-|δυνηθ-	δυνήσ-ομαι		δεδύνη-μαι	ἐδυνήθ-ην 'I was able'
ἐά-ω 'allow'	ἐασ-	ἐάσ-ω	εἴασ-α	εἴακ-α	εἰάθ-ην
ἐγείρ-ω 'arouse'	ἐγειρ-	ἐγερέ-ω	ἤγειρ-α	ἐγρήγορ-α 'I am awake'	ἠγέρθ-ην
ἐθέλ-ω 'wish'	ἐθελησ-	ἐθελήσ-ω	ἠθέλησ-α	ἠθέληκ-α	

Verb	Main stem (no aug.)	Future	Aorist	Perfect	Aorist passive
εἰμί 'be'	ὀντ-|εἰ-	ἔσ-ομαι	ἦ(ν) (impf.)		
εἶμι 'shall go'	ἰ-	εἶμι	ἦα (impf.)		
ἐκπλήττ-ω 'terrify'	ἐκπληξ-	ἐκπλήξ-ω	ἐξέπληξ-α	ἐκπέπληγ-μαι (pass.)	ἐξεπλάγ-ην
ἐλαύν-ω 'drive'	ἐλασ-|ἐλα-	ἐλά-ω	ἤλασ-α	ἐλήλακ-α	ἠλάθ-ην
ἕλκ-ω 'drag'	ἑλκυσ-	ἕλξ-ω ⎫ ἑλκύσ-ω ⎭ εἵλκυσ-α		εἵλκυκ-α	εἱλκύσθ-ην
ἐλπίζ-ω 'hope, expect'	ἐλπισ-	ἐλπιέ-ω	ἤλπισ-α		
ἐπίστα-μαι 'know, understand'	ἐπιστα-|η-	ἐπιστήσ-ομαι			ἠπιστήθ-ην 'I knew'
ἕπ-ομαι 'follow'	σπ-	ἕψ-ομαι	ἑσπ-όμην		
ἐργάζομαι 'work' (pass. 'be made')	ἐργασ-	ἐργάσ-ομαι	εἰργασά-μην	εἴργασ-μαι	εἰργάσθ-ην
ἔρχ-ομαι 'go'	ἐλθ-	ἐλεύσ-ομαι ⎫ εἶμι ⎭	ἦλθ-ον	ἐλήλυθ-α	
ἐρωτά-ω 'ask'	ἐρ-|ἐρωτησ-	ἐρήσ-ομαι ⎫ ἐρωτήσ-ω ⎭	ἠρ-όμην ⎫ ἠρώτησ-α ⎭	ἠρώτηκ-α	ἠρωτήθ-ην
ἐσθί-ω 'eat'	ἐδ-|φαγ-	ἔδ-ομαι	ἔφαγ-ον	ἐδήδοκ-α	ἠδέσθ-ην
εὑρίσκ-ω 'find'	εὑρ-	εὑρήσ-ω	ηὗρ-ον	ηὕρηκ-α	ηὑρέθ-ην
ἔχ-ω 'have, hold'	σχ-	ἕξ-ω ⎫ σχήσ-ω ⎭	ἔσχ-ον	ἔσχηκ-α	ἐσχέθ-ην
ζά-ω 'live'	ζήσ-|ζω-	ζήσ-ω	ἔζων ⎫ ἔζην ⎭ (impf.)		
ἥδ-ομαι 'be pleased, enjoy'	ἡσθ-	ἡσθήσομαι			ἥσθ-ην 'I enjoyed'
-ἧμαι(καθ-) 'be seated'	ἡμ-		ἥμην|ἐκαθήμην		
ἠμί 'say'	------		ἦν δ' ἐγώ, ἦ δ' ὅς, ἦ - - - - - - - - - 'I said' 'he said'		- - - - -
θάπτ-ω 'bury'	θαψ-	θάψ-ω	ἔθαψ-α	τέθαμ-μαι (pass.)	ἐτάφ-ην
-θνῄσκ-ω(ἀπο) 'die'	θαν-	θανέ-ομαι	ἔθαν-ον	τέθνηκ-α	
ἵη-μι 'shoot, let go, send'	ἱε-|ἑ-|εἱ-	ἧσ-ω	ἧ-κα	εἷκ-α	εἵθ-ην
ἵστη-μι 'set up' (mid. 'stand')	στησ-|στα-|στη-	στήσ-ω	ἔστησ-α ἔστη-ν (mid.)	ἕστηκ-α (mid.)	ἐστάθ-ην
καί-ω 'burn'	καυσ-	καύσ-ω	ἔκαυσ-α	κέκαυκ-α	ἐκαύθ-ην

Verb	Main stem (no aug.)	Future	Aorist	Perfect	Aorist passive
καλέ-ω 'call'	καλεσ-, κληθ-	καλέ-ω	ἐκάλεσ-α	κέκληκ-α	ἐκλήθ-ην
κάμν-ω 'toil'	καμ-	καμέ-ομαι	ἔκαμ-ον	κέκμηκ-α	
κεῖ-μαι 'lie, be placed'	κει-	κείσ-ομαι	ἐκεί-μην (impf.)		
κλαί-ω 'weep'	κλαυσ-	κλαύσ-ομαι	ἔκλαυσ-α	κέκλαυ(σ)-μαι (pass.)	ἐκλαύσθ-ην
κλέπτ-ω 'steal'	κλεψ-	κλέψ-ω	ἔκλεψ-α	κέκλοφ-α	ἐκλάπ-ην
κλίν-ω 'cause to lean' (pass. 'lean, lie')	κλιν-|κλιθ-	κλινέ-ω	ἔκλιν-α	κέκλι-μαι	ἐκλίθ-ην ⎫ ἐκλίν-ην ⎬
κόπτ-ω 'hit'	κοψ-|κοπ-	κόψ-ω	ἔκοψ-α	κέκοφ-α	ἐκόπ-ην
κρίν-ω 'judge'	κριν(α)-|κριθ-	κρινέ-ω	ἔκριν-α	κέκρικ-α	ἐκρίθ-ην
κτά-ομαι 'gain'	κτη-	κτήσ-ομαι	ἐκτησά-μην	κέκτη-μαι	ἐκτήθ-ην
κτείν-ω(ἀπο) 'kill'	(ἀπο)κτειν-|κταν-	(ἀπο)κτενέ-ω	(ἀπ)έκτειν-α (ἀπ)έκταν-ον	(ἀπ)έκτον-α	
λαγχάν-ω 'obtain by lot'	λαχ-	λήξ-ομαι	ἔλαχ-ον	εἴληχ-α	ἐλήχθ-ην
λαμβάν-ω 'take'	λαβ-	λήψ-ομαι	ἔλαβ-ον	εἴληφ-α	ἐλήφθ-ην
λανθάν-ω 'escape notice of' (mid. 'forget')	λαθ-	λήσ-ω	ἔλαθ-ον	λέληθ-α	
λέγ-ω 'say'	λεξ-|εἰπ-|ἐρ-	λέξ-ω ⎫ ἐρέ-ω ⎬	ἔλεξ-α ⎫ εἶπ-ον ⎬	εἴρηκ-α	ἐλέχθ-ην
λείπ-ω 'leave'	λιπ-	λείψ-ω	ἔλιπ-ον	λέλοιπ-α 'I have left/have failed'	ἐλείφθ-ην
μανθάν-ω 'learn'	μαθ-	μαθήσ-ομαι	ἔμαθ-ον	μεμάθηκ-α	
μάχ-ομαι 'fight'	μαχεσ-	μαχέ(σ)-ομαι	ἐμαχεσ-άμην	μεμάχη-μαι	
μέλλ-ω 'intend'	μελλ(ησ)-	μελλήσ-ω	ἐμέλλησ-α		
μέλ-ει 'it concerns'	μελησ-	μελήσ-ει	ἐμέλησ-ε	μεμέλη-κε	
μέν-ω 'remain'	μειν-	μενέ-ω	ἔμειν-α	μεμένηκ-α	
μιμνήσκ-ω 'remind' (mid. 'remember')	μνησ(θ)-	μνήσ-ομαι	ἔμνησ-α	μέμνη-μαι (mid.)	ἐμνήσθ-ην (mid.)
νέμ-ω 'distribute'	νειμ-	νεμέ-ω	ἔνειμ-α	νενέμηκ-α	ἐνεμήθ-ην
νομίζ-ω 'think, consider'	νομισ-	νομιέ-ω	ἐνόμισ-α	νενόμικ-α	ἐνομίσθ-ην

Verb	Main stem (no aug.)	Future	Aorist	Perfect	Aorist passive
οἶδα 'know'	εἰδ-	εἴσ-ομαι	ᾔδη (impf.)		
οἴ-ομαι 'think'	οἰη-	οἰήσ-ομαι	ᾤ-μην (impf.)		ᾠήθ-ην 'I thought'
ὄλλυ-μι(ἀπ) 'destroy' (mid. 'perish')	ὀλεσ-/ὀλο-	ὀλέ-ω	ὤλεσ-α ὠλό-μην (mid.)	ὀλώλεκ-α ὄλωλ-α (mid.)	
ὄμνυ-μι 'swear'	ὀμοσ-	ὀμέ-ομαι	ὤμοσ-α	ὀμώμοκ-α	ὠμό(σ)θ-ην
ὁρά-ω 'see'	ἰδ-	ὄψ-ομαι	εἶδ-ον	ἑώρακ-α	ὤφθ-ην
ὄρνυ-μι 'raise' (mid. 'rise, rush')	ὀρσ-/ὀρμ-	ὄρσ-ω	ὦρσ-α ὠρό-μην (mid.)	ὄρωρ-α (mid.)	
ὀφείλ-ω 'owe'	ὀφε(ι)λ-	ὀφειλήσ-ω	ὠφείλησ-α ὤφελ-ον ('would that')		
ὀφλισκάν-ω 'incur charge of'	ὀφλ-	ὀφλήσ-ω	ὦφλ-ον	ὤφληκ-α	
πάσχ-ω 'experience, suffer'	παθ-	πείσ-ομαι	ἔπαθ-ον	πέπονθ-α	
πέμπ-ω 'send'	πεμψ-	πέμψ-ω	ἔπεμψ-α	πέπομφ-α	ἐπέμφθ-ην
πίν-ω 'drink'	πι-	πί-ομαι	ἔπι-ον	πέπωκ-α	ἐπόθ-ην
πίπτ-ω 'fall'	πεσ-	πεσέ-ομαι	ἔπεσ-ον	πέπτωκ-α	
πίμπλη-μι 'fill'	πλησ-	πλήσ-ω	ἔπλησ-α	πέπληκ-α	ἐπλήσθ-ην
πίμπρη-μι 'burn up'	πρησ-	πρήσ-ω	ἔπρησ-α	πέπρη-μαι (pass.)	ἐπρήσθ-ην
πλέ-ω 'sail'	πλευσ-	πλεύσ-ομαι	ἔπλευσ-α	πέπλευκ-α	ἐπλεύσθ-ην
πράττ-ω 'act, fare'	πραξ-/πραγ-	πράξ-ω	ἔπραξ-α	πέπραχ-α πέπραγ-α ('I have fared')	ἐπράχθ-ην
πυνθάν-ομαι 'hear, inquire'	πυθ-	πεύσ-ομαι	ἐπυθό-μην	πέπυσ-μαι	
πωλέ-ω 'sell'		πωλήσ-ω	ἀπεδό-μην	πέπρακ-α	ἐπράθ-ην
ῥήγνυ-μι 'break'	ῥηξ-	ῥήξ-ω	ἔρρηξ-α	ἔρρωγ-α 'I am broken'	ἐρράγ-ην
ῥίπτ-ω 'throw'	ῥιψ-/ῥιφ-	ῥίψ-ω	ἔρριψ-α	ἔρριφ-α	ἐρρίφ(θ)-ην
σκοπέ-ω (σκέπτ-ομαι) 'view'	σκεψ-	σκέψ-ομαι	ἐσκεψά-μην	ἔσκεμ-μαι	
σπένδ-ω 'pour a libation'	σπεισ-	σπείσ-ω	ἔσπεισ-α	ἔσπεισ-μαι	
στέλλ-ω 'send'	στειλ-	στελέ-ω	ἔστειλ-α	ἔσταλκ-α	ἐστάλ-ην

Verb	Main stem (no aug.)	Future	Aorist	Perfect	Aorist passive
σῴζ-ω 'save'	σωσ-	σώσ-ω	ἔσωσ-α	σέσωκ-α	ἐσώθ-ην
τέμν-ω 'cut'	τεμ-	τεμέ-ω	ἔτεμ-ον	τέτμηκ-α	ἐτμήθ-ην
τίθη-μι 'place, put, make'	τιθε-|θε-	θήσ-ω	ἔθη-κα ἐθέ-μην (mid.)	τέθηκ-α	ἐτέθ-ην
τίκτ-ω 'bear'	τεκ-	τέξ-ω|-ομαι	ἔτεκ-ον	τέτοκ-α	
τίν-ω 'pay'	τισ-|τεισ-	τ(ε)ίσ-ω	ἔτ(ε)ισ-α	τέτ(ε)ικ-α	ἐτ(ε)ίσθ-ην
τιτρώσκ-ω 'wound'	τρωσ-	τρώσ-ω	ἔτρωσ-α	τέτρω-μαι (pass.)	ἐτρώθ-ην
τρέπ-ω 'turn'	τρεψ-|τραπ-	τρέψ-ω	ἔτρεψ-α ἐτραπό-μην ('I was turned')	τέτροφ-α	ἐτρέφθ-ην } ἐτράπ-ην }
τρέφ-ω 'rear, nourish'	θρεψ-	θρεψ-ω	ἔθρεψ-α	τέτροφ-α	ἐθρέφθ-ην
τρέχ-ω 'run'	δραμ-	δραμέ-ομαι	ἔδραμ-ον	δεδράμηκ-α	
τυγχάν-ω 'happen, chance'	τυχ-	τεύξ-ομαι	ἔτυχ-ον	τετύχηκ-α } τέτευχ-α }	
τύπτ-ω 'strike'	τυπ-	τυπτήσ-ω	ἐτύπτησ-α		ἐτύπ-ην
ὑπισχνέ-ομαι 'promise'	ὑποσχ-	ὑποσχήσ-ομαι	ὑπεσχό-μην	ὑπέσχη-μαι	
φαίν-ω 'reveal' (mid. 'appear, seem')	φαν-	φανέ-ω	ἔφην-α	πέφαγκ-α } πέφην-α (mid.) }	ἐφάν(θ)-ην
φέρ-ω 'bear, carry'	ἐνεγκ-	οἴσ-ω	ἤνεγκ-ον } ἤνεγκ-α }	ἐνήνοχ-α	ἠνέχθ-ην
φεύγ-ω 'flee, run off'	φυγ-	φεύξ-ομαι	ἔφυγ-ον	πέφευγ-α	
φημί 'say'	φα-	φήσ-ω	ἔφησ-α ἔφη-ν (impf.)		
φθάν-ω 'anticipate'	φθα(σ)-	φθήσ-ομαι	ἔφθασ-α } ἔφθη-ν }		
φθείρ-ω(δια) 'destroy, corrupt'	φθειρ-|φθαρ-	φθερέ-ω	ἔφθειρ-α	ἔφθαρκ-α	ἐφθάρ-ην
φύ-ω 'produce' (mid. 'be, be naturally')	φυ-|πεφυ(κ)-	φύσ-ω	ἔφυσ-α ἔφυ-ν (mid.)	πέφυκ-α (mid.)	
χαίρ-ω 'rejoice, bid farewell'	χαρ-	χαιρήσ-ω		κεχάρηκ-α	ἐχάρ-ην 'I rejoiced'
χρά-ομαι 'use; consult oracle' (act. 'give oracle')	χρησ(θ)-	χρήσ-ομαι	ἐχρησά-μην	κέχρη-μαι	ἐχρήσθ-ην
χρή 'it is necessary'			(ἐ)χρῆν (impf.)		
ὠνέ-ομαι 'buy'	ὠνε-|πρια-	ὠνήσ-ομαι	ἐπριά-μην	ἐώνη-μαι 'I have bought|I have been bought'	ἐωνήθ-ην

○ F. Prepositions

It is worth noting that prepositions were originally adverbs and so used in conjunction with verbs; e.g. εἰσ-φέρω, ἐκ-βάλλω. The original meaning (where it is possible to determine it) is indicated in the first column. Observe how the original adverbial meaning is modified according to the case the preposition takes.

	Accusative	Genitive	Dative
ἀμφί ('around')	'about, near' ἀμφὶ δείλην 'about evening' οἱ ἀμφὶ Πλάτωνα 'those around Plato', i.e. 'followers of Plato'		
ἀνά ('up')	'up, through, by' ἀνὰ τὸν πόταμον 'up the river' ἀνὰ τὸν πόλεμον 'through the war' ἀνὰ ἑκατόν 'by hundreds'		
ἀντί ('against')		'instead of, for the sake of' ἀντὶ πολέμου 'instead of war' ἀντὶ ἀδελφοῦ 'for the sake of a brother'	
ἀπό ('from')		'from' ἀπὸ τῆς πόλεως 'from the city'	
διά ('through')	'because of, through' διὰ τοῦτο 'because of this'	'through' (time, place) διὰ νυκτός 'through the night' διὰ τῆς τραπέζης 'through the table'	
εἰς|ἐς ('into')	'into, until, up to' εἰς Σικελίαν 'into Sicily' ἐς ἠῶ 'until dawn' εἰς ἑκατόν 'up to 100'	'to the house of' εἰς Ἅιδου 'to the house of Hades'	

	Accusative	Genitive	Dative
ἐν ('in')		'at the house of' ἐν Κροίσου 'In Croesus' house'	'in, in the power of' ἐν Σπάρτῃ 'in Sparta' ἐν χειμῶνι 'in winter' ἐν ἐμοί 'in my power'
ἐκ|ἐξ ('from out of')		'from' ἐκ Σπάρτης 'from Sparta' ἐκ τῶν παρόντων 'from, with an eye on, present circumstances'	
ἐπί ('at, on')	'at, against, over' ἐπὶ βασιλέα 'against, at the king' ἐπὶ πέντε ἔτη 'over five years'	'on; in the time of; at' ἐπὶ βωμοῦ 'on the altar' ἐπὶ ἐμοῦ 'in my time' ἐπὶ σχολῆς 'at leisure'	'on; for the purpose of, because of' ἐπὶ τῇ θαλάττῃ 'on the sea' ἐπὶ δείπνῳ 'for dinner' ἐπὶ τούτοις 'because of these things, on these conditions'
κατά ('down')	'down, by; according to' κατὰ τὸν πόταμον 'down river' κατὰ θάλατταν 'by sea' κατὰ τοὺς νόμους 'according to the laws'	'down from, beneath, against' κατὰ τῆς πετρᾶς 'down from the rock' κατὰ χθονός 'beneath the earth' κατὰ ἐμοῦ 'against me'	
μετά ('among')	'for, after' μετὰ χρύσον 'for, after gold' μετὰ τὸν πόλεμον 'after the war'	'with, in company with' μετὰ τῶν φίλων 'with his friends'	
παρά ('alongside')	'to, throughout, against' παρὰ τοὺς φίλους 'to my friends' (house)' παρὰ τὸν ἐνίαυτον 'throughout the year' παρὰ τὸν νόμον 'against the law'	'from beside, from' παρὰ τῶν νεῶν 'from beside the ships' παρὰ τῶν μαθητῶν 'from the students'	'with, near' παρὰ ἡμῖν 'with us, at our house'
περί ('around, about')	'about, near' περὶ τὸ τεῖχος 'near the wall' περὶ τοῦτον τὸν χρόνον 'about this time'	'concerning' περὶ πατρός 'concerning father' περὶ πολλοῦ ποιεῖσθαι 'to value highly'	'about, concerning' δείσαντες περὶ τῇ στρατιᾷ 'fearing for (concerning) the army'

	Accusative	*Genitive*	*Dative*
πρό ('before')		*'in front of, before'* πρὸ τῶν θυρῶν 'in front of the doors' πρὸ δείπνου 'before supper'	
πρός ('to, at, by')	*'towards; with a view to'* πρὸς τὴν πόλιν 'towards the city' πρὸς τὰ πάροντα 'with a view to the present'	*'in name of; from; under the protection of; to the advantage of'* πρὸς θεῶν 'in the name of the gods!' πρὸς Διός 'from Zeus' *or* 'under Zeus' protection' πρὸς ἡμῶν 'to our advantage'	*'by, in addition to'* πρὸς τῷ πυρί 'by the fire' πρὸς τούτῳ 'in addition to this'
σύν ('with the help of')			*'with the help of; in company with'* σὺν τοῖς θεοῖς 'with the help of the gods' σὺν ἡμῖν 'with us'
ὑπέρ ('over')	*'over, exceeding'* ὑπὲρ τὴν θάλατταν 'over the sea' ὑπὲρ δύναμιν 'beyond one's power'	*'on behalf of; over'* ὑπὲρ τῆς πόλεως 'on behalf of the city' ὑπὲρ τῆς κεφαλῆς 'over my head'	
ὑπό ('under')	*'up to and under, at'* ὑπὸ τὰ τείχη 'under the walls' ὑπὸ νύκτα 'at night'	*'under, by'* ὑπὸ τῆς γῆς 'under the earth' ὑπὸ τούτου τοῦ ἀνδρός 'by this man'	

⭕ G. Particles*

General remarks

1. Particles are short invariable words which

(i) connect an item of utterance to a preceding item, whether that item is uttered by the same speaker or by a different speaker ('and', 'but', 'so . . .' etc.)

(ii) qualify an item ('even', 'also', 'anyway', etc.)

(iii) 'colour' an item, expressing what is commonly expressed in spoken

---

* This section was contributed by a member of the Advisory Panel (see *Reading Greek (text)*, p. xii).

O   G. *Particles*   293

English by volume and tone of voice ('he *told* me!', 'he told *me*', etc.) and in written by, e.g., italics, exclamation-marks, inverted commas, etc.

ἆρα, ἤ, ἀλλά, καί

2. Four particles – ἆρα, ἤ, ἀλλά, καί – normally come first in the sentence or part of the sentence to which they belong. ἆρα and ἤ introduce questions, e.g.

> ἆρ' ἤκουσας; 'Did you hear?'
>
> ἀλλὰ τίς σοι διηγεῖτο; ἤ αὐτὸς Σωκράτης; 'But who told you? Socrates himself?'

3. ἀλλά 'but' and καί 'and' are widely used as in English, e.g.

> οὐχ ἡμεῖς ἀλλ' ἐκεῖνοι 'not we, but they'
>
> ἀλλὰ τίς σοι διηγεῖτο; 'but who told you?'
>
> ἡμεῖς καὶ ἐκεῖνοι 'we and they'
>
> καὶ ταῦτ' ἀποκρινάμενος ἀπῆλθεν 'and with that answer he went away'

4. καί may be repeated to give the sense 'both . . . and . . .', e.g.

> καὶ ἡμᾶς ἐζήτει καὶ ἐκείνους 'he was looking both for us and for them'

5. καί is also used in the senses 'actually, also, even', etc., and where English raises the volume of the voice, e.g.

> ἐζήτουν καὶ ἐκεῖνον 'I was looking for him too' (or ' . . . for him also', ' . . . also for him')
>
> ἐκεῖνον καὶ ἐζήτουν 'I was (actually) *looking* for him'
>
> τί καὶ βούλεσθε; 'What do you (actually) want?' (or, 'What is it that you *want?*)
>
> τὰ τοιαῦτα αἰσχρὸν καὶ λέγειν 'it's disgraceful (even) to *speak* of things like that'
>
> οὐδὲν ἄν μοι μέλοι εἰ καὶ ἀποθάνοι 'I wouldn't care (even) if he *did* die'

δέ, γάρ, οὖν

6. Most other particles are postpositives, i.e. they cannot come immediately after a pause, and usually come close after the word which does follow the pause. The three most important are δέ, γάρ and οὖν.

7. δέ is translatable by 'and', 'but', or not by anything, according to context; one might call it the 'basic connective' between sentences, e.g.

> τί δ' εἰ ἀποθάνοι; 'But what if he were to die?'
>
> καθεύδει, ἐγὼ δ' ἀγρυπνῶ 'he's asleep, and/but *I'*m awake'
>
> ἀκούσας δ' ἀπῆλθεν '(and) having heard it he went away'

8. When δέ is combined with a negative, the form οὐδέ/μηδέ is used if the preceding item is negative, but otherwise οὐ/μή follows δέ, e.g.

οὐ ταῦτ' εἶπον οὐδ' ἂν ἐπαινοίην 'that isn't what I said, nor would I commend it' (or '... and I wouldn't commend it')

ταῦτ' εἶπον, ὁ δὲ Σωκράτης οὐκ ἐπῄνει 'that is what I said, but Socrates did not commend it'

9. οὐδέ/μηδέ is the opposite of καί in some of the senses of §5 above, e.g.

οὐδ' ἐκεῖνον ἐζήτουν 'I wasn't looking for him either'

τί ἐρεῖς ἐὰν μηδ' ἀποκρίνηται; 'What will you say if he doesn't even answer?'

10. γάρ introduces the reason for the previous utterance ('for, because'), e.g.

ἔφευγεν· ἐδίωκον γάρ 'he ran away, for/because they were pursuing him'

11. In a response to a previous speaker γάρ is sometimes translatable as 'Why, ...', 'Yes, ...', 'No, ...', e.g.

τί γὰρ ἂν ποιοίη; 'Why, what would he do?'

πῶς γὰρ οὔ; 'Yes, of course' (or 'Yes, indeed'; lit., 'For how not?')

οὐ γάρ μ' ἐῶσιν 'No, they don't let me'

12. οὖν is the converse of γάρ, introducing the consequence of the previous utterance ('therefore, so, then'), e.g.

ἐδίωκον· ἔφευγεν οὖν 'they were pursuing him, so he ran away'

13. The consequential sense of οὖν is, however, sometimes very 'faded', so that it approximates to 'then' in the sense 'next', or to 'Well, ...' or 'So ...' in colloquial English narrative.

ἄρα, δῆτα, μήν, τοίνυν

14. Other important particles with a connective sense are ἄρα, δῆτα, μήν and τοίνυν.

15. ἄρα is often translatable as 'then' or 'so', especially (though not only) when the speaker perceives a conclusion to be drawn from a situation or preceding argument, or when he envisages a possibility, e.g.

οὐκ ἄρ' ἀγαθὸν ὁ πλοῦτος 'so wealth is not a blessing after all'

ἤκουσα αὐτῶν ὡς ἄρ' οὐδὲν ἔλαβεν 'I'm told by them that he didn't receive anything, it seems'

εἰ δ' ἄρα καὶ ἀδικεῖς ... 'but if by any chance you are in the wrong ...' (or '... if ... actually', 'if ... after all')

16. δῆτα is commonest in questions or negations responding to a previous speaker, e.g.

πῶς δῆτ' ἔπραξεν; 'So how did he manage?' (or, 'How did he manage, then?')

οὐ δῆτα 'No indeed!' (according to context, 'No, I won't!', 'No, he didn't!', etc.)

17. μήν is mostly found in combinations with other particles (see below), but note one independent usage with interrogatives and one with negatives, e.g.
(ἀλλά) τί μήν; '(but) what, then(, if not that)?'
οὔτε Καλλίας οὔτε Φιλῖνος οὐ μὴν οὐδὲ Σωκράτης 'neither Kallias nor Philinos nor, indeed, Socrates'
18. τοίνυν introduces an exposition or a stage in an exposition, like English 'Now, . . .', 'Well, now, . . .', 'Well, then, . . .'

τε

19. τε is a peculiar particle in that it may either connect an item to what precedes or look forward to what follows (the former usage is not very common in prose), e.g.
τέθνηκέ τε 'and he is dead'
ἐγώ τε καὶ σύ '(both) I and you'
20. οὔτε/μήτε is used in pairs or series in the sense 'neither . . . nor . . .', 'not . . . or . . .', 'not . . ., nor . . ., nor . . .' e.g.
οὔθ' ἡμᾶς εἶδες οὔτ' ἐκείνους 'you didn't see us or them' (or 'you saw neither us nor them')

γε, δή, μέν, τοι

21. The commonest particles of which the main function is to 'colour' the item with which they occur rather than to connect it with what precedes are γε, δή, μέν and τοι.
22. γε sometimes has a limiting sense, like 'anyway, at least, at any rate' in English, but is used in Greek far more than those expressions in English, e.g.
ἐκεῖνόν γε ἐνίκησας 'you defeated him' (implying 'even if you didn't defeat anyone else' or 'I don't know if you defeated anyone else')
23. γε is also common in responses to a previous speaker's utterance, especially to a question, e.g.
'τί σοι δοκεῖ ποιεῖν;' – 'What do you think he's doing?'
'μέμφεσθαί γε τῷ στρατηγῷ.' – 'Criticising the general.'
'ἔστι τις ἔνδον;' – 'Is anyone in?'
'οὐδείς γε.' – 'No, nobody.'
24. Thirdly, γε corresponds to an exclamation-mark with words which convey praise, blame or some other emotional reaction, e.g.
ἀμαθής γ' εἶ 'Why, you are stupid!'
εὖ γε 'Well done!'
25. δή is equivalent to an increased volume of voice on the preceding word, or to an emphatic gesture designed to sustain or revive the hearer's attention. It is used especially with quantitative words ('most', 'many', 'least', 'often', 'only',

etc.), with points of time (giving 'then' and 'now' a colouring of 'then at last' and 'just now'), and with expressions such as 'it is obvious' or 'now, consider . . .' It is rarely translatable. There is one special usage in which it has the effect of showing that the word which it accompanies is quoted from someone else, or represents someone else's way of thinking, and this usually imparts a tone of scepticism or sarcasm.

26. μέν accompanies the first item of a pair, usually when there is a contrast, but when the word which it accompanies is repeated the effect may be cumulative rather than contrastive, e.g.

οἱ μὲν Λακεδαιμόνιοι ἐπαινοῦσιν αὐτόν, τοῖς δὲ Θηβαίοις οὐκ ἀρέσκει 'the Spartans praise him, but he doesn't please the Thebans'

τὰ μὲν μάλ᾽ ἀκριβῶς ἐργάζεται, τὰ δ᾽ ἀμελεῖ 'some things he produces very carefully, but there are other respects in which he is careless'

πολλοὶ μὲν ἀπέθανον, πολλοὶ δ᾽ ἐζωγρήθησαν 'many were killed and many captured'

27. τοι expresses the speaker's feeling that the hearer's attitude or conduct ought to be affected by what is said: a threatening 'Let me tell you!', a firm but friendly 'do remember' or a gentle 'You *do* realise, don't you?' Sometimes, however, it conveys little more than 'Look, . . .', '. . ., you know, . . .', '. . ., you see, . . .' or 'after all' in English.

Particle combinations

28. A very large number of combinations of particles occur, and some of them are written as a single word: γε + οὖν as γοῦν, καί + τοι as καίτοι and μέν + τοι as μέντοι. οὐ + τοι is also written οὔτοι, and οὐ + οὖν as οὔκουν or οὐκοῦν (see §32 below).

29. γοῦν is an emphatic 'at least, at any rate'.

30. καίτοι is an emphatic 'and', sometimes implying 'and yet' (a contrast with what precedes) and sometimes 'and moreover' (the second premise of an argument from which a conclusion is going to be drawn).

31. μέντοι can function as a connective, meaning 'but, however', but also as emphasising a demonstrative or personal pronoun, e.g.

'ἐγώ;'   – 'What, me?'

'σὺ μέντοι.'   – 'Yes, *you*!'

32. When the sequence of letters ουκουν occurs, the sense sometimes requires 'therefore . . . not' but sometimes 'therefore'. The latter sense can often be got by punctuating the utterance as a question, not as a statement (turning 'so he was not successful' into 'wasn't he successful, then?'), but ancient grammarians recognised a usage οὐκοῦν = οὖν, with οὔκουν (accented on the negative) = οὐ + οὖν.

33. In other combinations the second element is most commonly γάρ, γε, δή, μήν or οὖν.

34. ἀλλά+γάρ may = ἀλλά, e.g.

βουλοίμην ἄν, ἀλλ' οὐ γὰρ οἷός τ' εἰμί 'I'd like to, but I can't'

35. In καί+γάρ, γάρ has its normal sense (§11) and καί as in §5.

36. καί+γε and δέ+γε, usually found in response to a previous speaker, correspond to 'Yes, and . . .' and 'Yes, but . . .' respectively.

37. γὰρ δή and μὲν δή are not distinguishable in translation from γάρ and μέν respectively, but καὶ δή imparts a lively tone, 'Look, . . .!', 'See, . . .!', sometimes 'And, what's more . . .'

38. καὶ μήν is an emphatic 'and'; there is considerable overlap of meaning between καὶ δή and καὶ μήν.

39. The combination μὲν οὖν, when it does not combine the usual senses of μέν and οὖν (§§12f., 26) – as it very often does – has a special sense, in which the speaker corrects previous words of his own or of another speaker, e.g.

ὀψὲ λέγω; χθὲς μὲν οὖν καὶ πρώην 'Did I say "lately"? Why, it was
   only the other day!' (lit., 'yesterday and the day before yesterday')
   (Demosthenes)

This correction often takes the form of suggesting that the previous speaker has not gone far enough, and thus expresses emphatic agreement, e.g.

'οὐ ταῦτά σοι δοκεῖ;'   – 'Don't you think so?'
'πάνυ μὲν οὖν.'   – 'Very much so.' (or 'Yes, certainly!')

O   H. ὡς (ὥς)

This word has a wide range of meanings, which are summarised here:
   (i) = 'as, when, since, because' (+ind. or part.) e.g. ὡς ἀφίκετο, εἰσῆλθεν 'when he came, he entered'; ὡς ἔμοιγε δοκεῖ 'as it seems to me';
   (ii) = 'how!' e.g. ὡς καλὰ τὰ δένδρα 'how fine are the trees!';
   (iii) = 'that' e.g. ἔλεγεν ὡς 'he said that . . .' (cf. ὅτι);
   (iv) = 'to, in order to' (+fut. part.), e.g. εἰσῆλθεν ὡς μαθησόμενος τὰ γένομενα 'he came in to learn what had happened';
   (v) = 'to, in order to' (+subj./opt.), e.g. εἰσῆλθεν ὡς μάθοι τὰ γενόμενα 'he came in to learn what had happened' (cf. ἵνα);
   (vi) = 'as – as possible' (+superlatives), e.g. ὡς πλεῖστοι 'as many as possible';
   (vii) = 'to' (+acc.), e.g. ἦλθεν ὡς Φιλόστρατον 'he came to Philostratos' (house)';
   (viii) (as ὥς) = 'so, thus';
   (ix) = 'so as to' (+inf.; see Reference Grammar J (iv)).

O I. Participles

The main uses of the participle are as follows:

(i) as an adjective, when it may best be translated by a relative clause, e.g.

ἀνὴρ καλῶς πεπαιδευμένος 'a well-educated man', *or* 'a man who has been well educated'

(ii) as a noun, when it is used with the definite article, e.g.

οἱ τρέχοντες 'those who run, runners'

(iii) to show the aspect of an action, e.g.

ταῦτ' ἐποίησε βασιλεύων 'he did this *when he was basileus*'

(iv) to denote cause, e.g.

ταῦτ' ἐποίησε βουλόμενος νικῆσαι 'he did this *because he wished to win*'

(n.b. ὡς and ἅτε are often attached to these usages)

(v) to denote purpose (usually +future participle), e.g.

ταῦτ' ἐποίησε (ὡς) νικήσων 'he did this *to win*'

(vi) conditionally, e.g.

νικήσας ἀπέφυγεν ἄν 'winning (i.e. *if he had won*) he would have escaped'

(n.b. negative is μή when such participles are conditional)

(vii) concessively, when they mean 'although', and are often used with καίπερ, e.g.

(καίπερ) δυνάμενοι φυγεῖν, ἐμείναμεν 'being able (i.e. *although we were able*) to escape, we stayed'

Note

In all the above cases, the participle and its noun go into the genitive when the clause which they form plays no other part in the sentence, e.g.

τῶν πολεμίων ἀπελθόντων, οἱ στρατιῶται ἐστρατοπεδεύσαντο 'when the enemy departed, the soldiers pitched camp'

(viii) Observe the following idioms:

φθάσας 'sooner' ('anticipating')

λαθών 'secretly' ('escaping notice')

κλαίων 'to one's regret' ('weeping')

ἔχων, φέρων, ἄγων, λαβών, χρώμενος 'with'

τί παθών . . .; 'what has one experienced to . . .? what has made one . . .?' (lit. 'suffering what?')

(ix) A number of verbs take a participle to complete their meaning. Among these are:

τυγχάνω 'happen, chance, actually to'; e.g. ἔτυχε φυγών 'he actually did escape' λανθάνω 'escape the notice of'; e.g. ἔλαθέ με φυγών 'I did not see him escaping'

φθάνω 'anticipate, do something first'; e.g. φθάνω σε φεύγων 'I escape before you'

φαίνομαι 'seem, appear'; e.g. φαίνονται φεύγοντες 'they seem to be in flight (and *are*)'

δῆλός|φανερός εἰμι 'be obviously, openly'; e.g. δῆλός ἐστι φεύγων 'he is obviously running away'

(x) In indirect speech; see Reference Grammar K (iii).

O J. Infinitives

The main uses of the infinitive are as follows:

(i) to express the English 'to –' in certain contexts controlled by verbs, e.g.

ἀγαθόν ἐστι μάχεσθαι 'it is good to fight' (where 'fight' is the subject of the sentence)

βούλομαι μάχεσθαι 'I wish to fight' (where 'fight' is the object of 'wish')

κελεύομεν σε μένειν 'we order you *to stay*'

ἐκώλυεν αὐτοὺς ἐλθεῖν 'he prevented them *from going*'

οὐ πέφυκε δουλεύειν 'he is not born *to be a slave*'

ὥρα ἐστὶν ἀπιέναι 'it is time *to depart*'

δεῖ }
χρή } ἡμᾶς ἐλθεῖν 'it is necessary for us *to go*'

ἔξεστι μοι λέγειν 'it is permitted for me *to speak*'

δοκεῖ εἶναι σοφός 'he seems *to be* wise'

φαίνεται ἀγαθὸς εἶναι 'he appears *to be* good' (but *isn't*)

(ii) in certain constructions with adjectives, e.g.

δεινὸς λέγειν 'clever at speaking'

δυνατὸς ποιεῖν τοῦτο 'able to do this'

ἐπιστήμων λέγειν καὶ σιγᾶν 'knowing how to speak and be silent'

(iii) to limit the extent of application of a word, e.g.

λόγοι χρήσιμοι ἀκοῦσαι 'words useful to hear'

πρᾶγμα χαλεπὸν ποιεῖν 'an action difficult to do'

θαῦμα ἰδέσθαι 'a wonder to behold'

(iv) in certain parenthetical phrases (usually with ὡς|ὅσον), e.g.

ὡς εἰπεῖν 'so to speak'

ὡς ἀπεικάσαι 'to make a guess'

ὀλίγου δεῖν 'almost' (lit. 'to want a little')

(v) as an imperative, e.g.

μὴ ἤπιος εἶναι 'Don't be soft!'

(vi) with the definite article, standing as a noun, e.g.

τοῦτό ἐστι τὸ ἀδικεῖν 'this is injustice'

διὰ τὸ ξένος εἶναι 'because of his alienness'

τοῦ πιεῖν ἐπιθυμία 'desire for drink'

τῷ μάχεσθαι 'by fighting'

(vii) note the number of possibilities with verbs of prevention or hindrance:

εἴργει σε τοῦτο ποιεῖν
εἴργει σε τοῦ τοῦτο ποιεῖν
εἴργει σε μὴ τοῦτο ποιεῖν
εἴργει σε τοῦ μὴ τοῦτο ποιεῖν

} 'he prevents you from doing this'

(N.b. τὸ μή is quite common in expressions implying hindrance, prevention, denial.)

(viii) in indirect speech; see this Reference Grammar K (iii).

Note

The negative with an infinitive is nearly always μή.

Impersonal verbs

These verbs have only 3rd s. forms in finite tenses, an accusative s. n. participle, and a regular infinitive (e.g.

δεῖ, δεήσει, ἔδει; δέον; δεῖν and ἔξεστι, ἔξεσται, ἐξῆν; ἐξόν; ἐξεῖναι)

The subjects of such verbs appear in the accusative or dative; and the verb which follows the impersonal goes into the infinitive, e.g.

ἔξεστί μοι ἐλθεῖν 'it is possible for me to go'

δέον με ἐλθεῖν 'it being necessary for me to go'

νομίζω ἐξεῖναι αὐτῷ ἐλθεῖν 'I think that he is permitted to go'

The most common impersonal verbs are:

δεῖ   +acc. and inf. 'must, ought'
χρή   ,,   ,,   'must, ought'
ἔξεστι +dat. and inf. 'it is permitted, possible'
πρέπει ,,   ,,   'it is proper'
προσήκει ,,   ,,   'it is appropriate'
δοκεῖ   ,,   ,,   'it seems best' ⎫ these also appear in regular forms and
συμβαίνει ,,   ,,   'it happens'   ⎭ are not restricted to impersonal use only

Result clauses

These express the idea 'so that' or 'so . . . that' and indicate the result of an action. The 'that' clause is expressed in Greek by ὥστε, which can take either an infinitive (change of subject in the accusative) or an indicative. The infinitive usage is best translated 'as to', but the difference between the two is often marginal, e.g.

οὕτως ἀνόητός ἐστιν ὥστε ἐπιλανθάνεται τῶν βιβλίων
'he is so foolish that he forgets his books'
ὥστε ἐπιλανθάνεσθαι τῶν βιβλίων
'he is so foolish   as to forget his books'.

These clauses are usually set up by οὕτως 'so', or by a word such as τοσοῦτος, τόσος ('so great', 'so many'), τοῖος ('of such a kind').

O K. Indirect speech

One can distinguish between three basic types of utterance – statements, questions, and commands (i.e. orders). These can be quoted directly (when, as a rule, inverted commas will be used; e.g. he said, 'What shall I do? I shall go . . .'), or indirectly (e.g. he wondered what to do, and decided that he would go . . .). In Greek, indirect questions and orders are expressed in largely the same way as English; so too are those indirect statements introduced by the Greek ὅτι 'that', but there are a number of verbs which use different methods of expressing indirect statements.

(i) *Verbs taking ὅτι (ὡς), and indirect questions*

Verbs taking ὅτι, and indirect questions, quote what was originally said, only changing the person, e.g.

ἔλεγεν ὅτι ἀφίξεται 'he said that he would come'
The original statement was 'I shall come'. Changing the person only, Greek writes 'he said that *he shall come*'; this converts to the English form 'he said that he would come'.

ἤρετο ὅποι Σωκράτης βαίνει 'he asked where Socrates was going'
The original question was 'Where is Socrates going?' This becomes indirectly 'he asked where Socrates *is going*' (no need to change persons here); English changes this to 'he asked where Socrates was going'.

Note that, in *secondary* sequence, verbs in such clauses can be turned into the *optative* without affecting the meaning, e.g.

ἔλεγεν ὅτι ἀφίξοιτο⎫
                    ⎬ 'he said that he would come'
ἀφίξεται⎭

(ii) *Indirect orders*

Indirect orders are expressed as in English, i.e. by the use of the infinitive, e.g.

κελεύω σε ἀπιέναι 'I order you to depart'

Accusative + infinitive or participle

More difficult are those cases in which a 'that' clause is expressed in Greek not by ὅτι 'that', but by putting the verb of the 'that' clause into an infinitive form (cf. Latin accusative and infinitive) or a participle form. There is an English parallel for the infinitive usage here; e.g. 'he knows that I am wise', or 'he knows me to be wise'. In these cases, the infinitive will show the time at which the action took place by its tense, e.g.

ἔφη με ἐλθεῖν 'he said that I had gone' (orig. 'you went')

ἔφη με ἰέναι 'he said that I was going' (orig. 'you are going')

ἔφη με ἀφίξεσθαι 'he said that I would come' (orig. 'you will come')

Some verbs take a participle in the 'that' clause rather than an infinitive, e.g.

οἶδα σε μῶρον ὄντα 'I know that you are stupid'

ἐπύθετο Νέαιραν ἀφιξομένην 'Αθήναζε 'he learnt that Neaira would come to Athens'

N.b. all the above examples have put the subject of the 'that' clause into the accusative. Where the subject of the 'that' clause is the *same* as that of the main verb, no subject in the 'that' clause will be stated; or if it is, it will be in the nominative, e.g.

ἔφη ἐλθεῖν 'he said he had gone' (both 'he's are the *same* person)

ἔφη αὐτὸν ἐλθεῖν 'he said that he had gone' (the 'he's are *different* people)

Indirect speech is *very common* in Greek; and it is very likely suddenly to emerge in a quite unexpected context. WATCH OUT FOR THE ACCUSATIVE AND INFINITIVE/PARTICIPLE CONSTRUCTION ALL THE TIME. When you come across it, begin your translation with the English 'that . . .' – this will remind you that you are in indirect speech.

(iii) Verbs taking infinitives and participles

The following verbs generally take the **infinitive** in indirect speech:

φημί 'say that . . .'

οἴομαι ⎫
νομίζω ⎬ 'believe, think that . . .'
ἡγέομαι ⎬
δοκέω ⎭

ὑπισχνέομαι 'promise to'

ἐλπίζω 'hope to'

Cf. γιγνώσκω 'determine how to, recognise how to'

μανθάνω 'learn how to'

οἶδα ⎫
ἐπίσταμαι ⎬ 'know how to'

The following generally take the **participle:**
ἀκούω 'hear that . . .'
πυνθάνομαι 'ascertain that . . .'
αἰσθάνομαι 'perceive that . . .'
οἶδα 'know that . . .'
γιγνώσκω 'ascertain that . . .'
ἀγγέλλω 'announce that . . .'
μανθάνω 'learn that . . .'
Note the distinction between φαίνομαι, δῆλος, φανερός + participle (which all
mean 'it seems to be the case that', with the strong implication that it really *is* the
case), and φαίνομαι, δῆλος, φανερός + infinitive (where the implication is that
what seems to be the case is not really the case).

○   L. Temporal clauses

Definite temporal clauses

'Definite' temporal clauses express the time at which an event took
place; the verb goes into the indicative, e.g.
ἕως ἔμενε, ἀπήλθομεν 'while he waited, we left'
ἐπεὶ ἐδίωξαν, ἀπέφυγον οἱ πολέμιοι 'when they pursued, the enemy
    fled'
ἐμείναμεν ἕως ἐκέλευε ἡμᾶς ἀπελθεῖν 'we waited until he told us to go'
πρίν 'before' takes an infinitive (change of subject in the accusative), e.g.
πρὶν ἀπελθεῖν, εὔξατο 'before departing, he offered up a prayer'
πρὶν ἡμᾶς ἀπελθεῖν, εὔξατο 'before we departed, he offered up a
    prayer'

Indefinite temporal clauses

'Indefinite' temporal clauses express the idea of generality (i.e. not
'when', but 'whenever'), or of uncertainty about the actual completion of the
event, which is made to seem to lie in some indefinite future. In these cases, the
verbs in the temporal clause go into the subjunctive + ἄν in primary sequence,
or the optative in secondary sequence, e.g.
ἐξίασιν ὅταν βούλωνται 'they go out whenever they wish'
ἐξῆλθον ὅτε βούλοιντο 'they went out whenever they wished'
ἐμείναμεν ἕως κελεύοι ἡμᾶς ἀπελθεῖν 'we waited until such time as he
    should tell us to leave'
μὴ λέγε τοῦτο πρὶν ἂν μάθῃς τὰ γενόμενα 'do not say this before/until
    you learn what has happened'

Observe that the rules for 'definite' or 'indefinite' utterance apply equally to relative clauses, e.g.

ὅστις ἂν τοῦτο ποιῇ, ἀνόητός ἐστιν 'whoever does this is stupid'
ἐκέλευεν αὐτὸν ἄγεσθαι ἰατρὸν ὃν βούλοιτο 'he ordered him to bring a doctor, whomever he wished/he ordered him to bring whichever doctor he wanted'

Note
It must be said that Greek is, as usual, flexible in its usages on this point: sometimes one finds the subjunctive where one would expect the optative, and sometimes ἄν drops out.

M. Purpose clauses and verbs of fearing

Purpose Clauses

A purpose clause indicates an intention in the mind of the speaker, and is often expressed by the English 'in order to', or simply 'to', e.g. 'he has come here *in order to insult us*', or '*To cross the railway*, passengers are asked to use the bridge.'

Perhaps because an intention is expressed of which the fulfilment is quite uncertain Greek uses a quasi-indefinite construction in one instance, i.e. ἵνα + subjunctive in primary sequence (no ἄν) and optative in secondary, e.g.

ἀφικνεῖται ἵνα ἡμᾶς πείθῃ 'he is coming to persuade us'
ἀφίκετο ἵνα ἡμᾶς πείθοι 'he came to persuade us'

But Greek also expresses the idea of purpose in two other common ways, i.e.
(i) ὡς + future participle (lit. 'as intending to –'), e.g.
   ἀφικνεῖται ὡς ἡμᾶς πείσων 'he is coming to persuade us'
(ii) ὅς + future indicative (lit. 'who will/intends to –')
   ὁ ἀνὴρ ἀφικνεῖται ὃς ἡμᾶς πείσει 'the man is coming to persuade us' (lit. 'who will persuade us')

Notes
(i) ὅπως, ὡς can be used in place of ἵνα.
(ii) When ἵνα takes an indicative, it means 'where'.

Verbs of fearing

Fearing in case something may happen *in the future* attracts the same sort of construction as purpose clauses, i.e. subjunctive in primary sequence, optative in secondary, e.g.

φοβοῦμαι μὴ Σωκράτης ἔλθῃ 'I am afraid that/lest Socrates may/will come' ἐφοβήθην μὴ Σωκράτης ἔλθοι 'I was afraid that/lest Socrates might/ would come'

But if the fear is expressed for something that has happened already, the simple indicative is used, e.g.

φοβούμεθα μὴ ἔπεισεν ἡμᾶς 'we are afraid that he persuaded us'

N. Polite (potential) ἄν

ἄν with the optative expresses a future action as dependent on circumstances or conditions, and is best translated by the English 'may, might, could, would, can, would like to', or 'possibly, perhaps'. But there are times when it is very difficult to differentiate between this 'potential' use and the straight future 'will, shall'; e.g.

λέγοις ἄν μοι 'can you tell me?/would you tell me?/tell me!/would you like to tell me?/will you tell me?'

δὶς ἐς τὸν αὐτὸν ποταμὸν οὐκ ἂν ἐμβαίης 'you could not/would not/ cannot step twice into the same river'

O. Conditionals

Conditional sentences (i.e. sentences with an 'if' clause) should be translated by some form of English 'would' or 'should' when they show ἄν in the main clause, as follows:

(i) optatives in the 'if' clause (called the 'protasis') and the main clause (called 'apodosis', or 'pay-off'), with ἄν in the apodosis too, make the condition refer to the FUTURE, and should be translated 'if . . . were to, . . . would', e.g.

εἰ κελεύοις, πειθοίμην ἄν 'if you *were to* order, I *would* obey'

(ii) imperfects in the protasis and apodosis, with ἄν in the apodosis, should be translated 'if . . . were (now), . . . would' (as referring to the *present*), e.g.

εἴ με ἐκέλευες, ἐπειθόμην ἄν 'if you *were (now)* ordering me, I *would* obey'

(iii) aorists in the protasis and apodosis, with ἄν in the apodosis, should be translated 'if . . . had, . . . would have' (as referring to the *past*), e.g.

εἴ με ἐκέλευσας, ἐπιθόμην ἄν 'if you *had* ordered me, I *would have* obeyed'

Notes
(i) These conditions can be mixed. Greek will then treat each clause on its merits. E.g.

εἴ με ἐκέλευσας, ἐπειθόμην ἄν. *'If you had ordered me, I would (now) be obeying.'*

(ii) When there is no ἄν, translate normally without 'would/should', e.g.

εἰ ἁμαρτάνεις, μῶρος εἶ *'if you make a mistake, you are a fool'.*

(iii) Observe that when a non-'would/should' refers to future time, Greek will treat the 'if' clause as an indefinite clause (since there can be little certainty about the outcome of a future conditional event) and use ἐάν with subjunctive, e.g.

ἐάν με πείθῃς, οὐκ ἄπειμι *'if you (will) persuade me, I shall not go away'.*

O   P. Wishes

Wishes for the future in Greek are expressed by the *optative* (e.g. ἀπολοίμην 'may I perish!'), or by εἴθε/εἰ γάρ/εἰ+optative (e.g. εἰ γὰρ πείθοιμι τὸν ἄνδρα 'if only I could persuade the man!').

Unattained wishes for the present or past use the imperfect or aorist indicative (cf. unfulfilled conditions, which they closely resemble), e.g.

εἴθε τοῦτο ἐποίει 'if only he were doing this!'

εἰ γὰρ τοῦτο ἐποίησε 'if only he had done this!'

Alternatively, they can be expressed by using a form of ὤφελον+infinitive, e.g.

(εἴθε) ὤφελον ποιεῖν τοῦτο 'would that I were doing this!'

(εἰ γὰρ) ὤφελε ποιῆσαι τοῦτο 'would that I had done this!'

Observe the difference to the tense which the infinitive makes here.

N.b. ἄν is NEVER used with wishes.

O   Q. Commands (orders)

Greek uses one set of forms for 2nd person imperatives ('Do this!' 'Do that!') and another for 3rd person orders ('Let him/them do this!') and another for 1st person commands ('Let us do this!'). The 2nd and 3rd person forms appear under the imperative forms in the verb tables.

The distinction between orders using the aorist form and the present form is one of aspect – the aorist form suggests the order applies to a particular instance, the present to a continued or repeated occurrence (cf. 'Pick up that book!' and, 'Pick up all the litter!'). But when the order is negative ('Don't do that!' 'Let him

not do that!') Greek uses μή + aorist *subjunctive* to express the *aorist aspect*, NOT
μή + aorist imperative, e.g.

μὴ ποιήσῃς τοῦτο 'don't do this (once)'

μὴ ποίει τοῦτο 'don't do this (at all, ever)'

Observe also that the subjunctive is used after certain words to express an order
or a quasi-order, e.g.

φέρε ποιήσω τοῦτο 'come, let me do this'

βούλει ποιήσω τοῦτο 'do you wish I should do this?'

ποιήσω here is aor. subj., NOT future.

The subjunctive is used to express the idea 'let us . . .', e.g.

ἴωμεν 'let us go'

O   R. Deliberatives

When a first-person question appears in the subjunctive, it carries the idea
'(What) am I to . . .?', e.g.

ποῖ τράπωμαι; 'Where am I to turn?'

τί γένωμαι; 'What is to become of me?' (lit. 'What am I to become?')

If such a 'deliberation' occurs in past time, Greek uses ἔδει + infinitive, i.e. 'what
ought I to have . . .?', e.g.

ποῖ ἔδει με τραπέσθαι; 'Where was I to turn?' (lit. 'Where ought I to
have turned?')

If a deliberation in the subjunctive is reported, in *secondary* sequence, it will turn
into the optative, e.g.

ἤρετο με ποῖ τράποιτο 'he asked me where he was to turn to'.

C *Language surveys**

O Language Survey (1): a brief history of the Greek language

Greek belongs to the great family of Indo-European languages, which includes English and most modern European languages as well as Persian and the languages of north India. It has the longest recorded history of any of them, running from the fourteenth century down to the present day. Its apparent similarity to Latin is due, not to any specially close relationship, but to the fact that both languages are recorded at an early date; in some ways, Greek is also close to the ancient language of India, Sanskrit.

The earliest record of the Greek language is contained in the clay tablets written in the Linear B syllabic script in the Mycenaean palaces of Knossos and the mainland (fourteenth to thirteenth centuries). This represents an archaic form of the language, but demonstrates firmly that Greek had developed as a separate language well before this date. The alphabet was introduced from Phoenicia, probably in the early eighth century, and although the shape of the letters and the pronunciation has changed, this script has been in use ever since. The two great poems of Homer were probably composed during this century, but their written form is a modernisation of Hellenistic (third century) date. The earliest inscriptions are mostly brief records of names, but before the end of the eighth century someone had scratched on a vase at Athens a line and a bit of verse, given here in modernised spelling:

ὃς νῦν ὀρχηστῶν πάντων ἀταλώτατα παίζει,
τοῦ τόδε . . .

* These surveys were contributed by members of the Advisory Panel, as indicated in *Reading Greek (text)*, p. xii.

'Who now of all the dancers sports most delicately,
   this is his . . .'
The early inscriptions show that down to the end of the fourth century every Greek city had its own dialect and often its own peculiar form of alphabet. We can group the dialects into four main types:
   (i) West Greek, or Doric, the type spoken by most of Athens' enemies in the Peloponnesian War; it was used in literature for choral lyric poetry
   (ii) Arcadian and Cypriot, without any literary use
   (iii) Aeolic, spoken in Thessaly, Boiotia and Lesbos; the personal lyric poetry of Sappho and Alkaios (c. 600) is in a form of Lesbian.
   (iv) Ionic, spoken in the central and east Aegean, used by Homer and all epic poets, and also by Herodotus; together with Attic, the speech of Athens, which is the first dialect you will meet in learning Greek. The amount and quality of Attic Greek vastly outweighs the surviving Greek of other dialects.
   Attic Greek was used in modified form by Thucydides and the tragedians, and in its purer form by Aristophanes, Plato and the orators. But in the third century it yielded to another slight modification, which became the standard language of Hellenistic Greece and most of the eastern part of the ancient world; this was called ἡ κοινὴ διάλεκτος 'the common speech'. Its grammar and syntax changed little for over a thousand years, though there was some development in vocabulary; but the pronunciation underwent major changes, while retaining the old spellings. Thus a knowledge of Attic will not only enable you to read Athenian literature; it supplies a key to the other dialects used in literature and to the whole of later Greek literature.
   After the fall of Constantinople to the Turks in A.D. 1453, Greek was still maintained as the language of the Orthodox Church, and continued to be spoken widely. With the liberation of Greece in the early nineteenth century attempts were made to revive the old language for official purposes, and Greeks today still respect ancient forms as 'more correct' than those they use colloquially. Despite its many changes, modern Greek is much closer to ancient Greek than Italian is to Latin. The difference in pronunciation will prevent you from understanding the spoken language, but many public notices will be intelligible, and there is a real sense of continuity in the modern language.
   For example, some of the signs to be seen on shops and offices in Greece today will be easily understood, such as παντοπωλεῖον 'General store' (i.e. where everything is sold), or Ἐθνικὴ Τράπεζα τῆς Ἑλλάδος 'National Bank of Greece' (τράπεζα 'table' had already in antiquity acquired the sense of 'bank'). A notice sometimes to be seen in parks or woodland reads
   ΑΓΑΠΑΤΕ ΤΑ ΔΕΝΔΡΑ 'Be kind to the trees'
Words found on Mycenaean documents (the earliest Greek we know, dateable

to c. 1400) but still in use today with only slight change of pronunciation include:

ἔχω 'I have'
θεός 'god'
μέλι 'honey'
παλαιός 'old'

○ Language Survey (2): active, middle and passive

Grammarians traditionally use the term 'voice' to describe those verb-forms of which the basic function is to signal the relationship between the subject and the action denoted by the verb. Thus many languages, Greek included, have an *active* voice, used when the subject is doing the action (e.g. 'Dikaiopolis goes to the agora', 'Neaira hates Phrastor', 'Socrates deceived the young'); and a *passive* voice, used when the subject is having something done to it ('Phrastor was hated by Neaira', 'the young were deceived by Socrates').

In addition to these, Greek also has a so-called *middle* voice. It has a variety of meanings, but the most important is that of doing something *for oneself*. Thus αἱρεῖν means 'to take, capture'; its middle αἱρεῖσθαι means 'to take for oneself, to choose'. Again, προσάγω means 'to bring x up to y', but προσάγεσθαι means 'to bring x to oneself, to win x over to one's own side'. The act of engaging in a lawsuit is δικάζειν (active), seen from the point of view of the judges, but δικάζεσθαι (middle) from that of the litigants, who are in it for their own benefit. Consequently, the active forms mean 'give judgment', the middle forms mean 'go to law'.

The forms of the middle and passive are the same in the present, imperfect and perfect, but differ in the aorist and (usually) in the future. Many verbs occur only in the middle or only in the passive; others, such as ἀκου- 'hear', have an active form in the present (ἀκούω 'I hear'), but a middle form in the future (ἀκούσομαι 'I will hear'). Quite a number of middle verbs use the passive forms in the aorist (see **206**).

○ Language Survey (3): aspect

The tenses of the Greek verb fall into four *systems:*
System (i): present, including imperfect
System (ii): future

System (iii): aorist

System (iv): perfect, including pluperfect and future perfect.

Each of these systems carries its own particular meaning and this applies to all moods in the system, including participle, imperative and infinitive.

Only one of these systems has an *exclusively* temporal force, and that is the future. Each of the three other systems *may* refer in time to either the present or the past. Observe that in Attic Greek, past time is normally marked by the presence of the augment, though this is optional in certain kinds of verse.

(i) The present system

This conveys what is known as the 'imperfective' aspect. This means that the system shows the action of the verb to be a continuing action, a process, e.g. ποιεῖ 'he is (in the process of) making'; or the process may consist of repetition, e.g. ἤστραπτε 'there were several flashes of lightning, it went on lightning for some time'.

(ii) The aorist system

The aorist system, by contrast, conveys that the action is regarded as an event or a fact, not a process, e.g. ἐποίησε 'he made' (often used on vases with the maker's signature); ἤστραψε 'there was (a flash of) lightning'.

(N.b. if the speaker so wishes, he is quite at liberty, of course, to regard any action as imperfective (i.e. continuing) or aoristic (i.e. happening as a fact or event). Thus some makers write on their vases ἐποίει 'he was the maker'; and lists of Olympic victors can have ἐνίκα 'he was the victor'.)

It is often stated that the aorist participle has reference to past time, e.g. ταῦτα εἰπὼν ἀπῆλθε *can* be translated 'having said this he went away'. But this arises naturally from the fact that one action must have preceded the other; it would be equally correct to translate 'saying this he went away; he said this and went away; with these words he went away'. That the aorist participle does not *have* to refer to past time is evident from the common phrase ὑπολαβὼν ἔφη 'he said in reply' (not 'having replied'!).

(iii) The perfect system

The perfect is not a past but a present tense; past time is indicated by the pluperfect. The perfect indicates a present state resulting from a past action, e.g.

ἀποθνήσκει	(present)	'he is on his death-bed'
ἀπέθανε	(aorist)	'he died'
τέθνηκε	(perfect)	'he is (now) dead'
ἐτεθνήκει	(pluperfect)	'he was (at that time) dead'

This explains why some perfects are used with present meaning (see Language Survey (8)), e.g.

οἶδα 'I have perceived, (therefore) I know'

μέμνημαι 'I have called to mind, (therefore) I remember'

The first sentence of Thucydides' history is an excellent example of the aspectual systems at work:

Θουκυδίδης Ἀθηναῖος ξυνέγραψε τὸν πόλεμον τῶν Πελοποννησίων καὶ Ἀθηναίων, ὡς ἐπολέμησαν πρὸς ἀλλήλους, ἀρξάμενος εὐθὺς καθισταμένου καὶ ἐλπίσας μέγαν τε ἔσεσθαι καὶ ἀξιολογώτατον τῶν προγεγενημένων, τεκμαιρόμενος ὅτι ἀκμάζοντές τε ἦσαν ἐς αὐτὸν ἀμφότεροι παρασκευῇ τῇ πάσῃ καὶ τὸ ἄλλο Ἑλληνικὸν ὁρῶν ξυνιστάμενον πρὸς ἑκατέρους, τὸ μὲν εὐθύς, τὸ δὲ διανοούμενον.

'Thucydides of Athens wrote the history *(event)* of the war between the Peloponnesians and Athenians, how they fought *(event)* each other. He began *(event)* as soon as it started *(process)* and expected *(event)* it would be *(future)* important and more notable than any that had occurred previously *(perfect)*, drawing conclusions *(process)* from the fact that they were undertaking *(process)* it at the height of their powers *(process)* in every department and seeing *(process)* that the rest of the Greek nation were inclining *(process)* to one side or the other, some at once, others having only the intention *(process)*.'

○ Language Survey (4): optative

(i) Forms

The distinguishing feature of the optative mood is the presence of -ι- preceding the personal endings (occasionally the iota will be written subscript, but it is always there). In the 3rd s. active forms there is usually no personal ending, so that the word ends with -οι or sometimes -αι. The full set of endings (other than duals) is as follows:

Active (also aorist passive)

1st s.	-μι	παύοιμι, παύσαιμι, εἴποιμι, παύσοιμι, ἴοιμι
	-ην	τιμῴην, φιλοίην, εἴην, τιθείην, θείην, παυσθείην
2nd. s.	-ς	παύοις etc.
	-ας	παύσειας (this ending only in wk. aor. act.)
	-ης	τιμῴης etc.

3rd s.   παύοι etc.
    -ε(ν) παύσειε(ν) *(this ending only in wk. aor. act.)*
    -η   τιμῴη etc.
1st pl. -μεν   παύοιμεν, παύσαιμεν, τιμῷμεν, τιθεῖμεν etc.
2nd pl. -τε   παύοιτε, παύσαιτε, τιμῷτε, τιθεῖτε etc.
3rd pl. -εν   παύοιεν, τιμῷεν, τιθεῖεν etc.
    -αν   παύσειαν *(this ending only in wk. aor. act.)*

Middle

1st s.   -μην παυοίμην, παυσαίμην, λαβοίμην, μεθείμην etc.
2nd s. -ο   παύοιο etc.
3rd s. -το   παύοιτο etc.
1st pl. -μεθα παυοίμεθα etc.
2nd pl. -σθε παύοισθε etc.
3rd pl. -ντο παύοιντο etc.

You will observe that these endings resemble the endings of the *past* indicative tenses (e.g. ἐπαυόμην, ἐπεπαύμην) – a fact which it may be helpful to connect with the use of the optative in 'secondary sequence' (**167**) governed by *past* main verbs.

(ii) Uses

In very broadest outline, the indicative is the mood for what is *factual*, the subjunctive for what is *prospective* (i.e. sometime in the future), the optative for contingencies which are *more remotely prospective*. This basic force of the optative surfaces in three ways:

(a) in subordinate clauses of various kinds, the optative replaces the subjunctive (sometimes the indicative) when the clause is in secondary sequence. See Running Grammar **167, 186–8, 194–5, 211.**

(b) the optative is used to express a *wish for the future*, e.g.

ἀπολοίμην 'may I perish! damn me!'
δοίη τις πέλεκυν 'if only someone would give me an axe!'
γενοίμην αἰετός 'would I were an eagle!'

(c) the optative with ἄν is used to characterise some event or situation as a *future* possibility (the so-called 'potential' use of the optative in which, with trifling exceptions, it is always in Classical Greek accompanied by ἄν); English usually employs for this purpose such words as 'may', 'might', 'can', 'could', 'would', 'should', (sometimes) 'will', e.g.

λέγοις ἄν 'you might tell me' (i.e. 'please tell me')
λέγοιμι ἄν ἤδη 'I will tell you now'

εἰ ἐκεῖσε ἔλθοις, ἐγὼ ἄν σοι ἐποίμην 'if you were to go there, I would follow you'

ἀλλὰ εἴποι τις ἄν ὅτι . . . 'but someone may say that . . .'

Note that while a potential optative virtually always has ἄν accompanying it, the ἄν may very well not be adjacent to the verb. Note also that the optative usages of types (a) and (b) never have an ἄν, i.e. an optative accompanied by an ἄν is *always* potential.

○   # Language Survey (5): subjunctive and optative usages

As remarked under the optative (Language Survey (4)), the subjunctive mood is appropriate to events and situations viewed not as actual but as *prospective*. In several constructions, accordingly, the dividing line between the subjunctive and the future indicative can be rather fine; on the whole, the difference is that the future indicative gives an impression of greater definiteness and certainty.

In independent sentences

The subjunctive is used only

(i) in first person exhortations (ἴωμεν 'let us go')

(ii) in deliberative questions (τί εἴπω; 'what am I to say?')

(iii) in prohibitions (aorist only) (μή με ἐπιτρίψῃς, ὦ Ἑρμῆ 'do not destroy me, O Hermes')

In subordinate clauses

The subjunctive is found in many types of clause which have an indefinite or prospective sense, e.g.

indefinite relative clauses with ἄν (**175**)

indefinite clauses of time, place (etc.) with ἄν (**175, 193**)

conditionals relating to the future (introduced by ἐάν, ἤν, ἄν) (**176**)

'fear' clauses relating to the future (**182**)

'purpose' clauses (sometimes with ἄν, though ἵνα 'in order that' never takes ἄν; ἵνα ἄν, if it occurs, will mean 'wherever') (**186**).

Observe that, where ἄν accompanies a subjunctive, the particle will almost always come directly after the conjunction or relative introducing the clause (often the two fuse together into one word, e.g. ὅταν, ἐάν, ἐπειδάν).

In secondary sequence (**167**), the subjunctive in all these subordinate usages is generally replaced by the optative; this use of the optative is NOT 'potential', and accordingly there is NO ἄν.

O   Language Survey (6): the uses of ἄν

The particle ἄν has two entirely different fields of usage, which fortunately need never be confused because in one field the verb associated with ἄν *will always be subjunctive*, while in the other field the verb *will never be subjunctive*. In a rather vague sense the two usages may be thought to have some elements in common, but it is better to treat them quite separately.

(a) Attached to a conjunction or relative (with the verb in the subjunctive)

ἄν has the effect of making the clause *indefinite* (like the English '-ever'), or *prospective* (referring to future contingencies rather than present facts), e.g.

(i) ἐπειδὴ εἰσῆλθεν, ἐχαίρομεν 'when he came, we were glad'

(ii) ἐπειδὰν εἰσέλθῃ, χαιρήσομεν 'when he comes (whenever that will be) we will be glad'

(i) refers to a known time in the past; (ii) refers to an unknown time in the future.

(iii) ᾧ τρόπῳ ἐβούλοντο 'in the way they wanted'

(iv) ᾧ ἂν τρόπῳ βούλωνται 'in whatever way they want'

(iii) refers to a particular type of treatment that was applied; (iv) gives *carte-blanche* to apply any kind of treatment.

(v) εἰ μὴ ἀπέδωκε, διώξομαι αὐτόν 'if he hasn't paid, I'll sue him'

(vi) ἐὰν μὴ ἀποδῷ, διώξομαι αὐτόν 'if he doesn't pay, I'll sue him'

In (v), the debtor has already *in fact* either paid or defaulted, though the speaker does not know which; in (vi) it is still a matter of speculation whether he will pay or not. An alternative to (vi) is:

(vii) εἰ μὴ ἀποδώσει, διώξομαι αὐτόν 'if he is not going to pay, I'll sue him'

(vii) suggests, in contrast with (vi), that the speaker has already half-decided that the debtor will *not* pay voluntarily, so the process of law is all the more certain.

(b) Accompanying a verb in the optative (typically, though not always, in an independent clause)

ἄν signals that the optative is 'potential' (see Language Survey (4) (ii) (c)).

(c) Accompanying a verb in past tense (impf., aor., plup. INDICA-TIVE)

ἄν signals a hypothetical statement (or question) based on a condition contrary to fact ('unfulfilled'), e.g.

εἰ Λακεδαιμόνιοι ταῦτα ἐποίησαν, εὐθὺς ἂν καθειλκύσατε διακοσίας ναῦς 'if the Spartans had done that, you would have launched 200 ships at once'

εἰ ἄδικος ἦν, οὐκ ἂν ἐνθάδε νῦν ἠγωνιζόμην, ἀλλὰ ἑκὼν ἂν ἔφευγον 'if I were in the wrong, I would not now be standing trial here, but would be in voluntary exile.'

Observe that you will sometimes find ἄν accompanying an infinitive or participle. In such cases (usually in indirect speech), the force of ἄν will be potential or occasionally hypothetical (i.e. (b) or (c)); the verb of a clause containing an ἄν of type (a) MUST be *subjunctive,* otherwise the ἄν simply cannot stand.

Often in Homer you will find κε or κεν performing just the same functions as ἄν; but the strict principles laid down above for the use of ἄν and of the subjunctives and optatives do not apply in their entirety to Homer, where there is much more freedom in the use of moods.

Language Survey (7): verbs in -μι

We divide all Greek verbs into thematic or -ω verbs and athematic or -μι verbs. The two classes mainly differ in the present and imperfect (sometimes in the aorist too); also the conjugation of the -μι verbs is far less predictable than that of the -ω verbs.

In the pres. and impf. the -ω verbs (παύω, φέρω, τιμάω etc.) show an -ο- or -ε- vowel (the so-called thematic vowel) between the root and the personal endings, while the -μι verbs do not: contrast παύ-ο-μεν, παύ-ε-τε (παύω) or τιμῶμεν, τιμᾶτε which derive from τιμά-ο-μεν, τιμά-ε-τε (τιμάω) with τίθε-μεν, τίθε-τε (τίθη-μι), δείκνυ-μεν, δείκνυ-τε (δείκνῡ-μι), φα-μέν, φα-τέ (φη-μί), ἐσ-μέν, ἐσ-τέ (εἰ-μί). The -μι verbs have different endings from the -ω verbs in the singular of the ind. pres. active: contrast παύω, παύεις, παύει with τίθη-μι, τίθη-ς, τίθη-σι or δείκνῡ-μι, δείκνῡ-ς, δείκνῡ-σι (but notice the irregular patterns of εἰμί, εἶ, ἐστί 'I am . . .' and εἶμι, εἶ, εἶσι 'I shall go'). The 3rd pl. ind. pres. of the -μι verbs tends to end in -ασι(ν) (but εἰσί 'they are' is again irregular).

In the impf. and aorist active the -μι verbs have a 3rd pl. in -σαν: cf. ἐτίθε-σαν (impf.), ἔθε-σαν (aor.), ἐδίδο-σαν (impf.), ἔδο-σαν (aor.), ἐδείκνυ-σαν (impf. of δείκνυμι; the aorist ἔδειξαν is like ἔπαυσαν), ἦσαν 'they were', ᾖσαν 'they were going'.

In the middle the -μι and -ω verbs have similar endings but in the -μι verbs the 2nd s. indicative ends in -σαι in the present (τίθε-σαι etc.) and in -σο in the imperfect (ἐτίθε-σο); it may be helpful to remember that the equivalent forms of the -ω verbs, παύῃ and ἐπαύου are contracted from παύεαι and ἐπαύεο.

In the -μι verbs the infinitive active pres. ends in -ναι (and not in -ειν as in the -ω verbs): τιθέναι, διδόναι, δεικνύναι, εἶναι, ἰέναι etc. The middle inf. ends in -σθαι as in the -ω verbs: τίθεσθαι, κεῖσθαι etc.

Most -μι verbs preserve in the present and impf. active – some also in the aorist – a contrast in the vowel of the stem; the s. has a long vowel or diphthong and the dual and plural have a short vowel: cf. τί-θη-μι (1st s.) vs. τί-θε-μεν (1st pl.), δί-δω-μι (1st s.) vs. δί-δο-μεν (1st pl.), δείκνῡ-μι (1st s.) vs. δείκνῠ-μεν (1st pl.), φη-μί (1st s.) vs. φᾰ-μέν (1st pl.), εἶμι (1st s.) vs. ἴ-μεν (1st pl.) etc. The 'short' stem normally appears in the optative and in all the middle forms.

There is no 'regular' conjugation of the -μι verbs parallel to the conjugation of e.g. παύω. This is partly because most of the -μι verbs are archaic formations which have undergone a number of changes (remember how irregular is the inflection of 'I am' in English). The most 'regular' type is that of the -νυμι or -ννυμι verbs (δείκνυμι, κεράννυμι etc.), which all inflect in a similar manner, differ from the -ω verbs only in the present and imperfect, and form the other tenses from the root without the -(ν)νυμι suffix (the aorist is mostly sigmatic; cf. δείκ-νυμι vs. ἔδειξα). These verbs have present optatives similar to those of the -ω verbs (cf. δεικνύοιμι, δεικνύοις, δεικνύοι etc., just like παύοιμι, παύοις, παύοι etc.). The other -μι verbs like τίθημι, δίδωμι etc. follow the type: 1st s. τιθείην, 2nd s. τιθείης, 3rd s. τιθείη, 1st pl. τιθεῖμεν, 2nd pl. τιθεῖτε, 3rd pl. τιθεῖεν (cf. διδοίην, pl. διδοῖμεν from δίδωμι; ἱσταίην, pl. ἱσταῖμεν from ἵστημι; εἴην, pl. εἶμεν from εἰμί). The opt. of εἶμι 'I shall go' follows the normal pattern of the -ω verbs (ἴοιμι, pl. ἴοιμεν etc.).

Among the -μι verbs which do not belong to the δείκνυμι type (and are not defective like εἰμί 'I am' and εἶμι 'I shall go') τίθημι, ἵστημι, δίδωμι and ἵημι are the most frequent and show very similar inflections. ἵστημι has a sigmatic aorist ἔστησα 'I set' with a transitive meaning and an aorist ἔστην 'I stood' used intransitively. τίθημι, δίδωμι, ἵημι, and only these three verbs, form aorists in -κα (ἔθηκα, ἔδωκα, ἧκα) where the -κ- appears in the singular only (ἔθηκα, ἔθηκας, ἔθηκε, pl. ἔθεμεν, ἔθετε, ἔθεσαν). It is important not to confuse these forms with the perfect which would have a reduplication (τέθηκα, δέδωκα, -εικα) rather than an augment and would keep the -κ- all through the inflection of the indicative.

○ Language Survey (8):
verbs with perfect force

As you have seen (165) the earliest function of the perfect in Greek was to describe a situation in the present arising from some past event. The tendency as the language developed was to lay more emphasis on the past event, so that in Classical Greek the perfect is often to be translated 'I have –ed'; but there remain considerable relics of its older function. In addition to what was said at 165, note the following:

(a) the perfect passive is often to be rendered 'it is –ed', as against 'it has been –ed' e.g.

ταῦτα ἐν τοῖς Σόλωνος νόμοις γέγραπται 'this is written in the laws of Solon' (i.e. 'it has been written down and *can still be read*')

τέτρωται 'he is wounded' (i.e. 'he has received a wound and *still suffers from it*')

τὰ κρέα ἐξώπτηται 'the meat is cooked' (i.e. 'has been cooked and *is ready to serve*')

(b) a number of verbs which are perfect in form have virtually the sense of the simple present. You have already met ἕστηκα 'I stand', οἶδα 'I know'.

Some others are:

μέμνημαι   'I remember'

πέφυκα   'I am – by nature'

οἱ βάρβαροι ἐχθροὶ πεφύκασι τοῖς Ἕλλησιν 'The barbarians are natural enemies to the Greeks'

κέκραγα   'I shout'

γέγηθα   'I am glad'

δέδοικα   'I am afraid'

ἐγρήγορα   'I am awake'

εἴωθα   'I am accustomed to'

ἔοικα   (i) 'I seem to – ' (ii) 'I resemble' (+dat.)

κέχηνα   'I gape'

(c) another relic of an earlier state of the language is seen in the use of active forms of the perfect of a few verbs in what seems like a middle or passive sense. Sometimes these active perfects actually parallel middle or passive present tenses, e.g.

γίγνομαι 'I become, come to be, come into existence'

γέγονα 'I am – by birth'

τί γέγονεν; 'What has happened?'

ἁλίσκομαι 'I get captured, I get convicted'
ἑάλωκα 'I have been captured/convicted'
Note also:
    κατέαγε 'it is broken' (κατάγνυ-μι)
    πέπηγε 'it is fixed' (πήγνυ-μι)

◯ Language Survey (9): the negatives οὐ and μή

Greek has two negative particles, οὐ and μή. They are both normally translatable as 'not', and the main difference between them is simply the contexts in which they are used. These may be summarised as follows, but note the qualifications and further points at the end of the summary:

    with the *indicative*, οὐ is used (except after εἰ, ἵνα)
    with the *imperative*, μή is always used
    with the *subjunctive*, μή is generally used
    with the *optative expressing a wish*, μή is always used
    with all forms of *potential*, οὐ is always used
    with all forms of the *infinitive*, μή is generally used.

Notes
    (i) In accordance with the above, in conditional sentences μή is used in the 'if' clause, and οὐ with the statement based on it. e.g.
        ἐὰν μὴ εἰσέλθῃ, οὐ λήψεται τὸ ἀργύριον*'if he doesn't come, he won't get the money'*
    (ii) The infinitive is usually negatived by μή, except mainly in indirect speech, where the negative is the one used in the direct *context.*
    (iii) A participle (and this is one of the few cases where the distinction between the two negatives matters for the understanding of the text), may be negated by either οὐ or μή. The difference here is that the use of μή gives the participle a conditional *flavour, so that the sentence above could have an alternative form, i.e.*
        οὐ λήψεται τὸ ἀργύριον μὴ εἰσελθών *'he won't get the money unless he comes'*
It is thus necessary to distinguish between, e.g.
    τί δράσω, τοῦ πατρὸς οὐκ εὖ φρονοῦντος (=ἐπεὶ οὐκ εὖ φρονεῖ) 'What shall I do, seeing that my father is not in his right mind?'
    τί δράσω τοῦ πατρὸς μὴ εὖ φρονοῦντος (=ἐὰν μὴ εὖ φρονῇ) 'What shall I do if my father is not in his right mind?'

(iv) Where the same negative is repeated in a clause, the negatives either reinforce each other or cancel one another (see 38).

But combinations of different negatives (οὐ μή or μὴ οὐ) have special meanings:

(a) μὴ οὐ with an infinitive means the same as μή alone, e.g.

οὐ μισοῦμεν τὰς 'Αθήνας μὴ οὐ μεγάλας εἶναι *'We do not hate Athens (wishing) that it should not be great'*

(b) μὴ οὐ with verbs of fearing:

φοβοῦμαι μὴ νικήσῃ *'I fear he may win'*

φοβοῦμαι μὴ οὐ νικήσῃ *'I fear he may not win'*

(c) οὐ μή with future indicative expresses a strong prohibition, *e.g.*

οὐ μὴ φλυαρήσεις *'Do stop talking nonsense!'*

(d) οὐ μή with subjunctive expresses a strong denial, *e.g.*

οὐ μή ποτε ἁλῶ *'I shall certainly never be caught'*

Observe that (c) and (d) are easily confused; but remember that in the second person (which is by far the most frequent), the meaning is always prohibitory *(i.e. 'don't . . .', 'do stop . . .' as in (c)).*

○ Language Survey (10): morphology of the cases

At first sight the Greek declensions give the impression of a bewildering variety of forms. In order to recognise the cases it is useful to concentrate on the similarities and to notice that some of the differences are due to later changes (contractions etc.).

Nom. and acc. s.

In all declensions the nom. s. of m. and f. nouns and adjectives either ended in -ς (ναύτης, νεανίας, ἄνθρωπος, πόλις, πρέσβυς, ὀφρῦς, βασιλεύς) or was equal to the stem, though mostly the last vowel was lengthened (βοή, λιμήν, πατήρ). Accented words ending in consonants, end only in -ς, -ν, -ρ so that if any other consonant occurred in final position this was dropped; that is why we have nom. like λέων vs. the gen. λέοντ-ος or ὤν vs. the gen. ὄντ-ος.

In type 1 the nom. s. f. ends in -ā, -ă or -η; normally -ā appears after -ε-, -ι-, -ρ- (κόρη is an exception).

The acc. s. m. and f. ends in -ν in types 1 and 2 (the preceding vowel is the same as in the nom.). In type 3 the ending tends to be -ν after vowel, as in πόλιν, and -α after consonant, as in λιμένα. Forms like τριήρη and βασιλέα are due to contraction (-εα→-η) or to a switching round of the quantity of the vowels, the so-called quantitative metathesis (-ηα→-εā).

In type 2 the nom./acc. n. ends in -ον like the acc. m./f.; in type 3 it has no
ending of its own and is like the stem (allowing for the dropping of final
consonants different from -ς, -ν, -ρ), cf. πρᾶγμα, gen. πράγματος. Notice that
words like πλῆθος, ἀμελές do not break the rule by introducing an -ς ending:
the -ς is part of the stem.

Gen. s.

The gen. s. ends in -ου in type 2 and in the m. of type 1; the other nouns
of type 1 add -ς to the final vowel of the stem *(-ᾱ- or -η-, never -ᾰ-)*. Type 3 has
an -ος ending. The terminations -ους and -εως of e.g. τριήρους, πλήθους and
πόλεως, βασίλεως are due to contraction *(-εος→-ους)* or to quantitative
metathesis *(-ηος→-εως)*. The accent of πόλεως is comprehensible if one thinks
of the older form πόληος.

Dat. s.

The dat. s. always ends in -ι, which follows a long vowel in types 1 and
2 and is written subscript *(βοῇ, ἀνθρώπῳ)*. Notice that in πλήθει, τριήρει, πόλει,
βασιλεῖ etc. the -ε- is part of the stem (observe the contraction and metathesis in
the gen.).

Nom. and acc. pl.

In the plural the nom. of the m. and f. ended in -αι or -οι in types 1 and
2 and in -ες in type 3. -ες sometimes contracted with a preceding vowel of the
stem to yield -ης or -εις *(βασιλῆς but πόλεις, τριήρεις)*.

The acc. pl. (m. and f.) always ends in -ς; the endings are -ᾱς and -ους in types
1 and 2; in type 3 normally an acc. s. in -α calls for an acc. pl. in -ας. Other types
are either equal to the nom. *(πόλεις)* or have forms closely related to the acc. s.
(ὀφρῦς vs. ὀφρῦν, βασιλέᾱς vs. βασιλέᾱ).

The nom.–acc. n. pl. ended in -α in all types. In forms like πλήθη and ἄστη (3c
and 3f) -η derives from a contraction of -εα.

Gen. pl.

The gen. pl. of all types ended in -ων; in type 1 this ending always
carries a circumflex accent because it is contracted from -άων.

Dat. pl.

For the dat. pl. we have endings in -αις and -οις in types 1 and 2 and in
-σι in type 3; some -σι datives alter the shape of their stem mainly in order to
avoid consonantal groups not admitted in Greek (e.g. οὖσι where we expect
*ont-si).

Voc.

The pl. vocative is always identical to the nominative; in the s. the vocative is either identical to the nom. (in all neuters, the f. of type 1 and in most nouns of type 3) or appears in a form which is identical to the stem (i.e. without the -ς- of the nom. in the m. and f.) though the final vowel may change (cf. ναύτᾱ, ἄνθρωπε, τριῆρες, πάτερ, βασιλεῦ etc.).

Dual forms

The dual is not found very frequently but unlike the other dialects Attic preserved it up to Hellenistic times. It has only two forms for each noun-type, one for the nom./acc./voc. and one for the gen./dat. In type 1 these end in -α and -αιν (nom./voc./acc. βοά, ναύτᾱ, gen./dat. βοαῖν, ναύταιν), in type 2 in -ω and -οιν both for m., f. and n., and in type 3 in -ε and -οιν again in all genders. Normally the -ε- of the nom./voc./acc. contracts with a preceding vowel; hence forms like nom./voc./acc. dual τριήρει, πόλει etc.

Language Survey (11): use of the cases

Greek has five cases: nominative, vocative, accusative, genitive and dative. The last three may – though they need not – occur in close association with a preposition but the first two cannot.

Vocative case

The vocative may be treated separately from the other cases; its position is peculiar in that (a) often it is not morphologically distinguished from the nominative, and (b) need not occur in a sentence but can be used on its own in exclamations or when addressing a person or thing *(ὦ Ζεῦ, ὦ Δικαιόπολι)*. Even when it occurs in a sentence its link with it is tenuous; it could be removed without making the sentence ungrammatical. In Attic it is normally used after the particle ὦ; if ὦ is absent this denotes strong emotion or a desire to keep the person addressed at a distance.

Nominative case

As in Latin, the nom. indicates the subject of a sentence; syntactically this is defined by the fact that the verb agrees with it in number (an exception is the nom. pl. n. which can take a s. verb): cf. 8. The nom. is also the case of all nouns, adjectives, articles etc. which agree with the subject, either as appositions or as attributes or complements. Finally, Greek may use the nom. as the citation case or as a title or heading: cf. the numerous inscriptions which start with the phrase τύχη ἀγαθή.

Accusative case

The acc. is the case which most closely defines and specifies the meaning of the verb. It indicates the 'object' of the sentence and in English it corresponds to the noun which immediately follows the verb (without any intermediate preposition). Notice, however, that if we had to translate into Greek a sentence like 'He gave John the toy', we would use the acc. for 'toy' but not for 'John', which would go in the dative (the sentence is equivalent to 'He gave the toy to John' but not to *'He gave John to the toy'). On the other hand Greek has some verbs which take a double accusative; αἰτέω 'I ask', κρύπτω 'I conceal', διδάσκω 'I teach' etc.; cf. δίδασκέ με τὸν σὸν λόγον 'teach me your argument'. In other instances, when we find a verb joined to two independent accusatives one of the two has predicative value: ἑαυτὸν δεσπότην πεποίηκεν 'he made himself master'.

The link with the verb is less close when the acc. is used (with transitive, intransitive or even passive verbs) to indicate extent of space or time or in adverbial function: ἀπέχει ... σταδίους ἑβδομήκοντα 'it is seventy stades distant'; ἐβασίλευσε πεντήκοντα ἔτεα 'he was king for fifty years'. It is often difficult to draw a line between these uses and those of the so-called acc. of respect: πόδας ὠκὺς ᾿Αχιλλεύς 'swift-footed Achilles', δεινοὶ μάχην 'terrible in battle' etc. Some accusatives used in adverbial function often became fossilised: cf. ἀρχήν 'initially', πρόφασιν 'under the pretext of', χάριν 'for the sake of, on behalf of, on account of'; cf. also τρόπον τινά 'in some way' etc.

The acc. can also indicate movements towards or direction; in prose this usage calls for a preposition (εἰς, ἐπί, πρός etc.) or for a construction where the acc. is followed by the particle -δε (᾿Αθήναζε = ᾿Αθήνας + δε).

[For the so-called acc. absolute, see **184**.]

Genitive case

Some uses of the gen. have been listed in **92**. It is customary to distinguish first the so-called adnominal gen. which is used in close connection with a noun, just as phrases introduced by 'of' are in English; its meaning varies according to the meaning of the nouns in question, so that it can indicate possession, origin, part etc. (cf. **26** for the relative order of the gen. and the noun on which it depends).

We often find the gen. in close connection with the verb in the grammatical slot normally reserved for the acc. With verbs which mean 'to eat', 'to take' etc.

324 C. Language Surveys

the gen. indicates that a part only of what the noun refers to is taken, eaten etc.: cf. τῆς γῆς ἔτεμον 'they ravaged (part of) the land' vs. τὴν γῆν πᾶσαν ἔτεμον 'they ravaged all the land' and compare the similar use of 'de', 'du' etc. in French ('j'ai mangé du pain'). In this partitive function we expect the gen. to alternate with all cases and not only with the acc.; this does in fact happen but less frequently in Attic than in e.g. Homer.

The gen. comes to be regularly associated with some verbs; in most instances this may be explained by its partitive function but we must also make allowance for the fact that the gen. can indicate origin, cause, movement from etc. (this is because it continues both an ancient gen. and an ancient ablative case which had these functions).

Some of the most frequent verbs which take the gen. belong to the following meaning-types:

to touch, to come in contact or to fail to do so; cf. ἅπτομαι, ἔχομαι, ἁμαρτάνω etc.

to share, to participate; cf. μέτεστι, μετέχω, κοινωνέω etc.

to aim at, to desire; cf. ἐπιθυμέω, ἐράω etc.

to reach, to obtain, cf. ἐφικνέομαι, τυγχάνω etc.

to start, to begin; cf. ἄρχω, ἄρχομαι etc.

to remember, to care for, to forget, to despise; cf. μιμνήσκω, φροντίζω, μέλει, ἀμελέω, καταφρονέω etc.

to admire, to be amazed at, to envy, to reproach, to be angry; cf. θαυμάζω, ζηλόομαι, ὀργίζομαι, ὀνειδίζω etc.

to hear, to perceive, to come to know; cf. ἀκούω, αἰσθάνομαι, πυνθάνομαι etc.

to order, to dominate; cf. ἄρχω, κρατέομαι etc.

to need, to lack; cf. ἀπορέω, στερίσκω, δέω, δέομαι etc.

Notice that the adjectives which have these or similar meanings also can take the gen.

Like the acc., the gen. can be used to indicate time or place (less frequently) normally with a partitive nuance; cf. ἡμέρας 'by day', νυκτός 'by night' and see 104 for the difference in meaning between dat., acc. and gen. in these constructions.

In more specialised contexts the gen. indicates price or value (especially with verbs which mean 'to buy', 'to sell' etc.), crime and penalty (with verbs which mean 'to convict', 'to punish', 'to bring to trial etc.): cf. πόσου; 'how much?', ἐργάζεσθαι μισθοῦ 'to work for pay' etc.; ἀσεβείας γράφειν 'to prosecute for impiety', ἀσεβείας φεύγειν 'to be tried for impiety'.

The gen. is regularly construed with comparatives and superlatives: cf. μέλιτος γλυκίων 'sweeter than honey', σοφώτατος ἀνθρώπων 'wisest among men'.

After prepositions the gen. is used in a number of functions, but whenever separation, or movement from, is indicated the preposition takes the gen. (cf. ἐκ, ἀπό etc.).

Finally we should notice the use of the gen. in the so-called genitive absolute constructions: see **139**.

Dative case

The dative case may indicate the indirect object of a verb, where English would normally have a phrase introduced by 'to' or 'for' (cf. **104**): ταῦτα δίδωσιν αὐτοῖς 'he gives these things to them', λέγει ταῦτα αὐτοῖς 'he says these things to them'. Words which refer to things or persons or abstractions are put in the dative to indicate that something is done to their advantage or disadvantage: ἥδε ἡ ἡμέρα τοῖς Ἕλλησι μεγάλων κακῶν ἄρξει 'this day will be the start of great sorrows for the Greeks'. Related to this usage is that of the possessive dative with the verb 'to be' or related verbs: ταῦτά μοί ἐστι/γίγνεται/ὑπάρχει 'I have these things'. Notice also the idioms τί ταῦτ' ἐμοί; τί ἐμοὶ καὶ σοί; literally 'what (are) these things to me?', 'what (is) there to me and you?', i.e. 'what have I to do with . . .?'

Since the Greek dative continues an ancient dative but also two other cases which have merged with it, the instrumental and the locative, we may expect to find traces of the functions of these two cases in its usage. In fact, the dat. may be used (as the ancient instrumental) to indicate the manner in which something is done, or means or tools used: ταῖς μαχαίραις κόπτοντες 'smiting them with swords' etc. To indicate accompaniment or association prose normally uses a preposition (σύν) with the dat. but a survival of the ancient usage is found in the constructions of αὐτός with the dat.: τῶν νεῶν μία αὐτοῖς ἀνδράσιν 'one of the ships with its men'.

In poetry the dative without a preposition was used (with its earlier locative value) to indicate place *at which* or time *when;* in prose this usage survives in a limited number of instances (it is more frequent with place names and time expressions), but the normal construction calls for ἐν and the dative: cf. Σαλαμῖνι 'in Salamis' but ἐν Σπάρτῃ 'in Sparta'; τριτῷ μηνί 'in the third month' but ἐν τῷ χειμῶνι 'in the winter'.

Some verbs are regularly construed with the dative where English would have a non-prepositional phrase in equivalent sentences. The most frequent meanings are:

to help, to please, to displease, to blame, to envy: cf. βοηθέω, ἀρέσκω, εὐνοέω, ὀργίζω, φθονέω etc.

to obey, to serve, to trust, to advise: cf. πείθομαι, δουλεύω, πιστεύω, αἰνέω etc.

to meet: cf. ἀπαντάω, περιτυγχάνω etc.
to follow, to accompany: cf. ἕπομαι, ἀκουλουθέω etc.

Addenda. In passive constructions the 'agent' is normally indicated by ὑπό with a genitive if the word refers to a person, or by a simple dative if it refers to a 'thing'; cf. the examples given in 138 πείθεται ὑπὸ ἐμοῦ 'he is being persuaded by me', ἐβαλλόμην τοῖς λίθοις 'I was being pelted by/with stones'. However, sometimes the simple dative can indicate the personal agent, especially when the passive verb is perfect or pluperfect and is used impersonally: ἐμοὶ πέπρακται 'it has been done by me'.

Language Survey (12): use of the definite article

General features

Greek has only one article, ὁ ἡ τό 'the'. When English uses 'a' Greek either has the simple noun without an article or (less often) makes use of the indefinite pronoun τις 'a, a certain, some'.

There is a certain amount of agreement in the Greek and English use of the definite article but the overlap is by no means complete. Here are some of the main differences:

(a) Greek can (but need not) use the article with personal names and place names: ὁ Σόλων 'Solon', ἡ Ἀσία 'Asia'.

(b) Greek can use the article with abstract nouns: ἡ ἀρετή 'courage', ἡ χάρις 'grace'.

(c) In general statements Greek may use the article where English would omit it: ὁ ἄνθρωπος 'man' (i.e. the class of all men).

(d) Greek uses the article before possessive adjectives: ὁ ἐμὸς υἱός 'my son'.

(e) Greek does not use the articles with nouns used as predicates: νύξ ἡ ἡμέρα ἐγένετο 'the day became night' (νύξ could not have the article).

The article as noun

One of the main features of classical Greek is that the article can be used with almost any part of speech (adjectives, adverbs, participles, infinitives, whole phrases) to form noun phrases: ὁ σοφός 'the wise man', ὁ λέγων 'the man who is speaking', τὸ θανεῖν 'the fact of dying, death'. In this way Greek introduces the aspectual distinctions of verbs into nominal constructions and can distinguish for instance between ὁ θάνατος 'death' and τὸ θνῄσκειν or τὸ θανεῖν. An article may also be followed by an adverb, or a genitival or prepositional phrase: cf. οἱ ἐκεῖ 'the men there', οἱ περὶ Ἡράκλειτον 'those round Herakleitos' (i.e. 'Herakleitos and his school'), τὰ τῶν Ἀθηναίων, lit. 'the things of the Athenians' (the meaning of τὰ is determined by the context), τὰ ἐν Λακεδαίμονι 'the things/events in Sparta'. The article also allows a noun to be determined by an adverb: ὁ ὀρθῶς κυβερνήτης 'he who is really a pilot, a real pilot'.

Finally the neuter article may introduce phrases which though not nominal in origin are treated as such: τὸ λίαν ἧσσον ἐπαινῶ τοῦ μηδὲν ἄγαν 'I approve the "too much" less than the "nothing in excess" ', i.e. 'I approve of excess less than of moderation'; θαυμαστὸν δέ μοι φαίνεται καὶ τὸ πεισθῆναί τινας 'I also find it amazing that some people may have been convinced.' This use of the article allowed an immense stylistic and semantic flexibility which Greek literature and philosophy exploited in full.

The position of the article

Normally the article precedes the noun but notice that in a simple phrase of article, adjective, noun the article can take various positions even though the meaning does not change substantially: ὁ σοφὸς ἀνήρ, ὁ ἀνὴρ ὁ σοφός, ἀνὴρ ὁ σοφός (rare) all mean 'the wise man' (cf. 60). However in the phrases σοφὸς ὁ ἀνήρ and ὁ ἀνὴρ σοφός, σοφός is used as a predicate and the meaning is 'the man is wise'.

Some adjectives (often of pronominal origin) – οὗτος, ὅδε, ἐκεῖνος, πᾶς – take the predicative position: οὗτος ὁ ἀνήρ, ὁ ἀνὴρ οὗτος 'this man'. Notice, on the other hand, the contrast between ὁ αὐτὸς ἀνήρ 'the same man' and ὁ ἀνὴρ αὐτός, αὐτὸς ὁ ἀνήρ 'the man himself'.

Demonstrative uses

Attic preserves only a few traces of the original demonstrative value of the article: cf. ὁ μὲν . . . ὁ δέ 'the one . . . the other' and also the expressions καὶ ὅς, ἦ δ' ὅς 'and he . . .', 'he said' (notice that in these phrases the nom. is ὅς and not ὁ though the form must not be confused with that of the relative pronoun).

O Language Survey (13): vocabulary building

The following list of prefixes and suffixes attached to nouns, adjectives, adverbs and verbs will help you to determine the meaning of roots or stems which you recognise but the shape of which may be slightly unfamiliar. Following this list of prefixes and suffixes a table of useful common roots/stems is given.

(i) Formation of nouns

The following suffixes will be frequently met:

(a) to denote *actions:*

-σις *f. (3e)* παίδευσις 'training' *(παιδεύω)*

-σια *f. (1b)* ἐργασία 'work' *(ἐργάτης)*

-μός *m. (2a)* διωγμός 'pursuit' *(διώκω)*

(b) to denote the *result of an action:*

-μα *(-ματος) n. (3b)* πρᾶγμα 'thing (done)' *(πράττω)*

(c) to denote *the agent:*

-τήρ *m. (3a)* σωτήρ 'saviour' *(σῴζω)*

-τωρ *m. (3a)* ῥήτωρ 'orator' (cf. ἐρῶ)

-τής *m. (1d)* ποιητής 'maker, poet' *(ποιέω)*

(d) to denote *means or instrument:*

-τρον *n. (2b)* ἄροτρον 'plough' *(ἀρόω)*

(e) to denote *profession or class of a person:*

-εύς *m. (3h)* ἱερεύς 'priest' *(ἱερός)*

-της *m. (1d)* πολίτης 'citizen' *(πόλις)*

(f) to denote *quality:*

-της *(-τητος) f. (3a)* ἰσότης 'equality' *(ἴσος)*

-σύνη *f. (1a)* σωφροσύνη 'moderation' *(σώφρων)*

-ία *f. (1b)* σοφία 'wisdom' *(σοφός)*

(g) to denote *place where an activity occurs:*

-τήριον *n. (2b)* δικαστήριον 'law-court' *(δικάζω)*

-εῖον *n. (2b)* κουρεῖον 'barber's shop' *(κουρεύς)*

(h) to denote a *small example* (familiar or contemptuous):

-ιον *n. (2b)* παιδίον 'child' *(παῖς)*

-ίδιον *n. (2b)* οἰκίδιον 'small house' *(οἶκος)*

-ίσκος *m. (2a)* νεανίσκος 'youth' *(νεανίας)*

-ίσκη *f. (1a)* παιδίσκη 'young girl' *(παῖς)*

(i) to denote 'son of' (often used as a person name, cf. English names in '–son')

-άδης *m. (1d)* Βορεάδης 'son of Boreas' *(Βορέας)*

-ίδης *m. (1d)* Πριαμίδης 'son of Priam' *(Πρίαμος)*

(j) to denote the *feminine form:*

-ις *(-ιδος) f. (3a)* νεᾶνις 'young girl' *(νεανίας)*

(ii) Formation of adjectives

Adjectives are formed either by derivation (i.e. the addition of suffixes), or by composition (in which two elements are compounded, or juxta-posed) and the meaning is deduced from the sense of the two elements. These elements may come from nouns or verbs or prepositions. If the first element is a *noun* or *adjective*, it has either the bare stem (e.g. εὐρύ-πορος, from εὐρύς 'broad'), or a vowel -ο- inserted (e.g. ψυχ-ο-πομπός 'escorting souls' from ψυχ-ή). If the first element is a *verb*, the form sometimes ends in -ε or -σι, e.g.

> φερέ-νικος 'bringing victory'
>
> ἑλκεσί-πεπλος 'trailing robes'

The prepositions are very commonly used in compounds and sometimes have special meanings (see below under 'Formation of verbs').

Note especially:

(i) the frequent adjective formation with εὐ- 'good'

> εὐδαίμων 'having good deities, happy'

(ii) the prefix ἀ- or ἀν- which carries a negative force, e.g.

> ἄγαμος 'unmarried'
>
> ἀνώνυμος 'unnamed'

But beware of the small number of words where ἀ- means 'together with', e.g.

> ἄλοχος 'wife' (lit. 'bedfellow').

Some of the more common adjectival suffixes are listed here:

(a) to denote a *general relationship:*

> -ιος: πολέμιος 'enemy' *(πόλεμος)*
>
> -ικός, φυσικός 'natural' *(φύσις)*

(b) to denote *material:*

> -ινος: λίθινος 'of stone' *(λίθος)*
>
> -εος: -ους: χρυσοῦς 'golden' *(χρυσός)*

(c) to denote *inclination, or tendency:*

> -μων: μνήμων 'mindful' (cf. μέ-μνη-μαι)

(d) to denote *aptitude:*

> -ιμος: χρήσιμος 'useful' *(χράομαι)*

(e) to denote *passive force* or *capability:*

> -τος: σχιστός 'divided' *(σχίζω)*
>
> ὁρατός 'visible' *(ὁράω)*

(f) to denote *obligation:*

> -τεος: τιμητέος 'that is to be honoured' *(τιμάω)*

(iii) Formation of adverbs

Most adjectives form adverbs by adding -ως e.g. κακός – κακῶς, ἀληθής – ἀληθῶς. Those in -υς add -εως, e.g. ἡδύς – ἡδέως. The neuter accusative may be used adverbially as well, e.g.

πολύ 'much'
μεγάλα 'greatly'
μόνον 'alone'
There are also many adverbs that do not fall into a regular pattern, e.g.
τάχα 'quickly'
εὐθύς 'at once'
παντάπασι 'in every respect'
Special types are:
-δόν, -αδόν, -ηδόν   κυνηδόν 'like a dog'
                      ὁμοθυμαδόν 'unanimously'
-δήν, -αδήν   κρυβδήν 'secretly' (cf. κρύπτω 'hide')

(iv) Formation of verbs

Verbs are formed from nouns (or adjectives) by such suffixes as these:

-άω	τιμάω	'honour'	(τιμή)
-έω	πονέω	'work'	(πόνος)
-όω	δουλόω	'enslave'	(δοῦλος)
-εύω	βασιλεύω	'reign'	(βασιλεύς)
-ζω	ἀγοράζω	'buy'	(ἀγορά)
-ίζω	πλουτίζω	'enrich'	(πλοῦτος)
-ύνω	ἡδύνω	'sweeten'	(ἡδύς)

To denote a wish:

-ιάω	στρατηγιάω	'to want to be a general'	(στρατηγός)
-σείω	γελασείω	'to want to laugh'	(γελάω)

Verbs are frequently compounded with prepositions, the sense of which is sometimes subtle and difficult to render. Apart from their normal senses, note the following *special* senses of prepositions as compounded to form both verbs and adjectives:

ἀνα-	withdrawal	ἀναχωρέω	'retreat'
	repetition	ἀναβιόω	'come to life again'
ἀντι-	exchange	ἀντιδίδωμι	'give in return'
	equality	ἀντίθεος	'god-like'
	against	ἀντίδικος	'opponent at law'
ἀπο-	return	ἀποδίδωμι	'give back'
	completion	ἀπεργάζομαι	'finish off'
	for the defendant	ἀπολογέομαι	'defend oneself'
δια-	separation	διαλύω	'break up'
	disagreement	διαφωνέω	'disagree'
	succession	διαδέχομαι	'take the place of'
	completion	διαπράττω	'accomplish'

ἐπι-	opposition	ἐπιστρατεύω	'march against'
	addition	ἐπιμανθάνω	'learn besides'
	superiority	ἐπιβιόω	'survive'
κατα-	thoroughness	καταμανθάνω	'learn thoroughly'
	to destruction	καταλύω	'destroy utterly'
μετα-	change	μεταγιγνώσκω	'change one's mind, repent'
	share	μέτεστι	'share in'
παρα-	deviation	παραβαίνω	'overstep, transgress'
περι-	intensity	περικαλλής	'very beautiful'
προ-	abandonment	προδίδωμι	'betray'
	anteriority	προοράω	'foresee'
ὑπερ-	excess	ὑπερβάλλω	'overshoot, exceed'
ὑπο-	subjection	ὑπήκοος	'subject'
	moderation	ὑπόλευκος	'whitish'
	stealth	ὑποσπάω	'withdraw secretly'

(v) Changes in root syllables

You will have noticed that the root syllables of Greek words are sometimes modified, especially in their vowels. This is familiar in English, where we have such patterns as 'sing', 'sung', 'sang' or 'foot', 'feet'. The details in Greek are very complicated, but it is worth noting the pattern which replaces -ε- by -o- or by zero. i.e. this vowel disappears completely. However, the zero vowel is in some contexts, especially where λ, μ, ν, or ρ are involved, replaced by α. The following table gives a few examples:

ε	o	zero
πέτομαι 'fly'	ποτάομαι 'hover'	πτερόν 'wing'
λείπω 'leave'	λέλοιπα (perf.)	ἔλιπον (aor.)
φεύγω 'run away'		ἔφυγον (aor.) φυγή 'flight'
φέρω 'bring'	-φορος '-bringing'	
πατέρα (acc.) 'father'		πατρός (gen.) πατράσι (dat. pl.)
βέλος 'missile'	βόλος 'cast'	βάλλω 'throw'
τέμνω 'cut'	τόμος 'slice'	ἔταμον (aor.)
πένθος 'grief'	πέπονθα 'suffer' (perf.)	ἔπαθον (aor.)
θείνω 'kill'	φόνος 'murder'	ἔπεφνον (aor.)

The last example shows another strange feature, the replacement of θ by φ. Similarly we find τ replaced by π, e.g.

τίς 'who?' | ποῦ 'where?'
τίνω 'pay' | ποινή 'penalty'
πέντε 'five' | πέμπτος 'fifth'

(vi) Latin transcriptions

The Greek words that have been borrowed into English have normally come by way of Latin; only a few (e.g. 'kudos') are taken directly from the Greek form. Similarly, the proper names of Greek are frequently given a Latin form in English, which is occasionally different from the Greek (e.g. Achilles for Ἀχιλλεύς), but usually follows a regular rule of transcription. Most equivalents are obvious, but note the following:

θ = th

ϕ = ph

χ = ch

κ = c

v = y

ov = u

Thus, for example, Θουκυδίδης appears as 'Thucydides'.

Vowel-length is not shown and the corresponding English vowels are often different. Thus Ὅμηρος becomes 'Hŏmērus', English 'Hōmer'. Cf. also Σόλων becomes English Sōlŏn. For transcriptions in this course, see p. 260.

(vii) Useful stems

Here is a list of useful stems from which many words can be guessed:

ἀγγελ-	announce, proclaim, report	ἀπολογ-	defend
ἀ-	(prefix) no, not	ἀπορ-	want; ignorance, doubt
ἀγορ-	gather, frequent; talk	ἀποστα-	revolt, part from, stand away
ἀγρ-	country, field; hunt, savage	ἁρπ-	seize, plunder
ἀγων-	contest, fight	ἀρχ-	rule; office; begin
αἰσθ-	feel, apprehend, notice	ἀσθεν-	weak, ill
αἰτι-	cause, accuse, blame	ἀστ-	city; clever
ἀκο(υ)-	hear	βα|βη-	go, walk, stand
ἁλ-	be captured	βαλ|βολ-	throw, strike
ἀληθ-	true	βαρ-	heavy, serious
ἁμαρτ-	miss, err, fail, do wrong	βια-	force, violence
		βιο-	life, livelihood
ἀναγκ-	compel, force, necessity	βοα|βοη-	shout, demand, roar
		βοηθ-	cry for help, help, assist
ἀνδρ-	man, manliness, bravery	βουλ(ε)(υ)-	plan, advise, resolve
ἀπατ-	deceive, trick	βουλ-	wish
ἀποκρι-	reply, answer; separate	γαμ-	marry

γεν-	become, be, be born	ἡγε-	lead; think
γνο|γνω-	perceive, be aware, decide	ἡδ-	sweet, pleasant, pleased
γραφ-	write, propose; lawsuit	ἡσυχ-	calm, rest, silence
		θαν-|θν-	die, death
γυναικ-	woman, female	θαυμ-	wonder, amazement
δεικ|δειξ-	show, reveal, demonstrate	θεα-	see, wonder
		θεραπ-	cure, look after, serve
δημ-	people, live, inhabit	θνητ-	mortal, death
διατριβ-	spend time, waste time	θυ-	sacrifice
διαφθερ-	destroy, corrupt	θυμ-	heart, anger, enthusiasm, courage, purpose, will
διδασκ|διδαξ-	teach		
δικ-	justice; law; penalty; court		
δο-	give	ἰατρ-	cure, medicine, doctor
δρα-	do, act	ἰδ-	see
δυνα-	be able, possible	ἱερ-	holy, sacred, priest, temple
δυσ-	bad, poor, evil		
εἰδ-	see; know; shape, figure	κακο-	evil, wicked, bad, corrupt
εἰκ-	reasonable; yield; twenty	κατηγορ-	accuse, charge, prove
		κελευ-	order
εἰπ-	say, speak	κηρυγ|κηρυξ-	announce, herald, proclaim
ἐλεγχ-	disprove, examine, test		
		κινδυν-	danger, risk
ἐλευθ-	free	κλεπ-|κλοπ-	steal
Ἑλλ-	Greece	κλη-	call, summon
ἐλπ-	hope	κοιν-	common, shared, united
ἐξεταζ-	question, search		
ἐοικ-	be like; be reasonable	κρατ-	power, sway, control
ἐπαιν-	praise	κριν|κρισ-	judge; reply; discern
ἐργ-	do, work	κτ-	kill; gain
ἑταιρ-	friend, companion	λαβ-	take
εὐ-	well, good	λαθ-	secret
εὑρ-	find, discover; broad	λεγ|λογ-	speak; words; reason
εὐχ-	pray	λιπ|λοιπ-	leave, abandon
ἐχθρ-	hostile, enemy	μαθ-	learn
ζα|ζω-	live	μαρτυ(ρ)-	witness, evidence
ζημ-	fine, penalise	μαχ-	fight
ζητ-	seek, search	μεγ(αλ)-	large, size

μελ-	care, concern	σιγ-	silence
μηχαν-	device, contrive	σκεπ|σκοπ-	see, review, consider
μνη(μ)-	remember, mention	σκευ-	prepare; gear, furniture
μισ-	hate		
ναυ-	ship, nautical	σοφ-	wise, intelligent
νικ-	conquer	σπενδ|σπονδ-	libation, pour
νο(ε)|νοι-	notice; plan; intend; mind	σπευδ|σπουδ-	hurry; enthusiasm; serious
νομ-	custom; law; think, be used to	στρατ-	army, march, camp
νοσ-	disease, illness	σω-	safe, sound
ξεν-	stranger; guest; alien	ταχ-	speed, hurry
οἰκ-	live, house, inhabit, serve	τεκμαιρ-	witness, evidence
		τελ(ευτ)-	end, finish, death
ὀλ-	destroy	τεχν-	art, skill, means, trade
ὀμ-	swear, take an oath	τιμ(α)-	honour; value; punish, penalty
ὁμο-	at one with		
ὀργ-	anger, passion	τιμωρ(ε)-	vengeance
ὀψ-	sight, vision	τρεφ|τροφ-	rear, nurture
παθ-	experience, suffering	τυχ-	chance, happen
παι(δ)|παιζ-	child; educate; play	ὑβρ-	violence
παν-	all, every	φασ|φαν-	appear, seem
πειθ-	persuade	φιλ-	love, respect
πειρ-	try, experience, test	φοβ-	fear
πεμπ|πομπ-	send	φρην|φρον(τ)-	mind; worry; thought
πεσ-	fall	φυγ-	flight
πιστ-	faithful, trust	φυλακ-	guard, protect
πλε(υ)|πλοι-	sail, voyage	φυ-	nature, naturally
ποιε|ποιη-	make, do	φων-	voice, speech
πολεμ-	war, enemy	χαρ-	please; charm; welcome
πραγ|πραξ-	act, do, accomplish	χρη-	use; useful; ought
πρεσβ-	old, embassy	χωρ-	go, place
πυθ-	learn, inquire	ψευδ-	false
σαφ-	clear	ψηφ-	vote, decree
σημ-	sign, show, signify	ψυχ-	soul, life

D. *A total vocabulary of all words to be learnt*

Finding the lexicon form of a verb

The essence is to isolate the present stem, since it is most often this form which will be shown in the lexicon.

(i) Look at the front of the word, and remove any augment, or reduplication.

η could be the augmented form of α, ε, η

η	,,	,,	αι, ει
ηυ	,,	,,	αυ, ευ
ω	,,	,,	ο
ῳ	,,	,,	οι
ῑ, ῡ	,,	,,	ι, υ
ει	,,	,,	ε, ει

Bear in mind that the augment might be hidden by a prefix such as κατά, ἐκ, πρό, εἰς, ἐν, so check the prefix as well.

προὔβαλον = προ-έ-βαλον
ἐξέβαλον = ἐκ-έ-βαλον
ἐνέβαλον from ἐμβάλλω

Here is a list of common prefixes, with their various forms:

ἀνά ἀν᾽	ἐν ἐμ- ἐγ-	παρά παρ᾽
ἀπό ἀπ᾽ ἀφ᾽	ἐπί ἐπ᾽ ἐφ᾽	πρό προε- πρου-
διά δι᾽	κατά κατ᾽ καθ᾽	σύν συμ- συγ-
ἐκ ἐξ	μετά μετ᾽ μεθ᾽	ὑπό ὑπ᾽ ὑφ᾽

(ii) Having made an adjustment for augment/reduplication and prefix, examine the stem and the ending. Remove any personal endings.

(iii) If the remaining stem ends in σ, ξ, ψ, especially if an α follows, it is probably an aorist. Try dropping the σα (e.g. ἔ-λυ-σα = λύω) or converting σ to ζ

(ἐ-νόμισ-α=νομίζω).   Try   restoring   a   terminal   ξ→κ   or   →ττ
(ἔ-πραξ-α=πράττω), and a terminal ψ to π *(ἔ-πεμψ-α=πέμπω)*.

If the stem ends in some form of θη, remember that χ may hide ττ or κ
(ἐπράχθην=πράττω), φ may hide π or β *(ἐπέμφθην=πέμπω)*.

(iv) If there is no augment, check the endings for some sign of σ *(ξ, ψ)* or
ε-contract in the stem, when it may be future. Check also endings for signs of
participle, infinitive, etc. and remember that the stem you so isolate may be
present or aorist or perfect or future (see Reference Grammar E.2).

(v) If you are still stumped, isolate the stem and look that up in the vocabulary
or the stem list (Language Survey (13) (vii)). Highly irregular stems have been
placed there for your peace of mind.

Total Vocabulary

† for Principal Parts see Reference Grammar E.4 (pp. 284ff.)

†† these forms only appear with the prefix as shown, but should still be looked up without the prefix in E.4.

* see appropriate sections of Reference Grammar or Language Survey.

A

ἀγαγ- aor. stem of ἄγω

ἀγαθός ή όν good; noble; courageous

ἄγαλμα (ἀγαλματ-), τό image, statue (3b)

†ἀγγέλλω (ἀγγειλ-) report, announce

ἄγγελος, ὁ messenger (2a)

ἄγε come! (s.)

ἄγομαι bring for oneself; lead; marry

ἀγορά, ἡ gathering (-place); market-place; agora (1b)

ἀγορεύω speak (in assembly); proclaim

ἄγρη, ἡ hunt (1a)

ἄγροικος ον from the country; boorish

ἀγρός, ὁ field; country (side) (2a)

†ἄγω (ἀγαγ-) lead, bring; live in, be at

εἰρήνην ἄγω live in/be at peace

ἀγών (ἀγων-), ὁ contest; trial (3a)

ἀγωνίζομαι contest, go to law

ἀδελφός, ὁ brother (2a)

ἀδικέω be unjust; commit a crime; wrong

ἀδίκημα (ἀδικηματ-), τό crime, wrong (3b)

ἄδικος ον unjust

ἀδύνατος ον impossible

†ἄδω = ἀείδω

ἀεί always

†ἀείδω sing

ἀέκων = ἄκων

ἀθάνατος ον immortal

Ἀθήναζε to Athens

Ἀθῆναι, αἱ Athens (1a)

Ἀθηναῖος, ὁ Athenian (2a)

Ἀθήνησι at Athens

ἄθλιος α ον pathetic, miserable, wretched

ἀθροίζω gather, collect

ἀθυμέω be downhearted, gloomy, disheartened

ἀθυμία, ἡ lack of spirit, depression (1b)

αἰδώς, ἡ respect for others, shame (acc. αἰδῶ; gen. αἰδοῦς; dat. αἰδοῖ)

αἰεί = ἀεί

αἱρέομαι (ἑλ-) choose

†αἱρέω (ἑλ-) take, capture; convict

†αἰσθάνομαι (αἰσθ-) perceive, notice (+acc. or gen.)

αἰσχρός ά όν ugly (of people); base, shameful (comp. αἰσχίων; sup. αἴσχιστος)

†αἰσχύνομαι be ashamed, feel shame (before)

αἰτέω ask (for)

αἰτία, ἡ reason, cause; responsibility (1b)

αἴτιος α ον responsible (for), guilty (of) (+gen.)

αἰχμή, ἡ spear-point (1a)

ἀκήκοα perf. ind. of ἀκούω

ἀκηκοώς υἷα ός (-οτ-) perf. part. of ἀκούω

ἀκοή, ἡ hearing (1a)

ἀκολουθέω follow, accompany (+dat.)

ἀκόσμητος ον unprovided for

†ἀκούω hear, listen (to) (+gen. of person, gen. or

acc. of thing) (fut.
ἀκούσομαι)
ἀκριβῶς accurately, closely
ἀκρόπολις, ἡ Acropolis,
citadel (3e)
ἄκυρος ον invalid
ἄκων ἄκουσα ἆκον
(ἀκοντ-) unwilling(ly)
ἁλ- aor. stem of ἁλίσκομαι
ἀλήθεια, ἡ truth (1b)
ἀληθῆ, τά the truth
†ἁλίσκομαι (ἁλ-) be
convicted; be caught
ἀλλ᾽ οὖν well anyway;
however that may be
ἀλλά but
ἀλλήλους each other, one
another (2a)
ἄλλος η ο other, the rest of
ἄλλος . . . ἄλλον one . . .
another
ἀλλότριος α ον someone else's;
alien
ἄλλως otherwise; in vain
ἄλογος ον speechless; without
reason
ἅμα at the same time
ἀμαθής ές ignorant
†ἁμαρτάνω (ἁμαρτ-) err; do
wrong; make a mistake;
miss (+gen.)
ἅμαρτε 3rd s. (str.) aor of
ἁμαρτάνω (no augment)
ἀμείβομαι answer, reply to
(+acc.)
ἀμείνων ἄμεινον (ἀμεινον-)
better
ἀμελής ές uncaring
ἀμήχανος ον impossible,
impracticable
†ἀμύνω keep off, withstand
ἀμφέρχομαι
(ἀμφηλυθ-) surround
(+acc.)
ἀμφίπολος, ἡ handmaiden (2a)
ἀμφότερος α ον both
•ἄν (+ind.) conditional
(+opt.) potential; (+subj.)
indefinite

ἀναβαίνω (ἀναβα-) go up,
come up
ἀναβάς (ἀναβαντ-) aor. part
of ἀναβαίνω
ἀναγκάζω force, compel
ἀναγκαῖος α ον necessary
ἀνάγκη, ἡ necessity (1a)
ἀνάγκη ἐστί it is obligatory
(for x (acc. or dat.)
to – (inf.))
ἀναιρέω (ἀνελ-) pick up
ἀναίτιος ον innocent
ἀναλαμβάνω (ἀναλαβ-) take
back, up
†ἀναλίσκω (ἀναλωσ-) spend,
use, kill
ἀναμένω (ἀναμειν-) wait,
hold on
ἄναξ (ἀνακτ-), ὁ lord, prince,
king (3a)
ἀναπείθω persuade over to
one's side
ἄνασσα, ἡ princess (1c)
ἀναχωρέω retreat
ἀνδρεῖος α ον brave, manly
ἄνεμος, ὁ wind (2a)
ἀνέστην I stood up (aor. of
ἀνίσταμαι)
ἀνέστηκα I am standing (perf.
of ἀνίσταμαι)
ἀνεστώς ὦσα ός
(ἀνεστωτ-) standing (perf.
part. of ἀνίσταμαι)
ἄνευ (+gen.) without
†ἀνέχομαι put up with
(+gen.)
ἀνήρ (ἀνδρ-), ὁ man (3a)
ἄνθρωπος, ὁ man, fellow (2a)
ἀνίσταμαι (ἀναστα-) get up,
stand up, emigrate
ἀνόητος ον foolish
ἀνομία, ἡ lawlessness (1b)
ἀντί (+gen.) instead of, for
ἀντίδικος, ὁ contestant in
lawsuit (2a)
ἄνω above
ἄξιος α ον worth, worthy of
(+gen.)

ἄοπλος ον unarmed
ἀπαγγέλλω
(ἀπαγγειλ-) announce,
report
ἀπαγορεύω (ἀπειπ-) forbid
ἀπάγω (ἀπαγαγ-) lead, take
away
ἄπαις (ἀπαιδ-) childless
ἀπαιτέω demand (x (acc.)
from y (acc.))
ἀπάνευθε(ν) afar off
ἅπας ἅπασα ἅπαν
(ἁπαντ-) all, the whole of
ἀπέβην aor. of ἀποβαίνω
ἀπέδωκα aor. of ἀποδίδωμι
ἀπέθανον aor. of ἀποθνῄσκω
ἄπειμι be absent
ἄπειρος ον inexperienced in
(+gen.)
ἀπελεύθερος, ὁ, ἡ freedman,
freedwoman (2a)
ἀπελθ- aor. stem of
ἀπέρχομαι
ἀπέρχομαι (ἀπελθ-) go
away, depart
ἀπέχομαι (ἀποσχ-) refrain,
keep away from (+gen.)
ἀπῆλθον aor. of ἀπέρχομαι
ἀπιέναι inf. of
ἀπέρχομαι/ἄπειμι
ἄπιθι imper. of
ἀπέρχομαι/ἄπειμι
ἀπικνέομαι=ἀφικνέομαι
ἀπιών οὖσα όν part. of
ἀπέρχομαι/ἄπειμι
ἀπό (+gen.) from, away
from
ἀποβαίνω (ἀποβα-) leave,
depart
ἀποβλέπω look steadfastly at
(and away from everything
else)
ἀποδίδωμι (ἀποδο-) give
back, return
ἀποδο- aor. stem of
ἀποδίδωμι
ἀποδραμ- aor. stem of
ἀποτρέχω

ἀποδώσειν fut. inf. of
   ἀποδίδωμι
ἀποθαν- aor. stem of
   ἀποθνῄσκω
†ἀποθνῄσκω (ἀποθαν-) die
ἀποκρίνομαι
   (ἀποκριν-) answer
ἀπόκρισις, ἡ reply, answer
   (3e)
ἀποκτείνω (ἀποκτειν-) kill
ἀπολαβ- aor. stem of
   ἀπολαμβάνω
ἀπολεσ- aor. stem of
   ἀπόλλυμι
†ἀπόλλυμι (ἀπολεσ-) kill,
   ruin, destroy; mid./pass. be
   killed (aor. ἀπωλόμην);
   perf. mid. I have been
   killed, I am done for
   (ἀπόλωλα)
ἀπολογέομαι make a speech
   in defence, defend oneself
ἀπολογία, ἡ speech in one's
   defence (1b)
ἀπολ- aor. stem of ἀπόλλυμαι
ἀπολύω acquit, release
ἀπόλωλα perf. of ἀπόλλυμαι
ἀποπέμπω send away,
   divorce
ἀπορέω have no resources, be
   at a loss
ἀπορία, ἡ lack of provisions,
   perplexity (1b)
ἀποτρέχω (ἀποδραμ-) run
   away, run off
ἀποφαίνω reveal, show
ἀποφέρω (ἀπενεγκ-) carry
   back
ἀποφεύγω (ἀποφυγ-) escape,
   run off
ἀποχωρέω go away, depart
ἀποψηφίζομαι vote against;
   reject; acquit (+gen.)
ἅπτομαι touch (+gen.)
†ἅπτω light, fasten, fix
ἀπώλεσα aor. of ἀπόλλυμι
*ἄρα then, consequently
   (marking an inference);

straightaway
*ἄρα ? (direct q.)
ἀργύριον, τό silver, money
   (2b)
†ἀρέσκω please (+dat.)
ἀρετή, ἡ courage, excellence,
   quality (1a)
ἄριστος η ον best, very good
†ἁρπάζω seize, plunder,
   snatch
ἄρτι just now, recently
ἀρχή, ἡ beginning; rule,
   office, position; board of
   magistrates (1a)
ἄρχομαι (mid.) begin
   (+gen./inf./part.); (pass.)
   be ruled over
†ἄρχω rule (+gen.); begin
   (+gen.)
ἄρχων (ἀρχοντ-), ὁ archon
   (3a)
ἀσέβεια, ἡ irreverence to the
   gods (1b)
ἀσεβέω (εἰς) commit
   sacrilege upon
ἀσεβής ἐς impious, unholy
ἀσθένεια, ἡ illness, weakness
   (1b)
ἀσθενέω be ill, fall ill
ἀσθενής ἐς weak, ill
ἀσπάζομαι greet, welcome
ἀστή, ἡ female citizen (1a)
ἀστός, ὁ male citizen (2a)
ἄστυ, τό city (3f)
ἀσφαλής ἐς safe, secure
ἀτάρ but
ἅτε since, seeing that (+part.)
ἀτιμάζω hold in dishonour,
   dishonour
ἀτιμία, ἡ loss of citizen rights
   (1b)
ἄτιμος ον deprived of citizen
   rights
αὖ again, moreover
αὐδάω speak, say
αὖθις again
αὐλή, ἡ courtyard (1a)
αὔριον tomorrow

αὐτάρ but, then
αὐτίκα at once
αὐτόν ἥν ὁ him, her, it, them
αὐτός ἥ ὁ self
ὁ αὐτός the same
ἀφαιρέομαι (ἀφελ-) take x
   (acc.) from Y (acc.), claim
ἀφειλόμην aor. of ἀφαιρέομαι
ἀφεῖναι aor. inf. of ἀφίημι
††ἀφέλκω (ἀφελκυσ-) drag
   off
ἀφελ- aor. stem of ἀφαιρέομαι
††ἀφίημι (ἀφε-) release, let
   go
†ἀφικνέομαι (ἀφικ-) arrive,
   come
ἀφικόμην aor. of ἀφικνέομαι
ἀφίσταμαι relinquish claim to
   (+gen.), revolt from
   (+gen.)

B

βαδίζω walk, go (fut.
   βαδιοῦμαι)
βαθύς εῖα ύ deep
†βαίνω (βα-) go, come, walk
†βάλλω (βαλ-) hit, throw
βάλλ' εἰς κόρακας go to
   hell!
βάρβαρος, ὁ barbarian,
   foreigner (2a)
βάρος, τό weight, burden (3c)
βαρύς εῖα ύ heavy, weighty
βαρέως φέρω take badly,
   find hard to bear
βασιλεύς, ὁ king, king archon
   (3g)
βασιλεύω be king, be king
   archon; be queen
βέβαιος (α) ον secure
βέλτιστος η ον best
βελτίων βέλτιον (βελτιον-)
   better
βιάζομαι use force
βίος, ὁ life; means, livelihood
   (2a)
βλέπω look (at)

βληθείς εἶσα ἐν
(βληθεντ-) aor. part. pass.
of βάλλω
βοάω shout (for)
βοή, ἡ shout (1a)
βοήθεια, ἡ help, rescue
operation (1b)
βοηθέω run to help (+dat.)
βουλεύομαι discuss, take
advice
βουλευτής, ὁ member of
council (1d)
βουλή, ἡ council (1a)
†βούλομαι wish, want
βραδέως slowly
βραχύς εῖα ύ short, brief
βροτός, ὁ mortal, man (2a)
βωμός, ὁ altar (2a)

Γ
'γαθέ=ἀγαθέ
γαῖα (1c)=γῆ, ἡ (1a)
†γαμέω (γημ-) marry
γάμος, ὁ marriage (2a)
*γάρ for
γὰρ δή really, I assure you
*γε at least (denotes some sort of
reservation)
γεγένημαι perf. of γίγνομαι
γεγενημένα, τά events,
occurrences (2b) (perf. part.
of γίγνομαι)
γέγονα perf. of γίγνομαι
(part. γεγονώς or γεγώς)
γείτων (γειτον-), ὁ neighbour
(3a)
†γελάω (γελασ-) laugh
γεν- aor. stem of γίγνομαι
γένεσις, ἡ birth (3e)
γενναῖος a ον noble, fine
γεννήτης, ὁ member of a genos
(1d)
γένος, τό genos; race, kind (3c)
γέρων (γεροντ-), ὁ old man
(3a)
γεῦμα (γευματ-), τό taste,
sample (3b)
γεύομαι taste

γεωργός, ὁ farmer (2a)
γῆ, ἡ land, earth (1a)
γημ- aor. stem of γαμέω
†*γίγνομαι (γεν-) become,
be born, happen, arise
†γιγνώσκω (γνο-) know,
think, resolve
γίνομαι=γίγνομαι
γλαυκῶπις (γλαυκωπιδ-), ἡ
grey-eyed
γλυκύς εῖα ύ sweet
γνήσιος α ον legitimate,
genuine
γνούς γνοῦσα γνόν
(γνοντ-) aor. part. of
γιγνώσκω
γνώμη, ἡ judgment, mind,
purpose, plan (1a)
*γοῦν at any rate
γοῦνα, τά knees (2b)
(sometimes γούνατα (3b))
γραῦς (γρα-), ἡ old woman
(3a; but acc. s. γραῦν; acc. pl.
γραῦς)
γραφή, ἡ indictment, charge,
case (1a)
γραφὴν γράφομαι indict x
(acc.) on charge of y (gen.)
γράφομαι indict, charge
†γράφ-ω propose (a decree);
write
γυνή (γυναικ-), ἡ woman,
wife (3a)

Δ
δαίμων (δαιμον-), ὁ god,
demon (3a)
†δάκνω (δακ-) bite, worry
δάκρυον, τό tear (2b)
δακρύω weep
*δέ and, but
δεήσει fut. of δεῖ
†δεῖ it is necessary for x (acc.)
to – (inf.)
†δείκνυμι (δειξ-) show
δεινός ή όν terrible, dire,
astonishing, clever; clever
at (+inf.)

δέκα ten
δέμνια, τά bed, bedding (2b)
δένδρον, τό tree (2b)
δεξιά, ἡ right hand (1b)
δεξιός ά όν right, clever
†δέομαι need, ask, beg
(+gen.)
δέον it being necessary
δέρμα (δερματ-), τό skin (3b)
δεσμός, ὁ bond (2a)
δέσποινα, ἡ mistress (1c)
δεσπότης, ὁ master (1d)
δεῦρο here, over here
†δέχομαι receive
*δή then, indeed
δῆλος η ον clear, obvious
δηλόω show, reveal
δημιουργικός ή όν technical,
of a workman
δημιουργός, ὁ craftsman,
workman, expert, (2a)
δῆμος, ὁ people; deme (2a)
δήπου of course, surely
*δῆτα then
*διά (+acc.) because of
(+gen.) through
διὰ τί; why?
διαβαίνω (διαβα-) cross
διαβάλλω (διαβαλ-) slander
διαβολή, ἡ slander (1a)
διάκειμαι be in x (adv.) state,
mood
διακρίνω (διακριν-) judge
between, decide
διακωλύω prevent
διαλέγομαι converse
διαλείπω (διαλιπ-) leave
διανοέομαι intend, plan
διάνοια, ἡ intention, plan (1b)
διαπράττομαι (διαπραξ-) do,
perform, act
διατίθημι (διαθε-) dispose,
put x (acc.) in y (adv.) state
διατριβή, ἡ delay, pastime,
discussion, way of life (1a)
διατρίβω pass time, waste
time
διαφέρω differ from (gen.);

make a difference; be
superior to (gen.)
διαφεύγω (διαφυγ-) get
away, flee
††διαφθείρω (διαφθειρ-)
corrupt; destroy; kill
διαφυγή, ἡ means of escape,
flight (1a)
διδάσκαλος, ὁ teacher (2a)
†διδάσκω teach
†δίδωμι (δο-) give, grant
δίκην δίδωμι be punished,
pay the penalty
διεξέρχομαι (διεξελθ-) go
through, relate (fut.
διέξειμι)
διέρχομαι (διελθ-) go
through, relate
διεφθάρμην plup. pass. of
διαφθείρω
διηγέομαι explain, relate, go
through
δικάζω be a juror; make a
judgment
δίκαιος α ον just
δικαιοσύνη, ἡ justice (1a)
δικανικός ή όν judicial
δικαστήριον, τό law-court
(2b)
δικαστής, ὁ juror, dikast (1d)
δίκη, ἡ lawsuit; justice;
penalty (1a)
δίκην δίδωμι be punished,
pay the penalty
δίκην λαμβάνω punish,
exact one's due from
(παρά + gen.)
διοικέω administer, run
δῖος α ον godlike
διότι because
διώκω pursue, prosecute
δο- aor. stem of δίδωμι
δοκεῖ it seems a good idea to x
(dat.) to do y (inf.); x (dat.)
decides to – (inf.)
δοκέω seem, consider (self) to
be
δόμοι, οἱ house, home (2a)

δόξα, ἡ reputation, opinion
(1c)
δοῦλος, ὁ slave (2a)
δούς δοῦσα δόν (δοντ-) aor.
part. of δίδωμι
δρᾶμα (δραματ-), τό play,
drama (3b)
δραχμή, ἡ drachma (coin)
(pay for two days' attendance
at ekklesia) (1a)
†δράω (δρασ-) do, act
†δύναμαι be able
δύναμις, ἡ power, ability,
faculty (3e)
δυνατός ή όν able, possible
δύο two
δυστυχής ές unlucky
δῶκαν 3rd pl. aor. of δίδωμι
δωρέω bestow, give as a gift
δῶρον, τό gift, bribe (2b)

E

ἐ- augment (remove this and try
again under stem of verb)
*ἐάν (+subj.) if (ever)
ἑαυτόν ήν ό himself/herself/
itself
†ἐάω allow
ἐγγράφω enrol, enlist,
register
ἐγγυάω engage, promise
ἐγγύς (+gen.) near, nearby
ἐγκλείω shut in, lock in
ἔγνων aor. of γιγνώσκω
ἐγώ I
ἔγωγε I at least, for my part
ἐδόθην aor. pass. of δίδωμι
ἔδομαι fut. of ἐσθίω
ἔδωκα aor. of δίδωμι
†ἐθέλω (ἐθελησ-) wish, want
ἔθεσαν 3rd pl. aor. of τίθημι
ἔθηκα aor. of τίθημι
ἔθος, τό manner, habit (3c)
*εἰ if
εἶ 2nd s. of εἰμί
εἰασ- aor. stem ἐάω
εἰδείην opt. of οἶδα
εἰδέναι inf. of οἶδα

εἶδον aor. of ὁράω
εἰδώς εἰδυῖα εἰδός
(εἰδοτ-) knowing (part. of
οἶδα)
εἶεν very well then!
*εἴθε (+opt.) I wish that!
would that! if only!
εἰκός probable, reasonable,
fair
εἴκοσι(ν) twenty
εἰκότως reasonably, rightly
εἴληφα perf. of λαμβάνω
εἱλόμην aor. of αἱρέομαι
εἱμαρμένος η ον allotted,
appointed
εἵματα, τά clothes (3b)
†*εἰμί be
†*εἶμι I shall go (inf. ἰέναι;
impf. ᾖα I went)
εἶναι to be (inf. of εἰμί)
εἰπ- aor. stem of λέγω
εἰπέ speak! tell me!
εἶπον aor. of λέγω
εἴρηκα I have said (perf. act.
of λέγω)
εἴρημαι I have been said (perf.
pass. of λέγω)
εἰρήνη, ἡ peace (1a)
εἰρήνην ἄγω live in, be at
peace
*εἰς (+acc.) to, into, onto
εἷς μία ἕν (ἑν-) one
εἰσαγγελία, ἡ impeachment
(1b)
εἰσαγγέλλω
(εἰσαγγειλ-) impeach
εἰσάγω (εἰσαγαγ-) introduce
εἰσεληλυθώς υἶα ός
(-οτ-) perf. part. of
εἰσέρχομαι
εἰσελθ- aor. stem of
εἰσέρχομαι
εἰσέρχομαι (εἰσελθ-) enter
εἰσήγαγον aor. of εἰσάγω
εἰσῄα impf. of
εἰσέρχομαι|εἰσειμι
εἰσῆλθον aor. of εἰσέρχομαι
εἰσιδ- aor. stem of εἰσοράω

εἰσιέναι inf. of
εἰσέρχομαι/εἴσειμι
εἰσιών οὖσα όν (-οντ-) part.
of εἰσέρχομαι/εἴσειμι
εἴσομαι fut. of οἶδα
εἰσοράω (εἰσιδ-) behold,
look at
εἰσπεσ- aor. stem of εἰσπίπτω
εἰσπίπτω (εἰσπεσ-) fall into,
on
εἰσφέρω (εἰσενεγκ-) bring,
carry in
εἶτα then, next
εἴτε . . . εἴτε whether . . . or
εἶχον impf. of ἔχω
ἐκ (+gen.) out of
ἕκαστος η ον each
ἑκάτερος a ον each (of two)
ἐκβαλ- aor. stem of ἐκβάλλω
ἐκβάλλω (ἐκβαλ-) throw
out, divorce; break down,
break open
ἐκβληθείς εἶσα ἐν (-εντ-) aor.
part. pass. of ἐκβάλλω
ἐκδέχομαι receive in turn
ἐκδίδωμι (ἐκδο-) give in
marriage
ἐκδο- aor. stem of ἐκδίδωμι
ἐκδύομαι undress
ἐκεῖ there
ἐκεῖνος η ο that, (s)he
ἐκεινοσί that there (pointing)
ἐκεῖσε there, (to) there
ἐκκλησία, ἡ assembly,
ekklesia (1b)
ἐκπέμπω send out, divorce
ἐκπεσ- aor. stem of ἐκπίπτω
ἐκπίπτω (ἐκπεσ-) be thrown
out, divorced
ἐκπορίζω supply, provide
††ἐκτίνω (ἐκτεισ-) pay
ἐκτρέχω (ἐκδραμ-) run out
ἐκφέρω (ἐκενεγκ-) carry out;
(often: carry out for burial)
ἐκφεύγω (ἐκφυγ-) escape
ἐκφορέω carry off
ἐκφυγ- aor. stem of ἐκφεύγω
ἐκών οὖσα όν

(ἑκοντ-) willing(ly)
ἔλαβον aor. of λαμβάνω
ἔλαθον aor. of λανθάνω
ἐλάττων ἔλαττον (ἐλαττον-)
smaller; fewer; less
ἔλαχον aor. of λαγχάνω
ἔλεγχος, ὁ examination,
refutation (2a)
ἐλέγχω refute, argue against
ἐλ- aor. stem of αἱρέω/ομαι
ἐλευθερία, ἡ freedom (1b)
ἐλεύθερος α ον free
ἐλευθερόω set free
ἐλήλυθα perf. of ἔρχομαι
ἐλήφθην aor. pass. of λαμβάνω
ἐλθέ come! (s.)
ἐλθ- aor. stem of ἔρχομαι
ἔλιπον aor. of λείπω
Ἑλλάς (Ἑλλαδ-), ἡ Greece
(3a)
Ἕλλην (Ἑλλην-), ὁ Greek
(3a)
†ἐλπίζω hope, expect (+fut.
inf.)
ἐλπίς (ἐλπιδ-), ἡ hope,
expectation (3a)
ἔμαθον aor. of μανθάνω
ἐμαυτόν ήν myself
ἐμβαίνω (ἐμβα-) embark
ἔμεινα aor. of μένω
ἐμεωυτόν=ἐμαυτόν
ἔμμεναι=εἶναι
ἐμός ή όν my, mine
ἔμπειρος ον skilled,
experienced
ἔμπεσ- aor. stem of ἐμπίπτω
ἐμπίπτω (ἐμπεσ-) (ἐν)
(εἰς) fall into, on, upon
ἐμφανής ές open, obvious
*ἐν (+gen.) in the house of
(+dat.) in, on, among
ἐν τούτῳ meanwhile
ἐν- stem of εἷς one
ἐναντίον (+gen.) opposite, in
front of
ἔνδον inside
ἐνεγκ- aor. stem of φέρω
ἔνειμι be in

ἕνεκα (+gen.) because, for
the sake of (usually follows
its noun)
ἐνέπεσον aor. of ἐμπίπτω
ἐνέχυρον, τό security, pledge
(2b)
ἔνθα there, where
ἐνθάδε here
ἐνθυμέομαι take to heart, be
angry at
ἐνί=ἐν
ἐνταῦθα here, at this point
ἐντεῦθεν from then, from
there
ἐντίθημι (ἐνθε-) place in, put
in
ἐντυγχάνω (ἐντυχ-) meet
with, come upon (+dat.)
ἐξ=ἐκ
ἐξάγω (ἐξαγαγ-) lead, bring
out
ἐξαίφνης suddenly
ἐξαπατάω deceive, trick
ἐξέβαλον aor. of ἐκβάλλω
ἐξεδόθην aor. pass. of ἐκδίδωμι
ἐξέδωκα aor. act. of ἐκδίδωμι
ἐξελέγχω convict, refute,
expose
ἐξελθ- aor. stem of ἐξέρχομαι
ἐξέρχομαι (ἐξελθ-) go out,
come out
ἔξεστι it is possible for x (dat.)
to – (inf.)
ἐξετάζω question closely
ἐξευρ- aor. stem of ἐξευρίσκω
ἐξευρίσκω (ἐξευρ-) find out
ἐξῆλθον aor. of ἐξέρχομαι
ἐξήνεγκα wk. aor. of ἐκφέρω
ἐξιέναι inf. of
ἐξέρχομαι/ἔξειμι
ἐξόν it being permitted,
possible
ἔξω (+gen.) outside
ἔοικα seem; resemble (+dat.)
ἔοικε it seems, is reasonable; it
is right for (+dat.)
ἐπαγγέλλω
(ἐπαγγειλ-) order

ἔπαθον aor. of πάσχω

††ἐπαινέω (ἐπαινεσ-) praise, agree

ἐπανελθ- aor. stem of ἐπανέρχομαι

ἐπανέρχομαι (ἐπανελθ-) return

ἐπανῆλθον aor. of ἐπανέρχομαι

ἐπεί since, when

*ἐπειδάν (+subj.) when(ever)

ἐπειδή when, since, because

ἐπεισέρχομαι (ἐπεισελθ-) attack

ἔπειτα then, next

ἐπείτε when, since

ἐπέρχομαι (ἐπελθ-) go against, attack

ἐπέσχον aor. of ἐπέχω

ἐπέχω (ἐπισχ-) hold on, restrain, check

*ἐπί (+acc.) against, at, to (+gen.) on; in the time of (+dat.) at, near; for the purpose of

ἐπιδείκνυμι (ἐπιδειξ-) prove, show, demonstrate

ἐπιδημέω come to town, be in town

ἐπιεικής ές reasonable, moderate, fair

ἐπιθόμην aor. of πείθομαι

ἐπιθυμέω desire, yearn for (+gen.)

ἐπικαλέομαι call upon (to witness)

ἐπιλανθάνομαι (ἐπιλαθ-) forget (+gen.)

ἐπιμέλεια, ἡ concern, care (1b)

ἐπιμελέομαι care for (+gen.)

ἐπιμελής ές careful

ἐπισκοπέομαι (ἐπισκεψ-) review

†ἐπίσταμαι know how to (+inf.); understand

ἐπισχ- aor. stem of ἐπέχω

ἐπιτήδειος α ον suitable, useful for

ἐπιχειρέω undertake, set to work

†ἕπομαι (σπ-) follow (+dat.)

ἔπος, τό word (3c) (uncontr. pl. ἔπεα)

ἐρ- see ἐρωτάω or ἐρέω

†ἐργάζομαι work, perform

ἔργον, τό task, job (2b)

ἐρέω fut. of λέγω

ἐρῆμος ον empty, deserted, devoid of

†ἔρχομαι (ἐλθ-) go, come

†ἐρωτάω (ἐρ-) ask

ἐς = εἰς

ἐσθής (ἐσθητ-), ἡ clothing (3a)

†ἐσθίω (φαγ-) eat

ἐσθλός ή όν fine, noble, good

ἔσομαι fut. of εἰμί (be) (3rd s. ἔσται)

ἐσπόμην aor. of ἕπομαι

ἔσσι = εἶ you (s.) are

ἔσται 3rd s. fut. of εἰμί (be)

ἔσταν they stopped (3rd pl. aor. of ἵσταμαι)

ἐστερημένος η ον perf. part. pass. of στερέω

ἑστηκώς υῖα ός (-οτ-) standing (perf. part. of ἵσταμαι)

ἔσχατος η ον worst, furthest, last

ἔσχον aor. of ἔχω

ἑταίρα, ἡ prostitute, courtesan (1b)

ἑταῖρος, ὁ male companion (2a)

ἕτερος α ον one (or the other) of two

ἕτερος . . . ἕτερον one . . . another

ἔτι still, yet

ἔτι καὶ νῦν even now, still now

ἕτοιμος η ον ready (to) (+inf.)

ἔτος, τό year (3c)

ἐτραπόμην aor. of τρέπομαι

ἔτυχον aor. of τυγχάνω

εὖ well

εὖ ποιέω treat well, do good to

εὖ πράττω fare well, be prosperous

εὐδαίμων εὔδαιμον (εὐδαιμον-) happy, rich, blessed by the gods

εὐθύς at once, straightaway (+gen.) straight towards

εὔνοια, ἡ good will (1b)

εὔνους ουν well-disposed

ἐϋπλόκαμος ον with pretty hair

εὐπορία, ἡ abundance, means (1b)

εὐπρεπής ές seemly, proper, becoming

εὑρ- aor. stem of εὑρίσκω

εὕρηκα perf. of εὑρίσκω

†εὑρίσκω (εὑρ-) find, come upon

εὐρύς εῖα ύ broad, wide

εὐσεβέω act righteously

εὐτυχής ές fortunate, lucky

εὐχή, ἡ prayer (1a)

εὔχομαι pray

ἐφ' = ἐπί

ἐφάνην aor. of φαίνομαι

ἔφην impf. of φημί

ἐφοπλίζω equip, get ready

ἔφυν be naturally (aor. of φύομαι)

ἔχθρα, ἡ enmity, hostility (1b)

ἐχθρός, ὁ enemy (2a)

ἐχθρός ά όν hostile, enemy

†ἔχω (σχ-) have, hold (+adv.) be (in x (adv.) condition)

ἐν νῷ ἔχω have in mind, intend

ἐών = ὤν being

ἑώρα 3rd s. impf. of ὁράω

ἕως, ἡ dawn
*ἕως (+ἄν+subj.) until
(+opt.) until
(+ind.) while; until
ἑωυτόν=ἑαυτόν

Z

Ζεύς (Δι-), ὁ Zeus (3a)
ζημία, ἡ fine (1b)
ζημιόω fine, penalise, punish
ζητέω look for, seek
ζῷον, τό animal, creature, living thing (2b)

H

ἠ- augment (if not under ἠ- look under ἀ- or ἐ-)
ἤ or; than
ἦ 1st s. impf. of εἰμί (be)
ἤ or
ἦ δ' ὅς he said
ᾖα impf. of ἔρχομαι/εἶμι
ἡγεμών (ἡγεμον-), ὁ leader (3a)
ἡγέομαι lead (+dat.); think, consider
ἠδέ and
ᾔδει 3rd s. past of οἶδα
ᾔδεσαν 3rd pl. past of οἶδα
ἡδέως with pleasure, sweetly
ἤδη by now, now, already
ᾔδη past of οἶδα
†ἥδομαι enjoy, be pleased with (+dat.)
ἡδονή, ἡ pleasure (1a)
ἡδύς εῖα ύ sweet, pleasant (sup. ἥδιστος)
ἥκιστα least of all, no, not
ἥκω come
ἦλθον aor. of ἔρχομαι/εἶμι
ἥλιος, ὁ sun (2a)
ἦμαρ (ἡματ-), τό day (3b)
ἡμεῖς we
ἦμεν 1st pl. impf. of εἰμί
ἡμέρα, ἡ day (1b)
ἡμέτερος α ον our
ἡμίονος, ὁ mule (2a)
ἦν 3rd s. impf. of εἰμί

ἦν δ' ἐγώ I said
ἤνεγκον aor. of φέρω
ἠπιστάμην impf. of ἐπίσταμαι
'Ηρακλῆς, ὁ Herakles (3d uncontr.)
ἠρόμην aor. of ἐρωτάω
ἦσαν 3rd pl. impf. of εἰμί
ἦσθα 2nd s. impf. of εἰμί
ἠσθόμην aor. of αἰσθάνομαι
ἡσυχάζω be quiet, keep quiet
ἡσυχία, ἡ quiet, peace (1b)
ἥσυχος η ον quiet, peaceful
ἦτε 2nd pl. impf. of εἰμί or 2nd pl. subj. of εἰμί
ἥττων ἧττον (ἡττον-) lesser, weaker
ηὗρον aor. of εὑρίσκω
ἠώς, ἡ (=ἕως, ἡ) dawn (acc. ἠῶ; gen. ἠοῦς; dat. ἠοῖ)

Θ

θάλαμος, ὁ bedchamber (2a)
θάλαττα, ἡ sea (1a)
θαν- aor. stem of θνῄσκω
θάνατος, ὁ death (2a)
θαυμάζω wonder at
θε- aor. stem of τίθημι
θεά, ἡ goddess (1b)
θεάομαι watch, gaze at
θεατής, ὁ spectator, (pl.) audience (1d)
θεῖος α ον divine
θεῖτο 3rd s. aor. opt. of τίθεμαι
θέμενος η ον aor. part of τίθεμαι
θεός, ὁ ἡ god (2a)
θεράπαινα, ἡ maidservant (1c)
θεραπεύω look after, tend
θεράπων (θεραποντ-), ὁ servant (3a)
θές place! set! put! (aor. imper. (s.) of τίθημι)
θέσθαι aor. inf. of τίθεμαι
θέω run

θῆκε(ν) 3rd s. aor. of τίθημι (no augment)
θηρίον, τό beast (2b)
θήσεσθε 2nd pl. fut. of τίθεμαι
†θνῄσκω (θαν-) die
θνητός ἡ όν mortal
θορυβέω make a disturbance, din
θόρυβος, ὁ noise, din, clamour, hustle and bustle (2a)
θυγάτηρ (θυγατ(ε)ρ-), ἡ daughter (3a)
θυμός, ὁ heart; anger (2a)
θύρα, ἡ door (1b)
θυσία, ἡ sacrifice (1b)
θύω sacrifice
θώμεθα 1st pl. aor. subj. of τίθεμαι

I

ἰατρικός ἡ όν medical, of healing
ἰατρός, ὁ doctor (2a)
ἰδ- aor. stem of ὁράω
ἰδιώτης, ὁ layman, private citizen (1d)
ἴδον 1st s. aor. of ὁράω (no augment)
ἰδού look! here! hey!
ἰέναι inf. of ἔρχομαι/εἶμι
ἱερά, τά rites, sacrifices (2b)
ἱερόν, τό sanctuary (2b)
ἴθι imper. s. of ἔρχομαι/εἶμι
ἱκανός ἡ όν sufficient; able to (+inf.); capable of (+inf.)
ἱκάνω come, come to/upon (+acc.)
ἱκετεύω beg, supplicate
ἱκέτης, ὁ suppliant (1d)
†ἱκνέομαι (ἱκ-) come to, arrive at
ἱκόμην aor. of ἱκνέομαι
ἱμάτιον, τό cloak (2b)
*ἵνα (+subj./opt.) in order to/that; (+indic.) where
ἵππος, ὁ horse (2a)

ἴσασι(ν) 3rd pl. of οἶδα
ἴσμεν 1st pl. of οἶδα
ἴστε 2nd pl. of οἶδα
†ἵστημι (στησ-) set up, raise
ἴσταμαι (στα-) stand
ἰσχυρός ά όν strong, powerful
ἴσως perhaps
ἴω subj. of ἔρχομαι/εἶμι
ἰών ἰοῦσα ἰόν (ἰοντ-) part. of
  ἔρχομαι/εἶμι

K

κάδ = κατά
καθαίρω (καθηρ-) cleanse,
  purify
καθέστηκα I have been put
  (perf. of καθίσταμαι)
καθεστώς ῶσα ός
  (καθεστωτ-) having been
  made (perf. part. of
  καθίσταμαι)
καθεύδω sleep
††κάθημαι be seated
καθίζομαι sit down
καθίζω sit down
καθίσταμαι (καταστα-) be
  placed, put, made
καθίστημι (καταστησ-) set
  up, make, place, put x (acc.)
  in (εἰς) y
καθοράω (κατιδ-) see, look
  down on
*καί and, also, even
*τε . . . καί both A and B
*καὶ γάρ in fact; yes, certainly
*καὶ δή and really; as a matter
  of fact; look! let us suppose
*καὶ δὴ καί moreover
*καὶ μήν what's more; look!;
  yes, and; and anyway
καίπερ although (+part.)
*καίτοι and yet
κακοδαίμων κακόδαιμον
  (κακοδαιμον-) unlucky,
  dogged by an evil daimon
κακός ή όν bad, evil,
  cowardly, mean, lowly

κακὰ (κακῶς) ποιέω treat
  badly, do harm to
καλεα- aor. stem of καλέω
†καλέω (καλεσ-) call,
  summon
κάλλιστος η ον most (very)
  fine, good, beautiful
καλός ή όν beautiful, good
κάρη (καρητ-), τό head (Attic
  κάρα (κρατ-), το (3b))
*κατά (+acc.) in, on, by,
  according to; down,
  throughout, in relation to
  (+gen.) below, down from,
  against
καταβαίνω (καταβα-) go
  down, come down
καταδικάζω condemn;
  convict x (gen.) of y (acc.)
καταδίκη, ή fine (1a)
καταθε- aor. stem of
  κατατίθημι
καταθνῄσκω (καταθαν-) die
  away
κατακλίνομαι lie down
καταλαβ- aor. stem of
  καταλαμβάνω
καταλαμβάνω
  (καταλαβ-) overtake,
  come across, seize
καταλέγω (κατειπ-) recite,
  list
καταλείπω (καταλιπ-) leave
  behind, bequeath
καταλήψομαι fut. of
  καταλαμβάνω
καταλύω bring to an end,
  finish
καταμαρτυρέω give evidence
  against (gen.)
καταστάς ᾶσα άν
  (κατασταντ-) being
  placed, put (aor. part. of
  καθίσταμαι)
καταστῆναι to be put (aor.
  inf. of καθίσταμαι)
καταστήσομαι fut. of
  καθίσταμαι

κατατίθημι (καταθε-) put
  down, pay, perform
καταφέρω (κατενεγκ-) carry
  down
καταφρονέω despise, look
  down on (+gen.)
κατεγγυάω demand securities
  from (+acc.)
κατέλαβον aor. of
  καταλαμβάνω
κατέλιπον aor. of καταλείπω
κατέστην I was put (aor. of
  καθίσταμαι)
κατέστησα I put (aor. of
  καθίστημι)
κατηγορέω prosecute x (gen.)
  on charge of y (acc.)
κατηγορία, ή speech for the
  prosecution (1b)
κατήγορος, ὁ prosecutor (2a)
κατθανών aor. part. of
  καταθνῄσκω
κατιδ- aor. stem of καθοράω
κάτω below
κε (κεν) = ἄν (enclitic)
†κεῖμαι lie, be placed, be
  made
κεῖνος η ο = ἐκεῖνος
κέλευσαν 3rd pl. aor. of
  κελεύω (no augment)
κέλευσε 3rd s. aor. of
  κελεύω (no augment)
κελευστής, ὁ boatswain (1d)
κελεύω order
κεν = κε
κεφαλή, ή head (1a)
κῆρυξ (κηρυκ-), ὁ herald (3a)
κηρύττω announce, proclaim
κινδυνεύω be in danger, run a
  risk; be likely to (+inf.)
κίνδυνος, ὁ danger (2a)
κλαίω (κλαυσ-) weep
κλείω close, shut
κλέπτης, ὁ thief (1d)
*κλέπτω steal
κληθείς εἶσα έν
  (κληθεντ-) aor. part. pass.
  of κλλέω

κλοπή, ἡ theft (1a)
κλύον 3rd pl. aor. of κλύω (no
  augment)
κλῦτε 2nd pl. imper. of κλύω
κλύω hear
κοινός ἥ όν common, shared
κοῖος = ποῖος
κολάζω punish
κομίζομαι collect
†κόπτω knock on; cut
κόραξ (κορακ-), ὁ crow (3a)
  βάλλ᾽ εἰς κόρακας go to hell!
κόρη, ἡ maiden, girl,
  daughter (1a)
κόσμος, ὁ decoration,
  ornament; order; universe
  (2a)
κοτε = ποτε
κου = που
κούρη, ἡ = κόρη, ἡ girl,
  daughter (1a)
κρατέω hold sway, power
  over (+gen.)
κρείττων κρεῖττον (κρειττον-)
  stronger, greater
†κρίνω (κριν-) judge, decide
κρίσις, ἡ judgment, decision;
  dispute; trial (3e)
†κτάομαι acquire, get, gain
†κτείνω (κτειν-) kill
κτῆμα (κτηματ-), τό
  possession (3b)
κυβερνήτης, ὁ captain,
  helmsman (1d)
κύριος a ον able, with power,
  sovereign, by right
κύων (κυν-), ὁ dog (3a)
κωλύω prevent, stop
κως = πως

Λ

λαβ- aor. stem of λαμβάνω
†λαγχάνω (λαχ-) obtain by
  lot; run as a candidate for
  office
  δίκην λαγχάνω bring suit
  against

λαθ- aor. stem of λανθάνω
Λακεδαιμόνιος, ὁ Spartan (2a)
λαμβάνομαι (λαβ-) take hold
  of (+gen.)
†λαμβάνω (λαβ-) take,
  capture
  δίκην λαμβάνω punish, exact
  one's due from
  (παρά+gen.)
λαμπάς (λαμπαδ-), ἡ torch
  (3a)
†λανθάνω (λαθ-) escape
  notice of x (acc.) –ing
  (nom. part.)
λαός, ὁ people, inhabitant (2a)
λαχ- aor. stem of λαγχάνω
†λέγω (εἰπ-) speak, say, tell,
  mean
†λείπω (λιπ-) leave, abandon
λέληθε 3rd s. perf. of λανθάνω
ληφθ- aor. pass. stem of
  λαμβάνω
λήψομαι fut. of λαμβάνω
λίθος, ὁ stone (2a)
λιμήν (λιμεν-), ὁ harbour (3a)
λίσσομαι beseech
λογίζομαι calculate, reckon,
  consider
λογισμός, ὁ calculation (2a)
λόγος, ὁ speech, tale, word,
  reason, argument (2a)
λοιπός ἥ όν left, remaining
λούω wash (mid. wash
  oneself)
λύω release

M

μά by! (+acc.)
μαθ- aor. stem of μανθάνω
μαθήσομαι fut. of μανθάνω
μαθητής, ὁ student (1d)
μακρός ά όν large, big, long
μάλα very, quite, virtually
μάλιστα (μάλα) especially,
  particularly; yes
μᾶλλον (μάλα) . . . ἥ more,
  rather than
†μανθάνω (μαθ-) learn,

  understand
μαρτυρέω give evidence, bear
  witness
μαρτυρία, ἡ evidence,
  testimony (1b)
μαρτύρομαι invoke, call to
  witness
μάρτυς (μαρτυρ-), ὁ witness
  (3a)
μάχη, ἡ fight, battle (1a)
†μάχομαι (μαχεσ-) fight
μεγάλοιο gen. s. m. of μέγας
μέγας μεγάλη μέγα
  (μεγαλ-) great, big
μέγεθος, τό size (3c)
μέγιστος η ον greatest (sup. of
  μέγας)
μέθες 2nd s. aor. imper. of
  μεθίημι
μεθίημι (μεθε-) allow, let go
μείζων μεῖζον (μειζον-)
  greater (comp. of μέγας)
μέλας αινα αν (μελαν-) black
†μέλει x (dat.) is concerned
  about (+gen.)
†μέλλω be about to (+fut.
  inf.); hesitate; intend
  (+pres. inf.)
μέμφομαι blame, criticise,
  find fault with (+acc. or
  dat.)
*μέν . . . δέ on one
  hand . . . on the other
*μέντοι however, but
†μένω (μειν-) remain, wait
  for
μέρος, τό share, part (3c)
*μετά (+acc.) after
  (+gen.) with
  (+dat.) among, in
  company with
μεταυδάω speak to
μετελθ- aor. stem of
  μετέρχομαι
μετέρχομαι (μετελθ-) send
  for, chase after; go among
  (+dat.); attack (+dat. or
  μετά+acc.)

μετέχω share in (+gen.)
μετίημι=μεθίημι
μέτριος α ον moderate,
  reasonable, fair
*μή not
  (+imper.) don't!
  (+aor. subj.) don't!
μηδαμῶς not at all, in no way
*μηδέ ... μηδέ neither ... nor
μηδείς μηδεμία μηδέν
  (μηδεν-) no, no one
μηκέτι no longer
*μήτε ... μήτε neither ... nor
μήτηρ (μητ(ε)ρ-), ἡ mother
  (3a)
μηχανάομαι devise, contrive
μηχανή, ἡ device, plan (1a)
μιαρός ά όν foul, polluted
μικρός ά όν small, short, little
†μιμνήσκομαι (μνησθ-)
  remember, mention
μιν him, her (acc.) (enclitic)
μισέω hate
μισθός, ὁ pay (2a)
μῖσος, τό hatred (3c)
μνᾶ, ἡ mina (100 drachmas)
  (1b)
μνεία, ἡ mention (1b)
μνημονεύω remember
μνησθ- aor. stem of
  μιμνήσκομαι
μόνος η ον alone
  μόνον only, merely
  οὐ μόνον ... ἀλλὰ καί not
  only ... but also
μῦθος, ὁ word, story (2a)
μῶν surely not?
μῶρος α ον stupid, foolish

N
ναί yes
ναυμαχία, ἡ naval battle (1b)
ναῦς, ἡ ship (3 irr.)
ναύτης, ὁ sailor (1d)
ναυτικός ή όν naval
νεανίας, ὁ young man (1d)
νεανίσκος, ὁ young man (2a)
νεηνίης, ὁ=νεανίας, ὁ

νειμ- aor. stem of νέμω
νεκρός, ὁ corpse (2a)
†νέμω (νειμ-) distribute,
  allot, assign
νέος α ον young
νή by! (+acc.)
νῆσος, ἡ island (2a)
'νθρωπε=ἄνθρωπε
νικάω win, defeat
νίκη, ἡ victory, conquest (1a)
νοέω plan, devise; think,
  mean, intend, notice
νομή, ἡ distribution (1a)
νομίζομαι be accustomed
†νομίζω acknowledge, think
  x (acc.) to be y (acc. or
  acc.+inf.)
νόμος, ὁ law, convention (2a)
νοσέω be sick
νόσος, ἡ illness, plague,
  disease (2a)
νοῦς, ὁ (νόος) mind, sense
  (2a)
  ἐν νῷ ἔχω have in mind,
  intend
νυ=νυν
νυν now, then (enclitic)
νῦν now
νύξ (νυκτ-), ἡ night (3a)

Ξ
ξεῖνος=ξένος
ξένη, ἡ foreign woman (1a)
ξένος, ὁ foreigner, guest, host
  (2a)

Ο
ὁ ἡ τό the: in Ionic=he, she, it
ὁ αὐτός the same
ὁ δέ and/but he
ὁ μέν ... ὁ δέ one ... another
ὅτι; what? (sometimes in reply
  to τί;)
ὅδε ἥδε τόδε this
ὁδί this here (pointing)
ὁδοιπόρος, ὁ traveller (2a)
ὁδός, ἡ road, way (2a)

ὅθεν from where
οἱ=αὐτῷ to him, her (dat.)
  (Ionic)
οἱ (to) where
†*οἶδα know
  χάριν οἶδα be grateful to
  (+dat.)
οἴκαδε homewards
οἶκε=ἔοικε resemble, be like
  (+dat.)
οἰκεῖος, ὁ relative (2a)
οἰκεῖος α ον related, domestic,
  family
οἰκέτης, ὁ house-slave (1d)
οἰκέω dwell (in), live
οἴκημα (οἰκηματ-), τό
  dwelling (3b)
οἴκησις, ἡ dwelling (3e)
οἰκία, ἡ house (1b)
οἰκία, τά palace (2b)
οἰκίδιον, τό small house (2b)
οἴκοι at home
οἴκονδε home, homewards
οἶκος, ὁ household, house (2a)
οἰκός=εἰκός reasonable
οἰκτίρω (οἰκτιρ-) pity
†οἶμαι think
οἴμοι alas! oh dear!
οἷος α ον what a! what sort of
  a!
  οἷός τ' εἰμί be able to (+inf.)
οἴχομαι be off, depart
ὁκόθεν=ὁπόθεν
ὀλ- aor. stem of ὄλλυμαι
ὀλεσ- aor. stem of ὄλλυμι
ὀλίγος η ον small, few
ὀλίγωρος ον contemptuous
ὄλλυμαι (aor. ὠλόμην) be
  killed, die, perish
†ὄλλυμι (ὀλεσ-) destroy, kill
ὅλος η ον whole of
ὀλοφύρομαι lament
†ὄμνυμι (ὀμοσ-) swear
ὅμοιος α ον like, similar to
  (+dat.)
ὁμολογέω agree
ὁμόνοια, ἡ agreement,
  harmony (1b)

ὅμως nevertheless, however

ὄνειρος, ὁ dream (2a)

ὄνομα (ὀνοματ-), τό name (3b)

ὀξύς εῖα ύ sharp, bitter, shrill

ὅπλα, τά weapons, arms (2b)

ὁπόθεν from where

ὁποῖος a ον of what kind

ὁπόσος η ον how many, how great

*ὁπόταν whenever (+subj.)

*ὁπότε when; whenever (+opt.)

ὅπου where? where

*ὅπως how (answer to πῶς;); how (indir. q.)
   (+fut. ind.) see to it that (+subj. or opt.)=ἵνα in order to/that

†ὁράω (ἰδ-) see

ὀργή, ἡ anger (1a)

ὀργίζομαι grow angry with (+dat.)

ὄρεος=ὄρους gen. of ὄρος, τό

ὀρθός ή όν straight, correct, right

ὅρκος, ὁ oath (2a)

ὁρμάομαι charge, set off

ὄρος, τό mountain (3c)

ὅς ἥ ὅ who, what, which

ὅσος η ον how great! as much/many as

ὅσπερ ἥπερ ὅπερ who/which indeed

ὅστις ἥτις ὅτι who(ever), which(ever)

*ὅταν (+subj.) whenever

ὅτε when

ὅτι that; because

*οὐ (οὐκ, οὐχ) no, not

οὐ μόνον . . . ἀλλὰ καί not only . . . but also

οὐδαμῶς in no way, not at all

οὐδέ and not

οὐδείς οὐδεμία οὐδέν (οὐδέν-) no, no one, nothing

οὐδέποτε never

οὐδέπω not yet

οὐκ=οὐ no, not

οὐκέτι no longer

*οὐκοῦν therefore

*οὔκουν not . . . therefore

*οὖν therefore

οὔνομα=ὄνομα, τό

οὔπερ where

οὔποτε never

οὔπω not yet

οὐρανός, ὁ sky, heavens (2a)

οὐσία, ἡ property, wealth (1b)

*οὔτε . . . οὔτε neither . . . nor

οὔτις (οὔτιν-) no one

οὗτος αὕτη τοῦτο this; (s)he

οὗτος hey there! you there!

οὑτοσί this here (pointing)

οὕτως/οὕτω thus, so; in this way

οὐχ=οὐ

†ὀφείλω owe

ὀφθαλμός, ὁ eye (2a)

ὄφρα (+subj./opt.)=ἵνα (+ind./subj./opt.) while, until

ὄψις, ἡ vision, sight (3e)

Π

παθ- aor. stem of πάσχω

πάθος, τό suffering, experience (3c)

παιδίον, τό child, slave (2b)

παιδοποιέομαι beget, have children

παίζω play, joke at (πρός+acc.)

παῖς (παιδ-), ὁ, ἡ child; slave (3a)

πάλαι long ago

παλαιός ά όν ancient, of old, old

πάλιν back, again

πανταχοῦ everywhere

παντελῶς completely, outright

*πάνυ very (much); at all

*πάνυ μὲν οὖν certainly, of course

πανύστατος η ον for the very last time

πάρ=παρά

*παρά (+acc.) along, beside; against, to; compared with; except
   (+gen.) from
   (+dat.) with, beside, in the presence of

πάρα=πάρεστι it is possible for (+dat.)

παραγίγνομαι (παραγεν-) be present, turn up at (+dat.)

παραδίδωμι (παραδο-) hand over

παραδώσειν fut. inf. of παραδίδωμι

παραιτέομαι beg

παράκειμαι lie, be placed beside (+dat.)

παραλαβ- aor. stem of παραλαμβάνω

παραλαμβάνω (παραλαβ-) take, receive from; undertake

παρασκευάζω prepare, equip

παρασκευή, ἡ preparation, equipping; force (1a)

παρασχ- aor. stem of παρέχω

παρεγενόμην aor. of παραγίγνομαι

πάρειμι be at hand, be present (+dat.)

παρέλαβον aor. of παραλαμβάνω

παρελθ- aor. stem of παρέρχομαι

παρέρχομαι (παρελθ-) pass, go by, come forward

πάρεστι it is possible for (+dat.)

παρέχω (παρασχ-) give to, provide

πράγματα παρέχω cause trouble (to)

παρθένος, ἡ maiden (2a)

Total Vocabulary

349

πάριτε 2nd pl. imper. of
παρέρχομαι/πάρειμι
παριών οὖσα όν (-οντ-) part.
of παρέρχομαι
παροράω (παριδ-) notice
παρών οὖσα όν
(παροντ-) part. of πάρειμι
πᾶς πᾶσα πᾶν (παντ-) all
ὁ πᾶς the whole of
†πάσχω (παθ-) suffer,
experience
πατήρ (πατ(ε)ρ-), ὁ father
(3a)
πατρίς (πατριδ-), ἡ fatherland
(3a)
πατρῷος α ον ancestral, of
one's father
παύομαι stop (+part.); cease
from (+gen.)
παύω stop x (acc.) from y
(ἐκ+gen.); stop x (acc.)
doing y (acc. part.)
πείθομαι (πιθ-) believe, trust,
obey (+dat.)
πείθω persuade
πειράομαι (πειρασ-) test, try
πείσομαι fut. of πάσχω or
πείθομαι
†πέμπω send
πένης (πενητ-) poor man
(3a); (adj.) poor
πενία, ἡ poverty (1b)
πεντήκοντα fifty
*περί (+acc.) about,
concerning
(+gen.) about, around
(+dat.) in, on, about
περιφανής ές very clear,
obvious
πεσ- aor. stem of πίπτω
πέφυκα tend naturally to
(perf. of φύομαι)
πηδάω leap, jump
πιθ- aor. stem of πείθομαι
†πίνω (πι-) drink
†πίπτω (πεσ-) fall, die
πιστεύω trust (+dat.)
πιστός ή όν reliable,

trustworthy, faithful
πλεῖστος η ον very much,
most (sup. of πολύς)
πλέον more (adv.) (comp. of
πολύς)
†πλέω (πλευσ-) sail
πλέως α ων full of (+gen.)
πλῆθος, τό number, crowd;
the people (3c)
πλήν (+gen.) except
πλησίον nearby
πλησίος α ον near, close to
(+gen.)
πλοῖον, τό vessel, ship (2b)
πλούσιος α ον rich, wealthy
πλύνω wash
πόθεν; from where?
ποῖ; where to?
ποιέομαι make
ποιέω make, do
κακὰ (κακῶς) ποιέω treat
badly, harm
ποιητής, ὁ poet (1d)
ποιμήν (ποιμεν-), ὁ shepherd
(3a)
ποῖος α ον; what sort of?
πολεμέω make war
πολεμικός ή όν of war,
military, martial
πολέμιοι, οἱ the enemy (2a)
πολέμιος α ον hostile, enemy
πόλεμος, ὁ war (2a)
πόλις, ἡ city, city-state (3e)
πολιτεία, ἡ state, constitution
(1b)
πολιτεύομαι be a citizen
πολίτης, ὁ citizen (1d)
πολιτικός ή όν political
πολῖτις (πολιτιδ-), ἡ female
citizen (3a)
πολλά many things
πολλάκις many times, often
πολύς πολλή πολύ
(πολλ-) much, many
πολύ (adv.) much
πονηρός ά όν wicked,
wretched
πόντος, ὁ sea (2a)

πορεύομαι march, journey,
go
πορίζω provide, offer
πόρνη, ἡ prostitute (1a)
πόρρω far, afar off
Ποσειδῶν (Ποσειδων-), ὁ
Poseidon, god of sea (3a)
(voc. Πόσειδον; acc.
Ποσειδῶ)
πόσις, ὁ husband, spouse (3e)
ποταμοῖο gen. s. of ποταμός
ποταμός, ὁ river (2a)
ποτε once, ever (enclitic)
πότερον ... ἤ whether ... or
πότερος α ον; which (of two)?
που somewhere, anywhere
(enclitic)
ποῦ; where?
πούς (ποδ-), ὁ foot (3a)
πρᾶγμα (πραγματ-), τό thing,
matter, affair (3b)
πράγματα παρέχω cause
trouble
πρᾶξις, ἡ fact, action (3e)
†πράττω do, perform, fare
εὖ πράττω fare well, be
prosperous
πρέσβεις, οἱ ambassadors (3e)
πρεσβευτής, ὁ ambassador
(1d)
πρεσβύτερος α ον older,
rather old
*πρίν (+inf.) before
πρὶν ἄν (+subj.) until
πρίν (+opt.) until
πρό (+gen.) before, in front
of
προάγω lead on
πρόβατον, τό sheep (2b)
πρόγονος, ὁ forebear,
ancestor (2a)
προδίδωμι (προδο-) betray
προδο- aor. stem of
προδίδωμι
προθυμέομαι be ready, eager
πρόθυμος ον ready, eager,
willing
προίξ (προικ-), ἡ dowry (3a)

*πρός (+acc.) to, towards
(+gen.) in the name/under
the protection of
(+dat.) in addition to, near
προσαγορεύω address, speak
to
προσάπτω give, attach to
(+dat.)
προσδραμ- aor. stem of
προστρέχω
προσεῖπον I spoke x (acc.) to y
(acc.) (προσέειπον Ionic)
προσελθ- aor. stem of
προσέρχομαι
προσέρχομαι
(προσελθ-) go/come
towards, advance
προσέχω bring near, apply to
προσέχω τὸν νοῦν pay
attention to (+dat.)
προσήκει it is fitting for x
(dat.) to – (+inf.)
προσῆλθον aor. of
προσέρχομαι
πρόσθεν previously; before
(+gen.)
προσιών οὖσα ὄν
(προσιοντ-) part. of
προσέρχομαι/πρόσειμι
προσκαλέω summon, call
προσλέγω (προσειπ-) address
προσπίτνω fall upon,
embrace
προστάττω (προσταξ-) order
(+dat.)
προστρέχω (προσδραμ-) run
towards
προτείνω stretch out
προτεραῖος α ον of the
previous day
πρότερον formerly,
previously
πρότερος α ον first (of two);
previous
προτρέπω urge on, impel
πρύτανις, ὁ prytanis (3e)
πρῶτον first, at first
πρῶτος η ον first

πυθ- aor. stem of πυνθάνομαι
πύλη, ἡ gate (1a)
†πυνθάνομαι (πυθ-) learn,
hear, get to know
πῦρ (πυρ-), τό fire (3b)
πυρά, τά fire-signal (2b)
πυρά, ἡ funeral pyre (1b)
πύργος, ὁ tower (2a)
πω yet (enclitic)
†πωλέω sell
πως somehow (enclitic)
πῶς; how?
*πῶς γὰρ οὔ; of course

P

ῥᾴδιος α ον easy
ῥᾳδίως easily
ῥᾶστος η ον very easy
ῥαψῳδός, ὁ rhapsode (2a)
ῥήτωρ (ῥητορ-), ὁ orator,
politician (3a)
†ῥίπτω throw

Σ

σαφῶς clearly
σεαυτόν yourself (s.)
σελήνη, ἡ moon (1a)
σέο=σοῦ of you
σεῦ=σοῦ of you
σημαίνω (σημην-) tell, signal
σημεῖον, τό sign, signal (2b)
σιγάω be quiet
σιδηρέος η ον of iron, metal
σῖτος, ὁ food (2a) (pl. σῖτα, τά
(2b))
σιωπάω be silent
†σκέπτομαι examine, look
carefully at
σκεύη, τά gear, furniture;
ship's gear (3c)
σκοπέομαι look at, consider
†σκοπέω consider, examine
σμικρός ά όν small, short,
little
σός σή σόν your (s.)
σοφία, ἡ wisdom (1b)
σοφιστής, ὁ sophist, thinker
(1d)

σοφός ή όν wise, clever
†σπένδω pour a libation
σπεύδω hurry
σπονδαί, αἱ treaty, truce (1a)
σπονδή, ἡ libation (1a)
σπουδάζω be concerned; do
seriously
σπουδαῖος a ον serious,
important
σπουδή, ἡ zeal, haste,
seriousness (1a)
στάς στᾶσα στάν
(σταντ-) standing (aor.
part. of ἵσταμαι)
στείχω go, come
στένω groan
στερέω deprive of
στῆ=ἔστη he/she stood (aor.
of ἵσταμαι) (no augment)
στῆθ'=στῆτε
στῆτε stand! (2nd pl. imper.
aor. of ἵσταμαι)
στόμα (στοματ-), τό mouth
(3b)
στρατηγός, ὁ general (2a)
στρατιά, ἡ army (1b)
στρωμνή, ἡ bed (1a)
σύ you (s.)
συγγεγένημαι perf. of
συγγίγνομαι
συγγένεια, ἡ kinship (1b)
συγγενής, ὁ relation (3d)
συγγίγνομαι (συγγεν-) be
with, have intercourse,
dealings with (+dat.)
συγγνώμη, ἡ pardon,
forgiveness (1a)
συγγνώμην ἔχω forgive,
pardon
συγκόπτω beat up, strike
(aor. pass. συνεκόπην).
συγχωρέω agree with, to;
yield to (+dat.)
συλλέγω collect, gather
συμβουλεύομαι discuss with
(+dat.)
συμβουλή, ἡ discussion,
recommendation (1a)

σύμμαχος, ὁ ally (2a)
συμπέμπω send with (+dat.)
συμπροθυμέομαι share
  enthusiasm of (+dat.)
συμφορά, ἡ disaster, mishap,
  occurrence (1b)
συμφορή = συμφορά
*σύν (+dat.) with the help of,
  together with
συνέρχομαι (συνελθ-) come
  together
συνῆλθον aor. of συνέρχομαι
συνοικέω live with, together
  (+dat.)
συντυγχάνω (συντυχ-) meet
  with (+dat.)
σφεῖς they (Attic σφᾶς σφῶν
  σφίσι) (Ionic σφεῖς σφέας
  σφέων σφι)
σφι to them (dat. of σφεῖς)
σφόδρα very much,
  exceedingly
σχ- aor. stem of ἔχω/ἔχομαι
σχεδόν near, nearly, almost
σχολή, ἡ leisure (1a)
†σώζω save, keep safe
Σωκράτης, ὁ Socrates (3d)
σῶμα (σωματ-), τό body,
  person (3b)
σῶος a ον safe
σωτήρ (σωτηρ-), ὁ saviour
  (3a)
σωτηρία, ἡ safety (1b)
σωφροσύνη, ἡ good sense,
  moderation (1a)
σώφρων (σωφρον-) sensible,
  temperate, modest, chaste,
  discreet, prudent,
  law-abiding, disciplined

T
τάλας αινα αν wretched,
  unhappy
τᾶν my dear chap
  (condescending)
τάξις, ἡ order, rank,
  battle-array (3e)
ταχέως quickly

τάχος, τό speed (3c)
τε . . . καί both . . . and
τεῖχος, τό wall (of a city) (3c)
τεκμαίρομαι conclude, infer;
  assign, ordain
τεκμήριον, τό evidence, proof
  (2b)
τέκνον, τό child (2b)
τελευτάω die, end, finish
τέλος in the end, finally
τευ = τινος
τέχνη, ἡ skill, art, expertise
  (1a)
τήμερον today
τι a, something (enclitic)
τί; what? why?
†τίθημι (θε-) put, place
†τίκτω (τεκ-) bear, give
  birth to
τιμάω honour, value, reckon;
  (+dat.) fine
τιμή, ἡ privilege, honour (1a)
τίμημα (τιμηματ-), τό fine
  (3b)
τιμωρέομαι take revenge on
τιμωρία, ἡ revenge,
  vengeance (1b)
τις τι (τιν-) a certain,
  someone (enclitic)
τίς τί (τίν-); who? what?
  which?
τίτθη, ἡ nurse (1a)
*τοι then (inference)
τοι = σοι
τοί = οἵ (relative)
*τοίνυν well then (resuming
  argument)
τοιόσδε ἥδε όνδε of this kind
τοιοῦτος αύτη οὖτο of this
  kind, of such a kind
τοῖσι = τοῖς
τόλμα, ἡ daring (1c)
τολμάω dare, be daring,
  undertake
τοσοῦτος αύτη οὖτο so great
τότε then
τούτῳ dat. of οὖτος
ἐν τούτῳ meanwhile, during

this
τράπεζα, ἡ bank (1c)
τραπ- aor. stem of τρέπομαι
τρεῖς τρία three
τρέπομαι (τραπ-) turn (self),
  turn in flight
†τρέπω cause to turn, put to
  flight
†τρέφω (θρεψ-) rear, raise,
  feed, nourish
†τρέχω (δραμ-) run
τριηραρχέω serve as a
  trierarch
τριήραρχος, ὁ trierarch (2a)
τριήρης, ἡ trireme (3d)
τρόπος, ὁ way, manner (2a)
τροφή, ἡ food, nourishment
  (1a)
†τυγχάνω (τυχ-) chance,
  happen (to be –ing+nom.
  part.) be actually –ing
  (+nom. part.)
  (+gen.) hit, chance/happen
  on, be subject to
†τύπτω strike, hit
τυχ- aor. stem of τυγχάνω
τύχη, ἡ chance, good/bad
  fortune (1a)

Υ
ὑβρίζω treat violently,
  disgracefully; humiliate
ὕβρις, ἡ aggression, violence,
  insult, humiliation (3e)
ὑβριστής, ὁ violent, criminal
  person (1d)
ὕδωρ (ὑδατ-), τό water (3b)
υἱός, ὁ son (2a or, except for
  acc. s., like m. forms of
  γλυκύς)
ὑμεῖς you (pl.)
ὑμέτερος a ον your (pl.)
ὑπακούω reply, answer; obey
  (+dat.)
ὑπάρχω be, be sufficient;
  begin (+gen.)
*ὑπέρ (+gen.) for, on behalf
  of

ὑπηρέτης, ὁ servant, slave (1d)

†ὑπισχνέομαι (ὑποσχ-) promise (to) (+fut. inf.)

ὕπνος, ὁ sleep (2a)

*ὑπό (+acc.) under, along under, up under (+gen.) by, at the hand of (+dat.) under, beneath

ὑποδέχομαι welcome, entertain

ὑπόλοιπος ον remaining

ὗς, ὁ boar (3h)

ὑστεραῖος α ον of the next day

ὕστερον later, further

ὕστερος α ον later, last (of two)

ὑφ᾽ = ὑπό

ὑφαιρέομαι (ὑφελ-) steal, take for oneself by stealth

Φ

φαίνομαι (φαν-) appear, seem (to be) (+nom. part.), seem to be but not really to be (+inf.)

†φαίνω (φην-) reveal, declare, indict

φάμενος η ον aor. part. mid. of φημί (ἐφάμην)
οὐ φάμενος saying . . . not, refusing

φάναι inf. of φημί

φανερός ά όν clear, obvious

φάνη 3rd s. aor. of φαίνομαι (no augment)

φάσθ᾽ you say (2nd pl. mid. of φημί)

φάσκω allege, claim, assert

φάτο he spoke (3rd s. aor. mid. of φημί)

φέρε come!

†φέρω (ἐνεγκ-) bear, endure; lead; carry
χαλεπῶς φέρω be angry, displeased at

†φεύγω (φυγ-) run off, flee;

be a defendant, be on trial

φεύξομαι fut. of φεύγω

†φημί say

φής you say

φήσω fut. of φημί

φήσειεν 3rd s. aor. opt. of φημί

†φθάνω (φθασ-) anticipate x (acc.) by/in –ing (nom. part.)

φιλέω love, kiss; be used to (+inf.)

φιλία, ἡ friendship (1b)

φίλος, ὁ friend (2a)

φίλος η ον dear; one's own

φιλοσοφία, ἡ philosophy (1b)

φιλόσοφος, ὁ philosopher (2a)

φίλτατος η ον most dear (sup. of φίλος)

φοβέομαι fear, be afraid of, respect
φοβέομαι μή (+subj./opt.) fear that, lest

φοβερός ά όν terrible, frightening

φόβος, ὁ fear (2a)

φόνος, ὁ murder (2a)

φράζω utter, mention, talk

φράτηρ (φρατερ-), ὁ member of phratry (3a)

φρήν (φρεν-), ἡ heart, mind (3a)

φρονέω think, consider

φροντίζω think, worry

φροντίς (φροντιδ-), ἡ thought, care, concern (3a)

φυγή, ἡ flight (1a)

φύγον 1st s. aor. of φεύγω (no augment)

φυλακή, ἡ guard (1a)

φύλαξ (φυλακ-), ὁ guard (3a)

φυλάττω guard (Ionic φυλάσσω)

φύσις, ἡ nature, character, temperament (3e)

†φύω bear (aor. mid.) ἔφυν be naturally (perf.) πέφυκα be inclined

by nature

φωνέω speak, utter

φωνή, ἡ voice, language, speech (1a)

φῶς (φωτ-), τό light (3b)

φώς (φωτ-), ὁ man, mortal (3a)

Χ

χαῖρε greetings! hello! farewell!

†χαίρω (χαρ-) rejoice

χαλεπός ή όν difficult, hard
χαλεπῶς φέρω be angry, displeased at

χαλκοῦς ῆ οῦν of bronze

χαρίζομαι oblige, please; be dear to (+dat.)

χάρις (χαριτ-), ἡ thanks, grace (3a)
χάριν οἶδα be grateful to (+dat.)

χειμών (χειμων-), ὁ winter, storm (3a)

χείρ (χειρ-), ἡ hand (3a)

χείρων χεῖρον (χειρον-) worse (comp. of κακός)

χθές yesterday

χίλιοι αι α thousand

χορός, ὁ dance; chorus (2a)

†χράομαι use, employ (+dat.)

χρέα, τά debts (3c uncontr.)

†χρή it is necessary for x (acc.) to – (infin.)

χρῆμα (χρημα-), τό thing (3b)

χρήματα, τά money (3b)

χρηματίζω do business

χρῆσθαι pres. inf. of χράομαι

χρήσιμος η ον profitable, useful

χρηστός ή όν good, fine, serviceable

χρῆται 3rd s. pres. of χράομαι

χρόα acc. of χρώς

χροΐ dat. of χρώς

χρόνος, ὁ time (2a)
χροός gen. of χρώς
χρυσέος η ον golden
χρώς (χρωτ-), ὁ flesh, skin, body (3a) (Ionic acc. χρόα; gen. χροός; dat. χροΐ)
χωρέω go, come
χώρη, ἡ land (1a) (Attic χώρα, ἡ (1b))
χωρίον, τό place; space; region; farm (2b)
χωρίς apart, separately (from) (+gen.)

Ψ

ψευδής ές false, lying
ψεύδομαι lie, tell lies
ψευδῶς falsely
ψηφίζομαι vote
ψήφισμα (ψηφισματ-), τό decree (3b)
ψῆφος, ἡ vote, voting-pebble (2a)
ψυχή, ἡ soul, life (1a)

Ω

ὠ- augment (if not under ὠ-look under ὁ-)
ὤ what . . .! (+gen.)
ὦ Ο (+voc./nom.) (addressing someone)
ὧδε thus, as follows
ὠθέω push, shove
ὠλόμην aor. of ὄλλυμαι
ᾤμην impf. of οἶμαι
ὦμος, ὁ shoulder (2a)
ὤν οὖσα ὄν (ὀντ-) part. of εἰμί
ὦν=οὖν
†ὠνέομαι (πρια-) buy
*ὡς how! as; that (+acc.) towards, to the house of (+fut. part.) in order to (+sup.) as - as possible (+subj./opt.)=ἵνα in order to/that
ὡς thus, so
ὥσπερ like, as
*ὥστε so that, with the result that, consequently (+inf./indic.)

List of proper names

Most names of people(s) and all names of places will be found in the running vocabularies where they occur. The names which recur several times and are not repeated in the running vocabularies are listed here for convenience of reference.

Ἄδμητ-ος, ὁ Admetos (2a) (husband of Alkestis)
Ἄδρηστ-ος, ὁ Adrastos (2a) ('Unable to escape'; member of the Phrygian royal family and suppliant of Croesus)
Ἀθήν-η|-ᾶ, ἡ Athene (1a/b) (goddess of craftsmanship and protectress of Odysseus)
Ἀλκίνο-ος, ὁ Alkinoos (2a) (king of the Phaiakians and father of Nausikaa)
Ἀμφί-θε-ος, ὁ Amphitheos (2a) ('God on both sides'; goes to Sparta to get Dikaiopolis' private peace-treaty)

Ἀπολλόδωρ-ος, ὁ Apollodoros (2a) (prosecutor of Neaira and Stephanos; friend of Aristarkhos)
Ἀπόλλων (Ἀπολλων-), ὁ Apollo (3a: but voc. usu. Ἄπολλον; acc. Ἀπόλλω) (god of prophecy, with oracular shrine at Delphi)
Ἀρίσταρχ-ος, ὁ Aristarkhos (2a) (friend of Apollodoros, narrator of his legal troubles at the hands of Theophemos and Euergos)
Ἀφροδίτ-η, ἡ Aphrodite (1a) (goddess of love; used often as synonym for sexual pleasure)
Βδελυκλέων (Βδελυκλεων-), ὁ Bdelykleon (3a)

('Loathe-Kleon'; son of
Philokleon)
Δικαιόπολις, ὁ   Dikaiopolis (3e)
('Just citizen'; Attic farmer in search
of peace)
Διονυσόδωρ-ος, ὁ   Dionysodoros
(2a) (sophist, brother of
Euthydemos)
Ἐπιμηθ-εύς, ὁ   Epimetheus (3g)
('Aftersight'; brother of
Prometheus)
Ἑρμ-ῆς, ὁ   Hermes (1d) (Zeus'
messenger)
Εὐεργίδ-ης, ὁ   Euergides (1d)
(experienced dikast)
Εὔεργ-ος, ὁ   Euergos (2a) (brother of
Theophemos and his helper in
seizing Aristarkhos' goods)
Εὐθύδημ-ος, ὁ   Euthydemos (2a)
(sophist, brother of Dionysodoros)
Θεογέν-ης, ὁ   Theogenes (3d) *(basileus
archon* and for a short time husband
of Phano)
Θεόφημ-ος, ὁ   Theophemos (2a)
(enemy of Aristarkhos and
responsible for the seizure of his
goods)
Ἰλισ-ός, ὁ   river Ilisos (2a) (see map,
Text, p. 19)
Κινησί-ας, ὁ   Kinesias (1d)
('Sexually active'; husband of
Myrrhine)
Κλεινί-ας, ὁ   Kleinias (1d) (a young
friend of Socrates)
Κλεονίκ-η, ἡ   Kleonike (1a) (friend
and fellow-conspirator of
Lysistrata)
Κροῖσ-ος, ὁ   Croesus (2a) (king of
Lydia) (see map, *Text,* p. 157)
Κωμί-ας, ὁ   Komias (1d)

(experienced dikast)
Λάβης *(Λαβητ-),* ὁ   Labes (3a)
('Grabber'; dog indicted on a
charge of stealing cheese)
Λυδ-οί, οἱ   Lydians (2a) (Croesus'
people) (see map, *Text,* p. 157)
Λυσί-ας, ὁ   Lysias (1d) (the famous
orator, lover of Metaneira)
Λυσιστράτ-η, ἡ   Lysistrata (1a)
('Destroyer of the army';
prime-mover of the women's
sex-strike)
Μετάνειρ-α, ἡ   Metaneira (1b) (a
slave and prostitute in Nikarete's
brothel, loved by Lysias)
Μυρρίν-η, ἡ   Myrrhine (1a) (friend
of Lysistrata and wife of Kinesias)
Μυσ-οί, οἱ   Mysians (2a) (see map,
Text, p. 157)
Ναυσικά-α, ἡ   Nausikaa (1b)
(unmarried daughter of Alkinoos,
king of the Phaiakians)
Νέαιρ-α, ἡ   Neaira (1b) ('wife' of
Stephanos; indicted by
Apollodoros for living with
Stephanos as his wife and
pretending that her children were
citizens)
Νικαρέτ-η, ἡ   Nikarete (1a)
(brothel-keeper; former owner of
Neaira)
Ξανθί-ας, ὁ   Xanthias (1d) (slave of
Bdelykleon)
Ὀδυ(σ)σσ-εύς, ὁ   Odysseus (3g)
(cunning Greek hero, who
wandered for ten years after the
Trojan War before finally
returning to Ithaka, his kingdom)
Ὅμηρ-ος, ὁ   Homer (2a) (epic poet,
author of the *Iliad* and the *Odyssey*)

Πεισ-έταιρ-ος, ὁ   Peisetairos (2a)
('Persuade-friend'; friend of
Dikaiopolis; plans to leave Athens
with Euelpides)

Περικλ-ῆς, ὁ   Pericles (3d: uncontr.)
(political leader in Athens during
the mid-fifth century)

Προμηθ-εύς, ὁ   Prometheus (3g)
('Foresight'; brother of
Epimetheus)

Πῶλ-ος, ὁ   Polos (2a) (a rower on
board a trireme)

Στέφαν-ος, ὁ   Stephanos (2a)
('husband' of Neaira; indicted by
Apollodoros for living with a
foreigner as his wife and trying to
pass off her children as citizens)

Στρεψιάδ-ης, ὁ   Strepsiades (1d)
('Twist and turn'; debt-ridden
farmer, father of Pheidippides)

Στρυμόδωρ-ος, ὁ   Strymodoros (2a)
(inexperienced dikast)

Σωσί-ας, ὁ   Sosias (1d) (slave of

Bdelykleon)

Φαίηκ-ες, οἱ   Phaiakians (3a)
(Alkinoos' people)

Φαν-ώ, ἡ   Phano (acc. Φαν-ώ; gen.
Φαν-οῦς; dat. Φαν-οῖ) (daughter of
Neaira; married to Phrastor, then
Theogenes)

Φειδιππίδ-ης, ὁ   Pheidippides (1d)
('Son of Pheidon and horse';
chariot-racing, horse-mad son of
Strepsiades)

Φιλοκλέων (Φιλοκλεων-),
ὁ   Philokleon (3a) ('Love-Kleon';
jury-service-loving father of
Bdelykleon)

Φράστωρ (Φραστορ-), ὁ   Phrastor
(3a) (for a time husband of Phano)

Φρυνίων (Φρυνιων-), ὁ   Phrynion
(3a) (former lover of Neaira, from
whom Stephanos rescued her)

Χαιρεφῶν (Χαιρεφωντ-),
ὁ   Khairephon (3a) (good friend
of Socrates)

E   English–Greek vocabulary

Notes

(a) This vocabulary has been compiled from all the words needed to complete successfully all the English–Greek Exercises in Book One. If you find difficulty with a particular phrase, look in this vocabulary under the main word in the phrase. You will normally find some helpful suggestions as to how to tackle it. Remember that you may often have to rethink the English phrasing, particularly in the prose passages.

Please note that this vocabulary is for use with the Exercises in this book. It may be misleading to apply it to other prose exercises.

(b) Remember, especially if you try the prose passages, that Greek uses many more connecting and other particles than English. For this reason you will not find many particles given in this vocabulary. But they are important to the composition of good Greek. So try to use at least μέν . . . δέ, δέ, ἀλλά, γάρ, δή and οὖν in your writing, all of which you will meet very often in your reading. See further Reference Grammar G.

a (certain) τις τι (τιν-)
able, be able δύναμαι (+inf.)
about περί (+acc./gen.)
according to κατά (+acc.)
account, on x's ὑπέρ (+gen.)
accurately ἀκριβῶς
acquit ἀπολύω
actually *indicating definite*
   statement: use indicative verb
advocate ἀντίδικος, ὁ (2a)
afraid of, be φοβέ-ομαι
   (+acc.)

afraid that, be φοβέ-ομαι μή
   +subj./opt.
   afraid that . . . not μή . . . οὐ
after μετά (+acc.)
afterwards, not long οὐ διὰ
   πολλοῦ
again αὖθις
against one's will ἄκων
   ἄκουσα ἄκον (ἀκοντ-)
agree ὁμολογέω
all πᾶς πᾶσα πᾶν (παντ-)
all sorts of *use* πᾶς

at all πάνυ *or omit*
allow ἐάω (ἐασ-)
already ἤδη
although καίπερ +part., *or*
   plain part.
always ἀεί
amazed, be θαυμάζω
Amazon 'Αμαζών
   ('Αμαζον-), ἡ (3a)
ambassador πρεσβευτής, ὁ
   (1d)
and καί

and yet καίτοι
angry, be made ὀργίζομαι
(aor. ὠργίσθην)
announce, make an
announcement κηρύττω
another ἄλλος η ο
answer ἀποκρίνομαι
(ἀποκριν-)
anyone *in negative sentence use*
οὐδείς οὐδεμία οὐδέν
(οὐδεν-); *if no neg.*, *use* τις
any such thing τι τοιοῦτο
Apollodoros Ἀπολλόδωρος,
ὁ (2a)
appear φαίν-ομαι; δοκέω
archon ἄρχων (ἀρχοντ-), ὁ
(3a)
argument λόγος, ὁ (2a)
arrive ἀφικνέομαι (ἀφικ-)
as *use* ὤν οὖσα ὄν (ὀντ-); ὡς
+ind.; ὡς +noun
as – as possible ὡς +sup.
adv./adj.
ask ἐρωτάω (ἐρ-)
ask for αἰτέω
assembly ἐκκλησία, ἡ (1b)
astounded at, be θαυμάζω
(+acc.)
at εἰς (+acc.)
at once εὐθύς
at the hands of ὑπό (+gen.)
Athenian Ἀθηναῖ-ος, ὁ (2a)
attention, pay *use aor. of*
ἀκούω; προσέχω τὸν νοῦν
(+dat.)

bad κακός ή όν
bank τράπεζα, ἡ (1c)
Bdelykleon Βδελυκλέων
(-εων-), ὁ (3a)
be εἰμί
bear φέρω
find hard to bear βαρέως
φέρω (fut. οἴσω)
because διότι
because of διά (+acc.)
become γίγν-ομαι (γεν-)
before πρίν (+inf.)

do x before y φθάνω y (acc.)
doing x (nom. part.)
begin ἄρχομαι (+gen. or
part.); ὑπάρχω (+gen.)
behalf of, on ὑπέρ (+gen.)
beloved *use pass. of* φιλέω
best ἄριστος η ον
better, feel συλλέγω ἐμαυτόν
(1st pl. ἡμᾶς αὐτούς)
big μέγας μεγάλη μέγα
(μεγαλ-)
boat πλοῖον, τό (2b)
body νεκρός, ὁ (2a)
boy παῖς (παιδ-), ὁ (3a)
bribe δῶρον, τό (2b)
bring ἄγω (ἀγαγ-)
bring out ἐκφέρω (ἐξενεγκ-)
bring to an end καταλύω
bumpkin ἄγροικος ον
business, move χρηματίζω
(fut. χρηματιῶ: έω contr.)
but ἀλλά (*first word*); δέ
(*second word*)
by κατά (+acc.)
by land κατὰ γῆν
by! (oath) νή (+acc.)
by (agent) ὑπό (+gen.)

call upon ἐπικαλέομαι
captain κυβερνήτης, ὁ (1d)
capture αἱρέω (ἑλ-) (fut.
αἱρήσω); καταλαμβάνω
(-λαβ-) (fut. -λήψομαι)
carefully ἀκριβῶς
carry out ἐκφορέω
cast (a vote) τίθεμαι (θε-)
caught, be ἁλίσκομαι (ἁλ-)
charge, make a γραφὴν
γράφομαι (γραψ-)
chase διώκω
child παιδίον, τό (2b)
childless ἄπαις (ἀπαιδ-), ὁ
(3a)
citizen ἀστός, ὁ (2a)
city πόλις, ἡ (3e)
claim φάσκω (fut. φήσω)
clear δῆλος η ον
it is clear that δῆλόν ἐστιν ὅτι

clearly, be δῆλός ἐστι
(+nom. part.); *or use* δῆλόν
ἐστιν ὅτι
clever σοφός ή όν
closely πλησίον
collect λαμβάνω (λαβ-)
come ἔρχομαι (ἐλθ-)
have come ἥκω
come! ἐλθέ
come across καταλαμβάνω
(καταλαβ-)
come forward προσέρχομαι
(προσελθ-)
(to address
assembly) παρέρχομαι
(παρελθ-)
come in(to) εἰσέρχομαι
(εἰσελθ-)
come on! ἄγε
come upon εὑρίσκω (εὑρ-)
conceive διανοέομαι
condemn x (person) to y
(punishment) καταδικάζω
x (gen.) to y (acc.)
consequently ὥστε
consider σκοπέω
contest ἀγωνίζομαι
converse (with) διαλέγομαι
(πρός +acc.)
corpse νεκρός, ὁ (2a)
corrupt διαφθείρω
council βουλή, ἡ (1a)
countryside ἀγροί, οἱ (2a)
court (room) δικαστήριον, τό
(2b)
creditor χρήστης, ὁ (1d)
cross διαβαίνω

danger κίνδυνος, ὁ (2a)
danger (of), be in κινδυνεύω
(περί +acc.)
daughter θυγάτηρ
(θυγατ(ε)ρ-), ἡ (3a)
dear φίλος η ον
death θάνατος, ὁ (2a)
debts χρέα, τά (3c uncontr.)
deceive ἐξαπατάω
decree ψήφισμα, τό (3b)

deed ἔργον, τό (2b); or use n.
pl. adjectives
defeat νικάω (νικησ-)
defence speech ἀπολογία, ἡ
(1b)
make a defence
speech ἀπολογέομαι
defendant φεύγων
(φευγοντ-), ὁ (3a)
demand κελεύω
depart ἀπέρχομαι (ἀπελθ-)
deposited, be κεῖμαι
despair ἀπορία, ἡ (1b)
be in despair ἀπορέω
destroy διαφθείρω; ἀπόλλυμι
die ἀποθνῄσκω (ἀποθαν-)
difficult χαλεπός ή όν
Dikaiopolis Δικαιόπολις, ὁ
(3e)
dikast δικαστής, ὁ (1d)
din θόρυβος, ὁ (2a)
Dionysodoros Διονυσόδωρος,
ὁ (2a)
discover (ἐξ)ευρίσκω
((ἐξ)ευρ-)
disdainful ὀλίγωρος ον
disease νόσος, ἡ (2a)
dishonour ἀτιμάζω
divorce ἐκβάλλω (ἐκβαλ-);
ἐκπέμπω
do ποιέω; δράω (δρασ-);
πράττω
dog κύων (κυν-), ὁ (3a)
don't μή+imperative;
μή+aor. subj.
door θύρα, ἡ (1b)
downhearted, be ἀθυμέω
(ἀθυμησ-)
draft γράφω
drag away ἀφέλκω
duty translate 'must'

easy ῥᾴδιος α ον
most easy ῥᾷστος η ον
end, bring to an καταλύω
enemies πολέμιοι, οἱ (2a)
enmity ἔχθρα, ἡ (1b)

enough ... to οὕτω ... ὥστε
+inf.
enter εἰσέρχομαι (εἰσελθ-)
(εἰς+acc.)
equip παρασκευάζω
equipment σκεύη, τά (3c); or
use τά+gen. (of what it
belongs to)
escape ἀποφεύγω (ἀποφυγ-)
Euelpides Εὐελπίδης, ὁ (1d)
ever ποτε (enclitic)
in indef. sentences add ἄν to
conjunction and use subj. verb
everything translate 'all
(things)'
evidence τεκμήριον, τό (2b)
evil κακός ή όν
except πλήν (+gen.)
expect ἐλπίζω (+fut. inf.)
experience πάθος, τό (3c)
experienced (in) ἔμπειρος ον
(περί+acc.)

face the prospect of μέλλω
(+fut. inf.)
fall πίπτω
fall ill ἀσθενέω
family οἰκεῖοι, οἱ (2a)
farmer γεωργός, ὁ (2a)
father πατήρ (πατ(ε)ρ-), ὁ
(3a)
feel better συλλέγω ἐμαυτόν
(1st pl. ἡμᾶς αὐτούς)
fetch out ἐκφέρω (fut.
ἐξοίσω)
few ὀλίγοι αι α
fifty πεντήκοντα
fight μάχομαι
(μαχεσ-) (with,
against) πρός (+acc.)
finally τέλος
find εὑρίσκω (εὑρ-)
find out πυνθάνομαι (πυθ-)
fine τίμημα (τιμηματ-), τό
(3b)
fine (adj.) καλός ή όν
fire πῦρ (πυρ-), τό (3b)
flatter θωπεύω

follow ἕπομαι (σπ-)
(=accompany) ἀκολουθέω
(+dat.)
fool(ish) μῶρος α ον
for γάρ (second word)
for (prep.) ὑπέρ (+gen.)
force ἀναγκάζω (ἀναγκασ-)
forefather πρόγονος, ὁ (2a)
fortunate εὐδαίμων εὔδαιμον
(εὐδαιμον-)
free ἐλεύθερος α ον
freedom ἐλευθερία, ἡ (1b)
friend φίλος, ὁ (2a); φίλη, ἡ
(1a)
furniture σκεύη, τά (3c)

gaze out (into) ἀποβλέπω
(εἰς+acc.)
gear σκεύη, τά (3c)
general στρατηγός, ὁ (2a)
get λαμβάνω (λαβ-)
get back κομίζομαι
get hold of λαμβάνομαι
(+gen.)
get into καθίσταμαι
(καταστα-) (εἰς+acc.)
get up ἀναβαίνω (ἀναβα-)
give δίδωμι (δο-)
glance βλέπω (aorist aspect)
go ἔρχομαι (ἐλθ-) (fut. εἶμι;
subj. ἴω; perf. ἐλήλυθα)
go away (off) ἀπέρχομαι
(ἀπελθ-)
going to, be μέλλω (+fut.
inf.)
go up to προσέρχομαι (-ελθ-)
(πρός+acc.)
god θεός, ὁ (2a)
good καλός ή όν; χρηστός ή
όν; ἀγαθός ή όν or translate as
adverb, 'well'
grab λαμβάνομαι (λαβ-)
(+gen.)
great μέγας μεγάλη μέγα
(μεγαλ-)
govern πολιτεύομαι
grievously μεγάλα
guard φυλάττω

guard φύλαξ (φυλακ-), ὁ ἡ
(3a)

hand χείρ (χειρ-), ἡ (3a)
  at the hands of ὑπό (+gen.)
hand over παραδίδωμι
  (παραδο-)
happen (to be) τυγχάνω
  (τυχ-) (+nom. part.)
happen, occur γίγνομαι
  (γεν-) (perf. γεγένημαι)
harbour λιμήν (λιμεν-), ὁ (3a)
hard, find hard to
  bear βαρέως φέρω (fut.
  οἴσω)
hate μισέω
hated by the gods κακοδαίμων
  κακόδαιμον (κακοδαιμον-)
have ἔχω (σχ-); ἐστί (+dat.)
have in mind ἐν νῷ ἔχω
have to δεῖ x (acc.) to y (inf.)
hear ἀκούω (ἀκουσ-)
here ἐνθάδε
home(wards) οἴκαδε
hope ἐλπίζω (+fut. inf.)
horse ἵππος, ὁ (2a)
house οἰκία, ἡ (1b)
how? πῶς;
how (indir. q.) πῶς, ὅπως
how big ὅσος η ον; ὁπόσος η
  ον
hullo! χαῖρε
husband ἀνήρ (ἀνδρ-), ὁ (3a)

I ἐγώ (or just 1st s. of verb)
idea γνώμη, ἡ (1a)
  it seems a good idea to δοκεῖ
  to x (dat.) to do y (inf.)
if εἰ
if (fut. time) ἐάν (+subj.)
if ... were –, ...
  would – εἰ+opt., opt.+ἄν
if ... were –ing, ... would be
  –ing εἰ+impf., impf.+ἄν
if ... had –ed, ... would have
  –ed εἰ+aor., aor.+ἄν
if not εἰ μή
if only εἴθε, εἰ γάρ (+opt.)

ignoramus ἀμαθής ές
ill, be ill ἀσθενέω
impious, be ἀσεβέω
in ἐν (+dat.); ἔνδον (adv.)
  be in, present πάρειμι
inclined to, be naturally
  πέφυκα (+inf.)
inhabit οἰκέω
intend μέλλω (+fut. inf.)
  intending to ὡς+fut. part.
into εἰς (+acc.)
itself (reflexive) ἑαυτόν
  ἑαυτήν ἑαυτό

job ἔργον, τό (2b)
judge δικάζω
  give, pass judgment δικάζω
juror δικαστής, ὁ (1d)
just δίκαιος α ον
justly δικαίως

Khairedemos Χαιρέδημος, ὁ
  (2a)
kill ἀποκτείνω (ἀποκτειν-)
king (king archon) βασιλεύς,
  ὁ (3g)
knock (on) κόπτω (+acc.)
  gave a knock use aorist
know γιγνώσκω; οἶδα (part.
  εἰδώς; inf. εἰδέναι)

lady γυνή (γυναικ-), ἡ (3a)
Lampito Λαμπιτώ, ἡ (voc.
  Λαμπιτοῖ)
land γῆ, ἡ (1a)
  by land κατὰ γῆν
large μέγας μεγάλη μέγα
  (μεγαλ-)
last, at last τέλος
laugh γελάω (γελασ-)
law νόμος, ὁ (2a)
law-court δικαστήριον, τό
  (2b)
learn μανθάνω (μαθ-)
leave ἀπέρχομαι (ἀπελθ-)
  (ἀπό+gen.)
legal translate 'of the court'
legitimate γνήσιος α ον

let ἐάω (ἐασ-); or use 3rd
  person imper. or 1st pl. subj.
life ψυχή, ἡ (1a)
like φιλέω (φιλησ-)
liking, be to one's ἀρέσκει
  (+dat.)
listen (to) ἀκούω (+gen./acc.
  of thing)
live (in) οἰκέω (+acc.)
live together συνοικέω
live with συνοικέω (+dat.)
lock in ἐγκλείω (ἐν+dat.)
long after, not οὐ διὰ πολλοῦ
look (at) βλέπω
  (εἰς/πρός+acc.)
look! ἰδού (s.)
look after θεραπεύω
look for ζητέω
lot, a use πολλά
  a lot of πολύς πολλή πολύ
  (πολλ-)
loud μέγας
  very loud μέγιστος η ον
love φιλέω
love of wisdom φιλοσοφία, ἡ
  (1b)

maidservant θεράπαινα, ἡ
  (1c)
make ποιέομαι
man ἄνθρωπος, ὁ (2a); ἀνήρ
  (ἀνδρ-), ὁ (3a)
managed to (x) use aorist of
  (x)
many πολλοί αἱ ά
marry γαμέω (γημ-)
matter πρᾶγμα (πραγματ-),
  τό (3b)
messenger ἄγγελος, ὁ (2a)
mind, have in ἐν νῷ ἔχω
mistreat κακά (κακῶς) ποιέω
  (+acc.)
mock (at) παίζω (πρός+acc.)
money χρήματα, τά (3b)
mother μήτηρ (μητ(ε)ρ-), ἡ
  (3a)
move business χρηματίζω
  (fut. χρηματιῶ: -έω contr.)

much πολύς πολλή πολύ
(πολλ-)

mule ἡμίονος, ὁ (2a)

must δεῖ x (acc.) to do y (inf.)

my ἐμός ή όν

myself use αὐτός

name ὄνομα (ὀνοματ-), τό
(3b)

naturally inclined, to
be πέφυκα (+inf.)

Neaira Νέαιρα, ἡ (1b)

necessary, it is δεῖ (past. ἔδει)
for x (acc.) to y (inf.)

neighbour γείτων (γειτον-),
ὁ (3a)

neither if it means 'and not' use
οὐδέ (phrased so that another
οὐ precedes it)

neither . . . nor οὔτε . . . οὔτε

never οὐδέποτε

new use ἄλλος η ο

news ('the news') omit in
translating

next day τῇ ὑστεραίᾳ

not οὐ, οὐκ, οὐχ (accented οὔ
at end of sentence)
(with infinitives) μή, except
in indirect speech

notice use οὐ λανθάνω (λαθ-)
('x (nom.) does not escape
the notice of y (acc.) doing z
(nom. part.)')

notice of, take προσέχω τὸν
νοῦν (+dat.)

number πλῆθος, τό (3c)

oath ὅρκος, ὁ (2a)

obediently use part. of
πείθομαι

obey πείθομαι (+dat.)

obliged use δέον (acc. absol.)
('x (acc.) is obliged to y
(inf.)')
be obliged, compelled
to ἀνάγκη ἐστί for x (acc.)
to y (inf.)

obviously δῆλόν ἐστιν ὅτι

old man γέρων (γεροντ-), ὁ
(3a)

old woman γραῦς (γρα-), ἡ
(3a irr.)

on may indicate aorist aspect
(e.g. 'on seeing him')

on (preposition) κατά
(+acc.)

once, once and for all may
indicate aorist aspect (e.g.
'stop that once and for all!')
aorist aspect; or, use γίγνομαι
(γεν-) (e.g. 'once friends');
or use a gen. absolute (e.g.
'once this had
happened, . . .')

once, at see at once

only μόνον

or ἤ

order, give orders κελεύω
(κελευσ-)

our ἡμέτερος α ον

out of ἐκ (+gen.)

out with it! use aor. imper. of
λέγω

owe ὀφείλω

peace εἰρήνη, ἡ (1a)

Peisetairos Πεισέταιρος, ὁ
(2a)

people δῆμος, ὁ (2a); πλῆθος,
τό (3c)

perform διαπράττομαι

perplexed, be ἀπορέω
(ἀπορησ-)

Persian Πέρσης, ὁ (1d)

persuade πείθω (πεισ-)

persuasion use the verb

Phano Φανώ, ἡ (acc. Φανώ;
gen. Φανοῦς)

Philokleon Φιλοκλέων
(-εων-), ὁ (3a)

Philoxenos Φιλόξενος, ὁ (2a)

Phrastor Φράστωρ
(Φραστορ-), ὁ (3a)

Phrynion Φρυνίων
(Φρυνιων-), ὁ (3a)

pick up ἀναιρέω (ἀνελ-);
ἐκδέχομαι (ἐκδεξ-)

pious, be εὐσεβέω

Piraeus Πειραιεύς, ὁ (3g)

place χωρίον, τό (2b)

plague νόσος, ἡ (2a)

plan γνώμη, ἡ (1a); μηχανή, ἡ
(1a)

plan, make a μηχανὴν
ποιέομαι

pleasure, with ἡδέως

poet ποιητής, ὁ (1d)

politician ῥήτωρ (ῥητορ-), ὁ
(3a)

poor condition πονηρῶς

position turn qualifying adj.
into noun

possession κτῆμα (κτηματ-),
τό (3b)

possible for, it is ἔξεστι for x
(dat.) to y (inf.)
since it is possible ἔξον

praise ἐπαινέω (ἐπαινεσ-)

promise in marriage ἐγγυάω

property use τά+gen. of
person who owns it

prosecute κατηγορέω

prosecution κατηγορία, ἡ
(1b)

prosecutor κατήγορος, ὁ (2a):
διώκων (διωκοντ-), ὁ (3a)

prospect of, face the μέλλω
(+fut. inf.)

prostitute ἑταίρα, ἡ (1b)

prove δηλόω

prytaneis πρυτάνεις, οἱ (3e)

punish κολάζω

pursue διώκω

pursuer διώκων (διωκοντ-), ὁ
(3a)

put down κατατίθημι
(καταθε-)

put in(to) καθίστημι
(καταστησα-) x (acc.) in(to)
y (εἰς+acc.)
be put into καθίσταμαι
(καταστα-)

put x into such a y state,

condition διατίθημι
(διαθε-) x (acc.) οὖτω γ
(adv.)

question ... closely ἐξετάζω
quickly ταχέως
quiet, keep ἡσυχάζω

reason, for what διὰ τί; τί
βουλόμενος;
for x (gen.) reason ἕνεκα
(prep. after noun)
receive δέχομαι *(δεξ-)*
recover ἀνίσταμαι
refrain ἀπέχομαι (fut.
ἀφέξομαι)
(from) (+gen.)
relate διέρχομαι *(διελθ-)*
remember μνημονεύω
rescue-force βοήθεια, ἡ (1b)
responsible (for) αἴτιος a ον
(+gen.)
retreat ἀναχωρέω
return ἐπανέρχομαι *(-ελθ-)*
rhapsode ῥαψῳδός, ὁ (2a)
rich εὐδαίμων εὔδαιμον
(εὐδαιμον-)
risk κινδυνεύω (+inf.)
river ποταμός, ὁ (2a)
rogue ὑβριστής, ὁ (1d)
rule ἄρχω
run τρέχω
run away φεύγω
run off φεύγω
run out ἐκτρέχω *(ἐκδραμ-)*
run towards προστρέχω
(-δραμ-) *(πρός+acc.)*

sacrifice θύω
make sacrifices θυσίας θύω
safe σῶος a ον
sail πλέω
sailor ναύτης, ὁ (1d)
same ὁ αὐτός ἡ αὐτή τό αὐτό
say (that) λέγω *(εἰπ-)*+ὅτι;
φημί+acc./nom.+inf.
I said ἦν δ᾽ ἐγώ
Scythian Σκύθης, ὁ (1d)

sea θάλαττα, ἡ (1c)
by sea κατὰ θάλατταν
sea-battle ναυμαχία, ἡ (1b)
see ὁράω *(ἰδ-)*
don't you see? use λανθάνω
(e.g. 'doing γ (nom. part.)
does he avoid your
notice?' – *translating 'your
notice' as 'you' (acc.)*
seem δοκέω
seem a good idea δοκεῖ to x
(dat.) to γ (inf.)
seize λαμβάνω *(λαβ-)*
sell πωλέω
serious βαρύς εῖα ύ
set up ποιέομαι
share μέρος, τό (3c)
sheep πρόβατον, τό (2b)
ship πλοῖον, τό (2b); ναῦς, ἡ
(3a irr.)
short (of time) ὀλίγος η ον
should use ἄν+opt.
shout βοάω
gave a shout use aorist
shout, shouting βοή, ἡ (1a)
show δηλόω; ἀποφαίνω
shut in ἐγκλείω *(ἐγκλεισ-)*
since use ὤν οὖσα ὄν *(ὀντ-)* or
participle
sit (down) καθίζω; καθίζομαι
slander διαβάλλω
slave δοῦλος, ὁ (2a); δούλη, ἡ
(1a); ὑπηρέτης, ὁ (1d); παῖς
(παιδ-), ὁ (3a)
sleep καθεύδω
slowly βραδέως
so οὖν *(second word)*
so that
(intent) ἵνα+subj./opt.
someone τις *(τιν-)*
son υἱός, ὁ (2a)
soon as possible, as ὡς
τάχιστα
sophist σοφιστής, ὁ (1d)
space χωρίον, τό (2b)
Spartan Λακεδαιμόνιος, ὁ (2a)
speak λέγω
speak in assembly ἀγορεύω

speak up! *use aor. imper.*
spectator θεατής, ὁ (1d)
steal ὑφαιρέομαι *(ὑφελ-)*
Stephanos Στέφανος, ὁ (2a)
stop (doing) παύομαι
(+part.)
stop (someone doing) παύω
(acc.+part.)
(put a stop to) παύω (+acc.)
stranger ξένος, ὁ (2a)
strike τύπτω
student μαθητής, ὁ (1d)
stupid μῶρος a ον
such/so ... that οὖτω ... ὤστε
+inf./ind.
suffer πάσχω *(παθ-)*
suit δίκη, ἡ (1a); γραφή, ἡ
(1a); ἀγών *(ἀγων-)*, ὁ (3a)
sun ἥλιος, ὁ (2a)
suppliant ἱκέτης, ὁ (1d)
sure βέβαιος ον
sway, hoid κρατέω
swear ὄμνυμι *(ὀμοσ-)*
sweetly ἡδέως

take λαμβάνω *(λαβ-)*
take back ἀναλαμβάνω
(ἀναλαβ-) (fut.
ἀναλήψομαι)
take off ἄγω
take up ἐκδέχομαι
talk διαλέγομαι
teach διδάσκω *(διδαξ-)*
teacher διδάσκαλος, ὁ (2a)
tell λέγω *(εἰπ-)*
tell me! εἰπέ (s.)
terrible δεινός ή όν
than ἤ
that (conj.) ὅτι
that (adj.) ἐκεῖνος η ο
so that
(result) ὤστε+inf./ind.
their (belonging to
subject) ἑαυτῶν
them αὐτούς αὐτάς
themselves αὐτοί αὐταί
(reflexive) ἑαυτούς

then δή (emphasising previous word)

then, from then on ἐντεῦθεν

Theogenes Θεογένης, ὁ (3d)

Theophemos Θεόφημος, ὁ (2a)

there, over there ἐκεῖ

therefore οὖν (second word)

they ἐκεῖνοι/οὗτοι

thief κλέπτης, ὁ (1d)

thing πρᾶγμα (πραγματ-), τό (3b); or use n. of adj. or pronoun

this οὗτος αὕτη τοῦτο

though use ὤν οὖσα ὄν (ὀντ-) or καίπερ+part.

throw out ἐκβάλλω (ἐκβαλ-)

time χρόνος, ὁ (2a)

to (intention) ὡς+fut. part; ἵνα+subj./opt.

to, towards πρός (+acc.); εἰς (+acc.)

(of persons) ὡς (+acc.)

tolerable μέτριος α ον

too καί

torch λαμπάς (λαμπαδ-), ἡ (3a)

towards πρός (+acc.)

town, be in ἐπιδημέω

travel πορεύομαι

trial ἀγών (ἀγων-), ὁ (3a)

trierarch τριήραρχος, ὁ (2a)

trireme τριήρης, ἡ (3d)

trouble use κίνδυνος, ὁ (2a)

truce σπονδαί, αἱ (1a)

truth ἀληθῆ, τά; ἀλήθεια, ἡ (1b)

try πειράομαι (πειρασ-)+inf.

uncaring ἀμελής ές

unhappy κακοδαίμων κακόδαιμον (κακοδαιμον-)

unjust ἄδικος ον

unlucky κακοδαίμων κακόδαιμον (κακοδαιμον-)

until ἕως ἄν+subj. (primary);

ἕως+opt. (past); ἕως+ind. (definite)

=before πρὶν ἄν+subj. (primary); πρίν+opt. (past)

urge on προτρέπω

use χράομαι (+dat.)

used to use imperfect

useful χρήσιμος η ον

vengeance on, take τιμωρέομαι (+acc.)

very ('this very thing') αὐτὸ τοῦτο

victorious, be νικάω

virtue ἀρετή, ἡ (1a)

vote ψῆφος, ἡ (2a)

wait μένω (fut. μενῶ: ἐω contr.)

wall τεῖχος, τό (3c)

want (to) βούλομαι (+inf.); ἐθέλω (ἐθελησ-)

war πόλεμος, ὁ (2a)

way τρόπος, ὁ (2a)

we ἡμεῖς (or just 1st pl. of verb)

well εὖ

well-disposed (to) εὔνους ουν (+dat.)

what? ὅ τι; (reply to question τί;)

what (indir. q.) ὅστις ἥτις ὅ τι

what sort of ὁποῖος α ον

whatever ὅστις ἄν, ἥτις ἄν, ὅ τι ἄν

when ὅτε, ἐπειδή, ἐπεί, ὁπότε

when(ever) (indef.) ἐπειδάν, ὅταν, ὁπόταν

where? ποῦ;

where (indir. q.) ποῦ, ὅπου

where(ever) (indef.) ὅπου ἄν+subj. (primary); ὅπου+opt. (past)

where to? ποῖ;

whether . . . or πότερον . . . ἤ

which use ὤν οὖσα ὄν (ὀντ-) or ὅς ἥ ὅ (relative)

while use μέν . . . δέ ('on the one hand (μέν) x is happening, while (δέ) y . . .'); or use gen. abs.

while, a ὀλίγον χρόνον

who? τίς; τί; (τιν-)

who use ὤν οὖσα ὄν (ὀντ-); or ὅς ἥ ὅ (relative)

why? διὰ τί; τί; τί παθών; τί βουλόμενος;

wicked πονηρός ά όν

wife γυνή (γυναικ-), ἡ (3a)

will, against one's ἄκων ἄκουσα ἄκον (ἀκοντ-)

win νικάω (νικησ-)

wisdom σοφία, ἡ (1b)

wise σοφός ή όν

wish βούλομαι

with (=by means of) use dative case

without being seen by use λανθάνω +acc.+nom. part.

woman γυνή (γυναικ-), ἡ (3a)

word λόγος, ὁ (2a)

worry φροντίζω

worth ἄξιος α ον (+gen.)

would use imperfect or ἄν+opt.

wrong ἀδικέω (ἀδικησ-)

yes ναί; or just repeat question as statement

yet, and yet καίτοι

yokel ἄγροικος ον

you (s.) σύ (or just 2nd s. of verb)

(pl.) ὑμεῖς (or just 2nd pl. of verb)

young νέος α ον

young man νεανίας, ὁ (1d); νεανίσκος, ὁ (2a)

your (s.) σός σή σόν

(pl.) ὑμέτερος α ον

zeal σπουδή, ἡ (1a)

Zeus Ζεύς (Δι-), ὁ (3a)

F   *Grammar Index*

Numbers in bold type refer to the running grammar; references by capital letter refer to the Reference Grammar (pp. 259–307); references prefixed by *Surv.* refer to the Language Surveys (pp. 308–34).
The Reference Grammar and Language Surveys give the general picture; the running grammar picks up points as they arise.

Grammar Index (Greek)

All nouns/adjectives and verbs are also summarised in the Reference Grammar *ad. loc*

NOTES

Errata in *Reading Greek* (Text)

page 9, line 9: *for* εἰσι *read* εἰσι
page 14, line 40: *delete* Ἕλληνες
page 60, caption to picture: *for* ἀνήρ *read* παῖς
page 69, line 25 and page 72, line 32: *for* ΔΕΛ. *read* ΒΔΕΛ.
page 69, line 25 and page 104, line 28: *for* οὐκ *read* οὐχ
page 77, caption to picture: *for* τυροκνήστιδι *read* τυροκνήστιδι
page 102, line 21: *delete* τε *and for* τήν *read* τὴν
page 115, line 23: *for* ἔφερεν *read* ἔφερον
page 117, line 14: *insert* τὸν Φράστορα *after* ὀμόσαι
page 139, line 10: *for* λήψοιμι *read* ληψοίμην
page 172, line 19: *for* 'Ηὼς *read* 'Ηὼς
page 174, line 37: *for* γαστὴρ *read* γαστήρ,

Errata in the *Morphology Charts*

Cover: *for* typical *read* atypical
page 3: *alongside* τί/τι, *for* m.f. *read* n.
page 8, Notes: *for* -δώσομαι *read* δώσομαι

NOTES

NOTES

NOTES

NOTES

NOTES

NOTES